Esposito, John L.

The Oxford Dictionary of Islam

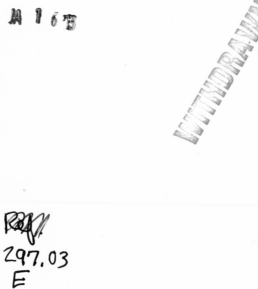

The Oxford
Dictionary of
Islam

The Oxford
Dictionary of
Islam

JOHN L. ESPOSITO
EDITOR IN CHIEF

OXFORD
UNIVERSITY PRESS

2003

OXFORD
UNIVERSITY PRESS

Oxford   New York
Auckland   Bangkok   Buenos Aires   Cape Town   Chennai
Dar es Salaam   Delhi   Hong Kong   Istanbul   Karachi   Kolkata
Kuala Lumpur   Madrid   Melbourne   Mexico City   Mumbai   Nairobi
São Paulo   Shanghai   Taipei   Tokyo   Toronto

Copyright © 2003 by Oxford University Press, Inc.

Published by Oxford University Press, Inc.
198 Madison Avenue, New York, New York 10016

www.oup.com

Oxford is a registered trademark of Oxford University Press

Library of Congress Cataloging-in-Publication Data
Esposito, John L.,
The Oxford dictionary of Islam / John L. Esposito,
editor in chief.
p.   cm.
Includes bibliographical references
ISBN 0-19-512558-4
1. Islam—Dictionaries
I. Title
BP40.095   2003
297.03—DC21   12-870919

9 8 7 6 5 4 3 2 1

Printed in the United States of America
on acid-free paper

For Our Parents

Contents

Preface

Publication of *The Oxford Dictionary of Islam* is the next logical step in a long-term partnership with Oxford to provide major reference works on Islam and the Muslim world. It began with the four-volume *The Oxford Encyclopedia of the Modern Islamic World*, a collection of entries authored by more than four hundred and fifty Muslim and non-Muslim scholars. This was followed by *The Oxford History of Islam*, which combined major articles with over four hundred illustrations. *The Oxford Dictionary of Islam* is a natural outgrowth of this process and adds to the growing library of scholarship on Islam to inform and educate the general public.

The emergence of Islam as the second largest religion globally and second or third largest religion in Europe and America, as well as the impact of 9/11, have made even more critical the need for a concise, accessible reference work. I have written a standard introduction to Islam, *Islam: The Straight Path*. I recently wrote *What Everyone Needs to Know About Islam* (in question and answer format), which addressed head-on many of the tough questions I had been asked after 9/11. It provides basic, direct answers that respond not only to professionals in the media and government but also to the many teachers and counselors who were bombarded by questions from their students. However, my experience with journalists, politicians, religious leaders, and the general public still forcefully demonstrated the critical need for a brief, basic, inexpensive reference providing essential information on Islam in the world today.

The Oxford Dictionary of Islam is designed for general readers with little or no knowledge of Islam. Organized in an easy-to-use, A-to-Z format, it provides more than two thousand entries that synthesize selected materials from *The Oxford Encyclopedia of the Modern Islamic World* with a large number of new entries, written by over one hundred contributors. The entries were selected and reviewed by an editorial board drawn from the full range of disciplines and areas covered in the *Dictionary* and was composed of scholars from the United States, Europe and the Islamic world.

Focusing primarily on the nineteenth and twentieth centuries, the *Dictionary* deals with the religion of Islam and its impact on history, politics, and society. Readers will find many entries on topics of current interest, such as terrorism and the Taliban, Osama bin Laden and al-Qaeda, the PLO and HAMAS. The *Dictionary's* scope, however, extends beyond recent headlines, ranging from major social and political movements and historical events to key Islamic beliefs, doctrines, rituals, and laws. A series of entries look at Islam in individual nations, such as Afghanistan, the West Bank and Gaza, Bosnia-Herzegovina, and the United States, and offer discussions of Islamic views on such issues as abortion, birth control, the Rushdie Affair, and the theory of evolution. Twelve featured entries cover topics of popular interest such as women and Islam, Sufism, Mosque and Hajj.

Following the readable style and format of *The Oxford History of Islam,* The dictionary implements standard transliteration but without diacriticals. The exception are words which have achieved currency in non-standard transliteration in English, including terms such as al-Qaeda and names like Hussein. Thus, the name Muhammad (standard transliteration) is sometimes spelled Mohamed, if for example, the person in question has published in English with this spelling. In addition, the dictionary lists entries alphabetically in the language the editors believed readers would most likely look for them. Thus, "fasting" appears rather than "sawm," but "hijra" rather than "emigration." "al-Qaeda" appears rather than "the Base" but Palestine Liberation Organization" rather that "Harakat al-Tahrir al-Filistin."

Cross-references are used to guide readers to related discussions elsewhere in the volume. Cross-references are indicated by "See Also" at the conclusion of an entry. In addition, blind entries of alternate spellings and synonyms provide cross-references to the articles they seek. For example, a reader looking up a term in English may be referred to its Arabic equivalent and vice versa. A chronology provides the reader with key events in the history of Islam throughout the world.

This kind of project requires a team of editors and researchers. The very professional and responsive editorial board and primary researchers are acknowledged separately. I owe them a great debt of thanks. In addition, I am indebted to Elda Rotor at OUP who has been there from conception to birth, supportively making a sometimes complicated and frustrating process easier. Catherine Humphries patiently and professionally shepherded the project through production. Tamara Sonn, associate editor, went beyond the call of duty and undertook an exhaustive review of the entire copyedited manuscript, reconciling the thousand and one inconsistencies of spelling and cross-references that a multi-authored work generates. Neither the magnitude of the task nor my debt to her can be over-estimated. Many thanks as well go to Susan Gray Eakin, our intrepid proofreader. As in so many things, my colleague and friend, John Voll, was there whenever I needed a quick review and response. Finally, Jeanette Esposito, my wife and collaborator in life, played a critical role from identifying the technology that would make our task more efficient to compiling lists of possible entries and reading and commenting on the manuscript at every stage.

Editorial Board

Contributors

Rula Jurdi Abisaab Assistant Professor of Middle Eastern/Islamic History and World Civilizations, University of Akron, Ohio

Khaled Abou El Fadl Acting Professor, The Omar and Asmeralda Alfi Distinguished Fellow in Islamic Law, School of Law, University of California, Los Angeles

Hibba Abugidieri Assistant Professor of History, Honors and International Affairs, The George Washington University

As'ad AbuKhalil Associate Professor of Politics and Public Administration, California State University, Stanislaus, Turlock, California

Asma Afsaruddin Assistant Professor of Arabic and Islamic Studies, Department of Classics, University of Notre Dame

Mumtaz Ahmad Professor of Political Science, Hampton University, Virginia

Engin D. Akarli Joukowsky Family Professor of Modern Middle Eastern History and Professor of History, Brown University

Shahrough Akhavi Professor, Department of Government and International Studies, University of South Carolina

Ejaz Akram Managing Editor, *The American Journal of Islamic Social Sciences*

Waddah Al-Khatib Assistant Professor of Arabic, University of Virginia

Roger Allen Professor of Arabic Language and Literature, University of Pennsylvania

Diane Apostolos-Cappadona Adjunct Professor, Center for Muslim-Christian Understanding, Georgetown University

Michael Bishku Assistant Professor of History, Augusta State University, Georgia

Amelie Blom Adjunct Professor, Lahore University of Management Sciences, Lahore, Pakistan

Issa Boullata Professor of Arabic Literature and Qur'anic Studies, Institute of Islamic Studies, McGill University

Kristen Brustad Associate Professor of Middle Eastern Studies, Emory University

Richard Bulliet Professor of History, Columbia University

François Burgat Director, French Centre for Yemeni Studies

Charles Butterworth Professor of Government and Politics, University of Maryland

Sandra Campbell Adjunct Professor of Islam, Occidental College

William Chittick Professor, Interdepartmental Doctoral Program in Anthropological Sciences, State University of New York at Stony Brook

Stephen Cory Doctoral Candidate, Department of History, University of California, Santa Barbara

Kathryn M. Coughlin Doctoral Candidate, Department of History, Georgetown University

Farhad Daftary Head, Department of Academic Research and Publications, Institute of Ismaili Studies, London

Ahmad Dallal Associate Professor of Middle Eastern History, Stanford University

Suleman Dangor Professor of Islamic Studies, School of Religion and Culture, University of Durban—Westville

Linda Darling Professor of Middle Eastern History, University of Arizona

Natana J. DeLong-Bas Doctoral Candidate, Department of History and Center for Muslim-Christian Understanding, Georgetown University

Yusuf Talal DeLorenzo Shariah Supervisory Board Member, The Dow Jones Islamic Market Indexes

Walter Denny Professor of Art History, Adjunct Professor of Middle Eastern Studies, University of Massachusetts at Amherst

Alnoor Dhanani Harvard University

Abdelwahab El-Affendi Senior Research Fellow, Centre for the Study of Democracy, Westminster University, London

John Entelis Professor of Political Science and Director of the Middle East Studies Program, Fordham University, Bronx, New York

Mohammad H. Faghfoory Independent Scholar, Alexandria, Virginia

Majid Fakhry Professor Emeritus of Islamic Philosophy, American University of Beirut, and Adjunct Professor, Georgetown University

Mamun Fandy Center for Contemporary Arab Studies, School of Foreign Service, Georgetown University

Sean Foley Doctoral Candidate in History, Georgetown University

Bruce Fudge Department of Near Eastern Languages and Civilizations, Graduate School of Arts and Sciences, Harvard University

Adam Gaiser Fulbright Commission, Amman, Jordan

Kambiz GhaneaBassiri Committee on the Study of Religion, Harvard University

Shaikh M. Ghazanfar Professor of Economics, University of Idaho

Ali Gheissari Adjunct Professor, Department of Theology and Religious Studies, University of California, San Diego

Dru Gladney Professor of Asian Studies, Center for Chinese Studies, University of Hawaii

Peter Gottschalk Assistant Professor of Religion, Southwestern University, Georgetown, Texas

Bassam Haddad Department of Government, Georgetown University

Juliane Hammer Independent Scholar, Berlin, Germany

Nomanul Haq Assistant Professor of Islamic Studies, Rutgers University

Mona Hassan Doctoral Candidate, Department of Near Eastern Studies, Princeton University

Meir Hatina Adjunct Professor of Middle Eastern and African History, Tel Aviv University, Israel

Marcia Hermansen Professor of Islamic Studies, Loyola University, Chicago

Thomas Emil Homerin Professor of Religion and Classics, University of Rochester, New York

Qamar-ul Huda Assistant Professor of Islamic Studies and Comparative Theology, Boston College

Toby Huff Professor of Sociology and Anthropology, University of New Hampshire, Dartmouth

George Irani Visiting Assistant Professor of Political Science, Washington College, Chestertown, Maryland

John Iskander Department of Religious Studies, University of California, Santa Barbara

Iftikhar Isma'il Independent Scholar, Lahore, Pakistan

Sherman Jackson Associate Professor of Islamic Studies, Department of Near Eastern Studies, University of Michigan

R. Kevin Jaques Assistant Professor of Islamic Studies, Indiana University

Anthony Johns Emeritus Professor, Department of Pacific and Asian History, Research School of Pacific and Asian Studies, The Australian National University

Amy Johnson Assistant Professor of History, Berry College, Georgia

Ibrahim Kalin Professorial Lecturer, Department of Religion, George Washington University

Haifa Khalafallah Professional Lecturer, Department of History, Georgetown University

Muqtedar Khan Assistant Professor of Political Science and Director of the International Studies Program, Adrian College, Michigan

Richard K. Khuri Council for Research in Values and Philosophy, Falls Church, Virginia

Charles Kurzman Assistant Professor of Sociology and Asian Studies, University of North Carolina at Chapel Hill

Todd Lawson Professor of Islamic Studies, McGill University

Keith Lewinstein Assistant Professor of History and Religion, Smith College, Massachusetts

Leonard Lewisohn Research Associate, Centre of Near and Middle Eastern Studies, School of Oriental and African Studies, University of London and Research Associate, The Institute of Ismaili Studies, London

Fedwa Malti-Douglas The Martha C. Kraft Professor of Humanities in the College of Arts and Sciences, Indiana University

Peter Mandaville Assistant Professor of Public and International Affairs, George Mason University, Virginia

Richard Martin Professor of Islamic Studies and History of Religion, Emory University

Mohsen Milani Professor of Political Science and Chair, Department of Government and International Affairs, University of South Florida

Mustansir Mir Professor of Philosophy and Religious Studies, Youngstown State University, Ohio

Ebrahim Moosa Associate Research Professor of Religion, Duke University

David Nancekivell   Doctoral Candidate in Arabic and Islamic Studies, Harvard University

Azim Nanji   Director and Professor, Institute of Ismaili Studies, London

Seyyed Vali Reza Nasr   Assistant Professor of Political Science, University of San Diego

Jorgen Nielsen   Professor of Islamic Studies, Centre for the Study of Islam and Christian-Muslim Relations, University of Birmingham, United Kingdom

Farish Noor   Institute for Strategic and International Studies (ISIS), Malaysia.

Sulayman Nyang   Professor of African Studies, Howard University, Washington, D.C.

Jason Anthony Odem   Doctoral Candidate, Georgetown University

Robert Olson   Professor of Middle Eastern and East Asian History, University of Kentucky

Ghada Osman   Doctoral Candidate in History and Middle Eastern Studies, Center for Middle Eastern Studies, Harvard University

G. John Renard   Professor of Theological Studies, St. Louis University

Monica Ringer   Mellon Fellow of Middle Eastern History, Williams College, Massachusetts

Andrew Rippin   Professor of History, Specialist in Islamic Studies, University of Victoria, Canada

Michael Rouland   Doctoral Candidate in History, Georgetown University

Abdulaziz Sachedina   Professor of Religious Studies, University of Virginia

Omid Safi   Assistant Professor of Islamic Studies, Colgate University, New York

Sara Scalenghe   Doctoral Candidate in History, Georgetown University

Emad Shahin   Associate Professor of Political Science, The American University in Cairo, Egypt

M. Nazif Shahrani   Professor of Anthropology and Central Asian and Middle Eastern Studies, Indiana University

Andrew Sharp   Instructor of Religious Studies, Virginia Commonwealth University

Jane I. Smith   Professor of Islamic Studies and Co-Director of the Macdonald Center for the Study of Islam and Christian-Muslim Relations, Hartford Seminary

Amira el-Azhary Sonbol Associate Professor of Islamic History, Law, and Society, Center for Muslim-Christian Understanding, School of Foreign Service, Georgetown University

Tamara Sonn William R. Kenan Distinguished Professor of Humanities, The College of William and Mary

Marston Speight Independent Scholar, Cromwell, ConnecticutT

Ewan Stein Doctoral Candidate, Edmond A. Walsh School of Foreign Service, Georgetown University

Barbara Stowasser Director, Center for Contemporary Arab Studies, Georgetown University

Suriani Suratman Assistant Professor of Malay Studies, National University of Singapore

Liyakat Takim Professor of Religious Studies, University of Denver

Colin P. Turner Lecturer in Islamic Studies and Persian Language and Literature, Centre for Middle Eastern and Islamic Studies, University of Durham, United Kingdom

Nada Unus Georgetown University

Gabrielle van den Berg Researcher, Institute of Ismaili Studies, London

John O. Voll Associate Director and Professor of Islamic History, Center for Muslim-Christian Understanding, School of Foreign Service, Georgetown University

Fred von der Mehden Professor Emeritus of Political Science, Rice University, Texas

Brannon M. Wheeler Assistant Professor of Near Eastern Languages and Civilization, University of Washington, Seattle

Theodore P. Wright Jr. Professor Emeritus of Political Science, Graduate School of Public Affairs, State University of New York at Albany

M. Hakan Yavuz Assistant Professor of Political Science, The Middle East Center, University of Utah

Imtiyaz Yusuf Head, Department of Religion, Graduate School of Philosophy and Religion, Assumption University

Muhammad Qasim Zaman Robert Gale Noyes Assistant Professor of Religious Studies, Brown University

The Oxford
Dictionary of
Islam

A

Abd Slave. Common element in Muslim names, followed by one of the divine names of God—for example, Abd al-Rahman, Abd al-Halim, Abdullah. Also an epithet of the Prophet. Denotes total subservience and obedience to God.

Abd al-Aziz, Shah (d. 1824) Indian Islamic scholar and son of Shah Wali Allah (d. 1762), the foremost alim of eighteenth-century India. Prolific author of a wide range of works. Known primarily for his epistles refuting Shiism, the most important and controversial of which is *Tuhfah-i ithna ashariyah* (1789–90).

Abd al-Jabbar, Qadi (d. 1024) Prominent Mutazili theologian. An adherent of the Shafii school of law, he was appointed chief justice (qadi) under the Buwayhids. His *Fadl al-itizal wa tabaqat al-mutazilah* is a major source of Mutazili hagiography, and his *Al-mughni fi abwab al-tawhid wa'l-adl* is our major source for Mutazili doctrine.

Abd al-Malik ibn Marwan (r. 685–705) Umayyad caliph responsible for standardizing imperial coinage and collecting a corpus of hadith to be interpreted by appointed faqihs (Muslim jurists), causing hadith to emerge as a cornerstone of Islamic scholarship. Arabized and centralized the state administration, creating a new class of bureaucrats; the Arabization program led to the development of Arabic-language sciences, particularly adab literature, and the emergence of Arabic as the empire's official language. Sponsored public art featuring Islamic themes. During his reign, the Dome of the Rock was constructed, Jerusalem was appropriated as a holy place for Islam, and the first Arabic-script coinage of the Islamic empire was struck.

Abd al-Muttalib ibn Hashim (d. ca. 578) Muhammad's grandfather. Cared for Mu-hammad after the deaths of his parents. Died when Muhammad was eight. Credited by hadith with receiving a command from God to dig up the well of Zamzam, over which he maintained control and from which he sold water to pilgrims coming to the Kaaba in Mecca.

Abd al-Qadir (d. 1883) Algerian independence leader, Sufi mystic, and poet. Born in Algeria to a notable Moroccan family. Became involved in the Algerian independence movement after the French occupation of Algiers (1830). In 1834 assumed the title amir al-muminin (commander of the faithful). Surrendered in the wake of successive French military victories (1847). Originally a Qadiri Sufi, but joined the Naqshbandis in Damascus, where he lived in self-exile after his surrender. Known works include *Kitab al-mawaqif* (Book of stages), a commentary on the doctrines of Ibn al-Arabi, and a collection of mystical poems. *See also* Salafi

Abd al-Rahman, Aisha (b. 1913) Also known as Bint al-Shati. Egyptian writer and professor of Arabic language and literature and Quranic studies. Wrote more than sixty books on Arabic literature, Quran interpretation, lives of women in the early Muslim community (especially members of Muhammad's family), and contemporary social issues, as well as works of fiction. Is recognized and respected throughout the Arab world. Takes a literary, rather than traditional, approach to Quranic exegesis, arguing against multiple interpretations of verses in favor of single interpretations based on the use of the word in the Quran as whole. Rejects the use of external sources in Quran interpretation. Insists that women's liberation does not abandon traditional Islamic values.

Abd al-Raziq, Ali (d. 1966) Egyptian qadi, intellectual, and author. Born to a powerful and wealthy landowning family in Minya, Abd al-Raziq received both Western and traditional Islamic educations at Oxford and al-Azhar. In 1925 he published the highly controversial and influential *Al-Islam wa-usul al-hukm* (Islam and the sources of political authority), which argued against the idea of a specifically Islamic notion of government. Most contentious was his assertion that Muhammad's role was that of a prophet and spiritual—not political—leader. His writings continue to inspire debate, illustrating the extent to which these issues dominate contemporary Muslim political thought. *See also* Law: Modern Legal Reform

Abd Allah Slave of God. Muslim name, often transliterated as Abdullah. It is common for Muslim personal names to consist of the word *Abd* followed by one of the ninety-nine special names for God. Other examples include Abd al-Rahman and Abd al-Wahid. *See also* Abd

Abd Allah ibn Saba Enigmatic alleged founder of Shii Islam (advocating rule by Muhammad's nephew Ali). His origins and political role are contested in early sources. To him are attributed extremist ideas of Ali's divinity and divine appointment, and the belief that Ali was not dead but would return to bring righteousness on earth.

Abd Allah ibn Umar ibn al-Khattab (d. 693) Companion of the Prophet Muhammad and son of the second caliph, Umar ibn al-Khattab. Prominent authority in hadith and law. Known for neutrality toward factions engaged in first civil war (656–61). *See also* Sammani Tariqah

Abd el-Krim, Muhammad ibn Abd al-Karim al-Khattabi (d. 1963) Moroccan leader of the Rif Rebellion and Islamic reformer. Eldest son of a notable family in a Berber-speaking tribe of northern Morocco, Abd el-Krim and his Moroccan troops soundly defeated Spanish forces under General Silvestre at the Battle of Anual (1921), initiating the Rif Rebellion. Influenced by Salafi ideas, he declared a republic based on

Islamic law (1923) and sought to eliminate Sufism. At its zenith, the Rifian state included most of the Spanish protectorate and a portion of the French protectorate. In 1926 Spanish and French armies defeated Abd el-Krim's forces and disbanded the republic. He died in self-exile in Cairo.

Abdali Dynasty *See* Durrani Dynasty

Abdel Rahman, Omar (b. 1938) Egyptian religious scholar, spiritual guide of al-Jamaah al-Islamiyyah, and radical Islamist. Accused of leading the Egyptian Jihad Organization, which assassinated President Sadat. Encouraged overthrow of the secular state in order to restore Quranic principles. Convicted of inspiring his followers to bomb the World Trade Center in New York City in 1993.

Abduh, Muhammad (d. 1905) Egyptian scholar, journalist, theologian, jurist, grand mufti, and reformer, regarded as an architect of Islamic modernism. Educated at al-Azhar University. Adherent of the Shadhili Sufi order, although he later renounced his Sufi background. Disciple of Jamal al-Din al-Afghani (d. 1897). Supported pan-Islamism and political activism. Edited the journal *Al-urwah al-wuthqa* (The strongest bond) in the 1880s. Exiled from Egypt 1882–88, during which time he traveled to Syria, North Africa, and France. Upon returning to Cairo, focused thoughts and efforts on education and the renewal of Islamic theology. Strove to emancipate Muslims from the mentality of taqlid (adherence to tradition) while retaining Islamic authenticity. Taught that reason and revelation are inherently compatible and harmonious. Most popular work was *Risalat al-tawhid* (The theology of unity), which asserts belief in God as a rational act and the need for rational analysis of revelation. Declared that any reluctance to apply rationality to social issues or refuse its scientific fruits was a disavowal of divine creation, constituting shirk (associationism). Bitterly opposed by some academics and legal scholars. Ideas found continuing expression through the journals *Al-manar*, published by his disciple Muhammad Rashid Rida (d. 1935), and *Al-manar al-jadid* (est. 1998).

Abdul Rahman, Tunku First prime minister of independent Malaysia and leader of United Malays National Organization. Was committed to a secularist vision of the Malaysian nation and power sharing with Chinese and Indians. Was blamed for the worsening plight of Malays and the racial riots of 1969. After 1969, led PERKIM and won the Faisal Award for his contribution to the propagation of Islam among non-Muslims in Malaysia. *See also* PERKIM; United Malays National Organization

Abdulhamid II (d. 1918) Thirty-fourth Ottoman sultan (r. 1876–1909). His reign faced overwhelming difficulties: an insolvent treasury, violent nationalist movements in the Balkans, antireform movements among some Muslims, and increasing foreign intervention. A disastrous military defeat by the Russians (1877) resulted in major territorial concessions and an influx of Muslim refugees from the ceded lands. Nevertheless, Abdulhamid's reign expanded public works, including highways, railroads, and telegraph lines. Education, literacy, and judicial services improved significantly. In the wake of rising nationalist sentiments and alienated religious and army groups, Abdulhamid was dethroned in 1909 and spent the rest of his life under house arrest.

Abdullah, Sheikh Muhammad (d. 1982) Kashmiri political leader, twice chief minister of Jammu and Kashmir State in India (1948–53, 1975–82) after persuading the Hindu maharaja to opt for belonging to India, not Pakistan, at partition (1947). Deposed and imprisoned by Indian prime minister Jawaharlal Nehru (1953–64) under suspicion of secessionism; restored in 1975 by Indira Gandhi.

Abdulmejid, Sultan (r. 1922–24) Descendant of Ottoman dynasty installed as caliph by Turkish Grand National Assembly, although not acknowledged as sultan. Appointment led to opposition by supporters of the caliphate on the grounds that the division of spiritual and temporal authority contradicted the Islamic theory of state. Sent into exile in 1924 when the Grand National Assembly abolished caliphate.

ABIM Angkatan Belia Islam Malaysia or Malaysian Islamic Youth Movement. Founded in 1972. Major objectives include establishment and propagation of Islamic tenets and principles enshrined in the Quran and Sunnah; spread and defense of the Islamic message, with particular emphasis on its universal dimensions; and mobilization of Muslim youth. Has been critical of the government over issues of corruption, abuse of power, and westernization. Promoted a systematic and comprehensive approach to Islamic propagation that emphasized the relevance and efficacy of Islam in confronting modern problems. Has been the most organized force in Islamic revivalism in Malaysia since the late 1970s. Many ABIM activists have occupied key leadership positions in religious, social, educational, and political arenas, giving it access to the decision-making channels of government and bureaucracy as well as the ability to affect policy directions and the intensification of the Islamic ethos in the country. Most instrumental figure in the party is the former deputy prime minister Anwar Ibrahim. *See also* Ibrahim, Anwar

Ablutions *See* Wudu

Abortion Muslim jurists uniformly hold abortion to be blameworthy but permissible under certain conditions. Ensoulment of the fetus is understood to occur 120 days after conception; after ensoulment, abortion constitutes homicide and requires a juridical punishment. The four Sunni schools of law provide certain rights to the ensouled fetus: the right to be born and live as long as God permits, a right to inheritance, and a right to burial. When a pregnant woman dies, the Shafii tradition mandates that the unborn child be removed in an attempt to save that life. If a pregnant woman is condemned to die, the death sentence must be postponed until after she has given birth. An unborn child cannot inherit while in the womb; the inheritance is held until after the birth. Miscarried and stillborn children are given a name, placed in a white cloth, and buried. *See also* Birth Control/Contraception

Abraha Ruled in sixth-century Yemen on behalf of the Negus of Abyssinia. Attacked Mecca in 570. His assault was, according to the Quran (surah 105), foiled by God, who sent a flock of birds that bombarded his army with clay pellets. The event is important for the traditional dating of Muhammad's birth. *See also* Year of the Elephant

Abraham Arabic Ibrahim. Original monotheist, purifier of God's house, builder of the Kaaba, and first Muslim. Preached against idolatry and sin. Rewarded by God for his faith and given a position of spiritual leadership, to be passed down to his descendants. The Quran records God's covenant with Abraham and his son by Hagar, Ishmael, as well as the covenant with Abraham and his son by Sarah, Isaac. Abraham's faith was so great that he prepared to obey God's command to sacrifice his son. At the last minute, God permitted him to substitute a ram. As father of both Ishmael and Isaac, Abraham is the common ancestor of Jews, Christians, and Muslims.

Abrogation *See* Naskh

Abu Father. Initial part of the nickname or familiar name by which a man is known after becoming a father. Followed by the name of his oldest son or daughter.

Abu al-Tayyib Ahmad ibn al-Husayn *See* Mutanabbi, al-

Abu Bakr, Yasin Leader of radical Black Muslim organization Jamaat al-Muslimin in Trinidad. Led July 1990 storming of the parliament building in Port of Spain, taking the prime minister hostage; demanded government reforms. Reportedly financed by Libyan leader Muammar Qaddafi. *See also* Jamaat al-Muslimin (Trinidad)

Abu Bakr al-Siddiq (r. 632–34) First Sunni caliph, father of Muhammad's wife Aishah, and one of four "rightly guided" caliphs in Sunni Islam. Elected to the caliphate by leaders of the early Muslim community upon Muhammad's death (the caliphate is not recognized by Shiis). Known for egalitarian distribution of the spoils of war. Believed that religious and political leadership of Muslims was the right of the Meccan Companions of Muhammad, rather than Muhammad's family. Unified Arabia. Fought Muslims who refused to pay zakah. Asserted the legitimacy of leadership via adherence to the principles of shura (consultation), aqd (contract between ruler and ruled), and bayah (oath of allegiance), forming the basis for modern theories of Islamic democracy.

Abu Dharr al-Ghifari (d. 652) Companion of the Prophet and subject of modern ideological debate. Shiis emphasize his criticism of the Umayyads and his early liaison with Ali and posit him as an Alid supporter; Sunnis stress his asceticism, piety, and advocacy for the poor. The Egyptian scholar Muhammad Sharqawi called al-Ghifari an ideal Muslim socialist.

Abu Hanifah, al-Numan ibn Thabit ibn Zuta (d. 767) Founder of Hanafi school of Islamic law. Native of Kufa, Iraq, although of Persian descent. Studied jurisprudence under a student of Muhammad's Companion Ibn Masud while working as textile merchant. His training in jurisprudence combined with his experience as a merchant led to his use of reason and logic in applying rules to practical questions of life and broadening those rules through use of analogy (qiyas) and preference (istishan). He emphasized personal reasoning and free judgment in legal interpretation. Reliance on his opinion resulted in his eponymous school being referred to as "People of Opinion," as opposed to "People of Traditions" (those more dependent on hadith). His legal doctrines were noted for their liberality and respect for personal freedom. He was the first jurist to formulate rules pertaining to contracts, such as the price of goods for future deliveries and reselling purchased goods at a higher price provided that usury is not involved. The school of law he founded is the most widespread in the Islamic world.

Abu Hurayrah Companion of Muhammad and important transmitter of hadith. Nickname (meaning "father of the little female cat") given to him by Muhammad due to his affection for his cat. Converted from sun worship to Islam at age thirty. Scholars have noted that hadith he transmitted tended to restrict rights of women and refer to their capacity to cause ritual uncleanliness, leaving them outside the political sphere and often confining them to the home. His hadith figure prominently in prestigious religious texts such as Sahih al-Bukhari despite the fact that they sometimes disagree with hadith transmitted by Muhammad's wife Aishah, particularly on purification rituals.

Abu Jahl (d. 624) Member of the ruling Quraysh of Mecca and one of early Islam's staunchest enemies. Attempted to do physical harm to the Prophet. Name means "father of ignorance/savagery"; his real name was Amr ibn Hisham. Killed in the Battle of Badr.

Abu Lahab Enemy of the Prophet Muhammad, he was the brother of Muhammad's father. Name means "father of fire" and is one of the few Meccan personal names mentioned in the Quran (surah 111), where he and his wife are assured punishment in hell. Died shortly after the Battle of Badr, frustrated by Islam's stunning success.

Abu Muslim al-Khurasani (d. 755) Semilegendary Iranian revolutionary who led the rebellion that toppled the Umayyad caliphate in 750 and brought the Abbasid dynasty to power. A freedman convert using the nom de guerre Abu Muslim, he mobilized Arab and Iranian forces in Khurasan (northeast Iran) and governed there under Abbasid authority until executed by the caliph.

Abu Sayyaf An extremist separatist movement in southern Philippines. Known for cruelty, violence, kidnapping, extortion, and ransom demands. Has targeted foreign tourists in particular. Since spring 2000 it has fought the government over successive hostage takings. Their claim to representing Filipino Muslim interests is now in question. Their ideology is unknown.

Abu Sufyan Wealthy and powerful seventh-century leader of Mecca and tribe of Quraysh. Led caravan that fought and was defeated by forces of Muhammad in the Battle of Badr. Also led forces opposed to and victorious over Muhammad at the Battle of Uhud and those defeated by Muslims at the Battle of the Trench.

Abu Talib (d. ca. 619) Muhammad's uncle, protector, and guardian after the death of his parents. According to tradition, he was present when Muhammad was recognized as a prophet by the Christian monk Bahira. Did not convert to Islam but offered his own protection, as well as that of the Banu Hashim clan, to Muhammad when his preaching was opposed, permitting survival of the early Muslim community.

Abu Ubayda ibn al-Jarrah (d. 639) Companion of the Prophet and one of the ten to whom paradise was promised by him. Played an important role in the election of Abu Bakr as Muhammad's successor, and later led military campaigns in Syria. Said to have been caliph Umar ibn al-Khattab's choice as his successor, but predeceased him.

Abu Yusuf (d. 798) Nickname for Yaqub ibn Ibrahim al-Ansari. Student of legist Abu Hanifah. Spread influence of Hanafi school through his writings and the government positions he held. Appointed judge in Baghdad, later chief justice (qadi al-qudat) under Abbasid caliph Harun al-Rashid with authority to appoint judges in the empire. Some of his opinions differ from those of Abu Hanifah, probably on the basis of traditions not available to the earlier scholar.

His most famous work is *Kitab al-kharaj*, a treatise on taxation and fiscal problems of the state prepared for the caliph. He compiled the earliest known work of principles of Islamic jurisprudence (usul al-fiqh). Portion of work devoted to international law.

Abu Zahra, Muhammad (d. 1974) Conservative Egyptian public intellectual, scholar of Islamic law, and author. Educated at the Ahmadi Madrasa, the Madrasa al-Qada al-Shari, and the Dar al-Ulum, he taught at al-Azhar's faculty of theology and later, as professor of Islamic law, at Cairo University. He also served as a member of al-Azhar's Academy of Islamic Research. His more than forty books include biographies of Abu Hanifah, Malik, Shafii, Ibn Hanbal, Zayd ibn Ali, Jafar al-Sadiq, Ibn Hazm, and Ibn Taymiyyah, as well as works on personal status, pious endowments (waqf), property, and crime and punishment in Islamic law.

Aceh Province of Indonesia in northern Sumatra. Some historians believe that Islam first came to Indonesia through Aceh in approximately the ninth century and that Aceh was the site of the first Muslim sultanate in the islands. It became a regional power in the seventeenth and eighteenth centuries but was conquered by the Dutch at the beginning of the twentieth century after a lengthy war. After Indonesia declared its independence in 1945 the Acehnese frequently challenged the republic's legitimacy and continue to demand autonomy or independence. Approximately 98 percent of Acehnese are Muslims and are known for their strong devotion to Islam.

Ad The name of a people frequently mentioned in the Quran to whom a prophet had been sent by God and whose disobedience to God's law brought about their extinction. Their arrogance, materialism, and attitude toward their prophet are compared with that of Muhammad's own tribe, the Quraysh.

Adab Medieval anecdotal form of prose designed to be both edifying and entertaining.

Can include Quranic verses, poetry, and the traditions of Muhammad (hadith). Often written in the form of manuals for behavior, protocol, conducting affairs of state, and carrying out the duties of office with advice embedded in tales and anecdotes about rulers, judges, misers, and other characters. The word *adab* thus also came to mean "proper conduct and etiquette." Initially a Persian genre, it was synthesized with Arabic literature in the ninth century, reflecting the expansion of the Islamic empire and borrowing from other cultures. The greatest master of Arabic adab was the ninth-century writer al-Jahiz. In contemporary Arabic, *adab* refers to literature in general. *See also* Tarbiyyah

Adab al-Tabib *See* Bioethics

Adalet Partisi *See* Justice Party

Adam First human being. Created to be God's vicegerent (steward) on earth. The Quran records Adam's fall from grace as the result of disobedience to God's commands but, unlike Christian tradition, the fall carries no accompanying "original sin" passed down to all mankind. God forgave Adam when he repented and turned away from disbelief.

Adat Customs, accepted practice. The functional equivalent of urf (sing., pl. *araf*); a known, common usage. No consensus exists in Islamic jurisprudence regarding the place of adat/urf as a source of law. The Quran directs believers to use socially accepted practices in organizing details pertaining to a variety of legal issues (e.g., dowry sums, settling certain financial obligations). While generally scholars insisted that customs were not a fundamental source of jurisprudence, fiqh relied heavily on adat/urf to formulate cultural rules (e.g., dress, mannerisms). In time many pre-Islamic beliefs and worship practices were also adopted without reference to primary sources. The reliance on adat/urf in law is highly contested by reformers. Some reformers associate custom with being reactionary, while others see it as a necessary instrument for achieving public interest. *See also* Urf

Adhan Ritual call to prayer. Consists of three iterations of "God is the greatest" followed by two repetitions each of "I witness that there is no god but God," "I witness that Muhammad is the messenger of God," "Come to prayer," "Come to prosperity," and "God is the greatest." At the end, "There is no god but God" is repeated.

Adil Düzen A central program (the name means "just order") of Turkey's Welfare Party. Consists of a secure social and economic environment, the protection of state property, an end to nepotism and corruption, cooperation between state and society to cope with poverty, and an end to undue Western influence over Turkey. The Welfare Party was banned in 1998. *See also* Welfare Party

Adl wa'l-Hasan, al- *See* Yasin, Abd al-Salam

Adoption Formal adoption is forbidden by the Quran (33:4–5), which calls for children to carry their own names since children need to know their origins. Adopted children cannot legally inherit under Islamic law. However, informal adoption, known as "embracing the child," exists, enabling Muslims to bestow monetary gifts upon such children during their lifetime.

Aesthetics Arabic *ilm al-jamal*. Until modern times there has been no systematic Islamic theory of aesthetics or of fine arts, although historically poetry, music, and the visual arts often demonstrate commonly held ideals of beauty based on rules of poesy, harmony, or ideal form. Aesthetic concepts such as unity, harmony, symmetry, spirituality, ideal form, and rationality often appear in Islamic critical writing, although without a systematic philosophical approach.

Afghani, Jamal al-Din al- (d. 1897) Thinker and political activist. Born and raised in Iran, although claimed to be of Afghan origin. Educated in Iran and Iraq. Traveled to India, where he came into contact with British colonialism. Lived in Afghanistan, Istanbul, and Egypt but was expelled due to his anti-British stance and supposedly heretical teachings. Returned to India, where he wrote his most famous works. With Muhammad Abduh, published the influential journal *Al-urwah al-wuthqa* (The strongest bond), emphasizing pan-Islamism and the need for active opposition to British rule in Muslim lands. Advocated Sunni-Shii unity. Believed in reason and natural law, although he preached orthodox religion for the masses. Stressed the need for internal reform and self-improvement, particularly technical and scientific education. One of the first modern politically activist reformist Muslim figures to use Islam to promote a primarily political program; his political activism included public speeches, newspaper articles, use of the Masonic lodge for political purposes, opposition to foreign concessions, formation of secret opposition organizations, publication of leaflets, and participation in the assassination of the Iranian king. Remains popular in the Muslim world today due to his political activism, emphasis on Muslim solidarity against the Christian and imperial West, and modernist, pragmatic, and anti-imperialist reinterpretation of Islam. *See also* Osmania University

Afghanistan, Islam in Approximately 88 percent of modern-day Afghanistan's population is Sunni; 12 percent is Shii. Islam arrived in the eighth century during the expansion of the Islamic empire. Various rulers have legitimized their rule based on protection of Islam and personal piety. From the 1920s until the 1970s Afghanistan was dependent upon the Soviet Union. Communist parties were supported, and Islam was restricted to rituals and legal injunctions. The Communist government ruled 1978–92 after a Soviet-sponsored coup d'etat, resulting in a crackdown on Islamist movements, which became the opposition. During Communist rule Islamists emerged among university faculty and students who sought an Islamic state; they joined with traditional tribal and religious leaders to form the mujahidin and fought a nationwide jihad to drive out the Soviets (achieved in 1989) and Afghan Communists. An Islamic state was declared in 1992. The country then fell into bloody interethnic and sectarian warfare. The Islamist movement split from within; two major factions were led by Burhanuddin Rabbani and Gulbuddin Hekmatyar and were funded by Pakistan and Iran. Continued corruption and disorder in the country led to the takeover of Kabul by the Taliban in 1996. The Taliban consolidated control over approximately 90 percent of Afghanistan and placed the country under an extremist interpretation of Islam, including strict enforcement of segregation of sexes, full veiling in the burqa for women, a prohibition against women working outside the home or seeking education, and destruction of idols, such as the fifth-century Buddha statues destroyed in 2000. *See also* Durrani Dynasty

AFIC *See* Australian Federation of Islamic Councils

Aflaton *See* Plato

African-Americans *See* Nation of Islam; America, Islam in

African Islamic Center *See* National Islamic Front (Sudan)

Afsharid Dynasty Of Turkic origin, the Afsharids ruled Iran 1736–96; at its zenith, the dynasty stretched from Iraq to northern India. Founder Nadir Shah Afshar (r. 1736–47), backed by an army of mostly Sunni Afghans, routed the armies of the Shii Safavid dynasty. Nominally Shii, Nadir Shah forced compromises between Shii and Sunni religious leaders in order to legitimize his claims to Mughal India and Ottoman Iraq. The Shii ulama agreed to renounce explicitly anti-Sunni practices, and the Sunni ulama agreed to acknowledge certain precepts of Shii law. Nadir Shah's religious and political

attempts to eradicate Shii Safavid tradition ultimately failed.

Afterlife In Islam, one's condition in the afterlife, whether in heaven or hell, is determined by the degree to which one has affirmed the unity and justice of God, acted with mercy and justice toward others, and been ethically responsible. Heaven will be achieved by those who have faith in God's revelations and have lived out that faith through their good works and moral conduct. Unbelievers and evildoers will be punished eternally in hell. Every individual will be held accountable for his or her own actions on the Day of Judgment. In the twentieth century, discussions about the afterlife address the interconnection between human action and divine judgment, the need for moral rectitude, and the eternal consequences of human action in this life and world. *See also* Day of Judgment; Heaven; Hell

Afwaj al-Muqawamah al-Lubnaniyah *See* AMAL

Aga Khan Title of the Nizari Ismaili imams since Hasan Ali Shah (d. 1881). The Aga Khan represents direct lineal descent and succession from the first Shii imam, Ali, and his wife Fatimah, Muhammad's daughter. The present imam, Prince Karim al-Husayni, is the forty-ninth hereditary imam of the worldwide Nizari Ismaili community. *See also* Assassins; Ismailis; Khojas; Nizaris

Aga Khan Award for Architecture Established in 1977 by the Aga Khan to enhance the understanding and appreciation of Islamic culture as expressed through architecture. It seeks out and recognizes examples of architectural excellence that successfully address the needs of societies in which Muslims have a significant presence. *See also* Aga Khan

Aga Khan Foundation A private philanthropic institution founded by the Aga Khan in 1967 to provide "the Muslim ethic of care and compassion for those of society in greatest need" and to address economic and social needs through Islamic ideals and ethics. Funding is provided by the Aga Khan, the Nizari Ismaili community, international and local donor agencies, foundations, and individuals. Since its inception, the Aga Khan Foundation has become a recognized international development agency with programs in Asia, Europe, Africa, and North America. Headquartered in Geneva, the foundation has three major foci: health, education, and rural development. *See also* Aga Khan

Agha In Algeria, chief officer of the Janissaries, who eventually undermined Ottoman-appointed provincial governors. In 1659 the Agha became the ruler of Algeria. Tribute was sent to Istanbul, but Algeria remained independent.

Aghlabids Hereditary Islamic dynasty of the ninth and early tenth centuries in North Africa, centered in Qayrawan. Came to power in 800 when Ibrahim ibn Aghlab, governor for the Abbasid caliph Haroun al-Rashid, quelled Khariji uprisings. He was rewarded with relative independence in exchange for tribute. Independence eventually grew, and Aghlabid territory extended into Sicily, Malta, and southern Italy. Qayrawan became an important crossroads of commercial and intellectual activity, the center of Maliki jurisprudence, and home to an outstanding mosque. Aghlabids also constructed many forts and waterways. Their sovereignty ended in 909 when the Ismaili leader al-Mahdi and a coalition of Berbers conquered the Maghreb, establishing the Fatimid dynasty.

Ahd Covenant or compact, as in agreement or swearing of allegiance. Describes various relationships between early Muslims and other groups with whom they were allied. Also used by Sufis as part of the initiation ceremony into a Sufi order. In orders where a shaykh is intended to be the intercessor between God and the order initiate, ahd is sworn to give allegiance to that shaykh alone. Actions accompanying ahd typically consist of swearing of obedience, handclasp with the shaykh patterned after Muhammad's practice, and investiture of the initiate with the habit of the order. Upon declaration of ahd, the initiate is instructed in his responsibilities.

Ahidjo, Ahmadou Muslim premier (1958) and president (1960–82) of Cameroon. Founded Union Camerounaise in 1958, combining five small, predominantly Muslim political groups from the north. Initiated an affirmative action program aimed at underprivileged areas of the country; the north was the major beneficiary of government development programs. Departed from office suddenly. Implicated in coup attempts of 1984.

Ahl al-Adl wa'l-Tawhid *See* Mutazilis

Ahl al-Bayt People of the house, or Muhammad's family and descendants. Shiis are particularly devoted to the Prophet's family, believing that they embody special holiness, spiritual power, and knowledge due to their blood relationship to Muhammad. However, Sunnis also revere the family of the Prophet. The phrase is often associated with both Shii descendants (sayyids) and Sunni descendants (sharifs).

Ahl al-Hadith People of the traditions (of the Prophet). Also *ashab al-hadith*. The characterization refers to the adherents of the powerful movement of the late second and third centuries of Islam (late eighth and ninth centuries C.E.) that insisted on the authority of the traditions (hadith) attributed to the Prophet Muhammad, as against the informed "opinions" (ray) on which many contemporary juristic schools based their legal reasoning. This movement played a critical role in the emergence of Sunni Islam.

Ahl al-Hall wa'l-Aqd Those qualified to elect or depose a caliph on behalf of the Muslim community. In medieval political theory, the term refers to legal scholars whose task it was to offer the caliphate to the most qualified person. Because, in practice, most rulers designated their successors, the task was generally a mere formality.

Some modern thinkers have tried to accommodate this task to that of a parliament.

Ahl al-Kitab Quranic term referring to Jews, Christians, and Sabaeans as possessors of books previously revealed by God. Sometimes applied to Zoroastrians, Magians, and Samaritans. The books associated with Jews and Christians are the Torah, Psalms, and Gospels, all of which are recognized by the Quran as God's revelation, although the Quran declares that they were abrogated and superseded by Muhammad's book since they were corrupted. The Quran recognizes the special relationship of Jews with God and grants both Jews and Christians a special legal status in Muslim communities as dhimmis (protected scriptural minorities), permitting them to practice their faith, defend themselves from external aggressions, and govern their own communities in return for paying a special tax (jizyah). Many twentieth-century scholars are concerned that dhimmis enjoy only second-class citizenship in Muslim states. Some modern thinkers call for recognition of the ties binding the People of the Book together as a means of promoting interfaith dialogue and cooperation. *See also* Dhimmi

Ahl al-Quran Nineteenth-century Indian movement led by Abdullah Chakralavi. Advocated total reliance on the Quran as the perfect source of guidance. Taught that Muslims were free to decide on matters not covered by the Quran. Opposed to the Ahl-i Hadith movement of the same time, which emphasized reliance on hadith over the Quran. *See also* Ahl al-Hadith

Ahl al-Sunnah wa'l-Jamaah People of the Prophet's Way and the Community. Also known as Barelvis and Barelwis. Founded in northern India in 1880s, based on the writings of Mawlana Ahmad Reza Khan Barelwi. Believe themselves South Asia's heirs and representatives of the earliest Muslim community. Triggered by the failure of the Indian revolt of 1857 and the subsequent formal colonization of India by the British, which led to the final dissolution of the Mughal Empire. Emerged as part of the religious debate among Islamic legal scholars as to how Muslim identity and action should be used to redeem India. Emphasizes primacy of Islamic law over adherence to Sufi practices and personal devotion to the Prophet Muhammad. Since partition of India and Pakistan in 1947, has addressed leading political issues for Muslims. Largely rural phenomenon when begun, but currently popular among urban, educated Pakistanis and Indians. *See also* India, Islam in; Pakistan, Islam in

Ahl-i Hadith Offshoot of nineteenth-century Indian Tariqah-i Muhammadiyyah movement. Tied to the tradition of Shah Wali Allah and the eighteenth-century Wahhabi movement. Favors direct use of Islamic sources and exercise of ijtihad (independent reasoning), rather than following schools of law (taqlid). Heavy reliance on hadith and "concealed" revelation contained within led to polemical war with Ahl al-Quran, a countergroup that advocated total reliance on the Quran as the perfect source of guidance. Reportedly had two thousand local branches and two million adherents in Bangladesh in the mid-1980s. Particularly prominent in the north. Avoids exclusive, sectlike behavior and is open to relationships with Muslims of other persuasions. *See also* Ahl al-Quran

Ahl-i Haqq People of the truth. Also known as Ali Ilahis, "deifiers of Ali." Members of a sect centered in northwest Iran, incorporating certain Shii and Sufi ideas, associated with Sultan Sohak (fourteenth or fifteenth century). Believe in seven successive incarnations of God, hierarchy of angels, metempsychosis, no single primary scripture. Resemble Sufi dervishes in some practices, such as dhikr sessions, master-disciple relations, and initiation rites.

Ahmad, Israr (b. 1932) Founder amir of Tanzeem-i Islami (Islamic Organization). Born in the Indian Punjab; graduated from King Edward Medical College, Lahore, in 1954. Joined the Jamaat-i Islami–affiliated student organization Islami Jamyat-e Talaba and served as its president. Joined the

Jamaat-i Islami but resigned in 1957 because of the Jamaat's decision to participate in democratic elections, which, he believed, was antithetical to the "revolutionary methodology" of Islam. Popular for his Quranic lectures. Believes that Islamic renaissance is possible only by revitalizing iman (faith), which can come from reflecting on the wisdom of the Quran. Founded several Islamic organizations, including Tanzeem-i Islami (1975) and Tahreek-i Khilafat (1991). Author of over sixty tracts and books on Islamic topics in Urdu. Believes that reforming society according to Quranic principles will lead to the reestablishment of the Islamic khilafah (caliphate).

Ahmad, Jalal al-e (d. 1969) Iranian writer and social critic, noted for his polemical booklet *Gharbzadegi* (Westoxification), published in 1962, the title of which became a popular term expressing anti-Western sentiment. Criticized Iranian secular reformists for having passively subscribed to Western cultural values and political theories. Further prescribed that Iran, as part of the Muslim world, should rely more confidently on its own traditional heritage, including religious identity. Made an early break with his family's Shii clerical tradition that was marked by a short-lived association with the pro-Soviet Tudeh Party. Viewed as important to the alliance of the left and Shii clerics that led to the Iranian revolution.

Ahmad, Khurshid (b. 1932) Pakistani Islamic scholar, activist, and economist who attempted to develop Islamic economics using Quranic value patterns to provide an alternative to capitalism and socialism. Teaches that social responsibility takes precedence over individual rights. Proposes cooperation and mutual obligations, rather than competition. Promotes human resource development as an objective of economic policy. Critical of West but recognizes the importance of science and technology. A lifelong follower of Mawlana Abul Ala Mawdudi and translator of his major works into English. Served as minister of planning in the military regime of General Zia-ul-Haq. Founding chairman of the Islamic Founda-

tion, Leicester (UK), Institute of Policy Studies, Islamabad, and vice president of the Jamaat-i Islami Pakistan. Was a member of Pakistan's senate.

Ahmad, Qazi Husayn (b. 1938) Leader of Jamaat-i Islami of Pakistan since 1987. Born into a Pathan family of Deobandi ulama. Joined the Jamaat in 1970. In the 1980s played an important role in Pakistan's Afghan policy, especially by creating ties between the Jamaat and Gulbuddin Hekmatyar's Hizb-i Islami. After 1987 pushed to popularize the Jamaat's message by adopting populist causes, downplaying ideological posturing in favor of pragmatic politics, and introducing new electoral strategies. Responsible for forging Jamaat's links with Muslim resistance movements in Kashmir, Bosnia, Palestine, and Chechnya.

Ahmad Khan, Sayyid (d. 1898) Indian Islamic modernist writer, educationist, and political activist. He promoted an Indian Muslim nationalism that gave rise to the All-India Muslim League. Writings emphasized a rational approach to Islam and modern education for Muslims. Founder of the Aligarh Mohammadan Anglo-Oriental College (now Aligarh Muslim University). In recognition of his accomplishments, the British government knighted him in 1888. *See also* Aligarh; Muslim League

Ahmad Reza Khan, Mawlana *See* Barelwi, Sayyid Ahmad Reza Khan

Ahmadis Controversial messianic movement founded by Mirza Ghulam Ahmad in Qadian, Punjab (British-controlled India), in 1889. Founder claimed to be a "nonlegislating" prophet (thus not in opposition to the mainstream belief in the finality of Muhammad's "legislative" prophecy) with a divine mandate for the revival and renewal of Islam. Dedicated to peaceful propagation of faith, production of literature, and establishment of mosques and missionary centers. Rejected by the majority of Muslims as heretical since it believes in ongoing prophethood after the death of Muhammad. Currently based in

Pakistan, but forbidden to practice, preach, or propagate their faith as Islam or their places of worship as mosques. Consists of two factions: Qadiani and Lahori (who stress Ghulam Ahmad's claim to be a "renewer" of the faith rather than a prophet). Current head, Mirza Tahir Ahmad, resides in London. *See also* Ghulam Ahmad, Mirza

Ahmed, Akbar Twentieth-century Pakistani Islamic scholar. Understands fundamentalism through the context of postmodernity, globalization, failure of modernist ideologies, revival of ethnic conflicts, and conflict between Islam and the West. Believes the greatest challenge facing Muslims is the preservation of Muslim identity and Quranic messages of tolerance, equality, and love of knowledge.

Ahmed Shahid, Sayyid *See* Barelwi, Sayyid Ahmad Reza Khan

Ahsai, Shaykh Ahmad (d. 1826) Theologian and founder of Shaykhi branch of Twelver Shiism. Born in Bahrain. Known for mystical experiences and spiritual visions. Spent fifteen years in Iran, where he was highly esteemed by the Qajar rulers. Opposed by many ulama. Doctrine of spiritual resurrection only, rather than physical, led to his forced departure for Mecca. Influenced by the Akhbari school and the teachings of Mullah Sadra and his disciples. Stressed the importance of the Shii traditions of the Twelve Imams. Believed that he had a special revelatory mission as the singular spokesperson for the Imam in Occultation. *See also* Akhbaris; Shaykhis; Shii Islam

Aishah Daughter of first caliph, Abu Bakr; youngest and reputedly favorite wife of Muhammad. With Muhammad when he died. Renowned for knowledge of medicine, history, and rhetoric. Important transmitter of hadith. When she was accused of adultery, Muhammad received a revelation vindicating her of the charges. She opposed Ali's bid for the caliphate and led her forces against Ali's in the Battle of the Camel but lost. Because this was first time one Muslim army opposed another, this incident is often cited by conservatives as proof that women should be kept out of politics.

Aisyiyah Auxiliary of the Indonesian Muhammadiyyah movement, named after the Prophet's wife Aishah and concerned with women's affairs. Founded in 1914 and originally named Sapa Tresno (those who love), the association's objective was to spread Islam among women. The Aisyiyah has built numerous women's mosques, kindergartens, and schools. *See also* Muhammadiyyah

Ajal The appointed time of death that Muslims believe God has determined for every individual; cannot be delayed or hastened. General linguistic usage can refer to other times established by God, such as the moment of birth, the precision of lunar and solar phases, and the Day of Judgment.

Ajam People unable to speak properly. Refers to non-Arabs. Connotes cultural and ethnic inferiority. Adjectival form: *ajami*. Principally used to designate (and eventually synonymous with) Persians.

Ajami *See* Ajam

Ajmer City in the Rajasthan state of northwestern India. Founded around 1100, it became an important center of trade and a military base during the Muslim Mughal rule in India. It hosts the mausoleum of the most important Muslim saint of India, Muin al-Din Muhammad Chishti (d. 1236), the founder of the Chishti Sufi order, and the palace of Akbar, the most celebrated of all the Mughal kings who ruled India from 1556 to 1605. Chishti's tomb in Ajmer, visited by Akbar on foot, remains to this day one of the most crowded centers of pilgrimage in l..dia.

Akbar I, Abu al-Fath Jalal al-Din Muhammad (r. 1556–1605) First great Mughal emperor. Upon his father Humayun's death, the adolescent Akbar, third in the Timurid line, conquered and diplomatically integrated all but south India. Initially claiming ideological legitimation by applying Islamic law, leading prayer, and honoring the Sufi shaykh Muin al-Din Chishti, he later perfected absolute power and subjugated the religious scholars. Repealing the tax paid by non-Muslims and including non-Muslims throughout his administration and the military, Akbar established an enduring, indigenously rooted state that nurtured a unique Islamic civilization in South Asia. Some of his administrative and revenue systems were later adopted by the British.

Akhbar Reports. In Shii Islam, rulings of the early imams in the form of hadith, which were systematically compiled and consulted as a source of law. *See also* Hadith

Akhbaris Twelfth-century Twelver Shii school of thought in Iran. Stressed the literal interpretation of the Quran and hadith of both Muhammad and the Twelve Imams as a source of religious authority. Restricted the authority of individual scholars for interpretation, declared ijtihad (independent reasoning) an unsound and unnecessary innovation, and denied the role of the mujtahid (practitioner of ijtihad) in guiding Shii society. Saw the role of ulama as a matter of reviewing fundamental sources for answers to problems, rather than developing new solutions. Became the dominant school in intellectual studies in Shii holy cities. Engaged in major debate with Usulis, who accorded greater authority to mujtahids and interpretion of law according to individual reasoning. *See also* Usulis

Akhirah *See* Afterlife

Akhlaq *See* Ethics

Akhund A word of disputed etymology, generally accepted to mean "religious leader." In Pahlavi Iran (1925–79), the word came to have a pejorative connotation; in the government-sanctioned press there, the term was applied to those who were anachronistic and opposed to modernization. *See also* Mullah

Alam World. Worlds spoken of in the Quran refer to the realms of the three species of rational creatures: humans, jinn, and angels.

Alamut Name of a mountain fortress in northern Iran. Situated about forty-five kilometers northeast of the city of Qazwin, Alamut was built on the summit of an inaccessible rock in the central Alborz mountains. According to legend, an eagle indicated the site to a Daylami ruler, whence its name in the Daylami dialect, derived from *aloh* (eagle) and *amukht* (taught). The fortress was constructed by a Justanid ruler of Daylam in 860. Subsequently the area came under the influence of Zaydi Alid rulers. The Ismaili leader Hasan-i Sabbah seized the fortress in 1090 and made it the headquarters of his Nizari Ismaili state. The fortress became the focal point of Sabbah's challenge to Seljuk authority in Iran. It became infamous for its assassins. The Mongols took Alamut in 1256 and partially demolished it, also burning its famous library. It was restored under the Safavids, who used it as a prison until the seventeenth century. After that Alamut was abandoned, and it was gradually destroyed by the elements and local inhabitants searching for treasures. *See also* Nizaris; Sabbah, Hasan-i

Alawi, Abu Abbas Ahmad ibn Mustafa al- (d. 1934) Algerian Sufi and poet. Joined the Darqawi tariqah during a period of intense French colonization. By 1916, established an independent Sufi order. Denounced westernization, secularism, modernization, and Algerians who accepted French citizenship. Authored fifteen works on Sufism and poetry.

Alawi, Mawlay Muhammad ibn al-Arabi al- (d. 1964) Moroccan reformist, educator, and opponent of the French colonial regime. Major figure in the spread of the Salafi reform movement, which was opposed to popular religion. Supported Arabic and Islamic education, encouraging the development of Moroccan nationalism. Opposed to the religious practices of Sufi tariqahs cooperating with the colonial government.

Nationalists translated this into religious opposition to the Christian colonial regime. Student of Abu Shuayb al-Dukkali.

Alawi Dynasty Also known as Filalis or Filalians. Family of religious notables who became the royal house of Morocco from the seventeenth century through the present. Claim descent from Muhammad. Migrated from the Arabian Peninsula to southeastern Morocco in the thirteenth century. Financed jihad against Christian holdings along the Atlantic and Mediterranean coasts in the seventeenth century. Adhere to Sunni interpretation of Islam. Assert role as interpreters of shariah and are strong supporters of Islamic scholarship and education.

Alawis Secretive Shii school of thought located in a mountain range in northwestern Syria. Believe in the absolute oneness of God and that God appeared on earth seven times in human form with Ali as the last manifestation. Interpret the Quran and hadith allegorically, emphasizing good and evil, symbolized by light and darkness. Celebrate both Muslim and Christian festivals. Also known as Nusayris, after their founder Muhammad ibn Nusayr, a ninth-century follower of the eleventh Shii imam.

Alawite See Alawis

Alawiyyah See Alawi Dynasty; Alawis

Albania, Islam in Albania was part of the Ottoman Empire and is the only European country with a Muslim majority. It is home to 800 mosques and 360 Bektashi Sufi holy places. The head of the Bektashi Sufi order reestablished his headquarters there in 1928 when he was expelled from Turkey. Islamic religious leaders were persecuted and killed under the Communist regime, and the state was declared officially atheist in 1967, resulting in the closure and destruction of mosques and churches and a ban on wearing religious symbols. The ban was lifted in 1990, leading to the return of religious worship, rededication of mosques, and display of religious works of art. Muslim missionary

organizations and charities have provided funds to restore mosques and promote Islam, but unrest among Muslims in Kosovo and disturbances within the country have made the restoration of normal religious life difficult. See also Kosovo, Islam in

Alchemy Arabic *ilm al-kimiyah*. The science of alchemy combined occult practices, such as the transformation of the spirit, with scientific concerns and methodologies, but retained a strong technological dimension. These included the preparation of compounds and chemical products, chemical operations such as distillation and crystallization, and the invention of technical apparatus for laboratory use. Most of the known works of alchemy, including those of Jabir ibn Hayyan (eighth century) and Abu Bakr al-Razi (ninth century), contain considerable sections on practical chemistry. This aspect of the practice of alchemy in Muslim societies characterizes it as the precursor to the modern science of chemistry. See also Razi, Abu Bakr Muhammad ibn Zakariyya, al-

Alcoholic Beverages See Intoxicants

Alevis See Alawis

Alexander the Great (d. 334 B.C.E.) Arabic *al-Iskandar*. Conqueror of Egypt and the Persian Achaemenid Empire and founder of cities. Often identified with Dhu al-Qarnayn, "the two-horned" of the Quran (18:83–94), who figures prominently in Muslim eschatology by serving the cause of the righteous. Considered a Muslim believer and by some a prophet.

Algeria, Islam in Ottoman Algeria enjoyed strong traditions of religious and political autonomy, and it took the French fifty-two years to conquer the country (1830–82). The combination of French colonial policies and indigenous population increase impoverished the traditional rural population and created a new urban society. Upon Algeria's independence (1962), the country was poor and overwhelmingly rural. One million Algerians (out of nine million) had died in the fight for independence; two million were homeless. The National Liberation Front (FLN) established industrialization and education programs, but the state-controlled economy stagnated due to low oil prices in the 1980s. In response to widespread riots, the FLN instituted multiparty elections (1988), and the Islamic Salvation Front (FIS) became the strongest challenger of the FLN, demanding the establishment of an Islamic state and economic privatization. The military intervened and invalidated the election results. The FIS was outlawed in 1992. A constitutional revision (1996) yielded a bicameral parliament: the National People's Assembly (380 seats; elected by popular vote; members serve four-year terms) and the Council of Nations (144 seats; the president appoints one-third, indirect vote elects two-thirds; members serve six-year terms). In the 1997 elections the overwhelming majority of seats elected were from the Democratic National Rally (RND), whose chairman is Mohamed Benbaibeche. *See also* Islamic Salvation Front

Algerian People's Party *See* Parti du Peuple Algérien

Alhambra Al-Qasr al-Hamra, "red castle," fourteenth-century palace of the Nasrid dynasty in Granada, Spain. Set atop the Sabikah hill along with the Alcazaba fortress and the Generalife gardens, the surviving parts of the palace include the famous Court of the Lions and the Court of the Myrtles.

Alhamdu Lillah Praise be to God. Used in everyday speech as expression of thanks and praise for something good that has happened.

Alhazen *See* Ibn al-Haytham, Abu Ali al-Hasan

Ali, Shaukat Co-leader of the Indian Khilafat movement and the Society for the Servants of the Kaaba, uniting Muslims in defense of Mecca, Medina, and Jerusalem during World War I. Resisted British colonial regime's division of the Indian population along confessional lines. As leader of the Muslim League, emphasized pan-Islamic themes and cooperation with the Indian National Congress.

Ali ibn Abi Talib (d. 660) Cousin and son-in-law of Muhammad, fourth caliph of Sunni Muslims, and first imam of Shii Muslims. First male convert to Islam and second convert after Muhammad's wife Khadijah. Married Muhammad's daughter Fatimah. Father of sons Hasan and Husayn and daughters Zaynab and Umm Kulthum. Participated in most expeditions during Muhammad's lifetime. Distinguished judge, pious believer, and brave warrior. Shiis believe that he was appointed by Muhammad as successor (the appointment is celebrated as the Festival of Ghadir on 18 Dhu al-Hijjah) and place him next to God and Muhammad as the center of religious belief. Sunnis acknowledge him only as the fourth caliph. His rule as caliph was marked by political crisis and civil strife. Assassinated while praying in a mosque in 660. Ali serves as the paradigm for political activism for redress of social and political injustices for the downtrodden. His political discourse, sermons, letters, and sayings have served as the Shii framework for Islamic government.

Ali Ilahis *See* Ahl-i Haqq

Alids In early Islam, those who contended that only a member of the Prophet's clan of Hashim (descendants of Ali) should rule and that political legitimacy lay in genealogy; the Shii community. Others, such as the Umayyads, held that consensus of the Muslim community was necessary to establish a legitimate claim to head the Islamic community. Alids fomented numerous uprisings in the last years of Umayyad rule (661–750). By the late eighth century, some Shiis had developed the imamate concept, which held that only an Alid could rightfully claim leadership of the Muslim community.

Aligarh Large town in western India associated with major Muslim educational, political, and ideological movements since the late nineteenth century. Headquarters of Aligarh Scientific Society and Mohammadan Anglo-Oriental College (Aligarh Muslim University), both of which were established to make contemporary European education available to a primarily Muslim public.

Aligarh Muslim University Established in 1920 by Sayyid Ahmad Khan as the Mohammadan Anglo-Oriental College to educate Indian Muslims in contemporary European disciplines and Islamic heritage. Many students became prominent government officials, lawyers, and journalists in the early twentieth century. Served as an arena for social and political controversy and as the center of Indian nationalism. *See also* Ahmad Khan, Sayyid

Alim *See* Ulama: Shii; Ulama: Sunni

Alimony *See* Nafaqah

Al-Khoei Benevolent Foundation Established in the late 1980s in the name of Ayatollah Abol-Qassem al-Khoi (d. 1992), marja al-taqlid (authority to be followed) for the majority of Shii Muslims worldwide and superintendent of their religious assets, to provide Islamic education through religious centers and institutions, engage in humanitarian activities, and supervise religious endowments and assets throughout the world. The foundation was set up in New York so that his governance over these assets would be recognized by Western law. Its two major administrative branches are in New York and London. Upon his death, the assets became treated as pious endowments (waqfs) to be supervised by appointed trustees in various countries. The foundation today is managed by businessmen who have registered it as a nonprofit corporation that solicits, raises, accepts, holds, administers, invests, and reinvests funds and other property. Its objective is the representation of Shii interests worldwide, but all goals are defined and executed by the board. Ceremonial patrons since al-Khoi's death have tended to be successors to the position of marja al-taqlid.

Allah God. Worshiped by Muslims, Christians, and Jews to the exclusion of all others. Revealed Himself in the Quran, which is self-described as His book. Defined in the Quran as creator, sustainer, judge, and ruler of the material universe and the realm of human experience. Has guided history through the prophets Abraham (with whom He made a covenant), Moses, Jesus, and Muhammad, through all of whom He founded His chosen communities, People of the Book (ahl al-kitab). The Quran asserts God's omnipotence but allows for human free will. Worshiped at the Kaaba in Mecca as "high god" over all other gods prior to rise of Islam. Only god in Mecca not represented by idol. Muhammad called Muslims not only to belief in or worship of Allah but also to exclusion of all other deities, forbidding their association (shirk) with Allah. The Quran lists ninety-nine names for Allah, defining His attributes, such as merciful (Rahman) and compassionate (Rahim). Muslims developed the science of theology (kalam) to investigate the nature, attributes, and operations of God. Many theologians hold that these attributes are metaphorical rather than real, since comparison of God to human beings is strictly forbidden due to fears of associationism. Some early Sufis sought union with God as the purpose of mystical experiences.

Allahu Akbar God is greater. Phrase, known as takbir, that implies God is greater than anything that can be named. Part of the call to prayer. Used as a slogan and as a chant in political rallies and for religious causes.

All-India Mohammedan Educational Conference Forum organized from 1886 through 1937 by Sayyid Ahmad Khan to promote modern education among Muslims and Muslim nationalism geared toward separation from India. Opposed to the All-India National Conference. Eventually gave rise to the All-India Muslim League, which spearheaded the movement for the creation of Pakistan. *See also* Ahmad Khan, Sayyid

All-India Muslim League *See* Muslim League

All-Indonesian Association of Muslim Intellectuals *See* ICMI

All-Malaysia Muslim Welfare Association *See* PERKIM

Almohads (r. 1130–1269) Also known as al-Muwahhidun, or Unitarians. Movement begun in southern Morocco by Muhammad ibn Abdullah ibn Tumart. Preached moral reform, supremacy of the Quran and hadith, and tawhid. Rejected authority of law schools, anthropomorphism, adoption of pagan Berber customs, consumption of wine, music, and luxurious clothing. Sought to restore early Islamic community. Used Islam to legitimate new political elites and unify tribes. Political regime consisted of a leader advised by a council of ten disciples, which in turn was advised by an assembly of fifty tribal delegates. Religious administration included a keeper of morals, muezzins, and Quran instructors. Conquered Morocco, influenced part of Spain, and invaded Algeria and Tunisia.

Almoravids (r. 1046–1157) Also known as al-Murabitun (those bound by allegiance to the cause of defending the faith). Coalition of Western Saharan Berbers united by religious doctrine and leadership. Spread forcibly into Spain and Morocco. Major teacher was Abdallah ibn Yasin. Focused on the Quran, hadith, and Maliki law. Preached a message of repentance, strict discipline, reinstatement of Quranic legal penalties, and warnings about the Last Day. Taught internal and external jihad. Closed taverns, destroyed musical instruments, enforced Islamic law in distributing war booty, and abolished taxes not prescribed by Islamic law. Opposed to Sufism and theology. Laid the foundation for the flowering of North African civilization through patronage of scribes, poets, philosophers, and architects.

Almsgiving *See* Zakah

Alp Arslan, Adud al-Dawlah Abu al-Shuja Second Seljuk Turkish sultan (r. 1063–72/3). United the region from Syria to Iran and developed its administration under the grand vizier Nizam al-Mulk. His 1071 defeat of the Byzantines at Manzikert and his threat to Jerusalem (captured that year by Turkish raiders) provoked the Crusades and opened Anatolia to Turkish settlement.

Amal Arabic pl. Acts, works, deeds, actual practice. One of many terms referring to a multifaceted concept of precedent. Malik ibn Anas (d. 796) first introduced the amal (practice) of the people in Medina as a highly authoritative source of making rules. Maliki scholars of later times recognized this concept. In time other schools recognized amal (to varying degrees) as legal authority. In legal theory, *amal* (sing.) refers to the acts of the Prophet.

AMAL Acronym, meaning "hope," for Afwaj al-Muqawamah al-Lubnaniyah (Lebanese Resistance Detachments). Populist Lebanese Shii political movement. Emerged in 1975 as a branch of the Harakat al-Mahrumin under the leadership of Sayyid Musa al-Sadr. Became prominent during 1978 hostilities between Israel and Lebanon, as it acted to reduce the influence of the Palestine Liberation Organization in southern Lebanon and to protect Shiis against Israeli retaliatory strikes. Became the largest Shii organization in Lebanon and the most dynamic force in its politics by the 1982 Israeli invasion. Has played a central role in the quest of Lebanon's Shiis for dignity and political power. Current head, Nabih Berri, ascended to the position of parliamentary speaker in 1991, indicating AMAL's willingness to work within the parliamentary system. *See also* Harakat al-Mahrumin; Lebanon, Islam in

Amaliyyah Foundation *See* Jamiat al-Khairiyyat al-Islamiyyah

Aman *See* Diplomacy; Diplomatic Immunity

Amarah, Muhammad (b. 1931) Egyptian Islamic intellectual and prolific writer. Has written more than one hundred books on Islamic philosophy, the Quran, politics, and intellectual issues. Has compiled and commented on the works of major Muslim reformers such as Jamal al-Din al-Afghani, Muhammad Abduh, and Abd al-Rahman al-Kawakibi. Considered an independent Islamic intellectual activist, not linked to organized Islamist groups, who attempts to give rise to a comprehensive, rationalist, and contemporary Islamic model. Criticizes secular intellectuals and their attempts to separate Islam from state affairs and the ideological orientations of society. Has gained recognition and respect throughout the Arab world on the basis of his extensive research.

Ameer Ali, Syed (d. 1928) Indian jurist and Shii modernist. Educated at Hooghly College, Calcutta, and in London. Lectured in Islamic law at Calcutta University and was appointed to the Bengal Legislative Council (1881) and the Bengal High Court (1890). Established the Central National Muhammadan Association (1877) and the All-India Muslim League in London (1908). A prolific author who wrote English-language books and articles on religion and history, arguing Islam as the vehicle of rationality and dynamism during the age of European barbarism and Muhammad as a messenger of moral humanism and progress. His most well-known book is *Spirit of Islam*. *See also* Muslim League

America, Islam in The first Muslims to arrive in America were black African slaves, most of whom were forced to convert to Christianity. Beginning in the late 1800s some Muslims came to America as part of a predominantly Christian group of immigrants from greater Syria. Most were poor, working-class males who hoped to return home to their families financially successful. In many cases they stayed to settle, and as they were joined by Muslims from other areas they began to establish communities in many parts of America, including both cities and rural areas. By the second half of the twentieth century immigrant Muslims were coming not only from the Arab world but also from South and Southeast Asia, Turkey, Iran, and Africa, many representing higher educational and economic classes than earlier arrivals. Most recent immigrants have been numbers of Muslim refugees from politically unstable regions of the Islamic world. Meanwhile, in the middle of the twentieth century significant numbers of African-Americans assumed an Islamic identity through the Nation of Islam (NOI). After 1975 many NOI members began the transition from sectarian to Sunni Islam, although the NOI continues today with a small membership. African-Americans, along with other converts to Islam, represent somewhat less than half of American Muslims. Shiis make up about a fifth of the total Muslim community. Others who consider themselves Muslim, such as Druze, Ahmadis, some Sufis, and members of sectarian movements, are often not accepted as such by mainstream Muslims. Muslim organizations have proliferated at both local and national levels to provide structure and identity for the community. The building of mosques, Islamic centers, and Muslim schools has increased greatly over recent years, as has the production of promotional and educational literature and the use of the Internet. Many Muslims today, unlike earlier generations, advocate active public and political participation for both men and women in American society. *See also* Nation of Islam

American Muslim Council American Muslim political action committee working to raise awareness of international Muslim concerns, particularly the fate of Muslims in Cyprus, Kashmir, Bosnia, Kosovo, Bulgaria, and Somalia. Leadership has been invited to the White House for Islamic celebrations. Sponsors petitions and issues joint statements with both Muslim and non-Muslim political and religious organizations.

American Muslim Mission Formerly known as World Community of Islam in the West, but changed its name in 1978 and came into closer relationship with mainstream Sunni Islam. Led by Warith Deen Muhammad. Largest indigenous Muslim organization in the United States. Now known as the Muslim American Society. *See also* Nation of Islam; World Community of Islam in the West

Amidi, Sayf al-Din al- (d. 1233) Influential Shafii jurist who integrated theology (kalam) with jurisprudential methods. Raised and educated in Baghdad and Damascus, he moved at an early age to Egypt, where his fame spread. Accused of adopting heretical rationalist methods, he moved back to Damascus, where he died. His most famous work is *Al-ihkam fi usul al-ahkam* on Islamic jurisprudence.

Amili Ulama Shii scholars from Jabal Amil (south Lebanon). Founders of eminent madrasas in the regions of Jabal Amil, Karak Nuh, and Balabak in Syria. Most noteworthy were al-Shahid al-Awwal (d. 1384); al-Shahid al-Thani (d. 1558), his son Sahib al-Maalim (d. 1602), and his nephew Sahib al-Madarik (d. 1600); al-Muhaqqiq al-Karaki (d. 1533) and his two grandsons, al-Mujtahid (d. 1592) and Mir Damad (d. 1631/32); Husayn ibn Abd al-Samad (d. 1576) and his son Bahai (d. 1621); Ahmad ibn Zayn al-Abidin (d. 1644); Lutfullah al-Maysi (d. 1622/23); and Muhammad al-Hurr (d. 1699). Numerous sixteenth- and seventeenth-century Amili scholars migrated to Mecca, Iraq, Iran, and India. Rose to the highest religious offices of the Safavid Empire (1501–1736). Divided between Akhbaris (traditionists) and Usulis (rationalists), the Amilis shaped clerical authority in Iran. *See also* Akhbaris; Usulis

Amin, Qasim (d. 1908) Egyptian lawyer, writer, advocate of women's rights. Earned legal license in Cairo and Montpellier. Served in various Egyptian judicial posts. Signature publications, *Tahrir al-marah* (The liberation of women) (1899) and *Al-marah al-jadidah* (The new woman) (1900), advocated greater rights for women and spawned great debate over women's issues throughout the Arab world. Critiqued veiling, female seclu-

sion, early marriage, and lack of education. Considered the restructuring of Egyptian culture and legal reform as remedies to social ills. Historically viewed as a pioneer of Egyptian feminism, though revisionist scholarship has criticized Amin's work as pro-Western and as treating Egyptian women as objects through which nationalist issues were deliberated.

Amina bint Wahab (d. ca. 576) Muhammad's mother. Died when Muhammad was six years old. Some histories record light shining from her face during pregnancy, indicating the coming birth of the Prophet. Some histories also record the face of his father, Abd Allah, shining prior to consummating the marriage, indicating that he would father the Prophet.

Amir Traditionally, a military commander, leader, governor, or prince. Historically used in the title for caliphs, amir al-muminin (commander of the faithful). In modern times, the title denotes membership in the ruling families of the monarchs governing Muslim countries (i.e., Saudi Arabia, the Gulf countries, Brunei) and means "prince."

Amir al-Muminin Commander of the faithful. Title first attributed to the second caliph, Umar ibn al-Khattab (r. 634–44), and adopted by numerous Muslim leaders throughout history. Use of the title waned after the thirteenth-century Mongol invasions, and Ottoman sultans rarely invoked it; West African Muslim communities employed the term through the early nineteenth century.

Ammah *See* Khassah

Amr bi al-Maruf wa'l-Nahy an al-Munkar, al- Enjoining the right/honorable and forbidding the wrong/dishonorable. Used in the Quran nine times, referring to the collective duty of the Muslim community to encourage righteous behavior and discourage immorality, as recognized by reason and the Islamic moral and legal system. Aims to remove oppression from society and instead establish justice. Applied to moral, social, political, and economic facets of life. It is, ideally, the distinguishing trait of the Muslim nation.

Amr ibn al-As (d. ca. 663) Conqueror and governor of Egypt. Invaded Egypt from Hijaz in 639; established control over the whole country in 642. Founded Fustat as capital instead of Alexandria. Replaced as governor by Caliph Uthman. Fought with Muawiyah in the Battle of Siffin, 657, and earned reinstatement in Egypt. Remained governor until his death.

Amr ibn Ubayd (d. 761) One of the earliest leaders of the "rationalist" theological movement of the Mutazilis. A student of the famous early theologian Hasan al-Basri, he led the Mutazilis during the early years of the Abbasid caliphate. He generally followed a quietist political stance toward the Abbasid political establishment.

Amrullah, Hajji Abdul Malik Karim See Hamka

Amsar See Misr

Amulets In popular religion, worn or hung object on which Quranic verses, holy texts, or numerical or symbolic formula is written. Intended to ward off evil spirits, slander, and gossip; offer protection from ailments and physical dangers; provide security while traveling; ensure success and influence; protect pregnancy; promote intelligence; cure diseases; and provide therapeutic benefits.

Analogy See Qiyas

Andalus, al- Those parts of the Iberian peninsula governed by Muslims from 711 to 1492. Locus of the most prolonged encounter between Islam and Christendom, traces of which can be found in the Spanish and Portuguese languages, art, and architecture, and the governance models of colonial Mexico and South America. Some of the finest cultural accomplishments of Islam emerged in al-Andalus: the great mosque of Córdoba, the Alhambra of Seville, the Cuenca school

of ivory carving, the philosophy of Ibn Rushd (Averroës), and the medicine of Ibn Zuhr. The period also held significant Jewish cultural productivity (Maimonides). The golden age ended around the eleventh century; thereafter, Christian military might pushed the frontier south to Granada, conquered in 1492 (the Reconquista). See also Alhambra; Europe, Islam in; Umayyad Caliphate

Andalusia See Andalus, al-

Angels God's messengers who may intercede with Him, but only with His permission. The Quran describes them as having hands and two, three, or four wings, and not eating. Some have specific functions, such as Gabriel (Jibril) bringing divine revelation to Muhammad and the angel of death (traditionally known as Izrail). Michael (Mikail) is believed to be the same rank as Gabriel. May serve as messengers, guardians over humans, and keepers of the inventory of good and bad deeds. Some traditionists make belief in angels an article of faith. Made of light, but not necessarily perfect, they are distinct from satans and jinn.

Angkatan Belia Islam Malaysia See ABIM

Anglo-Muhammadan Law Applied in British colonial courts in India, it included criminal and civil law and was based on an interpretation of Islamic texts and practices. A comprehensive penal code (1860) ended its criminal application, but it continued to be applied in personal status law until the Muslim Personal Law Application Act (1937).

Anjuman Persian. Assembly, meeting, or association. An organization initially formed by government officials and intellectuals who wanted to emulate European concepts of government to modernize Iran. Played a leading role in the Constitutional Revolution (1905–11). Advocated and opened modern schools and libraries to disseminate European ideas. Coordinated the activities of different groups seeking political change. The term is also used generically to refer to religious associations serving as political opposition groups. Particularly popular among students and educated members of the lower and middle classes in the years preceding the Islamic revolution of 1979. Literary anjumans also served to disseminate European literary and cultural ideas and literature but did not adopt political stands. *See also* Majlis

Ansair *See* Ansar

Ansar Companions or supporters. The term applied to people of Medina who supported Muhammad after the hijrah and was appropriated as the name for the supporters of the Sudanese Mahdi, Muhammad Ahmad ibn Abd Allah (d. 1885). The movement was declared illegal following the conquest of the Mahdist state by the Anglo-Egyptian army in 1898. In the twentieth century the Mahdi's son reorganized the Ansar, and by Sudanese independence in 1956 the Ansar were the largest Muslim association and the basis for the Ummah Party. Since independence, the Ansar have represented an identification with the Mahdist tradition and leadership by the Mahdi family rather than a separate organization. *See also* Ummah Party

Ansari, Abu Madyan Shuayb ibn al-Husayn al- (d. 1198) First influential Sufi teacher from North Africa. Born in Spain. Initiated into Sufism in Fez, Morocco. Established the distinctive Madyani Way, although few orders following it developed. Taught the founder of the Shadhili Sufi order. Most of the great Maghrebi Sufis of his lifetime and after acknowledged him as master. Many saints who performed miracles included him in their spiritual genealogies. His influence in religious matters led the ruling Almohads to summon him to court to defend his doctrines to their religious scholars, but he died en route. The mosque, school, public baths, and ancillary buildings built around his tomb are popular points of veneration and pilgrimage.

Ansari, Murtada (d. 1864) First scholar universally recognized as supreme authority (marja al-taqlid) in matters of Shii law. Proclaimed that the clergy were vested with a modicum of the Hidden Imam's authority, privileging them to serve as guardians of the infirm, the needy, widows, and orphans and to supervise religious expenditures. Developed a notion of "rule of the jurist," later converted by Ayatollah Ruhollah Khomeini into political ideology.

Anthropology, Islamic According to the "Islamization of knowledge" model of modern learning, believed to be based on and validated by the Quran: "Travel throughout the world and see how God did originate creation" (29:20); the Prophet said, "Seek knowledge, even unto China." Ismail al-Faruqi (d. 1986) warned anthropologists to avoid the Western paradigm—to "stop looking at people of the world as if they were specimens in a zoo"—and called for a universalizing model of knowledge based on the belief that truth, like God and humankind, are one. Today Muslim anthropologists examine and address major social problems such as AIDS, alcoholism, drug abuse, and famine. *See also* International Institute of Islamic Thought

Anthropomorphism Assignment of physical attributes to God, forbidden by the Quran according to orthodox Muslims. Because God is utterly unique, there can be no similarity between Him and created entities. Quranic references to God's attributes are typically understood metaphorically as a tool for learning about God and His actual nature. Sufis also use metaphors and allegories with reference to God in mystical poetry to describe their desired relationship to Him. God's attributes are usually listed as seven in number: knowledge, power, life, will, speech, hearing, and sight. Theological disputes about God's attributes center on whether or not God's essence and attributes are identical and eternal.

Antichrist Known as Dajjal (the deceiver). Supposed to appear during the age of injustice preceding the end of the world, causing corruption and oppression to sweep over the earth for a period of either forty days or forty years. Appearance is one of the sure signs of the last days. Will deceive many by false teachings and miracles, bringing with him food and water to tempt those who have been suffering. Not mentioned in the Quran, but prominent in hadith and later Islamic literature. Correlates to Christian apocalyptic legends about the Antichrist. Medieval Christians often portrayed Muhammad as the Antichrist. Many evangelical Christians today portray Muslims as agents of the Antichrist. *See also* Eschatology

Apostasy Renunciation of one's religion. The Arabic terms (*riddah, irtidad*) are not used in the Quran, but it promises dire consequences in the afterlife for those who "turn from" or "renounce" (*yartaddu*, 2:217; 5:54) and "those who disbelieve after having believed" (3:81ff.; 5:61; 9:66; 4:137; 16:106). Hadith reports introduce the teaching that renunciation of Islam is punishable by beheading, burning, crucifixion, or banishment. Some traditions allow an apostate to repent. Islamic legal codes agree on the death penalty (traditionally by the sword) for an adult male in full possession of his faculties who has renounced Islam voluntarily. Thus apostasy was included among crimes for which there were punishments believed to be divinely mandated (*hadd* pl. *hudud*, "offenses"). Some schools of law allow imprisonment instead of death for apostate women. The schools vary on the question of whether or not an apostate may be allowed, encouraged, or disallowed to repent, as well as on the status of an apostate's property after death or banishment, but they agree that the marriage of an apostate is void. Based on the Quranic prohibition of coercion in matters of religion (2:257), many modern thinkers argue against capital punishment for apostasy, and the legislation is rarely invoked today. *See also* Kufr; Murtadd

Aqd Contract or legal transaction. The term is used to refer to the conclusion of contracts of sale, loan, and marriage, and it denotes legal action that becomes effective upon the acceptance of an offer. The contract should reflect the mutual understanding and agreement of the parties and must be entered into freely and without coercion. The term is also used to refer to legal documents or deeds,

such as title to property or a will. In political uses, it refers to a contract for governance between ruler and ruled as evidenced by the convocation of a session or meeting.

Aqidah Islamic creed or articles of faith. Quranic formulation includes belief in God, angels, prophets, scriptures, and the Day of Judgment. Early creeds reflected Shii-Sunni polemics: Shiis upheld the notion of the designated imamate, and Sunnis responded that the community elected the imam and that the historical order of the caliphates of Abu Bakr, Umar, Uthman, and Ali was theologically proper. More detailed formulations stress a triad—belief in God, the Prophet, and the Day of Judgment—as constituting the essential belief system in Islam.

Aqiqah Birth ritual involving shaving of the child's head, distribution of money to the poor, animal sacrifice, and naming of the child. The call to prayer is spoken in the child's right ear and the summons to prayer in the left. *See also* Birth Rites

Aql, al- Intelligence. In Islamic theology, natural human knowledge. In philosophy, the intellect. In Neoplatonic speculation, God's First Creation. In Ismaili thought, the intellect as divine emanation. In jurisprudence, reason as source for shariah. For modern Islamic reformers, aql as rationality is an integral aspect of Islam. Thus Islam is not antithetical to reason.

Aqqad, Abbas Mahmud al- (d. 1964) Egyptian Islamic modernist thinker. Discussed place of Islam in ongoing history of religions. Wrote books about Muhammad, early Muslim leaders, and heroic days of Islam. Contributed to dialogue on nationalism, feminism, and social and cultural issues. Teacher of Sayyid Qutb. Teachings later rejected by Qutb as overly intellectualized.

Aqsa, al- Seventh-century mosque in the Haram al-Sharif, Jerusalem. Known as the "Farther Mosque" to distinguish it from the "Holy Mosque" of Mecca. Mentioned in connection with the Prophet's Noctural Journey in the Quran (17:1). A first version was founded around 637 after the conquest of Jerusalem, but in 715 Umayyad caliph al-Walid built a much larger structure at the south end of the Haram, later destroyed and again rebuilt. In its present form the building largely dates to the eleventh century. In 1969 an arsonist's fire destroyed the twelfth-century pulpit (minbar) given to the mosque by Salah al-Din (Saladin). *See also* Haram al-Sharif; Jerusalem

Arab-Israeli Conflict Ongoing conflict between Arabs and Israel over Palestinian territory. The origins of the conflict lie in the Balfour Declaration (1917), which promised "a national home for the Jewish people," and in Arab-Jewish conflict during the British mandate period. Since the creation of Israel in 1948, Arabs and Israelis have fought wars in 1948, 1956, 1967, and 1973. In 1978 Egypt and Israel signed a peace treaty (Camp David accords). In 1982 Israel invaded Lebanon. In December 1987 Palestinians launched the intifadah (uprising) in an attempt to liberate the West Bank and Gaza. In 1988 the Palestine Liberation Organization (PLO) expressed a desire to reach a peace with Israel based on a two-state solution. The United States and Russia sponsored the Madrid peace talks (1991) with Israel, Palestinian representatives, Syria, Jordan, and Lebanon: no agreement was reached. Two years later in Oslo, Israelis and Palestinians signed a Declaration of Principles in which the parties agreed to resolve issues over a timeline, but the most intractable matters still remain unresolved: the status of Jerusalem, Palestinian state boundaries, sovereignty, and water control issues. In late 2000 a new intifadah erupted amid calls for a Palestinian state after Israeli general and hard-liner Ariel Sharon visited the al-Aqsa mosque in Jerusalem. To date, only Jordan and Egypt have signed full peace treaties with Israel, though many other Arab nations have informal relations. *See also* Palestine Liberation Organization

Arab League Founded in Cairo in 1945. Goals include close cooperation of member states in political, security, economic, communications, cultural, social, and financial matters. Outlawed use of force in settling disputes between member states but has been ineffective in resolving inter-Arab conflicts. Supports Palestinian cause and Arab and Islamic issues in international arenas.

Arab Nationalism Defined by an anticolonial ethos and the glorification of origins and history in the face of Western dominance experienced by Arab countries in the nineteenth and twentieth centuries. Aims at political reunification of all Arabic-speaking states. Roots traced by some scholars to eighteenth-century reform movements or nineteenth-century anticolonial movements; others consider it a twentieth-century phenomenon based on Arabic language and culture. Manifested in the Arab revolt against the Ottoman Empire during World War I to protest its Turkification program, and in the short-lived United Arab Republic (merger between Egypt and Syria from 1958 to 1961). Invoked by Saddam Hussein during the Gulf War in a failed attempt to unite Arabs and Muslims against Western powers. *See also* Nationalism and Islam

Arab Socialism In the Arab context, defined as state-sponsored economic development, as manifested in Nasserism and Baathism as state ideologies of Egypt in the 1950s and 1960s and of Iraq and Syria from the 1960s until the mid-1980s. Developed after World War II when a consensus emerged among the educated middle class and the unofficial opposition that the most urgent national needs were independence and economic development. The state was understood to be the natural vehicle to carry out transformations. Stringent land reforms were introduced, and banking, insurance, foreign trade, large industries, and large private and foreign-owned companies were all nationalized. The economic program was accompanied by expansion in social, welfare, health, and educational services. *See also* Socialism and Islam

Arafat Mountain located outside of Mecca, on whose plain pilgrims gather on the ninth day of Dhu al-Hijjah. There they pray continuously from just after noon until shortly after sunset. Many believe that God's spirit descends closest to earth at this spot at this time, making it easier for human prayers to attract His attention. A sermon is also preached there during the pilgrimage, commemorating Muhammad's final pilgrimage and farewell sermon from this site. Standing at Arafat is one of the three minimum requirements of the hajj. Some believe that one of the greatest sins is standing at Arafat and doubting God's forgiveness. *See also* Hajj

Arafat, Yasir *See* Palestine Liberation Organization

Arbitration In Islamic law greater emphasis is placed on arbitration and mediation than on establishing guilt. Muhammad saw himself as an arbitrator. In the early days of Islam, diplomatic missions were exchanged for the purpose of negotiating or arbitrating particular issues. Codes of Islamic personal status law require the appointment of arbitrators to reconcile spouses seeking judicial divorce.

Architecture The most distinctive form of Islamic architecture is the mosque. The Friday mosque with minaret (tower) indicates the presence of a Muslim community and permits worship and education for both adults and children. Mosques typically include domes and minarets; minarets are used for the call to prayer, and domes signal a place of prayer and Islamic education. Domes and minarets vary in shape, construction materials, and size according to region and political dynasties. The Ottoman use of multiple minarets per mosque symbolized the sultan's patronage, his construction of the mosque, and the expansion of Ottoman rule and power. Prior to the twentieth century, hammams (bathhouses) were often built near mosques to facilitate ritual purity requirements for Friday prayers. Other typical architectural styles include storage spaces for merchants and traders, known as khans and caravanserais, and covered marketplaces with formal entrances. Khans and caravanserais usually had two floors so that animals could be stabled on the ground floor and

goods stored and merchants housed on the second floor. Islamic domestic spaces typically include public, male, communal spaces separate from private, female spaces, which are reserved for women, children, and close male relatives. Major twentieth-century architectural developments include the construction of state and national mosques, airports, and university campuses, often combining Western and traditional Islamic architecture.

Ardabili, Shaykh Safi al-Din (d. 1334) Founder of Safavid Sufi order, the origin of the later Safavid dynasty (1501–1722) in Iran. Given to visions of angels and visits by saints. Disseminated religious ideas from his base in Tabriz to Anatolia, Syria, and India. A Sunni follower of the Shafii rite at a time of religious syncretism and ferment.

Aristotle (d. 322 B.C.E.) Greek philosopher whose writings on logic, natural science, psychology, mathematics, metaphysics, and ethics were translated from Greek into Syriac and then into Arabic by the ninth century C.E. They were commented on by Arab and Persian philosophers and scientists throughout the medieval period, and formed the basis of falsafah (philosophy) in the Muslim world. The commentaries of Ibn Sina (Avicenna) and Ibn Rushd (Averroës) were widely read and disseminated, along with those of al-Farabi. Hebrew and Latin versions of the Arabic translations formed the basis of learning in the Western Jewish and Christian traditions, since direct translations from the Greek were not available in the West until the thirteenth century. Some scholars in the Muslim world erroneously attributed certain Napoleonic works to Aristotle, resulting in confusion about his ideas. His *Politics* seems to have been unknown in the Muslim world; scholars relied on the *Rhetoric* and *Nicomachean Ethics* for his political thought, and sometimes Plato's *Republic*. *See also* Philosophy

Aristu *See* Aristotle

Aristutalis *See* Aristotle

Arithmetic *See* Mathematics

Arkan al-Din *See* Pillars of Islam

Arkan al-Islam *See* Pillars of Islam

Arkoun, Mohammed (b. 1928) French intellectual who, using sophisticated hermeneutics based on contemporary Western critical methodologies, critiques classical Islamic religious, legal, and philosophical traditions. Trained as a medievalist and has written on topics ranging from the twelfth-century Andalusian philosopher Ibn Tufayl to orientalism. Argues in the highly influential *Lectures du Coran* the importance of distinguishing revelation from the written text and commentaries.

Army *See* Jaysh

Arsalan, Shakib (d. 1946) Druze reformist, activist, and writer. Played an important role in Arab/Islamic politics between the two world wars. Served as Ottoman administrator and in the Ottoman parliament in 1914. Loyalty to the Ottoman Empire led him to oppose Sharif Husyan's Arab revolt in 1916, warning of the advent of European imperial powers. Exiled after World War I to Geneva, where he founded the anti-European journal *Le Nation arabe*. Died as an advocate of the Axis powers.

Art and Islam *See* Architecture; Calligraphy and Epigraphy; Carpets; Dance; Devotional Art; Painting

Articles of Faith *See* Aqidah

Asaba In legal terminology, refers to the male relatives who inherit upon the death of a male family member. The order of inheritance is generally: sons and grandsons of the deceased, father and brothers, uncles and cousins, and then descendants of the grandfather of the deceased. Also refers to those who have the right to demand exaction of blood money in case of physical injuries. *See also* Inheritance

Asabiyyah Social solidarity with an emphasis on group consciousness, cohesiveness, and unity. Familiar in the pre-Islamic era, the term became popularized in Ibn Khaldun's (d. 1406) *Muqaddimah*. Asabiyyah is neither necessarily nomadic nor based on blood relations. In the modern period, the term is analogous to *solidarity*. *See also* Ibn Khaldun, Abd al-Rahman ibn Muhammad

Asad, Muhammad (d. 1992) Statesman, journalist, author. Born Leopold Weiss into a Jewish family in Austria. Studied philosophy and the history of art. Traveled extensively in the Middle East and North Africa as a journalist. Regarded as an expert on Middle East affairs and the Arabic language. Embraced Islam in 1926. Spent many years among the Bedouins in Saudi Arabia. Later moved to British India. Represented Pakistan at the United Nations as an envoy. Wrote four books and translated the *Sahih al-Bukhari* and the Quran into English. Favored a rationalist interpretation of the Quran. Produced a monthly journal, *Arafat*. Buried in Granada, Spain.

Asadabadi, Jamal al-Din al *See* Afghani, Jamal al-Din al-

Asbab al-Nuzul Reasons for the revelations. Refers to a field of study and genre of literature devoted to recounting the circumstances of the Prophet Muhammad and his followers when particular verses from the Quran were revealed. Perhaps the best-known of these texts is the *Asbab al-Nuzul* of Ali ibn Ahmad al-Wahidi, which is regularly reprinted alongside the text of the Quran. Legal scholars regard this study as of great importance, on the principle that sound understanding of the revelation proceeds from knowing the reasons God revealed the Quran and how the Prophet Muhammad applied the revelation when he received it.

Ascetic Arabic *zahid*. One renouncing worldly comforts by undertaking specific practices, including fasting, seclusion, and night prayer vigils, in order to discipline selfishness and curb temptation. Having only a limited appeal to most Muslims today, asceticism forms an essential initial stage within Islamic mysticism, fostering the purification and self-control necessary for spiritual illumination.

Asceticism *See* Ascetic; Zuhd

Asfar Sing. *safar.* Journey travel. In Sufi (mystical) Islam, signifies the spiritual journey of the novice, with a great variety of stages or divisions. One of the most famous divisions is the fourfold journey, which constitutes a complete circle of spiritual realization and mystical experience. The first part is the journey from everyday life (creation) to the Truth (min al-khalq ilal-haqq), referring to the beginning of the journey. The second is the journey with the Truth in the Truth (bil-haqq fil-haqq), referring to the further perfection of the soul of the traveler. The third is the journey from the Truth to the created with the Truth (min al-haqq ilal-khalq bil-haqq), corresponding to the first journey at a higher level. The fourth is the journey with the Truth in the created (bil-haqq fil-khalq), signifying the return of the traveler from the stage of spiritual ecstasy to the world of creation.

Ashab al-Hadith *See* Ahl al-Hadith

Ashab al-Nabi *See* Companions

Ashairah *See* Asharis

Ashari, Abu-al-Hasan Ali ibn Ismail al- (d. 935) Muslim theologian who bridged the gap between a literal, legalistic interpretation of the Quran and hadith and rationalism. Postulated that the Quran as revelation was uncreated, but any physical copy of the Quran is created, asserting the difference between essence and existence. Held that all human acts are decided, created, and governed by God, but that people participate in decision making and actions. Stressed the importance of divine power over free will

and rational faculties. Reason is to be used to determine meanings of the Quran and hadith, to defend religious truth, and to persuade others of the validity of revelation.

Asharis Classical Sunni theological school (tenth to twelfth centuries), founded by Abu al-Hasan al-Ashari, that became an important religious movement forming a middle ground between the rationalism of the Mutazilis and the literalism of the Hanbalis. Used a rational approach to religious truth but preserved the primary importance of scriptural revelation as the sole source of certainty. Acknowledged that reason may play a role in defending truth, convincing others, and participating in moral actions, but held that all moral actions are governed by God. Associated with the Shafii school of law. Assimilated into the Maliki school of law in the tenth century. Opposed by Hanbalis in the eleventh century. *See also* Theology

Ashmawi, Muhammad Said al- (b. 1932) Egyptian judge, intellectual, lecturer, and former head of the State Security Tribunal. Has written several books on philosophical, legal, and Islamic issues. Contributes articles regularly to Egyptian newspapers and magazines. Holds a secular orientation and advocates the separation of religion and politics. Articulates critical views of political Islamist movements.

Ashraf *See* Sharif

Ashtar, Malik ibn al-Harith al-Nakhai al- (d. 657) Commander under Caliph Ali ibn Abi Talib during the Battles of the Camel (656) and Siffin (657). He opposed the truce with Muawiyah, ruler of Syria and a relative of Uthman, suspecting him of trying to sabotage Ali's impending victory in Siffin. Ali appointed him governor of several cities in Iraq and Syria, but this provoked opposition from Muawiyah. In 657 Ali appointed him governor of Egypt. En route to Egypt al-Ashtar was poisoned in al-Arish, apparently on orders from Muawiyah. *See also* Siffin, Battle of

Ashura Tenth day of the Muslim month of Muharram. Commemoration of the martyrdom in 680 of Husayn, Muhammad's grandson and the third imam of Shii Islam. Shii communities annually reenact the tragedy in a passion play, including self-mortification and displays of sorrow and remorse intended to unite them in Husayn's suffering and death as an aid to salvation on the Day of Judgment. Shii communities experiencing deprivation, humiliation, or abuse today understand Husayn's martyrdom as a paradigm for the struggle against injustice, tyranny, and oppression. Became a major symbol and slogan during the Iranian Islamic revolution, during the Iran-Iraq war (1980–88), and in Lebanon.

Ashurkhanah *See* Husayniyyah

Asia *See* Central Asia, Islam in

Askari, Hasan al- (d. 874) Eleventh imam of the Twelver (Ithna Ashari) Shiis. Born in Medina. Became the imam following the death of his father, Ali al-Hadi, in 868 and is believed to have left a son named Muhammad, the last imam of the Twelvers. Lived a life of strict seclusion and was kept under surveillance by the Abbasid caliph. Died in Samarra, Iraq, where he is buried beside his father.

Asma bint Abu Bakr (d. 693) Daughter of the first caliph, Abu Bakr, and the elder half-sister of Muhammad's wife Aishah. During the hijrah (622), when Muhammad and Abu Bakr took shelter in a cave to evade the Meccans who were in pursuit, Asma lowered to them food tied to her belt, which she had torn into two, thus giving her the nickname Dhat al-Nitaqayn (she of the two belts). Married al-Zubayr ibn al-Awamm; their son Abd Allah is considered to be the first Muslim child to be born in Medina.

Asmau, Nana (d. 1864) Daughter of Uthman Dan Fodio and leader in the Sokoto caliphate. Collected, edited, and translated her father's works and wrote works basic to the development of the ideology of the West

African jihad movement. A leading figure in scholarship and Sufi piety as well as politics.

Asnaf *See* Guilds

Asqalani, Ahmad ibn Hajar al- (d. 1447) Medieval Islamic scholar who is best known for his massive work *Fath al-bari bi-sharh sahih al-Bukhari*, which is considered to be the most important commentary on the hadith collection of Imam al-Bukhari (d. 870).

Assassins *See* Nizaris

Assembly *See* Majlis

Association of Algerian Ulama Founded in 1931 by Abd al-Hamid ibn Badis and other religious scholars to educate Algerians, promote the Arab-Islamic heritage and national identity of Algeria, revive and reform Islam, and critique Sufi orders and assimilationism. Protested French occupation. Demanded religious freedom, restoration of charitable endowments, and recognition of Arabic as official language. *See also* Algeria, Islam in; Ibn Badis, Abd al-Hamid

Association · of Muslim Professionals (AMP) Singapore Islamic association. Established in 1991 due to the perception within the Singapore-Malay community that Malay political leaders are ineffective in representing the interests of the community. Headed by volunteer Malay Muslim professionals. Presents a potential mechanism for Singapore Malay Muslims to express their needs and interests. Sees its role as a think tank, mobilizer, and problem solver in the development and progress of the Singapore Malay Muslim community. Carries out research and publishes its findings. Conducts programs in early childhood development, enrichment classes for students, courses in parental education, and skill training for workers. *See also* Southeast Asia, Islam in

Association of Muslim Social Scientists (AMSS) Academic association founded in 1972 that aims to generate cooperation among Muslim scholars and social scientists seeking to unify revealed knowledge with acquired knowledge. Holds an annual national conference and hosts seminars and regional meetings. Publishes *The American Journal of Islamic Social Sciences*.

Astarabadi, Mir Muhammad Baqir ibn Shams al-Din Muhammad al-Husayn al- *See* Mir Damad

Astrolabe Arabic *asturlab*. A family of astronomical instruments based on the projection of the celestial sphere onto its plane. Served to measure the positions and altitude of celestial bodies. Dramatic and fundamental improvements in the relatively crude Greek models were made in the medieval Islamic world, and from here the astrolabe reached Latin Europe. The most common form is the flat (musattah) astrolabe, but at least two other forms are also known: linear (khatti) and spherical (kuri).

Astrology Arabic *ilm al-nujum* or *ilm al-falak*. In early Arabic sources, *ilm al-nujum* was used to refer to both astronomy and astrology. In medieval sources, however, a clear distinction was made between *ilm al-nujum* (science of the stars) or *ilm al-falak* (science of the celestial orbs), referring to astrology, and *ilm al-haya* (science of the figure [of heavens]), referring to astronomy. Both fields were rooted in the Greek, Persian, and Indian traditions. Despite consistent critiques of astrology by scientists and religious scholars, astrological prognostications required a fair amount of exact scientific knowledge and thus gave partial incentive for the study and development of astronomy.

Astronomy Arabic *ilm al-haya*. Astronomy in the Muslim world integrated Indian, Persian, and Greek elements and built upon the second-century astronomer Ptolemy's system, making dramatic improvements upon it. In the thirteenth century Nasir al-Din al-Tusi developed the mathematical device called the "Tusi couple," enabling astronomers to explain observed planetary motions without violating the principle of uniform circular motion, as Ptolemy had done. A timekeeper of a Damascene mosque, Ibn al-Shatir (fourteenth century), refined Tusi's innovations further and developed models for the moon and Mercury that reappear in the works of Copernicus two centuries later.

Atabat Thresholds. The Shii shrine cities of Iraq—Najaf, Karbala, Kazimayn, and Samarra (location of the tombs of the six imams)—are important centers of devotion, pilgrimage, scholarship, and political activism. Pilgrimage to these tombs, especially in Karbala, is believed desirable, and these cities remain a place of Shii scholarship today.

Atatürk, Mustafa Kemal (d. 1938) Founder of the Turkish Republic (1923). Former brigadier general and Young Turk. Served as the first president of modern Turkey. Sought to establish a capitalist, secular nation-state based on popular sovereignty. Oversaw a massive social revolution that addressed education and gender inequity, among other issues.

Atomism A theory adopted in Sunni and Shii theology proposing that the world consists of two kinds of primary entities: atoms, which are conjoined to form bodies, and the accidents that reside in these atoms, each of which contains a single discrete instance of a characteristic or its contrary. Atoms exist through many instants, whereas accidents, since they exist for only an instant, must constantly be created anew by God.

Attar, Farid al-Din (d. ca. 1220) Persian mystic poet. Worked as a pharmacist in Nishapur. Said to have been killed by invading Mongols. Known for mystical epic poems narrating the soul's progression to inner perfection, as well as couplet poems, the most famous of which is the *Simurgh*. Wrote a widely read Sufi hagiography. Portrayed the controversial martyr al-Hallaj (d. 922) as an exemplary model. His stories uphold the idea that the release of the soul is attainable in life by eliminating the self, that the universal soul is found within. Notable for lively presentations full of anecdotes and didactic digressions. Numerous lesser attributed works are of questionable authenticity.

Attas, Syed Muhammad Naquib al- (b. 1931) Malaysian thinker. Trained at Sandhurst Military Academy in Britain and the University of Malaya. Defended Malay identity and as such served as mentor to ABIM in the 1970s. Best known for his works on the Islamization of knowledge. Rejects secularism as a Western product that leads to the "leveling" of the Muslim mind. Founder-director of the International Institute of Islamic Thought and Civilization (ISTAC) since 1987. *See also* ABIM

Aurangzeb Sixth emperor of Mughal India (r. 1658–1707) at the height of Mughal power and wealth. His policies of military expansion and Islamic orthodoxy undermined the effects of his father Shah Jahan's diplomacy and his brother Dara Shukoh's attempted reconciliation of the monotheistic religions. His strict construction of Islamic government alienated non-Muslim nobles, stultified Mughal culture, and inspired temple destruction and discriminatory taxation. Constant warfare, failure against the southern Marathas, and his distance from his northern officials weakened Mughal unity. Aurangzeb's legacy to India was factionalism, sectarianism, decentralization, and vulnerability to European encroachment.

Australia and New Zealand, Islam in The first Muslims came in the late nineteenth and early twentieth centuries on camel drives. Today more than 80 percent are of Turkish or Lebanese origin, although South Asians and Indians from Fiji are also represented. Muslims account for 1–2 percent of the total population. The majority live in urban centers and belong to the working class. Local Islamic associations were first organized in the mid-1950s along ethnic lines. The Australian Federation of Islamic Councils and the Federation of Islamic Associations of New Zealand are national associations founded to provide educational, cultural, community, and religious services, certify halal slaughter of animals, and coordinate financial requests and overseas dealings. Muslims in these countries share a perception of discrimination and negative stereotyping, stemming from conflicts between their customs and local ways.

Australian Federation of Islamic Councils Founded in 1975 to provide educational, cultural, and religious services in conjunction with state councils and local associations. Represents Australian Muslims to both Australian and overseas agencies. Certifies halal slaughter of animals. Supports local associations and their imams. Channels financial assistance for building mosques.

Avempace *See* Ibn Bajjah

Averroës *See* Ibn Rushd, Abu-i-Walid Muhammad ibn Ahmad ibn Muhammad

Avicenna *See* Ibn Sina, Abu Ali Husayn ibn Abd Allah

Awami League Major political party in Bangladesh. Led country's war of independence against Pakistan in 1971 under the leadership of Shaykh Mujibur Rahman. Secular and nationalist in orientation. Asserts national unity on basis of linguistic-cultural, rather than religious, identity. Current leader is Shaykh Hasinah Vajid.

Awang, Haji Abdul Hadi ibn Haji (b. 1947) Malaysian religious and political activist. Chief minister of Trengganu since 1999. Deputy president, Parti Islam Se-Malaysia (PAS). Has long supported the establishment of an Islamic state in Malaysia while also advocating justice and equality for all.

Awdah, Abdal-Aziz (b. 1948) Palestinian Islamic fundamentalist leader. Born in Bir al-Sab but settled in the Jabaliyyah camp in Gaza after the creation of Israel. Received a degree from Dar al-Ulum in Egypt. In Egypt, was close to the most militant fundamentalist groups (some of which were linked to the assassination of Anwar Sadat). Returned to Gaza in 1981 and lectured at the Islamic University of Gaza. One of the founders of Islamic Jihad of Palestine, which, along with HAMAS, represents the Islamic fundamentalist ideology among the Palestinians and perpetrates violent acts against Israeli targets. Awdah was arrested by Israeli forces in 1984 and deported in 1993 to south Lebanon.

Aws, al- Tribe that, with the Khazraj, invited Muhammad to Yathrib to settle a feud between the two groups. Both tribes (called ansar [helpers] of the Prophet), along with emigrants from Mecca on the hijrah, established the first Islamic community. Afterward Yathrib was renamed Medina (city of the Prophet) and became the paradigm for Islamic civic and religious life.

Awzai, Abu Amr Abd al-Rahman ibn Amr al- (d. 774) Chief representative and eponym of the Awzai school of Islamic law, which descended from the ancient Iraqi school. Apparently born in Damascus. Very little of his writings survive, but his style of jurisprudence is preserved in Abu Yusuf's *Al-radd ala siyar al-Awzai*, in particular his reliance on the "living tradition," the uninterrupted practice of Muslims handed down from preceding generations. For Awzai, this is the Sunnah of the Prophet. Awzai's school flourished in Syria, the Maghreb, and Spain but was eventually overcome by the Maliki school in the ninth century. However, given his authority and reputation as a Sunni imam and pious ancestor, his views retain potential as a source of law and a basis for alternative legal approaches and solutions. Died and was buried near Beirut, where his tomb is still visited.

Aya Sofia Mosque Major imperial mosque of Ottoman Istanbul. Originally the Church of Holy Wisdom (Hagia Sophia) erected by Byzantine emperor Justinian in 537, converted into a mosque by the Ottoman Sultan Mehmed II in 1453, extensively restored by the Ottomans. Became a museum under the Turkish Republic in 1935. *See also* Istanbul

Ayah/Ayat Usually translated as "verse" or "sign." Refers to divisions within surahs (chapters) of the Quran. Also used within Quranic texts to refer to evidence of God in nature, miracles confirming truth of prophetic message, revealed messages in general, or a fundamental point within a surah. *See also* Quran

Ayan wa Ashraf Notables; a social distinction. In the later Ottoman empire the term *ayan* came to be applied more specifically to the local notables. The meaning of *ashraf* (sing. *sharif*) has changed through time and place in the Islamic world, sometimes indicating descent from the Prophet Muhammad or, more generally, persons of nobility and importance. In Turkey and Persia today, *sharif* denotes high social and economic status, while *sayyid* is used for descendants of the Prophet. In South Asia the term is applied specifically to Muslims of foreign descent as opposed to indigenous Indian Muslim lineages.

Ayat al-Kursi, al- Verse of the Throne, Quran 2:256. One of the principal verses of refuge and protection. Its recitation is believed to protect one from evil; before sleep, to keep house and family safe; after each prayer, to pave the way to paradise. Often used for amulet inscriptions. Its power is also praised in hadith.

Ayatollah Sign of God. Honorific title in Twelver Shii Islam. Popularly assigned to outstanding legal scholars. General use of the title appeared in the late Qajar period in Iran. It is not used among Shiis of Lebanon, Pakistan, or India. Its use in Iraq is restricted to legal scholars of Iranian origin. An ayatollah must be a fully qualified mujtahid, serve as marja al-taqlid, and assert authority over peers and followers. The title became increasingly common in the second half of the twentieth century, particularly in postrevolutionary Iran, where it indicates hierarchical status. The leading Iranian ayatollah is known as ayatollah al-uzma, reflecting the temporal and spiritual power initially held by Ayatollah Ruhollah Khomeini. *See also* Marja al-Taqlid; Mujtahid; Shii Islam

Ayb Arabic word roughly meaning "disgrace,""defect," or "shame" resulting from dishonorable behavior, which may range from the shirking of familial responsibilities by a man to resorting to provocative clothing or being seen in the company of unrelated men for a woman. Mischievous or disrespectful children are often reproved by adults with this powerful admonition.

Ayn, al- *See* Evil Eye

Ayn Jalut According to tradition, the site in Palestine where David killed Goliath. According to chronicles of the Crusades, the opposing armies of Salah al-Din (Saladin) and the Franks camped there face-to-face in 1183 but departed without military engagement. In 1260 Egyptian Mamluks and Mongols battled there, and the Mongols experienced their first defeat, initiating their decline. Arabic, particularly Egyptian, chronicles regarded this victory as decisive in saving Islam and Cairo from the Mongols. The Mamluk victory resulted in the expulsion of the remaining Christian Crusader states by 1291 and expanded the boundaries of the Mamluk empire to unify Egypt and Syria.

Ayodhya Incident December 1992 destruction of the Babri Masjid in Ayodhia. Ayodha is an ancient city in northern India and an important pilgrimage site. A mosque was built there in 1528 by the Mughal conqueror Babur, supposedly on the site of a demolished temple at Rama's birthplace. The city became the focus of the Hindu campaign to restore the temple after Indian independence (1947). After Hindu militants succeeded in destroying Babri Masjid, Hindu-Muslim riots followed throughout north India and Bombay. The incident helped popularize the Hindu nationalist Bharatiya Janata Party.

Ayyub *See* Job

Ayyubids Governing dynasty in Egypt, Muslim Syria, Upper Mesopotamia, and Yemen from the end of the twelfth to the middle of the thirteenth century; established by the Kurdish officer Salah al-Din (Saladin). Promoted Sunnism and returned Egypt to the Abbasid fold after two centuries of Fatimid (Shii) rule; greatly reduced the power of the Crusader principalities of Syria. Organized with territories (outside of Egypt) divided among the various family princes who supported military officers and troops with revenue grants (iqta). Regime usually integrated by the dominance of the sultan of Egypt; collapsed in Egypt in 1250 and elsewhere over the next decade after an army of Turkish slave-soldiers (Mamluks) supplanted the last Ayyubid ruler in Egypt.

Aza *See* Mourning

Azad, Abu al-Kalam (d. 1958) Indian Islamic thinker. Received a traditional Islamic education and was considered a child prodigy. As a journalist in Calcutta, argued that Muslim nonviolent resistance against the British was a religious duty. Eventually joined forces with Gandhi. Was imprisoned by the British numerous times; spent one-seventh of his life in prison. Served as president of the All-India National Congress (1940). In 1947 joined the Indian government as minister of education and later as vice president. *See also* Tarjuman al-Quran

Azakhanah *See* Husayniyyah

Azerbaijan, Islam in Conquered by the Russian Empire in the early 1800s, Azerbaijan remained under Russian rule until 1918. The first Republic of Azerbaijan (1918–20) was a secular state that guaranteed freedom of religion; it was conquered by the Red Army and remained under Soviet rule until 1991, when it declared its independence. Ninety-four percent of the eight million residents are Muslim; 6 percent belong to various Christian denominations. The constitution was adopted in November 1995 and established a unicameral National Assembly with 125 seats; members serve five-year terms. Heydar Aliyev has been chief of state since 18 June 1993. *See also* Central Asia, Islam in

Azhar, al- Founded in 969/970, this Cairene university may have been named for the prophet Muhammad's daughter Fatimah "al-Zahra"(the brilliant), the eponymous ancestor of the Fatimids, founder of Cairo. Premodern al-Azhar had no formal admissions procedures, academic departments, written examinations, grades, or degrees; the curriculum focused on Quranic exegesis, hadith, jurisprudence, grammar, rhetoric, and the sciences. The early modern period ushered in attempts to reform and modernize the university through the addition of new subjects and required yearly examinations, but students and faculty protested and forced the cancellation of these measures. Starting in 1961 the usually conservative university has adopted modern higher educational standards and has expanded its curricular base to include colleges of agriculture, engineering, medicine, commerce, science, and education. Women students are admitted albeit educated in separate colleges. Outside Egypt, al-Azhar is prized as a champion of Sunni Islam and the Arabic language.

Azl *See* Birth Control/Contraception

Bab See Shirazi, Sayyid Ali Muhammad

Bab-i Ali Ottoman Sublime Porte. Term refers to palace, court, and government of ruler; initially referred to the dwelling of the grand vizier. The Porte housed the Ministry of the Interior, the Ministry of Foreign Affairs, the former Department of Chief of Secretaries, and the Council of State.

Babism Nineteenth-century militant Iranian Shii messianic movement for radical religious and social change, led by Sayyid Ali Muhammad Shirazi (d. 1850), self-proclaimed bab (gate) to "innate" knowledge of the Quran. Babism became a mass movement supported by merchants and government officials. It sought intensified observance of Islamic law and military preparation for imminent reappearance of the Hidden Imam, expected in 1845–46. Bab was arrested and imprisoned, leading to his claim to be the Hidden Imam. Babism abrogated the laws of the Quran. The state fought and killed most of its leadership. Bab was executed in 1850, leaving behind a substantial body of writing believed by followers to be divine revelation. Babism's teachings were refashioned by the later Bahai movement. Most Muslims label the movement heretical. See also Shirazi, Sayyid Ali Muhammad

Babur, Zahir al-Din Muhammad First Mughal ruler of India (r. 1526–30). Descended from Timur, he fought most of his life for tribal holdings in Central Asia. Invited to India as a warrior and ally, he occupied Delhi (1526), initiating the Mughal Dynasty. He wrote poetry in Turkish and authored the first major Muslim autobiography, the *Baburnama*.

Badawah See Bedouin

Badawi, al-Sayyid Ahmad (d. 1276) Moroccan-born founder of Ahmadi Sufi order, one of the four largest in Egypt. Influenced by Ahmad al-Rifai and Abd al-Qadir al-Jilani and their Sufi orders. Received a vision instructing him to go to Egypt, where he won many followers and reputedly worked miracles. Fought against the Crusaders. The annual celebration of his birth (mawlid) is among the most popular feasts in Egypt. By the early nineteenth century, three feasts were being held in his honor, coinciding with the agricultural cycle of the Nile Delta. The shrine and mosque built over his tomb are popular sites for devotees.

Badr, Battle of Battle fought in 624 by Muhammad and followers against the larger Meccan army led by Abu Sufyan. Seen as a symbol of the victory of Islam over polytheism and unbelief and as a demonstration of divine guidance and intervention on behalf of Muslims, even when outnumbered. Egyptians used "Operation Badr" as a code name for the 1973 Egyptian-Israeli war.

Baghdad Known as the City of Peace. Construction was begun by the Abbasid caliph al-Mansur in 762. Was the Abbasid capital until 1258, and became a center of international trade, medicine, communication with provinces, immigration, and industry, as well as the largest city in the Middle East. Home to a variety of religious and ethnic groups. Integrated Arabs and non-Arabs into a single society. Symbol of wealth, Arab imperial authority, majesty of caliphate, and Islamic civilization. Home of Bayt al-Hikmah, a center for the scientific study and translation of Syriac and Greek works into Arabic. Maintained its position as the capital of Islamic religious and Arabic literary studies after the fall of Abbasid caliphate. Capital of present-day Iraq.

Baha Allah (d. 1892) Glory of God. Title used by Mirza Husayn Ali Nuri, prophet-founder of the Bahai faith, who was an early adherent of the Bab movement, leading to his arrest and exile. He experienced divine visions during the period 1853–63 and announced his mission during the years 1863–68 through a series of letters to heads of state. Followers consider his works in Persian and Arabic divine revelation. He broke off from the Bab movement over a leadership dispute and claimed that Bab foretold him as future divine messenger. He called for world unity, the establishment of a world tribunal, adoption of a universal auxiliary language, and the belief that all religions come from the same God and teach the same essential truth with differences due to historical, linguistic, and social factors. He was condemned as a heretic in Iran and banished by the Ottomans to Acre, where he is buried. *See also* Bahai

Bahai Follower of Iranian Baha Allah, Mirza Husayn Ali Nuri (d. 1892). Bahais believe in progressive revelation, with Muhammad as the last prophet, and a continual process of revelation and divine manifestations, based on the conviction that God never leaves humanity without guidance. Bahais believe in the oneness of God, humanity, and religion. They reject prejudice and superstition and believe in the harmony of science and religion, equality of men and women, universal education, social and economic justice, and a spiritual basis for society. The faith has about five million adherents worldwide; the largest community is in India. The movement is considered heretical by most Muslims. *See also* Babism; Baha Allah

Bahira Christian monk believed to have recognized signs of prophethood in the child Muhammad, affirming the continuity of his prophethood with that of Moses and Jesus and the continuity of Muhammad's message with Jewish and Christian scriptures.

Bahithat al-Badiyah *See* Nasif, Malak Hifni

Bakkai al-Kunti, Ahmad al- (d. 1865) West African religious and political leader. One of the last principal spokesmen in precolonial Western Sudan for an accommodationist stance toward the threatening Christian European presence. The last of the great Kunta shaykhs, whose prestige and religious influence were interwoven with the Qadiri brotherhood and the economic fortunes of the Timbuktu region. His voluminous correspondence provides a rare, detailed glimpse into political and religious thought in nineteenth-century West Africa regarding three primary concerns: the nature of the imamate/caliphate in Sahelian and Sudanese communities, issues surrounding the encroaching Christian powers, and the growing politicization of Sufi tariqah affiliation.

Bakri, Mustafa ibn Kamal al-Din al- (d. 1748) Sufi teacher of the Khalwati order. Had through his students, particularly Muhammad al-Hifni and Muhammad al-Sammani, a significant impact on movements of Islamic renewal, especially in Africa. Born in Damascus and spent much time in Jerusalem and Cairo. Wrote a widely used prayer manual, poetry, mystical treatises, and accounts of spiritual travel. His reorganization of the Khalwati tradition involved more effective coordination of the followers' activities and greater scope for participation by common people.

Bakri Tariqah Special branch of the Khalwati Sufi order established in the mid-eighteenth century in Egypt by Mustafa ibn Kamal al-Din al-Bakri. Served as a parent organization to subgroups of activist, revivalist tariqahs (orders) throughout the Islamic world, since major disciples began their own orders after his death. Al-Bakri taught exclusive affiliation to tariqah, strict discipline in performance of litanies, greater participation of common people in tariqah rituals, and strict adherence to the Quran, Sunnah, and shariah. Leaders were heavily involved in hadith studies. The order split into different groups after al-Bakri's death. Some of his students became major hadith teachers in the latter part of the eighteenth century.

Bakshish Gratuity given for services; not payment. Not, as commonly mistranslated, "bribe." Derived from Persian root meaning "to give." Used in Persian, Turkish, Arabic, and South Asian Muslim languages to mean a gift given by a superior to an inferior, including, in Sufism, God's gifts to His worshipers.

Baladhuri, Ahmad ibn Yahya al- (d. 892) Early Muslim historian. Wrote a history of Arab conquests (*Futuh al-buldan*) arranged by areas conquered and based on documents, excerpts of which were included; this work is an important source of information on local administration and chief Muslim families. Also wrote *Ansab al-ashraf*, which included extensive biographical information, emphasizing the importance of family tradition and ancestry as sources of loyalty and examples for descendants. His discussions of the rise and fall of powerful dynasties provide a political moral. His commentaries on methodology are sparse, other than assertions of accuracy.

Baligh In legal terminology, refers to a person who has reached maturity and has full responsibilities under the law. Legal theorists assign different ages and criteria for reaching this state for both males and females.

Balkan States, Islam in the The Muslim population of the Balkan states, including Hungary, Romania, Greece, Bulgaria, Albania, and the former Yugoslavia, consists of a variety of ethnic groups speaking about ten different languages. Social and political conditions vary according to the size of the population and the ideology professed by successive regimes of each state. Most are Sunnis following the Hanafi school of Islamic law. Populations can be traced to three origins: Turkish-speaking settlers who arrived in the wake of Ottoman invasion or later, Muslim settlers from other parts of the Islamic world who were established in the region by Ottoman power, and indigenous people who converted to Islam. Conversion was most common in Albania, Bosnia-Herzegovina, Bulgaria, and Crete. During the Ottoman era, Muslims enjoyed privileged status, since non-Muslims were denied full citizenship. After the Christian reconquest,

Muslims were reduced everywhere but in Albania to the status of an inferior religious and/or ethnic minority in predominantly Eastern Orthodox or Catholic societies.

Balya ibn Malkan *See* Khidr, al-

Bangladesh, Islam in Eighty-five percent of the population in Bangladesh are Sunni Muslims; the rest are mostly Hindus. Islam arrived with Turkic invaders around 1200; in 1576 the region was conquered by the Mughals, who ruled until the arrival of the British (1747). At independence from Britain (1947), India was divided along religious lines into India and Pakistan; East Bengal became a province of Pakistan. The lack of economic and political parity with western Pakistan caused resentment. In 1971 a rebellion led by the separatist Awami League created an independent Bangladesh. The unicameral National Parliament has 330 seats, with 300 elected by popular vote and 30 reserved for women; members serve five-year terms.

Bani Sadr, Abol-Hasan (b. 1933) Iranian dissident and major theorist of the revolutionary movement who supported and served as adviser to Ayatollah Khomeini in the 1979 Iranian revolution. Elected Islamic Republic of Iran's first president in 1980. Impeached in June 1981 on charge of being a pro-American liberal; fled to exile in France.

Banking (Islamic) Islamic banking is interest-free banking inspired by Islamic law. Its uses include mudarabah (profit sharing), murabahah (advance purchase with later sale at marked-up price), ijarah (leasing or long-term credit), and musharakah (equity sharing). The first modern Islamic banking institutions were farmer credit unions in Pakistan in the 1950s and the Mit Ghamr Savings Bank in Egypt (1963). Major expansion came in the 1970s due to oil revenues and growing economies in the Persian Gulf and the rising desire for implementation of Islamic values in all spheres, including economic and financial. Gulf business interests strongly supported the Islamic banking movement, which has spread beyond the Muslim world into the West. Islamic banking today is particularly strong in Malaysia and Indonesia. Islamic financial instruments increasingly are accepted internationally, even in non-Islamic countries. In Iran and Pakistan, the financial system was reorganized in the 1980s to bring it into conformity with Islamic law. *See also* Economics (Islamic); Islamic Develoment Bank

Banna, Hasan al- (d. 1949) Egyptian founder of the Muslim Brotherhood (Jamiat al-Ikhwan al-Muslimun) in 1928. Held absolute personal authority over the movement and required personal loyalty and obedience from all adherents. Transformed it into a political movement in 1933. Active in the underground movement with the Free Officers in plotting to overthrow the Egyptian monarchy. In the 1930s and 1940s, founded Muslim schools and a publishing house that produced daily and weekly newspapers and Muhammad Rashid Rida's scholarly journal *Al-manar*. Proclaimed Islam as a comprehensive system of life and the Quran as the only acceptable constitution and law, with Muhammad as model. Rejected secularism and Arab nationalism because he considered all Muslims to be members of a single country. Declared that Muslims had an obligation to engage in individual, rather than collective, jihad. Advocated major principles of Islamic social justice, such as use of zakah exclusively for social expenses. Declared that the establishment of a just society would not occur through righteous thinking and good works alone, but required institutions, state intervention, and progressive taxes on income and wealth. Advocated implementation of Islamic law only after achievement of an Islamic society of social justice. Assassinated by Egyptian secret police in February 1949.

Banu al-Nadir Jewish tribe of Medina. Contributed significantly to Medinan economy. Entered into a pact with Muhammad known as the Constitution of Medina. Besieged and expelled after the Battle of Uhud in 625 for suspected disloyalty. Chapter 59 in the Quran concerns their expulsion. In 627, planned siege of Medina with Quraysh against the Muslims.

Banu Hashim (Quraysh) Descendants of Hashim ibn Abd Manaf, common ancestor of Muhammad, Ali, and Abbas, members of the Quraysh tribe. The term is also applied to the Prophet's family. Most Hashimis supported Muhammad's mission; they were boycotted and persecuted by other Quraysh in Mecca. Abbasids used the term to rally support for revolution. Due to the close relationship to Muhammad that it implies, Hashimi descent is considered meritorious. Also known as Hashemites. Prominent members ruled Hijaz (western Arabia) until World War I. After the war, they were established as kings of Jordan, Syria, and Iraq by the European Mandate powers. Only the ruling family of Jordan remains in power today. *See also* Ahl al-Bayt

Banu Israil Phrase that occurs forty times in the Quran, referring to the historical Jewish community as the recipient of God's various favors, including being saved from Pharaoh and being preferred over other nations. Also refers to Jews contemporary to Muhammad, who are accused in the Quran of wrongful behavior, forging scripture, hiding truth, and refusing to accept Islam. *See also* Judaism and Islam

Banu Qurayza Prosperous Jewish tribe of Medina. Initially agreed to support Muhammad; later negotiated with the Quraysh against the Muslims during the siege of Medina in 627. As a consequence, the Muslims besieged them. Sad ibn Muadh, an ally of the Qurayza, ruled that their men should be killed and the women and children sold as slaves, with their property divided among Muslims.

Baqa Abiding or remaining in God. Used by Sufis to describe the state of perfected soul following annihilation of self (fana), which is the ultimate goal of a person performing dhikr (spiritual exercise of remembrance).

Also refers to immortality or subsistence in the Unity of God sought by Sufis.

Baqarah, al- The Cow. Title of the second surah (chapter) in the Quran. It takes its name from a passage that begins at ayah (verse) 67, where Moses reports to the children of Israel that God has commanded them to sacrifice a cow. The theme of the surah is divine guidance.

Baqi, al- He who remains, the Everlasting One. One of the ninety-nine special names of God. Identification of God as al-Baqi is evident in the mystical process of gnosis whereby the ego (fana) is annihilated and replaced with God (baqa).

Baqillani, Abu Bakr Muhammad al- (d. 1013) Ashari theologian and Maliki jurist of Iraq. Instrumental in propagation of Ashari kalam, though his own doctrinal contribution is difficult to distinguish. Debated at Buwayhid and Byzantine courts. Was appointed teacher of the Buwayhid ruler's son, Samsam al-Dawla. Supported the doctrine of the apologetic miracle being proof of prophecy, the noncreation of the Quran, intercession, and the possibility of seeing God. Wrote a major work on the superiority of the Quran to poetry, arguing that the doctrine of Quranic inimitability (ijaz) is part of its structural composition, not dependant on rhetorical figures.

Baqir Muhammad, al- (d. ca. 732–43) Fifth Shii imam. Called al-Baqir, "the splitter" or "the opener" (of knowledge). Began teaching of distinctive Imami Shii law and doctrine. Opposed individual reasoning, stressing the authority of the imam. Respected as a scholar and traditionist by some non-Shiis. Personally ascetic, politically quietist, did not support revolts against Umayyads, but held that the imamate was explicitly designated by God. Politically overshadowed by his half-brother Zayd, whose revolt failed, and by proto-Abbasid forces. Had his authority claimed by some Shii extremist groups. Means and date of death are disputed; there are reports of poisoning by Umayyads or rivals for imamate. Buried in Medina.

Barakah Blessing conferred by God upon humankind. The term has a wide range of meanings depending on context. Uncommonly pious individuals are endowed with it (as is the Quran). In popular Islam, merely possessing barakah is not sufficient to enter the ranks of the saints (living and dead)—one must be able to transmit it to ordinary mortals, who benefit both materially and spiritually. One of the most visible manifestations of barakah in popular Islam is the ability to perform miracles. In popular Islam, barakah has long been viewed as hereditary. It may be associated with specific places, things, and acts, such as certain foods, animals, plants, events, words, and gestures. *See also* Popular Religion

Barawi, Shaykh Umar Uways al- *See* Uwaysi Tariqah

Barelvi *See* Ahl al-Sunnah wa'l-Jamaah

Barelwi *See* Ahl al-Sunnah wa'l-Jamaah

Barelwi, Sayyid Ahmad Reza Khan (d. 1831) North Indian reformer and activist. Educated and well-born. Associated with the family of Shah Wali Allah of Delhi from 1806 to 1811. Opposed to practices derived from Sufism, Shii doctrine, and local customs that were said to compromise God's unity. Launched a mass-based jihad movement to fight against the Sikh domination of Punjab. Died in Balakot (Northwest Frontier Province, Pakistan) with some six hundred followers while conducting jihad against Sikhs. Also known as Sayyed Ahmed Shadid. *See also* Ahl al-Sunnah wa'l-Jamaah

Barmakids Powerful family (originally Buddhist priests) from Balkh, Khurasan, that moved west at the time of the Abbasid revolution. Produced generals, provincial governors, and tutors of young princes. Became leaders of important kuttab (bureaucrats) pressure group. Largely responsible for the coup that brought Harun al-Rashid to power in 786. Responsible for centralizing the Abbasid administration. But their power depended largely on the pleasure of the caliph, and in 803 Rashid executed leading members of the family. Conflict over the successor to Rashid, together with a lack of independent military support, led to the family's downfall.

Barzakh, al- Mentioned briefly in the Quran. Understood in the popular imagination as the time between individual death and resurrection. Barrier between deceased and realm of living. Some questionable traditions suggest that circumstances experienced in barzakh are conditioned by the behavior of the deceased while alive. Modern Muslim thinkers deemphasize barzakh, focusing instead on individual accountability and the Day of Judgment.

Bashir, Hassan See Turabi, Hassan al-

Bashir, Omar Hassan al- (r. 1989–) Sudanese general who took control of the country's government from Sadiq al-Mahdi in 1989. His government was initially identified with the National Islamic Front due to support from Hassan al-Turabi and the Muslim Brotherhood, but Bashir relieved Turabi of all posts in 1999–2000. Fundamentalist-style Islamization projects were implemented in the 1990s to legitimize the regime. Bashir was opposed by older civilian political parties and the southern Sudanese in a major civil war.

Basmachis Bandit. Term applied by the Soviets to their Muslim opponents active in Central Asia between the Russian revolution and the 1930s. Basmachis included disparate groups of people who did not operate as a unified movement and who did not refer to themselves by this pejorative. The Soviets were able to exploit Basmachi internal divisions to quell them fairly rapidly once the Red Army had consolidated power elsewhere in Russia and Central Asia. Legacy is that of opposition to foreign rule in Central Asia generally, but they were highly dis-

organized, deeply divided, and readily susceptible to manipulation by outside forces. See also Central Asia, Islam in

Basmala See Bismillah

Basmallah See Bismillah

Bast Spiritual expansion. A profound involuntary spiritual state that overtakes a spiritual seeker, as a result of which he or she feels the divine presence directly. Described by Sufis as a state when the veils between them and God are lifted. Taken as a sign of God's mercy, pleasure, and acceptance. Accompanied by a sense of joy, exaltation, hope, and compassion. Opposite state is qabd (contraction). The terminology is based on a Quranic verse: "God contracts and He expands, and to Him you shall return" (2:245). See also Qabd; Sufism

Bastami See Bistami, Abu Yazid al-

Batin Inner, interior, inward, hidden, secret. In Shii, Ismaili, and Sufi thought, the Quran is held to contain two aspects: an outer or apparent meaning (zahir) and an inner or secret meaning, often allegorical or symbolic (batin). While the apparent meanings of the Quran are accessed through the traditional discipline of tafsir or exegesis, the batin is made known only through the hermeneutical process known as tawil (interpretation). The notion of secret meanings underlying the Quranic verses is connected to the notion of God as al-Batin, the Hidden One (Quran 57:3), whose absolutely nonmanifest Being underpins the created realm. The Ismailis were also known as the Batinis, presumably on account of their predilection for esoteric interpretations of the divine revelation. See also Zahir

Batini See Batin; Ismailis

Bayah Oath of allegiance to a leader. Unwritten pact given on behalf of the subjects by leading members of the tribe with the understanding that, as long as the leader abides by certain responsibilities toward his subjects, they are to maintain their allegiance to him. Representatives usually include religious scholars and political leaders. Bayah is still practiced in countries such as Saudi Arabia and Morocco. Like other concepts of classical tribal Islam, bayah is experiencing change as traditional tribal communities transform themselves into modern administrative states.

Bayan Clearness, lucidity, manifestation. Ilm al-bayan (the art or science of eloquence) is a branch of Arabic rhetoric dealing with metaphorical language, connecting idea and verbal expression or writing, and interpreting knowledge, and is close to balagha, eloquence. Based on the sanctity of Arabic as the Quranic language, the Quran is sometimes called al-Bayan, the ultimate manifestation.

Baybars I Third Mamluk sultan of Egypt (r. 1260–77). Turkish military slave of the last Ayyubid ruler. Won early victories over Louis IX's Crusaders (Mansura, Egypt, 1250) and Mongols (Ayn Jalut, Syria, 1260), taking Egypt's throne by violence. Defeated the Mongols several times, suppressed the Assassins, reconquered much Crusader territory, and extended Egyptian control into Anatolia and Nubia. Founded the Abbasid "shadow" caliphate (not universally accepted) to support the Mamluks' Islamic legitimacy. Created an effective military machine, training program, and intelligence service; centralized land administration and the judiciary; promoted anti-Mongol diplomacy and Indian trade. Inspired the popular epic romance *SiratBaybars*.

Baydawi, Abd Allah al- (d. probably 1286, perhaps as late as 1316) Shafii jurist, Ashari theologian. Educated in Baghdad, lived in Shiraz. Most famous for a concise commentary on the Quran with a special focus on grammar and variant readings, *Anwar al-tanzil wa-asrar al-tawil* (The lights of revelation and the secrets of interpretation), based on the earlier work of al-Zamakhshari (d. 1144),

Al-kashshaf (The unveiling). This work became standard in the Muslim world, receiving many supercommentaries and commonly being studied in madrasa courses on Quranic interpretation, and was one of the first Quran commentaries published in Europe (1846–48). Baydawi also wrote works on history, jurisprudence, grammar, and theology.

Bayezid *See* Bistami, Abu Yazid al-

Bayram *See* Id al-Adha; Id al-Fitr

Bayrami Tariqah Turkish Sufi order established in the fifteenth century by Haci Bayram Veli. Adherents follow the Shii traditions of the Twelve Imams and an extreme interpretation of the doctrine of unity of being. Reject dhikr, wearing of distinctive clothing, and most external trappings of Sufism. Virtually eradicated by the twentieth-century Turkish Republic's ban on Sufi orders, although traces exist in the Balkans.

Bayt al-Hikmah House of wisdom. Until recently, considered a celebrated institution of learning founded in Baghdad by the Abbasid ruler Harun al-Rashid (r. 786–809) and given a powerful impetus under his son al-Mamun (r. 813–33), housing the monumental activity of the translation of Greek works into Arabic. But this long-held view has now been called into question. The Bayt al-Hikmah apparently was a bureau of sorts established under al-Mansur (r. 754–75), modeled after the royal libraries of the Sasanian rulers of Persia, the primary function of which was to translate works of Sasanian history and culture from Persian into Arabic and to hold them.

Bayt al-Mal House of money. Historically, a financial institution responsible for the administration of taxes. Acted as royal treasury for caliphs and sultans, managing personal finances and government expenditures. Administered distribution of zakah (obligatory alms) revenues for public works. Modern Islamic economists deem the institutional framework appropriate for Islamic society. *See also* Diwan

Bayyumi Tariqah Egyptian successor to the Badawi tariqah (Sufi order). Departed from the spirit of the Khalwati tariqah, which emphasized individualism, strict training of dervishes, and reverence for a powerful leader. Founded by hadith scholar Ali ibn al-Hijazi al-Bayyumi (d. 1769), a student of Abd al-Rahman al-Halabi and a member of the branch of the revivalist Khalwati order. Linked to butchers' guild. Championed rights of poor. Popular order that served as a religious counterculture, defending the lower classes from the conservatism of establishment ulama.

Bazaar Persian. Market or shop. The bazaar is a place of personal, ethical struggle (jihad) for moral business practices, fair prices, negotiated justice, provision of services on behalf of the communal good, and enforcement of Islamic codes of commerce by judicial officers, judges, and experts in religious law. The credit system and social institutions tied to bazaars, such as guilds, mosques, and religious circles, enable them to play an active social, cultural, and political, as well as economic, role in society. Bazaars are central to the economy, particularly in traditional agricultural and craft systems, as an outlet for goods and for extension of credit.

Bazaaris Small shopkeeper/merchant sector of the traditional middle class of Iran. Historically have participated in and financially supported various religious organizations. Have also funded mosques, educational programs, and religious leaders speaking out against state policies affecting the marketplace. Joined forces with ulama, using their economic power and a broad population base, to support the 1870s Tobacco Revolt, the 1905 Constitutional Revolution, Mosaddeq's 1950s coalition against the shah, and the 1979 Islamic revolution. These actions were all opposed to the state's support and protection of Western interests, to the perceived detriment of the interests of the Iranian people and Islam.

Bazargan, Mehdi (b. 1907) Iranian modernist, university professor, reformer, and major voice of the Islamic opposition in the pre- and post-1979 revolutionary eras. Founded or cofounded many professional Islamic organizations. Headed the supervisory committee for nationalization of Iranian oil. First prime minister of the Islamic Republic of Iran and member of Council of the Islamic Revolution. Elected to parliament in 1980. Policies represent a synthesis of nationalism, positivism, and Islam. Prior to 1979 revolution, emphasized unity of religion and politics.

Bazzaz, Abdul-Rahman al- (b. 1913) Iraqi Arab nationalist politician. Born in Baghdad, educated at Baghdad University and King's College, London. Served as dean of the law school of the University of Baghdad, Iraqi ambassador to London, and secretary general of the Organization of Petroleum Exporting Countries (OPEC). Selected by Iraqi leader Abd al-Salam Arif in September 1964 to serve as deputy prime minister and minister of oil and foreign affairs. Served as prime minister for several months in 1966. Was a candidate for the presidency of the republic after the death of Abd al-Salam in 1966 but was defeated by the latter's brother, Abd al-Rahman.

Bedouin Nomads or desert dwellers. The name comes from Arabic *badawi*, "one who lives in the desert" (*badiyyah*), and is sometimes generically used to refer to any nomadic desert dweller, from West and North Africa to Central Asia, but more specifically refers to nonsedentarized tribally organized Central Arabian nomads or their descendants. From a culturally rich society, Bedouin were renowned for their complicated oral traditions and metered poetry. As late as the 1950s traditional Bedouin society comprised 25 percent of the Arabian peninsula's population. Today, Saudi government sedentarization policies have settled most of the nomadic population in the kingdom into modern cities and towns and incorporated them into the sedentary economy.

Beheshti, Muhammad Hossein (d. 1981) Leading Iranian Shii intellectual, cleric, and political organizer. Instrumental in the consolidation of clerical rule after the Islamic revolution in 1979. Head of the Revolutionary Council of Iran. Founder and secretary general of the Islamic Republican Party (IRP). Rejected efforts to reconcile liberal democracy, nationalism, and socialism with Islam, affirming a purely Islamic alternative represented by Khomeini's "rule of the jurist" instead. Killed in bombing of IRP headquarters.

Being *See* Dhat

Bektashi Tariqah Sufi order founded in the thirteenth century in Anatolia by Hajji Bektash Veli. Emphasizes the role of the spiritual teacher as mediator of prayers and blessings, intercession by earlier spiritual teachers, saints, the Twelve Imams, and Ali ibn Abi Talib as revealer of the mystical understanding of the Quran. Understands Muhammad and Ali as a single personage, emphasizing the complementarity and unity of God's word and its mystical dimension. Celebrates the Shii festivals of Ashura and Nawruz. Historically, criticized by Sunnis for ritual laxity, immorality, and heresy for its elevation of Ali and its comparisons of Ali and Muhammad to God. Widespread in the Ottoman Empire, particularly among townspeople and Ottoman military forces in the Balkans. Mobility and simplicity of organization, relaxed attitude toward literal legalism, and tolerance of non-Muslims facilitated the gradual conversion of part of the Balkan population, particularly in Albania. Moved its headquarters from Anatolia to Albania in 1925 when Atatürk abolished all Sufi orders in the Republic of Turkey. Suffered restrictions and confiscations of property under Communist rule in Albania. Today has communities in Turkey, in Albanian regions of the Balkans, and among Albanian immigrants to North America. Headquarters reopened in Albania in 1990. Turkey has recognized Bektashi contributions to Turkish culture through spiritual poetry in the Turkish language.

Bel Hadj, Ali (b. 1956) Leader in the Islamic Salvation Front (FIS) of Algeria. Best known for his fiery speeches at the al-Quba and al-Sunnah mosques in Algiers. Contributed theological articles to the movement's magazine, *Al-munqidh*, reflecting his Salafi orientation. His thorough religious knowledge, modest lifestyle, and remarkable oratorical skills enabled him to build a large constituency of followers. Viewed as representing the radical wing of the FIS, and some of his views, especially on democracy, dialogue with the regime, and armed struggle, have raised controversy. Still commands tremendous influence, particularly over the militant elements of the FIS, despite being imprisoned since 1990. *See also* Islamic Salvation Front

Belief *See* Iman

Ben Maimon, Moshe (d. 1204) Also known as Maimonides. Medieval Jewish legal scholar, community leader, philosopher, and physician. He is best known for his commentary on a rabbinic law code, the *Mishnah*; his codification of the whole of Jewish law, the *Mishneh Torah*; and his extraordinarily complex explanation of scripture and theology for one of his favorite students, the *Guide for the Perplexed*. In addition, he is known for his *Treatise on the Art of Logic* and for several epistles written in response to particular requests. These, like the *Mishnah* and the *Guide*, were written in Arabic but in Hebrew letters. Though he was a highly accomplished student and exegete of Aristotle, he wrote no commentaries on Aristotelian works. His work is studied by scholars of medieval philosophy today for his philosophical treatment of Jewish thought and for the light he sheds on predecessors and near contemporaries such as Al-Farabi, Ibn Sina, and Ibn Bajjah, as well as on Islamic dialectical theology (kalam).

Bengal, Islam in *See* Bangladesh, Islam in

Bequest Arabic *wasiyyah*. A testamentary disposition. Bequests are limited to one-third of the decedent's total estate. The remainder of the estate is divided according to Quranically prescribed rules to specific heirs. The bequest may exceed one-third of the estate only if the Quranically designated heirs grant their consent. The beneficiaries of bequests take their share after the payment of outstanding debts owed by the decedent. In Sunni law, a bequest in favor of a Quranically designated heir is invalid. Several Muslim countries such as Egypt, Sudan, and Iraq do not follow this rule as long as the bequest does not exceed one-third of the estate. *See also* Inheritance

Berbers Indigenous inhabitants of North Africa, with the largest concentrations in the mountainous areas of Morocco and Algeria and on the fringes of the Sahara. Their origins are disputed. They are divided into tribes and separated by vast deserts and different dialects, preventing their evolution into one nation. Converted to Islam after a fierce resistance to conquering Muslim armies, and many became Arabized (eighth to eleventh centuries). Supported the Arabs in conquering Spain (eighth century). Two confederations of Berber tribes, Almoravids and Almohads, established Islamic empires in northwestern Africa and Spain (eleventh and twelfth centuries). In modern times Berbers have expressed aspirations for political inclusion and recognition of their language.

Berri, Nabih (b. 1938) Lebanese Shii political leader. Head of AMAL and current speaker of the Lebanese parliament. Born in Sierra Leone, he received a law degree from the Lebanese University and was active in Lebanese politics in the 1970s as a lieutenant of Imam Musa al-Sadr. Succeeded al-Sadr as AMAL leader in the 1980s. Led AMAL during the critical years of Shii ascendancy after the Iranian revolution. His unwavering loyalty to the Syrian regime also helped his position. *See also* AMAL

Bhashani, Abdul-Hamid (d. 1978) Legendary leader and activist on behalf of peasants in Bengal and Assam. Received a traditional Islamic education in north India. Joined the freedom struggle through working in the Khilafat movement, the All-India National Congress, and later in the Muslim League to mobilize Muslim peasants in Assam and rural Bengal in support of the demand for the creation of Pakistan. He was jailed several times in British India and in independent Pakistan for his oppositional activities. Blending Islam and socialism, Bhashani became a major figure in Pakistan's left-wing politics in the 1950s and 1960s.

Bhutto, Benazir *See* Women and Islam

Bibi Fatimah *See* Fatimah, Hazrat-i-Masumah

Bible The Islamic tradition considers the Jewish and Christian scriptures to be divinely revealed, and the Quran refers frequently to the Hebrew scriptures (tawrat) and the Gospels (injil). The text and/or the interpretation of these scriptures is, however, held to have become "distorted" or "corrupted" (the doctrine of tahrif), finally to be superseded by the Quran. In debates with Christian missionaries, polemicists such as the Indian Rahmat Allah Kayranawi (d. 1891) drew on modern Western biblical criticism to further bolster ideas of tahrif in the Bible, contrasting this with the textual integrity of the Quran. A contemporary of Kayranawi, the Indian modernist Sayyid Ahmad Khan (d. 1898), rejected the idea (as had some premodern Muslim scholars) of textual corruption in the Bible, and he remains exceptional among Muslim scholars for undertaking an ambitious commentary on the Bible, *Tabyin al-kalam* (The Mahomedan commentary on the Holy Bible), which, however, remained incomplete. *See also* Christianity and Islam; Judaism and Islam; Torah

Bidah *See* Innovation

Bihbihani, Ayatollah Muhammad Musavi (d. 1963) Leading Iranian Shii cleric of the Pahlavi period. Son of one of the principal ulama leaders of the Constitutional Revolution (1905–11). Studied under Mirza Hasan Ashtiyani. Opposed government attempts at deveiling and enfranchisement of women, as well as land redistribution. Allegedly facilitated a coup against the popular prime minister Mohammed Mosaddeq in 1953.

Bihzad (d. 1535) Painter of Persian Timurid and early Safavid dynasties. Director of royal library. Supervisor of workshop producing illuminated manuscripts. Founded painting schools in Herat and Tabriz. Noted for liveliness of paintings, sense of movement, reality of figures, individualization of faces, and subtlety of colorings, particularly shades of blue and green.

Bila Kayfa Without asking/knowing how. Used in Islamic theological texts and discussions to avoid anthropomorphical discussions of God by delineating the manner in which God exists, acts, and so on, positing instead that God's mode of being is beyond human comprehension.

Bilal Also known as "The Black." Muhammad's former slave, who became a close associate and supporter of Islam in the seventh century. Appointed by Muhammad as first muezzin. In the twentieth century, Bilal became an important symbol of honor and dignity for early African-American Muslims.

Bilalians Name used by early African-American Muslims. Refers to Bilal, former black slave of Muhammad. Bilal's importance as the first Muslim muezzin, his ardent support for early Islam, and his favored status under Muhammad made him an important symbol of black honor and dignity, major themes of early African-American Islam.

Bilqis According to Arab tradition, the biblical Queen of Sheba. Sheba was a wealthy country whose god was represented by the sun. The Quran records that Solomon (Sulayman) wrote to Bilqis demanding her submission to him and to God. Bilqis responded by sending him a gift. Solomon then insisted

that she come to visit him, at which point she accepted Islam.

Bimaristan In medieval Islam, a hospital; in modern usage, this Persian appellation is applied especially to a mental hospital. One of the greatest and original institutional achievements of classical Islamic society, the bimaristan provided a wide range of services, sometimes without fee, and also functioned as a medical research and teaching school. The first bimaristan was established in Baghdad under Harun al-Rashid (r. 786–809). Among the most illustrious were the twelfth-century Adudi hospital in Baghdad and the Mansuri hospital in Cairo, completed in 1284, which had a huge administrative staff, lecture halls, a mosque, a chapel, a rich library, both male and female attendants, and separate networks of wards for fevers, ophthalmia, surgery, and dysentery; it also had a pharmacy, a dispensary, and an outreach division. *See also* Medicine: Traditional Practice

Bin Laden, Osama (b. 1957) Militant extremist believed to be a major financier of international terrorism and head of the al-Qaeda network. Educated in economics and public administration at King Abdul Aziz University in Jeddah, Saudi Arabia. Made a fortune in the family construction business. Fought for and financed the mujahidin in Afghanistan, 1979–89. Returned to his native Saudi Arabia in 1990. Offered his own troops, trained in Afghanistan, to drive Iraq out of Kuwait during the Gulf War, since he opposed the presence of U.S. troops in Saudi Arabia. Became an opponent of the Saudi royal family after they rejected his offer. Stripped of Saudi citizenship in 1994. Exiled to Sudan 1993–96. Returned to Afghanistan in 1996 and became a supporter of the Taliban regime. Issued a fatwa declaring that jihad against Americans and Zionists was a duty incumbent upon all Muslims due to the continued U.S. presence in Saudi Arabia, U.S. support for economic sanctions against Iraq, and unequivocal U.S. support for Israel, which he accuses of terrorism against Palestinians. Implicated in funding or masterminding attacks against the United States in Somalia and New York in 1993, Saudi Arabia in 1995, Tanzania and Kenya in 1998, the USS *Cole* in 2000, and New York and Washington in 2001.

Bin Nabi, Malik (d. 1973) Algerian thinker and writer. Wrote over twenty books on Islamic, cultural, societal, and developmental issues. Produced all his books under the series title The Problems of Civilization, which he held central in understanding the Muslim peoples' current state of decline. Urged Muslims to reconstruct themselves individually, change their state of "colonizability," and elevate themselves to higher standards of civilization. His ideas influenced segments of Algerian intellectuals, who later became active members of the contemporary Islamic movement.

Bint al-Shati *See* Abd al-Rahman, Aisha

Bioethics A field of inquiry dealing with the moral obligations of health professionals and society in meeting the needs of the sick and injured, providing a framework for moral judgment and ethical decision making in the wake of phenomenal advancements in medicine. Muslim jurists employ the principles of public interest (maslahah) and equity (istihsan) in making the majority of decisions dealing with health care policies in general. In dealing with patient rights and the obligations of medical professionals, the two principles of protection against distress and constriction (usr wa haraj) and refraining from causing loss or harm to oneself or to others (la darar wa la dirar) predominate. Issues such as genetic engineering and human cloning are debated, but no consensus of religious authorities has been reached.

Birgewi, Mehmed *See* Muhammadi Tariqah

Birth Control/Contraception In contrast to Christian and Jewish traditions, from earliest times family planning and contraception found acceptance in Islamic tradition. The Quran contains no clear or explicit text re-

garding birth control. However, the traditions (hadith) of Muhammad do. Though some traditions forbid birth control, the majority permit it. The vast majority of Sunni and Shii jurists believed that birth control through use of coitus interruptus (azl) was permissible, although a minority disagreed. However, because this procedure deprived a woman of her rights to children and to sexual satisfaction, her consent was required. Sunni and Shii jurists, employing the legal principle of reasoning by analogy (qiyas), have argued that since birth control in the form of coitus interruptus has been accepted for so long in Islam, then by analogy other, more modern forms of birth control such as use of the diaphragm, contraceptive pill, and IUD are acceptable. *See also* Abortion; Sexuality

Birth Rites A hadith holds that a child is born Muslim; it is the child's parents who make him or her a Jew or Christian, and so there is no need for a rite of initiation such as baptism or circumcision. Consequently the relatively few Islamic birth rites are recommended rather than juridically obligatory. In customary practice, often an animal is sacrificed (one for a girl, two for a boy) and the child is named; any name is acceptable unless it is particularly "heathen." Popular culture stipulates male circumcision and, more rarely, female circumcision. It also includes many other rituals connected with childhood and birth, but most of these have no foundation in normative Islamic sources. *See also* Aqiqah; Circumcision

Birthday *See* Mawlid

Biruni, Abu Rayhan Muhammad ibn Ahmad al- (d. 1048) Also known as al-Khwarizmi. Persian philosopher and one of Islam's greatest scientists. Wrote more than 150 works on astronomy, mathematics, mathematical geography, minerology, metallurgy, pharmacology, history, and philosophy. Most important philosophical contributions were criticism of Ibn Sina's natural philosophy and introduction of Hindu philosophy to the Islamic world. Interested in trigonometry and its application to astronomy. Astronomical works are a synthesis of Greek, Indian, and Arabic traditions. Invented practical machines and tools to determine specific weights of metals as well as compositions of compounds and alloys as part of his work on theoretical statics and hydrostatics. Wrote important work on India surveying Hindu culture, history, social customs, and doctrines.

Bismillah In the name of God. First word in opening chapter of the Quran. Also refers to formula used by Muslims to dedicate written works, "Bismillah al-Rahman al-Rahim" ("In the name of God, the Merciful, the Compassionate"). Generally also the first phrase taught in Quran recitation and in Quranic schools. Often used to open speeches. Use is shorthand for the full opening chapter of the Quran. Sometimes followed by phrases praising God and wishing blessings upon Muhammad and his family.

Bistami, Abu Yazid al- (d. 874) Also known as Bayezid. Prominent paradigm of "intoxicated" Sufism from the northeastern Iranian town of Bistam. Early education included Hanafi legal thought. Best known for "ecstatic utterance" (shath), several hundred of which are attributed to him by Sufi historians and theorists. The most famous is "Glory be to me! How exalted is my state!" Identified himself metaphorically as the Divine Throne, the Divine Footstool, and the heavenly archetype of the Quran (Preserved Tablet). Reported a vision in which the Kaaba circumambulated him, reversing the hajj ritual in which pilgrims circumambulate the sacred shrine. Described the experience in terms of Muhammad's "ascension" (miraj). Some read Abu Yazid's exclamations as theologically unacceptable; others see them as irrepressible expressions of divine intimacy. *See also* Shath

Black Muslims *See* Nation of Islam

Black Stone *See* Hajar al-Aswad, al-

Blasphemy *See* Apostasy; Kufr

Blessing *See* Barakah

Blood Money *See* Diyyah

Bohras Group numbering approximately one million, residing in India, Pakistan, the Middle East, East Africa, and the West (the name means "traders"). Trace their spiritual ancestry to eleventh-century Indian Hindu converts to Ismaili Shiism. Divided into several subgroups. Most prominent, best-organized, and wealthiest are the Daudi Bohras. Led by dais, currently Muhammad Burhanuddin, who are well known for their prolific written works and as orators. Oath of allegiance to shariah, imam, and dai is first given at puberty and is renewed annually on the feast of Gadir al-Khumm. Follow Fatimid school of jurisprudence, recognizing seven pillars of Islam (rather than the standard five), in which love of God, Prophets, imam, and dai is first and most important. Other pillars are purity, prayers, charitable dues, fasting, pilgrimage to Mecca, and jihad. Pilgrimages to saints' shrines are an important part of devotional life. Have a strong tradition of religious learning. Wear distinctive dress: beards and gold-rimmed white caps for men, colorful two-piece head-to-toe dress for women. Group also includes some Sunnis. Sulaymani Bohras are a smaller group, located in Yemen. *See also* India, Islam in; Ismailis; Shii Islam

Borujerdi, Mohammad Hosayn (d. 1962) Iranian cleric. Advocated a quietist attitude toward politics. Supported the return of the shah to power in 1953. Encouraged the shah to purge Bahais from government positions and seize their assets. Opposed the 1963 land reform bill, which appropriated religious endowments. Reinvigorated the practice of independent investigation of hadith. Worked to establish closer ties between Sunnis and Shiis.

Bosnia-Herzegovina, Islam in Islam arrived in Bosnia-Herzegovina between the late fourteenth and the sixteenth centuries, when Ottoman military and administrative officials settled there. Other Muslim immigrants also established themselves there, including Turks and non-Turkish Muslims. The Islamic population is mostly Serbo-Croatian-speaking Slavic Muslims. Under the Yugoslav government, Muslims were granted freedom of action and material advantages in 1960. In 1967 the Muslims of Bosnia-Herzegovina were recognized as one of the country's constituent peoples and became known as the Muslim Nation. Their privileged status deteriorated as ethnic and religious tensions grew following the downturn of the Yugoslav economy and the collapse of its Communist regime. Islam was politicized by the Democratic Action Party of Alija Izetbegovic, which encouraged religious and political activism among Bosnian Muslim communities. Hostilities between Muslims, Orthodox Serbs, and Catholic Croats resulted in combat and civil war beginning in 1992. Killings of Muslims remain under investigation by the United Nations.

Bouhired, Djamila (b. 1937) Algerian National Liberation Front (FLN) activist. Was sentenced to death for FLN bombings in Algiers in 1957. After Algeria gained independence, she ran unsuccessfully for the National Assembly and then returned to private life.

Brazil, Islam in Muslims in Brazil are descendants of African slaves and of emigrants from Ottoman Syria and Lebanon. The majority of Muslims in Brazil today are descendants of Sunni Muslims who left Lebanon after World War II. Most are engaged in commerce and follow Muslim ways through mosques, Islamic centers, periodicals, and social clubs.

Brethren of Purity See Ikhwan al-Safa

Bribe See Bakshish

Brothers See Ikhwan

Brunei, Islam in Islam is Brunei's national religion. Sixty-five percent of the population is Muslim, mostly Sunnis of Malay origin who follow the Shafii school of Islamic law. Most other Muslims are Kedayans (converts from indigenous tribal groups) and Chinese converts. Islam was adopted in the fifteenth century when a Malay Muslim was installed as sultan. The sultan traditionally was responsible for upholding the Islamic way of life, although the responsibility usually was delegated to appointed officials. Since the 1930s sultans have used rising oil revenues to provide an extensive social welfare system and promote Islam, including subsidizing the hajj, building mosques, and expanding the Department of Religious Affairs. The current sultan promotes the Malay Islamic monarchy as a national ideological alternative to Islamic theocracy.

Bucaille, Maurice (b. 1920) French surgeon, historian, spiritualist, and popular author of *The Bible, the Quran, and Science.* Claims that every scientific fact and phenomenon known today was anticipated in the Quran; therefore all scientific predictions can and should be based on the study of the Quran. Work has been translated into several languages and is widely read by Muslims.

Bukhara Khanate A Central Asian state that existed from circa 1500 to 1920. Ousting the Timurids, Uzbeks formed a decentralized polity based in several cities including Bukhara, Samarqand, and Tashkent. Late-sixteenth-century Bukhara emerged as the effective capital of a more centralized state, retaining its status through the political and economic decline of eighteenth-century Central Asia. The late nineteenth century saw commercial and diplomatic ties with Russia give way to armed conflict soon after the Russian conquest of Tashkent (1865). In 1920 the former khanate became the Bukharan People's Soviet Republic, dissolving into the Soviet republic of Uzbekistan in 1924. *See also* Central Asia, Islam in

Bukhari, Muhammad ibn Ismail ibn Ibrahim ibn al-Mughirah al- (d. 870) Major collector and transmitter of *Sahih al-Bukhari*, one of six works of hadith widely recognized as authentic and canonical and considered the most authoritative source of hadith along with *Sahih Muslim*. Noted for careful testing of genuineness of hadith reports. Gave definitive shape to the body of hadith as well as the means of determining accuracy and tracing genealogy, giving rise to the methodology of ilm al-rijal ("science of the men," i.e., authorities in hadith transmission). Organized hadith by topics, covering faith, purification, prayers, pilgrimage, fasting, commerce, alms, wills, inheritance, oaths, vows, murders, crimes, war, hunting, judicial proceedings, and wine. Offers anecdotes of Muhammad's dealings with same. *See also* Sahih al-Bukhari

Bulgaria, Islam in Thirteen percent of Bulgaria's population is Muslim (mostly Hanafi Sunnis). Ottomans ruled the region from the fourteenth century until 1878 in the north, 1908 in the south. Bulgarian Muslims are composed of four distinct ethnic groups whose identification with and practice of Islam varies significantly: Pomaks, Turks, Tatars, and Gypsies. *See also* Europe, Islam in

Bulugh *See* Baligh

Bunyad Persian. Base, root, origin, or foundation. Refers to a certain type of grassroots, nonprofit institution organized after the 1979 Iranian revolution. Although a few bunyads predated the revolution, they never gained the size or social significance of postrevolutionary ones. Most engage in functions such as trade, manufacturing, banking, and social services. Some also function as vehicles for patronage, mass mobilization, ideological indoctrination, and even repression. Three types exist in contemporary Iran: public, private, and waqf (pious endowment). They are exempt from taxes and organized into an elaborate network of functional and spatial offices.

Buraq Winged creature, usually depicted as a horse, which Muhammad mounted and

rode to Jerusalem, through seven heavens, hell, and paradise, into the presence of God, and back to earth, according to the story of his Night Journey. Legends state that other prophets before Muhammad also rode Buraq. Used prominently in West African folk art as a symbol of Muhammad's mystical powers.

Burckhardt, Ibrahim Titus (b. 1908) Author and expert on Islamic art and culture. Born in Florence. Embraced Islam in 1934. Edited and published ancient manuscripts. In 1972 was appointed by UNESCO to help preserve the cultural legacy of Fez. Wrote in German and English on Islamic art and culture and on Sufi doctrine. Translated Arabic religious and philosophic works.

Burhami Tariqah *See* Dasuqi Tariqah

Burhan Family Abbasid-era family of ulama from Bukhara who served as local governors. Collaborated with successive nomadic regimes, which conquered eastern Iran and Transoxiana. Represented a break from the past tradition of ulama resisting involvement in politics. Demonstrated the breakdown of power of the Abbasid caliphate.

Burhani Tariqah *See* Dasuqi Tariqah

Burhanuddin, Sayyidna Muhammad (b. 1915) Head of Daudi Bohra Ismaili community and fifty-second "absolute summoner" (representative of Hidden Imam). Resides in Bombay, India. Promotes blending of secular and religious studies in Islam-oriented schools. Scholar, author of several books on Ismaili religious thought, and poet. Internationally recognized for charitable, educational, and cultural endeavors, especially restoration of Fatimid-era architecture and relics.

Burma *See* Myanmar, Islam in

Burqa *See* Chador

Bu Said Dynasty Founded in Oman in 1741 by Imam Ahmad ibn Said of the Ibadi imams after expelling the Persians. Ruler was imam, formally elected by ulama. Continues to rule through the present, although the title of imam is no longer used and rulers are no longer elected. Religious prestige is based on ties to the Ibadi tradition. Established a trade-based empire encompassing East Africa and the Indian Ocean region. Ruled Zanzibar until 1964. Current ruler is Sultan Qabus ibn Said, who has modernized the political regime and crushed political and religious opposition.

Buti, Muhammad Said Ramadan al- (b. 1929) Syrian Islamic leader. Born in Jilka, Turkey. Attended the Institute of Islamic Guidance and al-Azhar University (Egypt). In 1960 was appointed dean of the Faculty of Religion at Damascus University. Continues to teach at Damascus University and is currently chair of the Department of Theology. Is a prolific scholar and continues to be actively engaged in the field, lecturing frequently at mosques throughout Syria, regularly attending international conferences, writing for numerous newspapers and journals, and maintaining his own website.

Buwayhids Also known as Buyyids. Dynasty of mercenary soldiers from the Caspian province of Daylam who controlled western Iran and Iraq from the mid-tenth to the mid-eleventh century, dominating the Abbasid Caliph until the arrival of the Seljuks. Established courts in Baghdad, Shiraz, and Isfahan; for most of the period the three power centers rivaled one another. Despite their Shii affiliation, for practical reasons the Buwayhids maintained the Abbasid Caliph in power, ruling in his name and exacting titles from him. Pioneered use of revenue grants (iqta) to pay soldiers, establishing a pattern of military dominance of the civilian administration later brought to completion by the Seljuks.

Buyyids *See* Buwayhids

Byzantine Empire Eastern, Greek-speaking part of the Roman Empire from 330 B.C.E. to 1453 C.E. At its height, the Byzantine Empire encompassed the Balkans, Greece, Anatolia, the Levant, and parts of North Africa. In 1204 the Fourth Crusade conquered Constantinople (Istanbul), and a severely weakened empire fell to the Ottoman Turks in 1453.

C

Cairo Arabic *al-Qahira* (meaning "victorious"). Capital of Egypt, largest city in Africa (sixteen million inhabitants), and a major cultural, religious, and political center. Located on the Nile banks. Founded by the Fatimids in 969; Fatimid Cairo contains al-Azhar (established 970), the renowned Islamic university. Fortified with the hilltop Citadel in 1176 by Salah al-Din (Saladin). Flourished under the Mamluks (thirteenth to sixteenth century), who erected splendid mosques, khans, khanaqahs (Sufi lodges), and madrasas for religious education. Contains hundreds of mosques, educational institutions, and magnificent architectural structures dating back to medieval times. Largely transformed in the nineteenth century with the building of European-style structures. Remains a major cultural and educational center for the Arab and Islamic worlds.

Cairo Declaration on Human Rights in Islam The Organization of the Islamic Conference (OIC) issued the Cairo Declaration in 1990, asserting that "fundamental rights and universal freedoms in Islam are an integral part" of Islam. Rule 24 holds that all rights and freedoms stipulated in the declaration are subject to shariah. *See also* Human Rights

Calendar *See* Islamic Calendar

Caliph/Caliphate Term adopted by dynastic rulers of the Muslim world, referring to the successor to the Prophet Muhammad as the political-military ruler of Muslim community. The first four successors to that office were chosen by consensus of the Muslim community's elders and were known as leaders of the believers. After them, the caliphate became hereditary. Two principal dynasties, the Umayyads and Abbasids, dominated the caliphate until 1258. The Mamluk sultanate kept members of the Abbasid family as tit-

ular caliphs in Cairo until the Ottoman conquest of Egypt in 1517. Ottoman sultans were then widely recognized as caliphs until abolition of the caliphate in 1924. The caliph's functions classically are the enforcement of law, defense and expansion of the realm of Islam, distribution of funds (booty and alms), and general supervision of government. It is not a spiritual office, but the institution was imbued with political and religious symbolism, particularly regarding the unity of the Muslim community. *See also* Khalifah

Call of Islam (COI) A breakaway group from the Muslim Youth Movement of South Africa (MYMSA). Formed in 1984 and led by Farid Esack and Ebrahim Rasool. Divisions took place when a small group advocated that MYMSA affiliate with the United Democratic Front (UDF), the internal wing of the then exiled African National Congress. COI articulated an Islamic message against racial discrimination (apartheid) that was in line with the strategies and vision of the UDF. In postapartheid South Africa the organization is effectively in decline.

Call to Prayer *See* Adhan

Calligraphy and Epigraphy A hadith claims that a person who writes beautifully "in the name of God the Merciful, the Compassionate" (the bismillah) will enter paradise. The belief that God's own word, the Quran, should be written in a style worthy of its contents led to the development of elegant calligraphic styles. Special attention was given to large, complicated scripts used in chancelleries to discourage imitation or forgeries of important documents. Though there are basic classical styles of writing used throughout the centuries, regional variants arose throughout the Islamic world. Maghrebi script was restricted to North Africa and

Andalusia, where writers often used colorful ornamentation. A similar development can be observed in the Bihari script used in medieval India for Quranic texts. Often faces, flowers, or animals are formed by sentences written in highly decorative scripts. To write an invocation to Ali in the shape of a lion is particularly admired by Shiis because Ali is often called Asad Allah, or "God's lion." Interest in calligraphy is increasing in Muslim countries such as Bangladesh, Malaysia, Indonesia, and Turkey, which use scripts other than Arabic for their languages, thus producing modern interpretations of traditional forms and calligraphic paintings. *See also* Naskh; Nastaliq; Taliq

Cambodia, Islam in Cambodia's Muslim community consists of descendants of Arab and Indian merchants and artisans as well as converts. Muslims there tend to be employed in trading, agriculture, and fishing and are primarily Sunnis with practices and beliefs similar to other orthodox Southeast Asian Muslims. The Muslim population was decimated by the Khmer Rouge. Religious education and understanding were severely weakened by the loss of teachers and leaders.

Camel, Battle of the Battle that took place in 656 between followers of Caliph Ali ibn Abi Talib and Meccan aristocrats led by Muhammad's wife, Aishah, protesting Ali's failure to capture and punish the murderers of his predecessor, Uthman. Named for the camel on which Aishah sat. First battle in which the caliph led troops against other Muslims.

Cameroon, Islam in Muslims comprise 16 percent of Cameroon's 13.1 million inhabitants; Christians are 33 percent and practitioners of indigenous African religions 51 percent. The Fulani, a pastoral nomadic group, spread Islam in early-nineteenth-century West Africa through commercial activity and Sufi brotherhoods (Qadiri and Tijani). Colonized by the Germans (1884–1916) and the British and French (1916–60), northern Cameroonians strongly resisted westernization; at independence in

1960, the developmental imbalance between the Muslim north and the south, where indigenous African religions and Christianity predominate, was obvious. In the last elections (1997) the Cameroon People's Democratic Movement (CPDM) won overwhelmingly; it is government-controlled and was the only party until legalization of opposition parties in 1990. There are no active Islamic political parties.

Canada, Islam in The majority of Canadian Muslims are post-1965 immigrants. Numerically, the most dominant are Indo-Pakistanis, followed by West Asians and North African Arabs. The population is generally young, educated, and professional. All major Canadian cities have mosques or other public spaces for religious observances. Important Canadian Muslim institutions include the Council of Muslim Communities of Canada, the Canadian Council of Muslim Women, the Ismaili National Council for Canada, the Canadian Muslim Education and Research Institute, and the Muslim Research Foundation. Particular challenges facing Canadian Muslims are prejudice, stereotyping, Muslim unity, the difficulty of practicing Islam in a predominantly Christian environment, gender issues, and preservation of Islamic cultural and spiritual heritage while assimilating into the Canadian secular mainstream.

Capitalism and Islam Islamic concepts of capitalism can be found in Quranic support for and protection of individual rights to private property, commercial honesty, and competition tempered by concern for the disadvantaged, and in hadith reports on the virtues of pious merchants. Some Muslims are opposed to Western capitalism because it served as the means by which the imperial West destroyed indigenous commerce and industries, blocking the paths of independence and prosperity. Muslims also denounce the primary concern for profit making over human welfare. The current trend in Islamic economics is the quest for identification of Islamically authentic concepts and trends. Islamic economics has developed since the 1970s. Current theories stress the primacy of private property, free enterprise, cooperation between the private sector and the state, cooperation between Muslim firms and governments internationally, the need for just redistribution of wealth within and between Muslim nations, and environmental preservation. Major state-supported Islamic banks seek to centralize investment and power while sharing risk and profit and avoiding interest payments at fixed rates. Rather, they offer depositors shares in gains and losses. *See also* Economics (Islamic)

Capitulations Commercial privileges granted by Muslim states, especially the Ottoman and Persian Empires, to Christian European states to conduct trade. Based on the principle of aman (safe conduct), capitulations set custom rates; established the security of life, property, and religion; and established channels to settle legal disputes. As the balance of power shifted toward western Europe, they were used to obtain privileges and extraterritorial status for Europeans and their clients in Muslim lands, so that by the nineteenth century they became instruments of imperialist exploitation. They were abolished in the Ottoman Empire in 1914, in Iran in 1928, and in Egypt in 1937.

Carmithians *See* Qaramita

Carpets Carpet weaving most commonly takes place in lands marked by dry and temperate climates, an abundance of marginal grazing land, and nomadic or seminomadic pastoral traditions. Both pile carpets and flat-woven types are made from Morocco to western China. Anatolia, Iran, Transcaucasia, and Turkic Central Asia boast the four most important weaving traditions. *See also* Sajjadah

Caucasus *See* Central Asia, Islam in

CDLR *See* Committee for the Defense of Legitimate Rights

Central Asia, Islam in Present-day Armenia, Azerbaijan, Chechnya, Dagestan, Georgia, and Abkhazia comprise the region historically known as the Caucasus; Central Asia

proper consists of Uzbekistan, Kazakhstan, Kyrgyzstan, Tajikistan, and Turkmenistan, but the two regions share many affinities. Most Muslims in the region are Sunni and follow the Hanafi school, though Shiism can be found among the Azeris, Ironis, and Tats of Dagestan. The majority are Turkic peoples; exceptions include the Uighurs and Kazakhs in Chinese Xinjiang and the Tajiks, who are ethnically and linguistically Indo-Iranian. By the mid-seventh century, conquering Arabs had imposed Islamic rule in the eastern Caucasus. From 800 to 1200 Islam spread further through merchants and traders. By the mid-sixteenth century Crimea, the southern Russian steppes, the Kazakh steppes, and western Siberia had come under Islamic law. Russia began conquest of the region in the sixteenth century. Sufi brotherhoods were important in preserving Islam during Russian domination and in many areas led the struggle against Russian rule. The Qadiri order in particular gave birth to several militant Sufi organizations that forcibly opposed Russian rule until the disintegration of the Soviet Union, treating the struggle as a jihad. *See also* Kazakhstan, Islam in; Kyrgyzstan, Islam in; Tajikistan, Islam in; Turkmenistan, Islam in; Uzbekistan, Islam in

Cevdet Pasha, Ahmad (d. 1895) Ottoman administrator and reformer of the Tanzimat period who tried to balance secular and religious influences in the empire. Received an Islamic education in Istanbul. In 1851 he collaborated with the Porte's translator, Fuad Pasha, to publish a standard grammar of modern Ottoman Turkish. During the 1860s he oversaw the implementation of reforms, first as inspector general in Bosnia-Herzegovina and later as governor of Aleppo in Syria. From 1868 to 1876, as president of the Council of Judicial Ordinances and later as minister of justice, he completed work on a new civil code, known as the Mecelle (law collection), that combined Islamic and Western elements. In 1873 became minister of pious foundations (awqaf) and the following year minister of education. After 1876 served as head of a number of ministries during the reign of Abdulhamid II.

Chad, Islam in Islam arrived before the eleventh century via Berbers, Muslim traders, and itinerant Sufi preachers whose organizations later played a key role in resisting nineteenth-century French colonization efforts. Before colonization the socioeconomic center was located in the Muslim north; by independence (1960) the Christianized south was more politically and economically developed. The Muslim-Christian power shift was magnified when bloody riots broke out in 1965 over oppressive taxation. Recent Islamic revivalism is inspired by the ideas of the National Islamic Front in neighboring Sudan. Hissein Habré (r. 1982–90) was indicted in Senegal for 97 political killings, 142 cases of torture, and 100 disappearances while governing Chad.

Chador Persian. Veil. Full-length garment covering a woman from head to foot, typically black in color. Not mandated by the Quran, although it symbolizes modest dress in Islamic culture. Historically worn by urban upper-class women for protection, honor, and distinction. Western feminists point to it as a symbol of backwardness and women's oppression and inferior status in Islamic societies. Westernized elites discarded it in favor of Western dress. Like the hijab, the chador has become popular among women in Islamist movements wishing to visibly identify themselves as Islamists and as an assertion of dignity and Islamic culture. Mandated in Saudi Arabia. *See also* Hijab

Chagatai Khanate Central Asian subdivision of the Mongol Empire ruled by descendants of Genghis Khan's second son, Chagatai. The family, becoming independent after 1259, adopted Islam but retained the nomadic organization and way of life. Declining around 1334, the khanate became the setting for the rise of the conqueror Timur Lang (Tamerlane). *See also* Mongols; Timur Lang

Chakralavi, Abdullah *See* Ahl al-Quran

Chaldiran, Battle of Battle in 1514 between the Ottoman Empire and the Persian Safavid dynasty. The Ottoman victory resulted in annexation of eastern Anatolia and northern Mesopotamia, Ottoman control over trade routes between Tabriz, Aleppo, and Bursa, and conquest of Arabian Peninsula and Mamluk territories in Egypt and Syria by 1517. The Safavid defeat permanently discouraged Safavid aspirations in Anatolia and shattered belief in the shah's invincibility.

Chapter *See* Surah

Charity *See* Sadaqah; Zakah

Charlemagne (d. 814) King of the Franks and head of the Holy Roman Empire in western Europe. Contemporary of Abbasid caliph Harun al-Rashid, with whom he established technological and economic exchange. Drove Muslims out of Gaul (France). Formed an alliance with the unconquered population of Spain to support Christian-ruled kingdoms in the north against the Muslim-ruled south.

Charter of Medina *See* Constitution of Medina

Chechnya, Islam in Chechnya is a Russian republic in the heart of the Tatar region. Although the majority of the non-Russian population is Muslim, recent population fluctuations prevent the calculation of exact demographic figures. Sunni Islam was introduced from the southeast in the late eighteenth century by Sufis. Chechen and other Caucasian tribes mounted a prolonged resistance to Russian conquest beginning in the early nineteenth century under Imam Shamil. In the twentieth century the Soviets launched an assault on organized religious faith that undermined the influence of Islam. Nevertheless, Islam remained an important component of Chechen identity, especially as an element in the resistance movement of the 1990s. In 1997 Chechnya officially embraced Islam as the state religion, ostensibly to restore order in a country plagued by war and anarchy. As a result, the Chechen population is experiencing both a revival and a transformation of Islam. Islam and Sufi orders have served as the backbone of a ferocious separatist movement since 1997. *See also* Russia, Islam in

Child Marriages Arabic *zawaj al-qasir*. Classical Islamic law allows child marriage on the condition that the marriage is contracted by the legal guardian and that the marriage not be consummated prior to the child's reaching the age of maturity. The child, upon reaching the age of maturity, may renounce the marriage prior to its consummation. Most Muslim countries have enacted minimum age requirements for marriage. At present the minimum age requirements in the various Muslim countries range from sixteen to eighteen for females and seventeen to twenty-one for males. Child marriage continues to be a problem, however, because of the difficulty of enforcement in rural areas.

China, Islam in Islam has been in China for over thirteen hundred years, with a current Muslim population of more than thirty million. Muslims first came to China as traders and itinerant teachers. Chinese expansion into Central Asia incorporated Muslim peoples such as the Uighars into the state, so that Muslims in China include both Hui (Chinese Muslims) and people from Muslim ethnic groups. Throughout history, Muslims have served as prominent imperial officers as well as opponents of imperial expansion. Under Communist rule Muslims experienced suppression, but they received support from Muslim countries in the international context of the Islamic resurgence at the end of the twentieth century.

Chinghez Khan *See* Genghis Khan

Chiragh Ali (d. 1895) Indian modernist author who rose to prominence as a supporter of Sayyid Ahmad Khan and the Aligarh movement. Served as revenue and political secretary in Hyderabad (1877). Agreed with Sir Sayyid that there was no conflict between the Quran and modern science. Produced modernist apologetics designed to refute missionary and orientalist criticisms of Islam as incapable of reform, and to argue that Islam requires no particular political or social system. Championed women's education and criticized polygyny and divorce. Works were influential among Western-educated Muslims in the late nineteenth and twentieth centuries.

Chishti, Muin al-Din Muhammad (d. 1236) Founder of the Chishti Sufi order, the most important and widespread Sufi order in India. Born in Sistan (Sijistan) and died in Ajmer. Came to India in 1193 after traveling in Khurasan and Baghdad. Freely adopted local Indian practices into his order, including the use of music in Sufi rituals, which then became an important point of contact between Muslims and the indigenous people of India. His tomb in Ajmer is one of the most popular shrines in northwestern India, visited by Muslims, Sikhs, Hindus, and Christians alike. *See also* Chishti Tariqah

Chishti Tariqah One of the most popular Sufi brotherhoods of South Asia. Founded in thirteenth-century India by Muin al-Din Chishti (d. 1236), it spread throughout present-day India, Pakistan, and Bangladesh. The order's members portray themselves as embracing poverty and avoiding contact with temporal rulers. Its golden age was the thirteenth to fourteenth centuries, when its leadership focused on practical and emotional mysticism and the close relationship between elder and disciple, rather than academic or intellectual sophistication. It was revitalized in the late seventeenth and early eighteenth centuries by Shah Wali Allah of Delhi, who declared their excellence in adapting early Muslim preaching to contemporary conditions. Under nineteenth-century British rule, the order was often associated with unsuccessful attempts to reform Islamic institutions. The shrine of its founder is the most important Muslim pilgrimage center in India. The Chishtis have developed a musical culture called qawwali— a group song genre of Hindustani light classical music presenting mystical poetry in

Persian, Hindi, and Urdu—performed in Sufi assemblies at shrines to produce religious emotion and ecstasy. The brotherhood is particularly devoted to Ali ibn Abi Talib as Muhammad's first successor in the initiatory chain of masters.

Christianity See Muslim-Christian Dialogue

Christianity and Islam The early Islamic empire included Christians in its bureaucracies; the first language of the Umayyad administration was Greek. Early relations were good, though there is evidence of discontent (Coptic uprising, 829–30). Islam inherited the Greek intellectual tradition, translating and elaborating on scientific, philosophical, medical, and religious texts, including the Bible. Legal rights for non-Muslims were established. The Crusades (1095–1291) and Reconquista (1085–1492) resulted in sustained military engagements and an exchange of knowledge that eventually led to the European Renaissance. Christians and Jews studied with Muslims at the universities of Córdoba (established 968) and Cairo (972), perhaps influencing the development of western European universities (Paris, 1150; Bologna, 1119). Religious tolerance varied with social, political, and economic circumstances. After the Middle Ages, the religious dimension of Christian-Muslim relations became secondary to economic and political interests. The Industrial Revolution ensured military supremacy of the Western powers, whose colonial influence affected most of the Muslim world. Colonial policies and the emergence of nineteenth-century Christian missionary movements affected the social, economic, educational, cultural, and religious institutions of Muslim communities worldwide. The reaction to Western hegemony has been a struggle to create independent nation-states reflecting varied interpretations of Islamic and Western political thought. Some emphasize minimal involvement with secular society; others promote Islam's reconciliation with the contemporary world. The Islamist trend advocates the complete integration of shariah, causing intercommunal discord in places such as Nigeria, Sudan, Afghanistan, and Pakistan. Creation of the state of Israel (1948) and the subsequent displacement of Palestinians have had a profound effect on Muslim-Christian relations everywhere. See also Muslim-Christian Dialogue

Church See Kanisah

Çiller, Tansu See Women and Islam

Circumcision Rite of passage conveying status change for males, from young boys to responsible men. Opinions differ as to whether it is legally obligatory (fard) or the practice of Muhammad (Sunnah). It is not mentioned in the Quran, but many Muslims believe it is a requirement for conversion to Islam. It is often identified as part of rites of purification (taharah) or traced to the Old Testament practice of Abraham. Circumcision has been variously interpreted as an outward symbol of self-discipline in God's requirements, the inner growth of reason, the submission of base passions to higher spiritual requisites, the physical acknowledgment of God's hegemony over uncontrolled instincts, and the deeper religious commitment expected of a mature Muslim. The practice is not universal. In Europe and North America, it is typically done in a hospital immediately after birth. Among traditional societies in the Middle East, a separate rite occurs between the ages of two and twelve as a part of ritual celebration, and older circumcised boys are immediately required to join older relatives in public prayer and are restricted from moving freely between the male and female parts of the house.

Commander of the Faithful See Amir al-Muminin

Commentator See Mufassir

Commercial Law In their broad outline, the fundamental principles of Islamic law in the area of contract and business law do not differ much from their counterparts in Western legal systems. From the nineteenth century, the influence of Western legal systems is largely found in the process of codification, intended to express legal norms in an accessible form, rather than in the substantive content of those norms. The Egyptian civil code (1948), based on Islamic law, Egyptian court decisions from 1883, and various modern Western codes served as a model for the new civil codes of Syria (1949), Iraq (1951), Libya (1953), Algeria (1975), Yemen (1979), and Kuwait (1980). There is no consensus regarding the Islamic legal prohibition against riba (interest) on paper money, although conservative Islamists condemn it; the validity of insurance contracts continues to be debated throughout the Muslim world. *See also* Contract Law; Economics (Islamic)

Committee for the Defense of Legitimate Rights First independent human rights organization in Saudi Arabia. Founded out of concern about a decline in Islamic standards after the Gulf War of 1990–91. Stated objectives reflect the diversity of membership and include release of political prisoners, accountability of the royal family to the people, reforms in human rights, purification of Islam from tribal customs, strict application of Islamic law, and elimination of oppression and injustice. Established in 1993 by Muhammad al-Masari and based in London in 1994 after being officially banned in Saudi Arabia for alleged ties to terrorist and extremist groups. Members have been arrested, removed from jobs, and imprisoned. Split occurred with formation of Movement for the Islamic Revolution in Arabia (MIRA). *See also* Masari, Muhammad al-

Communism and Islam Communists in the Muslim world have generally proclaimed official atheism and opposed established religious hierarchies. From the 1940s through the 1960s, Communists and Islamists sometimes joined forces in opposing colonialism and seeking national independence. Communists were most successful in Central Asia, where Soviet rule in 1920s led to secularization, destruction of patriarchal family

structures, and the creation of a proletarian workforce and social ownership via industrialization. Detachment from other Islamic societies was caused by the Soviet emphasis on ethnicity, territorial frontiers, and standardization of languages. The antireligious policies of the Soviet state combined with relative isolation from historic Islamic centers of learning drastically reduced the number of ulama in Central Asia and transformed Islamic identification into a set of customary observances coupled with ethnicity. Islamic identity as a form of ethnicity was also found in Communist-ruled China, Yugoslavia, Albania, and Afghanistan. The collapse of the Soviet Union in 1991 led to the reemergence of independent states with renewed Muslim identity across Central Asia.

Community *See* Ummah

Companions Those believed to have lived, interacted with, heard, or seen the Prophet Muhammad. In Sunni Islam, they are considered to be the most authoritative sources of information about the conduct of Muhammad and normative examples in their own right, immune from major sins and beyond criticism. The Shiis view many of the Companions as guilty of preventing their first imam, Ali ibn Abi Talib (d. 661), from succeeding to the caliphate, and hence morally culpable.

Compensation *See* Diyyah

Congresses (Islamic) Islamic congresses were proposed by late-nineteenth-century Muslim reformists to promote internal reform of Islam and resist Western imperialism. The dismemberment of the Ottoman Empire and abolition of the caliphate after World War I created a void that Muslim leaders and activists sought to fill by convening these congresses. Purposes included seeking an Islamic consensus for their own ambitions; garnering Muslim support against non-Muslim enemies, particularly in the Arab struggle against the British mandate and Zionism in Palestine; and claiming the caliphate. Issues were more political than religious. The competition for authority in Islam continued into the 1990s and 2000s with congresses seeking to legitimate policies and bring together Islamic opposition movements in pursuit of power.

Conseil National des Français Musulmans Founded in 1989 and reformed in 1992. Includes 190 associations with 14,000 members (as of 2001). Headquarters is in Dole. Acts as a lobby for an end to social and economic discrimination against Muslims in France and full integration of Muslims into French society. Provides assistance to Muslims in housing, education, and welfare; opposes xenophobia, racism, and anti-Semitism. Desires government recognition of French Islamic institutions as the equal of those of the Catholic, Protestant, and Jewish faiths, including appointment of an imam as army chaplain and reservation of burial areas in cemeteries for Muslims.

Consensus See Ijma

Constantinople See Istanbul

Constitution of Medina Charter set up by Muhammad, outlining the rights and duties of all citizens and the relationship of the Muslim community to other communities on the basis of religious confession rather than tribal ties or ethnicity. Recognized Jews as an integral part of the community, allied with Muslims but with religious and cultural autonomy. Considered the ideal model for an Islamic state.

Constitutional Revolution (Iran) Iranian revolution, 1905–11, caused by dissatisfaction with economic stagnation, influence of Western power, and results of the Russo-Japanese War of 1904–05 and the Russian revolution of 1905. It was sparked by the beating of a merchant accused by Tehran's governor of raising prices. Mullahs and merchants took sanctuary in Tehran's royal mosque, demanding justice from the shah. Radical preaching and violence ensued, as well as the demand for establishment of a

parliament. The first majlis were created as a result in 1906, granting power to popular-class guilds. The intent was to set up a constitutional monarchy with power held by a parliament and chosen ministers. Majlis produced the Iranian constitution that remained in effect, albeit largely ignored by the monarchs, until the 1979 Islamic revolution.

Consultation See Shura

Consultative Council of Indonesian Muslims See Masjumi

Contract See Aqd

Contract Law The classical law of contracts and obligations adopted the principle of freedom of contract and elaborated various requirements for the formation and validity of contracts. For example, according to the Quran, contracts must be entered into and applied in good faith, preferably be in writing, and avoid riba, the definition of which remains a subject of contention to date. The model contract is the contract of sale (bay). Most Muslim countries codified contract law by the late nineteenth or early twentieth century. The Ottoman Mecelle (Arabic majallah), enacted between 1869 and 1886, became the model for widespread codification of contract law. The Egyptian civil code (1948), developed under the guidance of Abd al-Razzaq al-Sanhuri (d. 1971), became the model for, among others, the Syrian, Kuwaiti, and Libyan commercial codes. States that have not devised a unified civil code (such as Saudi Arabia) interpret contract law in light of classical jurisprudence. In all Muslim jurisdictions, valid contracts are binding. See also Commercial Law

Convention Nationale des Musulmans Français Branch of Conseil National des Français Musulmans. Politically active in pursuit of the national and economic integration of Muslims in France and the reintroduction of religion into public life. Seeks the creation of Islamic colleges and universities directed by French Muslims. *See also* Conseil National des Français Musulmans

Conversion Conversion to Islam entails declaring in the presence of at least one witness that "there is no god but God and Muhammad is the messenger of God." Performance of other required duties—paying zakah, five daily prayers, pilgrimage to Mecca, and fasting during Ramadan—is expected to follow. Male converts are expected to be circumcised. Female converts are expected to adopt modest dress. Both sexes often adopt Muslim names and no longer eat pork or drink alcohol. Because the Quran states, "There is no compulsion in religion" (2:256), many twentieth-century scholars and activists argue against forced conversions, emphasizing instead Muhammad's practice of inviting people to Islam through preaching, teaching, and warning. Historically, some forced conversions under threat of exile or death did occur, but these are considered deviations from the rule. Nevertheless, pressure for conversion existed because conversion to Islam meant the right to own land and slaves, lower taxes, and privileges in certain types of trade, as well as polygyny and the attainment of higher social positions. Since the mid-sixteenth century conversions have been achieved largely though traveling merchants, Sufis, and popular preachers. In the twentieth century, emigration has played an important role in spreading Islam. Contemporary conversion approaches emphasize Islam as the fulfillment of Judaic and Christian teachings, Muhammad as last in the line of prophets including Abraham, Moses, and Jesus, and the divinity of Muhammad's message.

Copts/Coptic Church Copts are Orthodox Christian followers of the Coptic Church, headed by the pope and the patriarch of Alexandria, Egypt, the latter chosen from among three priests nominated by an electoral college formed of leading Coptic priests and laity. They constitute about 7 percent of Egypt's population. The Coptic Church traces its roots back to the apostle Mark, who brought the message of Christ to Egypt, and Egyptians consider the Coptic Church to be the first church outside Palestine founded by Christ's apostles. In the fifth century Egyptian Copts refused to follow the decrees of the Council of Chalcedon (451) defining the nature of Jesus Christ as "dual," at once divine and human. Because Egypt was under Roman rule at that time, Copts suffered from severe Roman persecution. When Muslim armies invaded Egypt, they were welcomed by the Egyptian Copts as liberators from Byzantine oppression. Accepted the authority of the Roman pope in the eighteenth century. The Copts' Greek name for themselves, Aigyptos (Westernized as *Copt*), is the source for Europe's name for Egypt (which is called Misr in Arabic).

Córdoba, Caliphate of After the fall of the Umayyad dynasty in Damascus, Abd al-Rahman ibn Muawiyah, an Umayyad prince, established himself in Córdoba in 756 as ruler of al-Andalus. The Córdoban cultural and scientific flowering peaked in the tenth century under Abd al-Rahman III, who took the title of caliph, and his son al-Hakam II, who was a well-known bibliophile and patron of the arts and sciences. Following several ineffectual caliphs and political disintegration of the country, the Córdoban caliphate finally collapsed in 1016, and several puppet caliphs appeared throughout the tumultuous eleventh century in an era of small competing states. *See also* Andalus, al-

Cosmology Science of the cosmos. Theocentric in Islam, since the cosmos is inseparable from the Quranic conception of God as creator and ruler of the cosmos. Holds that God is the central reality, so the cosmos did not come into existence by chance or without ultimate purpose. Traditionally extends the cosmos to the nonphysical world, including heavens and angels. Important contributor to natural and mathematical studies of the physical cosmos, including alchemy. Highest goal is to visualize the cosmos as a book of symbols for meditation and contemplation for spiritual upliftment or as a prison from which the human soul must escape to attain true freedom in the spiritual journey to God.

Council *See* Diwan; Majlis

Council for the Education of Muslim Children *See* Mendaki

Council of Experts (Iran) Also known as Assembly of Experts. Elected to advise the Revolutionary Council (dissolved 1980) and faqih (chief legal scholar) in the Islamic Republic of Iran. Dominated by clerics. Drafted a constitution that was ratified in 1979, establishing the authority of clerics in management and guidance of the republic. Made permanent in 1983 to select Khomeini's successor and oversee the orderly transfer of power.

Council of Masajid of the United States Established in 1978 by representatives of the Muslim World League to oversee mosques in the United States. Sponsored by Saudi Arabia. Consolidated with the Council of Masajid of Canada as Continental Council of Masajid of North America. Goals are to aid local mosques in educational and outreach programs, acquire permanent mosque buildings, perpetuate Islamic culture, and facilitate communications with non-Muslims.

Council on American-Islamic Relations (CAIR) Islamic advocacy group based in Washington, D.C., that challenges the prejudicial treatment of Islam and Muslims by the media, government agencies, and private organizations. Basically a civil rights organization defending the right of Muslims to live and practice Islam in America without having to suffer discrimination.

Court *See* Mahkamah

Court System The traditional Islamic court is the qadi's (judge's) court. Historically, there were no specialized court buildings and laws were not codified in the Western style. Judges were appointed by the ruler and typically heard cases in marketplaces, mosques, palaces, or private homes and were sometimes assisted by a consultative council (majlis) of legal scholars. Nineteenth-century European colonial administrations accelerated the institutionalization of courts and substitution of codified European laws for Islamic laws in all but personal status law. Twentieth-century Islamists seeking the re-Islamization of law assert that Islamic legal norms should replace European law codes in all areas. *See also* Shariah Courts

Courts *See* Mazalim Courts

Covenant *See* Ahd

Creed *See* Aqidah

Crimea Khanate Established by Muslim Tatars and Turks in the mid-fifteenth century. Although not completely independent of Ottoman sultans, its political and social institutions developed autonomously, blending Tatar steppe traditions with Ottoman bureaucratic and dynastic practices. Its economy was largely trade-based: slaves from the northern Slavic settlements, foodstuffs, and fine finished goods; Jews and Christians played important economic roles. Eighteenth-century Russian expansion and Crimean-Ottoman decline brought about its defeat by Russian armies between 1768 and 1774. Under Catherine II, the entire peninsula was annexed to the Russian empire.

Criminal Law Islamic criminal law recognizes three categories of wrongs punishable by the state: hudud crimes (sing. *hadd*; contravention of limits set by God), which lead to a prescribed and mandatory punishment; tazir (chastisement) crimes, involving discretionary punishment inflicted by the ruler; and qisas (retribution) crimes, concerned with injuries against the person such as homicide, infliction of wounds, and battery. In cases of qisas, the victim or the victim's next of kin may waive retribution in exchange for financial compensation (diyyah). However, in some cases the state retains the jurisdiction to punish the offender, despite the victim's or kin's acceptance of diyyah. Except for Saudi Arabia and a few other countries that continue to use traditional Islamic law in penal matters, most Muslim countries have adopted French-based criminal codes: Algeria, 1966; Kuwait, 1960; Libya, 1953; Morocco, 1962; and Pakistan, 1979. *See also* Hadd; Qisas; Tazir

Crusades Expeditions by Latin Christians, primarily in the late twelfth and thirteenth centuries, to reconquer the Christian Holy Lands of Syria-Palestine, which had been conquered by Muslims. Several Crusader states, lasting for two centuries, were established during this time. Campaigns were mostly aggressive and brutal, with cities pillaged and civilians massacred. Local quarrels among Muslims limited united efforts against the Crusaders. However, anti-Crusade sentiment was an important factor in the rise of the international Sunni movement. Muslim military heroes such as Salah al-Din (Saladin) recovered some territory, but Crusader rule did not fully end until 1291. Though the Crusades placed the Christian Holy Lands exclusively under Christian control for a time and enriched several Frankish lords, they did little for Christianity in the region. The relative tolerance previously extended to Christians faded as Muslims suspected native Christians of collaboration with the crusaders. The Crusades also damaged inter-Christian relations. The fourth Crusade, which sacked Constantinople, introduced a period of Latin domination and solidified the separation of Eastern and Western Christianity. Since the Crusades, Muslim-Christian relations have often been characterized by aggression, intolerance, and misunderstanding, and the Crusades are frequently identified as a symbol of the conflictual relations.

Cumhuriyet Halk Partisi *See* Republican People's Party (Turkey)

Custody *See* Hadana

Custom *See* Sunnah; Urf

D

Daftar *See* Defter

Dahlan, Kiyai Hadji Ahmad (d. 1923) Founder of Indonesian Muhammadiyyah movement. Born Mohammad Darwisi. Trained by Muhammad Abduh in Cairo. Supported modern scientific education combined with traditional religious learning, particularly for women. Sought to purify Islam from syncretic mysticism, animism, Hinduism, Buddhism, feudalism, and colonialism. Neither violent nor revolutionary. Remained official at court mosque until death.

Dai One who invites people to the faith, to the prayer, or to Islamic life. The invitation or "call" to Islam is known as dawah. In modern Islam, many Muslim groups around the world actively engage in dawah. *See also* Dawah

Dajjal, al- *See* Antichrist

Dakwah (Malaysia) General Malaysian term for missionary work, proselytization, and Islamization. Specifically refers to the political Islamist movement that emerged in the 1970s through the activities of youth organizations. Seeks greater application of Islamic laws and values in national life and articulates a holistic Islamic perspective of social, economic, and spiritual development. Became particularly prominent politically in 1979–82 at height of the Iranian Islamic revolution. Incorporated into the government in the 1980s through the appointment of Anwar Ibrahim of ABIM. Led to creation of the Islamic Bank and establishment of the International Islamic University and the International Institute of Islamic Thought and Civilization, reflecting the institutionalization of Islamization process. Particularly active in educational programs and initiatives. *See also* Dawah

Dalil Term that generally means "proof" but is not limited to logical deduction. Also includes reasoning based on analogy, called "proof by example." For example, the world must have been produced in time because, like a waterwheel, it is composed of parts, and we know that things containing multiple parts were produced in time. Dalil also includes inference. For example, a smile is a sign of happiness; a woman who is smiling must therefore be happy. Dalil in natural science and law has an empirical aspect, whereby material evidence is required to establish the relevant claim, such as an experiment, event, or document.

Damascus Capital of the Arab Republic of Syria. Cosmopolitan metropolis of very ancient origins; has been a major center of Islamic culture ever since its conquest by the Muslims in the seventh century. Was the center of the Umayyad caliphate.

Damm *See* Hadana

Dan Fodio, Uthman (d. 1817) Nigerian religious leader and reformer. Led Fulani efforts to spread Islam among the Hausa aristocracy in present-day northern Nigeria. The Fulani demanded political and cultural surrender to the strictly orthodox practice of Sunni Maliki Islam. Hostilities broke out in 1804 when the Hausa refused to abandon traditional religious practices. Uthman's brother, Shaykh Abd Allah ibn Muhammad, led the successful military campaigns that established the Sokoto caliphate, established new trade patterns, and transformed Islam into the official state religion. The present-day significance of the jihad rests more with Uthman's brother, Abd Allah, whose platform was strict adherence to Islamic law and who is admired by the present generation of Islamic radicals in northern Nigeria. *See also* Fulani Dynasty

Dance There is no specific theory or tradition of religious dance in Islamic civilization. Some Sufis (mystical Muslims) use dance to visually represent the Islamic principle of tawhid, emphasizing the oneness, peerlessness, and utter transcendence of God. Non-individuation of content, structured gestures, and symmetrical repetition of motifs within a prescribed spatial plan invoke the elaboration of arabesque patterns. Most famous is that of the "whirling dervishes," performed by the Mawlawi Sufi order, founded by Jalal al-Din Rumi. Other types of dance found in the Muslim world include solo dances, line dances performed by one-gender groups, and martial and combative dances.

Dandarawi Tariqah See Ibn Idris, Ahmad

Daoud See David

Daoud Khan, Muhammad (d. 1978) Afghan minister of interior (1949–50) and prime minister (1953–63). Encouraged social reforms and in 1959 permitted women to abandon the veil and encouraged their participation in the economic life of Afghanistan. Deposed his cousin, King Zahir, in July 1973 and was president of the Republic of Afghanistan until he and his family were executed in April 1978.

Dar al-Arqam Grassroots Malaysian Islamic dawah movement founded in 1968 by Shaykh Imam Ashari Muhammad al-Tamimi. Aims to revive Islamic religious belief and values for comprehensive practice in everyday life. Emphasizes self-assessment, self-correction, and formation of the Islamic personality. Uses the Sufi teacher-disciple bond to reinforce obedience to leadership. Sponsors lectures, concerts, and cultural shows, publishes books, magazines, and newspapers, and produces videos and cassette tapes showing the Islamic way of life. Expanded to an international arena in 1979 through missionary programs and diplomatic contacts. Has established self-contained Islamic villages throughout Malaysia to demonstrate the viability of the Islamic sociopolitical and economic system. Operates schools, clinics, businesses, agricultural complexes, and advertising and service agencies.

Dar al-Harb Territory of war. Denotes the territories bordering on dar al-Islam (territory of Islam), whose leaders are called upon to convert to Islam. Refers to territory that does not have a treaty of nonaggression or peace with Muslims; those that do are called dar al-ahd or dar al-sulh. Jurists trace the concept to Muhammad, whose messages to the Persian, Abyssinian, and Byzantine emperors demanded that they choose between conversion and war. When the leaders of dar al-harb accept Islam, the territory becomes part of dar al-Islam, where Islamic law prevails; conversely, according to the majority of jurists an Islamic territory taken by non-Muslims becomes dar al-harb when Islamic law is replaced. Like other classical legal concepts, dar al-harb has been affected by historical changes, and with the fragmentation of the Muslim world into numerous states, the concept has little significance today. See also Dar al-Islam; Dar al-Sulh

Dar al-Islam Territory of Islam. Region of Muslim sovereignty where Islamic law prevails. The Hanafi school of law holds that territory conquered by nonbelievers can remain dar al-Islam as long as a qadi administers Islamic laws and Muslims and dhimmis are protected. During the colonial period the status of colonized territories was debated, and Indian Muslims argued that British India was dar al-harb. There seemed to be no connection between the status of dar al-harb and an obligation to wage jihad against the British. Muslim scholars held that colonized Algeria was dar al-harb, and discussion arose about the obligation to emigrate to dar al-Islam.

Dar al-Islam Movement Also known as Darul Islam. Indonesian Islamic insurgent movement that challenged the legitimacy and authority of the newly independent Republic of Indonesia between 1948 and 1962.

Led by Sukarmadji Maridjan Kartosuwiryo. Consisted of military forces known as the Indonesian Islamic Army, which sought to enforce a proclaimed Islamic state. Initially supported by villagers and rural Muslim leaders of West Java. Support deteriorated with the rise of national resistance to Dutch colonialism in the 1950s and as military activities turned into rural terrorism; security problems created by extremism led political leaders to limit tolerated opposition to secular nationalism. Eradicated by government military forces. *See also* Kartosuwiryo, Sukarmadji Maridjan

Dar al-Mazalim *See* Mazalim Courts

Dar al-Musannifin *See* Nadwi, Sayyid Sulayman; Shibli Numani, Muhammad

Dar al-Shifa *See* Bimaristan

Dar al-Sulh Territory of treaty. Non-Muslim territory that has concluded an armistice with a Muslim government, agreeing to protect Muslims and their clients in that territory and often including an agreement to pay (or receive) tribute. Some modern writings equate dar al-sulh with the territory of friendly nations. *See also* Dar al-Harb; Dar al-Islam

Dar al-Taqiyyah Territory of dissimulation. In Khariji and Shii theology, used to indicate a region with imperfect living conditions under hostile governments where minorities such as Shiis and Kharijis must exercise caution in revealing their beliefs or expectations.

Dar al-Ulum Egyptian university established in 1872 to train teachers of modern subjects. Offered a mix of religious and secular subjects. Initially recruited students from the mosque-university of al-Azhar and preferred learning by rote memorization; eventually modernist ulama and laymen moved it in new directions. Had its budget deliberately restricted during the era of British control to prevent challenges to London's rule by modern-educated Egyptians. Never lost its hybrid quality as an institution influenced by both al-Azhar and the state but did eventually lose its rationale as Egypt's public universities began to train teachers. Merged with Cairo University. *See also* Deobandis

Darar Legal term meaning harm, prejudice, or cruelty. As an example, during illness, fasting could cause harm, so some schools of law allow an exemption from prescribed fasting during illness. In marriage, darar may be grounds for divorce. For instance, traditional Maliki jurisprudence granted a wife the right to divorce if her husband did not treat her and her co-wives equally or if the husband married a second wife.

Darqah *See* Tombs

Darqawi, Abu Hamid (Ahmad) al-Arabi al- (d. 1823) North African Sufi reformer and preacher. Stressed noninvolvement in worldly affairs and spoke against other Sufi orders exploiting claims of barakah (blessings). Was imprisoned by the Moroccan ruler Mawlay Suleyman (r. 1792–1822) for supporting revolts against the throne; released by Abd al-Rahman (r. 1822–1859). A Sufi order was organized around his teachings after his death, with members coming from a wide range of social groups; though once the most important tariqah in Morocco, its power waned as it spread throughout North Africa. *See also* Darqawi Tariqah

Darqawi Tariqah Revivalist branch of the Shadhili tariqah, originally emphasizing emotional fervor and the contemplative life as exemplified by wandering dervishes. Most widespread, largest, and most influential tariqah in North Africa, branching into derivatives. Established by followers of Ahmad al-Arabi al-Darqawi after his death. Opposed to the exploitation and abuse of barakah by established orders and the excessive repetition of prayers. Promoted the restoration of communication with God through ecstasy achieved via a combination of prayer and dance. Became an important politico-religious movement opposed to Ottoman rule in North Africa. Hostile to contemporary Tijani order. Allowed women to serve in leadership positions. *See also* Shadhili Tariqah

Darul Arqam *See* Muslim Converts' Association of Singapore (Darul Arqam)

Darul Islam *See* Dar al-Islam Movement

Darura In legal terminology, a state of necessity on account of which one may omit doing something required by law or may do something illegal. The conditions allowing this license and the extent of the license are stipulated variously by different legal scholars. Most legal theorists agree that murder or other gross physical harm is never legitimate.

Darwish *See* Dervish

Dasuqi Tariqah Sufi order founded in Egypt by Ibrahim ibn Abi al-Majd al-Dasuqi (d. 1288). Also known as Ibrahimi tariqah until the sixteenth century or Burhani or Burhami tariqah. Spread to Syria, Hijaz, Yemen, and Hadramawt. Focused on need for inner purity and self-denial. Emphasized adherence to shariah in one's heart and actions, rather than just through words, wearing Sufi garments, or living in a zawiyah. Celebrated three mawlids annually.

Daudis *See* Bohras

Daudiyah Sufi zawiyah founded in Damascus by Hanbali jurist Abu Bakr ibn Daud in the late fourteenth and early fifteenth centuries. Developed by his son, Abd al-Rahman. First zawiyah in Damascus of the Qadiri order. Functioned as pious meeting place. Contained waterwheel, well, grotto, mosque, library, and quarters for both men and women.

David Arabic *Daoud*. In the Quran, father of Solomon, shepherd, warrior, king, wise man, poet, prophet, and composer of psalms. As a youth, killed the giant Goliath with three pebbles and a slingshot. Used as a paradigm in the twentieth century for colonized Muslim nations, since his story shows that faith, determination, and God's blessing are more important than size and strength.

Dawah Call. God's way of bringing believers to faith and the means by which prophets call individuals and communities back to God. Militant submovements interpret dawah as calling Muslims back to the purer form of religion practiced by Muhammad and the early Muslim community. Historically, missionary dawah accompanied commercial ventures or followed military conquests. Dawah was also the function of the caliph, extending authority over Muslims outside Islamic lands and promoting Islamic unity. In the twentieth century, dawah has become the foundation for social, economic, political, and cultural activities as well as domestic and foreign policy strategies; jusitification for breaking away from the secular and colonial West; legitimation for claims to independent authority within the nation-state; and a call to membership in the righteous Islamic community. Four major modern trends are political orientation, interiorization, institutional organization, and social welfare concerns. Politically oriented national and transnational organizations seek the Islamization of laws and societies. Major international organizations are the World Council of Mosques and the Organization for the Distribution of the Quran. Modern movements focus on universal invitation within faith, rather than conversion of non-Muslims. Transnational organizations are usually reformist in orientation and most successful in places where local cults and cultures are no longer influential. Those with little political content have had the most lasting influence. Some states, such as Saudi Arabia and Libya, consider dawah a state responsibility. Others focus on dawah as the work of individual Muslims or private Muslim organizations.

Dawud *See* David

Day of Judgment Muslims believe that at the end of time, all human beings will have to face God and account for their deeds, good and bad. God will judge them accordingly, assigning reward or punishment. The time of the Day of Judgment is not specified in the Quran but is understood to be near. Its depiction is similar to biblical accounts, with earthquakes, moving mountains, the sky splitting open, heaven being rolled back, the sun ceasing to shine, stars being scattered and falling upon the earth, oceans boiling over, graves opening, the earth bringing forth hidden sins as well as lost stories and the dead themselves, and people vainly trying to flee divine wrath. Everyone will bow before God. Traditional Islamic thought portrays the Day of Judgment as preceded by a cosmic battle between Satan's forces, represented by the false messiah al-Dajjal and Gog and Magog, and God's forces, led by the Mahdi and Jesus. *See also* Afterlife

Death Referred to as "the certainty" in the Quran. Muslims believe that death should be contemplated throughout life as the most critical stage in the soul's progress. Suicide is considered sinful. At the onset of death, Quranic surahs, preferably surah 36, should be recited. The dying person should repent and perform ablutions, if possible. Relatives and companions should be present to pray and provide solace. The Islamic profession of faith (shahadah) should be recited in the dying person's ear in the hope that he or she will remember it and other fundamental principles of Islam when questioned in the grave by the angels Munkar and Nakir. Muslims are required to bury the dead as soon as possible, preferably before nightfall on the day of death.

Deedat, Ahmad (b. 1918) South African lecturer and writer, founding member and president of the Islamic Propagation Centre International in Durban in 1957. Largely self-taught and controversial; nonetheless, widely respected for his efforts to defend Islam against Christian efforts to debunk it. Received the King Faisal Award from the

Saudi Arabian government in 1986 for outstanding service to Islam.

Defter Also spelled *daftar*. A bound or stitched notebook, booklet, or register. After the ninth century the term is used primarily in reference to fiscal, military, and diplomatic administrative registers and record books. All extant collections of defters are those of the Ottoman Empire, although individual ones from elsewhere have survived.

Delhi Sultans (r. 1206–1526) First Islamic state centered in South Asia. Included the Mamluk, Khalji, Tughluq, Sayyid, and Lodi dynasties, which dominated the Indian subcontinent's north. Qutbuddin and his ethnically Turkish successors made Delhi their capital and patronized artists fleeing the Mongols, which stimulated a growing composite tradition arising from Persianate and indigenous sources.

Democracy A form of government in which people choose their legislators and executive leaders. Many modern thinkers believe democracy is compatible with Islamic principles. For example, the Quran urges Muslims to consult with each other when conducting affairs, providing an Islamic precedent for election. The Quran forbids compulsion in religion, laying the groundwork for tolerance for religious and political pluralism and equality of Muslims and non-Muslims in civic rights and duties. Some thinkers point to the legal principle of ijma (consensus) as a foundation for democracy. The modern history of democracy in Islam begins with the Egyptian reformer Muhammad Abduh, who sought to strengthen the moral roots of Islamic society by returning to the past while recognizing and accepting the need for change and linking change to the teachings of Islam. He asserted Islam as the moral basis of modern, progressive society. In the early twentieth century, constitutional democracy was advocated by supporters of secularism. The political and socioeconomic failures of Arab governments and rising civil strife in the 1970s and 1980s led to a broader agenda of grievances against regimes and a larger public search for Islamic revival as the only valid basis for social and political life. *See also* Bayah; Maslahah; Shura

Democratic Party (Turkey) Demokrat Parti. Ruled Turkey 1950–60. Lifted prior ban on call to prayer in Arabic. Permitted radio broadcasts of religious programs. Reintroduced Islamic instruction in schools. Encouraged religious activity as a distraction from the economic downturn of the 1950s. Facilitated the resurgence of Islam, especially at the popular level, in Turkey.

Demokrat Parti *See* Democratic Party (Turkey)

Demons *See* Ifrit; Jinn

Deobandis Indo-Pakistani reformist ulama movement centered in the Dar al-Ulum of Deoband. The school was founded (1867) by scholars associated with the thought of Sayyid Ahmad Reza Khan Barelwi to preserve the teachings of the faith during non-Muslim rule. Deobandis educated Muslims in "correct practice" and emphasized individual responsibility for correct belief. The school emphasized hadith and the Hanafi legal tradition, and encouraged spiritual transformation through "sober" Sufism. Providing an alternative to an intercessory religion focused on shrines and elaborate customary celebrations, Dar al-Ulum educated imams, preachers, writers, and publishers of religious works. By 1967 Deobandis had founded 8,934 schools throughout India and Pakistan. Originally quiescent politically, the majority of Deobandis opposed the partition of India and saw Pakistan as the creation of Western forces. Since the 1920s the Deobandi apolitical stance has taken shape in the transnational movement Tablighi Jamaat, but Islamist trends such as those of Pakistan's Jamiatul Ulama-i Islam and Afghanistan's Taliban have also emerged from the ranks of the Deobandis. *See also* Barelwi, Sayyid Ahmad Reza Khan

Dervish Persian. Also spelled *darwish*. Poor or mendicant. Refers to ascetic Sufis who wear rough wool clothing as a reflection of their rejection of material luxuries and dedicate themselves to a life of prayer, meditation on the Quran, fasting, seeking hidden or deeper guidance, and imitating the example of Muhammad. *See also* Faqir

Desire *See* Iradah

Destiny *See* Jabr

Devil *See* Satan

Devotional Art Fine or folk art created or utilized specifically for protection, intercession, or votive offering. Must be evaluated within the context of its function in the daily activities of believers, not for its aesthetic or economic merits. Provides documentation of everyday religious practices and rituals of the average believer even within what is otherwise characterized as the aniconic religious culture of Islam. For example, amulets and talismans such as a hand-crafted "hand of Fatimah" divert the evil eye, protect women and children, and reverse infertility, while geometrically orchestrated designs of the name of Allah protect believers under any circumstance. May be identified by association, for example, pious objects from pilgrimage such as drawings, engravings, photographs, or hangings illustrating relics or buildings while pilgrimage sites locate devotionalism. Includes the careful and elegant transcription of the Quran, particularly the bismillah and scriptural passages about protective imagery such as surah 2:256; the resulting calligraphy is highly esteemed by believers. Examples such as modern Islamic iconography—for example, portraits of the Ayatollah Khomeini in Iran—attest to its inherent links with religion and politics, and to the ubiquitous presence of religion in everyday life.

Devotional Music Can include the call to prayer and recitation of the Quran, though strictly speaking, musical accompaniment is always subordinate to the text. Sufi music and dhikr vary in form throughout the Islamic world. Its practices include elaborate, virtuosic solo singing of supplications, the reciting and singing of religious poetry, and group singing of religious hymns—for example, songs of pilgrimage to Mecca or other shrines. In Shii communities, music accompanies the commemoration of Husayn's martyrdom and ritual reenactments of his death. The place of music in Islamic culture has been disputed for centuries, as has that of women's voices in public. *See also* Sama

Devotional Poetry Early Islam discouraged poetry, which was criticized in the Quran and often described negatively in hadith. Sufi poems composed in the tenth and eleventh centuries spoke of the poet's longing for his divine beloved, using imagery of profane love. The first major genre entirely confined to devotional expression was the mawlud, a poem recited on the Prophet's birthday. Parallel with the mawlud is a narrative that describes the wondrous acts of the Prophet, of the first four caliphs, or very often of Sufi saints. Both folk and "high" Muslim devotional poetry are found throughout the Islamic world.

Devshirme Ottoman practice of levying a "tax" of young Christian males from the Balkans to serve as soldiers, court officers, administrative officers, and royal pages in the sultan's household. Instituted in 1395. The most promising recruits received Arabic, Turkish, and Islamic education in the sultan's court and palace schools and often attained positions of great power.

Dhahabi, Shaykh Muhammad Husayn (d. 1977) Former Egyptian minister of religious endowments and shaykh of al-Azhar. Strong critic of Islamic extremists and militants. Kidnapped as a hostage by Takfir wa'l-Hijrah in July 1977 in order to exchange him for imprisoned members of the movement. Subsequently assassinated when the government failed to respond. His execution led to a government crackdown on militant Islamic organizations in Egypt.

Dhahabi Tariqah A branch of the Kubrawi order, founded by Najm al-Din Kubra (d. 1221) in the thirteenth century. Its line of succession goes back to Abd Allah Barzishabadi in the fifteenth century. The origin of the name Dhahabi is not known. The order is centered in Shiraz with sister khanaqahs (Sufi centers) in Tehran and Tabriz.

Dhat Essence or substance. Often used to refer to God and His attributes. Mutazilis and philosophers believe that God is pure essence and that His attributes serve to explain Him. Sufis proclaim that God has no actual attributes, but that names and attributes have been defined to help believers move toward communion with Him.

Dhawq Tasting. Refers to mystical intuition, that is, direct knowledge of invisible realities or of God. In a general sense, a synonym for *kashf* (unveiling) and *shuhud* (witnessing, contemplation). Connotes the incommunicability of unmediated knowledge. Often considered the initial stage of unveiling, to be followed by "drinking" (shurb) and "quenching" (ri).

Dhikr Remembering or reminding. In Islamic devotional practice, it represents the ways of reminding oneself of God, based on Quranic injunctions such as "O you who believe, remember Allah with frequent dhikr" (33:41). In Sufi devotions, the term is used both for the regular activity of remembrance and for the litanies and prayers involved in the acts of remembering. Dhikr may be an act of individual devotion, but the term usually refers to collective devotions whose specific formulas and prayers are defined by the devotional path or tariqah that identifies the group. Each Sufi brotherhood has its own distinctive poems and prayers for the regular dhikr meetings of the order and the personal devotions of its members.

Dhimmi Non-Muslim under protection of Muslim law. A covenant of protection was made with conquered "Peoples of the Book," which included Jews, Christians, Sabaeans, and sometimes Zoroastrians and Hindus. Adult male dhimmis were required to pay a tax on their income and sometimes on their land. Restrictions and regulations in dress, occupation, and residence were often applied. In return, Islam offered dhimmis security of life and property, defense against enemies, communal self-government, and freedom of religious practice. In the modern period, dhimmi status has declined in importance as a result of the formation of nation-states and Western or quasi-Western legal codes. *See also* Ahl al-Kitab

Dhu al-Kifl *See* Ezekiel

Dhu al-Qaranyn *See* Alexander the Great

Dhul-Nun al-Misri (d. 859) Famous Egyptian Sufi (full name Dhul-Nun Abu-Faid Thawban ibn Ibrahim al-Misri). Born in upper Egypt; died in Djiza near Cairo. Considered among the most prominent figures of early Sufism and holds a position in the Sufi chronicles as high as Junaid (d. 910) and Bayazid (d. 874). Wisdom sayings and poems, which are extremely dense and rich in mystical imagery, emphasize knowledge or gnosis (marifah) more than fear (makhafah) or love (mahabbah), the other two major paths of spiritual realization in Sufism. No written work has survived, but a vast collection of poems, sayings, and aphorisms attributed to him continues to live on in oral tradition.

Dietary Rules The Quran and hadith expressly forbid Muslims from consuming carrion, spurting blood, pork, and food that is consecrated to any being other than God. Date wine was repudiated gradually; the strongest condemnation of it was among the last revelations received by Muhammad (632). Ritual slaughter and sacrifice are required for domestic cattle, sheep, goats, and fowl, which must be killed in God's name by making a fatal incision across the throat. The Quran permits fishing and hunting wild animals as long as the creature is lawful; it forbids the consumption of any animal strangled, beaten, or gored to death, or animals that have died by falling. Other dietary rules apply to specific ritual occasions. During Ramadan, Muslims are obliged to abstain completely from food and drink during daylight hours. Pilgrims are prohibited from slaughtering or hunting lawful animals as long as they remain in a sacral state. *See also* Halal

Din Way of life for which humans will be held accountable and recompensed accordingly on the Day of Judgment. The word is the root of the Arabic terms for "habit," "way," "account," "obedience," "judgment," and "reward,"and is often translated as "religion." It implies that living in obedience to God is an obligation owed to Him, for which people will be taken to account, judged, and recompensed. Din can refer generally to any path that humans follow for their lives or more specifically to Islam as the comprehensive way of life chosen by God for humanity's temporal and eternal benefit. Din encompasses beliefs, thought, character, behavior, and deeds. Thus, if these aspects of life are derived from God's guidance, as originally taught by the prophets, then they comprise Islam. However, if they are taken from human innovations or are deviations from what the Prophets taught, then they are only generally considered as the different ways that individuals or groups have chosen for themselves. Therefore Islam, or peaceful submission to God in belief, character, rituals, and sociopolitical and economic interactions, is termed the "way of truth" (din al-haqq), which is accepted by God. This sincere worship of none but Him is the "straight path" established for human life (al-din al-qayyim).

Din wa-Dawlah Phrase first used by Ali ibn Rabban al-Tabari (d. 870) as the title of his book *Al-din wa'l-dawlah fi ithbat nubuwwat Muhammad* (Religion and the state). Indicates that Islam addresses both the religious and political affairs of the Muslim community. Utilized by contemporary Muslims to emphasize that Islam is not solely a religion (din) in the Western secularized sense of the word, but that it also affects matters of state and government (dawlah).

Dinshaway Egyptian village northwest of Cairo. In June 1906 an incident between villagers and British soldiers hunting pigeons led to the death of a British soldier. A special tribunal imposed harsh sentences on the villagers, and the incident became a major symbol for emerging Egyptian nationalism.

Dipanegara (d. 1855) Son of a Javanese sultan; led a peasant rebellion against the Dutch and the Dutch-supported government in the name of Islam, 1825–30. Devoted himself to religious studies. Allied with ulama. Known for visions. Opposed corruption of aristocracy. Sought to purify Islam. Became a symbol of national resistance to foreign rule despite the ultimate failure of the rebellion.

Diploma See Ijazah

Diplomacy The principle of diplomacy appeared in early Islamic history in Muhammad's treaties with the Medinans and with the Jews and Christians of the Arabian Peninsula, and in his dispatch of envoys to other rulers. Muhammad's conclusion of the Hudaybiyyah Treaty with the Meccans has become the prototype of truce between combatants. Abbasid caliphs routinely concluded treaties with foreigners and received foreign envoys as representatives of fellow sovereigns. The Ottoman sultan Suleyman the Magnificent and the French king François I signed a treaty in 1535 endorsing a valid and sure peace between the countries for the duration of their lifetimes. Muslim majority states have increasingly recognized the need for diplomatic relations and the pursuit of diplomatic solutions to international conflicts.

Diplomatic Immunity Guarantees the protection of a diplomat's person, property, and premises. Medieval Muslim jurists argued this was commanded by Muhammad, who is reported to have strictly forbidden the molestation of envoys. By the 1960s most Muslim nations had acceded to the Vienna Conventions and have maintained a good record in observing diplomatic immunities.

Disbelief See Kufr

Divination Art of knowing that which cannot be known by empirical or rational means. The Quran condemns practices connected with pagan cults, and divination is officially abrogated in Islam, but many Islamic thinkers consider it a divine gift and a type of prophecy. Considered a part of folk religion, it incorporates astrological and magical methods. Types include interpretation of dreams, observation of footprints, morphoscopic and genealogical lines, chiromancy, observation of shoulder blades, invocation of celestial bodies, making oneself invisible, incantations, recitation of beautiful divine names, science of Islamic personal prayers, conjuring, catarchic astrology, geomancy, and omens. Its characteristic feature in Islamic practice is its consideration as a systematic art and science.

Divorce See Khul; Marriage and Divorce: Legal Foundations; Marriage and Divorce: Modern Practices

Diwan Central administration of Islamic state or specific branch of government, typically headed by a vizier. States typically had chancellery, financial, and military diwans, with separate diwans for pious foundations, fiefs, taxes, alms, customs, and administration. In literary circles, the term refers to a collection of poetry or prose. In the bureaucratic world, it refers to an archival register.

Diyyah Blood money. Financial compensation payable to the victim or the victim's next of kin in cases of crime against an individual, such as homicide, infliction of wounds, or battery, in place of retribution. Diyyah for killing is typically set and standard, while diyyah for injury varies according to the type and severity of injury. Encouraged by the Quran in place of retribution.

Djibouti, Islam in Ninety-six percent of Djibouti's 490,000 people are Sunni

Muslims who follow the Shafii legal tradition; many belong to the Qadiri, Ahmadi, and Salihi Sufi brotherhoods. Sixty percent of the population are ethnic Somalis; 35 percent are Afar. After independence from France (1977), the republic constructed a legal system based on French jurisprudence, customary practices, and Islamic law.

Dogs Considered impure and unclean in many traditional Islamic societies. A hadith mandates ritual ablution for anyone or anything that comes in contact with dog saliva. But the Quran mentions dogs favorably five times, including surah 5:4, which states, "Lawful for you are all good things, including what trained dogs . . . catch for you."

Dome of the Rock See Qubbat al-Sakhra

Dowry See Mahr

Dreams Dreams and visions were important in the life of the Prophet Muhammad and have received considerable attention in Islam. As a result, a highly developed science of oneiromancy (interpretation of dreams) existed within the Muslim world by the mid-ninth century. Dreams are viewed either as coming from God or as deriving from human desires. This distinction is so important that different Arabic words are used for a dream inspired by God (ruya) and for one inspired by desire (hulm). Dreams have often been seen as vehicles of divine communication in the lives of famous Muslims.

Dress (Islamic) Varies according to gender, age, marital status, geographical origin, occupation, religiosity, and political sentiment. Long and flowing garments have been worn by both genders for centuries for modesty, comfort, and practicality. Traditionally, men cover their heads and their bodies from waist to knees, typically wear beards, and wear appropriate outerwear in public. Women cover their bodies from neckline to ankles and wrists; they also cover their hair and neck and sometimes wear a face veil. The degree of covering depends on whether one is alone or with one's spouse, among friends or relatives of the same sex, or in a mixed setting. Materials are generally plain and somber in color. Hijab (head covering) is outlawed in Turkey, Tunisia, and France but tolerated in Egypt, Syria, and Jordan. See also Modesty

Drew, Timothy See Noble Drew Ali

Druze Millenarian offshoot of Ismaili Shiism, founded by Hamzah ibn Ali, a Persian missionary, in the tenth century in Cairo. Named for the eleventh-century missionary Muhammad al-Darazi. Considered a separate religion rather than a sect of Islam. Followers believe in the imamate of Fatimid caliph al-Hakim ibn Amr Allah and call themselves al-Muwahhidun (unitarians) due to a strict emphasis on monotheism. Missionary activities ended in 1043, after which no conversions were accepted. The faith is largely kept secret from outsiders. It forbids polygyny and concubinage, which are allowed in mainstream Sunni Islam, and temporary marriage, which is allowed in Shii Islam. Believers hold that ultimate truth is contained in revelations to their teachers, particularly Baha al-Din, contained in their scriptures Al-hikmah al-sharifah. A distinctive belief is that souls transmigrate (are reincarnated) from generation to generation. Largest populations today are in Lebanon, Syria, and Israel. Population totals slightly over one million worldwide.

Dua An appeal or invocation; usually refers to supplicatory prayers in Islam. These are often performed kneeling at the end of the formal ritual prayers (salat) and are accompanied by a gesture of outraised hands with the palms facing up. Special duas follow formulas established by the Prophet and other significant religious leaders. Examples of these special supplications are dua al-qunut, a supplication requesting guidance and protection, which is often recited during the dawn or single evening (witr) prayer, and dua al-komayl, which Shiis recommend reciting every Thursday night. In some cases communal supplications are uttered collectively; for example, a special prayer for rain may be performed during drought periods.

Duali, Abul Aswad al- *See* Nahw

Dualism Arabic *thanawiyyah*. Usually the (heretical) doctrine that upholds two divinities or creative or fundamental principles such as light and darkness. Entered the Islamic world through the mass conversion of Persians after the Abbasid ascent (750). Evident in the work of Ibn al-Muqaffa (d. ca. 760). Also perceived by some in the profession of the independence of the material substratum (Ibn Sina, d. 1037) and the indestructibility of material bodies (al-Jahidh, d. 868). Tawhid, the doctrine of the Transcendent One, is the essence of Muslim theology. All dualisms are therefore held in contempt by Islam.

Dunya Near or nearest; commonly translated as "world," "earth," or "this world." In matters of religious belief and practice, refers to earthly concerns, contrasted with those of God or heavenly concerns (din).

Duri, Abd al-Aziz al- (b. 1919) Iraqi educator and Arabist social historian. Focuses on Arab nationalism and identity as a cultural and linguistic matter rather than an ethnic, regional, or religious issue. Considers Islam and Arabism as a single unit, since Islam unified Arabs and gave them the intellectual and ideological basis for state formation, enabling the spread of Islam abroad.

Durr, Shajar al- (d. 1257) Born a Turkish slave, was the concubine and then the freed wife of the Ayyubid ruler al-Salih Ayyubi. After her husband's death in 1249 and the murder of the heir apparent, she became the queen of Egypt in 1250, the second woman in Islamic history to rule in her own right.

Durrani, Ahmad Shah (d. 1772) Founder of Durrani dynasty in Afghanistan. Charismatic leader, warrier, poet, and skilled diplomat. Tied to Sufi orders. Treasury official and commander of Afghan cavalry force under Iranian monarch Nadir Shah. Upon Nadir Shah's murder, launched an ambitious military campaign, ultimately dominating most of the territories of the former Mughal, Safavid, and Shaybanid dynasties.

Durrani Dynasty Afghani dynasty. In the conflicts following the death of the Iranian ruler Nadir Shah in 1747, a former commander in his army, Ahmad Khan Abdali, emerged as the ruler of much of Afghanistan. He adopted the title of Durr-i Dowran (pearl of pearls), which gave the name to the dynasty he established, the Durrani. His clan provided rulers of Afghanistan for more than two centuries, including Abd al-Rahman Khan, who established Afghanistan's international position at the end of the nineteenth century, and the last king, Muhammad Zahir Shah, who was overthrown by a military coup in 1973.

E

Economics (Islamic) Promoted as an alternative to neoclassical economics, Marxism, and other Western economic doctrines. Based on teachings of the Quran and Sunnah and aims to rediscover and revive the economic values, priorities, and mores of the early Muslim community. The movement to establish Islamic economic doctrine was born in India in the decades preceding partition (1947) as part of a plan to establish a full range of distinctly Islamic disciplines. Its most prominent promoter was Sayyid Abu al-Ala Mawdudi. Major emphases are economic justice, the failures of existing economic systems, and the need for an Islamic revival if Muslims are to recover the prosperity of the past. Theorists insist that true adherence to Islamic principles does not allow for selfishness, waste, extravagance, destructive competitive behavior, or immoral activities such as gambling, speculation, and hoarding. Interest is strictly prohibited. Profit sharing and investment based on risk taking are encouraged instead. A truly Islamic society will emphasize generosity toward the needy, hard work, fair prices, and protection of private property. Its four ethical bases are the unity of the Muslim community, equilibrium between supply and demand, free will of consumer and investor, and responsibility of the individual to the Muslim community. *See also* Banking (Islamic)

Edict *See* Farman

Education: Educational Institutions Historically, there are two major types of Islamic educational institutions: elementary Quranic schools (kuttab or maktab) and higher religious schools (madrasas). Elementary Quranic schools emphasized memorization of the Quran in Arabic, reading, and writing. Madrasas were endowed residential colleges that taught Quranic exegesis, hadith, juris-

prudence, theology, Arabic grammar, and logic. Upon completion of studies, students received a document indicating what texts had been studied and with whom (ijazah). Less-formal education was available from Sufi lodges, literary circles in princely courts, private tutors, and apprenticeships in state bureaus and craftsmen's shops. Western-style institutions introduced after 1800 became rivals to kuttab and madrasas. After independence, Islamic and Western school systems were unified, maintaining Western models and curricula. Islamists are presently working to Islamize education as part of the broader goal of Islamization of society.

Education: Educational Reform The nature of postcolonial educational reform varied among Muslim countries, depending on the development model adopted and the role played by oil-rich countries and their international benefactors. Malaysia adopted a largely coeducational secular curriculum, expanding education in science, mathematics, and technology-related disciplines; current literacy rates are 89.1 percent (male) and 78.1 percent (female). Saudi Arabia, Algeria, and Pakistan have indirectly restricted the intellectual development of women by emphasizing sex segregation. Literacy rates reflect this: Saudi Arabia, 71.5 percent (male) and 50.2 percent (female); Algeria, 74 percent (male) and 49 percent (female); Pakistan, 50 percent (male) and 24.4 percent (female).

Effendi Ottoman title of respect. In some Arab countries in the nineteenth and twentieth centuries it was similar to *Mr.* or *Esquire* and often referred to literate townspeople.

Egypt, Islam in The British occupation of Egypt (1882) did not end until Egyptian independence (1952). Under British domination, secular and Islamic reform movements emerged; Jamal al-Din al-Afghani, Muhammad Abduh, and Muhammad Rashid Rida articulated divergent reform ideologies that have greatly influenced modern Islamic thought. The early twentieth century saw the emergence of strong nationalist sentiments under leaders such as Saad Zaghlul. In 1928 Hasan al-Banna founded the Muslim Brotherhood, which sought to meet the religious and sociopolitical needs of an economically devastated country. In 1952 the Free Officers coup overthrew the British and established a republic under Gamal Abdel Nasser. Sayyid Qutb, a disciple of al-Banna, promoted radicalism and armed resistance; he was executed under Nasser, and various Islamic groups were suppressed. After defeat by Israel (1967), Nasser's death (1971), and peace with Israel (1979), Islamic militants assassinated Nasser's successor, Anwar Sadat (1981). In the 1990s a loosely linked group called the New Islamic Current expressed commitments to democracy and pluralism. It includes Yusuf al-Qaradawi, Kamal Abu al-Majd, and Shaykh Muhammad al-Ghazali and presents an alternative Islamic reformist agenda. Muslims comprise 93.7 percent of the sixty-eight million inhabitants of Egypt; Copts and other Christians are 6 percent. The Egyptian constitution of 1971 guarantees freedom of religion, although tensions along religious lines have risen sharply since the 1970s. *See also* Muslim Brotherhood in Egypt

Eid *See* Id

Eid al-Adha *See* Id al-Adha

Eid al-Fitr *See* Id al-Fitr

Elections The compatibility and permissibility of elections in Islam are the subject of a long-running debate. The consensus of most modern scholars is that there exists no explicit sanction against elections in the Quran and Sunnah. Although the textual sources specify no particular mechanisms of governance, many point to the Quran's emphasis on shura (consultation) as evidence of the essentially democratic character of

Islam. Indeed, the first caliphs or successors to the Prophet Muhammad were chosen from and by the leaders of the Muslim community through a form of electoral process. A number of more recent thinkers affirm the compatibility of Islam and elections. Rashid al-Ghannoushi, in particular, has argued that Islamist parties should act as government or loyal opposition depending on the will of the ballot box. The contemporary experience of elections in Islamic states varies. Pakistan and Iran have recently held elections with near universal suffrage, and in the case of the latter, popular dissent overwhelmingly handed victory to reformist candidates in 1997 and 2000. *See also* Democracy

Elias Arabic *Ilyas*. In the Quran, a preacher of truth and a prophet of the desert. Has been compared to Zachariah, John, and Jesus, and listed in the ranks of the righteous. Denounced worship of the sun god Baal, calling people back to Allah alone.

Elijah *See* Elias

Elisha Arabic *al-Yasa*. Listed in the Quran with Ishmael, Jonah, and Lot as favored by God above all nations, chosen by God for guidance along the straight path. Elisha inherited the mantle of the prophet Elijah. He served as an example of faith, constancy, and patience under suffering.

Enver Pasha (d. 1922) Ottoman Turkish general and commander of the Otttoman armies during World War I. Member of the Committee of Union and Progress (CUP). Married to Naciye Sultan, a daughter of Prince Suleyman. Died in battle in Tajikistan, where he had organized Muslims against the Bolsheviks following the Ottoman defeat in World War I.

Erbakan, Necmettin (b. 1926) Turkish politician. Elected to the National Assembly from Konya in 1969. In 1970 founded the neo-Islamist Milli Nizam Partisi (MNP, National Order Party), which called for a spiritual reawakening combined with technical development programs; it was banned from politics in 1972. Served as deputy prime minister in three coalition governments (1973–78) in the Milli Selamet Partisi (MSP, National Salvation Party). The formulation of an Islamist political program within the limits of parliamentary democracy owes much to Erbakan. He has been a major influence in the formation of the MNP, MSP, and the Refah Partisi (Welfare Party). *See also* Welfare Party

Eritrea, Islam in Islam has been linked to Eritrea since the seventh century, when followers of the Prophet Muhammad sought refuge in the Aksumite Empire because of Meccan persecution. Today almost half of the population is Muslim, and Muslims have been central to recent Eritrean developments, including the 1961–91 independence movement. Islam developed indigenously after the arrival of Arabs in the ninth century and under Imam Ahmed Gran in the sixteenth century. Nineteenth-century reformers changed Islamic practices and founded the first Islamic schools and courts in Eritrea. During the past century, Islam flourished in Eritrea under Italian rule (1882–1941) but was repressed under Ethiopian rule (1951–91).

Eritrean Liberation Front Leading movement for Eritrean independence from 1961 through the 1970s. Largely Muslim; received substantial support from Syria, Saudi Arabia, and other Arab states. Although plagued by Eritrea's regional and sectarian divisions, the organization was a catalyst for Eritrean nationalism, and most well-known Eritrean nationalists served in the movement.

Eritrean People's Liberation Front Leading force of Eritrean nationalism after the 1970s and in the current Eritrean government. Stresses secular nationalism, centralization, social reform, and self-reliance. Founders Ramadan Muhammad Nur and Isaias Afwerki left the Eritrean Liberation Front because of socioreligious differences and allied with organizations dedicated to the over-throw of the Dergue (the military government) in Ethiopia.

Ersoy, Mehmed Akif (d. 1936) Turkish Islamist poet. Gifted linguist in Turkish, Arabic, Persian, and French. Wrote poetic social commentary illustrating his vision for an Islamic society. His "Independence March" was adopted as the Turkish national anthem (1921) but, disappointed in the emergence of a secular Turkish republic, Ersoy moved to Egypt.

Eschatology The study of "last things" incorporates two related concepts: the afterlife and world's end. The Quran emphasizes the inevitability of resurrection, judgment, and the eternal division of the righteous and the wicked. On the day of resurrection, humans will be judged by their faith in God, their acceptance of God's revelations, and their works. The wicked will be consigned to eternal torment; the righteous will enjoy paradise. Later commentators include a belief in an intermediate state (barzakh) between death and the resurrection and final judgment. Before the final resurrection, the terrible tribulation of the last days occurs, during which the Great Deceiver, al-Dajjal, will appear. Though not mentioned in the Quran, al-Dajjal is prominent in hadith and later Islamic literature, as is the Mahdi (also absent in the Quran). The Mahdi will appear to bring justice and truth to all, the entire world will accept Islam, and his death (before the day of resurrection) will bring turmoil, uncertainty, and temptation. There are disagreements over the Mahdi's precise relationship to Jesus; some deny there will be a Muslim Mahdi, claiming that Jesus' second coming will fulfill this role. Some believe that Jesus will return as a just judge; he will die after forty years and be buried in a spot beside Muhammad's tomb in Medina that has been reserved for him. *See also* Mahdi

Essence *See* Dhat

Ethics In Islamic theology and philosophy, ethical theories were constructed on two closely related questions: the ontological status of value in ethics, and the sources of human knowledge of such value. Two theories of ethics emerged from these discussions: rationalist ethics, in which human reason is given a substantive role in judging what is right and wrong (maintained by the Mutazilis and the Shiis), and divine command ethics, in which right action is that which is commanded by God (maintained by the Asharis). In the modern debates on social and political ethics, it is mainly the rationalist theory that is finding support among activist reformers because of the doctrine of human capacity to know right through reason. *See also* Bioethics

Ethiopia, Islam in Almost half of Ethiopia's population is Muslim; Christians total approximately 40 percent, and the rest practice indigenous religions. Unlike many other African states, Christian-Muslim unrest is not the legacy of colonialism: Ethiopia is historically one of the oldest Christian states and the oldest independent country in Africa. Early Muslim communities were established by merchants, teachers, and migrating tribes. A jihad in the sixteenth century led by Ahmad Gran spread Islam, but Portuguese-aided Ethiopian rulers restored Christian power. Migrations of Oromo peoples beginning in the fifteenth century established a strong Muslim presence. Oromo liberation movements challenged Christian and leftist governments in the late twentieth century.

Ethnicity The Quran stresses the unity of the Islamic community and emphasizes the primacy of bonds created through Islam over those based on shared identities of kinship, region, and language—bonds that the medieval philosopher Ibn Khaldun (d. 1406) called asabiyyah. Nevertheless, when Muslims first conquered peoples who neither spoke Arabic nor could claim Arab descent, concerns regarding ethnicity frequently surfaced. Even today, Muslims claiming descent from Muhammad, called sharifs in North Africa and sayyids in Yemen and parts of

Asia, often enjoy religious prestige and legal entitlements.

Eunuch Castrated male slaves or captives of war who traditionally guarded wealthy women's residences or harems. The practice of guarding wealthy or upper-class women with eunuchs arose in the first Christian centuries in the Mediterranean Middle East, Byzantium, and Persia and was eventually absorbed into the upper echelons of Islamic society. Castration, however, is forbidden in Islamic law.

Europe, Islam in In the late twentieth century there were about eighteen million Muslims in Europe, with approximately nine million each in the western and southeastern parts of the continent. The largest group is in the Balkan states and consists of all social levels, including religious, intellectual, artistic, and commercial elites. In western Europe, Islam is essentially a religion of migrants, unskilled laborers, small merchants, and lower-level white-collar workers; large numbers have come from former colonies and most are not citizens, though there is a small number of converts. The historical antagonism between western and eastern Europe is apparent in the history of Islam there. During the late Middle Ages, Western Christian powers reconquered the last Muslim territories in Spain and the Mediterranean. During the sixteenth and seventeenth centuries, the last vestiges of Islam were removed from western Europe. Meanwhile, Ottoman Turks conquered Constantinople in 1453 and expanded into the Balkans. In the twentieth century the dismantling of the Ottoman Empire, dominance of Communist rule, and revival of nationalism caused the suppression of Islam in southeastern Europe and destroyed much of its ancient heritage and infrastructure. In western Europe, a stream of Muslim migrants and refugees arrived, resulting in significant Muslim populations in all countries there today. Mosques are the most important centers of Islamic education in western Europe and also serve as Muslim community centers, where feasts, wedding parties, circumcisions, and mourning rituals are held and where counseling services and social services are provided. Numerous national and international organizations for the promotion and protection of Muslim interests have been founded. Their major concern is legal pluralism and the right of Muslims to adhere to Islamic law both privately and publicly.

Eve Arabic *Hawwa*. Wife of Adam. She is not named in the Quran; her name is known through oral tradition (hadith). Unlike the Old Testament, the Quran does not present her as responsible for tempting Adam, although some later Islamic interpretations do.

Evidence *See* Dalil

Evil Eye Popular belief that a person can glance or stare at someone else's favorite possession and, if envious of the other person's good fortune, hurt, damage, or destroy it.

Evolution, Theory of, and Islam Debate about the theory of evoluation has pitted traditional religious scholars against modernists. The theory is denounced by most Muslim scholars, even some early modernists such as Afghani, as a refutation of Quranic theories of creation. Today the theory is taught in Turkey, Egypt, Iraq, Iran, Indonesia, and several other countries. It has ben removed from the syllabus in Pakistan and is forbidden in Saudi Arabia and Sudan.

Exegesis *See* Tafsir

Ezekiel The Quran mentions Hizqil (21:85, 38:48, also known as Dhu al-Kifl), a name that is thought to be the Arabic form of Ezekiel. Hizqil was noted for faithfulness and patience, a description that matches the biblical prophet Ezekiel, who was imprisoned by Nebuchadnezzar after attacking Jerusalem. Also known for reproaching evils among the people of Israel and denouncing false leaders.

Ezra Arabic *Uzayr*. The Quran mentions Ezra once (9:30), recording that Jews called him the son of God, much as Christians call Jesus the son of God. The title is problematic for Muslims because it associates another person with God and equates the words and actions of humans with those of God. Uzayr of the Quran may or may not refer to the fifth-century B.C.E prophet of the Hebrew Bible.

F

Fadail *See* Hagiography

Fadlallah, Muhammad Husayn (b. 1935) Lebanese Shii cleric and leader of Hizb Allah. Born and educated in Iraq. Since 1985, president of the Lebanese council of Hizb Allah and vice president of the central council of international Hizb Allah in Tehran. Named marja al-taqlid (source of imitation) by Khomeini in 1986. Opposed to American-brokered Arab-Israeli peace negotiations. Favors use of ijtihad in modern circumstances. Maintains the option of violent revolution but prefers change rather than sudden revolution, and favors a reformist path. Does not support restoration of the caliphate or Khomeini's principle of vilayat-i faqih on the grounds that it could lead to autocratic personal power. Rejects the distinction between political and religious power. Commends peaceful coexistence with the Christian population of Lebanon, maintaining that both Christians and Muslims must renounce political sectarianism. Played a central role in Hizb Allah's rise to power, its role in international hostage talks, and the confrontation with Israel in south Lebanon. *See also* Hizb Allah (Iran); Hizb Allah (Lebanon)

Fai In classical Islam, wealth taken peaceably from an enemy, either under the terms of a peace settlement or after fighting has ended. Fai was considered the right of the Prophet originally. Later it was distributed by the community leaders according to what was considered to be in the best interests of Islam and Muslims. *See also* Ghanimah

Faith *See* Iman

Faiz, Ahmad Faiz (d. 1984) Born in Sialkot, Pakistan. One of the most famous Urdu poets and an important political dissident in Pakistan. A student of philosophy and literature, but better known for his rebellious Urdu poetry and leftist politics. Inspired by Marxist ideology; wrote for the masses. Was awarded the Lenin Peace Prize. His poetry has been translated into all major languages of the world.

Fakhreddin, Rizaeddin (d. 1936) Volga-Ural Muslim scholar. Prolific writer who published more than sixty books and left many unpublished manuscripts in a wide range of disciplines including history, politics, law, and education. Writings emphasized the integrative capacity of Islam and advocated codification of Muslim legal practices in Russia.

Falsafah *See* Philosophy

Family Basic social unit of Islamic society. In Arabic, *ahl* or *aila* is a comprehensive term that may include grandparents, uncles, aunts, and cousins on both sides of the family. The Quran enjoins mutual respect and responsibility between spouses and among family members. Spouses and children have duties and rights protected by law. Men and women remain members of their natal families even after marriage. In modern times, the family has been subjected to economic and social pressures that have disrupted the traditional extended-family patterns, including changing responsibilities for women. Nevertheless, it remains a flexible unit of social organization in Muslim societies. *See also* Family Law; Marriage and Divorce: Legal Foundations; Marriage and Divorce: Modern Practices

Family Law A marriage contract requires an offer and acceptance before witnesses. The groom is required to give his wife a dowry (mahr), which is her property alone, to dispose of as she wishes. The groom may pay a portion of the dowry at the time of contract and the rest at a time specified in the marriage contract. Men may marry up to four wives, but women may marry only one man at a time. In most Muslim countries, divorce by the husband is effected by a unilateral pronouncement known as the talaq, which severs the legal relationship, although this is in violation of Quranic teachings and one of the subjects of modern reform efforts. After the talaq, the couple must refrain from sexual intercourse for three months. At the end of this time, the marriage is terminated. During the marriage, the wife is entitled to maintenance and support, which includes food, clothing, and accommodation; with divorce, this entitlement terminates. Legal adoption is not permissible under traditional Islamic law. The specifics of Islamic family law differ widely depending on place and time as well as school of law. The past two centuries have seen major reforms in Islamic family law: Tunisia rendered polygyny illegal on Islamic grounds and established equal rights for men and women in divorce; Turkey also forbade polygyny, but as a result of a wholesale adoption of the Western legal code. See also Adoption; Marriage and Divorce: Legal Foundations; Marriage and Divorce: Modern Practices; Polygyny

Family Planning See Birth Control/Contraception

Fana Passing away. In Sufi Islam, refers to the desired state of mystical annihilation of self, which is the state just prior to experiencing union with God. For early Sufism, this was the goal of following the Sufi path (tariqah). Some later orders have argued that human beings are not on the same level as God and therefore cannot be united with him; they focus on union with the spirit of the Prophet instead. Fana is the goal of dhikr (devotional exercises of remembrance) and is believed to be attainable by following tariqah under the guidance of the shaykh of the order or by loss of personality in him.

Faqih Pl. fuqaha. An expert in Islamic jurisprudence (fiqh). When Islamic legal theory emerged in the early tenth century, the term referred to a specialist in case law. The fuqaha constituted a major segment of the religious elite (ulama) and were considered the guardians of the community and its religion. They functioned as judges (qadis) and jurisconsults (muftis). As judges, they acted as trustees of the property of orphans, supervisors of charitable trusts, and marriage guardians for women who had no male relative to serve in this capacity. As jurisconsults, they issued opinions (fatwas) on legal questions addressed to them by members of the community. As a result of massive twentieth-century legal reforms in Muslim countries, the importance of the fuqaha has steadily declined. They have substantially lost not only their influence as a religious elite but also their functions as jurists, judges, legal guardians, and to a lesser degree jurisconsults. They have largely been replaced by modern lawyers, jurists, and judges, and their function is limited to the narrow sphere of family law, though this is not without the encroachment of state secular legislation. See also Fatwa; Fiqh; Law: Modern Legal Reform; Usul al-Fiqh

Faqir Poor one. Term that describes the tendency of many Sufis to live a poor or mendicant lifestyle. Used by Sufis to refer to one who is in need of God. Also a general term for dervish. Sometimes used to describe a Sufi leader or one who practices the Sufi way, carrying out rituals of the Sufi order. Can mean "spiritual slave." General term used throughout the Islamic world but often is imprecise in meaning. Loosely used in the Eastern Islamic world to describe wandering Sufis. Historically, faqirs have fulfilled a missionary role in spreading Islam.

Farabi, Abu Nasr Muhammad ibn Tarkhan al- (d. 950) Founder of Islamic political philosophy and formal logic in the Islamic world. Wrote important commentaries on Aristotle and works of philosophy, the most famous of which addresses the question of the virtuous city, characterized by division and protection of all good things among people and by the relationship between (and mutual duties of) ruler and ruled. Also synthesized the political philosophy of Plato and Islamic political thought. Integrated religion and science in written works. Understood philosophy as a quest for personal excellence, particularly in terms of intellect and moral character. Asserted that prophecy and philosophy are essentially one; the major difference is that the prophet perceives truth suddenly, by inspiration, whereas the philosopher must gain wisdom through a long and arduous struggle. A prophet possesses a special capacity to put the pure and abstract truth sought by philosophers in terms that ordinary people can understand. Revelation is thus philosophy for the masses, and prophets serve as popular examples of obedience to moral law. His views on the nature of prophecy were unpopular among religious scholars. Among his major works was *The Virtuous City* (Al-madinat al-fadilah). *See also* Madinat al-Fadilah, al-

Farahi, Hamiduddin (d. 1930) Indian Quran exegete. Viewed nazm (thematic and structural coherence) as the most significant organizing principle of the Quran. Held that the Quranic surahs are unities, each possessing a distinctive and systematically developed theme and yielding new insights in a contextualized interpretation.

Faraid Sing. *fard*. Obligatory ritual duties commanded by God. Generally refers to the five daily prayers, charity, fasting, and pilgrimage. Also refers to distributive shares in estates under Islamic inheritance laws as stipulated in the Quran. In Sufi orders, includes rituals specific to the order, including meditation, contemplation, movement, singing, recitation, prayer, repetition, music, and dance. *See also* Fard al-Ayn; Fard al-Kifayah

Faraidi Movement Nineteenth-century Bengali movement influenced by the ideas of the Wahhabi movement of Arabia, and led by Hajji Shariatullah (d. 1840). Considered India to be dar al-kufr (region of unbelief) but, rather than declaring jihad against it, initially resorted to the symbolic posture of

suspending public rituals such as Friday congregational prayers there, since an Islamic political order was not present. Attempted to implement Meccan standards of belief and practice consistent with orthodoxy and the five pillars of Islam. Emphasized religious obligations and individual practice in the context of British colonial power. Called upon local Muslims to abandon saint worship and Hindu-influenced customs and beliefs. After the death of its founder, took up the cause of Muslim peasantry against Hindu landlords and resorted to military uprisings, which were suppressed in the 1830s with British aid but which added a religious communal element to the social and political antagonisms spreading in the Bengali countryside at the time. Disseminated their teachings in pamphlets written in Bengali, spreading Islamic teachings to a broader portion of the population.

Faraizi *See* Faraidi Movement

Faraj, Muhammad Abd al-Salam (d. 1976) Ideologue and head of Islamic Jihad in Egypt. Claimed that Muslims must engage in armed revolt against the Egyptian government because it has replaced adherence to Islamic law alone with Western-inspired legal codes; such a government is not Islamic, so it must be forcibly replaced by an Islamic regime. *See also* Jihad, al-

Farangi Mahall A family of religious scholars in Lucknow, named after an estate bestowed on them by the Mughal emperor Aurangzeb. One of the most distinguished members of the family, Mulla Nizam al-din Ahmad (d. 1748), is credited with helping standardize the curriculum of the madrasas in South Asia. Scholars of this family distinguished themselves in the study of law, logic and philosophy, and mysticism, and maintained extensive intellectual and spiritual ties with scholars, students, and disciples throughout South Asia. Mawlana Abdul Bari (d. 1926), a member of this family, was one of the most important leaders of the Indian Khilafat movement (1918–24), but the

family's intellectual and religious prominence gradually faded away after that. *See also*
India, Islam in

Farazdaq, al- (d. ca. 728) Arab poet. Lived
primarily in Basra, but his poetry retained
Bedouin values and style. His panegyrics are
regarded as his best work. His poems are
among the last attempts to imitate pre-
Islamic poetry. Had an eccentric personality
and maintained a great literary rivalry with
his contemporary Jarir ibn Atiyya. Probably
held Alid sympathies.

Fard, Wallace D. (d. 1934?) Believed to be
the original founder of the Nation of Islam.
Preached Islam as the true identity of
African-Americans. Recognized by followers
as the Great Mahdi (savior) who came to
bring the message of salvation to African-
Americans. Later considered by followers to
be divine. Taught followers that they were
not Americans and therefore owed no allegiance to the state. Disappeared mysteriously
in 1934. *See also* Nation of Islam

Fard al-Ayn In Islamic law, refers to legal
obligations that must be performed by each
individual Muslim, including prayer, charity,
fasting, and pilgrimage. Individual obligation is contrasted with communal obligation
(fard al-kifayah). The question of whether
the obligation of "reproaching the unjust
ruler" or, more generally, the obligation to
"command the good and forbid the reprehensible" is an obligation on each individual
or can be satisfied by part of the community
is debated, particularly among Shii scholars.
See also Fard al-Kifayah

Fard al-Kifayah Defines a communal obligation in Muslim legal doctrine. In juxta-
position to fard al-ayn, fard al-kifayah is a
legal obligation that must be discharged by
the Muslim community as a whole, such as
military struggle; if enough members in the
Muslim community discharge the obligation, the remaining Muslims are freed from
the responsibility before God. However, if a

communal obligation is not sufficiently discharged, then every individual Muslim must
act to address the deficiency. In recent Islamic literature, this terminology is used to
discuss social responsibility, such as feeding
the hungry, commanding good, and forbidding evil. *See also* Fard al-Ayn

Fard Muhammad *See* Fard, Wallace D.

Farid al-Din Masud Ganj-i-Shakar (d.
1265) Also known as Baba Farid. A seminal
personality in the medieval Indian mystical
tradition, the Sufi saint and poet consolidated the Chishti order, and his verses elevated Punjabi to a literary status. Numerous
Punjabi tribes attribute their conversion to
him, and his shrine in Ajodhan (presently
Pakpattan, Pakistan) is a major pilgrimage
center.

Farman Persian. Command, edict, document, authority, or royal wish. In Turkish,
firman denotes any order or edict of the Ottoman sultan.

Farq Dispersion or separation. One of the
mystical states (ahwal) in Sufism, contrasted
with "gathering" (jama). As a positive attribute, it is discernment, or the recognition
of God's lordship and the acceptance of the
obligations of servanthood; negatively, it is
to lose perception of the One and to be
overcome by ignorance and confusion.

Farrakhan, Louis (b. 1933) Born Louis Eugene Wolcott. Controversial leader and charismatic preacher of the Nation of Islam.
Preaches black unity, self-knowledge, independence, and black nationalist and separatist doctrines central to the teachings of
Elijah Muhammad. Concentrates on establishing a strong economic system for the
African-American community, particularly
through small-business ownership, in which
members can be free of dominant white
structures. Allows members to participate by
voting and running for elected office. Has
sharply criticized the role of Jews and whites

in the oppression of black people. Since being diagnosed with cancer in 1999, has worked to bring the Nation of Islam into closer adherence to mainstream Sunni Islam and has eased antiwhite rhetoric. *See also* Nation of Islam

Farsi Indo-European language. Also known as New Persian. Replaced Pahlavi following the Islamic conquest of the Persian Sasanian Empire. Written in Arabic script and consists of as much as 70 percent Arabic loan words. Second language of Islam and the courtly language in Iran, the Ottoman Empire, Central Asia, and the Mughal Empire.

Faruqi, Ismail Raji al- (d. 1986) Palestinian Islamic scholar, writer, and activist. Governor of Galilee 1945–48. Professor at universities in Africa, Europe, the Middle East, and South and Southeast Asia. Works focus on a comprehensive vision of Islam and its relationship to all aspects of life and culture. Presented Islam as a religion of reason, science, and progress, emphasizing action and the work ethic. Combined the classical affirmation of God's oneness (tawhid) with a modernist interpretation and application of Islam to modern life through the exercise of ijtihad. Established Islamic studies programs, recruited and trained Muslim students, organized Muslim professionals, and was an active participant in international ecumenical dialogue. Cofounded the International Institute for Islamic Thought in the United States in 1981. Regarded the political, economic, and religio-cultural malaise of the Islamic community as a product of the bifurcated state of education in the Muslim world, which has resulted in a loss of identity and world vision. Believed the cure was the compulsory study of Islamic civilization and the Islamization of modern knowledge. Murdered in 1986.

Fasad/Mufsid fil-Ard Corruption; one who engages in spreading corruption on earth. In Quranic usage the term means corrupt conditions, caused by unbelievers and unjust people, that threaten social and political well-being. Among jurists, the term signifies the nullity of a legal act that is not valid in the eyes of the law.

Fasi, Muhammad Allal al- (d. 1973) Moroccan historian, teacher, poet, and political leader. Taught Islamic history at al-Qarawiyin University (1930). In 1934 he and other activists issued a Moroccan Reform Plan. Arrested and exiled to Gabon by the French (1937–46) but continued to influence the Moroccan reform movement. Upon return from Gabon, served as head of the Istiqlal (Independence) Party but in 1947 was forced to flee to Cairo and remained there until Moroccan independence in 1956. Most important writings include *The Independence Movements in North Africa* (1947) and *Self-Criticism* (1951). Advocated Arabic language reform and avoiding imitation of the West.

Fasting In Islam fasting is required during Ramadan, the ninth month of the Muslim lunar calendar, during which all Muslims are required to abstain during daylight hours from eating, drinking, or engaging in sexual activity. Through heightened awareness of their bodily needs, Muslims come to greater awareness of the presence of God and acknowledge gratitude for God's provisions in their lives. Abstinence during Ramadan is required of all Muslims, except children, those who are ill or too elderly, those who are traveling, and women who are menstruating, have just given birth, or are breastfeeding. In such cases, one may make up days of fasting at a later time. Various traditions recommend voluntary fasting: the fast of Ashura (tenth day of the month of Muharram); fasting for six days in Shawwal, the month after Ramadan; fasting three days of each month; and fasting on Mondays and Thursdays. Expiatory fasting (kaffarah) atones for certain transgressions or compensates for omissions of duty; fasts may be undertaken for failing to fulfill an oath (see Quran 5:89, 58:4) or the accidental killing of a believer (4:92). Some Sufis undergo fasts as part of their spiritual exercises.

Fatah *See* Palestine Liberation Organization

Fatalism Belief of pre-Islamic Arabs that humanity was left to an inexorable fate that determines the course of life, regardless of human desire. Islam replaced impersonal fate with a sense of divine direction of all of life, as well as of personal moral accountability. Nonetheless, affirmations of God's absolute power in the Quran and traditions led some to affirm a different kind of fatalism, sometimes called predestination, in which God's foreknowledge supersedes human free choice. The prevailing theological compromise posited a middle position whereby God's created actions are appropriated by humans. Contemporary Islam stresses the Quranic support of human potential and responsibility under God's guidance. *See also* Qismah

Fatawa al-Alamgiriyya A compilation of the authoritative doctrines of the Hanafi school of law. The work was commissioned by the Mughal emperor Aurangzeb Alamgir (r. 1658–1707) and was carried out by a team of religious scholars led by Shaykh Nizam Burhanpuri. The Fatawa is among the most comprehensive compendia of Hanafi law. It continues to be extremely influential in South Asia.

Fate *See* Qismah

Father *See* Abu

Fathi, Hasan (d. 1989) Egyptian architect, teacher, and reformer. Systematically opposed to the official architectural discourse in Egypt, he deplored the attempt to alter what was perceived as the decadent status quo of Muslim societies by enforcing universalizing modern technology and standardized architectural expression. Advocated the regeneration and esthetic adaptation of indigenous building techniques.

Fatihah "The Opening," title of the first surah of the Quran, also called Umm al-Kitab (mother of the book) or Surat al-Hamd (chapter of praise). It is regarded as the essence of the Quran and sums up the relation of humans to God. With recitation in each standing (rakah) of the five canonical prayers each day, it is repeated seventeen times a day and always concludes with *amin* (amen). It is also repeated over sick people for a blessing as well as recited for the deceased, upon visiting graves, when attending funerals, while visiting holy places, and upon marriage. Fatihah is an important part of dua, individual and purposeful noncanonical prayers. In folk religion, it is believed to be a powerful prayer for the making of amulets. *See also* Quran

Fatimah Daughter of Muhammad and Khadijah, wife of the fourth caliph, Ali ibn Abi Talib, and mother of Hasan and Husayn. Known as "Mother of the Imams," in accordance with Shii belief that only descendants of Muhammad through Fatimah could be imams. Believed by many to have been sinless. Often portrayed as a woman of sorrow due to the rejection, disinheritance, and martyrdom of her husband and sons. Role as exemplary daughter, wife, and mother is often juxtaposed with Aisha's problematic role in politics, which led to divisions within Muslim community. Only female among Fourteen Perfect or Pure Ones in Shii tradition.

Fatimah, Hazrat-i Masumah Also known as Bibi Fatimah. Daughter of seventh Shii imam, Musa al-Kazim, and sister of eighth imam, Ali al-Rida. Died in Qom, Iran. Grave is second most important shrine and pilgrimage site in Iran.

Fatimid Dynasty (909–1171) Ismaili Shii empire in Egypt and parts of North Africa. Named after Muhammad's daughter, Fatimah, since rulers claimed descent from her. Initially established in Qairawan, Tunisia, in 909. Conquered Egypt in 969 and made Cairo its new capital. Ruler adopted title of caliph, splitting the religious leadership and political power of the Islamic world between the Abbasid and Fatimid caliphates. Established al-Azhar mosque in Cairo as a training center for missionaries. Sponsored elaborate celebrations of Muhammad's birthday and construction of numerous shrines for his descendants, which became popular pilgrimage sites. Rivaled and opposed by Sunni Seljuks in the mid-eleventh century. Overthrown by Salah al-Din (Saladin) in 1171. *See also* Muhammad ibn Ismail; Qaramita

Fatwa Authoritative legal opinion given by a mufti (legal scholar) in response to a question posed by an individual or a court of law. A fatwa is typically requested in cases not covered by the fiqh literature and is neither binding nor enforceable. Its authority is based on the mufti's education and status within the community. If the inquirer is not persuaded by the fatwa, he is free to go to another mufti and obtain another opinion; but once he finds a convincing opinion, he should obey it. Theoretically, muftis should be capable of exercising legal reasoning independently of schools of law (ijtihad), although followers of tradition (muqallids) are also allowed to issue fatwas. Historically, fatwas were independent of the judicial system, although some muftis were officially attached to various courts. In the Ottoman and Mughal political systems, the chief mufti was designated shaykh al-Islam. Other muftis were appointed to positions as market inspectors, guardians of public morals, and advisers to government on religious affairs. Under colonial rule, madrasas took over the role of religious guides, and special institutions were established to issue fatwas. In modern times, print and electronic media have reinforced the role and impact of fatwas by making them instantly available to the public. Present-day Muslim states have tried to control fatwas through official consultative/advisory organizations within religious ministries. *See also* Mufti

Fazilet Partisi *See* Virtue Party

Federal Shariat Court Instituted in 1980 as part of Pakistan's Islamization scheme with appellate jurisdiction over verdicts of district courts involving Islamic laws and exclusive jurisdiction to hear petitions challenging state laws as repugnant to Islam. The court was staffed with retired judges and ulama, and its operation was modified twenty-eight times between 1980 and 1985 through twelve presidential ordinances. Between 1980 and 1987 some five hundred laws were either amended or changed by the court. After 1985 much of the court's mandate to Islamize the judiciary was taken up by the parliament and "shariat bills."

Fédération Nationale des Musulmans de France Established in 1985 as the official voice and protector of Muslims in France. Founded by a French convert to Islam, Daniel Youssof Leclerc, to coordinate the actions of and defend approximately one hundred Muslim associations, facilitate the practice of the Muslim faith in a non-Islamic country, and free the French Muslim community from Algerian influence. Seeks a friendly relationship with French society and hopes to instill better knowledge of Islam. Wishes to implement Islamic standards in all aspects of life. Does not demand the opening of specifically Muslim schools and universities or the legalization of polygyny. Assisted by the Muslim World League.

Federation of Islamic Associations North American organization originally known as the International Muslim Society. Founded in 1952 by first-generation, American-born Lebanese and Syrian Muslims to help maintain ties among scattered Muslim communities in the United States and Canada. Initial focus was recognition of Islam in the American armed services, holding annual meetings and conventions, and providing opportunities for young people to meet potential marriage partners with a common religious and cultural heritage. Hampered by lack of funds and lack of trained indigenous leadership. Condemned for its assimilationist tendencies by more conservative Muslims. Membership has decreased drastically in recent years due to disagreement over politics, particularly public attacks against other Muslim organizations.

Federation of Islamic Associations of New Zealand Formed in 1979 as a national organization to coordinate financial requests and other dealings overseas and to provide other services, such as halal certification. Tries to address discrimination, negative stereotyping, conflicts between Islamic and local ways, and legal concerns with marriage and divorce.

Feminism Muslim feminists work as independent agents to redefine their own lives as women, counter patriarchal hegemony, and strive for more egalitarian arrangements in families, communities, and nations in accordance with their views on the Quran's egalitarianism. The articulation of awareness of the unequal construction of gender and of the domination of males over females began in the late nineteenth century in the Muslim world. Feminists insist on equality of men and women as citizens in the public sphere and accept the complementarity of roles in the family sphere. Modes of expression include creative and scholarly writings, everyday activism, and organized movement activism. In the late nineteenth and early twentieth centuries, the major issues addressed were domestic seclusion and veiling, the need for female education, and elimination of women's oppression. In the second half of the twentieth century, major issues were gender roles and relations in family and society, sexual abuse and exploitation, misogyny, patriarchy, and women's gender and class oppression linked with imperialist oppression. At the end of the century, major trends were the construction of modern women citizens, reform of Muslim family law, respect for women's bodies, access to education as well as health care and family planning, confrontation of issues related to women's dress and mobility, and official recognition of the changing role of women in the public sphere and the workplace.

Festivals *See* Ashura; Mawlid; Mawlid al-Husayn; Mawlid al-Nabi

Feyzullah Effendi (d. 1703) Appointed Şeyhülislam in 1695 by the Ottoman sultan Mustafa II (r. 1695–1703) and soon became the real power behind the throne following the signing of the Treaty of Karlowitz (Karlofça) in 1699. Worked to create a dynasty of leaders within the ulama from among his own family. His policies made him the focus of discontented elements within the empire, including soldiers, ulama, and merchants. These factions joined forces in July 1703, compelling Mustafa II to execute Feyzullah in September in what became known as the Edirne Event (Edirne Vakasyi). The whole affair weakened the power of the imperial household in relationships with the major pashas.

Fez First capital and spiritual center of Morocco. Most prominent legacy of the Idrisid dynasty (788–974). Home of Qarawiyin University. In the medieval period, rivaled al-Azhar as a center of Sunni learning. Remains a provincial capital today, but Rabat has supplanted its administrative role, while Casablanca has superseded it as the nation's commercial center.

Fidaiyan-i Islam Commandos of Islam. Iranian religio-political organization founded in Tehran in 1945 by Sayyid Mujtaba Navvab Safavi. Active against the shah's regime. Financed by bazaaris and clerics. Ultimate goal was creation of a new order based on Islamic law, with clerics as judges and educators. Combined encouragement of business with a strong sense of social welfare and charity. Assassinated politicians and intellectuals in the 1940s and 1950s. Lost strength after Safavi was executed in 1956. Reemerged briefly during the Islamic revolution of 1979 but quickly disappeared, though a Tehran street carries Safavi's name and a stamp his likeness.

Fihrist Catalogue of books arranged by subject matter with varying degrees of detail regarding author, compilation, contents, commentaries, refutations, and so on. May also be arranged according to the Islamic scholars with whom the works were studied.

Prominent classical examples include the tenth-century Baghdad bookseller Ibn al-Nadim's *Fihrist*, the twelfth-century Andalusian Ibn Khayr al-Ishbili's *Fahrasah*, the fifteenth-century Egyptian Ibn Hajar al-Asqalani's *Al-Mujam al-Mufahras*, and the seventeenth-century Ottoman Hajji Khalifah's *Kashf al-Zunun*. Modern usage of the Arabicized word *fahrasah* includes the table of contents, bibliography, and various indexes of a book, in addition to a variety of indexed reference works.

Filalian *See* Alawi Dynasty

Fiqh Conceptually, the human attempt to understand divine law (shariah). Whereas shariah is immutable and infallible, fiqh is fallible and changeable. Fiqh is distinguished from usul al-fiqh, the methods of legal interpretation and analysis. Fiqh is the product of application of usul al-fiqh, the total product of human efforts at understanding the divine will. A hukm is a particular ruling in a given case. *See also* Hukm; Usul al-Fiqh

Fiqh al-Tabib *See* Bioethics

Firawn Pharaoh. Ruler of Egypt, pre-Islamic or non-Islamic. In the Quran, used in stories about Moses (Musa) and Harun, and symbolically for evildoers who ask forgiveness from God only directly before death. In the Muslim tradition, refers to Egyptian kings and is associated with Abraham and Joseph and the tower of Babel.

Firdawsi (d. ca. 1020) National poet of Iran. Born, died, and buried in Tus, northeastern Iran. Most famous for his epic story of Persian kings and dynasties, *Shahnameh* (Book of kings). Although there is a long tradition of writing epic stories in Persian under the rubric of shahnameh, Firdawsi's is unmatched in quality and popularity.

Firman *See* Farman

FIS *See* Islamic Salvation Front

Fitnah Trial or testing, temptation; by extension, treachery, persecution, seduction, enchantment, or disorder resulting from these things. A hadith states that the greatest fitnah for men is women. Though the term *fitnah* is generally negative, a girl may be named Fatin or Fitnah in the hope she will not be a seductress and in recognition of her beauty. In modern political terminology, allegation of fitnah can be used to discredit the actions of opponents. The first Muslims to write about the French revolution (1789) identified it as fitnah.

Fitra According to the Quran, the original state in which humans are created by God. In the Quran, God is called Fatir, that is, creator of heaven and earth, and the verb *fatara* is also used to mean "to create." However, the commonly accepted meaning of the word derives from the traditions of Muhammad, according to which God creates children according to fitra, and their parents later make them Jews or Christians. As such, every child is born a Muslim. The concept of fitra was commonly invoked by Sufis, who often viewed their own quest as the means for restoring the original harmony of creation.

Five Hidden Things *See* Mughayyabat al-Khamis, al-

Forbidden *See* Haram

Forgiveness *See* Repentance

Fornication Sexual act occurring outside of the legal relationship of marriage or concubinage, punishable by stoning. The Quran specifies that there must be four witnesses to the actual act in order to convict. Historically, incidents of punishment are relatively rare. Modern states often reinstate hudud punishments such as this as a visible sign of the Islamic nature of the state. *See also* Zina

France, Islam in Islam is the second largest religion in France, and the country has the largest number and percentage of Muslims in western Europe. The majority of Muslims are either immigrants or their descendants from the former French colonies of North Africa. Most are under thirty years old and either unskilled or semiskilled blue-collar workers living in major industrial centers, but there are rising numbers of students, professionals, and businesspeople. Visible signs of religious affiliation, such as head scarves, were banned in public schools in 1989 as a violation of the separation of church and state. Many French fear the growing number of Muslim immigrants, particularly exiled opposition politicians and movements, as a potential domestic security threat. Others accuse Muslims of resisting assimilation into secular society and of being the root of many social problems. Such fears have led to the increased popularity of extremist racist politicians.

Francis of Assisi (d. 1226) Founder of the Franciscan monastic orders and advocate of renunciation of worldly goods. Among the first Europeans to attempt to convert Muslims to Christianity in the thirteenth century. Visited Egypt during the Crusades and preached to the sultan, who, while not persuaded, was impressed with Francis' piety and sincerity.

Free Will Muslims believe that God gave human beings the ability to distinguish between and choose either good or evil and that in the hereafter all people will be recompensed for those choices. Muslims also believe that God has determined other aspects of people's lives for which they are not held accountable, for example, their place of birth and physical appearance. See also Fatalism; Qismah

Freedom See Hurr

Freedom Movement (Iran) See Liberation Movement of Iran

Front Islamique du Salut See Islamic Salvation Front

Fruit of Islam Elite male group of adherents of the Nation of Islam who provide security for Nation of Islam leaders and enforce dis-

ciplinary rules. Dismantled by Warith Deen Muhammad in 1975 after he assumed leadership of the Nation of Islam and reformed it to adhere more closely to mainstream Sunni Islam. Re-created by Louis Farrakhan. See also Nation of Islam

Fuad See Qalb

Fulani Dynasty West African Muslim leaders in the nineteenth and twentieth centuries. The Fulani, a major ethnic group in the region, came together under the leadership of Uthman Dan Fodio in a jihad begun in 1804 against the local rulers of Hausa states. The movement established the Sokoto caliphate under the leadership of Dan Fodio's son, Muhammad Bello. The dynasty and commanders in the state dominated northern Nigeria until the British took control in 1903. The British used the dynasty in their policy of indirect rule, and a descendant of Dan Fodio, Sir Ahmadu Bello, the sardauna of Sokoto, was prime minister of the northern region in the first Nigerian republic. See also Dan Fodio, Uthman; Sokoto Caliphate

Fundamentalism Term used to refer to early-twentieth-century American Christian Protestant movement based on affirmation of faith that defines belief in an absolutist and literalist manner. Involves an effort to purify or reform adherents' beliefs and practices in accord with self-defined fundamentals of faith, and a self-conscious effort to avoid compromise, adaptation, or critical reinterpretation of basic texts and sources of belief. In the Islamic context, the term typically refers to revivalist movements. Modern Islamic fundamentalist movements reject copying of Western methods, affirming instead the comprehensive and effective nature of the Islamic message. Some scholars believe that Islamic fundamentalism is a distinctively modern phenomenon, while others argue that activist movements advocating a return to pristine fundamentals of faith are evident throughout Islamic history.

Funerary Rites The tasks of preparing the body for funerary washing, performing the washing, and leading funerary prayers fall to the family of the deceased. The body is washed three times, the orifices are sealed with cotton, and the body is enshrouded and perfumed. If death occurs during the hajj, a man's shroud must be seamless and a woman's face must be uncovered. If the person is martyred or its equivalent (death during childbirth, by plague, or from an accident), the body is not cleansed and is buried as it fell. Special prayers (salat al-janazah) are offered, often at a mosque. Throughout washing, prayers, and burial, the body is to face Mecca. The body is carried to the grave in an open bier, followed by the funeral party, which is all male. The body is buried without a coffin in a grave deep enough to conceal odor and prevent abuse by animals. Close male relatives of the deceased descend into the grave with the body to turn the face toward Mecca. Muslims are required to bury the dead as soon as possible, preferably before nightfall on the day of death.

Funj Sultanate Around 1500 the Funj sultanate united much of the northern Nile Valley in Sudan. The Funj drew on older Sudanic traditions of statecraft and depended on the institution of matrilineal kinship inherited from medieval Christian Nubia, although the processes of Arabization and Islamization of northern Sudan accelerated under their rule. They opened the country to unprecedented commercial relations with neighboring lands; a middle class emerged in the mid-eighteenth century in a town-based money economy. By the eighteenth century, sultans faced many local revolts and came under the control of their military commanders; in 1820 the remnants of the Funj sultanate fell to the armies of Muhammad Ali, Ottoman viceroy of Egypt.

Fuqara *See* Faqir

Furqan, al- A solemn synonym for the Quran. *Furqan* means "discrimination," "separation," "criterion," "salvation," and "proof." The term appears in the Quran and was used by the Prophet. The furqan or proof is said to have been "sent down" to humankind, as were all scriptures revealed by Allah.

Furuq Sing. *farq*. Discrepancies, differences. A field of jurisprudence according to which the reasons for disagreements and differences in legal opinions are analyzed and evaluated. The independent legal thinker (mujtahid) looks for the fine discrepancy that another may have overlooked when applying qiyas (legal reasoning by analogy or syllogism) to discover a rule. If a structural difference (farq) exists, the qiyas is held faulty. The sum of these discrepancies is furuq.

Fustat, al- Old Cairo, first capital of the conquering Arab armies of Egypt. Built in 643 on the eastern side of the Nile River. Contains the oldest mosque in Egypt, Jami Amr. Evolved into a commercial, economic, and cultural center. Successive famines, epidemics, and revolts caused its deterioration. Attempts to revive the city proved unsuccessful, especially as new capitals were built. Currently one of the populous residential areas of metropolitan Cairo.

Futa Jallon Site in central Guinea, West Africa. Location of seventeenth- and eighteenth-century popular uprisings that sought to unseat non-Muslim rulers and institute Islamic reform. In the 1720s two Fulbe leaders, Karamoko Alfa and Ibrahima Sori, led a jihad against the non-Muslim rulers; the almaamate (Fula, from Arabic, meaning "imamate") was created. By the mid-eighteenth century the rulers became part of an oligarchy whose principal goal was to control trade from the Upper Niger to the coast. Uthman Dan Fodio, founder of one of the greatest states of nineteenth-century Africa, the Fulani empire of Sokoto, was born to one of these ruling families.

Futa Toro The successor state to the medieval Takrur kingdom, located in the Senegal River basin, West Africa. Nasir al-Din began a popular movement of Islamic reform here in the 1660s. His demand that rulers submit to him as imam was met with military force; Nasir al-Din was killed in battle in 1673. In the 1780s Abdul Kader became almaami (religious leader or imam) but his forces were unable to spread revolution to the surrounding states. In 1806 he and the original goals of the reform-minded revolution died, defeated by the non-Muslim Kaarta kingdom, the Bundu state, and a subversive element within Futa Toro itself.

Futuwwah Ideal of youthful manhood and chivalry based on the example of Ali ibn Abi Talib, Muhammad's cousin and the first youth to convert to Islam. Historically associated with popular forms of revivalist Islam, Sufi orders, craft guilds, and elite chivalric guilds. Contemporary radical Islamic cells are sometimes compared to futuwwah since they share elements of popular political resistance, opposition to state authority, class struggle, espousal of a purist and righteous Islamic ideology that justifies whatever actions are necessary for the good of the group, a required oath of loyalty, and strict obedience to the recognized leader.

Fyzee, Asaf Ali Asghar (d. 1981) Indian Islamic modernist, educator, and internationally known scholar of Islamic law. His most famous work, *Outlines of Muhammadan Law*, argues that in order to understand the system of Islamic jurisprudence, one ought to be familiar with the historical and cultural background of the law.

G

Gabriel Arabic, Jibril. According to the Quran (2:97–98), archangel sent by God to reveal the Quran to Muhammad. Also mentioned as protector of Muhammad (66:4). Hadith record him testing Muhammad on doctrinal questions.

Gadd al-Haqq (d. 1996) Egyptian shaykh of al-Azhar who issued a fatwa declaring female circumcision (clitoridectomy) part of the legal body of Islam and a laudable practice that honors women. The fatwa was issued in response to a public declaration by Egyptian muftis that clitoridectomies are not stipulated by the Quran and that hadith attributing the practice to Muhammad are unreliable.

Galiyev, Sultan Mir Said (d. ca. 1930) Tatar Muslim Communist intellectual from Volga who reinterpreted Communism for the Muslim context during the 1917 Bolshevik revolution in Russia. Understood Communism as a practical doctrine for organizing underground movements, educating and agitating the masses, articulating national rights, and gaining political support. Supported revolutionary national government as a necessary prerequisite to proletarian rule, deemphasizing the concept of class struggle. Declared all Muslims proletarians due to oppression suffered under colonialist governments. His philosophy, known as Sultangaliyevism, served as a rallying point for Muslim nationalist sentiments. Expelled from the Communist Party in 1923 for deviations from the party line. Imprisoned, exiled, and disappeared.

Gambia, Islam in Gambia became a Muslim state largely because of the efforts of nineteenth-century Muslim proselytizers and because of the state of peace brought about by British colonization. A republic governed by multiparty democratic rule,

Gambia achieved its independence from Great Britain in 1965. The Muslim sense of tolerance in Gambia is largely the work of the present leadership, which has decided to build on the colonial legacy of religious pluralism. In 2000, 90 percent of Gambia's 1.4 million people were Muslim; 9 percent were Christian. The constitution was repromulgated in 1997; a unicameral parliament serves in a democratic, multiparty system.

Gambling The Quranic expression is maysir (2:119, 5:90), but the term often used in Islamic law is qimar. All activities involving betting for money or property or undue speculation are prohibited in Islamic law. Most juristic discussions focus on defining precisely which activities are unduly speculative and hence unlawful.

Gaspraly, Ismail Bey *See* Gasprinski, Ismail Bey

Gasprinski, Ismail Bey (d. 1914) Crimean Tatar reformer, educator, and publicist. Also known as Ismail Bey Gaspraly. Regarded as an architect of modernism among Muslim Turkic subjects of the Russian empire. Educated in Muslim schools, a Russian military academy, and abroad (France and the Ottoman Empire); returned to Crimea to found one of the most important ethnic periodicals in Russian history, Terjuman (The interpreter). Posited that the influence of a misdirected religious orthodoxy condemned Muslims to cultural inferiority under modern Western technological, military, political, and intellectual hegemony. Believed that progress required educational reform, teaching a modern curriculum by modern methods, encouraging social and economic cooperation, and cultural borrowing. Spread his ideas by means of numerous pamphlets and periodicals. Inspired the movement known as Jadidism. Had an intellectually moderate and practical influence, which by the 1920s was felt throughout Turkic Russia as well as in Turkey, Egypt, and Muslim India. *See also* Jadidism

Gaylani Family Religious notables of Afghanistan, also known as the Naqib or Effendi family. Descendants of Sayyid Hassan Gaylani (d. 1941), the younger brother of the Naqib al-Ashraf of Baghdad. Gaylani came to Afghanistan in 1905. Welcomed among Pushtun tribes and by Amir Habibullah (r. 1901–19), he settled initially in Chaharbagh, near Jalalabad, then moved to Kabul. As leader of the Qadiri Sufi order with close ties to the rulers, he enjoyed great respect and political influence. He was succeeded by his sons, Sher Agha Jan (Sayyid Ali Gaylani, b. 1923) and then Effendi Jan (Sayyid Ahmad Gaylani, b. 1932), who left Kabul in 1978 and headed the National Islamic Front, Mahaz-e Milli-ye Islami-ye Afghanistan, in Peshawar during the jihad against the Soviet occupation.

Genealogy *See* Nasab

Genghis Khan (d. ca. 1227) Creator of the Mongol Empire. Genghis united the Mongol and Turkish tribes of the Siberian steppe in a supratribal military force (horde) that conquered northern China, northern Iran, and southern Russia. His descendants, governed by his collected edicts (yasa), created an empire stretching from the Mediterranean to the Pacific, crossed by traders such as Marco Polo. Although the Mongols killed the Abbasid caliph (1258) and caused great destruction, the Russian and Iranian portions of the empire became Muslim, restored what they had ruined, and sponsored history writing and Persian miniatures. *See also* Yasa

Genies *See* Jinn

Geomancy From the Latin *geomantia,* "divination by earth." In Arabic, the term is *ilm al-raml,* "science of sand." Pre-Islamic divination, accomplished by forming and then interpreting a design in earth or sand;

still a part of folk religion in many Islamic lands.

Geometry Arabic *ilm al-handasa.* Medieval Islamic geometrical works often appeared as introductions to books on astronomy. Mathematicians in the medieval Islamic world developed the use of geometry to solve algebraic problems, and vice versa; the mathematician Umar al-Khayyam (d. 1131) was the first to solve cubic equations, by the geometrical method of the intersection of two conic sections. Muslim mathematicians made lasting contributions to the discipline. For example, Ibn al-Haytham (Latin name Alhazen, d. 1039) constructed what is now known as the "strong Hilbert axiom of parallels," and some of the modern theorems of hyperbolic and elliptic non-Euclidean geometries were proved first by medieval Muslim mathematicians, who also used geometry in geodesic measurements, cartography, and astrolabe construction.

Germany, Islam in Approximately three million Muslims were in Germany in 2001. Germany's significant contacts with the Islamic world include exchanges during the Middle Ages between the Carolingian court and the Abbasid caliphate, the Crusades, and the Ottoman conquest of large parts of southeastern Europe. Prussia and the Ottoman Empire formed an alliance in 1790 that continued until the end of World War I. The Muslim population consists mainly of "guest workers," mostly of Turkish and Yugoslavian origin, who arrived en masse in the 1960s, and an important number of Turkish, Lebanese, Syrian, Bosnian, and Iranian citizens seeking political asylum. After World War II the German government sought to prevent the assimilation of migrant workers by maintaining them in separate housing and schools apart from German citizens and denying them citizenship. In 2000, recognizing the need for coexistence due to a continuing labor shortage and integration into the European Union, a commission was appointed to recommend an integrative immigration policy. The Bundestag passed a

2001 law granting citizenship to children of German-born foreigners who have lived in Germany for at least eight years. The most important Islamic organization is the Islamic Council of Germany, which is an umbrella group of thirty-eight Muslim groups.

Ghadir Festival Festival celebrating Muhammad's designation of Ali ibn Abi Talib as his successor, according to Shii Islam. Celebrated on 18 Dhu al-Hijjah.

Ghadir Khumm Place between Mecca and Medina where the Prophet Muhammad is reported to have pronounced Ali ibn Abi Talib the mawla (patron, master) of those for whom Muhammad was patron. Shiis interpret this statement as an affirmation of Ali's rightful position to lead the Muslim community after the Prophet, and annually celebrate the incident on the eighteenth of Dhul-Hijjah. Sunnis, however, view the Prophet's words as merely one of many expressions of his Companions' merits and note that this confirmation of the Prophet's esteem was needed to dissipate the ill feelings and accusations arising from Ali's strict handling of Yemeni booty immediately before. *See also* Ghadir Festival

Ghamidi, Javid Ahmad (b. 1951) A former member of the Jamaat-i Islami, this influential Pakistani Islamic scholar has, in his Urdu translation of the Quran and commentary, extended the work of his tutor, Amin Ahsan Islahi. Is frequently labeled a modernist for his insistence on the historical contextualization of Muhammad's revelation in order to grasp its true moral import. Has established two research centers in Lahore, al-Mawrid and Danish Sara, and teaches at the Civil Service Academy.

Ghana, Islam in Thirty percent of Ghana's nineteen million people are Muslim, 24 percent are Christian, and 38 percent practice indigenous religions. The Muslim presence is the result of extensive migration, rather than mass conversion or conquest. The Ghana Ahmadiyya Movement has been ac-

tive since 1885 and has operated a number of Western-style schools designed to spread their influence: one missionary training college, seven secondary schools, and about one hundred elementary schools. The Qadiri and Tijani Sufi orders also have followings among Ghana's Muslims. The constitution prohibits religion-based political parties; the only Muslim political party in the nation's history was the Muslim Association Party, disbanded after independence from the United Kingdom in 1957.

Ghanimah In classical Islam, wealth taken by force from an enemy in times of war. There were considerable differences among the classical jurists concerning rights to, and possession of, such wealth. All were agreed, however, that ghanimah was to be distributed in accordance with the shares specified in the Quranic directive in surah 8:41. *See also* Fai

Ghannoushi, Rashid al- (b. 1941) Tunisian Islamic thinker, activist, and political leader. Head and chief theoretician of Hizb al-Nahdah (Renaissance Party). Imprisoned for Islamic activism 1981–84 and 1987–88. Exiled to Europe in the early 1990s. Combines Western and Islamic philosophies to reconcile Islam with modernity and progress. Desires coexistence and cooperation between Islam and the West, rather than total rejection of the West. Understands democracy as a method of government rather than a philosophy. Rejects secular and nationalistic values typically associated with democracy in favor of "Islamic democracy" guided by moral content derived from shariah. Links westernization to dictatorship, noting that westernized elites typically resort to violent and repressive means to impose foreign-inspired models and perpetuate rule. Advocates the right of women to education, work, choice of home and marriage, ownership of property, and political participation. Considers the veil a matter of personal choice, not to be imposed by the state. Takes a gradualist approach to social and political change. Influential among Muslim activists and intellectuals. *See also* Hizb al-Nahdah (Tunisia); Tunisia, Islam in

Gharbzadegi *See* Ahmad, Jalal al-e; Westoxification

Ghaybah *See* Hidden Imam; Occultation

Ghazal Functional equivalent of musical sonatas in Persian poetry. Characteristically brief mosaics of words, sensibilities, and imagery highly admired in Persianate culture. Masters include Sanai (d. 1130), Nizami (d. 1209), and Sadi (d. 1292).

Ghazali, Abu Hamid al- (d. 1111) Influential Ashari theologian, jurist, and mystic. Born in Khurasan, he studied theology and law. While teaching law at Nizamiyya College in Baghdad, he suffered a spiritual crisis, withdrew from public life, and spent eleven years in travel and Sufi studies. Best-known work is *Ihya ulum al-din* (Revival of the religious sciences), an attempt to integrate theology and law, ethics and mysticism. Other important works include *Al-munqidh min al-dalal* (Delivery from error), a spiritual guidebook, and *Tahafut al-falasafah* (Destruction of the philosophers), an effort to debunk philosophy. His vast learning, systematic thought, and lucid style continue to ensure a wide audience.

Ghazali, Muhammad al- (d. 1996) Egyptian religious scholar and former leading member of the Muslim Brotherhood. Served as director of the Mosques Department, director general of Islamic Call, and undersecretary of the Ministry of Awqaf in Egypt. Taught at al-Azhar University (Egypt), at King Abd al-Aziz and Umm al-Qura Universities (Saudi Arabia), and in Qatar, and was academic director of Amir Abd al-Qadir Islamic University (Algeria). Favored the formation of an Islamic party in Egypt. Author of more than forty books on Islam's public role in politics and economics. Promoted the reduction of reliance on hadith in contemporary jurisprudence in favor of looking to both the Islamic past and contemporary societies, whether Muslim or non-Muslim, as a source of inspiration.

Ghazali, Zaynab (b. 1917) Prominent Egyptian writer, teacher of Muslim Brotherhood, and founder of the Muslim Women's Association as an Islamic alternative to the Egyptian Feminist Union. Educated and certified in hadith, preaching, and Quranic exegesis. Lectures weekly to crowds of up to five thousand women at the Ibn Tulun Mosque in Cairo. Instrumental in regrouping the Muslim Brotherhood in 1960s. Imprisoned 1965–71. Condemned tactics of murder, torture, and terrorism. Actively involved in writing and editing magazines for women and children. Proclaims that Islam allows women to be active in all aspects of public life as long as it does not interfere with their duties as wives and mothers.

Ghazan Khan, Mahmud (d. 1304) Celebrated Mongol ruler. Converted to Islam and recognized it as the state religion. Ruthlessly eliminated opposition and extended his reign over all Persia. Introduced major fiscal reforms, under which the country prospered. Admired the arts and sciences and mastered several languages. At his suggestion, the famous historian Rashid al-Din (d. ca. 1182) composed *Jami al-Tawarikh*, a history of the Mongols.

Ghaznavids South Asian dynasty, 962–1186. With Ghazna (in eastern Afghanistan) as its constant base and capital, this dynasty, at its height under Mahmud of Ghazna (r. 998–1030), encompassed much of Afghanistan, Iran, and the Indus and Ganges Valleys. Mahmud's father, the slave commander Sabuktigin, established a dynasty that demonstrated its affinity for Persianate culture by declaring a Persian lineage despite its Turkish ethnicity. Its members cast themselves as Sunni protectors of orthodoxy against the Shii Buwayhids and Ismailis. Its highly mobile military plundered the subcontinent and established indirect rule through local proxies. Replaced by Ghurids in the East and Seljuks in the West.

Ghaznawi, Mahmud ibn Sabuktigin al- *See* Mahmud of Ghazna

Ghazw Expeditionary raids by Bedouin tribes against another tribe. In modern linguistic usage, the word is used to connote raid, invasion, and aggression. The 1982 Israeli invasion of Lebanon is sometimes called *ghazw Lubnan*, and *al-ghazw al-fikri* (cultural invasion) is used to connote cultural imperialism.

Ghazwani, Shaykh Abdullah *See* Muhammadi Tariqah

Ghulam Young boy or slave; pl. *ghilman*. Associated with the system of military organization in the second half of the tenth and first half of the eleventh centuries. Ghilman were generally Turkish in origin, fought in bands, and demanded high pay for their services. Used by Fatimids, Buwayhids, and lesser societies of the Muslim world. *See also* Abd

Ghulam Ahmad, Mirza (d. 1908) Founder of Ahmadi movement in Punjab, India, in 1889. Claimed to be the Mahdi of Muslims, the Messiah of Christians, and the avatar of Krishna for Hindus. Also claimed to have received revelation from God. Denied that Muhammad was the last prophet. Prolific writer. Devoted to the organization and expansion of his movement; debates with Sunni ulama, Christian missionaries, and Hindu revivalists; and the publication of periodicals that propagated the Ahmadi interpretation of Islam. Built an effective social organization with economic cooperatives and other establishments designed to benefit followers. The movement is labeled non-Muslim and fiercely opposed by Muslims, although the group considers itself Muslim. *See also* Ahmadis

Ghulam Azam (b. 1922) Dhaka-born amir of the Jamaat-i Islami of Bangladesh from 1971 to 2000. Opposed the imposition of Urdu as the official language of united Pakistan as a student leader, and supported Pakistani army action against the Bangladesh independence movement in 1971. Spearheaded the revival of Jamaat-i Islami in post-independence Bangladesh against considerable odds.

Ghulat Extremists. Refers to those Shii groups critical in opposition to the centrist tendencies of Islamic doctrine and government during the first few centuries of Islam. Their speculations concerning the elevated status of Ali and subsequent Shii imams were rejected by Sunnis. As Shii groups within Islam developed into orthodoxies, they also condemned these early "exaggerators," although some of their doctrines were adopted. The term is used of several historical and contemporary Shii sects, such as the Bektashis (Turkey), Qizilbash (Turkey), Ali-Ilahis (Iran), and Nusayris or Alawis (Syria and Lebanon).

Ghurids Eastern Persian Sunni dynasty of the mid-twelfth to early thirteenth centuries. Tribal mountain chiefs who defeated the Ghaznavids in Afghanistan and India and the Khwarazmis in Iran. Generous patrons of literature, architecture, and the arts. Made regular incursions into India, conquering as far east as Bengal. Their slave generals became the first Muslim sultans of Delhi.

Ghusl Major purification ritual in Islam, to be contrasted with wudu, which is the minor purification ritual. Consists of washing hands and sexual organs, performing wudu, rubbing water into roots of hair, and pouring water over entire body, beginning with the right side; the water used must be clean, colorless, and odorless and cannot have been used for previous ritual. Necessary for all forms of worship, entrance into mosques, upon conversion to Islam, and after sexual relations, ejaculation, and menstrual or postpartum bleeding. In Shii Islam, also required after washing a corpse. Recommended by Sunnis. Also recommended prior to Friday prayers, days of major festivals (id), pilgrimage, and entering Mecca. *See also* Wudu

GIA *See* Groupe Islamique Armé

Gilani, Abd al-Qadir al- *See* Jilani, Abd al-Qadir al-

Ginans A popularization of the Sanskrit word *jnan*, which is generally defined as "contemplative or reflective knowledge." Among Ismailis originating in the Indian subcontinent, the word refers to the part of their tradition whose authorship is attributed to those who converted and preached beginning in the eleventh century. The languages in which the ginans exist reflect the areas from which they originate, including Sind, Punjab, and Gujarat. Recognized as important in preserving in local languages the devotional spirit of Islam.

Gnosticism Name given to a variety of movements or trends in various Near Eastern religions that emphasized esoteric knowledge (Greek *gnosis*) as a prerequisite for salvation. Gnostic ideas influenced many Shii movements of Iraq during the eighth and ninth centuries, including Ismaili-Shii thought. Gnosticism is characterized by a dichotomy of the exoteric (zahir) and the esoteric (batin). It is reflected in the Ismaili cosmology, letter symbolism, and cyclical views of history. The anonymous tenth-century *Rasail Ikhwan al-Safa* (Epistles of the brethren of purity) also reveals the impact of gnosticism. Various strands of Sufi thought and teachings have also been influenced by, and contributed to the further development of, ideas of a Gnostic origin. *See also* Neoplatonism

God *See* Allah

Gokalp, Mehmet Ziya (d. 1924) Turkish writer and nationalist. One of the most influential minds in twentieth-century Turkish political and intellectual history. Presented a version of Turkish nationalism that was a synthesis of secular Western and Islamic reform movements. Never published a major work, but his *Principles of Turkism* (1923) articulates his nationalist theories.

Goliath Arabic *Jalut*. Identified in the Quran (2:249–51) as the giant leader of the army opposing Talut (Saul). Talut's forces are presented as Muslims believing that God will grant victory to the faithful. Jalut was killed by David in accordance with God's will. In modern Islamic rhetoric, Jalut is typically used as a symbol of the West.

Government *See* Hukumah; Islamic State; Majlis

Granada Last Muslim stronghold in western Europe and last remnant of al-Andalus (Muslim Spain). Ruled by Nasrid dynasty, 1230–1492. Center of export trade in ceramics, silks, weapons, and porcelain. Home of Alhambra Palace, one of the greatest achievements of Islamic urban art. Fell to Spain's Christian rulers, Isabella and Ferdinand, in 1492, marking the end of Muslim rule in western Europe and the end of the Muslim population in Spain (Christian pressure on the Muslim population in Spain led to mass Muslim emigration to North Africa). Remains a powerful symbol in the collective Muslim memory of Western aggression.

Grand Mufti Also known as shaykh al-Islam. The term refers to the leading mufti serving in an advisory capacity to state and court. The position was first institutionalized by the Ottoman Empire in 1433. The grand mufti originally served as personal religious adviser to the sultan; he became head of ulama under Mehmed II and was given the power to appoint other ulama in the mid-sixteenth century.

Grand Vizier The sultan's absolute deputy in the Ottoman Empire; acted for the sultan in military and civil matters and presided over the imperial diwan (royal court), which consisted of ordinary viziers (ministers) as well as other officers of state. Lived in the Bab al-Ali (Sublime Porte), which quickly became synonymous with the state.

Great Britain, Islam in Approximately 1.5 million Muslims live in Britain. Muslim migration to Britain began with British colonial expansion in India in the late eighteenth and early nineteenth centuries. The first mosque was founded in 1889. The growth of British industry after World War II led to the recruitment of workers from colonial and former colonial territories, especially the Caribbean, India, and Pakistan. Britian tried to halt the influx of immigrant laborers in 1962 but did not prevent family reunion. Many refugees have arrived since the 1970s, as well as a number of extremely wealthy individuals from the Arab Gulf states. Major concerns are Islamic education, the right to practice Islamic law, and assimilation into British society.

Greater Bayram See Id al-Adha

Green Book See Qaddafi, Muammar al-; Third Universal Alternative

Groupe Islamique Armé The Armed Islamic Group (GIA) was formed in the early 1980s to challenge the socialist and secular policies of Algeria's ruling elites. Following the military coup d'etat of January 1992, which put a halt to the parliamentary election of an Islamist party (Islamic Salvation Front or FIS), the GIA went underground, from where it launched a terror campaign involving the killing of thousands of Algerian officials and ordinary citizens, including foreigners. Some of this terrorism has been exported abroad, especially to France, where nearly a million Algerians live.

Groupement Islamique en France Founded in 1979 to expand Islamic preaching to immigrant workers. Sponsors cultural, social, and sports activities to create and reinforce solidarity among Muslim workers. Emphasizes Islamic identity and compatibility of Islam with French republican values. Seeks better integration of Muslims into French society.

Guardian See Wakil

Guardianship The concept of guardianship (wilayah) is particularly important in Twelver Shii political theory, where it signifies the legitimacy of Ali's claim, together with that of the successor imams, to lead the Islamic community. In Islamic law, the term refers to guardianship of minors. For minors or the mentally ill, the father serves as legal guardian in most systems of Islamic law. In Maliki, Hanbali, and Shafii Islamic law, a guardian has the legal authority to contract marriage on behalf of a previously unmarried Muslim woman. Hanafis and the Shii Jafaris permit the interference of a guardian only if the bride's dowry is insufficient or in the event she wishes to marry someone who is not her equal according to law.

Guidance See Hidayah

Guide See Murshid

Guilds Urban organizations based on trade, commerce, and artisanal activities, and grouped in clearly delineated zones inside the city. Thus a guild corresponded to a trade as well as a specific urban zone. The origin of guilds in the Arabo-Islamic world is disputed. No Arabic equivalent exists for the English term guild, but the historical record demonstrates they were thriving from the sixteenth to the eighteenth centuries. Traditional guilds disappeared as a result of social, political, and administrative changes in countries undergoing profound transformations.

Guinea, Islam in Eighty-five percent of Guinea's 7.8 million people are Muslim; a sizeable Christian minority coexists in this democratic, multiparty republic. Most Muslims are Sunnis who follow the Maliki legal tradition and Qadiri and Tijani Sufi orders. Although the French established a colony in 1891, their control of the region was weak. After independence (1958), the nominally Muslim Marxist president Sékou Touré discouraged Islamization; only after his popularity waned in the 1970s did Touré seek to co-opt Muslim institutions to legitimize his rule. Since Touré's death in 1984, cooperation between the Muslim community and the government has continued.

Gülen, Fethullah (b. 1938) Founder of Turkey's largest faith-oriented Islamic movement, and an important Muslim thinker and prolific writer. Identifies knowledge, tolerance, and justice as the three core Islamic virtues. Led a movement that developed a sector of activities with a dense web of networks for the realization of these virtues, including founding more than two hundred private high schools and several universities in more than thirty countries and engaging in transnational media activities to empower Muslims.

Gulf States, Islam in the The Islamic Gulf states include Bahrain, Kuwait, Qatar, and United Arab Emirates (UAE). All four have experienced pronounced tensions between moderate Islamist reformers and Islamist radicals who advocate more fundamental changes of the ruling order. Rulers of all four base the legitimacy of their regimes on their interpretations of Islam. Bahrain and Kuwait have sizeable Shii communities who became more politically active after the Iranian revolution of 1979; the Shiis of UAE are not sympathetic to Iran. Most of Qatar's population adheres to the Hanbali school of Islamic law; about 16 percent of the population is Shii. The ruling families of Bahrain, Kuwait, and UAE favor Sunni Islam and the Maliki school of Islamic law. Bahrain tolerates considerable flexibility in applying law for the benefit of the community as a whole; Shiis constitute 70 percent of the population, but the advisory council appointed by the ruler in 1993 includes prominent representatives from both Sunni and Shii communities. In Kuwait, Shiis constitute 25 percent of the population, but after the Gulf War of 1990–91, the ruling family was forced to form the National Assembly; both Sunni and Shii Islamists were elected to the assembly in 1992, advocating shariah as the basis of Kuwaiti law. Kuwaiti Islamists are split into two groups: those seeking constitutional reform and conservatives. For UAE, Shiis constitute about 20 percent of the total population of the federation. Most of the influential families in Dubai are Sunni immigrants from southern Iran; Dubai also has a significant population of Shiis. Sharjah is predominantly inhabited by Shiis

of South Asian origin. Abu Dhabi is primarily Sunni but has a growing number of Twelver Shiis.

Gulf War War in 1990–91 between Iraq and a U.S.-led coalition acting to force Iraq to withdraw from Kuwait, which it had invaded and occupied in 1990. The coalition campaign had two phases: extensive bombing of Iraq and then a rapid ground offensive in which the Iraqi military was defeated with heavy casualties. The ceasefire agreement imposed severe economic and military sanctions on Iraq and required Iraq to submit to arms control inspections. Saddam Hussein, Iraq's leader, declared the conflict a jihad and protested against the stationing of non-Muslim troops in Saudi Arabia. In many parts of the Muslim world, there were demonstrations in support of Iraq.

Gulhane Rescript of 1839 Also known as the Charter of Gulhane. Declaration made as part of Ottoman reforms protecting the rights and property of subjects. Affirmed the restoration of shariah as law; instituted protections of life, honor, and property; fixed taxation according to wealth; granted all subjects the right to public trial and verdict; promised an even distribution of military service across the population; and extended rights to all subjects, whether Muslim or non-Muslim. Often cited as a hallmark of religious pluralism within the Ottoman Empire, demonstrating the protection of the rights of all subjects, regardless of religious creed, despite the state's affiliation with Islam. It is viewed as a major document of the Ottoman Tanzimat (reorganization). *See also* Tanzimat

Gumi, Shaykh Abubakar (d. 1992) Leader of the Izalah fundamentalist movement in Nigeria. Grand qadi of northern Nigeria during the First Republic. Taught and preached a return to the Quran and hadith after retiring in the 1960s. Became a popular radio star. Criticized traditional Sufi orders, local religious practices, and modernizing secularism. Translated the Quran into Hausa. Emphasis on non-Arabic Quranic interpretation helped to develop a specifically modern and Nigerian interpretation of Islam. Took a legalistic approach to Islam, opposing innovation and emphasizing the necessity of direct individual access to the Quran. Revived interest in re-creating either the Sokoto caliphate or the Medina model in the lives of individuals and political communities in Nigeria. Revived the early Islamic emphasis on education of women. *See also* Muslim Student Association (Nigeria)

Gus Dur *See* Wahid, Abdurrahman

H

Hadana Care of a child by the mother. Custody of a child belongs to the mother or other women relatives until the child no longer needs a woman's care, can drink and eat unassisted, can learn about other bodily functions, and can perform ablutions or purification unassisted. For a boy this is estimated at seven years of age. A girl remains under the custody of women relatives until she reaches puberty (hadd al-shahwa), when she must move to the protection of men; this is estimated to be from nine to eleven years of age, in the opinion of various legal authorities. When boys reach seven and girls nine to eleven, they are handed over to their father (or the closest male relative, according to their order of inheritance) to begin the second stage of custody, known as damm. This is according to the Hanafi code applied in most Islamic countries today. Other schools of law differ; for example, the Malikis allow a boy to remain with the mother until he reaches puberty and a girl to remain with her mother until she is married. Hadana belongs primarily to the mother, but if she remarries, she loses custody over her daughter unless the court decides otherwise. If a mother loses hadana, the child moves to the maternal grandmother; if that is not possible, then to the paternal grandmother, the maternal aunts, the paternal aunts or sisters, and so on. Damm belongs to male relatives: first the father, then the grandfather, uncle, and so on. Damm, which is enforced by the authorities if the mother refuses to surrender her children, is rationalized on the basis of a boy's need for male discipline and a girl's need for male protection at a vulnerable age before her marriage.

Hadd Limit or prohibition; pl. hudud. A punishment fixed in the Quran and hadith for crimes considered to be against the rights of God. The six crimes for which punishments are fixed are theft (amputation of the hand), illicit sexual relations (death by stoning or one hundred lashes), making unproven accusations of illicit sex (eighty lashes), drinking intoxicants (eighty lashes), apostasy (death or banishment), and highway robbery (death). Strict requirements for evidence (including eyewitnesses) have severely limited the application of hudud penalties. Punishment for all other crimes is left to the discretion of the court; these punishments are called tazir. With the exception of Saudi Arabia, hudud punishments are rarely applied, although recently fundamentalist ideologies have demanded the reintroduction of hudud, especially in Sudan, Iran, and Afghanistan. *See also* Criminal Law

Hadith Report of the words and deeds of Muhammad and other early Muslims; considered an authoritative source of revelation, second only to the Quran (sometimes referred to as sayings of the Prophet). Hadith (pl. *ahadith; hadith* is used as a singular or a collective term in English) were collected, transmitted, and taught orally for two centuries after Muhammad's death and then began to be collected in written form and codified. They serve as a source of biographical material for Muhammad, contextualization of Quranic revelations, and Islamic law. A list of authoritative transmitters is usually included in collections. Compilers were careful to record hadith exactly as received from recognized transmission specialists. The six most authoritative collections are those of al-Bukhari, Muslim, al-Tirmidhi, Abu Daud al-Sijistani, al-Nasai, and al-Qazwini. The collections of Malik ibn Anas and Ahmad ibn Hanbal are also important. Shiis also use these collections but recognize only some Companions as valid authorities; they consider hadith reports from descendants of Muhammad through Ali and Fatimah as fully authoritative. Other important Shii collections are those of al-Kulayni, al-Qummi, and al-Tusi. The science of hadith criticism was developed to determine authenticity and preserve the corpus from alteration or fabrication. Chains of authority and transmission were verified as far back as possible, often to Muhammad himself. Chains of transmission were assessed by the number and credibility of the transmitters and the continuity of the chains (isnad). The nature of the text was also examined. Reports that were illogical, exaggerated, fantastic, or repulsive or that contradicted the Quran were considered suspect. Awareness of fabrication and false teaching has long existed but became a major issue in academic circles in the twentieth century due to early reliance on oral, rather than written, transmission. Traditionally, the body of authentic hadith reports is considered to embody the Sunnah of the Prophet Muhammad. Muslim reformers encourage Muslims to be more discerning in acceptance of hadith.

Hadith Nabawi *See* Hadith Qudsi

Hadith Qudsi Sacred tradition or report. Also called hadith rabbani or hadith ilahi (divine hadith). Refers to a saying (hadith) of the Prophet Muhammad in which the meaning is revealed by God and the phrasing is formulated by the Prophet. Unlike prophetic hadith (hadith nabawi), the chain of transmission is traced back directly to God instead of ending with the Prophet. In contrast to the Quran, which is considered divine revelation in both meaning and wording, the authenticity of sacred hadith varies from one narration to another, and they may not be recited in prayer. They function as extra-Quranic revelation.

Hadrah Presence. The Friday Sufi communal gathering for dhikr (prayer of remembrance) and its associated liturgical rituals, prayers, and song recitals, whether private or public; in earlier orders, the "presence" referred to was that of God, but since the eighteenth century it has been considered the spiritual presence of Muhammad. Typically begins with a reading of the office of order and prayers, followed by dhikr and its

rituals. Also celebrated on special Islamic festivals and at rites of passage. May be held at home, in a mosque, in a Sufi hospice, or elsewhere.

Hafiz, Shams al-Din Muhammad (d. 1389) Also called al-Shirazi. Considered the greatest Persian poet, a master of the lyric form called ghazal, stressing the Sufi theme of an unrequited lover desperately seeking a divine beloved. Crafted metaphors of love's intoxication and of irresistible divine music; his artistic ambiguity inspired controversy as to whether his works suggest mystical longing or describe amorous liaisons. One of Shiraz's most popular personalities; his tomb attracts numerous visitors. Musicians continue to perform classical and contemporary settings of lyrics from some eight hundred poems in his collection (diwan).

Hafsa bint Umar (d. 665) Daughter of second caliph, Umar ibn al-Khattab. After being widowed at the Battle of Badr in 624, she became a wife of Muhammad (625). He may have divorced her but then taken her back. She is traditionally associated with surah 66:1–5. Segments of the earliest manuscript of the Quran were in her possession when she died.

Hafsids Dynasty of North Africa, centered in Tunis; reigned 1229–1574. The family was able to gain independence and support because of the role it played in establishing Almohadism. Tunis became the intellectual center of the Maghreb under Hafsid rule, and an important madrasa system was established. Maliki law and mysticism were strong. Andalusian and Christian merchant communities also thrived and were influential under the Hafsids. Though the dynasty survived the onslaught of a Crusade led by St. Louis, it eventually declined and fell under Ottoman rule because of the excesses of its rulers, the plague, revolts, and infighting.

Hagar Mother of Abraham's son Ishmael (Ismail). Servant of Abraham and Sarah. Not mentioned in the Quran. According to tradition, Hagar and Ishmael were abandoned by Abraham in the desert due to Sarah's jealousy, and God revealed the well of Zamzam to save them. The hajj ritual reenacts her search for water, with pilgrims running seven times between two small hills.

Hagia Sophia *See* Aya Sofia Mosque

Hagiography Accounts of lives of saints, prophets, and Companions of the Prophet Muhammad as portrayed in popular folk literature, performances in regional languages, and academic and officially sponsored works. Types of literature in Islam include manaqib (genealogies of holy people and histories of their merits and miracles), fadail (discussions of the virtuous qualities of important people), khasais (outlines of the special merits of prophets and their Companions), sirah (biographies of Muhammad and saints), tabaqat (classical-age collective biographical dictionaries organized by region, time period, Sufi order, or lineage), and tadhkirah (later collective biographies). Sufi biographical collections particularly emphasize lineage relationships, hierarchies of saints, karamah (capacity to perform miracles, which confirms a saint's high rank), and barakah (blessings emanating from a saint). In modern times, hagiographical literature has sometimes been used to highlight national, regional, and political themes, as well as to legitimate the religious authority of those claiming descent from saints. Biographies of early Islamic figures have on occasion been rewritten to make past role models more relevant to younger generations. Some governments, such as Pakistan's, have published popular saints' biographies to reinforce policy objectives, such as Islamic activism and social reform.

Hairi Yazdi, Abd al-Karim (d. 1936) Prominent Shii cleric, responsible for the importance of Qom as a center of Shii learning after 1921. Founded Hawzah-yi Ilmiyah Seminary. Taught that Shiis could follow more than one marja al-taqlid on different aspects of law since no one individual can master the full complexity of Islamic jurisprudence. Maintained a position of strict noninvolvement in political matters and a policy of nonopposition toward the government. Teacher of Ayatollah Ruhollah Khomeini.

Hajar *See* Hagar

Hajar al-Aswad, al- A stone set within a silver ring in the outer east corner of the Kaaba in Mecca. According to legend, the stone was brought to Abraham (Ibrahim) by the angel Gabriel while Abraham was building the Kaaba by God's command. During the hajj, pilgrims circumambulate the Kaaba and salute, touch, or kiss the stone, considered variously a symbol of the hereafter and divine presence. *See also* Kaaba

Hajj The annual pilgrimage to Mecca during the month of Dhu al-Hijjah. Approximately two million Muslims worldwide participate annually. Performance of the hajj is one of the five pillars of Islam, and all adult Muslims are required to perform it at least once in their lives if they are physically and financially able. Pilgrims dress modestly and simply, proclaiming the equality and humility of all believers before God, regardless of worldly differences in race, nationality, class, age, gender, or culture.

The hajj consists of the reenactment of a series of events in the lives of Abraham (Ibrahim), Hagar, and Ishmael (Ismail). It begins with the tawaf, seven circumambulations of the Kaaba, which imitates the angels circumambulating God's throne in heaven. Many pilgrims approach the corner of the Kaaba that holds the Black Stone, saluting, touching, or kissing it as a gesture of their renewed covenant with God and for purification from sin.

The tawaf is followed by the say, or running back and forth seven times between two small hills near the Kaaba in imitation of Hagar's search for water for Ishmael after being abandoned there by Abraham. The nearby well of Zamzam is believed to have miraculously appeared to save them from death. Pilgrims drink the well's water and wash and relax there.

The climax is the procession to the plains

of Arafat on the ninth of Dhu al-Hijjah. The pilgrims gather in tents, praying and conversing from just after noon until shortly after sunset. Many believe that God's spirit descends closest to earth at this place and time, making prayers more likely to attract His attention.

Although some pilgrims scale the sides of the Mount of Mercy, where Muhammad delivered his farewell message, most remain in the tent area to exchange international news and ideas about Islam. Promptly after sunset, the pilgrims travel through the mountain pass of Muzdalifa, where they spend the night under the open sky. The complete lack of accommodations at Muzdalifa makes this one of the most ascetic and inspiring phases of the hajj for many pilgrims. At sunrise on the tenth day, the pilgrims proceed to the valley of Mina, where they reenact Abraham's rejection of Satan's temptation to disobey God's command to sacrifice his son, Ishmael, by throwing seven pebbles at a tall stone pillar (jamarah). Afterward, each pilgrim offers an animal sacrifice (qurban), commemorating the sheep that God accepted in place of Ishmael. Muslims throughout the world participate vicariously in this ritual by performing their own sacrifices at home on this day, the feast of Id al-Adha.

During the following two or three days, the pilgrims shuttle back and forth between Mina and Mecca, performing at least six more stonings in Mina and at least one more tawaf and say in Mecca. National or local dress is gradually resumed, symbolizing the gradual return to the profane world.

Properly performed, the hajj absolves the pilgrim from all previous sins. However, the hajj is valid only if God accepts it—a judgment that cannot be known with certainty. A valid pilgrimage requires the sincere intention (niyah) of coming closer to God. If the intent is spiritually sound, most breaches of ritual formality can be corrected via additional animal sacrifices in Mecca or special acts of charity and fasting after returning home.

The hajj often serves as a rite of passage, coinciding with life events such as adulthood, marriage, career change, retirement, illness, or death. It may serve as an initiation for new converts to Islam or as spiritual rejuvenation after a personal crisis or loss.

The hajj links pilgrims with Muslims around the world symbolically, ritually, and politically. As a celebration of the annual reunion and renewal of the worldwide community of Muslims (ummah), it is the most powerful reminder of Islam's ideal of unity across space, culture, and time.

The government of Saudi Arabia currently oversees the hajj. Many Muslims have encouraged the Organization of the Islamic Conference (OIC) to establish an international agency to centralize and regulate hajj management so as to avoid favoritism, resentment, and heightened conflict among parties, regions, classes, and ethnic groups.

Hajj, Messali al- *See* Parti du Peuple Algérien

Hajjah *See* Hajji

Hajji Pilgrim. Often adopted as an honorific title preceding the name of Muslims who have made the pilgrimage to Mecca (*hajji* for men, *hajjah* for women). In some Muslim communities the title confers honor, respect, and special status.

Hakim (1) A generic term indicating a ruler, sovereign, or governor. The Arabic root of the word usually connotes judgment or adjudication. Historically, a common title taken by persons in positions of juridical authority. Principal term for a judge. (2) One blessed with profound understanding of the divine guidance for human life and perspicacity born from knowledge and experience and characterized by the undertaking of good deeds; one whose pronouncements are consistent with the truth. Also a traditional physician, theosophist, or philosopher.

Hakim, Khalifa Abdul (d. 1959) Scholar, educationist, and philosopher of Islam. Formerly head of the Department of Philosophy and dean of Osmania University, India, and director of the Institute of Islamic Culture,

Lahore, Pakistan. Compared Islam with Western ideologies in *Islam and Communism* (1951) and *Islamic Ideology: The Fundamental Beliefs and Principles of Islam and their Application to Practical Life* (1953).

Hakim, Muhammad Baqir al- (b. 1939) Iraqi political activist and Shii scholar. Son of the Grand Ayatollah Muhsen al-Hakim (d. 1970) and close associate of Ayatollah Mohammed Baqir al-Sadr (d. 1980). Since the 1970s, a key opposition figure advocating the establishment of an Islamic state in Iraq. Currently chairman of the Tehran-based Supreme Council for Islamic Revolution in Iraq (SCIRI).

Hakim, Muhsen al- (d. 1970) Influential Iraqi Shii cleric of the 1960s. A theological moderate, Hakim offered initiatives that were educational and political, and led an offensive against Communism. Tortured for opposition to the government. Many of his ten sons and their sons were executed by the Baath government of Saddam Hussein during the 1980s.

Hakim, Tawfiq al- (d. 1987) Egyptian dramatist, novelist, essayist, and short-story writer. His plays, including *People of the Cave* (1933), *Muhammad* (1936), and *The Tree Climber* (1962), show a concern for spiritual and social themes. Influential and controversial, he succeeded in establishing drama as a major genre in modern Arabic literature.

Hakimah Daughter of the tenth Shii imam, Ali al-Hadi. The shrine over her grave in Samarra is an important pilgrimage site for both Sunnis and Shiis.

Hal Condition or state of being; pl. *ahwal*. Used by Sufis to refer to the transitory spiritual state of enlightenment or ecstasy resulting from passage along the way to mystical knowledge of God. Considered a gift from God, as opposed to an acquired stage (maqam). Although the recipient may not have deliberately sought this state, reception of it is typically understood to be the

result of a definite, disciplined rule of life. Hal is often described as a trancelike state and can be either voluntary or involuntary. Some Sufis engage in ecstatic behavior while in this state, making it suspect to more legalistic interpreters of Islam. *See also* Maqam

Halal Quranic term used to indicate what is lawful or permitted. Most legal opinions assert the presumption that everything is halal (permissible) unless specifically prohibited by a text. Often used in conjunction with established dietary restrictions, halal can refer to the meat of permitted animals that have been ritually slaughtered, hunted game over which the name and praise of God have been pronounced, and fish and marine life. Prohibited categories (haram) include pork, blood, alcoholic beverages, scavenger animals, carrion, and improperly sacrificed permitted animals, although these may be eaten in cases of extreme necessity.

Halaqah Circle. In general, refers to a group of students studying under a particular professor. In Sufism, refers to the circle formed around a spiritual leader, and to the circle of students or devotees adhering to a specific course of study or set of rituals. Also refers to the circle that may be formed by followers for contemplation.

Halimah bint Abi Dhuayb Muhammad's nursemaid from infancy until he was four years old. According to hadith, she was unable to nurse her own son prior to taking Muhammad in due to drought and starvation in the desert. Once she started nursing Muhammad, she was able to produce enough milk for both Muhammad and her son.

Hallaj, Abu al-Mughith al-Husayn ibn Mansur ibn Muhammad al- (d. 922) Persian Sufi preacher and missionary. Ideal of piety and spiritual valor in Sufi tradition and broader Islamic cultural context. Claimed to have experienced an ecstatic sense of spiritual oneness with God, declaring, "Ana al-haqq" (I am Truth [i.e., God]). Claimed a religious authority greater than that of caliphs and religious scholars due to his possession of divine presence. Executed in spectacular fashion in Baghdad for heresy, with his remains cremated so that no tomb could be erected and serve as the center of a cult. Revered by Sufis as a martyr.

Hamadani, Ayn al-Qudat al- (d. 1131). Scholar and mystic. Native of Hamadhan, Iran. Born to a scholarly family; an early convert to Sufism. Disliked by orthodox Muslims and imprisoned in Baghdad for heresy; eventually released but later tortured and executed. Wrote in an elegant Arabic and Persian style on extreme forms of mystical love, such as Satan's pure love of God, and on the nature of sainthood.

Hamallah, Shaykh (d. 1943) Founder of Hamalli Sufi order. Born in Mali. Lived a secluded life spent in meditation with a few selected students. Widely known for asceticism and mysticism but not scholarship. Preached pacifism and social and religious reform. Led civil disturbances against the French, making him a symbol for Muslims opposed to French rule. Arrested and exiled. *See also* Hamallism

Hamallism Malian offshoot of Tijani Sufi brotherhood. Advocated social reform programs, stressed equality of all people, supported liberation of women, and opposed wealth of establishment religious leaders. Distinguished by veneration of its founder, Shaykh Hamallah. Some followers changed shahadah to declare, "There is no god but God and Hamallah is our shaykh." Despite its leader's espousal of pacifism, some followers were involved in the massacre of a rival nomadic group, resulting in harsh suppression by the French. Two types of movements grew out of the massacre experience: a series of enthusiastic but short-lived jihads and a quietist Sufi tradition that became the prototype for African socialism, nationalism, and mobilization of the masses.

HAMAS Acronym (meaning "zeal") for Harakat al-Muqawamah al-Islamiyyah (Movement of Islamic Resistance). Most important Palestinian Islamist organization in the occupied West Bank and Gaza. Established in December 1987 at the beginning of the Palestinian uprising (intifadah) as the organizational expression of Muslim Brotherhood participation in the armed anti-Israeli resistance. Founded by Abd al-Aziz al-Rantisi with Shaykh Ahmad al-Yasin as spiritual guide. Has an armed wing, called Izz al-Din al-Qassam Forces or Brigades. Explains the anti-Israeli engagement in terms of jihad, which is specified as an individual religious duty. Accuses Jews of seeking to destroy Islam; the consequent threat to Islam means that no Jewish state (Israel) can legitimately exist. Portrays the military option embodied in its interpretation of jihad as the only one available for the liberation of Palestine. Characterizes Palestine as an Islamic waqf (pious endowment), so no portion of it can be relinquished. Heavily emphasizes the religious importance of Palestine and Jerusalem, making land a major religious issue that cannot be compromised for political reasons. Rejects the political program adopted by the PLO. Refuses to recognize the peace process. Claims the support of 30 to 40 percent of Palestinians as members. Devotes the majority of its budget to educational and social welfare activities.

Hamasah Enthusiasm; courage; zeal. Also refers to a genre of Arabic poetry that recounts chivalrous exploits in the context of military glories and victories. Also, Persian and Turkish heroic and martial epic poetry. In late-twentieth-century usage, it has come to mean a sort of heroism in which the wider Islamic nation can take pride.

Hamd Noun from the Arabic root hmd, "to praise." The word is often used with the name Allah, hence "al-hamdu lil-Allah," often abbreviated as hamdila or hamdala, meaning "praise God" or "thanks to God." The phrase appears at the beginning of the first surah in the Quran. Thus a Muslim will utter it at least twice during any of the five daily prayers. The name Muhammad is derived from the same root as hamd.

Hamdala *See* Alhamdu Lillah

Hamdanids Arab nomadic Shii clan that undermined Abbasid rule from Mesopotamia (905–991). Its influence eventually extended from Mosul to Baghdad, westward to northern Syria, and northward into Armenia. The ascendance of the Hamdanids marks the ninth-century emergence of pastoral dominance over sedentarized communities.

Hamdard Foundation Pakistani charitable society and pharmaceutical company. Formed in 1953 by Hakim Mohammed Said. Provides free medical treatment to the poor. Said interpreted Islam as an eternal code of life based on love, equality, and respect for all human beings. The foundation's proclaimed mission is the worldwide propagation of the scientific nature of Eastern medicine. The foundation sponsors lectures, scientific conferences, the creation of an international network of scholars, and the publication of journals, pamphlets, scholarly books, and children's magazines and storybooks. In 1991 it received a charter from the government of Pakistan to establish Hamdard University. *See also* Said, Hakim Mohammed

Hamka (d. 1981) Acronym of Hajji Abdul Malik Karim Amrullah. Indonesian religious scholar and author of more than a hundred works of fiction, politics, history, biography, Islamic doctrine, ethics, mysticism, and tafsir. Most famous religious scholar in Malay-speaking world. Leading figure in the revolutionary struggle for national independence in West Sumatra, 1945–49. Sought moral messages in history to be applied to the present. Concerned for human suffering and faith in transitional society. Wrote an influential interpretation of the Indonesian national ideology, Pancasila, making the first principle the recognition of the oneness of God (tawhid).

Hamzah ibn Abd al-Muttalib Muhammad's paternal uncle. Held a reputation as the bravest, strongest, and best warrior of the Quraysh tribe. Converted to Islam and offered protection to Muhammad and Muslims from the Quraysh. His conversion led to a reduction of harassment of Muhammad in particular, since his adherence to Islam reflected Muhammad's growing power. Killed in the Battle of Uhud (625).

Hanafi, Hasan (b. 1935) Egyptian reformist thinker, writer, and professor of philosophy. Believes in fusion of ideals with a revitalized, reinterpreted Islam in order to form an "Islamic left" and bring about unity in Egypt, social and economic justice for the downtrodden, a democratic state free from Western domination and Zionist influence, the unification of the Arab world, and the restoration of Islam to a central position in world culture. Argues that human beings and history are at the center of Islamic religious consciousness, so it is appropriate to integrate the needs of modern Muslims into Islamic theology to create a revolutionary liberation theology that will enable Muslims to face modern challenges and fight poverty, underdevelopment, coercion, westernization, and alienation.

Hanafi School of Law Islamic school of legal thought (madhhab) whose origins are attributed to Abu Hanifah in Kufa, Iraq, in the eighth century. Most widespread school in Islamic law, followed by roughly one-third of the world's Muslims. Dominant in the Abbasid caliphate and the Ottoman Empire. Remains the dominant legal authority in successor states for personal status and religious observances. Uses reason, logic, opinion (ray), analogy (qiyas), and preference (istihsan) in the formulation of laws. Legal doctrines are relatively liberal, particularly with respect to personal freedom and women's rights in contracting marriages. First school to formulate contract rules for business transactions involving resale for profit and payment for goods for future delivery.

Hanbali School of Law Islamic school of legal thought (madhhab) whose origins are attributed to Ahmad ibn Hanbal in ninth-century Baghdad. The official school in Saudi

Arabia and Qatar, with many adherents in Palestine, Syria, and Iraq. Recognizes as sources of law: the Quran, hadith, fatwas of Muhammad's Companions, sayings of a single Companion, traditions with weaker chains of transmission or lacking the name of a transmitter in the chain, and reasoning by analogy (qiyas) when absolutely necessary. Encourages the practice of independent reasoning (ijtihad) through study of the Quran and hadith. Rejects taqlid, or blind adherence to the opinions of other scholars, and advocates a literal interpretation of textual sources. Ritualistically, the Hanbali school is the most conservative of the Sunni law schools, but it is the most liberal in most commercial matters.

Hanif One who is utterly upright in all of his or her affairs, as exemplified by the model of Abraham (Ibrahim) with his pure monotheism, sincerity, and complete submission and obedience to God. These essential components comprise the upright path of Islam (al-din al-qayyim), which Muslims believe is the basic nature and goodness (fitrah) upon which humanity was created. Being hanif implies maintaining this monotheistic orientation throughout one's life and avoiding all forms of polytheism as well as the sectarianism introduced by religious communities, such as Jews and Christians. The term was used before Islam to designate pious people who accepted monotheism but did not join the Jewish or Christian communities.

Haqiqah Reality. In Sufi thought, refers to the inward vision of divine power achieved through mystical union with God. Approached by Sufis through the use of intuitive and emotional spiritual faculties trained under the guidance of a shaykh. Both Shiis and Sufis believe haqiqah can be reached through adherence to shariah and the principle of tawhid, although specific methods differ.

Haqiqah al-Muhammadiyyah, al- The Muhammadan Reality. Term popularized by the Sufi theoretician Ibn al-Arabi (d.

1240) and used as a synonym for expressions such as "the Reality of Realities" (haqiqah al-haqaiq), which is the logos, or prototype of creation in God's knowledge; "the Breath of the All-Merciful" (nafas al-rahman), which is the divine utterance that gives rise to creation; "the First Intellect" (al-aql al-awwal), which is the first thing created by God; and "the perfect human being" (al-insan al-kamil), who is the origin and goal of the universe.

Harakah Movement; pl. *harakat.* Political parties, liberation movements, and other social phenomena are often called harakah, such as Harakat al-Tahrir al-Islami (Islamic Liberation Movement), Sudan; Harakati Inqilab (Revolutionary Movement), Afghanistan; and Harakat al-Tawhid (Unity Party), Palestine. Al-harakat al-niswiyah means "the women's movement."

Harakat al-Mahrumin Movement of the Dispossessed. Created by Musa al-Sadr in 1974 in Lebanon in response to the needs of the Shii community, which had been denied proportional representation in government and was suffering from economic deprivation and social exclusion. Changed the interpretation of Shii history from the glorification of sacrifice, martyrdom, and passive acceptance of injustice into an activist ideology of social protest, emancipation, and struggle, resisting injustice, deprivation, tyranny, and oppression. Peacefully demanded the reform of the political system for greater Shii representation, proportional to the actual size of the population. Became a dynamic force in Lebanese politics. Forerunner to AMAL. *See also* AMAL; Sadr, Musa al-

Harakat al-Muqawamah al-Islamiyyah *See* HAMAS

Harakat al-Tawhid al-Islami Islamic Unity Movement. Militant Sunni movement that emerged in Tripoli, Lebanon, in the 1980s in response to the Lebanese civil war and the Israeli invasion of 1982. Had ties to Iran, radical Egyptian religious leaders, and Hizb Allah. Goal was to establish an Islamic state

through an Islamic revolution according to the Iranian model. Supported reinstatement of the caliphate in Mecca to achieve a broader Muslim unity. Preached individual morality as a basis for social transformation. Led by Shaykh Said Shaban. Greatly weakened after military defeat in October 1985.

Harakat ul-Ansar/Harakat ul-Mujahidin Militant Pakistan-based organization active in Indian-held Kashmir. Originated as a part of the Afghan Islamic resistance against the Soviet occupation of Afghanistan in the 1980s. Founded as Harakat ul-Ansar in October 1993 by Mawlana Fazlur Rahman Khalil, a Deobandi scholar and activist. Declared a terrorist organization by the U.S. State Department after it was blamed for the assassination of four Western tourists in Kashmir. Reorganized under the name Harakat ul-Mujahidin in 1997, with its headquarters in Muzaffarabad, Pakistani (Azad) Kashmir. Believes in pan-Islamic ideology of "one flag, one government, and one state" for the entire Muslim world. Banned by Pakistan's government in December 2001 as part of its efforts to suppress all extremist and militant organizations.

Haram Legal term for what is forbidden or inviolable under Islamic law. Also describes the area around the three holy cities of Islam—Mecca, Medina, and Jerusalem—indicating their role as sanctuaries where no one may be killed. Hunting, uprooting trees, harvesting grain, violence toward humans except in self-defense, and carrying weapons are forbidden in these areas. Entry of non-Muslims into Mecca and Medina is also forbidden. Haram is the root of the word *harem*, referring to women's quarters that are forbidden to any males except relatives and husbands. The word is used as an exclamation in Arabic in reaction to bad news, meaning "God have pity!"

Haram al-Sharif The Noble Enclosure. Muslim sacred precinct on Mount Moriah in Jerusalem and the site of two Islamic holy places, the al-Aqsa mosque and the Qubbat al-Sakhra (Dome of the Rock). After Mecca

and Medina it is the third holiest site in the Islamic world, a place of Islamic pilgrimage for fourteen centuries. It also contains the earliest major surviving Islamic architectural monument, the Dome of the Rock. Presently administrated by Islamic authority under Israeli control. Originally the site of the First and Second Jewish Temples, the precinct is today the subject of contention between Israelis and Palestinians.

Haramayn The two holy places. Refers to the cities of Mecca and Medina in modern-day Saudi Arabia. The word *haram* also means "forbidden," referring here both to the fact that non-Muslims are not permitted to enter them and to the role of the two cities as sanctuaries, so that bloodshed within them is prohibited. *See also* Mecca; Medina

Harb Warfare not sanctioned by Islamic law. *See also* Dar al-Harb; Jihad; Terrorism

Harem Term for forbidden or sacred place. Refers to women's quarters, which are off-limits to males other than husbands or male relatives. May house wives, daughters, sisters, and mothers.

Harun al-Rashid (r. 786–809) Abbasid caliph whose exploits are the subject of *The Thousand and One Nights*. The Abbasid caliphate reached its apogee under his rule, which was characterized by relative peace, prosperity, and unity of the Islamic community. Corresponded with and sent a diplomatic mission to the Holy Roman Emperor, Charlemagne, opening a period of technological and economic exchange with the West. Established a hostel for Christian pilgrims in Jerusalem. Set up the first hospital and observatory in Baghdad, which served as models for later rulers.

Hasan, Muhammad Abdallah (d. 1920) Somali Sufi and intellectual leader who guided his country's resistance to European and Ethiopian occupation from 1899 to 1920. By mediating clan disputes and preaching anticolonialism, he won the support of most Somalis and worked to preserve Islamic values and found a theocratic Muslim state. Declared a holy war against foreigners in 1899 and inflicted serious losses on foreign armies until British aircraft destroyed his fortress in 1920. Though many Somalis see him as a national hero, he convinced few to adhere to his rigid vision of Islam.

Hasan al-Basri (d. 728) Major religious figure of the Umayyad period. Produced writings and sermons that were extremely influential in all areas of Islamic piety, from theology to Quranic exegesis. Known especially for his asceticism and upholding the doctrine of free will and the believer's own responsibility for sin. Often critical of or opposed to Umayyad rulers, but did not approve of rebellion against tyrannical rule. His sermons contain some of the earliest and best examples of Arabic prose style.

Hasan ibn Ali (d. 669) Muhammad's grandson, oldest son of Ali and Fatimah, and second imam in the Shii tradition. Forced by Muawiyah ibn Abi Sufyan to abdicate the role of caliph in his favor. After his abdication, many Shiis were terrorized and persecuted and Ali was vilified, leading numerous Shiis to favor Hasan's brother, Husayn, over Muawiyah as leader.

Hasan-Somalia, Muhammad Abd Allah *See* Mahamad Cabdille Hasan

Hashemite *See* Banu Hashim (Quraysh)

Hashishiyun *See* Nizaris

Hashiyyah Glosses or supercommentaries written in the margin of texts. While originally meaning the margin itself, by the eleventh century the term had come to designate an established scholarly practice reflecting the cumulative nature of Muslim scholarship. Hashiyyah are used to indicate corrections, variants, explanations, references, criticisms, or additional information.

Hasina, Shaykh *See* Women and Islam

Hawashi *See* Hashiyyah

Hawwa *See* Eve

Hawwa, Said (d. 1989) Syrian Islamist activist. Born in Hamah. Earned a law degree from the University of Damascus in 1961. Joined the Muslim Brotherhood in Hamah in the mid-1950s, quickly rising in its ranks. Was an active participant in the 1964 protests against secular rule in Hamah. Began to gain a reputation as an Islamic thinker in 1968 with the publication of his first book. In 1973 convinced the ulama to unite in their opposition to the secularist constitution, and was imprisoned for five years as a result. Wrote an eleven-volume exegesis of the Quran and a series of books on Sufism from his cell. Upon his release in 1978, left Syria for Jordan, living the remainder of his life in exile. Was removed from the Muslim Brotherhood leadership after the Syrian government's violent and effective repression of the movement in 1982.

Haya *See* Modesty

Hayd *See* Menstruation

Haykal, Muhammad Husayn (d. 1956) Egyptian novelist. Used religious symbols appealing to traditional Muslims to introduce a framework of modern rational, scientific analysis designed to promote long-range ideological reform and demonstrate the compatibility between Islam, progress, and reason. Wrote a biography of Muhammad that attempted to synthesize Islamic piety and "scientific" historical method by presenting Muhammad as an ideal personality manifesting modern rational and ethical values. Argued that Islam supports modern ideals of freedom of opinion and democracy. Stressed that the "rightly guided" caliphs left a set of organizational principles whose specific political applications could change over time. Argued against restoration of the traditional Islamic legal system. Attacked the materialism of Western culture.

Hazrat *See* Hadrah

Heaven The reward in the afterlife for those who have faith in God's revelations, who are dutiful, truthful, contrite, penitent, and who do good works, such as feeding the needy and orphans. Described in the Quran as a garden (jannah) wherein inhabitants enjoy shade, fruits, cool drinks, wine, and meat as they desire; they recline on couches adorned with armlets of gold and pearls, wearing green and gold robes of embroidered silk, and are waited on by servants. Male inhabitants of the garden are to enjoy the company of beautiful dark-eyed companions (houris). Many interpreters consider these descriptions metaphorical; tradition suggests that the ultimate reward of heaven is dwelling in God's presence. *See also* Afterlife

Hejaz Western coastal province of modern-day Saudi Arabia. Home to the pilgrimage cities of Mecca and Medina. Historically, Hejaz linked the main caravan routes of northern and southern Arabia and served as a center of pre-Islamic worship where Zoroastrianism, Judaism, and Christianity came into contact with each other. It was the first region to become part of the Islamic world under Muhammad's leadership.

Hekmatyar, Gulbuddin (b. ca. 1947) Leader of the Hizb-i Islami and prime minister of Afghanistan in the post-Soviet government. As a political leader during the 1978–92 war against the Marxist government, he was respected for his organizational skills and oratory but has been criticized for promoting a divisive revolutionary Islamic ideology. *See also* Hizb-i Islami (Afghanistan)

Hell Also known as al-Nar and Jahannam. Punishment assigned to evildoers and unbelievers in the afterlife. Described in the Quran as a place of eternal fire with crackling and roaring flames, fierce boiling waters, scorching wind, and black smoke. Often depicted as having seven gates or levels. Evildoers will tumble from the Bridge of Sirat into the fire below. Inhabitants sigh and wail, drinking foul liquids in a hopeless effort to assuage their thirst. Scorched skins are exchanged for new ones so that pain can be experienced repeatedly. Boiling water is poured over heads, melting the insides. Iron hooks drag people back if they try to escape. Many commentators interpret these descriptions as metaphors for the awareness of guilt and deprivation of divine presence. *See also* Afterlife

Heresy *See* Zandaqah; Ilhad

Hermeticism In the early history of Sufism, a combination of ascetic practices, intensive prayers, and renunciation of worldly affairs was considered the only way to remove inner desires. This entailed fasting, celibacy, poverty, and living a reclusive life. Except for some exceptional mystics, the modern-day mystical tradition has hardly any traces of hermeticism, but fasting and living modestly are still prevalent.

Hezbollah *See* Hizb Allah (Iran); Hizb Allah (Lebanon)

Hibri, Azizah al- (b. 1943) Muslim professor of corporate law and Islamic jurisprudence. Received a doctorate and a law degree from the University of Pennsylvania. Former professor of philosophy and Wall Street lawyer. Founder of KARAMAH: Muslim Women Lawyers for Human Rights. Founding editor of *Hypatia: A Journal of Feminist Philosophy*. Has authored several articles and books and spoken internationally on women in Islam and Islamic law, Islamic constitutionalism and democracy, Muslims in the United States, and international law. Activism is diverse, including civil and human rights, interfaith dialogue, family and gender violence prevention, and ethics and public policy. Particularly active in reforming Muslim personal status laws.

Hidayah God-given guidance to guard humans against their natural tendency to follow their own whims and to go astray. This guidance is believed to have been primarily provided in the form of the Quran.

Hidden Imam Twelver Shii doctrine holds that the twelfth imam (in this usage meaning a descendant of the Prophet Muhammad through his cousin Ali and his daughter Fatimah) did not die but went into a spiritual form of existence known as occultation, and will return at the end of time as a messianic Mahdi to restore justice and equity on earth. The twentieth-century interpretation of Ayatollah Ruhollah Khomeini of Iran holds that, in the meantime, the position of ruler of state should be filled by the most learned faqih (jurist) as the imam's representative, a position Khomeini held until his death. Musa al-Sadr of Lebanon is also identified with the Hidden Imam since he mysteriously disappeared on a trip to Libya while serving as leader of Lebanon's Shii community. *See also* Shii Islam

Hijab Traditional Muslim women's head, face, or body covering, of numerous varieties across time and space, often referred to as the "veil." Hijab is a symbol of modesty, privacy, and morality. The practice was borrowed from elite women of the Byzantine, Greek, and Persian empires, where it was a sign of respectability and high status, during the Arab conquests of these empires. It gradually spread among urban populations, becoming more pervasive under Turkish rule as a mark of rank and exclusive lifestyle. Hijab became a central topic of feminist/nationalist discourse during the nineteenth-century British colonial occupation of Egypt. Western feminists view hijab as a symbol of the subordination and inferiority of women in Islam. Since the 1970s it has emerged as a symbol of Islamic consciousness and the voluntary and active participation of young women in the Islamist movement, a symbol of public modesty that reaffirms Islamic identity and morality and rejects Western materialism, commercialism, and values. In the 1980s hijab became an assertion of Islamic nationalism and resistance to Western culture.

Hijaz *See* Hejaz

Hijrah Migration or withdrawal. Typically refers to the migration of Muhammad and his Companions from Mecca to Medina in 622 C.E., the first year in the Islamic calendar.

Symbolizes the willingness to suffer for faith and the refusal to lose hope in the face of persecution. Can be undertaken individually or collectively in response to a threat to survival. In modern times, has been used to oppose colonial rule, legitimize Muslim migrations, settle Bedouin tribes, and consolidate power. Most recently, has referred to a form of withdrawal from the politics of secularism, capitalism, socialism, and modernization/Westernization. For Sufis, refers to the process of self-purification during the inner spiritual journey of returning to God.

Hikmah Wisdom. Refers to both revealed wisdom (the Quran identifies itself as a form of wisdom) and the sciences in general. Some thinkers, such as Ibn Sina, have classified major branches of knowledge as subdivisions of hikmah, including medicine and medical ethics. A religio-philosophical school developed by Shihab al-Din Yahya Suhrawardi (d. 1191) is known as Hikmat al-Ishraq or Illuminationism. The plural, *hikam*, refers to the aphorisms or "wisdom sayings" attributed to several important medieval Sufis, notably the Egyptian Ibn Ata Allah (d. 1309).

Hikmat al-Ishraq Wisdom by illumination. In the Sufi and later philosophical traditions in Islam, ishraq referred to the apprehension of truth through a light emanating from God, who is described in the Quran (24:35) as "the Light of the heavens and the earth." For the more mystically inclined philosophers, such as Ibn Sina (Avicenna), the ultimate stage in the process of philosophical development is a nondiscursive stage whose roots ought to be sought in the East (al-sharq). A century and a half later, al-Suhrawardi (d. 1191) made ishraq the pivotal point of his philosophy, embodied in a famous treatise entitled *Hikmat al-ishraq* (The wisdom of illumination). Here al-Suhrawardi claims to go beyond rational (Hellenistic) philosophical methods to more direct, experiential modes of insight deriving from ancient Eastern, predominantly Persian, sources. The Ishraqi tradition reached its zenith in the work of the Persian philosopher Sadr al-Din al-Shirazi, known also as Mulla Sadra (d. 1641), generally regarded as the greatest exponent of the philosophy of ishraq, which continues to have a significant following in Iran today. *See also* Neoplatonism

Hilah Device to stop, hinder, or trick; pl. *hiyal*. Stratagem to avoid or circumvent legal principles or rigid constructs. A book on hiyal attributed to Muhammad al-Shaybani led to the belief that the Hanafi school was the first to champion the use of hiyal. Initially other schools of thought condemned the practice, but later their fuqaha utilized hiyal to solve contradictions between the dictates of executive powers or cultural choices and Quranic principles.

Hilal The crescent moon, the sighting of which is important for the determination of when certain religious duties and practices must take place. The Quran says that new moons are "fixed seasons for humankind and for pilgrimage" (2:189). The need to determine the precise appearance of the hilal was one of the inducements for Muslim scholars to study astronomy. When it became apparent that sighting the new moon by the naked eye was not exact, some Muslims (primarily Ismailis) argued for calculating (hisab) the appearance of the new moon. The majority of Sunni Muslims have rejected calculation in favor of visual sighting.

Hilli, Jamal al-Din Hasan ibn Yusuf ibn Ali ibn al-Mutahhar al- (d. 1325) Scholar and jurist of the Imami Shiis. Wrote on grammar, logic, and hadith, but is best known for his writings on jurisprudence and theology. Integrated the theory of ijtihad into Shii jurisprudence; all subsequent Shii thought on ijtihad can be seen as a development of or a reaction to Hilli's ideas.

Hilli, Safi al-Din Abd al-Aziz ibn Saraya al- (d. 1348) Famous poet. Born into a Shii family from al-Hilla, Iraq. Became court poet in Mardin in 1302 under the Turkmen Artukids. Author of several works on literary forms. Famous for his collection of poetry

(diwan) and for his taqiyah-oriented life in the Sunni world, in which he spent the majority of his life.

Hind bint Abi Umayya (d. 679) Better known as Umm Salama. Meccan aristocrat. Emigrated to Abyssinia with her first husband, who died of wounds sustained at the Battle of Uhud (625). Became a wife of the Prophet Muhammad (626). Reputedly intelligent, politically astute, active for women's rights in Medina. Acted as the Prophet's adviser during negotiations concerning the al-Hudaybiyya treaty with the Meccans (628).

Hinduism and Islam Depicted commonly as antagonistic opposites, these religio-cultural traditions have interacted, usually peacefully, since the seventh-century Islamic conversion of Arab merchants settled in coastal Indonesia and South Asia. The ancient Persians originated the term *Hindu* for "those beyond the Indus River," referring to a population, not a religion. In 711 Muslim Arab armies arrived in Sind, and in 1001 Mahmud of Ghazna initiated a series of Turkish incursions from Afghanistan throughout the Indo-Gangetic plain. Although these invaders and their various indigenous enemies occasionally defined one another in terms of religion, they more commonly differentiated themselves through ethnicity. Religious sites were more likely to be destroyed for political and economic purposes than because of religious animosity. In both Indonesia and South Asia, conversion of Hindus to Islam occurred most often through conviction, as Sufis inculcated a native interest in Islam by bridging local and Islamic beliefs and practices, while the development of Muslim-dominated states encouraged conversion for status advancement. Local cultures flourished with integrated and composite communities of Hindus and Muslims, which often shared devotion at Sufi shrines but seldom at mosques and temples. While South Asians remained predominantly Hindu, Indonesians became overwhelmingly Muslim by the eighteenth century. During the nineteenth and twentieth centuries, British rule in India heightened political tensions through policies that defined and enumerated religious communities as competing constituencies. The nationalist movement aroused Muslim anxiety when it promoted the Hindu majority's interests (e.g., cow protection) and employed Hindu symbols (e.g., India as mother goddess). Apprehensive of Hindu cultural and religious hegemony, many Muslims supported Islamic reform movements (e.g., the Deobandis) and political parties (e.g., the Muslim League, which supported the establishment of the Muslim state of Pakistan in 1947). The religious nationalism of South Asian political groups such as Jamaat-i Islami and the Bharatiya Janata Party (BJP) increasingly threatens to sacrifice shared local cultures for polarized national politics. In India, the meteoric rise of the BJP and similar organizations has encouraged a hardening of anti-Muslim sentiment among rural and urban dwellers alike. In response to the demand that the very definition of "Indian" be "Hindu" and the claim that all who resist such identification are unpatriotic, many contemporary Indian Muslims respond with a more demonstrative Indian nationalism and an increasingly austere vision of Islam.

Hirabah *See* Terrorism

Hisbah Term referring to community morals; by extension, to the maintenance of public law and order and supervising market transactions. The functions of the muhtasib (person responsible for hisbah) cover duties regarding prayers, mosque maintenance, community matters, and market dealings. With the advent of Western colonialism, hisbah came under the purview of secular departments in many Muslim societies. *See also* Muhtasib

History Arabic *ilm al-tarikh*. Includes compilations of hadith, biographical literature, annalistic chronicles, and digests. In modern usage, the term often refers to European styles of history writing.

Hittin, Battle of Battle in 1187 between the Muslim leader Salah al-Din (Saladin) and

Crusaders. The Christians were defeated, ending the Latin occupation of Jerusalem and bringing about an effective end to the Christian occupation of the Holy Land. Muslims recovered Jerusalem and other territories held by Christians. The loss of Jerusalem prompted the third Christian Crusade in 1189.

Hiyal *See* Hilah

Hizb Negative Quranic term meaning "faction," though used twice (5:56 and 58:22) with approbation. In modern usage, refers to political parties. The reluctance in Islamic countries to accept the notion of political parties is due to the inherent implications of divisiveness and competition rather than national unity. The term *jamiyyah* (organization, association) is typically preferred. *See also* Jamiyyah

Hizb al-Dawah al-Islamiyyah Also known as the Islamic Call Party. Formed 1958–59 in Iraq by Shii ulama to work for social justice and foundation of Islamic state. Most prominent Shii activist group by late 1970s. Inspired by Muhammad Baqir al-Sadr, who criticized both capitalism and Communism in favor of an Islamic alternative. Used tawhid as the basis for modern politics, economics, and philosophy. Made significant intellectual and conceptual contributions to the contemporary Islamic revival. Outlawed and repressed by Saddam Hussein in 1980 due to suspected Iranian influence and its opposition to the government; its members were deported, tortured, imprisoned, and/or executed. Al-Sadr was executed in 1980.

Hizb al-Istiqlal Leading Moroccan nationalist party, 1943–62. Founded in 1943 by Ahmad Balafrej; together with King Muhammad V, it played a major role in ending the French and Spanish protectorates in 1956. Now an opposition party in the Moroccan parliament.

Hizb al-Nahdah (Tunisia) Renaissance Party. One of the most active and largest of the Islamist movements in Tunisia. Founded by Rashid al-Ghannoushi, a Tunis university professor and lawyer, and Abd al-Fattah Muru in 1981 as the Islamic Tendency Movement (Mouvement de la Tendance Islamique, MTI); renamed in 1988 when the government forbade the word *Islam* in the names of political parties. Its platform called for reconstruction of economic life on a more equitable basis, an end to single-party politics, acceptance of political pluralism and democracy, and a return to Islamic moral and religious values. The Tunisian government refused to recognize the party, and by early 1993 it had diminished in popular power.

Hizb al-Tahrir al-Islami Islamic Liberation Party. Founded in Jerusalem in 1953 by Taqi al-Din al-Nabhani and former Muslim Brothers to revive the Islamic nation and purge it of vestiges of colonialism. Upholds the classical model of the caliphate and its accompanying traditional institutions as the only authentic form of Islamic government. Seeks implementation of traditional Islamic law. Enjoyed modest successes in Jordan and the West Bank until its suppression in 1957. Attempted coups d'etat in Amman (1968 and 1969), Baghdad (1972), Cairo (1974), and Damascus (1976). Focuses exclusively on political and intellectual spheres. Has no social, religious, or educational projects.

Hizb al-Wasat Egyptian political party founded in 1995 by moderate Islamists from the Muslim Brotherhood and other groups including moderate Christians. Advocates democratization of the political order and a joint role for Muslims and Christians in Egyptian society and Islamic civilization. Some founders and members were arrested, tried, and imprisoned for acting as the voice of the Muslim Brotherhood.

Hizb Allah (Iran) Loosely formed, unofficial militant Iranian Shii organization of Ayatollah Ruhollah Khomeini's supporters, active in the late 1970s and early 1980s. Organized demonstrations and strikes leading to the downfall of the shah, and helped to consolidate the new regime. The party's slogan was "Only one party, the Party of God; only one leader, Ruhollah." Members were generally the urban poor, bazaaris, and the working class. Sometimes used violence to achieve its goals. Played a major role in the downfall of President Abol-Hasan Bani Sadr in 1981 and in closing universities, enforcing veiling, and silencing the opposition and the press. Many members fought in the 1980–88 war against Iraq. The party sometimes served as a private militia to powerful clerics. Supported the development of Hizb Allah in Lebanon.

Hizb Allah (Lebanon) Political and social movement founded in the early 1980s seeking to transform Lebanon into an Islamic state. Main groups of supporters are the large Shii clans of the Bekaa Valley and Shii refugees forced by civil war into the slums of southern Beirut. Supporters strongly identify with the Palestinians and deeply resent Israel. Became the major political force in Lebanon in the 1980s. Shaykh Muhammad Husayn Fadlallah is recognized as its spiritual leader, although he holds no formal office. Hizb Allah declared a jihad against the Western and Israeli presence in Lebanon in 1985, seeking the termination of American and French influence in Lebanon, Israel's complete departure from Lebanese territory, the submission of Lebanese Phalangists, and the right of the people to choose their own system of government. Violent activities are carried out by its clandestine branch, Islamic Jihad. Is a major rival of AMAL for Shii support. Gained international notoriety for attacks against American, French, and Israeli forces deployed in Lebanon in the 1980s and for holding Western hostages. With Iranian assistance, has financed a wide range of social, economic, and media projects, including a television station. The party participated in parliamentary elections in 1992, sweeping the Shii vote in the Bekaa Valley and producing a credible showing in the south. Within the parliament, it has organized the opposition movement, denouncing government negotiations with Israel. Has been credited with the departure of Israel from Lebanese soil in 2000, ending a twenty-two-year Israeli occupation, and its members have been rendered national heroes.

Hizb-i Islami (Afghanistan) Afghan political movement created and led by Gulbuddin Hekmatyar and Maulavi Yunus Khales. Active in the Afghan war, 1978–92. Broken into factions. Ideology combines scriptural fundamentalism with revolutionary practice. Was supported financially, logistically, and militarily by Iran, Pakistan, and the United States until the collapse of the Soviet occupation of Afghanistan. Was excluded from the Islamically oriented coalition government that came to power in 1992.

Hizb-i Wahdat Afghani Shii Islamist political party created in 1990 by Shaykh Ali Mazari. Initially supported a radical and ideological position but shifted to a policy emphasizing ethnicity during the Afghan civil war. Represents the Shii Hazara ethnic group. Allied itself with Persian-speaking Sunnis following Ahmad Shah Masud. Desires the implementation of Islamic law but is opposed to the idea of an Islamic revolution. *See also* Afghanistan, Islam in; Shii Islam

Hizbollah *See* Hizb Allah (Iran); Hizb Allah (Lebanon)

Hizbul Mujahidin Leading Pakistan-based Kashmiri Muslim separatist group advocating freedom from Indian control of Kashmir. One of three main separatist groups; the other two are Lashkar-i Taiba and Harakat-ul-Mujahidin. Founded in 1990 by Ahsan (also called Abdul Majid) Dar and Mohammad Abdullah Bangroo as an alternative to the Jammu and Kashmir Liberation Front; was established with assistance from Pakistan's intelligence service and received major political, diplomatic, moral, and military support from successive Pakistani governments. Recruited its members from sectarian forces of Sipah Sahabah Pakistan and trained them in al-Qaeda camps in Afghanistan. Currently headed by Sayyid Salahuddin in Pakistan. Mostly composed of natives rather than foreign recruits.

Hizbul Muslimin Also called Parti Orang Muslimin Malaya. First Islamic party of Malaya. Formed on 17 March 1948 under the auspices of Majlis Agama Tertinggi Malaya (MATA, Malayan Supreme Religious Council). First president was Ustaz Abu Bakar al-Bakir. Party's objective was to win independence from British rule and to create an Islamic state. In June 1948 the British colonial authorities declared a national emergency, and the party's president and six of its leaders were arrested. As a result the party was effectively terminated.

Hizqil *See* Ezekiel

Hojatalislam Proof of Islam. Title given to middle-ranking scholars of the Shii clergy who achieve the rank of mujtahid and can express legal opinions. Until the nineteenth century the term was applied only to leading ulama, but it began to be used by all mujtahid when the title of ayatollah was invented before the Constitutional Revolution of 1905–11.

Hojatallah (1) The term is used in the Quran (6:149) in the form of "God's decisive proof" (al-hujjat al-baligha). It has been interpreted by the commentators as the most decisive and final proof against the claims of nonbelievers concerning God's revelation, referring both to certain parts and the whole of the Quran. The best-known book bearing the title *Hujjat Allah al-baligha* was written by Shah Wali Allah of Delhi (d. 1762), the famous Muslim scholar and philosopher of the Indian subcontinent. (2) Title for an authoritative interpreter of revelation among Twelver Shiis, Ismailis, and Sufi orders. Refers to the Prophet Muhammad and the Twelver imams, leading figures of the Ismaili religious hierarchy, and the heads of Sufi orders, respectively.

Hojatiyyah Conservative Shii religiopolitical school of thought. Founded in the 1950s by Shaykh Mahmud Halabi in Iran to eradicate the Bahai faith. After the Islamic revolution of 1979, adherents were accused by fundamentalist clerics of opposition to vilayat-i faqih (rule of the jurist) and of not actively promoting the necessary conditions for the return of the Hidden Imam. The name has become a negative term applied to those who generally support less involvement of the clergy in government and less government taxation of business. In 1983 the Islamic regime mounted a public campaign against the movement's sympathizers. The society was suspended by the government, and the regime has practically ignored its existence since 1983. The whereabouts of Halabi and the extent of support for the movement today are unknown.

Holy Cities *See* Haramayn

Holy War *See* Jihad

Homosexuality Islamic law recognizes the sexual nature of believers, noting that sexuality provides a balance to the spiritual, material, and intellectual spheres of life. Sexual fulfillment is to be found within marriage for both partners in the ideal state of affairs. Because homosexual activity occurs outside of marriage and between members of the same sex, it cannot occur in a legal manner. Homosexuality exists in practice in the Muslim world but is considered unlawful, abnormal, and even punishable under Islamic law.

Honor Arabic *sharaf, ird, ihtiram, izzah,* or *namus.* Culturally understood as a sign of God's pleasure and part of one's Muslim identity. May be displayed through ownership of land and resources, family solidarity, the chastity of women, and the personal characteristics of courage, generosity, hospitality, independence, wisdom, honesty, self-control, actions guided by reason, disinclination to conflict, avoidance of degradation of others, mastery of culture, and verbal skill, particularly in poetry recitation.

Hostages Those seized, detained, or threatened with injury for political considerations. Most Muslim states have ratified the Geneva Conventions and observe the prohibition against hostage taking. It has continued to be an issue in the Islamic world because guerrilla groups or national liberation movements have used hostages as a means to secure compliance with their political demands. Islamic jurisprudence holds that captives may not be used to make demands on a third party. As throughout the world, hostage taking in the Islamic world is motivated by political considerations and has little to do with religious or legal injunctions.

Houris Beautiful dark-eyed companions who inhabit paradise. While the Quran makes no reference to a sexual role, a popular belief that they are virgins offered as rewards to martyrs has been used to motivate suicide bombers. Modern commentators tend to interpret the houris as virgins only in the sense of being pure or purified souls. *See also* Heaven

House of Wisdom *See* Bayt al-Hikmah

Hubal A pre-Islamic deity represented by an idol in Kaaba that was destroyed by Muhammad when he conquered Mecca in 630. Patron of the Quraysh, leading tribe of Mecca.

Hudud *See* Hadd

Hujatalislam *See* Hojatalislam

Hujatollah *See* Hojatallah

Hujjah Proof, incontestable evidence. In theology, the term is applied to a conclusive argument distinguishing truth from falsehood. In Shiism, the imam is the hujjah through whom God's presence becomes established for a believer. In Ismaili Shiism, it refers to a high-ranking representative of the imam, responsible for teaching and preaching the faith.

Hujjar Agricultural settlements established by Abd al-Aziz ibn Saud from 1911–12 through the 1920s in central Arabia to settle the Bedouin, provide them with religious and military training, and consolidate Saudi control over them. The move from nomadic life to settled life in a community founded on Islamic principles symbolized the migration (hijrah) from a land of unbelief (dar al-harb) to a land of belief (dar al-Islam). *See also* Ikhwan; Saud, Abd al-Aziz ibn Abd al-Rahman al-

Hujjat al-Islam *See* Hojatalislam

Hujjat Allah *See* Hojatallah

Hujjatiyyah *See* Hojatiyyah

Hujjatollah *See* Hojatallah

Hujwiri, Sayyid Ali al- (d. 1072) Medieval Sufi intellectual and theoretician. Wrote a major theoretical work entitled *Kashf al-mahjub* (Revealing the hidden), which enumerated twelve theoretical schools of Sufism, ten of which were approved and two of which were condemned. Outlined the doctrines of each sect. Declared that the ten approved sects asserted truth and belonged to the mass of orthodox Muslims. Condemned the Hululi sect for the adoption of beliefs about incarnation, incorporation, and anthropomorphism and the Hallaji sect for the abandonment of sacred law. Like al-Ghazali and Ibn al-Arabi, Hujwiri sought to establish balance among all dimensions of Islamic thought and practice, with Sufism as the animating spirit of the whole. He idealized celibacy and declared that women cause all evil in the world.

Hukm In the Quran hukm denotes arbitration, judgment, authority, God's will. With no central legal power in the post-Medina Muslim society, the noun acquired new meanings over time, with hukm coming to refer to temporal executive rule/power or to a court decision and the plural, *akham*, referring to specific Quranic rules, positive fiqh laws derived from Islamic legal methodology, and rules or edicts. Early in Muslim history, the Kharijis' declaration to accept only hukm of God gave the word a political connotation.

Hukumah Government, commonly distinguished from *dawlah* (state). Understood as the group of individuals who exercise the authority of the state; the term was adopted as Muslims became increasingly interested in European forms of government. Classically, hukumah referred to the dispensation of justice. Government itself was narrowly referred to as *wilayah*, *sultan*, or *imarah*. The state did not exist as an institution with legal identity; government was legitimate because God and divine law authorized it. In the modern period, the word connotes administration, political authority, and rule. Ali Abd al-Raziq (d. 1966) argued that Islam mandates no particular form of government. Muhammad Rashid Rida (d. 1935) stated that the caliphate was a spiritual institution, not a legal one. Abu al-Ala Mawdudi (d. 1979) held there is no essential difference between state, society, and government: all are part of the larger Islamic order anchored in shariah. Ayatollah Ruhollah Khomeini (d. 1989) argued for the establishment of political institutions underpinned by Islamic law and run by legal scholars.

Human Rights The Islamic legal tradition distinguishes between huquq Allah (the rights of God) and huquq al-insan (the rights of people). Some Muslim scholars have argued that huquq al-insan are akin to human rights or serve as the basis for developing a human rights discourse. In many Muslim countries, the independence struggle against European colonizers accentuated the importance of rights and democratic freedoms. After World War II, modern international formulations of human rights were produced, setting standards that became incorporated in public international law. The UN Universal Declaration of Human Rights (1948) provoked criticism from some Muslim countries, although only Saudi Arabia failed to support its passage. Muslims sometimes charged that international human rights had a Western bias that precluded their acceptance in Muslim milieus. Some Muslim countries argued that the West focused on civil and political rights and ignored economic, cultural, and social rights. Principles of the freedom of religion—notably the right to convert from Islam to another faith—and the full equality of persons regardless of sex or religion seemed to pose particular problems. The Organization of the Islamic Conference's charter affirmed its commitment to the UN Charter and to fundamental human rights. In 1990, however, it issued the Cairo Declaration on Human Rights in Islam, which diverged significantly from international human rights standards: absent were guarantees of freedom of religion, association, or the press, and assurances of equality and equal protection under the law. Muslim opinion remains divided on the relationship between international human rights principles and the Islamic legal heritage, and on the compatibility between the two. *See also* Cairo Declaration on Human Rights in Islam

Humanism and Islam Muslim scholars reject the basic philosophical premise that humans—rather than God—are the measure of all things and that all intrinsic moral values are derived from human desires and needs. Islam, like other Semitic religions, teaches that God is the ultimate source of all moral values. Some modern Muslim scholars argue that the core values emphasized by humanism, such as the dignity of each human being, individual liberty, freedom of choice consistent with the collective good, participatory democracy, human rights, social justice, and rational inquiry, are all compatible with the Islamic worldview. These scholars reject secular humanism's philosophical foundations but share humanism's quest for a more humane, just, and compassionate society.

Hunayn ibn Ishaq (d. 877) Nestorian Christian who headed the center for translation of Greek texts into Arabic, Bayt al-Hikmah, in Baghdad. Responsible for the creation of a body of work that fostered the spirit of critical inquiry and led to a rigorous approach to philosophy. The translated works were commented on by both Christian and Muslim scholars and disseminated both information and ideas.

Huquq al-Insan *See* Human Rights

Hurr Free. Also *hurriyyah*, freedom. Hurr and hurriyyah became important metaphysical concepts in Sufism, connoting freedom from everything other than God and devotion to Him. Since humans are the slaves of God, freedom, as Ibn al-Arabi put it, is the perfect form of slavery.

Hurra, Aishah al- *See* Women and Islam

Hurra, Sayyida al- *See* Women and Islam

Hurriyyah *See* Hurr

Hurufis Populist Sufi order founded by Fadlallah Astarabadi in fourteenth-century Iran. Astarabadi claimed direct revelation from God and Hidden Imam status. The order preached that only manual work could produce legitimate income and claimed that salvation was attainable through secret knowledge of the numerical values of the alphabet. It spread into Anatolia and Bulgaria among Muslims and Christians. Some of its ideas were perpetuated by the Bektashi order.

Husain, Zakir (d. 1969) Indian educator, founder of Jamia Milliya Islamiyyah in Delhi, and third president of India, 1967–69. Loyal Muslim ally of the Indian National Congress during the struggle for independence. Associate of Mahatma Gandhi and an active participant in the development of national education.

Husayn, Taha (d. 1971) Egyptian novelist, critic, and modernist reformer. One of the towering figures of twentieth-century Arabic literature. Became blind at a young age but rose to a position of leadership in Egyptian society and letters. Educated in Egypt and France. Served as adviser to Egyptian Ministry of Education and as minister of education 1950–52. Known for novels, short stories, historical and critical studies, and political articles. Claimed that pre-Islamic odes were inauthentic. Favored secularism over traditionalism and promoted intimate connections between Egypt and the West.

Best known for his autobiography, *Al-ayyam* (Days), which exposed weaknesses in traditional education, and *The Future of Culture in Egypt*.

Husayn ibn Ali (d. 680) Third Shii imam, son of Ali ibn Abi Talib and Fatimah, and grandson of the Prophet Muhammad. After the assassination of his father and the abdication of his older brother, Hasan, Husayn recognized Muawiyah as caliph, although he refused to pledge allegiance to him. Muawiyah's appointment of his own son, Yazid, as successor led the Shiis of Kufa, Iraq, to invite Husayn to claim his rightful position as caliph and lead an insurrection against Yazid. Husayn accepted the invitation and set out for Kufa with his family and a small group of followers. Intercepted by Yazid's troops in Karbala, Husayn and his followers were killed or taken prisoner on 10 Muharram 680 C.E. (the event is commemorated by the Shii mourning observance of Ashura). The martyrdom of Husayn gave Shiis the ethos of suffering and martyrdom. In the twentieth century, Husayn has become a symbol of political resistance, revolution, and eschatological hope, since the expected Mahdi (messiah) is supposed to avenge his blood and vindicate him and all others who have suffered at the hands of tyrannical rulers. Shiis consider pilgrimage to his tomb in Karbala second in importance only to the hajj. The interpretation of Husayn as a revolutionary fighting for social justice has inspired Shii resistance movements in Lebanon and Iran. *See also* Shii Islam

Husayni, Hajj Amin (d. 1974) Mufti of Jerusalem, president of the Supreme Muslim Council of Palestine, and Arab nationalist leader during British rule in Palestine (1917–48). Participated in violent anti-Zionist protests in Jerusalem in 1920. Sought British and Muslim support for a national government in Palestine with an Arab majority. Supported violent Palestinian revolt against the British (1936–39) after the proposed partition of Palestine between Arabs and Jews. Sought Hitler's support for Arab independence. Exiled after World War II.

Husaynid Dynasty (r. 1705–1957) Founded by Husayn ibn Ali, this dynasty ruled Tunisia during an era of increasing external pressures. The Bardo Treaty, signed after France invaded Tunisia (1881), left Muhammad al-Sadiq on the throne but without any real authority. This long period of political impotence, lack of interest in or sympathy for the nationalist movements, and enormous popularity for the nationalist leader Habib Bourguiba all contributed to the ease with which al-Amin Bey (r. 1943–57) was deposed and the monarchy abolished.

Husayniyyah Also known as *imambarah*, *ashurkhanah*, and *azakhanah*. Temporary or permanent site where ritual ceremonies commemorating the life and martyrdom of the Shii imam Husayn are held. Sustained by annual revenue or income from waqf. Typically decorated with black drapery and flags, which are often embroidered with the name of the organization sponsoring the festivities and words of lamentation for Husayn. Women prepare and distribute food to attendees and the poor. The central event is connected with Muharram recitations, along with the reading and chanting of poetry. In some places the courtyard of husayniyyah is used for the performance of taziyah and as the starting and ending point for mourning procession.

Husayniyyah-yi Irshad Shii institution founded in Tehran, Iran, in 1965 for private religious studies and education. Ali Shariati lectured there in the late 1960s and early 1970s, setting the stage for the later Iranian revolution. Closed by the shah in 1972 due to its opposition to his regime. Reopened in 1979 after the Islamic revolution with a more conservative and compliant tone. *See also* Shariati, Ali

Husri, Abu Khaldun Sati al- (d. 1968) Ottoman ideologist, educational reformer, secular Arab nationalist, and pan-Arabist. Saw secular educational reform as a means of instilling patriotism in youth. Developed a theory of Arab nationalism based on common language and history, rather than race, religion, will, economic circumstances, or geography. His works on education and nationalism are popular with Baathists and Nasserists.

Huwiyyah He-ness or it-ness; means "identity" in modern Arabic. In classical Islamic philosophy it functioned as a technical term designating a thing's ability to subsist on its own or to take on existence. It also signaled something's essential identity as opposed to its quiddity (mahiyyah). In mystical thought the term differentiated the identity of the divine being from the "I-ness" (aniyyah) of the mystic's ego.

Hypocrite Arabic *munafiq*. A polemical term applied to Muslims who possess weak faith or who profess Islam while secretly working against it. In the Quran, the term applies to a specific group of people headed by Abd Allah ibn Ubaiy, whose lukewarm support of Muhammad at critical moments, such as at the Battle of Uhud and the Battle of the Trench, caused great strain for the early Muslim community. The Quran equates hypocrisy with unbelief (kufr) and condemns hypocrites to hellfire for their failure to fully support the Muslim cause financially, bodily, and morally.

Ibadah Worship; acts of devotion; service; pl. *ibadat*. The religious duties of worship incumbent on all Muslims when they come of age and are of sound body and mind. They include the pillars of Islam—profession of faith (shahadah), canonical prayer (salat), charity (zakah), fasting (sawm), and pilgrimage to Mecca (hajj)—as well as striving to live in the path of God and the condition of purity (taharah) required for worship and Quran recitation. Because they are of central importance to the Muslim community, the ibadat form the first subject matter of Islamic jurisprudence and most collections of prophetic traditions (hadith).

Ibadi Dynasty Omani dynasty. Over the past twelve centuries, the Ibadi community of Oman has elected sixty-one imams of different dynasties. Ibadi political power in Oman began with the seizure of power by the first publicly elected imam, al-Julanda ibn Masud (r. 749–741), who was slain in battle by the Abbasids. The imamate was revived in 793 under Muhammad ibn Affan. The Ibadis continued to elect imams under Abbasid rule after 893 and exercise considerable authority. Imam Nasir ibn Murshid al-Yarubi (r. ca. 1624–49) established the Ibadi dynasty during the struggle against Portuguese colonial dominance. This dynasty was replaced by the present ruling family in 1959, currently headed by Sultan Qabus.

Ibadis Moderate subsect of Khariji Islam founded in the eighth century. Has its strongest presence in Oman, but is also found in North Africa and Zanzibar. Headed by an elected imam who holds absolute ruling authority over the community as long as he abides by Ibadi principles and law. The imam can be deposed if he has disobeyed and not repented. Ulama are held in high esteem and guide the process of electing the new imam. The imam is expected to obey them and abide by their rulings. Ibadis accept coexistence with other Islamic sects. When suppressed by enemies, the community exists in a state of secrecy in which there may be no imam.

Iblis *See* Satan

Ibn Son. Also written as *bin*. Often used as the first part of the patronymic for males, followed by the name of the father, in which case the term means "son of."

Ibn Abd al-Wahhab, Muhammad (d. 1791) Saudi Arabian conservative theologian, Hanbali jurist, reformer, and ideologue of the Wahhabi movement. Proclaimed the necessity of returning directly to the Quran and hadith, rather than relying on medieval interpretations. Denounced as heretical innovations the practices of shrine cults, saint worship, requests for intercession from anyone other than God, and assigning authority to anyone other than God. Promoted strict adherence to traditional Islamic law. Opposed taqlid (adherence to tradition). Called for the use of ijtihad (independent reasoning through individual study of scripture). Plans for socioreligious reform in society were based on the key doctrine of tawhid (oneness of God). Formed an alliance with ibn al-Saud in 1744 that allowed Ibn al-Saud control over military, political, and economic matters and Ibn Abd al-Wahhab responsibility for religious concerns. The alliance resulted in foundation of the first Saudi dynasty and state and remains the basis for Saudi rule today. Many conservatives claim inspiration from the movement he founded. *See also* Saud, Muhammad ibn al-

Ibn Abd Allah, Muhammad Ahmad (d. 1885) Sudanese militant revivalist and reformer. Proclaimed himself Mahdi (divinely appointed guide) in 1881. Led a jihad against the Egyptians and their European allies in the 1880s. Preached against corruption of Islam in Sudan and adoption of foreign (Turko-Egyptian, European, and local non-Islamic) practices. Established an Islamic state over most of Sudan patterned on the original seventh-century political entity founded by Muhammad. Interpreted his victories as a sign of God's favor. Declared shariah the only valid law. After his death, the state he created lasted until Sudan was conquered by Anglo-Egyptian forces in 1898–99.

Ibn Abdin, Muhammad Amin ibn Umar (d. 1836) Syrian scholar. Trained in Shafii jurisprudence but eventually became known as a scholar of Hanafi jurisprudence. Worked outside the official Ottoman religio-legal bureaucracy. His fatwas dealt with issues represented by his nineteenth-century context and exhibited the workings of the process of rulemaking; he disagreed with some key positions of his own school, arguing that rules continuously evolved, leading to differences even from those of Abu Hanifah, the eponymous founder of the school.

Ibn al-Arabi, Muhyi al-Din (d. 1240) Among the most influential and controversial Sufi thinkers, also known as al-Shaykh al-Akbar, "the greatest shaykh." Born and lived in Spain for thirty years before traveling east, where he wrote most of his major works. Best known for views on the unity of being (wahdat al-wujud) and knowledge, emanationist metaphysics, the theory of microcosmic return through mystical love, and the notion of the perfect person (al-insan al-kamil). His philosophy has been criticized as pantheistic, deifying Muhammad, making all religions equal, idolizing women, and interpreting the Quran in an unconventional and dangerous manner. He was accused of heresy during his lifetime and after; some of his works are still banned in Egypt. Major works include Futuhat makkiyah (Meccan revelations) and Fusus al-hikam (Bezels of wisdom), a commentary on prophets mentioned in the Quran.

Ibn al-Ashath, Abd al-Rahman (d. 704) Leader of a revolt against the governor of Iraq and Persia, al-Hajjaj ibn Yusuf, in 700–03. Discontented troops mutinied at the prospect of a distant campaign and, gathering various supporters, revolted in 700–3. Prominent sentiments of the rebellion were the discontent of Kufan notables with the new social order and religious complaints of the Quran reciters.

Ibn al-Athir, Abu al-Hasan Ali Izz al-Din (d. 1234) Historian who recorded history as a sequence of military engagements, such as the Mongol invasion of the Islamic Empire. Believed history had both religious and mundane value and that moral lessons could be drawn from it to reform kingdoms. Abridged al-Tabari's history and continued it through 1231, including the Crusades, in Al-Kamil fil-Tarikkh (Complete history).

Ibn al-Farid, Umar (d. 1235) Celebrated Arab poet, mystic, and saint. Composed quatrains, love poems (ghazals), and odes (qasidas) expressing a mystical view of life in which all of existence reveals the beauty and love of God. Most famous are his Al-khamriyyah (Wine ode), praising love and the beloved, and the Nazm al-suluk (Poem of the Sufi way), an ode of 760 verses detailing the mystic's ascent to enlightenment. Today remains venerated as a saint in Cairo, and his influence is heard in the songs of popular religious singers and the writings of Naguib Mahfouz.

Ibn al-Hajjaj See Muslim (Ibn al-Hajjaj)

Ibn al-Haytham, Abu Ali al-Hasan (d. 1039) Also known as Alhazen. Wrote seven books on optics that were translated into Latin and Italian and were among the first scientific books to be printed. Strongly influenced medieval Latin, Renaissance, and seventeenth-century thinkers. Attacked Ptolemy's planetary theory as a violation of the classical principle of uniform velocity for all celestial bodies.

Ibn al-Humam (d. 1457) Egyptian Hanafi jurist and theologian. Born in Alexandria, educated in Cairo, lived for some time in Aleppo. Appointed head shaykh of the Khanaqah Shaykhuniyyah in Cairo in 1443. Highly regarded in all fields of knowledge, including Sufism.

Ibn al-Jawzi, Abd al-Rahman ibn Ali ibn Muhammad Abu al-Farash (d. 1200) Scholar of Hanbali jurisprudence in Baghdad. Held several influential teaching posts and had generally good relations with the caliphate. Wrote numerous works in all Islamic sciences. Condemned all deviations from orthodoxy, especially Shii and Sufi practices. Important figure in the rise of Sunni Islam.

Ibn al-Muqaffa, Abd Allah (d. 756) Member of kuttab (secretarial) class, responsible for translation of historical works from Persian into Arabic under Abbasid dynasty. Wrote a series of essays and epistles and translated animal fables (kalila wa dimna) that characterize the style and spirit of adab literature. Argued that religious matters are so important that the state must hold control over religious scholars and judges. Supported the caliph as a promulgator of doctrine and appointer of judges. Open to foreign ideas and achievements, reflecting the expansion of the Islamic empire into non-Arab territories. Believed that ancient civilizations were superior to modern ones. Promoted reason over emotion. Executed by political opponents.

Ibn al-Nadim, Muhammad ibn Abi Yaqub (d. 995) Famous bookseller who produced a landmark bibliography entitled Al-fihrist, containing a description of every book he had seen, learned of, or handled. This work, produced in 987, is an important resource for the history of the literary culture of the classical era and includes citations for works by early scholars that have since been lost.

Ibn al-Zubayr, Urwah (d. ca. 712) Leading member of the Quraysh tribe in Medina. Major authority on hadith and jurispru-

dence. Counted among the founders of Islamic historical study, particularly the historical school of Medina.

Ibn Aqil, Abu al-Wafa Ali ibn Aqil ibn Muhammad ibn Aqil ibn Ahmad al-Baghdadi (d. 1119) Hanbali jurist with rationalist leanings. In traditionalist eleventh-century Baghdad, his admiration for the mystic al-Hallaj (d. 922) led to his persecution and forced him to recant. Among his works of jurisprudence that have survived are Wadih fi usul al-fiqh and (in part) Kitab al-funun.

Ibn Ata Allah, Ahmad ibn Muhammad (d. 1309) Third shaykh of Shadhili Sufi order. Responsible for systematizing the order's doctrines and recording the biographies of its founder, Sidi Abu al-Hasan, and his successor, Sidi Abu al-Abbas al-Mursi. Author of the first systematic treatise on dhikr. His compilation of aphorisms (hikam; sing. hikmah) made the order very popular, and his work has been referred to as the last Sufi miracle performed on the banks of the Nile. Circulation of his written works led to spread of the Shadhili order in North Africa, where its founder had been rejected. The Wafai Sufi order was derived from his works. See also Hikmah

Ibn Babawayh Muhammad (d. 991) Also known as al-Qummi and al-Saduq. Twelver Shii scholar and the leader of the traditionists in Qom, Iran. Recorded and preserved traditions transmitted from Muhammad and the imams in the cities of Qom, Rayy, Mashhad, Nishapur, Baghdad, Kufa, Mecca, Hamdan, Balkh, and Samarqand. Made a thorough scrutiny of hadith transmitters and integrated the principles of Islamic law exclusively contained in Imami hadith. Disapproved of the rationalist appraisal of religious questions, even in defense of Shii doctrine. His approach was denounced by his student al-Shaykh al-Mufid (d. 1022), a rationalist theologian. Composed more than two hundred works.

Ibn Badis, Abd al-Hamid (d. 1940) Islamic reformer, national leader, and head of the

Association of Algerian Ulama (AAU). Received a traditional education in Tunis and returned to Algeria to teach. Founded a weekly paper, The Critic, that disseminated Salafi ideas and attacked the "un-Islamic" practices of Sufi orders. In 1931 Ibn Badis and other religious scholars formed the AAU, which promoted the Arab and Islamic roots of the Algerian nation, reform and revival of Islam, and criticism of the Sufi orders and assimilationists. He blamed the decline of Muslims on internal weakness, disunity, despotism, and the adoption of non-Islamic practices, and stressed education to purify Islam from popular accretions and improve the condition of the individual as a step toward reviving the entire society. Offering a modernist interpretation of the Quran, Ibn Badis' major contribution lies in linking reform and education with the promotion of an Algerian nationalism.

Ibn Bajjah (d. 1138) Full name Abu Bakr Muhammad ibn Yahia ibn al-Sayigh (Latin name Avempace). Born in Saragossa, Spain, and died in Fez, Morocco. First notable philosopher and physician of Muslim Spain. Wrote paraphrases of Aristotle's Physics, Meteorology, parts of On Generation and Corruption, and the spurious De Plantis, as well as extensive glosses on the logic of al-Farabi. His original works include Conduct of the Solitary, a political treatise that deals with the plight of the philosopher and his thwarted aspirations in an imperfect state, and a short treatise titled Conjunction with the Active Intellect, which dealt with a favorite theme of Muslim Neoplatonists.

Ibn Battutah, Abu Abd Allah al-Lawati al-Tanji (d. ca. 1368) North African traveler who made a tour of Muslim communities from 1325 to 1354, covering West Africa through Southeast Asia. His Rihlah, a written record of his observations, is an important primary source of historical, social, cultural, and religious information for that time period, as well as for oral accounts of earlier periods. He recorded particularly detailed descriptions of Sufi orders and organizations, noting their important role in spreading Is-

lam and Muslim commerce, the spread of Islam, and the accommodation of Islam to the Hindu environment in India. Described the entire Islamic world as conscious of Islamic unity, despite varying emphases on different schools of law.

Ibn Baz, Abd al-Aziz ibn Abdullah See Ibn Baz, Shaykh Abd al-Aziz

Ibn Baz, Shaykh Abd al-Aziz (d. 1999) Head of Supreme Religious Council and notable religious scholar in Saudi Arabia. Demanded political and economic reforms to institutionalize Islam throughout government and society. Issued a fatwa declaring support for reconciliation with Israel for the sake of Palestinian security.

Ibn Gabirol, Solomon ben Judah (d. ca. 1070) Leading figure in Hebrew poetry and philosophy in Muslim Spain. Wrote poetry in Hebrew, and wrote on ethics and metaphysics in Arabic while adapting the genre for Jewish readers. Most of his Arabic works are no longer extant. He was known via Latin translation to Albert the Great and Thomas Aquinas.

Ibn Hanbal, Ahmad (d. 855) Eponym of Hanbali school of Islamic law. Native of Baghdad. Known for literal and legalistic interpretation of the Quran and hadith. Reputed to be the greatest hadith scholar of his time. Introduced the principle of istislah (the best solution in the public interest) as the purpose of legal rulings not clearly specified by the Quran and hadith. Taught that the written word of the Quran is authoritative over human interpretation, leading to a dispute with Caliph al-Mamun over the caliph's authority to interpret religious texts. Argued that Islamic religious obligations were derived from fundamental texts as interpreted by recognized leading scholars, not by caliphal decree. Believed the caliph's role was to serve as executor of the Islamic community, not as the source of its beliefs. Islamic scholars were to serve as advisers and admonishers to ruling elites to induce them to observe and implement Islamic law. This politico-religious alliance is the basis for the modern Islamic state of Saudi Arabia. His collection of the traditions is the Musnad.

Ibn Hayyad, Jabir *See* Alchemy

Ibn Hazm, Abu Muhammad Ali ibn Ahmad ibn Said (d. 1064) Andalusian jurist, theologian, philosopher, and author of one of the first Muslim works on comparative religion. Popularized the Zahiri literalist school of theology. Opposed the allegorical interpretation of texts, preferring instead a grammatical and syntactical interpretation of the Quran. Granted cognitive legitimacy only to revelation and sensation. Considered deductive reasoning insufficient in legal and religious matters. Held that the legal principle of consensus (ijma) was limited to the community of Muhammad's Companions. Advocated a return to reliance on tradition (hadith) and opposed the principles of imitation (taqlid), analogy (qiyas), judgment in the public interest (istihsan), and giving reason (taaqqul). Influenced future theologians as well as mystics such as Ibn al-Arabi.

Ibn Hisham, Abu Muhammad Abd al-Malik (d. 827) Editor of a shorter, annotated version of the biography of Muhammad by Ibn Ishaq, which became the standard biography in the Islamic world and the basis for most subsequent works. His work is the main source of knowledge of the original work by Ibn Ishaq. He made critical observations about the authenticity of the poetry contained in the work.

Ibn Idris, Ahmad (d. 1837) Moroccan Sufi teacher and founder of the Idrisi tradition. Opposed the schools of Islamic jurisprudence and all forms of philosophy; believed that God alone grants an individual Muslim understanding of the Quran and Sunnah. Teachings were antiauthoritarian, emphasizing the individual's duty to seek God; the object of the mystical path was union with God. Prayers and teachings show considerable traces of the influence of Ibn al-Arabi (d. 1240). His Idrisi Sufi tradition spread to the Balkans and Istanbul, Syria, Cyrenaica,

the central Sahara, Sudan, Somalia, Indonesia, and Malaysia. Principal students included Muhammad ibn Ali al-Sanusi, founder of the Sanusi order; Muhammad Uthman al-Mirghani, founder of the Khatmi order; and Ibrahim al-Rashid, from whom stemmed the Rashidi, Salihi, and Dandarawi orders. Forty years after his death, his son established the Ahmadi Idrisi order, which has remained a local order in Egypt and Sudan. *See also* Idrisi Tariqah

Ibn Ishaq, Muhammad ibn Ishaq ibn Yasar ibn Khiyar (d. 767) Author of a major biography of Muhammad that was later condensed by Ibn Hisham. The biography was an apology for the Abbasid revolution and a model for subsequent universal histories, most notably that of al-Tabari. His narrative began with creation and chronicled the history of the world up until the time of Muhammad, presenting Muhammad's life as the fulfillment of a divine mission.

Ibn Jamaah, Badr al-Din Abu Abd Allah Muhammad (d. 1333) A distinguished Shafii jurist of Mamluk Egypt and member of the prominent Banu Jamaah clan. Served as chief justice under the Mamluks of Cairo and twice in Damascus, during a period when Shafii jurisprudence was favored by the state. Of his many works, the best-known is *Expounding the Rules Governing the (Political) Organization of the Muslim People*. His work is an important specimen of the highly developed genre of writings by premodern Muslim jurists who combined the fields of law and political theory.

Ibn Jubayr, Muhammad ibn Ahmad (d. 1217) Spanish Muslim traveler best known for his work *Rihlat Ibn Jubayr* (The travels of Ibn Jubayr), among the earliest of medieval travelogues, which remains an important source of information about medieval society in the Mediterranean littoral and the Arabian peninsula.

Ibn Kathir, Imad al-Din Ismail ibn Umar (d. 1373) Syrian historian, traditionist, and Quran exegete under the Bahri Mamluks.

Influenced by Ibn Taymiyyah (d. 1328), his approach was conservative and strongly dependent on past authorities. His history, *Al-Bidaya wa-l-Nihaya*, begins with the Prophet's life and ends in a chronicle of Damascus. His *Al-Jami* compiles the Prophet's traditions from earlier works and arranges them alphabetically according to the names of those transmitting them. His *Tafsir al-Quran al-Adhzim* accepts the principle that the Quran is best interpreted by itself and next by the Prophet as reported by his Companions and their followers.

Ibn Khaldun, Abd al-Rahman ibn Muhammad (d. 1406) Influential Arab historian, historiographer, and social philosopher. Held numerous public positions in Tunis; moved to Cairo in 1392, where he taught and served as a judge until his death. His major works are his autobiography (*Al-tarif b'Ibn Khaldun*), a candid evaluation of his career, and the *Muqaddimah* (Introduction to history), which traces his thoughts on sednetary and desert populations, dynasties, and the caliphate. In the *Muqaddimah*, Ibn Khaldun stated that he had established a new science, ilm al-umran (science of social organization); he is accordingly regarded as the father of sociology. Asabiyyah (social solidarity) is the core of his thought on nomadism, urbanism, and the rise and decline of the state. Stressed the interdependence of the religious, political, economic, military, and cultural spheres of life and therefore the need for effective social control of human activity. His ideas later echoed in those of Machiavelli, Vico, Comte, Durkheim, Spengler, and Wirth.

Ibn Majah (d. 886) Sunni traditionist. Native of Qazvin, Iran. Author of *Kitab al-sunan*, which contains approximately four thousand traditions and is one of the six canonical collections of Sunni hadith. Though highly praised by some, his work is criticized as containing many questionable ("weak") traditions. The work was first given canonical status in the early twelfth century but was not widely recognized until a century

later. Some scholars, such as al-Nawwawi (d. 1277) and Ibn Khaldun (d. 1405), did not consider his collection of hadiths reliable enough to be authoritative.

Ibn Masud, Abdallah (d. ca. 652) Companion of Muhammad. Among the first converts to Islam. Held administrative and diplomatic duties under the caliphs Umar and Uthman, but eventually broke with the latter. One of the most prolific transmitters of hadith, especially via the transmitters of Kufa, where he settled. He is especially important for traditions on the interpretation of the Quran, having been present for many revelations. The Quranic reading differing from the official Uthmanic text, notably in omitting verses 1:113–14, is attributed to him. His career and reputation were marked by his humble Bedouin origins, personal loyalty to the Prophet, and subsequent conflict with the Meccan aristocracy.

Ibn Miskawayh, Abu Ali Ahmad ibn Muhammad ibn Yaqub (d. 1030) Persian philosopher and historian, influenced by Aristotle. Author of the first major Islamic work on philosophical ethics, *Tahdhib al-akhlaq* (Ethical instruction), focusing on practical ethics, conduct, and refinement of character. Separated personal ethics from the public realm. Contrasted the liberating nature of reason with the deception and temptation of nature. Emphasized the human ability to control will and the necessity for society to perfect human virtue. Tied prosperity to justice and destruction to injustice. Paid specific attention to fiscal management. Member of the class of state secretaries and fiscal experts who counseled caliphs. Was an accomplished poet and scientist.

Ibn Qayyim al-Jawziyah, Shams al-Din Abu Bakr (d. 1350) Hanbali jurist from Baghdad. Disciple of Ibn Taymiyyah and compiler of his works. Critic of popular religion and the excesses of Sufism. Member of Qadiri Sufi order. Compiled a collection of hadith of Muhammad's medical practices. Outlined the five sources of law acceptable to Hanbalis: texts of the Quran and Sunnah; fatwas of the Companions of Muhammad when they are not contradicted by the Quran or Sunnah; sayings of individual Companions when they conform to the Quran and Sunnah; traditions with a weak chain of transmission or lacking the name of the transmitter in the chain; and, when absolutely necessary, reasoning by analogy.

Ibn Qudama, Muwaffaq al-Din (d. 1223) Hanbali theologian and jurist. Born near Jerusalem; educated in Quranic and hadith studies at the al-Salahi madrasa in Damascus. Continued his studies in Baghdad, becoming a student of the mystic Abd al-Qadir al-Jili. Left treatises in which he censures human judgment (ijtihad) and speculation in matters of faith, especially the Mutazili method of allegorical interpretation (tawil) of the Quran, which removed any human personification of Allah from it (tajsim). In strict Hanbali tradition, Ibn Qudama advocated the unconditional acceptance of scriptural depictions of the divine attributes.

Ibn Qutaybah, Abd Allah Abu Muhammad Abd Allah ibn Muslim al-Dinwari (d. 889) Major contributor to the development of Arabic literature (adab). As a judge, wrote Kitab tawil mushkil al-Quran (On the problem of Quranic interpretation), a study of problematic aspects of Quranic style, and Kitab adab al-katib (The correct behavior for bureaucrats), but best known for literary works such as Kitab uyun al-akhbar (Book of choice narratives), an anthology divided into ten topics (such as eloquence, friendship, war, and women), and Kitab al-shir wal-shuara (Book of poetry and poets), containing his theory of literary criticism. Also wrote a handbook of history, Kitab al-maarif (Book of knowledge).

Ibn Rushd, Abu-i-Walid Muhammad ibn Ahmad ibn Muhammad (d. 1198) Greatest Aristotelian philosopher of the Muslim world. Also known by his Latin name, Averroës, and as "The Commentator," since his commentaries on Aristotle were for many medieval Europeans their source of knowledge of Aristotle. Made important contributions in theology, medicine, and jurisprudence as well. Served as physician and chief religious judge of Córdoba. Set out to harmonize faith and reason, Aristotelian philosophy with the teachings of the Quran. His best-known philosophical work was Tahafut al-tahafut (The incoherence of the incoherence), a response to al-Ghazzali's attack on philosophy, Tahafut al-falasifah (The incoherence of the philosophers). His influence in the West was greater than in the Islamic world, where his work was condemned by orthodox religious scholars who rejected his views that religious law and philosophy have the same goal and that creation is an eternal process.

Ibn Saad, Muhammad (d. 844) Author of one of the earliest biographies of Muhammad and the compiler of the earliest known biographical dictionary, Kitab al-tabaqat al-kabir (The great book of generations). Systematized and organized the collection and presentation of biographical materials. His biography of Muhammad became an archetype in structure, content, and source materials for later literature addressing Muhammad's life, virtues, merits, and proofs of his prophethood.

Ibn Sina, Abu Ali Husayn ibn Abd Allah (d. 1037) Latin name Avicenna. With Ibn Rushd, best-known philosopher in the Muslim world. Born in Bukhara. Worked as a physician; wrote on logic, physics, psychology, metaphysics, and astronomy as well. Also wrote philosophico-mystical treatises and "visionary recitals." Most famous works are Al-qanun fi'l tibb (The canon on medicine), known in Europe from its partial translation into Latin in the twelfth century, and Kitab al-shifa (The book of health), which deals with logic, the natural sciences, and metaphysics. A Neoplatonist, Ibn Sina taught creation as a timeless process of divine emanation. Well known in Europe, where his mixture of Aristotelian and Platonic thought was criticized. Like Ibn Rushd, his rationalist religious thought was condemned by orthodoxy and included in al-Ghazzali's Tahafut *al-falasifah* (The incoherence of the philosophers). *See also* Hikmat al-Ishraq

Ibn Suleyman, Muhammad ibn Muhammad (d. 1683) Premodern polymath who represents the internationalization of Islamic scholarship and the epitome of scholarly erudition. Born in Tarudant in present-day Morocco, he received his initial education in the Maghreb and then traveled to the main centers of Islamic learning (such as Cairo, Jerusalem, Damascus, Mecca, Medina, and Istanbul) to study with the great scholars of his time. Died in Damascus. Due to his extensive writings in numerous disciplines, including rhetoric, mathematics, astronomy, Arabic grammar and syntax, fiqh, Sufism, and Quranic, hadith, and tafsir studies, he had a profound influence on subsequent scholars.

Ibn Taymiyyah, Taqi al-Din Ahmad (d. 1328) Prominent and controversial Syrian thinker, theologian, Hanbali jurist, and political figure. His intellectual activities, preaching, and politics resulted in persecution and imprisonment. Main doctrine was the supremacy and authoritativeness of the Quran and Sunnah of Muhammad and the early Muslim community. Encouraged a literal interpretation of scripture and condemned the popular practices of saint worship and pilgrimages to saints' tombs as worship of other than God. Rejected theology, philosophy, and metaphysical Sufism, although he encouraged pietistic Sufism. Opposed to blind obedience to tradition (taqlid), he favored ijtihad (independent reasoning). Tied Islam to politics and state formation and made a sharp distinction between Islam and non-Islam, noting the difference between a public proclamation of Islam and actions that are inconsistent with Islamic teachings and values. Issued fatwas against the Mongols as unbelievers at heart despite public claims to be Muslim. Influenced later thinkers such as Muhammad ibn Abd al-Wahhab, Hasan al-Banna, and Sayyid Qutb. His authority has been used by some

twentieth-century Islamist groups to declare jihad against ruling governments.

Ibn Tufayl, Abu Bakr Muhammad (d. 1185) Andalusian physician and philosopher best known for his philosophical novel *Hayy Ibn Yaqdhan* (The life of Ibn Yaqdhan), describing the intellectual development of a man living isolated on a desert island; the book is an attempt to demonstrate that awareness of God is possible without education.

Ibn Tulun, Ahmad (d. 884) Founder of the Tulinid dynasty in Egypt and the first Muslim ruler of Egypt to annex Syria. Introduced administrative and agrarian reforms, encouraged industries, and supported cultural activities. Founded a new capital, al-Qatai (870), and established splendid buildings, the most famous of which is his mosque, which still stands in Cairo.

Ibn Tumart, Abu Abd Allah Muhammad (d. 1130) Berber religious reformer and founder of the Muwahiddun or Almohad movement of North Africa. Summoned Muslims to close observance of religious obligations based on strict study of the Quran and tradition. Criticized the scholarly and ruling elite for their hostility toward theology and preoccupation with the branches rather than the roots of faith. Vehemently affirmed God's unity (tawhid) as a principle of faith, rejecting any anthropomorphism. Attracted many followers, who eventually declared him the infallible, awaited mahdi (guide). After his demise, they gradually gained rule of much of North Africa and south Andalusia.

Ibrahim *See* Abraham

Ibrahim, Anwar (b. 1947) Malaysian political and religious activist. Formed an alliance with Mahathir Mohamed in 1969, advocating Malay educational and economic rights. Established Malaysian Islamic Youth Movement (ABIM) in 1972, making him the most influential young leader of Malaysia. Calls for the Islamization of Malaysian life and excellence in education. Stresses social justice, including safeguards for the rights of the non-Muslim population. Detained 1974–76 following demonstrations against poverty in Baling. Served as leader of Malaysian Youth Council, representative of the World Assembly of Muslim Youth (WAMY) for Southeast Asia, cofounder of International Institute of Islamic Thought (IIIT) in Herndon, Virginia, and chancellor of International Islamic University at Kuala Lumpur between 1983 and 1988. Joined the ruling United Malays National Organization (UMNO) in 1983. Served as deputy party leader, acting prime minister, deputy prime minister, agricultural minister, education minister, minister of finance, and minister of youth, culture, and sports. In 1998 was removed from power and tried for sedition and corruption.

Ibrahimi Tariqah *See* Dasuqi Tariqah

ICMI Ikatan Cendekiawan Muslim Se-Indonesia or Association for Indonesian Muslim Intellectuals. Established in 1990 during President Suharto's rule as a forum for Muslim modernist intellectuals. Headed by Suharto's research and technology minister, B. J. Habibie. Claimed a membership of forty-two thousand during the mid-1990s, including university teachers, journalists, professionals, and high-ranking state officials. Critics maintained that ICMI was formed to counter the influence of more traditional Islamic groups opposed to President Suharto and to provide an intellectual basis for Islamic legitimacy of his regime. Its daily newspaper, *Republika*, became the most prominent Islamic publication in Indonesia during the 1990s.

Iconography Islamic forms of iconography include calligraphy, geometry, arabesques, domes, minarets, arches, and mihrabs. They serve as visual manifestations of the universal spirit of the Muslim community. Calligraphy originated with copying of the Quran and has become the highest art form in the Islamic world. Quranic verses, geometric patterns, and arabesques are typically used in decorative arts. *See also* Calligraphy and Epigraphy

Id Feast or festival. Refers to religious holidays, most typically Id al-Adha and Id al-Fitr, two canonical festivals of the Muslim calendar. Ids are typically characterized by special prayers and sermons, family gatherings, visits of extended family and friends, special charitable acts, and distribution of gifts and sweets.

Id al-Adha Feast of the Sacrifice. Also known as Greater Bayram. Celebrated at the end of the annual pilgrimage to Mecca, on the tenth day of Dhu al-Hijjah, the month of pilgrimage. Unblemished animals are sacrificed in commemoration of the ram substituted by God when Abraham was commanded to sacrifice his son, Ishmael, as a test of faith. Only a portion, usually one-third, of this animal's meat is to be consumed by the family offering the sacrifice. The rest is to be distributed to the poor. For those not on pilgrimage, the celebration includes visits to mosques and to the graves of relatives. It lasts for three days and includes the distribution of gifts and sweets as well as receiving and visiting extended family. *See also* Hajj

Id al-Fitr Feast of the Breaking of the Fast. Also known as Lesser Bayram. Celebrated at the end of Ramadan, the month of fasting. Begins upon sighting of the crescent moon and lasts for three days. In Muslim-majority areas, businesses are closed and invitations are extended to family, neighbors, and friends to join in the celebrations. Children receive gifts and sweets. Almsgiving is required prior to attending the morning feast prayer, in remembrance of the poor.

Iddah The waiting period a woman must observe after the death of her spouse or a divorce, during which she may not remarry, based on the Quran 2:228 and 2:238. The waiting period after a divorce is three months, and after the death of a spouse it is four months and ten days. Any pregnancy discovered during this period is assumed to be the responsibility of the former husband.

Ideology and Islam Most Muslims claim that "Islam is one" and offers a blueprint for all aspects of life. Islam increasingly occupies a special place in school curricula, and states seek to control what is said in mosques. Catechism-like pamphlets and essays, often in question-and-answer format and popular language, offer believers quick, encapsulated formulations of belief and practice. Religious activists encourage Muslims to be able to explain why they pray and fast. Such organization reflects a conscious systemization of doctrine and practice, so that masses, rather than specialists, are able to formulate and answer questions about faith. The result is empowerment of Muslims and the creation of new patterns of religious authority free from reliance on traditionally educated religious elites. The concern with ideology in Islam stems from the recognition that other ideologies have been applied in social and political contexts. Islamists charge that Islam should play a central role in the social and political arenas, noting that the Islamic ideology upheld in many countries is not a reflection of genuine Islam, but rather principles that secure the interests of the ruling class. The formal ideologies of reformists and Islamists in particular have offered interpretations of Islam that appeal primarily to modern, educated elites, so that urban values have been incorporated into formalized doctrine and practice.

Idris ibn Abdullah, Mulay *See* Idrisid Dynasty

Idrisi Tariqah Refers both to various Sufi brotherhoods and schools established by students of Ahmad ibn Idris (d. 1837) and to the order established by his descendants after his death. The prayers and litanies of Ibn Idris were spread throughout Egypt, the Balkans, Sudan, India, Southeast Asia, and the Ottoman Empire. Most prominent among his students were Muhammad ibn Ali al-Sanusi and Muhammad Uthman al-Mirghani, who respectively founded the

Sanusi and Khatmi orders, which played important political roles. *See also* Ahmad, Ibn Idris, Khatmi Tariqah, Sanusi Tariqah

Idrisid Dynasty Important early ruling family in North Africa. Its eighth-century founder, Mulay Idris ibn Abdullah, sought refuge in present-day Morocco after being forced into exile and persecuted for anti-Abbasid activities. He united the Berber tribes of the area by claiming descent from Muhammad, leading to the emergence of the first independent Islamic dynasty in Morocco. His son, Idris II, stressed the Islamic-Arab character of Morocco, organized the first central government, and undertook construction of the Qarawiyin and Andalus mosques and Qarawiyin University, making Fez an important religious and cultural center. The last head of the dynasty was killed in 985. Its legacy was a foundation for independent Moroccan monarchic rule.

Idtirar Term meaning compulsion or coercion by means of physical rather than moral power. A theological expression used in connection with human actions carried out under compulsion and those carried out of free choice (ikhtiyar). The majority of Sunnis accept that all human actions, whether acquired skills (such as writing) or involuntary motions (such as breathing), are ultimately created by God. *See also* Jabr

Ifrit Pl. *afarit*. Rebellious and wicked spirit, although some afarit are believed to be helpful. Mentioned in the Quran and hadith in the context of jinn, particularly rebellious ones. The term was popularized in folklore such as *Alf laylat wa'l-laylah* (The thousand and one nights). Afarit are male and female and may be believers or nonbelievers; they may marry humans but usually marry among themselves. If the term is used to refer to animals and humans, it connotes shrewdness, strength, and resourcefulness.

Ifta Act of issuing a fatwa (legal opinion) by an authoritative consultant in matters of law. Initially a private vocation, this came to be the role of the public office of mufti in the eleventh century. The Ottoman Empire integrated muftis into the bureaucratic system.

Iftar The breaking of the fast every evening after sunset during Ramadan. Also, the breaking of the fast of Ramadan on the first sighting of the new moon on the evening of Id al-Fitr. According to the example of the Prophet, the fast should be broken by eating dates or salt.

Ihram State of purity necessary to perform pilgrimage (hajj and umrah), achieved through ritual cleansing (including haircut, shave, and manicure for men) and symbolized by a seamless two-piece white garment covering the upper and lower parts of the body for males and modest clothing for women. Sexual relations, killing of insects or animals, and removal of bodily hair are not permitted while in the state of ihram.

Ihsan Doing what is beautiful. In Sufism, it refers to a deepened understanding and experience that allow one to worship God as if one sees Him. This leads Sufis to be aware of God's presence both in the world and in themselves, guiding them to act according to His will.

Ihtiram *See* Honor

Ihya Revival; strengthening of the spiritual dimensions of faith and practice in response to a perceived lapse of observance. Since the nineteenth century, the term has been used for revivalist movements seeking to revive Islamic influences in the lives of formerly colonized Muslims, either through a synthesis of Islam and modernity or through rejection of the West in favor of more traditional Islamic practices and beliefs. *See also* Revival and Renewal

IIIT *See* International Institute of Islamic Thought

Ijarah Economic term for leasing, typically offered through Islamic banks with long-term credit facilities for capital equipment

purchases. May involve purchase or an installment sale, where a customer eventually acquires ownership of the equipment. Longer-term participatory finance may also be provided by the Islamic bank becoming a partner in business, according to the principle of mudarabah (profit sharing). The bank may provide all of the funding, acting as financier, with an active manager providing entrepreneurial skills and management. Funding may be provided to either a pre-existing company or a new company. One of the most active fields of Islamic banking activity. The leasing arrangement circumvents the charging of interest, which, according to many scholars, is forbidden in Islam.

Ijaz Inimitability; something wondrous or miraculous. Muslims regard the beauty of the Quran's language and the coherence of its message as a miracle, establishing the Quran's divine origin and inimitability and confirming Muhammad's prophethood.

Ijazah Certificate awarded to a student upon successful completion of the study of Quran, hadith, and law. Enables the student to teach these same texts. Typically these are included in biographies, making it possible to trace connections between teachers and students over several generations. In the past it was considered sufficient qualification for a respectable job. Its function is fulfilled today by school diplomas.

Ijhad *See* Abortion

Ijma Consensus or agreement. One of four recognized sources of Sunni law. Utilized where the Quran and Sunnah (the first two sources) are silent on a particular issue. There is considerable debate concerning whose opinions are relevant for ijma. Some argue that only the opinions of scholars are relevant. Others contend that ijma includes the consensus of the laity. Most agree that the consensus of Muhammad's Companions, the people of Medina, or the family of the Prophet is authoritative. Once an ijma is established, it serves as a precedent. According to the majority of jurists, a decision based on ijma generally cannot override a statement of the Quran or the Sunnah. The binding force of ijma is based on a hadith in which the Prophet Muhammad is reported to have said, "My community will never agree on an error." In Twelver Shiism, consensus is neither an infallible sanctioning instrument nor a source of law. Ideas of consultation (shura) and parliamentarianism are used in attempts to formulate a theory of consensus useful in the modern world.

Ijtihad Islamic legal term meaning "independent reasoning," as opposed to taqlid (imitation). One of four sources of Sunni law. Utilized where the Quran and Sunnah (the first two sources) are silent. It requires a thorough knowledge of theology, revealed texts, and legal theory (usul al-fiqh); a sophisticated capacity for legal reasoning; and a thorough knowledge of Arabic. It is considered a required religious duty for those qualified to perform it. It should be practiced by means of analogical or syllogistic reasoning (qiyas). Its results may not contradict the Quran, and it may not be used in cases where consensus (ijma) has been reached, according to many scholars. Sunnis believe ijtihad is fallible since more than one interpretation of a legal issue is possible. Islamic reformers call for a revitalization of ijtihad in the modern world

Ikhtilaf al-Fiqh Disagreement of jurists. Refers to the differing legal opinions of early authorities, usually compiled and compared according to topic, described in such works as the *Ikhtilaf al-fuqaha* (Disagreement among jurists) of Ibn Jarir al-Tabari (d. 932). May refer to conflicting opinions among schools of legal thought or among the authorities within the different schools. Hanafi law, for example, is based on the conflicting opinions of three early authorities: Abu Hanifah, Abu Yusuf, and Muhammad al-Shaybani.

Ikhwan Brothers. Term used by many organizations, such as that founded in 1911–12 in Arabia by Abd al-Aziz ibn Saud to settle Bedouins into agricultural communities called hujjar, based on a literal interpretation of the Quran and Sunnah by Muhammad ibn Abd al-Wahhab. Emphasized public worship and obedience to Islamic law. The Ikhwan formed the backbone of Ibn Saud's army, fighting against nonbelievers who were not part of the hujjar settlements. Forcibly disbanded in 1926 when it opposed the consolidation of the Saudi kingdom and became a threat to Ibn Saud. *See also* Hujjar; Saud, Abd al-Aziz ibn Abd al-Rahman al-

Ikhwan al-Muslimin, al *See* Muslim Brotherhood in Egypt

Ikhwan al-Safa Also known as the Brethren of Purity. Tenth-and eleventh-century secret brotherhood of philosophers and scientists who wrote *Epistles of the Brethren of Purity*, which is claimed by both Twelver Shiis and Ismailis as part of their teachings, despite the criticisms of the doctrine of the Hidden Imam contained in its text. The authorship of the *Epistles* has been variously ascribed to Ali, Jafar al-Sadiq, and some of the Hidden Imams. The brotherhood promoted the belief that religion strengthens group cohesiveness, or asabiyyah. It also worked to harmonize the pre-Islamic understanding of cosmos with the data contained in the Quran.

Iktisab *See* Kasb

Ilhad Heresy that distorts the fundamental teachings of Islam, especially within the community. Behavior does not become ilhad until it publicly manifests itself in the form of rebellion or blasphemy. The term is almost always employed in polemical texts or situations.

Ilham Inspiration. Term used by Sufis to refer to the transformation of the human soul by the power of universal Spirit. Also means personal revelation received by and for an individual, as opposed to impersonal prophetic revelation intended for all people.

Illah Cause; defect or malady. In Islamic jurisprudence, *illah* refers to the effective or operative cause behind a law. In order for a law to be applicable to a specific case, its operative cause must be triggered by the circumstances of the case.

Ilm *See* Science

Ilm al-Alkhlaq *See* Ethics

Ilm al-Falak *See* Astrology

Ilm al-Handasa *See* Geometry

Ilm al-Haya *See* Astronomy

Ilm al-Hisab *See* Mathematics

Ilm al-Huruf Science of letters. Mystical process of numerology similar to the Hebrew gematria, whereby numerical values assigned to Arabic letters are added up to provide total values for words in the Quran. Used to infer meanings and reveal secret or hidden messages.

Ilm al-Jamal *See* Aesthetics

Ilm al-Kimiya *See* Alchemy

Ilm al-Lugha *See* Lexicography

Ilm al-Nujum *See* Astrology

Ilm al-Rijal Study of the men. Refers to study of the people who transmitted hadith reports, manifested in the production of biographical dictionaries (tabaqat). Aimed to demonstrate their moral character as a means of validating the reliability of those reports. The details of the geographical and historical events in a person's life allowed a judgment to be made on the likelihood of a given transmitter having received a report from another transmitter. When this was combined with assessments of the transmitter's character, theological affiliation, and mental capacity, rankings of reliability were established. Chains of transmission (isnads) containing "weak links" were, in theory, eliminated. Assessments were codified starting in the tenth century in a specific genre often

called al-iarh wa'l-tadil (rejecting and admitting).

Ilm al-Tabiah *See* Natural Science

Ilm al-Tarikh *See* History

Ilm al-Tibb *See* Medicine: Traditional Practice

Iltizam Type of tax farming practiced in Egypt and the Ottoman Empire. Tax farms were assigned to holders who paid fixed annual sums to the empire's central treasury in exchange for use of the property and the right to collect taxes for the empire. Holders were allowed to keep the balance of collections as personal profit, encouraging them to be diligent and efficient in the collection of taxes. Iltizam became a means of controlling movable officials, a way to prevent the accumulation of large territories by individuals or families, and a guarantee of tax collection in regions far from the center.

Ilyas *See* Elias

Ilyas, Muhammad (d. 1944) Sufi scholar, Deobandi alim, and founder of Tablighi Jamaat in India in 1927. Believed that only a grassroots Islamic religious movement could counter the efforts of the Hindu proselytization movements, expunge Hindu influences from Islam, and properly educate Muslims about their own beliefs and rituals. Promoted organization, formal travel, and education as means for achieving the objectives of tabligh.

Imam One who stands in front; a role model for the Muslim community in all its spiritual and secular undertakings. The title is used interchangeably with the word khalifah for the political head of the Sunni Muslim state. In legal writings the term is applied to the leader of the congregational prayers in the mosque. Historically, Muslim rulers used to appoint the imam for the official function of leading the Friday services in the main mosque of capital cities. Sunni Muslims use the title for their prominent jurists, who are also regarded as the founders of their legal schools, such as Abu Hanifah and Shafii. In Shii Islam the imam is the divinely appointed successor of Muhammad and is regarded as infallible, with the ability to make binding decisions in all areas of human activity. In Twelver Shiism, following the disappearance of the twelfth and last imam, the jurists (fuqaha) have assumed the title imam. Hence, Khomeini after the Iranian revolution in 1979 was given the title imam, following the practice of the Arab Shiis, who have always called their religious authorities imams. In North America, in the absence of official ordainment, religious leaders connected with different Islamic centers often use the title to indicate their religious standing in the community.

Imamah Religio-political leadership. Known as *imamate* in English. A major practical issue since Muhammad's death in 632. Abu Bakr (first caliph, r. 632–34) and associates regarded the imamate as the right of Muhammad's Meccan Companions who belonged to the tribe of Quraysh (Sunni view). Muhammad's family regarded the imamate as divinely invested in Ali ibn Abi Talib (r. 656–61), Muhammad's cousin, son-in-law, and closest living male relative (Shii view). The dispute ultimately led to the first civil war among Muslims (657–61). The first four caliphs are considered "rightly guided" by Sunnis in their exercise of the imamate, rendering their actions and legal decisions authoritative for all Muslims. Zaydi Shiis believe that the imamate belonged to any member of Muhammad's family who rose against illegitimate rulers. The Imami or Twelver Shii understanding of the imamate is based on the need for an infallible leader and authoritative teacher to guide humanity to prosperous life. Consequently, disregarding and disobeying a rightfully appointed imam is the equivalent of disobeying Muhammad for Shiis.

Imamate *See* Imamah

Imambarah *See* Husayniyyah

Imamis *See* Ithna Asharis

Imamzadah A shrine-tomb of a male descendant of a Shii imam is reverently accorded this title to indicate the love for the household of the Prophet among the Shiis. Centers of popular Shii devotion and pilgrimages, many tombs are believed to have miraculous properties. Among the female descendants of the Prophet, the shrine-tombs of Zaynab (the daughter of Ali ibn Abi Talib, the first Shii imam) and Fatimah (the daughter of Musa al-Kazim, the seventh imam) enjoy great prestige.

Iman Faith or belief. Suggests security for believers against untruth and misguidance in this world and punishment in the afterlife. Assumes belief in the oneness of God, angels, prophets, revealed books, and the hereafter. Faith is a matter of free choice in Islam but is also considered a gift from God; no one is to be compelled to believe. The Quran establishes the close connection between faith and action, so that true faith manifests itself in right conduct. Believers are commanded to obey God, Muhammad, and authorities; fulfill their commitments; be truthful; perform ritual prayer; spend their wealth and struggle steadfastly to do the will of God; shun drinking, gambling, and exploitative business practices; and avoid treating people condescendingly.

Imran Father of Aaron, who became head of the priests. The Quran records that John the Baptist's mother, Elizabeth, and her cousin Mary, the mother of Jesus, were daughters of this family. According to tradition, Mary's father was also called Imran, making her mother, Hannah, both a descendant of the house of Imran and the wife of Imran.

Imru al-Qays (d. ca. 540) Pre-Islamic Arab poet and author of the first of the *Muallaqat*. He is remembered and evoked in Arabic literature as the "wandering king" for his relentless, lifelong effort to avenge the murder of his father, the king of Banu Assad. Born in Najd; died in Ankara.

Imtiyazat *See* Capitulations

Incarnation Notion that the divine spirit can enter into a human being, fusing the identity of divine and human. Incarnation has consistently been rejected by Muslim thinkers on the grounds of God's absolute transcendence. The Quran insists that the Christian claim of God's incarnation in Jesus is false.

Incest *See* Zina

Independence Party *See* Hizb al-Istiqlal

Independent Reasoning *See* Ijtihad

India, Islam in Fourteen percent of India's one billion people are Muslim. Characterized by economic and political diversity, they are further divided regionally and linguistically: Bengali, Deccani, Gujarati, Hindustani, Mappila, Oriyya, and Punjabi. Most are Sunni Muslims following the Hanafi legal tradition; about 10 percent are Twelver Shiis, and a smaller percentage are Ismaili Shiis. Most Indian Muslims supported the partition of British India at independence, but a substantial minority supported the Indian National Congress. In independent India Muslims have been politically active as one of the largest Muslim national communities in the world.

Indian Mutiny of 1857 Failed Hindu-Muslim revolt against British control in the Indian subcontinent. The revolt brought a formal end to the Mughal Empire, with the last Mughal emperor exiled. The British crown claimed sovereignty, replacing the East India Company.

Indian Ocean Societies, Islam in Seven islands or island groups in the Indian Ocean have Muslim populations: Comoros, Maldives, Madagascar, Sri Lanka, Mauritius, Reunion, and Seychelles. Islam is the state religion in Comoros and Maldives. Comoros is a federal Islamic republic with a population that is nearly 100 percent Muslim; the

majority are Sunni and adhere to the Shafii school of Islamic law. Islam was brought to Maldives by traders and itinerant holy men in the twelfth century; the people are 100 percent Sunni. Muslims in Sri Lanka are mostly the descendants of North African traders who settled there beginning in the eighth century; Sri Lanka's Muslim minority of 1.3 million is larger than the combined Muslim population of all other Indian Ocean societies. Islam reached Madagascar in the fourteenth century through trading colonies established by Muslim traders from East Africa. Mauritian Muslims are largely of Indian descent; about one-third of the Indian population there is Muslim. In Reunion Muslims are 2 percent of the population. Islam has no influence in Seychelles.

Indonesia, Islam in In 2001 Indonesia possessed the largest Muslim population of any country in the world. Between 85 and 90 percent of the population of more than 180 million is Muslim, mostly Sunnis who adhere to the Shafii school of Islamic law. Islam arrived in the thirteenth century and was the majority religion by the eighteenth century. Conversions occurred mainly through peaceful means, via traders accompanied by religious scholars and Sufis. Sufism and the general tolerance of local traditions aided the growth of Islam and accounts for Hindu and other non-Muslim elements in Islamic practices. The nineteenth and early twentieth centuries saw the rise of reformism, particularly criticism of non-Islamic elements of religious faith and practice. In the twentieth century, Islam provided a common sense of identity in the face of European colonialism and an ethnically and linguistically diverse population. Pancasila (the Five Principles) was proclaimed as the national ideology after 1945, reflecting a secular and pluralist view of the role of religion in the state. The 1960s witnessed the proliferation of missionary activities and the rise of Islamism. Beginning in the late 1970s, radical Muslims turned to violence to express opposition to the government, seeking a stronger role for Islam in Indonesian politics. This, combined with increasing antagonism over the perceived power of Christianity in the islands, led to the 1999 election of Abdurrahman Wahid, who promised to end violence and assert a stronger presence of Islam in government, a position he held until 2001, when he was forced from office by the parliament that had elected him.

Infanticide Pre-Islamic practice in tribal communities, usually targeting female babies. Explicitly prohibited by the Quran. On this basis, Islamic law protects the right to life of the unborn child after it receives its soul, traditionally considered to be at the end of the fourth month of pregnancy. Many consider prohibition of infanticide an indication of the improvement of women's status under Islam.

Inheritance Islamic law on inheritance (mirath), based on the Quran, requires that Muslim women receive specifically regulated inheritance shares and permits inheritance to pass through the femle line. The Quran contains more extensive and specific rules on inheritance than on any other subject, although Sunni and Shii law diverge on interpretations and applications of these rules. Sunni inheritance law holds that the Quran reformed the existing system of inheritance in western Arabia under which males inherited, and Sunnis reconcile the Quranic injunctions for fixed inheritance portions with the claims of the male relatives. Shiis believe that the Quranic system was designed to supplant the pre-Islamic system; they keep more of the inheritance within the nuclear family and often place the daughters of the deceased in a more favorable position than under Sunni law. *See also* Bequest; Property; Waqf

Innovation Arabic *bidah*. Any modification of accepted religious belief or practice. Based on the hadith "Any manner or way which someone invents in this religion such that that manner or way is not part of this religion is to be rejected," the term has a negative connotation in Islam. Conservatives extend the prohibition beyond strictly religious matters to social practice, while more liberal thinkers condemn only innovations judged to substantially alter the core of Islamic teaching.

Inqadh To save, rescue, bring relief or salvation. In Islamic law, there is a duty to rescue a person in distress as long as the rescuer does not unduly endanger her-or himself. Failure to rescue results in sin and accountability before God, but there are no criminal penalties imposed on the bystander.

Inqilab *See* Revolution

Insan al-Kamil, al- The perfect person. Within the Islamic mystical tradition this term was originally used to refer to the Prophet Muhammad, who was considered to be the first Islamic mystic. Some Sufi teachers adopted the title for themselves, believing that a perfect being with divine knowledge was essential in the present world to truly guide mystics. *See also* Ibn al-Arabi, Muhyi al-Din

Insha Allah If God wills. Used in statements of what one hopes will happen in the future, reminding the believer that nothing happens unless God wills it and that only what God wills will happen. Demonstrates the belief that God's will supersedes human will. Common phrase in everyday speech.

Inspiration *See* Ilham; Wahy

Institute for Social Studies *See* International Institute of Islamic Economics

Intention Arabic *niyyah*. Proper intent is necessary to make an act meritorious, so ritual action carried out without proper intent is believed to be meaningless in the eyes of God. Affirmation of intent is required prior to canonical prayers as well as all other ritual observances in Islam. Intention is defined simply as someone intending to perform the activity he or she is performing, as opposed to doing it accidentally.

Intercession Requesting assistance from a spiritual intermediary when seeking divine help. In conservative interpretations, only Muhammad can intercede with God on behalf of human beings because Islam teaches that every believer has direct access to God. In Sufism and popular practice, intercession is often asked of saints or holy people. Some reform movements oppose requests for intercession. *See also* Salat al-Hajah

Interest *See* Riba

Intermarriage In Islam, intermarriage refers to a man and a woman of different faiths marrying; race or national origin is not relevant. Islamic law provides that a Muslim woman cannot marry a non-Muslim man, though a Muslim man is entitled to marry a Christian or a Jew.

International Institute of Islamic Economics Formerly the Institute for Social Studies. One of several institutes that comprise the International Islamic University at Islamabad. The institute organizes senior officers' training programs and has developed a body of Ph.D. graduates with the help of the U.S. Agency for International Development. *See also* International Islamic University, Islamabad

International Institute of Islamic Thought Islamic think tank with global following cofounded in 1981 by Ismail al-Faruqi and Anwar Ibrahim. Located in Herndon, Virginia. Hosts scholars from throughout the Islamic world to work on the "Islamization of knowledge," an examination of each main academic discipline in light of Islam. Publishes a monograph series and *The American Journal of Islamic Social Sciences*. Faruqi stressed that Islamization means not the subordination of knowledge to dogmatic principles, but rather testing every truth claim by internal coherence, correspondence with reality, and enhancement of human life and morality. Offers a master's degree in Islamic studies and a master's program for imams.

International Islamic Federation of Student Organizations Worldwide organization of Muslim student associations founded

in Indiana in 1966. Provides direction to various student movements, steering them toward rejuvenation of Muslim thought. Provides continuing education to membership. Encourages women to participate in the Islamic movement. Helps to develop private enterprise through provision of loans and expertise to small businesses. Active in providing relief and reconstruction help in places where natural disasters have occurred. Publishes Islamic literature in more than eighty languages, making the works of Islamic thinkers available to a broad audience. Active in promoting human rights throughout the world. Maintains close ties with other international Islamic umbrella organizations.

International Islamic News Agency Official news agency of the Organization of the Islamic Conference. Created in 1979. Based in Jeddah, Saudi Arabia. Issues daily news bulletins in Arabic, English, and French. *See also* Organization of the Islamic Conference

International Islamic Relief Organization Organization within the Muslim World League responsible for the League's activities in the fields of social welfare and humanitarian aid. Provides assistance to areas that have experienced natural disasters or other calamities. *See also* Muslim World League

International Islamic University, Islamabad Pakistani institution established to provide advanced courses in Islamic studies. Founded in 1980 with Saudi and Pakistani funding. Focal point for dissemination of Islamic thought in Pakistan and Central and Southeast Asia. Provides courses in Islamic law for judicial officers, public prosecutors, prayer leaders, preachers of Friday sermons, and teachers of religious schools. Hosts the Islamic Research Institute. *See also* International Institute of Islamic Economics

International Islamic University, Kuala Lumpur Malaysian institution founded in 1983 to integrate the teaching of all knowledge with Islamic values. Offers courses in law, business, accounting, economics, psychology, political science, history, civilization, philosophy, mass communictions, English, Arabic, Islamic revealed knowledge and heritage, sociology, anthropology, engineering, architecture, applied and basic sciences, and medical sciences.

International Law *See* Siyar

Intifadah *See* Arab-Israeli Conflict

Intizar Waiting. Term popularized by Iranian reformer Ali Shariati (d. 1977) in his 1971 lecture entitled "Waiting: The Religion of Refusal." A play on the term *al-muntazar*, referring to the awaited imam and Mahdi of Shii Islam. For Shariati, waiting means saying no to the oppressive status quo and striving for a just society. *See also* Shariati, Ali; Shii Islam

Intoxicants The Quran prohibits fermented drinks because of their intoxicating effect. For Muslims all association with intoxicating drinks—including buying, selling, and delivering them—is forbidden. Drinking spread with Muslim territorial victories, leading Umar I to fix a punishment of eighty lashes for consuming intoxicating drinks. In Muslim courts such drinks became common nevertheless, and poetry in praise of wine blossomed as a literary tradition. *Nabidh* refers to wine or nonintoxicating drinks made from soaked fruits. *Khamr* refers to the product of fermentation. In the modern world, the prohibition on intoxicants has been extended to include narcotics.

Iqbal, Muhammad (d. 1938) Indo-Pakistani political and religious writer and leader, lawyer, professor, poet, and ideologue who supported the foundation of Pakistan as a homeland for the Muslims of India. Educated in Urdu, Arabic, English, and Farsi. Studied in India and Europe. Member of the All-India Muslim League. Elected member of the Punjab legislative assembly 1926–30. Delivered a presidential address to the All-India Muslim League in 1930 that became a landmark in the Muslim national movement for the creation of Pakistan, emphasizing Muslim nationalism, the necessity of Muslim self-determination, and national liberation for the Muslims of India. Promoted the exercise of ijtihad (independent reasoning) in interpretation of the Quran and Sunnah. Laid the groundwork for religion and science as cooperative studies. Encouraged Muslims to learn modern sciences and use modern technology to improve their material existence and expand human development. Regarded as the greatest Urdu poet of the twentieth century; his major poetic works are in Persian. Perhaps his most influential work on Islamic reformism is *The Reconstruction of Religious Thought in Islam.*

Iqrar The moment when a mystic is living outside of daily reality and within the mystical sensation, experiencing the total release of one's own feelings for the pleasure of being with God. Mystics use the concept of iqrar to describe their loss of the self when the divine acknowledges and affirms their established place with God.

Iqta System for paying off political debts during the Abbasid caliphate that involved tax collection and has been compared to the European fief. Developed further by Buwayhids in Iran and Iraq during first half of the tenth century; continued by Great Seljuks, Ayyubids, Mamluks, and Ottomans (though under the name *muqataa*). One type, tamlik, was a concession of land designated for agricultural reclamation; in return, the recipient was allowed tax reductions and the right to pass the property on to heirs. The other type, istighlal, allowed the recipient to pay a fixed rate to the treasury in return for a portion of peasants' crops that was greater in value. Under the Buwayhids the latter was given usually to soldiers in lieu of salary. Although this system of tax farming did not confer ownership of land or judicial, administrative, or personal control over the peasants, such was often the practice over the years. *See also* Iltizam

Iqtisad, al- *See* Economics (Islamic)

Iradah Desire. Refers to the journey of the soul on the road to God through the discipline of a Sufi order. Also refers to the rule of life once on the road to God. Novitiate proper or purpose of novitiate presenting candidacy for order. Used in Sufi poetry to describe the desire to be joined with God.

Iran, Islam in Islam arrived in Iran in 637 as Arab Muslim conquests spread into Persia. Zoroastrian beliefs, rooted in the idea of a never-ending struggle between the forces of good and evil, were replaced by Islamic monotheism. The majority of Iranians embraced Islam and many Zoroastrians fled to India, but traces of Zoroastrianism remained. For the first millennium after the arrival of Islam, Sunni Islam prevailed. The rise of the Safavid dynasty in 1501 led to the predominance of Twelver Shiism and the emergence of religious scholars as an important social force. Shii clerics increased their power significantly in the Qajar era (ca. 1785–1925). By the end of the nineteenth century, they had become key actors in the country's social movements and institutions. Clerics and the bazaari (merchant) class played a leading role in the 1905–11 Constitutional Revolution, protesting tobacco concessions to Western companies and demanding a constitution and accountability of the ruler. The Pahlavi dynasty (r. 1925–79) downplayed religion in favor of modernization, westernization, and secular, Iranian nationalism, policies that eventually led to the dynasty's overthrow and replacement by an Islamic republic headed by Ayatollah Ruhollah Khomeini. Khomeini called for rule by jurists (vilayat-i faqih) and implementation of Islamic law in all areas of life. Clerics generally have been united on cultural issues but divided on economic matters such as property ownership, nationalization of trade, land reform, and trade with the West. The election of Mohammad Khatami as president in 1997 evidenced a growing tendency to encourage cultural, economic, and scholarly exchanges between Iran and the West. Women are active in professional capacities and as elected representatives, appointed government officials, and judges, making Iran one of the most progressive Muslim countries with respect to women's rights.

Iran-Iraq War (1980–88) Immediately after Iran's Islamic Revolution, Iraq attacked Iran to contain the spread of the revolution within Iraq and regain territory ceded under duress to Iran in 1975 in the Shatt al-Arab. In September 1980 Iraq seized ninety square miles of Iranian territory in the Shatt al-Arab but failed to achieve a quick victory, and a bloody war of attrition ensued. Iraq's 1984 use of chemical weapons drew worldwide outrage. The scope of the conflict increased, affecting shipping in the Gulf and leading to some of the bloodiest battles of this century. By 1987 U.S. forces in the Gulf began flying limited sorties against Iranian oil rigs and naval vessels as the balance of power shifted from Iraq to Iran. Iran and Iraq finally accepted a UN peace plan, and fighting between the two nations ceased in August 1988. Estimates of the number of dead range up to 1.5 million. The war cost the two countries nearly $700 billion in direct costs, loss of oil revenue, and destruction of property.

Iranian Revolution of 1979 Revolution in which a coalition of forces opposed to the Western-oriented Pahlavi regime and dominated by Shii Muslim clerics overthrew the government of Muhammad Reza Shah Pahlavi. The acknowledged leader was Ayatollah Ruhollah Khomeini. Causes included the modernization/westernization programs undertaken since the 1920s, particularly the economic and social reform programs of the 1963 White Revolution; state control of religious institutions, which deprived clerics of power and income; and the perceived corruption and extreme wealth of the shah and the ruling class. The revolution began on 9 January 1978, when theology students in Qom protested a newspaper article accusing Khomeini of licentiousness and crimes against the state. Demonstrators and police entered into violent conflict, fostering other protests throughout country. Khomeini, in exile in France, preached that the shah had conspired with foreign powers, particularly the United States, to exploit the Iranian people and undermine Islam. The message appealed to a broad base of economic classes from all regions of the country. The shah was forced to leave Iran on 16 January 1979. Khomeini appointed his own provisional revolutionary government and returned to Iran on 1 February 1979, to great popular acclaim. Khomeini officially seized power on 11 February. In March a referendum was held to determine the form of the new government, and Iran became an Islamic republic. The constitution adopted in 1979 invested ultimate power in Khomeini as the chief jurisprudent (faqih), along with a five-person religious Council of Guardians. The revolution was a symbolically important event that demonstrated that Western-influenced secular regimes could be overthrown by opposition forces organized under Islamic reformers. It gave new impetus to Islamic revivalists and triggered a rise in Islamic fundamentalist activities from Morocco to Southeast Asia. See also Khomeini, Ruhollah al-Musavi

Iranian Revolutionary Guards See Sipah-i Pasdaran-i Inqilab-i Islami

Iraq, Islam in The present state of Iraq was founded in 1920 under British mandate. The population of Iraq is approximately 55–60 percent Arab Shii, 15–20 percent Arab Sunni, and 20 percent Kurdish Sunni. Iranian Shiis consider the Iraqi holy cities of Najaf and Karbala as critical to their own faith and culture and wield significant religious influence over Iraqi Shiis there. Shiis throughout the world come to Najaf as the center of Shii learning. Najaf was the center from which opposition to British rule was organized, where Lebanese Shii religious leaders were trained, and where Ayatollah Khomeini spent fourteen years in exile. Shii activism directed from Najaf contributed to opposition to the Communist threat in the 1960s and to the Baath regime since 1968.

Ird See Honor

Irfan See Gnosticism

Irtidad See Apostasy

Irving, T. B. Islamic scholar and Quranic translator. A prominent American Muslim and a leading expert on Islamic Spain. Most noteworthy achievement is his translation of the Quran into contemporary American English. Authored several scholarly treatises on Islam, Muslims, and Muslim Andalusia. Lectured and taught at several universities overseas. Retired as a professor of Spanish and Arabic.

Isaac Called Ishaq in the Quran. Son of Abraham and Sarah in old age. The Quran mentions him seventeen times, as righteous man, servant of God, prophet, and father of Jews. The Quran records God's blessing of Isaac and his progeny as long as they uphold their covenant with God. His half-brother Ishmael (Ismail) is believed by Muslims to be the object of the sacrifice that God demanded from Abraham, although the Quran does not specify this.

Isa ibn Maryam See Jesus, Son of Mary

ISESCO See Islamic Educational, Scientific, and Cultural Organization

Isfahan Name of a province in Iran and its capital city. The city has been known since pre-Islamic Sassanid times for its exquisite carpets, hand-printed textiles, and metalwork. Isfahan has served as an Arab provincial capital (mid-seventh century) and capital of the Seljuk Turkish empire (1051), was captured by the Mongols (1388), and was capital of the Safavid dynasty (seventeenth century).

Ishaki, Ayaz (d. 1954) Tatar political activist and writer who promoted Turkic unity and national autonomy for the Volga-Ural Muslims. His writings reflected the ideals of enlightenment, justice, and economic and political advancement associated with Jadidism (Islamic reformism). Composed numerous short stories, novels, and plays, and translated many historical essays.

Ishaq *See* Isaac

Ishaq, Hunayn ibn *See* Hunayn ibn Ishaq

Ishmael Called Ismail in the Quran. Son of Abraham (Ibrahim) and Hagar. In the Quranic account, God asked Abraham to sacrifice his son but did not specify which one. Muslim tradition generally identifies the son to be sacrificed as Ishmael, rather than Isaac (Ishaq). Ishmael accepted the command due to his faith in God. Called people to prayer and charity. Believed by Muslims to have built the Kaaba with his father as a sign of God's covenant with them. Evicted from his home as an infant along with his mother, Hagar, due to the jealousy of Abraham's wife, Sarah, and nearly died of thirst in the desert until God revealed the well of Zamzam. Today Ishmael is considered the father of the Arab nation, and the Isaac/Ishmael conflict is often used as a paradigm for the Jewish/Arab conflict.

Ishq Passion. One of the stages through which a Sufi must pass in working toward union with either God or Muhammad. Immediately precedes union with God or Muhammad. Also translated as "love" or "yearning for God."

Ishraq *See* Hikmat al-Ishraq

Iskandar, al- *See* Alexander the Great

Iskandari, al- *See* Ibn Ata Allah, Ahmad ibn Muhammad

Islah Reform. Typically used to describe reform movements from the eighteenth century through the present. Based on the belief that historical misunderstandings and misinterpretations have distorted the original meanings of texts, introducing harmful practices. Therefore reform consists of a return to Islam's original message, although implemented in ways consistent with changed circumstances. The thrust behind the current reform movement is the perceived need to fulfill the ethical requirements of Islam. The movement stresses continuity of the Quranic message, rejection of innovations believed to be incompatible with the interests of the community and with the teachings of the Quran and hadith, reform of educational and political systems, and improvement of the status of women. *See also* Revival and Renewal

Islahi, Amin Ahsan (d. 1998) Pakistani Quran exegete. Author of a complete Quranic commentary, expounding each surah as a coherent discourse, arranging surahs into pairs, and establishing seven major surah divisions—the entire Quran thus emerging as a well-connected and systematic book.

Islam, Yusuf (b. 1948) The former Cat Stevens, at one time a pop singer, now an Islamic organizer and educator. After his conversion to Islam, his interest in educating Muslim children led him to found the Islamiah School in Brent, London, in the late 1980s. Was a founder of the Muslim Council of Britain and a fundraiser for Muslim charities.

Islami Jamiat Tulaba Islamic Society of Students. Official student wing of Pakistani Jamaat-i Islami (one-third of the current leadership of Jamaat-i Islami initially belonged to its student wing). Generally works to spread teachings of revivalist ideologues among students and enforce a strict code of ethics on campuses. Has dominated campus elections since 1971. Often more outspoken than its parent organization in calling for Islamic revolution. Was at the forefront of battles against leftist activities on university campuses. In 1971, negotiated directly with the government to help the martial-law administration of East Pakistan launch counterinsurgency units against Bengali guerrilla forces. Has been the target of government repression. *See also* Jamaat-i Islam

Islamic Banking *See* Banking (Islamic)

Islam: An Overview

Islam is the second most widespread of the world's religions, with more than one billion adherents. Muslim countries extend from North Africa to Southeast Asia. Muslims constitute the majority in forty-eight countries and are a significant minority in many others. Though the Arab world is often regarded as the heartland of Islam, the majority of Muslims live in Asia and Africa. The largest Muslim communities are in Indonesia, Bangladesh, Pakistan, India, Central Asia, and Nigeria. Islam has grown significantly in the West in recent years, where it is now the second largest religion in many parts of Europe and the third largest in the United States.

The term *Islam* is derived from the Arabic root s-l-m, which means "submission" or "peace." Muslims are those who surrender to God's will or law, rendering them at peace with themselves and with God. To embrace Islam is to become a member of a worldwide faith community (ummah). Thus believers have a religious identity that is both individual and corporate as well as a responsibility or duty to obey and implement God's will in their personal and social lives.

Islam stands in a long line of Middle Eastern prophetic religious traditions that share uncompromising monotheism, belief in God's revelation, prophets, ethical responsibility, accountability, and the notion of a Day of Judgment. Jews, Christians, and Muslims are all considered children of Abraham (Ibrahim), although they belong to different branches of the same family. Jews and Christians are spiritual descendants of Abraham and his wife, Sarah, through their son, Isaac (Ishaq); Muslims trace their lineage back to Ishmael (Ismail), Abraham's firstborn son by his Egyptian servant, Hagar. Ishmael became the father of Arabs in northern Arabia. Muslims believe that Islam was the original monotheistic faith, making it the oldest of the Abrahamic faiths, with Judaism and Christianity as tolerated offshoots.

Islamic scripture, the Quran, was revealed by God to the Prophet Muhammad in Arabia in the seventh century. Muslims believe it was revealed verbatim. The center and foundation of Islam is God, whom Muslims call Allah, or "the God." Allah is believed to be the transcendent, all-powerful, and all-knowing creator, sustainer, ordainer, and judge of the universe. The absolute monotheism of Islam is preserved in the doctrine of unity (tawhid) and sovereignty (rabb, "ruler" or "lord") of God that dominates Islamic belief and practice. As God is one, His rule and will or law are comprehensive, extending to all creatures and in all aspects of life. God is not only powerful and majestic but also merciful and just. Reward and punishment follow from individual ethical responsibility and accountability before God. Islamic ethics follow from human beings' special status and responsibility on earth.

Islam emphasizes practice as well as belief. Law rather than theology is the central religious discipline and locus for defining the path of Islam and preserving its way of life. The essential duties of all Muslims, the Five Pillars, are profession of faith (shahadah, "There is no god but God and Muhammad is the messenger of God"), worship or prayer five times daily with community prayers at the mosque on Fridays, charity (zakah), fasting during the month of Ramadan, and pilgrimage (hajj) to Mecca at least once in a lifetime. Jihad, or struggle in the way of God, is sometimes considered the sixth pillar. Jihad includes both internal spiritual struggles and external war waged in defense of the Muslim community.

Contemporary revivalism is rooted in Islam's time-honored tradition of renewal (tajdid) and reform (islah) embodied in Muhammad's leadership of the first Islamic movement, seventeenth- and eighteenth-century revivalism, and nineteenth- and twentieth-century Islamic modernist

(continued)

Islam (continued)

movements. At the heart of the revivalist worldview is the belief that the Muslim world is in a state of decline owing to Muslims' departure from the straight path of Islam. The proposed cure is to return to Islam in personal and public life so as to ensure restoration of Islamic identity, values, and power. For Islamic political activists, Islam is a total or comprehensive way of life, stipulated in the Quran, mirrored in Muhammad's example and the nature of the first Muslim community-state, and embodied in the comprehensive nature of shariah, God's revealed law. Islamic activists or Islamists believe that renewal and revitalization of Muslim governments and societies require restoration or reimplementation of Islamic law, which they believe is a blueprint for an Islamically guided and socially just state and society. Revivalism continues to grow as a broad-based socio-religious movement, functioning today in virtually every Muslim country and transnationally. Its goal is creation of a just society through the Islamic transformation of individuals at the grassroots level.

Islamic Calendar Also known as hijrah calendar. Lunar calendar consisting of twelve months, each of which lasts from the first sighting of one crescent moon to the first sighting of the next, approximately twenty-nine or thirty days. The year is 354 days long. The months in order are Muharram, Safar, Rabi al-Awwal, Rabi al-Thani, Jumada al-Ula, Jumada al-Akhirah, Rajab, Shaban, Ramadan, Shawwal, Dhu al-Qadah, and Dhu al-Hijjah. Holidays occur during different seasons from year to year since the calendar is lunar rather than solar. Days run from sunset to sunset. Year 1 of the Islamic calendar begins with the Muslim emigration (hijrah) from Mecca to Medina in 622 C.E.

Islamic Call Party *See* Hizb al-Dawah al-Islamiyyah

Islamic Call Society Libyan government missionary organization, founded in 1972. Responsible for preparing preachers and missionaries for international prosetylization. Students come primarily from Asia and Africa. Little domestic activity. The number of members is unknown. Consists of administrative council of at least five members, which plans and oversees activities; a general secretary, who serves as the official external representative; and the general assembly, which meets annually and evaluates the work of the administrative council. Has as its main financial source state subsidies. Is exempt from all taxes and duties, is subject to no restrictions on capital transfers, and has the right to work with any organization if it furthers the spread of Islam. Has branch offices throughout the world. Tries to tie Muslims around the world to Libya and Muammar Qaddafi's interpretation of Islam. Also serves to counter other proselytization organizations, especially the Saudi Muslim World League. Sends missionaries and medical relief caravans throughout the world, grants financial aid, and publishes books, brochures, and periodicals.

Islamic Chamber of Commerce Organ of the Organization of the Islamic Conference. Established in 1977 to promote trade, industry, and agriculture throughout the Islamic world; preferential terms of trade for members; cooperation between Islamic nations in finance, banking, insurance, and communications; arbitration of industrial and commercial disputes; fairs and joint showrooms, exhibits, seminars, lectures, and publicity campaigns; and the eventual establishment of an Islamic economic community. Composed of federations, unions, and national chambers of commerce in forty-six countries. Consists of a general assembly, executive committee, general secretariat, president, and six vice presidents. Funded by contributions from member countries according to a formula based on per capita incomes.

Islamic Charter Front Sudanese organization founded by the Muslim Brothers in

1964 with Hassan al-Turabi as secretary general. Advocated an Islamic constitution to win a broader range of support. Cooperated with Sadiq al-Mahdi's wing of the Ummah Party from 1965 to 1968 in the anti-Communist drive and promotion of an Islamic constitution. Active on university campuses. Ceased to exist as a formal organization after the military coup of 1969.

Islamic Circle of North America (ICNA) Established in 1971, ICNA is the largest full-service Islamic movement in the United States. Has established roots within the community at a national level through its regional organizations and neighborhood networks. Seeks to propagate Islam and to establish the Islamic way of life among American Muslims. Organizes annual convention, publishes a monthly magazine, The Message, and offers Islamic financial services. Known for its dedicated cadre of workers and links to the Jamaat-i Islami of South Asia.

Islamic Conference Organization See Organization of the Islamic Conference

Islamic Council of Europe Organization established in 1973 to coordinate the work of Islamic centers and organizations in Europe, with headquarters in London. The council was formed pursuant to resolutions adopted at a conference of Muslim foreign ministers and was supported by King Faisal of Saudi Arabia. Salem Azzam was a longtime director.

Islamic Democratic Alliance Coalition of Islamic and right-of-center parties that emerged in Pakistan following the death of General Zia-ul-Haq. Parties largely favored Zia's regime. Major parties within it were the Muslim League and Jamaat-i Islami. Challenged the Pakistan People's Party, headed by Benazir Bhutto, in the 1988 elections. Came to power in the 1990 elections under the leadership of Nawaz Sharif.

Islamic Development Bank An international development bank that funds projects on an interest-free basis. Capital is provided by governments of Muslim states. Based in Jeddah. Forty-five states participate in the bank, which began operations in 1975. Particularly active in providing long-term interest-free loans for projects with significant socioeconomic impact, usually infrastructural work such as roads, irrigation schemes, hospitals, and schools. Makes considerable efforts to support the poorest Muslim countries. Has taken steps in recent years to harness new capital, develop internationally acceptable Islamic financial institutions, and build closer relationships with Islamic commerical banks. See also Organization of the Islamic Conference

Islamic Economics See Economics (Islamic)

Islamic Educational, Scientific, and Cultural Organization (ISESCO) Institution within the Organization of the Islamic Conference (OIC) designed to strengthen cooperation among member states in educational, scientific, and cultural research, make Islamic culture the focal point of educational curricula at all levels, support Islamic culture, and protect the independence of Islamic thought against cultural invasion, distortion, and debasement. Based in Rabat, Morocco. Cooperates with the United Nations High Commissioner for Refugees (UNHCR) in refugee assistance within the Muslim world.

Islamic Foundation Established in 1973 to encourage research into the implementation of Islam in the modern world, project the image of Islam in Britain and Europe, and meet the educational needs of Muslims, especially young people. Works with young people and publishes research, particularly about economics, Christian-Muslim relations, Muslim Central Asia, and Islam in the modern world. Registered as an educational institution in Britain, where it is located. Responsible for establishing twenty mosques and community centers in its early years. First Muslim organization in Britain to establish cooperative relations with institutions of higher education, particularly addressing multicultural education and Islamic economics. Focus shifted in the 1980s to publishing books and periodicals on Islamic subjects.

Islamic Jihad (Jihad al-Islami). Also called Organization of Islamic Jihad. Lebanese organization founded by members of Hizb Allah in 1982 and used by Hizb Allah for covert operations. Leadership is shared with Hizb Allah to the extent that some prominent leaders of Hizb Allah have claimed Islamic Jihad activities as their own. High profile and great prestige in challenging the United States and the West due to use of violent means, such as bombings and hostage taking. Goal is the establishment of an Islamic state in Lebanon. Support is limited to a segment of the Shii community. Claimed responsibility for the bombing of the U.S. embassy in Lebanon on 18 April 1983 and the bombing of the U.S. Marine Headquarters of Multinational Forces (MNF) and its French contingent there on 23 October 1983. Also responsible for kidnapping of American and European nationals in Lebanon, beginning with the abduction of the acting president of the American University of Beirut in 1982. Hostage taking continued until 1988; the last American hostage was released in 1991. Major patrons are Syria and Iran. Syria has consistently refused to disarm it and uses it to undermine Western influence in Lebanon and to dominate the country politically and militarily. Iran used its influence with Islamic Jihad to create the arms-for-hostages deal central to the Iran-contra affair; it has also used Islamic Jihad to gain a foothold in Lebanon and to exercise significant influence there among Shiis. Islamic Jihad shares organizational links and sometimes coordinates activities with the Palestinian Islamic Jihad organization, but the two are separate organizations.

Islamic Jihad Community See Jihad, al-

Islamic Jihad of Palestine Like HAMAS, operates primarily in Palestine and the occupied territories with the objective of establishing an autonomous Palestinian state, although it is also active in other parts of the Middle East, including Jordan and Lebanon. It was founded in 1979–80 by Palestinian students in Egypt highly influenced by the Islamic revolution in Iran, on one hand, and by the radicalization and militancy of Egyptian Islamic student organizations, on the other. The founders—Fathi Shiqaqi, Abd al-Aziz Odah, and Bashir Musa—were disappointed by the moderation of the Egyptian Muslim Brotherhood and by what they considered neglect by the Egyptian Islamists of the priority that should be given to the Palestinian problem. Islamic Jihad is a much smaller, less organized group of Islamist radicals with closer ties to Iran, which has provided financial assistance. Headquartered in Syria, from which it receives logistical assistance. Unlike HAMAS, it has no network of schools, clinics, or mosques, and focuses entirely on the use of violence and terror. One of Islamic Jihad's founders, Shiqaqi, was killed by Israeli agents in 1995 in Malta. Its current leader, Ramadan Shallah, who had previously lived and worked in Tampa, Florida, now operates in Damascus, Syria.

Islamic Liberation Organization See Jamiah Shabab Sayyidna Muhammad

Islamic Liberation Party See Hizb al-Tahrir al-Islami

Islamic Medical Association Formed in 1967 by the Muslim Student Association to allow Muslim health professionals to meet, exchange information, and provide services to community. Sponsors annual publications and conferences.

Islamic Movement of Uzbekistan (IMU) Begun in 1991 with the collapse of the Soviet Union and organized as the IMU by Tahir Yuldeshev in 1998. Seeks to establish a government based on shariah. Based in Uzbekistan but has branches in other Central Asian countries.

Islamic National Action Front Umbrella political party founded and registered in 1992 in Jordan in preparation for the 1993

Islamic Law

Two terms are used to refer to law in Islam: *shariah* and *fiqh*. *Shariah* refers to God's divine law as contained in the Quran and the sayings and doings of Muhammad (hadith). *Fiqh* refers to the scholarly efforts of jurists (fuqaha) to elaborate the details of shariah through investigation and debate. Muslims understand shariah to be an unchanging revelation, while fiqh, as a human endeavor, is open to debate, reinterpretation, and change.

Scholars and jurists developed the law by combining knowledge of the Quran, hadith, and analogical reasoning with local practice. Beginning in the mid-eighth century, the major Sunni schools of legal thought (madhhabs)—Hanafi, Maliki, Shafii, and Hanbali—and the Twelver Shii Jafari madhhab emerged. Other minor and short-lived schools also developed.

Sunnis and Shiis differed in their understanding of who held the power to interpret shariah. For Sunnis, the scholars had this right, as delegated by the actual ruler. Shiis initially believed that only an imam (in this case, a descendant of Muhammad) could interpret shariah because the imam, like Muhammad, was believed to be infallible. When the line of appropriate descendants ended, this tradition was reinterpreted to grant judicial authority to the fuqaha as the imam's representatives. In addition to the Quran and hadith of Muhammad, Shiis also use the rulings of the imams. Ijma, or consensus, is admitted only if it includes the infallible imam's opinion.

There are two types of fiqh literature: that dealing with usul al-fiqh (roots) and that dealing with furu al-fiqh (branches). Usul al-fiqh explores the four sources of the law—the Quran, hadith, consensus (ijma), and analogical reasoning (qiyas)—to provide structures for interpreting revelation. The Quran and hadith are considered to be equal in authority, although the Quran, as God's word, is superior in its nature and origins. Other issues include the principles of abrogation (naskh); the application, ramifications, and limitations of analogical argument; and the value and limits of consensus. This whole set of interpretative structures is brought together in the idea of ijtihad, or independent reasoning, which both recognizes and encourages a variety of interpretations on all but the fundamental structures of the law. Only those with sufficient educational background in the sources of the law are qualified to practice ijtihad.

Education in fiqh was a critical part of Islamic education from the tenth century forward. It provided training in systematic thought and controlled argument, serving the needs of the merchant classes and governing bureaucracies. In the modern period, exclusive training in the traditional Islamic sciences has become less relevant as legal education has been reconstituted along European lines and the jurisdiction of religious courts has been restricted or eliminated.

Furu literature, both legal manuals and collections of cases, discusses rules for rituals (ibadat) and social relations (muamalat). Ritual topics include purity, prayers, alms (zakah), pilgrimage, fasting, and jihad. Social relations topics include marriage, divorce, inheritance, buying, selling, lending, hiring, gifts, testamentary bequests, agency, deposit, crimes, torts, penalties, compensations for injury, judicial practice and procedure, rules relating to slaves, land ownership, land holding, contractual partnerships, slaughter of animals for food, and oaths and their effects. There are five categories of actions in furu literature: mandatory, recommended, permitted, abhorred, and prohibited.

Historically, there were two types of court systems: the qadi (judge) court, responsible for family law (marriage, divorce, inheritance, testamentary bequests), administration of charitable endowments (waqf) and the property of orphans, and

(continued)

Islamic Law (continued)

overseeing contracts and civil disputes, and the mazalim, a supplemental court system that administered criminal law and investigated complaints against government officials. Interpretation of fiqh was carried out on an informal level by muftis who produced fatwas (responses to legal questions). A mufti's rulings could be given to individuals, qadis, and/or agents of government, and could either legitimize policies or restrict their practical effect. Muftis typically remained outside the official government bureaucracy.

In the nineteenth and twentieth centuries, impetus for reform has come both from within the Islamic tradition itself, as specialists in Islamic law have sought to incorporate changing attitudes and social needs into law, and from without, as political leaders have imposed modernization programs. Many Sunni Muslim administrators and reformers felt that Islamic law ought to be practical and resemble Western codes. Some reformers advocated disregarding school traditions and reinterpreting ijtihad to create modern Muslim administrative and institutional forms. Most twentieth-century Islamic legal reform efforts have focused on personal status matters.

elections. Composed largely of members of the Muslim Brotherhood; various mainstream independent Islamist individuals and political groups participated initially (constituting approximately 15 percent of the consultative committee), but most have since resigned. Registration under another name permits the Muslim Brotherhood to continue to receive funding from and maintain ties with political parties outside Jordan. Internal divisions and factionalism have rendered its influence minimal, and it has not performed well in elections. It is opposed to the Jordanian government's participation in the Palestinian-Israeli peace negotiations.

Islamic Party (Afghanistan) See Hizb-i Islami (Afghanistan)

Islamic Party (Malaysia) See Partai Islam Se-Malaysia (PAS)

Islamic Party (South Africa) South African political party formed by Muslims who chose not to follow the Muslim Front founded in 1992 after formulation of Religious Charter by South African chapter of World Conference on Religion and Peace. Has not won any seats in the national assembly. Working to develop a Muslim South African political identity.

Islamic Propagation Centre International See Deedat, Ahmad

Islamic Renaissance Party Islamic revivalist party founded in the former Soviet Union in 1990. Fundamental goals are the spiritual revival, economic freedom, and political and legal awakening of Muslims with the aim of activating the basics of the Quran and Sunnah in daily living. Present in all republics of the former Soviet Union, although banned in Uzbekistan and Tajikistan.

Islamic Republican Party Founded in Iran in 1979 to mobilize the traditional and reactionary forces of Iranian society. Approved by Ayatollah Khomeini. Key founding members were among Khomeini's top clerical loyalists. Initial secretary general was Muhammad Bihishti. Organized rallies and demonstrations against other groups, advocated purges of government institutions and an overhaul of state bureaucracy, pushed for the execution of officials of the previous regime, and ordered confiscation of their property and takeover of some sectors of the Iranian economy. Played an important role in the seizure of the American embassy in Tehran in 1979. Headquarters were bombed in 1981, resulting in the deaths of many leaders. Internal factionalism led to its official dissolution in 1987.

Islamic Research Institute Founded in Pakistan in 1960. Merged with the International

Islamic University in Islamabad in 1980 and became its research wing. Responsible for interpreting the teachings of Islam within the context of the intellectual and scientific progress of the modern world. Directed from 1962 to 1968 by Fazlur Rahman, who noted the initial difficulties of attempting to fuse Western academic methods with Islamic content, since students and scholars in Pakistan were not trained in both. Its scholars have produced works of both sincere faith and vigorous scholarship (including books and critical editions of classical texts), continuing the modernist effort to define the meaning of Islamic experience in the modern world.

Islamic Revolution *See* Iranian Revolution of 1979

Islamic Salvation Front Algerian Islamist party (Front Islamique du Salut, FIS). Founded in 1989 by Abbasi Madani, Ali Bel Hadj, and al-Hashimi Sahnuni, the FIS eschewed democratic structures; Bel Hajj and Sahnuni in particular openly opposed democracy and the national constitution. FIS holds that the religious scholar alone is permitted to interpret religion and law and provide political leadership. Equality, expressed in coeducation, gender mixing at the workplace, and universal national citizenship rights, is the evil through which the West seeks to destroy Islam and maintain world dominance. The overwhelmingly popular party was poised to win the 1992 elections when the National Liberation Army (ALN) staged a coup d'etat and banned the FIS (April 1992); thousands of its members were sent to detention camps in the Sahara. After offering an amnesty in 1999, President Abdelaziz Bouteflika secured the disbanding of the Islamic Salvation Army (AIS), the armed wing of the FIS.

Islamic Society *See* Jamaah al-Islamiyyah, al-

Islamic Society of North America Formed in 1982 as an umbrella organization for several Muslim professional groups originating in the Muslim Student Association, including the Association of Muslim Social Scientists, the Association of Muslim Scientists and Engineers, and the Islamic Medical Association. Various Muslim communities and mosques have also affiliated themselves with the society. Headquartered in Plainfield, Indiana, the society includes the following units: Islamic Teaching Center, Islamic Schools Department, Membership and Field Services Department, Convention and Audiovisual Department, and Publications Department. Its policy-making bodies are the Consultative Council and Executive Council. The society has a membership and support base of about four hundred thousand, and the leadership is drawn primarily from Muslim immigrant communities, although the number of native-born American Muslims is growing.

Islamic Society of Students *See* Islami Jamiat Tulaba

Islamic State Modern ideological position associated with political Islam. In classical theory, the Islamic concept of state is based on the principles of group/community, justice, and leadership. The legitimacy of the ruler is derived from principles of shura (consultation), aqd (ruled-ruler contract), and bayah (oath of allegiance). The caliph acts as the guardian of the community and faith, religious scholars give religio-legal advice, and judges settle disputes according to religious laws. Obedience to ruler and the necessity of avoiding civil strife are emphasized. The modern concept of the Islamic state emerged as a reaction to the 1924 abolition of the caliphate in Turkey. In Pakistan, Abu al-Ala Mawdudi sought an Islamic, rather than Muslim, state, recognizing God, rather than people or law, as sovereign; he emphasized that Muslims are defined by active involvement in enforcing an Islamic moral order on the legislative, political, and economic affairs of society. Hasan al-Banna and the Muslim Brotherhood also claimed that religion and government are inherently part of Islam. Sayyid Qutb taught that an Islamic order must be established prior to worrying about detailed laws and systems of government, inspiring militant Islamic movements in the Arab world. Shiis, as exemplified by Ayatollah Khomeini of Iran, emphasize the special quality of leadership in establishing a pious government, requiring that the leadership come under vilayat-i faqih (rule of the jurist). Other important signs of the Islamic nature of the state in the modern era include implementation of Islamic law, including hudud punishments, and a prohibition against charging or paying interest. Islamists claim that the concept of an Islamic state is unambiguously enshrined in religious texts, but forms of Islamic governments vary widely.

Islamic Tendency Movement *See* Hizb al-Nahdah (Tunisia)

Islamic Unity Movement *See* Harakat al-Tawhid al-Islami

Islamist Term used to describe an Islamic political or social activist. Coined in preference to the more common term "Islamic fundamentalist." Islamists (al-Islamiyyun) are committed to implementation of their ideological vision of Islam in the state and/or society. Their position is often seen as a critique of the establishment and status quo. Most belong to Islamic organizations or social movements (al-harakat al-Islamiyyah). *See also* Fundamentalism

Islamization of Knowledge *See* International Institute of Islamic Thought

Ismah Refers to the inerrancy of prophets elaborated in the classical creeds of Islam. Reflected in their fidelity to divine commands, veracity in respecting what God gave them to communicate, sagacity in understanding its meaning, and transmission of the message itself. Shiis consider their imams to be infallible as well in interpreting the Quran and formulating juristic rulings.

Ismail *See* Ishmael

Ismailis A major Shii Muslim community. Currently number several million and are scattered as Muslim minorities in some twenty-five countries of Asia, the Middle East, Africa, Europe, and North America.

Named after Ismail, the eldest son of Imam Jafar al-Sadiq (d. 765), in whose progeny they have recognized a continuous line of Alid imams, they have had a complex history dating to the middle of the eighth century. Elaborated specific literary and intellectual traditions based on a fundamental distinction between the exoteric (zahir) and esoteric (batin) aspects of religious scriptures and prescriptions, and made important contributions to Islamic civilization, especially during the Fatimid period of their history, when they possessed an important state over which the Ismaili imams ruled as Fatimid caliphs. In the course of their long history, the Ismailis have been subdivided into a number of major branches and minor groupings. Today the Nizaris, who recognize the Aga Khan as their imam, and the Daudis, belonging to the Mustali-Tayyibi branch, who have acknowledged a line of dais in the absence of their imams, represent the two main Ismaili communities. The Nizari and Mustali-Tayyibi Ismailis of South Asian origins have been more commonly designated, respectively, as Khojas and Bohras. *See also* Aga Khan; Bohras; Khojas; Nizaris; Qaramita

Isnad Chain of authority. Refers to the line of transmitters of a particular saying or doctrine, particularly with respect to hadith. Developed as a science in hadith study, since the chain of transmitters indicates the authority of given hadith. Sunnis and Shiis have different isnad. Sufis also use term to refer to the chain of mystical initiation by renowned spiritual masters. *See also* Hadith

Istanbul Capital of the Ottoman Empire from 1453 to 1923, now the largest city of the Turkish Republic. Called Byzantium in antiquity, then Constantinople, it is strategically situated on the Bosporus, partly in Asia and partly in Europe. Istanbul is a cosmopolitan metropolis with rich architectural remains, including Ottoman imperial palaces and the splendid Aya Sofia mosque.

Istighfar Asking forgiveness. The Quran enjoins believers to earnestly seek God's forgiveness in order to achieve paradise in the afterlife. Contemporary reformists and revivalists maintain that renewed commitment to faith is required after requesting forgiveness, as a sign of the belief that forgiveness has been granted. In Sufi practice, repeating the formula "I ask forgiveness of God" is an important part of the dhikr ritual; the number of repetitions varies from order to order.

Istihsan Juristic preference. Refers to the principle that permits exceptions to strict and/or literal legal reasoning in favor of the public interest (maslahah). Guides decision making in cases where there are several potential outcomes. Allows jurists to abandon a strong precedent for a weaker precedent in the interests of justice. Prominent in the Hanafi school of Islamic law, but rejected by the Shafii school. Demonstrates the potential for multiple interpretations of texts and analogies based on context, revealed texts, necessity, and consensus (ijma). Particularly favored in cases where following qiyas (analogical reasoning) would lead to hardship for the believer, since the Quran and Sunnah instruct that hardship should be avoided or alleviated. Modified version used by modern reformers as a principle for reforming Islamic law.

Istiqlal Party See Hizb al-Istiqlal

Istishab Islamic legal term for the presumption of continuity, where a situation existing previously is presumed to be continuing at present until the contrary is proven. Typical examples are the presumption that a sixth daily prayer is not mandatory, since texts require only five, and that an inheritance cannot be claimed from a missing person until evidence is presented that he or she is dead. Accordingly, a person is presumed to be free from liability until the contrary is proven.

Istislah Public interest. Regarded as the object and purpose of Islamic law. Ibn Hanbal used this principle to seek the best solution in order to serve the general interest of the

Muslim community. Use is limited to necessity and specific circumstances, and often requires the reinterpretation of relevant Quranic verses, hadith, and fiqh materials. Permitted only in cases that are not related to religious observances, that involve necessities as opposed to luxuries, and in which its application does not contradict the principles of shariah. Not recognized by the Shafii school due to concerns about the possibility of reliance on unrestricted subjective human opinions and because public interests vary according to context and time. Particularly useful in modern cases for which there is no exact historical precedent, such as blood transfusions and organ transplants. Recognizes the sanctity of human life and enjoins human beings to take action against suffering and injustice.

Ithna Asharis Also known as Twelvers, since they recognize twelve imams, and Imamis, due to their belief in the necessity of an imam for establishment of an ideal Muslim community. Largest subdivision within Shii Islam. See also Shii Islam

Ittihad See Niqabah

Ittihad al-Islami, al- See Somalia, Islam in

Ittihad-i Muhammadi Cemiyeti Muhammadan Union, political and religious organization founded by Hafiz Dervis Vahdeti, a Naqshbandi Sufi from Cyprus, via the newspaper Volkan in 1909. Known for its role in the insurrection of April 1909 in Istanbul, which aimed to destroy the Committee of Union and Progress (CUP). It called for Islamic unity as the basis of the Ottoman state and opposed the reforms envisaged by the constitutional regime. The insurrection was crushed, the Ittihad was proscribed, and some of its leaders, including Vahdeti, were hanged. The Ittihad and events of 1909 have come to symbolize religious reaction in Turkish political life.

Izzah See Honor

Jabarti, Abd al-Rahman al- (d. 1826) Last of the traditional Egyptian Muslim historiographers. Witnessed and wrote about the self-destruction of the Mamluk regime in the eighteenth century, the shock of French occupation (1798–1801), and the changes implemented by Muhammad Ali. Viewed Napoleon's invasion as a reversal of natural order and as a clash between Christianity and Islam. Wrote within the chronicle/biographical dictionary framework used by classical historians.

Jabir ibn Hayyan, Abu Musa (d. ca. 815) Muslim alchemist. Synthesized cosmological and scientific ideas, including the Neoplatonic theory of emanation of the world and depiction of the cosmos as a hierarchy of concentric spheres, the Pythagorean concept of cosmic harmony arising from qualitative or symbolic properties of numbers, the Chinese magic square and numerical symbolism, and the Hermetic science of alchemical and astrological symbolism. Known as the father of Arab chemistry.

Jabiri, Muhammad Abid al- (b. 1936) Moroccan intellectual, writer, and professor of Arab and Islamic philosophy. Wrote over a dozen books and numerous articles focusing on contemporary Arab thought, education, sociology, and Arab and Islamic philosophy. Contributed a fresh contextual analysis of Ibn Khaldun's ideas. Views Arab and Islamic philosophy as having evolved in relation to other philosophies, particularly Greek, which Muslim philosophers used for ideological objectives to reconcile reason and text, religion and philosophy, the temporal and spiritual. Critical of contemporary Arab thought for being ahistorical and unable to reconcile the dichotomy of traditions and modernity.

Jabr Destiny. The Quran is not decisive on the question of free will and predestination.

Many passages uphold the former and many passages uphold the latter. The Quran is uncompromising, however, on the absolute power of God, without whose permission or creative act nothing at all occurs. Early Islamic theology developed several distinct understandings of destiny. The Qadari movement upheld the power of the individual; the Murjia tended to deemphasize the efficacy of human volition. Later discussions between Mutazili and Ashari theologians further refined the discourse to such a degree that it is difficult to determine from the theological works themselves just where the will of God ends and the will of the human being begins. Muslims believe that human beings are morally and ethically responsible for their actions but are utterly dependent upon God for the ability and power to act.

Jabriyyah Compulsionists. Name given to early Muslim theologians who denied human freedom of will. They held that all human acts occur under the compulsion of divine power. This doctrine was later upheld, with refinements, by the dominant Ashari school of theology. *See also* Jabr

Jacob Arabic *Yaqub*. Mentioned in the Quran sixteen times, as a righteous man, servant of God, son of Isaac, and grandson of Abraham. Passed Islam down to his sons, as Abraham had to his sons. Jews consider him a great Jewish patriarch, but the Quran depicts him as a Muslim patriarch.

Jadd al-Haqq Ali Jadd al-Haqq *See* Gadd al-Haqq

Jadidism Nineteenth- and early-twentieth-century Russian Muslim intellectual movement, inspired by Ismail Bey Gasprinksi, that developed in response to colonial hegemony and the modern age. Sought to reform education, raise the quality of life for Muslims, improve their economic and technical competitiveness, and restore something of the power, wealth, and dignity gradually lost over the previous decades and centuries. Began with Sufi brotherhoods stressing the inner awakening and moral reformation of the individual, and intellecuals reassessing the accepted traditions of Islamic civiliation. Both promoted renewal and a better future by authenticating and implementing fundamental traditions of the early Muslim community. Sought to empower women and grant them a more central status and a greater role in society.

Jafari: Shii Legal Thought and Jurisprudence Named after the sixth imam (in this case, descendant of Muhammad through the appropriate line), Jafar al-Sadiq (d. 748). Recognizes four sources of Islamic law: the Quran, the Sunnah (including traditions reported by the Prophet and the imams), consensus (which must include the Prophet's or an infallible imam's opinion to establish its validity), and human reason. Human reason is capable of inferring categorical judgments drawn from both pure and practical reason. Whatever is judged necessary by reason is also judged necessary by revelation. This correlation between reason and revelation has allowed Shii jurists to derive religious rulings on many issues not covered in normative sources such as the Quran and Sunnah. Since 1959 the Jafari school of jurisprudence has been afforded the status of "fifth school" along with the four Sunni schools by Azhar University in Cairo. The other two legal schools that share the Jafari origin are the Zaydi and the Mustali Fatimid Ismaili jurisprudences. These two are closer to Sunnism in their derivation of religious practice.

Jafr See Ilm al-Huruf

Jahangir (r. 1605–27) Second great Mughal emperor. Continued his father Akbar's cultural and religious policies, yet the empire's overextended foundations began to weaken due to rising administrative and military expenses. His favorite wife, Nur Jahan, exercised increasing control as he became more debilitated by alcohol and opium abuse. He is renowned as a patron of miniature painting.

Jahannum See Hell

Jahiliyyah Pre-Islamic period, or "ignorance" of monotheism and divine law. In current use, refers to secular modernity, for example in the work of Abu al-Ala Mawdudi, who viewed modernity as the "new jahiliyyah." Sayyid Qutb interpreted jahiliyyah as the domination of humans over humans, rather than submission of humans to God. The term denotes any government system, ideology, or institution based on values other than those referring to God. To correct this situation, such thinkers propose the implementation of Islamic law, values, and principles. Radical groups justify militant actions against secular regimes in terms of jihad against jahiliyyah.

Jahiz, Abu Uthman Amr ibn Bahr ibn Mahbub al- (d. 868) Master of Arabic literature (adab); considered the finest prose writer in Arabic letters. Adapted and edited major works of classical Arabic and Persian literature to establish a common culture for Arabs and Arabic-speaking Persians. Believed nature offered didactic lessons about the world of reason and God's existence; this reflects the Mutazili influence on his thought. Believed in Islam as the inheritor of the best of world civilizations' thought and accomplishments, and thus held that true Islam entails a spirit of open-mindedness in seeking wisdom from all potential sources; the political implications of this led him to support the Abbasid caliphate. Wrote the *Book of Misers* as a source of both entertainment and moral education; this book is still a critical component of children's literature in the contemporary Arab world.

Jalut See Goliath

Jama Gathering or all-comprehensiveness. One of the stages of spiritual development in Sufism, contrasted with separation (farq). Designates the perception of God's oneness, or seeing all multiplicity brought together in the divine presence. In later Sufism, jama is also discussed as the specific characteristic of the divine image, which is the human being.

Jamaah al-Islamiyyah, al- Islamic Society. Major Sunni organization founded in the early 1960s in Tripoli, Lebanon, as an off-shoot of the Muslim Brotherhood, although it quickly spread to other cities. Led by lay-people. Expanded its base of support after the 1982 Israeli invasion of Lebanon. Currently led by Shaykh Fathi Yakan. Major Sunni Islamist force in Lebanese electoral politics of the early 1990s. Enjoys a broader base of support than more militant movements supporting Islamic revolution. Yakan was elected in Tripoli in 1992, breaking the monopoly of old families over local politics.

Jamaat al-Jihad See Jihad, al-

Jamaat al-Muslimin (Egypt) See Jamaat al-Takfir wa'l-Hijrah

Jamaat al-Muslimin (Trinidad) Islamic group in Trinidad. Led by Yasin Abu Bakr, a former police officer, advocating justice for the poor and reformation of Muslim religious life in Trinidad. It drew support from poor urban blacks rather than established Syrian and South Asian Muslims. A land dispute in the 1980s escalated, with government takeover of the land and dismissal of legal appeals. The group occupied the television station and parliament, proclaiming a program of reform in July 1990; eventually the group surrendered and its leaders were jailed. The group remained active and was operating security and other companies when its members received amnesty in 1995–96. See also Abu Bakr, Yasin

Jamaat al-Takfir wa'l-Hijrah Group of radical Muslims based in Cairo who abducted and assassinated Shaykh Muhammad Husayn al-Dhahabi, former Egyptian minister of awqaf (religious endowments) and Azhar

affairs, in July 1977. Name was assigned by Egyptian media. Group calls itself Jamaat al-Muslimin, or Society of Muslims. Leader was Shukri Ahmad Mustafa (d. 1978), who taught that all present societies are un-Islamic and that only members of his group were true Muslims. Anyone seeking to leave the movement was declared an enemy of God and threatened with death for apostasy and desertion. The group claimed that the classical system of Islamic law must be rejected because it is not the word of God but only the work of humans; it also claimed to rely solely on the Quran. Its leader was executed in 1978.

Jamaat Ansar al-Sunnah See Mali, Islam in

Jamaat-i Islami Pakistani Islamic revivalist party founded by Mawlana Abu al-Ala Mawdudi in 1941 in pre-partition India. The party encourages the reformation of society through education and conversion rather than by coercion. Its political agenda was premised on a program of training the vanguard "Islamic elite" to oversee the revival of Islam on the national level and mobilize the masses using religious symbols and ideals. Its political activism in the 1940s and 1950s culminated in an open confrontation with the government over the role of religion in politics, and it began direct participation in politics via elections in 1951. The party tried to undermine Zulfikar Ali Bhutto's regime by appealing to religious sentiments, and under the subsequent regime of General Zia-ul-Haq it became a political and ideological force in government, occupying important government offices, including cabinet posts, and playing a direct role in the Islamization of the country (introduction of traditional Islamic law) and the articulation of state policy, although it has never achieved success in elections. The party was rendered politically vulnerable when it was perceived to have been co-opted by the regime, and as Zia fell out of favor with the masses, so did the party. Its social and cultural influence is based on its organizational structure and its ability to manipulate the religious factor in Pakistan's political balance; it developed ties with students and, consequently, with the bureaucracy and the military. The party played an important role in the Afghan resistance in the 1980s and remains active in the struggle for the freedom of Kashmir from India. It has developed extensive contacts in the Islamic revivalist movements in the Middle East. *See also* Islami Jamiat Tulaba

Jamaat-i Islami of Bangladesh A major Islamic movement of Bangladesh that was part of the Pakistani party Jamaat-i Islami until 1971, when East Pakistan seceded to become independent Bangladesh. It supported a united Pakistan during the 1971 civil war and, as a consequence, was banned by the Awami League government after Bangladesh became independent. In 1975, after the assassination of Shaykh Mujibur Rahman, it was once again allowed to operate. Under the leadership of Gholam Azam, the party rose from a pariah group to the third largest political party in Bangladesh. Currently headed by Mawlana Motiur Rahman Nizami, a former president of Islami Jamiat Tulaba of Pakistan. The party won seventeen seats in the parliamentary elections of September 2001 and, for the first time, was offered two cabinet positions in Khaleda Zia's government. Organized into 6,580 administrative units throughout Bangladesh, the Jamaat-i Islami of Bangladesh has dominated student politics on several important university campuses and has a considerable following among madrasa students as well as teachers and other professionals. Like its counterpart in Pakistan, the Jamaat-i Islami Bangladesh strives for the establishment of an Islamic state through educational work, social reform, and democratic elections.

Jamaat-i Islami of India The Indian branch of the Jamaat-i Islami, whose headquarters moved to Pakistan at partition (1947). It avoids electoral participation because Muslims are a minority, but the Pakistani party puts up candidates, although with little success. It enjoys influence out of proportion to its numbers because of disciplined organization, welfare work, its reputation for honesty, and street power.

Jamarah *See* Hajj

Jamatul Nasril Islam Also known as JNI and the Society for the Victory of Islam. An organization established in Nigeria in 1962 to provide a vehicle for transcending divisions among Muslims in Nigeria. The sardauna of Sokoto, Ahmadu Bello, supported its creation on the advice of Abubakar Gumi, an influential Islamic renewal advocate. It has survived the turmoil of Nigerian politics, acting as a bridge between the influential Sufi orders in northern Nigeria and the activist anti-Sufi movement led by Gumi. In a time of tensions within the Muslim community in 1988–90, the mediation of the JNI made possible a formal reconciliation of the major Muslim groups.

Jameelah, Maryam (b. 1934) Born Margaret Marcus in the United States. Converted from Judaism to Islam in 1961. Became a spokesperson for Islam, defending Muslim beliefs against Western criticism and championing Muslim causes. Corresponded with Sayyid Abu al-Ala Mawdudi from 1960 to 1962 and moved to Pakistan in 1962 at his invitation. Has written a number of books systematically outlining Jamaat-i Islami's ideology and serves as one of its chief ideologues, although she has never formally joined the party. Focuses in her written works on the debate between Islam and the West, offering a revivalist critique of Christianity, Judaism, secular Western thought, and Islamic modernism.

Jamia Millia Islamiyyah University in Delhi. Started as a rival to the Aligarh Muslim University by Zakir Husain and Muslim supporters of the Congress Party in 1917. Though it began as an Islamic university, its curriculum is now shaped by the government and largely caters to secular curricula.

Jamiah Muslim Missionary Society of Singapore. Singaporean Islamic association founded in 1931 by Moulana Abdul Aleem Siddiqui al-Qaderi, a missionary from India, together with religious leaders in Singapore and Malaya. Until 1965 it was known as the All-Malaya Muslim Missionary Society. Its activities focus on propagating Islam through religious classes, public lectures, and publications. The group currently has a membership of more than twenty-four thousand.

Jamiah Shabab Sayyidna Muhammad Also known as Society of Muhammad's Youth and Islamic Liberation Organization. Founded in Egypt in the 1970s by Salih Sirriyyah. Seized the Military Engineering College in Cairo in 1974 as part of an unsuccessful plan to assassinate President Sadat; its leaders were executed and adherents imprisoned, and as a result many members went underground and/or joined other militant movements. An earlier group carrying the same name was founded in 1939 in Egypt by Mustafa al-Sibai as an offshoot of the Muslim Brotherhood.

Jamiah-yi Ruhaniyat-i Mubariz Society of Militant Clergy. Iranian movement that sought to maintain the momentum of the 1963 uprising led by Ayatollah Khomeini. Most important organization involved in protests against the shah, Israel, and the United States, particularly in light of Khomeini's subsequent exile. Other important members included Murtaza Mutahhari (d. 1979).

Jamiat al-Dawah al-Islamiyyah *See* Islamic Call Society

Jamiat al-Dawah wa'l-Irshad Society of Call and Guidance. Society founded by Muhammad Rashid Rida in 1911 in Egypt to serve as the cornerstone of Ottoman pan-Islamic activities. Revived in 1931 at the General Islamic Congress of Jerusalem as a missionary organization to propagate Islam outside of the Muslim community as well as within it.

Jamiat al-Khairiyyat al-Islamiyyah Also known as Amaliyyah Foundation. Lebanese Shii foundation established in 1923 to finance a range of welfare activities and religious events, particularly ecumenical commemorations of the martyrdom of Husayn. Its most far-reaching program has been support of a number of schools, particularly in village settings where only Quranic schools existed previously.

Jamiat al-Shubban al-Muslimin A pan-Islamic Egyptian political association founded in 1927 in Cairo. Formed on the model of the YMCA, and often referred to as the Young Men's Muslim Association (YMMA), it was created following the nationalist revolution of 1919 as a social, cultural, and religious organization for Egyptian youth.

Jamiat-i Islami (Afghanistan) Islamic Society. Founded in 1967 by Burhanuddin Rabbani. Ethnically Tajik government officially recognized by most governments even after the Taliban took control of Afghanistan. Major figures included the official leader of the Northern Alliance, ousted president Burhanuddin Rabbani, and its military leader, General Muhammad Fahim Khan. Primarily composed of northern (non-Pashtun) membership. Supported by Pakistan and Arab states, it operated mainly in the Panjsher Valley under commanders such as Ahmad Shah Masud, who commanded a force of twenty thousand fighters.

Jamiatul Ulama-i Ahl-i Hadith Society of the Ulama of the People of the Hadith. Pakistani extreme right-wing political party of ulama. Preaches uncompromising monotheism, rejects all notions of intercession by spiritual mentors, and condemns visitation of Sufi shrines as polytheism. Only ulama organization that rejects democracy as antithetical to Islam and advocates autocratic rule by a "pious ruler" under the guidance of Islamic law. Places heavy emphasis on hadith as source of revelation and Islamic law. Similar in outlook to Saudi Arabian Wahhabi movement.

Jamiatul Ulama-i Hind Association of Indian Ulama. Established in New Delhi at the Khilafat Movement conference (1919). Supported a united India and opposed partition into India and Pakistan. Many of its members were associated with the Deoband school. Its main contribution to Indo-Muslim thought is the theory of composite nationalism, in which nations can be created by various factors such as religion, race, homeland, and language. According to this theory, India is a nation despite its religious diversity. The organization is a rare historical case in which an association of traditional Muslim religious scholars has bestowed legitimacy upon the policies of a non-Muslim, secular government, born out of conflict with the generally acknowledged leadership of their own community.

Jamiatul Ulama-i Islam Society of Muslim Ulama (JUI) of Pakistan. Origins lie in the Deoband movement in pre-partition India and with the Jamiatul Ulama-i Hind. Originally opposed to British imperialism, it supported the aims and policies of the Indian National Congress and opposed the Muslim League's struggle for an independent Pakistan. Had limited political significance following India's partition in 1947. Was revived by Mawlana Mufti Mahmud, who opposed President Ayub Khan's modernizing policies. Regarded as uncompromisingly rigid and insisting on the strict enforcement of traditional Islamic law. Currently divided into two factions, that of Mawlana Fazlur Rahman and that of Sami-ul-Haq. Controls the largest number of madrasas in Pakistan. Associated with the rise of the Taliban version of Islam in Afghanistan and Pakistan.

Jamiatul Ulama-i Pakistan Islamic political party in Pakistan; also known as JUP. Established in Karachi in 1948, the JUP follows the Barelwi school of Islamic thought, which emerged to counter the influences of the Deobandis. Emphasizes populist and devotional practices of religion. Clashes over party decisions have divided the JUP into factions, and since 1986 the JUP has lost much of its support. The two main factions are headed by Shah Ahmad Noorani and Abdussahar Niazi. Its students' wing has a considerable following in Barelwi madrasas.

Jamiyyah In modern Arabic, jamiyyah refers to an assembly, society, or association, and can be used to describe a broad range of literary, charitable, religious, and political groups and international organizations (e.g., Jamiat al-Umam, the League of Nations; Jamiat al-Ikhwan al-Muslimin, the Muslim Brotherhood, etc.). In Persian and Urdu, the term *anjuman* is often the functional equivalent of the Arabic jamiyyah and likewise refers to religio-political, educational, and literary associations. In Arabic-speaking societies, the term *hizb* has often been used to designate a political party or organization, with the more fluid term jamiyyah referring to a wider variety of voluntary associations and fora.

Janabah A state of major ritual impurity caused by any contact with semen. The state of janabah renders Muslims unfit for the performance of ritual duties, such as prayer, until they purify themselves through complete ablution (ghusl).

Janaza Corpse; bier; funeral. *See also* Funerary Rites

Janissaries From the Turkish *yeni cheri*, "new troops." An elite slave infantry established in the fourteenth-century Ottoman Empire. A quadrennial collection (devshirme) selected young boys from conquered regions, particularly the Christian Balkans. They received a thorough military education, learned Turkish, and assumed Muslim names and identities. The Sultan could depend on their loyalty, as disobedience meant summary execution while obedience resulted in enormous personal power and tax-exempt status. In the mid-seventeenth century the Ottoman government weakened, and control of the outlying regions increasingly fell into Janissary hands. Sultan Mahmud II, relying on the power of his newly formed military and public contempt for Janissary tyranny, massacred most of the Janissaries in 1826 and drove the remainder from the provinces.

Jannah *See* Heaven

JAS *See* Mali, Islam in

Jawzi, Bandali al- (d. 1942) Palestinian intellectual. Wrote on the Arabic language and

Islamic history. Best known for the 1928 work *Min tarikh al-harakat al-fikriyyah fil-Islam* (The history of intellectual movements in Islam), the first Marxist interpretation of the history and development of Islamic thought, which introduced the critique of Orientalism and reevaluated classical Muslim heresiography in terms of historical circumstances.

Jaysh Army, armed forces.

Jayshi-i Muhammad Army of Muhammad. Islamist militant separatist group whose main objective is to unite Kashmir with Pakistan. Emerged in Pakistan in February 2000 under the leadership of Masood Azhar, who was released from Indian detention in 1999 in exchange for 155 hijacked airline passengers in Afghanistan. Based in Peshawar and Mazaffarabad, Pakistan, has generally carried out actions in occupied Kashmir. Suspected to have had close relations with the Taliban and Osama bin Laden. Recently outlawed by the Pakistani government under pressure from the West and neighboring countries to more forcefully combat terrorist activity originating within its borders. Membership consists mostly of Kashmiris, particularly youth, but also Pakistani, Afghan, and Arab veterans who fought the 1980s Soviet occupation of Afghanistan. Politically aligned with the Jamiatul Ulama-i Islam.

Jerusalem Arabic *al-Quds*; the holy. One of Islam's three holiest cities. Muslim armies took Jerusalem from Byzantine control without resistance in 635 and immediately refurbished its chief holy place, the neglected Temple Mount. By 692 the Dome of the Rock mosque had been completed; it is revered as the terminus of Muhammad's Night Journey and the site of Abraham's sacrifice and Solomon's temple. Muslims later allowed Jews to return to the city to pray for the first time since their expulsion by the Romans in 135; the city's history was unremarkable until the Crusades. The Crusaders occupied Jerusalem (1099–1187) until Salah al-Din (Saladin) drove them out. Under the Mamluks, many Sunni religious schools and convents (khanaqahs) that sur-

round the Dome of the Rock were constructed. The Ottomans inherited the city (1517) and continued generous support for it, building the city walls that still stand today. Nineteenth-century Jerusalem hosted numerous European consulates, missionaries, and archaeological teams, all beyond the power of the weakened Ottoman authorities. Jerusalem fell, unharmed, to the Allied forces in 1917; British mandate authorities governed it from 1922 to 1948. The UN plan to partition Palestine between Jews and Arabs assigned Jerusalem to an independent UN trusteeship. When the British withdrew, Jordanians occupied the Old City after joining the Arab war against Israel; it remained under Jordanian control until the 1967 war, when Israelis took it. The whole city has been integrated into the state of Israel, which declared it its "eternal undivided capital"; few countries recognize Jerusalem as the legal capital of Israel, acknowledging its status as disputed territory, in accordance with UN Security Council resolutions 242 and 338. Its status remains among the most difficult issues in Middle East peace negotiations.

Jesus, Son of Mary Mentioned in the Quran twenty-five times, as righteous prophet, messenger to Israel, sign, Spirit from God, and Messiah. The Quran denies the Christian beliefs of the crucifixion and resurrection of Jesus, asserting instead that although he appeared to have been crucified, God actually took Jesus up unto Himself. The Quran declares Jesus human, not God or the son of God, although Muslims believe that Jesus was conceived miraculously (Quran 3:45) and so had no earthly father. Muslims believe that considering Jesus to be God is polytheistic. The Quran places Jesus in the same line of prophethood as Moses and Abraham. For Muslims, Jesus was a great spiritual leader and teacher.

Jews *See* Banu Israil; Judaism and Islam

Jibril *See* Gabriel

Jihad From the Arabic root meaning "to strive," "to exert," "to fight"; exact meaning depends on context. May express a struggle against one's evil inclinations, an exertion to convert unbelievers, or a struggle for the moral betterment of the Islamic community. Today often used without any religious connotation, with a meaning more or less equivalent to the English word *crusade* (as in "a crusade against drugs"). If used in a religious context, the adjective *Islamic* or *holy* is added. Jihad is the only legal warfare in Islam, and it is carefully controlled in Islamic law. It must be called by a duly constituted state authority, it must be preceded by a call to Islam or treaty, noncombatants must not be attacked, and so on. To justify the struggle against their coreligionists, extremists branded them unbelievers for their neglect in adhering to and enforcing a particular interpretation of Islam. Contemporary thinking about jihad offers a wide spectrum of views, including conservatives who look to classical Islamic law on the subject and radicals who promote a violent jihad against Muslim and non-Muslim rulers.

Jihad, al- Jamaat al-Jihad or Islamic Jihad Community. Egyptian Islamic group that assassinated President Anwar Sadat in 1981. Established in the late 1970s by former members of the group Shabab Muhammad, which attempted a coup in 1974. Attracted a following in urban areas and in Upper Egypt. Forged an alliance with the Islamic Community (al-Jamaah al-Islamiyyah) in 1980. Its main ideologue, Muhammad Abd al-Salam Faraj, considered Sadat's regime illegitimate for not implementing Islamic law and jihad as an obligation to establish an Islamic state. By the mid-1980s the group was seriously weakened. In the late 1990s it renounced violence and applied to be recognized as a political party. *See also* Faraj, Muhammad Abd al-Salam

Jihad al-Islami *See* Islamic Jihad

Jilani, Abd al-Qadir al- (d. 1166) Born in Persia. Studied Hanbali jurisprudence in Baghdad. Spent twenty-five years as a wandering ascetic in the deserts of Iraq. Became a popular preacher with his own Sufi school

and center. Served as a Hanbali jurist and part-time mufti. Most universally popular saint and holy man in Islam. Recognized as the patron and founder of the Qadiri order but did not actually propagate any tariqah (order) during his lifetime; the order named after him was developed by his descendants and followers posthumously and has spread throughout the Islamic world. Has a reputation for theological soundness that has led others to claim his work as the basis for their own insights and experiences. *See also* Qadari Tariqah

Jilbab Generic term for women's outer garment (shawl, cloak, wrap) in Arabian sedentary communities before and after the rise of Islam. The Quran (33:59) instructs Muslim women to cloak themselves as a mark of status and as a defensive measure against sexual harrassment in public places.

Jinn Creatures known in popular belief in pre-Islamic Arabia and mentioned numerous times in the Quran, parallel to human beings but made out of fire rather than clay. Believed to be both less virtuous and less physical than humans, but like humans, endowed with the ability to choose between good and evil. In folk religion, jinn are spirits invoked for magical purposes and are often held responsible for miraculous or unusual events and for a wide range of illnesses, which are popularly believed to be caused by an imbalance between internal and external jinn. Healers often speak directly to jinn prior to driving them out of patients.

Jinnah, Mohammad Ali (d. 1948) Also known as Qaid al-Azam (the great leader). First governor-general of Pakistan. A successful Bombay barrister; joined the Indian National Congress in 1906 and the Muslim League in 1913, and was instrumental in drafting the jointly adopted Lucknow Pact (1916). By 1940 had declared India's Muslims a "nation," not a minority; the demand for a separate, single Pakistan became his major focus. Lived long enough to preside over the birth of the new nation, but died before he could establish a secular democracy free of corruption and internal politics. *See also* Pakistan, Islam in

Jizyah Compensation. Poll tax levied on non-Muslims as a form of tribute and in exchange for an exemption from military service, based on Quran 9:29. Sometimes conceived as a graduated head tax in which the rich paid more than the poor and the penniless were exempt; other times, it was strictly applied. If a Muslim leader did not provide his subjects with adequate security, he was obliged to refund the tax; Salah al-Din (Saladin) returned the money to his Christian subjects when he was compelled to withdraw his army from Syria. There is no consensus about its applicability in the modern world.

JNI *See* Jamatul Nasril Islam

Job Arabic *Ayyub*. In the Quran, a righteous man who was greatly afflicted by Satan but who remained faithful to God. God relieved his distress, restored his people to him, and doubled their number as a sign to all who serve God of His grace and mercy. The Quran highlights his patience, faithfulness, and excellent service to God.

John the Baptist Arabic *Yahya ibn Zakariyya*. Son of Zakariyya and Elizabeth. Cousin of Jesus. Born as a blessing from God when his parents were old and barren. As in the Bible, the Quran records God's promise of a son to Zakariyya in response to his prayer for an heir. When Zakariyya asked for a sign, God deprived Zakariyya of speech for three days. The Quran states that John served as a witness to the truth of Jesus' teaching. Described as wise, noble, chaste, a prophet, righteous, devout, and kind to his parents.

Jonah Arabic *Yunus*. In the Quran, a prophet who symbolizes patience and perseverance. Jonah was swallowed by a fish when he tried to run away from God. According to tradition, he carried God's message of impending punishment to the people of Nineveh, who then repented their sins and were saved.

Jordan, Islam in After the Ottoman Empire's defeat by the Allied powers in 1918, the Allies divided the Middle East into spheres of influence, with Transjordan and Palestine under British mandate. Transjordan achieved independence (1946) to become the Hashemite Kingdom of Jordan. Ninety-six percent of Jordan's population is Sunni Muslim; the remaining 4 percent are Christian. Two types of organized Islamic movements exist in Jordan today: the first focuses on political goals, the second on religious revival. Some of the politically oriented parties are legal; the Muslim Brotherhood, registered as a socioreligious philanthropic organization, functions freely, as it openly supports the ruling family. Others, such as the Islamic Liberation Party, Islamic Holy War Party, Hamas, and the Muslim Youth Movement, have no legal status. Sufi orders, the Jamaat al-Tabligh, and the Jamaat al-Sulufiyyah are among Jordan's organized, nonpolitical Islamic groups.

Joseph Arabic *Yusuf*. In the Quran, son of Jacob, interpreter of dreams, and trusted adviser of Pharaoh. Sold into slavery by jealous brothers but forgave them and used his acquired position in Egypt to save them and his father from famine. Is used as an example of generosity, mercy, compassion, and faith in God's control over events in life.

Judaism and Islam Islam has had a long, intertwined relationship with Judaism. Quranic respect for Jews and Judaism is shown in the notion of "people of the book," inspired by the Jews and their tradition. As a protected minority, Jews were often autonomous in their internal communal life while also interacting with the majority culture. Until the early modern period, Muslim-Jewish cultural and intellectual interchanges were significant. In theology, exegesis, philosophy, law, and mysticism, Jews and Muslims contributed to and learned from one another. Harsh treatment, while not unknown, was the exception. Later, the situation of Jews and other minorities generally deteriorated, but this occurred unevenly in different times and places; these developments reflected a relative political and economic decline in parts of the Islamic world. In the modern period, Zionism's emergence, Israel's creation, and the subsequent migration of Jews from Arab lands to Israel all led to a worsening of historic Muslim-Jewish relations.

Judge *See* Hakim

Juma Mosque Built in 1606 in Delhi by the Mughal emperor Shah Jahan. Major center of Muslim political activity in India. Speeches made there typically reflect political crises. In recent years Hindus have claimed that the mosque was built over the site of a Hindu temple and have demanded destruction of the mosque in order to build a new temple.

Junayd, al- Abu al-Qasim ibn Muhammad (d. 910) Early Sufi shaykh who is regarded as the founder of several tariqahs, including Kubrawiyyah and Mawlawiyyah. Known as "master of all the Sufis" and the highest example of "sober" Sufism. Stressed that renunciation and mental struggle were needed to return to a preexisting state in which the human being is a concept in God's mind. Other hallmarks are an emphasis on constant ritual purity and fasting. Taught that the goal of mysticism was not loss of self but the return to daily life transformed by a vision of God through the loss of self and constant remembrance of God's presence. Devoted to the fulfillment of God's will as expressed in the Quran and Sunnah.

Jurisprudence *See* Fiqh

Jurist *See* Faqih

Justice *See* Justice, Concepts of; Justice, Social

Justice, Concepts of The Quranic terms for justice are qist and adl; justice is also implicit in the Quranic terms maruf (the known, the good) and ihsan (doing good). The concept of justice was hotly debated among medieval Islamic legal and theological schools. The debate centered on God's control over human acts. If God determines human actions,

then can He justly punish humans for acting wickedly? Some schools argued that people are in control of their own acts and thereby take full responsibility for their actions. Others state that God creates potentialities and people act in fulfillment of their potentialities. In either case, it is believed that people can justly be held accountable for their actions. The same schools also debated whether concepts such as justice are determinable objectively by reason or exclusively by revelation. A prominent set of scholars argued that the central features of justice are as follows: relationships among people and toward God are reciprocal in nature, and reciprocity should guide all interactions; and process and result ought to equate otherwise dissimilar entities, but because relationships are highly contextual, justice is to be grasped through enactments rather than as a single abstract principle. *See also* Justice, Social

Justice, Social In nineteenth-century Muslim thought, the concept of social justice was a product of two interchangeable factors: prevailing backward social and economic conditions that did not attract the serious attention of the traditional ulama class, and Western domination that neglected to ameliorate the social conditions of the dominated people as a whole. It focused on poverty, indigence, and helplessness among the Muslim population in the context of colonialism. In the twentieth century, the issue became more sharply defined, especially with the extensive migration of peasants from the countryside to urban areas; the Muslim Brotherhood was founded (1928) against the background of endemic social crises in Egyptian and Arab societies. Sayyid Qutb's *Social Justice in Islam* enumerates the following principles: absolute freedom of conscience, complete equality of all people, and the permanent mutual responsibility of society. According to him, justice is not always concerned solely with the interests of the individual; Islam is also against monopoly, usury, corruption, wastefulness, and luxury.

Justice Party Adalet Partisi. Major Turkish political party of center-right 1961–80. Seen as the successor to the outlawed Democratic Party (Demokrat Parti). Emphasized economic development and traditional values. Led until 1964 by Ragip Gumuspala and then for the remainder of its existence by Suleyman Demirel (prime minister 1965–71, 1974–78, and 1979–80). Was a coalition of industrialists, large landholders, small traders, and peasants whose major opposition was the center-left Republican People's Party (Cumhuriet Halk Partisi). Discouraged the membership of Islamists such as Necmettin Erbakan. Political violence and economic crisis forced a miltary coup in 1980 that outlawed all political parties.

Juwayni, Abu al-Maali al- (d. 1085) Famous Iranian Ashari theologian and political philosopher. Teacher of Abu Hamid al-Ghazali (d. 1111). Taught that the sultan or amir was more necessary than the caliph. Proclaimed the amir or sultan responsible for carrying out jihad, appointing officials and judges, and maintaining a standing army. Allowed the appointment of a vizier to administer the state bureaucracy and raise revenues for the army.

Juwayriyya bint al-Harith (d. 670 or 676) Arabian tribal princess, daughter of the chief of Khuzaa. Captured during the Muslim raid on Banu Mustaliq in 627, and although her relatives wished to ransom her, she accepted Islam. The Prophet Muhammad freed her and married her in that same year. At their wedding, the Prophet and his soldiers released a hundred families of her kin from captivity.

K

Kaaba Cube-shaped "House of God" located in Mecca, Saudi Arabia. Focal point of the hajj pilgrimage and a world spiritual center that all Muslims face during prayer. Muslims believe that it was built by Abraham (Ibrahim) and Ishmael (Ismail); some believe Adam built it and Abraham and Ishmael only rebuilt it. Often called the earthly counterpart to God's throne in heaven. Circumambulated seven times during the hajj ritual in imitation of angels circumambulating God's throne. Contains the Black Stone, which pilgrims often try to touch or kiss during circumambulations, believing that it physically absorbs sin; all pilgrims salute the stone as a gesture of their renewed covenant with God. Covered with a cloth called kiswah, which is embroidered with verses from the Quran.

Kabylia Rugged mountainous region east of Algiers, adjacent to the Mediterranean, in Algeria. One of North Africa's most densely populated areas, it is culturally and linguistically unique. Ancient Berber culture, languages, customary laws, social organization, and traditions predominate. Fiercely independent, Kabyles maintained their own political and administrative institutions under the Ottomans (ca. 1525–1830) and were the last stronghold against French colonization (conquered ca. 1847–57). A Kabylian political party that advocates minority rights, a secular state, and a pluralistic society (Socialist Forces Front, or FFS) placed second only to the Islamic Salvation Front (FIS) in the 1992 elections. A 1996 law mandating Arabic as the Algerian national language was met with violent uprisings in Kabylia.

Kafaah Equivalence. Refers to a tradition requiring husband and wife (or wife's family) to be of equal rank in religion, lineage, social status, and means. Of these four, only religion is consistently significant across schools of law, although Muslim men are allowed to marry Jewish or Christian women while Muslim women may marry only Muslim men. Traditional Hanafi law stressed the husband's occupation as critical; premodern Maliki law stressed piety. Kafaah was not crucial in Shafii jurisprudence; Hanbalis emphasized lineage and means. Though not a critical concept in modern Islamic legal discourse, spousal equality is still culturally relevant.

Kaffarah Reparation; expiation from wrongdoing; atonement; penance. To be preceded by remorse for having done wrong or forgotten religious requirements. Consists of self-inflicted punishments of a religious character, which courts are not authorized to enforce. The Quran provides numerous expiations for various sins, including fasting, emancipation of slaves, and donations to charity.

Kafir Unbeliever. First applied to Meccans who refused submission to Islam, the term implies an active rejection of divine revelation. All unbelievers are thought to face eternal damnation in the afterlife. Although there is disagreement about whether Jews and Christians are unbelievers, they have generally received tolerant treatment from Muslim governments. Islamic fundamentalists in the twentieth century applied the term to other Muslims who did not adhere to their strict interpretations of the Quran. *See also* Kufr

Kalam *See* Theology

Kalila wa Dimna An originally Indian allegory narrated by two jackals who tell stories aimed to guide humanity to ethical and moral ways of dealing with a wide range of issues, from parenting to policy making. Ibn al-Muqaffa (d. 759) translated the original Pahlavi manuscript into Arabic.

Kamil, Mustafa (d. 1908) Egyptian lawyer, nationalist, and orator who fought for Egyptian independence from British rule. Called for social and educational reforms and the creation of a national university, organized mass demonstrations, and founded the National Party and its newspaper, *Al-liwa*, which presented a nationalist and Islamic voice.

Kampulan Saudara Baru *See* Muslim Converts' Association of Singapore (Darul Arqam)

Kandhalavi, Muhammad Zakariya (b. 1898) Hadith scholar at the Saharanpur madrasa in India who supported the Tablighi Jamaat movement in India and Pakistan. Wrote seven essays, based on hadith, outlining the basic knowledge of Islam, that are required reading for Tablighi missionaries.

Kanisah Places of worship for non-Muslims, such as Christian churches, Jewish synagogues, or pagan temples. The term has been adopted by minority Christian groups in Muslim countries and appears in church names, Christian writings, and Bible translations.

Kanun *See* Qanun

Karamah (1) Grace. Refers to charismatic gifts or the capacity to perform miracles, as evidenced by the temporary suspension of natural order through divine intervention. Signifies a state of sanctity and confirms validity of the saint (wali) in Sufi circles, encouraging veneration of holy men. Sign of God's favor. Manifestation of possession of barakah (God's blessing). (2) Miracles. Historically, prophets are believed to have performed miracles as evidence of their divine mission. Muslims consider the Quran itself to be a miracle because of the inimitability of its style and language. Miracles are an important part of popular Islam and Sufism. Holy people are believed to possess karamah (the ability to perform miracles) as a sign of God's favor. Tombs of famous ancestors and Sufis masters are often popularly venerated as sites where miraculous help can be attained. Sufi claims to perform miracles are often regarded as suspect by conservatives out of fear that people will come to worship human beings rather than God as performers of miracles.

Karbala One of the holiest cities of Shii Islam, often visited on pilgrimage in Iraq. Derives its fame from the martyrdom of Husayn and his followers there in 680. Sunni Abbasids were concerned about the growing sanctity connected with Husayn's shrine and so destroyed the tomb and prohibited visits there. Later, because of millenarian hopes associated with the site by Shiis, the visitation of Karbala and mourning for Husayn became suspect to Sunni authorities, particularly Wahhabis, who destroyed shrines there in 1801. The shrines have become the center of the spiritual and commercial lives of the city's inhabitants and have served as a place of refuge for those fleeing tyrranical rulers in Iran and Iraq. Many aged pilgrims sojourn there to await death, since they believe it to be one of the gates to paradise, which the Quran promises to the righteous. Shii leaders, particularly Ayatollah Khomeini, have used Karbala as a paradigm of human suffering and emancipation from all kinds of exploitation in changing sociopolitical and religious circumstances.

Kartosuwiryo, Sukarmadji Maridjan (d. 1962) Leader of Darul Islam movement in West Java, Indonesia. Active in the struggle to liberate Java from the Dutch in 1947. Founder of the Suffah Institute in West Java, which combined a traditional Islamic school with a center for political indoctrination and military training, producing a mystical, militant interpretation of Islam. Proposed an Islamic Indonesian state based on the Quran and headed by an elected imam. Refused to accept the 1948 truce between the Dutch and Indonesia. Declared himself imam of the

Islamic provincial government, resulting in his trial and execution for armed revolt.

Kasb In legal terminology, refers to legitimate economic gain in commercial transactions, to be distinguished from illegitimate economic gain (riba, often translated as "usury" or "interest"). In general, legal theorists allow for profit, especially from financial partnerships, under the categories of shirkah (general partnership), qirad (loans), and mudarabah (limited partnership). All of these practices are based on the principle of profit gained from service or shared risk.

Kashani, Abd al-Razzaq (d. 1329) Medieval Sufi leader in Iran under Il Khanid rule (1256–1353). Defender and proponent of the thought of the mystic Ibn al-Arabi (d. 1240) while averting his master's goal of merging with the divinity. Adherent of esoteric (batini) metaphysics. Concerned with issues of predestination and free will, seeking to vindicate individual responsibility.

Kashani, Ayatollah Hajj Sayyid Abol-Qasem (d. 1962) Iranian cleric and nationalist. Political leader during the 1950s movement to nationalize the Iranian oil industry. Saw the separation of religion and politics as a colonial plot. Supported technological modernization, adoption of certain aspects of Western institutions, and political reform. Revived the traditional leadership role of ulama as spokespeople for popular discontent, as apparent in clerical opposition to the government after 1963 and in the developments leading to the 1979 revolution. Emphasized a messianic mission for ulama, which Ayatollah Khomeini expanded into the doctrine of vilayat-i faqih. Most important legacy was the idea of a nonaligned political bloc of all Muslim states, which Khomeini proclaimed as the policy of "neither East nor West."

Kashf Uncovering, revealing (what is hidden). Sufis use this term to refer to their personal effort toward illumination, or "re-moving the veil" from what is hidden, such as the secret or hidden meaning of the Quran, through a mystical approach to revelation and seeking a vision of God as ultimate reality.

Kashmir A disputed territory between India and Pakistan. In 1941, 77 percent of the population was Muslim. Three major political forces dominated: the National Conference, which wanted to join India; the Muslim Conference, which wanted to join an independent state for Muslims; and the Dogra dynasty, which wanted to remain independent. In 1947 Britain partitioned the subcontinent into Hindu-majority India and Muslim-majority Pakistan. Kashmir remained autonomous under the leadership of a Hindu maharaja. Muslim tribespeople invaded from Pakistan, and the maharaja acceded to India in 1948; Pakistani and Indian troops fought in Kashmir beginning in 1947. India appealed to the United Nations, which called for a cease-fire, withdrawal of Pakistani troops, and a plebiscite on the future of Kashmir. The plebiscite has never been held. Another war between India and Pakistan in Kashmir (1965) failed to resolve the dispute. India continues to hold the greater part of Kashmir; roughly one-third is a semiautonomous region of Pakistan known as Azad (free) Kashmir.

Kasravi, Ahmad (d. 1946) Historian and political thinker. Founder of Azadigan (Freedom) Society. Argued that Iran's backwardness was due to divisions along sectarian lines, rather than foreign intervention or despotic governments. Attacked tribalism, regionalism, linguistic communalism, religious sectarianism, and socioeconomic classes as divisive factions. Denounced Shiism as a dynastic power struggle and a tool of terrorism for the Safavid dynasty. Asserted that Shiism was a falsification of history due to its claims about the status of the twelfth imam, its opposition to the state's authority as well as to democracy and popular sovereignty, and its insistence that the faithful should blindly follow clerical leadership.

Strongly opposed by the ulama, who declared him an apostate. Assassinated in 1946 by a member of the fundamentalist Fidaiyan-i Islam.

Kawakibi, Abd al-Rahman al- (d. 1902) Also known as al-Sayyid al-Furati and Traveler K. Syrian Islamic revivalist and advocate of Arab caliphate. Influenced by reform ideas of Jamal al-Din al-Afghani (d. 1897) and Muhammad Abduh (d. 1905). Advocated a return to the original purity of Islam, claiming that alien concepts and distortions such as mysticism, fatalism, sectarian divisions, and imitation had led to ignorance and submission to stagnant theologians and despotic rulers who suppressed freedoms, promoted false religion, and corrupted the moral, social, educational, and financial systems of the Muslim nation, as exemplified by the Ottoman Empire. Advocated Arab independence and an elected Arab caliph with limited powers as the basis for the revival of Islam.

Kazakhstan, Islam in This Central Asian republic is bordered by Russia, the Caspian Sea, Turkmenistan, Uzbekistan, Kyrgyzstan, and China. Major ethnic groups are Kazakhs (46 percent) and Russians (34.7 percent), with Ukrainian, German, Uzbek, and Tatar minorities. Forty-seven percent of the population is Muslim, 44 percent Russian Orthodox, and 9 percent other; Sufi orders such as the Naqshbandi have grown since independence from the former Soviet Union in 1991. Catherine the Great introduced Sunni Islam to the Kazakh territories in an effort to pacify pastoral nomads. Soviet rule severely repressed most religious activity but had little effect on rural practices. After independence, many mosques and religious schools opened, financed in part by Saudis, Turks, and local believers. The republic's constitution (1993) specifically guarantees freedom of religious worship and forbids adoption of a state religion; Islamic holy days are not state holidays. *See also* Central Asia, Islam in

Kazan Khanate A successor state to Genghis Khan's Golden Horde, centered in the city of Kazan, located in present-day Tatarstan on the Volga River. Muslim Turkic culture and literature flourished after its founding (1438 or 1445). By the early sixteenth century the Crimean Khanate was actively interfering in Kazan affairs. Kazan had been an important mercantile center, but as relations with Muscovy worsened, the latter moved its commercial activities to deprive the khanate of revenue. Kazan was conquered in 1552; much of the population was resettled with Orthodox Christian settlers. Numerous campaigns followed to convert and assimilate the local Muslims.

Kazim, Musa al- (d. 799) Recognized by the Twelver Shiis as the seventh imam, following his father, Jafar al-Sadiq. He was the object of apocalyptic expectations, with some of his followers claiming that he could not have died without fulfilling those expectations. Others among his followers came to acknowledge his son, Ali al-Rida, as the imam after him.

Kedayans *See* Brunei, Islam in

Kelantan Predominantly ethnic Malay state in the northeast of peninsular Malaysia, bordering the majority Malay Muslim provinces of southern Thailand. Historically noted for its pondok (Muslim religious schools) and ulama. Ceremonially headed by a sultan, but executive powers lie with an elected state government. Kelantan is the political locus of the Partai Islam Se-Malaysia (PAS), which has ruled the state since 1959, losing in 1978, regaining through 1990 and 1999 elections. PAS aims to establish an Islamic state in Kelantan, enforcing Islamic law, in opposition to the United Malays National Organization's (UMNO) nationalist policy of Islamization at the federal level.

Kemal, Mehmet Namik (d. 1888) Ottoman Turkish poet and writer. His political ideas are a mixture of traditional Islamic concepts and liberal European ideals. Best remembered in Turkey for his impassioned patriotic poetry, though most ignore his concern that constitutionalism should be harmonized with Islam. He was a leading figure in the Young Ottomans.

Kemal, Mustafa *See* Atatürk, Mustafa Kemal; Kemalism

Kemalism Principles of Mustafa Kemal Atatürk (d. 1938), founder and first president of the Turkish republic. Constitutes the official state ideology and went publicly unchallenged until the 1980s. Its major points are republicanism, statism (in economic policy), populism, laicism, nationalism, and reformism, as enumerated in the Republican People's Party (Cumhuriyet Halk Partisi, CHP) statutes of 1935; these were incorporated into the 1937 constitution, which remained in effect until 1961 when it was reformulated slightly. Kemalism was politically authoritarian, intended to undermine the traditionally minded religious authorities in favor of secular society.

Khadijah bint Khuwaylid (d. ca. 618) First wife of Muhammad, and his only wife until her death. Mother of Fatimah and other sons and daughters of Muhammad. First person to believe in Muhammad's prophethood. Wealthy widow who hired Muhammad to oversee her commercial transactions. Married Muhammad when she was around forty and he was twenty-five. Revered as a good and faithful wife, mother, and Muslim.

Khadim al-Haramayn al-Sharifayn Custodian of the two holy cities. Title referring to those responsible for the upkeep of mosques and holy sites within Mecca and Medina and protection of pilgrims on the hajj. The title originated with the Ottoman rulers and was used by the sharif of Mecca; it is currently held by the king of Saudi Arabia.

Khaksar Movement *See* Tahrik-i Khaksar

Khalafallah, Muhammad Ahmad (d. 1991) Egyptian Islamic modernist thinker and writer. Wrote a controversial doctoral dissertation suggesting that Quranic accounts of prophets and events prior to Muhammad were literary and artistic, rather than historical, in nature. Argued that Arab socialism is consistent with Islam. Claimed that the social welfare of the Muslim community takes precedence over Quranic texts.

Khales, Yunus *See* Hizb-i Islami (Afghanistan)

Khalid, Khalid Muhammad (b. 1920) Egyptian writer. Initially supported secularly based social justice and reform, but by the 1980s was more concerned with Islamic authenticity. Believes that Islam has both a civil mission and a religious one and that the state should apply Islamic principles. Maintains that an Islamic state aims at liberty and opposes despotism. Interprets the Quranic concept of shura (consultation) as parliamentary democracy.

Khalidi *See* Naqshbandi, Khalid al-

Khalifah (1) Deputy or steward; sometimes translated as vicegerent. According to the teachings of Islam, each individual is a khalifah to God. Muslims in particular must strive to adhere to and advance God's will by establishing a society that reflects human dignity and justice. Accordingly, human beings have been given the necessary intelligence, strength, and divine guidance to benefit humanity. Adam was the first appointed khalifah. King David is also identified by the Quran as a khalifah since he modeled his actions on God's commands and moral laws. (2) Successor; the dynastic rulers of the Muslim empire. (3) Leader of a Sufi order. *See also* Caliph/Caliphate

Khalil, al- Also known as Hebron. Palestinian town on the West Bank of the river Jordan, under Israeli control since 1968. Revered by Muslims and Jews as the traditionally accepted location of the tomb of Abraham. Site of much tension between Jews and Muslims in the late twentieth century, including the 1994 shooting of Muslim worshipers by a fanatic Israeli settler.

Khalwah Place of seclusion or retreat. Sometimes refers to individual spiritual retreats, generally within a Sufi hospice, taken under the leadership of a spiritual director, but can also refer to the physical space of an individual cell intended for meditation, typically around the mosque square. Sometimes used to refer to specific rituals of individual meditation. The Khalwati order derived its name from this term due to the order's special emphasis on the need for retreat and individual asceticism. The Sanusi order also emphasizes the need to withdraw from the world periodically. *See also* Khanaqah; Tekke; Zawiyah

Khalwati Tariqah Sufi order known for the practice of periodic retreat. Derives its name from this practice. Originated in Central Asia and entered the Ottoman Empire in the fifteenth century; by the sixteenth century it had become the most widespread Sufi order in the empire. Stressed a combination of knowledge and practice, and required symbolically tying the heart of the disciple to that of the master so that the relationship between the two would be stronger than that between father and son. Also emphasized silence, vigil, participation in dhikr (collective prayer), and communal recital of wird al-sattar (a fifteenth-century composition that is the center of Khalwati ritual). Revived in the seventeenth century in Egypt, it became the dominant order in Egypt in the eighteenth century, holding this status for eighty years. Accommodated both leading scholars and common people. *See also* Rahmani Tariqah; Sammani Tariqah

Khamanahi, Sayyid Ali (b. 1939). Born in Mashhad, Iran. A student of Ayatollah Hadi Milani (d. 1975) in Mashhad and of Muhammad Husayn Burujirdi (d. 1962) and Ayatollah Ruhollah Khomeini (d. 1989) in Qom. Engaged in political agitation from 1963 to 1978 and was repeatedly arrested. Member of the Revolutionary Council, 1979–1980; briefly headed Sipah-i Pasdaran-i Inqilab-i Islami, 1979. Was the Friday mosque prayer leader in Tehran, 1979–1981. Served as president of the republic 1981–89.

Khamr *See* Intoxicants

Khan Title traditionally designating tribal nomadic leaders in an area from Central Asia to northern India, Iran, Anatolia/Turkey, and southern Russia, but which became widespread following Genghis Khan's thirteenth-century conquests. Not widely used in the Arabic-speaking world. The term has generally fallen into disuse except as a surname in Pakistan and in the title for the Ismaili spiritual leader, the Aga Khan.

Khan, Inayat (d. 1927) Sufi of the Chishti tariqah from India who established that order in the West. A talented musician, he came to the United States in 1910, initially as a performer and later as a spritual teacher. He married an American, Ora Ray Baker, and their son, Pir Vilayat Inayat Khan (b. 1916), currently heads the order. The teachings of the Sufi order are eclectic and interfaith, encouraging followers to connect to the universal spirit of guidance.

Khanaqah Persian. Place where the meal cloth is spread. Term for Sufi meetinghouse. Al-Maqrizi (d. 1461) wrote that khanaqahs first appeared in the tenth century and that these buildings were "exclusively dedicated to the worship of God almighty," although other reports refer to their existence as early as the ninth century. Some of the earliest recorded khanaqahs in Persia were established by Muhammad ibn Karram (d. 839), the founder of the Karrami sect, for his followers. Abu Said ibn Abil-Khayr (d. 1049) was the first to codify and record rules for Sufi novices in the khanaqah. Early classical Persian Sufi sources employ five different terms—*khanaqah, ribat, sumaa, tekke,* and *zawiyah*—practically interchangeably to denote the meetinghouse of the first Sufi fraternities. *See also* Khalwah; Tekke; Zawiyah

Khanqah *See* Khanaqah

Khansa, al- *See* Marsiyyah

Kharaj Tax on agrarian land owned by non-Muslims, distinct from the tax system for Muslim-owned agrarian land. First introduced after the Battle of Khaibar, when the

Prophet allowed Jews to return to their land on the condition they pay half of their produce as kharaj. The only taxes recognized by the Quran are the zakah (alms from Muslims) and jizyah (head tax from non-Muslims); kharaj is based on the legal principle of discretionary interests.

Kharijis/Kharijites Seceders. Early sectarian group in Islam, neither Sunni nor Shii, although they originally supported Ali's leadership on the basis of his widsom and piety. They turned against Ali when he agreed to submit his quarrel with Muawiyah to arbitration; a group of his followers accused him of rejecting the Quran. Ali was forced to fight them in 658; in revenge, Ali was murdered at the mosque in Kufa in 661. The group survives today, known as the Ibadis, with fewer than one million adherents. *See also* Ibadis

Khassah Specific. Refers to passages from the Quran believed to apply to specific persons, times, places, or circumstances. It is contrasted with those verses believed to have general (ammah) significance. The distinction between the two is usually determined on the basis of the historical context in which the verse was delivered. Scholars disagree about which verses are general and which are specific.

Khatam al-Nabiyyin Seal of the prophets. Phrase occurs in Quran 33:40, referring to Muhammad, and is regarded by Muslims as meaning that he is the last of the series of prophets that began with Adam. Some biographers of the Prophet mention that he had a physical mark (seal) of some sort between his shoulders that was regarded as one of the signs of his prophethood. According to some scholars, belief in the final prophetic mission of Muhammad is part of the basic Muslim creed (aqidah).

Khatami, Muhammad (b. 1942) Iranian reformist president. Son of Ayatollah Ruhollah Khatami (d. 1988). Studied religion in Qom and then studied philosophy at Isfahan University and education at Tehran University.

Was appointed director of the Hamburg (Germany) Islamic Institute in 1978, where he mobilized Iranian student political activity. Served as minister of Islamic guidance 1982–92 and director of the Iranian National Library 1992–97 before being elected president of Iran in 1997. A critic of imperialism, especially of the international capitalist system, but also an admirer of the achievements of Western civilization.

Khatib Orator. Person who preaches the Friday sermon (khutbah) at a mosque. Any person well versed in Islam is eligible for the position, although in practice only males preach. It became a government-appointed position under the Abbasid caliphate. In the twentieth and twenty-first centuries it is often a government-appointed and regulated position.

Khatmi Tariqah Sufi order founded in Sudan in 1817 by Muhammad Uthman al-Mirghani. Claimed to be the "seal" (khatm) of Sufi orders. Prescribes devotion and quiet contemplation of Muhammad's "light" (inspiration), as well as twice-weekly performance of ritual, such as the poetic biography of Muhammad (mawlid), to provide spiritual rejuvenation. Has a youth organization that brings young men into the order. Has a large urban base, and its educated members are particularly politically active. Under Turco-Egyptian rule, assumed the role of intermediary between followers and authorities. Refused to join the Mahdist state (1885–98) and regained prominence after the state's fall. Ali al-Mirghani (d. 1968), the great-grandson of the founder, played an important role in the nationalist movement for Sudanese independence. Since independence, the order has played a significant role in government, either in coalition or in opposition. Military regimes have tried to weaken its political influence, but its position has been strengthened by the failure of military rule and the one-party system.

Khatun, Kutlugh *See* Women and Islam

Khatun, Padishah *See* Women and Islam

Khawajah Persian title or form of address, especially designated for Christians and Westerners, equivalent to sir or mister. It is used with or without the name of the person addressed. Also refers broadly to Westerners or tourists.

Khawarij See Kharijis/Kharijites

Khayr al-Din al-Tunisi (d. 1890) Also known as Khayr al-Din Pasha. Tunisian Islamic modernist and grand vizier under Abd al-Hamid II. Prime minister of Tunisia (1873). Introduced economic and administrative reforms to address the country's financial crisis. Appointed grand vizier of the Ottoman Empire (1878) but was dismissed shortly thereafter for his support of parliamentary government. One of the early Muslim thinkers to become concerned with the decline of the community and the means to revive it. His book *Aqwam al-Maslaik fi Marifat Ahwal al-Mamalik* advocated constitutional government, the parliamentary system, and modernization of the educational system. Founded Sadiqi College (1875), which educated generations of Tunisia's modernist elite.

Khayzuran See Women and Islam

Khazraj, al- One of two ruling clans in early seventh-century Medina, from which some of the first converts to Islam came. Upon Muhammad's death, the Khazraj decided to elect their own chief; in response, Abu Bakr was appointed caliph, successor to Muhammad's political leadership. The Khazraj eventually accepted his rule.

Khezr See Khidr, al-

Khidr, al- The green one. Name given by tradition to a mysterious figure in the Quran (18:65–82) who guided Moses and his servant on a long journey. Muslim scholarship agrees on very little about the historical al-Khidr despite attempts to identify a corresponding real person, but al-Khidr is nonetheless popular throughout the Muslim world as a spiritual guide, an immortal guide

for travelers, a protector of sailors, etc. Also known as Balya ibn Malkan.

Khilafa See Caliph/Caliphate; Khalifah

Khilafat Majlis Caliphate Conference. Islamic political group in Bangladesh, founded by Shaykh-ul-Hadith Mawlana Azizul Haq in 1989. Has a following among ulama and madrasa graduates. Works toward establishing Islamic rule in Bangladesh and is known for its opposition to the influence of foreign nongovernmental organizations working in the country. Joined the four-party alliance with the Bangladesh Nationalist Party of Khalida Zia during the 2001 elections to defeat the Awami League.

Khilafat Movement Agitation on the part of Indian Muslims allied with the Indian nationalist movement, 1919–24. Its purpose was to influence the British government to preserve the spiritual and temporal authority of the Ottoman sultan as caliph of Islam. Leaders and ulama viewed the European attack on the caliph's authority as an attack on Islam and thus a threat to the religious freedom of Muslims under British rule. The failure of the British to support their cause resulted in increased anti-British sentiments among Indian Muslims. The religious focus of the Khilafat movement provided a means of achieving pan-Indian Muslim political solidarity against the British as well as a vehicle of communication between leaders and their potential mass following. The movement led to a Muslim-Hindu alliance in struggling for Indian independence in nonviolent ways.

Khirqah Sufi patched cloak symbolizing initiation into the Sufi way. Symbol of the Sufi shaykh's authority over the disciple and the disciple's vow of obedience to the rules of the order. Conferred when a Sufi is received into the order. Also symbolizes silsilah, or the chain of transmission of the order, as well as the order itself.

Khiva Khanate Formed in the early sixteenth century when Ilbars, a chieftain of

Uzbek descent, united local fiefdoms in the territory of the ancient Khwarem. By the early seventeenth century it had become an important regional power and extended its reach westward to the Caspian, northward to the Emba River, southward into Khurasan, and eastward into Bukharan lands. Literature, art, and architecture flourished during this time; political infighting and the need for defense against Russian military advances led to its decline. In 1920 a Communist-led coup established the Khorezm People's Soviet Republic, which was incorporated in 1924 into the newly formed Soviet socialist republics of Turkmenistan and Uzbekistan.

Khizr *See* Khidr, al-

Khoi, Abol-Qasem (d. 1992) Iraqi Shii mujtahid, teacher of jurisprudence and theology, writer, and spiritual leader. Was by 1970 the most widely followed Shii mujtahid in the world. Used religious tithes to provide stipends for seminary students and establish Islamic schools. Founded a publishing house in Karachi, Pakistan, and several mosques with cultural centers. Opposed to the political activism of high-ranking religious authorities. Objected to Ayatollah Ruhollah Khomeini's doctrine of vilayat-i faqih, (rule of the jurist) claiming that the authority of Shii jurists does not extend to the political sphere and cannot be restricted to one or a few jurists. Only ayatollah in Iraq after 1980, but placed under virtual house arrest until his death.

Khojas Hindu Indian converts to Shii Islam. Retained the Hindu caste system since they continued to live as Hindus. Three groups resulted: a small minority of Sunnis, some Twelvers, and a majority of Nizari Ismailis who follow the Agha Khan. Today they have formally abandoned Khoja status with Hindu elements in favor of a more universal Ismaili Shiism. Mostly concentrated in Karachi (Pakistan) and Gujrat (India). *See also* Aga Khan; Ismailis; Nizaris

Khojki Script Also Khwaja Sindhi. One of the earliest forms of written Sindhi. The name probably comes from *khoja*, a variant of the Persian *khwaja* (lord, master). The script was devised for the Ismaili community in the subcontinent, enabling converts to learn Islamic principles in their own language.

Khomeini, Ruhollah al-Musavi (d. 1989) Iranian Shii cleric, leader of the Islamic revolution, and ideologue of the Islamic Republic of Iran. Opposed the shah's secularization policies and imitation of the West. Advocated clerical leadership in countering the influence of Western ideology and culture. Mobilized opposition to the shah, particularly merchants (bazaaris) and students. Turned attention away from Islamic rituals and toward the social, political, and cultural aspects of Islam. Compared the shah's regime to that of the Umayyad caliph Yazid and the Iranian people to Muhammad's grandson Husayn, establishing the paradigm of suffering and protest against injustice. Gave a sermon denouncing the shah, Israel, and the United States that resulted in a wave of anti-shah marches in Tehran and Khomeini's arrest and removal from Qom to Tehran, where he became the undisputed opposition leader. Exiled 1964–79. Developed a strong relationship with left-wing, anti-shah Iranian student organizations abroad. During the 1970s, proclaimed the need to destroy the Iranian monarchy, replace it with an Islamic republic conforming to the Quran and Shii traditions, and implement Islamic law. Widely distributed his written statements and audiotapes, preparing the ground for his return to Iran to wide popular acclaim. Returned to Tehran in 1979 with the goal of controlling the forces unleashed by the revolution and the consolidation of the regime. Formulated the doctrine of vilayat-i faqih (rule of the jurist), which determined the structure of the new government, which he led. Believed that ideology was meaningful only when it was translated into power and that holiness could be achieved only through action. Engaged Iran in war with Iraq 1980–88 despite strong opposition within the nation. Reign marked by strict enforcement of traditional social norms and harsh measures against those considered a threat to Islam, such as Bahais. Excluded from government those who did not agree with political Islam and the doctrine of vilayat-i faqih. During the 1980s, proclaimed the spread of Islam and Islamic revolution as a foreign policy goal to be achieved via a combination of preaching, confrontation, and armed struggle. Called upon Muslims of the Persian Gulf and throughout the world to rise up and overthrow oppressive, un-Islamic, pro-American governments. Accepted a truce with Iraq in 1988 due to national concerns that continuation of the war would result in failure of the republic. Death in 1989 led to a popular outpouring of grief.

Khoqand Khanate Eighteenth- and nineteenth-century central Asian state in the central part of the Ferghana Valley, formed as a result of the political and economic decline of the Bukharan Khanate. Abd al-Karim Biy founded the capital city, Khoqand (also called Kukon or Kokand), in 1740. By the early 1840s it entered a period of uninterrupted civil wars and rebellions, caused by conflicts between the major ethnic groups of its population (Uzbeks, Sarts, Tajiks, Kipchaks, Kyrgyz, and Kazakhs). The khanate was abolished in 1876 and its territory annexed to the Russian governorate general of Turkestan.

Khorasani, Muhammad Kazim (d. 1911) Most distinguished religious scholar in Iran during the Qajar period (1796–1925). Teacher of many of the most prominent Iranian clerics of the early twentieth century. His books remain required reading in Iranian and Iraqi Shii madrasas, and his legal principles are followed by many leading mujtahids in Iran. Khorasani sent telegrams to Iran during the Constitutional Revolution (1905–11), guiding the involvement of ulama in politics.

Khul Removal. Usually refers to a divorce procedure under Islamic law whereby a woman may obtain a divorce without showing cause by returning her dowry or conceding other financial obligations to her husband. This divorce procedure is initiated by the wife and is usually not revocable within the waiting period (iddah) prescribed for women before remarriage is allowed. Muslim legal sources disagree as to whether the consent of the husband is necessary for this procedure to take effect.

Khums Tax based on one-fifth of the war booty given by Muslims to Muhammad and his family. After Muhammad's death, khums was interpreted as an Islamic tax on profits of various sorts. Most important in Shii Islam. In the thirteenth century khums was split into two portions—one portion went to support indigent descendants of Muhammad, and the other portion went to mujtahids, who were to give half to the imam and half to the poor and orphaned descendants of Muhammad. Gave the Shii clergy in Iran in particular a source of income that granted them independence from the state and helped fuel the Iranian revolution. *See also* Taxation

Khurasani, Abu Muslim al- *See* Abu Muslim al-Khurasani

Khutbah Sermon or speech given by an imam during the Friday midday service at the mosque and on the occasion of the two major festivals (Id al-Adha and Id al-Fitr). Consists of expressions praising God, blessings on Muhammad and his family and his Companions, and exhortation to the community about their responsibility in this world and in preparation for the hereafter. In the absence of freedom of expression in many parts of the Muslim world, this institution often has served as the only means of religious and moral criticism of the governments in power.

Khwarizmi, Abu Jafar Muhammad ibn Musa al- (d. ca. 850) Mathematician, astronomer, and geographer. Synthesized extant Hellenic, Sanskritic, and cuneiform traditions to develop algebra, a term derived from the title of one of his books (containing the term al-jabr, meaning "forcing" [numbers]). Introduced Arabic numerals into the Latin West, based on a place-value decimal system developed from Indian sources. The word *algorithm* is derived from a Latin corruption of his name.

Kihanah *See* Divination

Kindi, Abu Yusuf Yaqub ibn Ishaq al- (d. ca. 873) Philosopher-scientist whose work was a synthesis of Aristotelian Neoplatonic philosophy and the cosmological teachings of Islam. First to grapple with the problem of expression of Peripatetic thought in Arabic. Argued for a finite and closed cosmos. Believed in the doctrine of creation from nothing. Also attempted to harmonize faith and reason. Had a widespread influence in both the Arab world and medieval Europe.

King Faisal Foundation Saudi Arabian philanthropic organization established in 1976. Promotes the establishment of hospitals, orphanages, and schools, the expansion of Islamic missionary activities, and the fostering of solidarity among Muslim states. Consists of the King Faisal Center for Research and Islamic Studies, the King Faisal International Prize, and the King Faisal Foundation General Secretariat. The King Faisal International Prize is awarded annually to outstanding international figures in the fields of service to Islam, Islamic studies, Arabic literature, medicine, and science. Foundation encourages young Muslims from around the world, both men and women, to pursue medical and engineering studies in the advanced industrial countries. Also includes an investment section and a program and research section.

Kirmani, Hamid al-Din (d. 1021) Medieval Ismaili philosopher. Served Fatimid caliphs as missionary in Iraq and Iran. Upheld the Fatimid imamate but rejected attributions of divinity to the caliph, al-Hakim (d. ca. 1021), during a period of controversy over the nature of the Ismaili imamate. Made major contributions in the field of metaphysics.

Kisakurek, Necip Fazil (d. 1983) Turkish poet, playwright, and essayist. A striking figure in modern Turkish literature, but today he is remembered primarily for his political ideology. His periodical *The Great East* (1943–78) critiqued the emptiness of humanism.

Kishk, Shaykh Abd al-Hamid Abd al-Aziz Muhammad (b. 1933) Popular Egyptian preacher. Dissident under the Nasser regime, refusing to sanction the government's execution of Sayyid Qutb or assert compatibility between Islam and socialism. Boycotted by the official media under the Sadat regime (1970–81), but cassette tapes of his sermons were widely distributed. Held political views opposed to the modern bureaucratic state. Emphasized personal and private piety in his preaching. Concerned with the end of the world, miracles of Sufi saints, metaphysics of the soul, eschatology, and death. Imprisoned after Sadat's assassination. Released by Mubarak in 1982 under the condition that he end his career as a public preacher; his books and cassette tapes are still freely available, but the mosque in Cairo where he preached was transformed into a public health center.

Kismet *See* Qismah

Kiswah Drape covering the Kaaba, embroidered with verses from the Quran. Based on pre-Islamic practice in which the Kaaba was draped with a large cloth embroidered with poetry. Woven of silk and cotton, dyed black, and embroidered in gold thread. Changed each year, and the old one is cut up and given to pilgrims.

Kitab In early Arabic, something written; soon thereafter, book. The Quran, which refers to itself as the "clear kitab," is generally recognized as the earliest Arabic book. The Quran is sometimes referred to as "the Book" (al-kitab). Highly esteemed and sometimes lavishly decorated, books have remained central to the transmission of knowledge, often complemented by oral recitation and commentary.

Kitab al-Jafr Mystical book compiled, according to Shii belief, by Ali ibn Abi Talib. Contained secret teachings for his descendants. The first mention of the book is associated with the sixth imam, Jafar al-Sadiq.

In Sunni lore, the book is named *Kitab al-mughaybat* (The book of hidden things).

Komiteh Revolutionary committees active in the Iranian Revolution of 1979. Began before the revolution as neighborhood defense units against government-backed club wielders who attacked protesters. Ideologically diverse; the Komiteh members who supported a democratic outcome left as the youth of the committees came under religious influence. In 1991 they were incorporated into the police force and ceased to exist independently.

Koprulu, Mehmet Fuat (d. 1966) Turkish intellectual. A disciple of Ziya Gokalp. Taught at Istanbul University 1913–43 and was internationally renowned for his scholarship on Turkish history and literature. Founded the Institute of Turcology in 1924 and stressed Turkish cultural connections with Central Asia. Elected to the Turkish Grand National Assembly in 1935. Along with Celal Bayar, Adnan Menderes, and Refik Koraltan, founded the Democratic Party in 1946. Served as foreign minister 1950–56 and resigned from the Democratic Party the following year because of the Menderes government's undemocratic practices.

Kosovo, Battle of Battle in 1389 between the Ottoman and Serbian empires. Although the Ottoman sultan Murad was killed in the battle, the Serbian military force was destroyed, opening the way for Ottoman expansion in the western Balkans. In the Serbian nationalist consciousness, the battle symbolizes the choice of death rather than compromise.

Kosovo, Islam in Muslims in Kosovo are largely of Albanian descent, with a small number of Turks who remained after Yugoslav independence. Albanians arrived in Kosovo beginning in the late seventeenth century, during Ottoman occupation. Longstanding enmity between Christian Serbs and Muslim Albanians was raised to fever pitch during the Communist era and again in the 1990s. Public religious observances were forbidden by the Communist regime, and many of the Sufi brotherhoods were outlawed. The current religious situation of the Albanian community is difficult to determine because assertions of Albanian nationalism, particularly since the explosion of violence in the 1990s, have monopolized public discourse. The actual influence of mosques and Sufi brotherhoods is unknown. As of 2001, approximately 90 percent of the population were ethnic Albanians, most of whom identify themselves as Muslims. *See also* Albania, Islam in

Kuchuk Kaynarja, Treaty of Treaty signed in 1774 granting the Russians control over the Black Sea and occupation of Ottoman Crimea. Muslim Crimean Tatars remained under the religious authority of the Ottoman sultan, and the Russians became the protectors and representatives of Orthodox Christians throughout the Ottoman Empire.

Kufa Major city in Iraq. Became a center for political and cultural development during the first centuries of Islam. Has always had strong associations with Shiism and remains a Shii center today. Founded as a military city in 638 by the general Sad ibn Abi Waqqas and served as a base for Muslim expansion into Iran and the East. During the first civil war in 656, Caliph Ali ibn Abi Talib (the first Shii imam) made Kufa his capital. Ali's tomb is located close to the city in Najaf.

Kufic Dominant style of Arabic calligraphy (khatt). The word is an adjective derived from Kufa, a city in southern Iraq. The Kufic style was one of the earliest employed in transcribing holy texts. Its angular quality made Kufic the style of choice in many architectural endeavors and geometric designs. *See also* Calligraphy and Epigraphy

Kufr Disbelief. A significant concept in Islamic thought, the word kufr or one of its derivatives appears in the Quran 482 times. Also means "ingratitude," the willful refusal to appreciate the benefits that God has bestowed. Modern reform and revival movements vest the concept with new significance: current Muslim beliefs and practices have been so corrupted from true Islam that they constitute shirk (idolatry) or jahiliyyah (ignorance). Premodern reformers tended to see kufr in popular Islam, including Sufi practices; some modern reformers see the pervasive influence of the West as a cause of kufr.

Kulayni, Muhammad ibn Yaqub ibn Ishaq al- (d. 940) Major compiler of Shii hadith and elaborator of Shii law. Studied in Qom. His compendium *Kitab al-kafi* is considered one of the four most authoritative sources of hadith and law by the Twelver Shiis.

Kurds Ethnic minority group with sizeable populations in Turkey, Iran, and Iraq. The largest population lives in Turkey (eleven million), although several million live in Iran and northern Iraq, where they have struggled against and been persecuted by Saddam Hussein's regime. Small numbers of Kurds live in Syria. Iraqi Kurds are mainly Shafii Sunnis and members of the Naqshbandi Sufi tariqah. Turkish Kurds are largely Alawis. Many live today as refugees. Many Muslim countries, particularly Iran and Turkey, have resisted refugees historically. The Islamic Republic of Iran has reversed this policy and works with UN agencies to provide emergency relief for refugees.

Kuttab   *See*   Education: Educational Institutions

Kyrgyzstan, Islam in Bordered by Kazakhstan, China, Tajikistan and Uzbekistan, Kyrgyzstan has a population that is 75 percent Sunni Muslim and 20 percent Russian Orthodox, with a statistically insignificant minority of Shii Muslims; major ethnic groups are Kyrgyz, Russians, Uzbeks, Ukrainians, and Germans. Brought by Muslim traders, Islam was introduced into Kyrgyzstan in the eighteenth century. President Askar Akaev's recent autocratic measures (flawed parliamentary elections, suppressed media, and expanded presidential powers) have eroded Kyrgyzstan's reputation as a democracy with a market economy. Islam here is influenced by both Kazakh conservatism, reflected in the speeches of Imam Ratbek Nisanbayev, and Tajik extremism. Militants from Tajikistan and Uzbekistan threaten stability along its southern and western borders; in August 2000, heavy border clashes in the south with Tajik extremists were reported. *See also* Central Asia, Islam in

Labor Party of Egypt Only legal Islamist party in Egypt and from 1987 the leading opposition party. Immediate goal is ending one-party rule and chronic corruption. Links democracy to Islam: without a central priesthood to interpret scriptures, the existence of different interpretations is legitimate, as are different political programs and parties.

Lahoris *See* Ahmadis

Lalla Zaynab bint Shaykh Muhammad ibn Abi al-Qasim (d. 1904) Algerian female saint and head of Rahmania Sufi zawiyah. Opposed to French colonial order. Took vow of celibacy, which gave her spiritual authority, freedom of movement, social empowerment, and the opportunity to devote herself completely to the care of the indigent, overseeing the zawiyah's social services, and promoting the mission of cultural redemption.

Lashkar-i Taiba A Pakistan-based Islamic militant group active in armed struggle in Indian Kashmir. Founded by Hafiz Muhammad Saeed, an Ahl-i Hadith scholar and activist, in the mid-1990s; planned and conducted several deadly and suicidal missions in Kashmir, including an attack on the Red Fort in Delhi in December 2000. Was blamed for an attack on the Indian parliament in December 2001 and declared a terrorist organization by the U.S. State Department and banned by the Pakistan government that same month.

Lat, al- One of three pre-Islamic goddesses worshiped at the Kaaba in Mecca prior to the rise of Islam. The name means "goddess." Identified as "daughter of Allah," since she was supposed to be the offspring of Allah's marriage to a jinn, but she may have been considered consort to Allah. Usually represented in human shape. The idol representing her was destroyed in 630 when Muhammad and Muslims conquered Mecca. Denounced in the Quran (53:19–20).

Law: Modern Legal Reform Modern legal reforms originated both within the tradition and from political leaders who imposed changes in conjunction with government modernization programs. Encounters with the West led to extensive borrowing of substantive and systemic features from European legal models. Islamic procedural rules, criminal law, and commercial codes were often replaced by European ones instead of being reformed. The pace and scope of reform varied with time and place. Ottoman reforms began with the Tanzimat (1839) and Mecelle (1869). The Indian subcontinent assimilated British judge-made case law, resulting in Anglo-Muhammadan law. Egyptian reform integrated French and Islamic legal models; the civil code devised by Abd al-Razzaq al-Sanhuri was subsequently adopted by almost all of the Arab countries. Reform of the legal systems of Indonesia, the Malay states, the Philippines, and Singapore was heavily influenced by local customary law (adat). Reforms in personal status law greatly impacted the lives of Muslim women. Tunisia abolished polygyny and gave men and women equal rights to divorce in 1956; adoption (prohibited in traditional Islamic law) was legalized in 1958. Turkey's new secular legal code vested women with rights akin to those of their Western counterparts. Recently, extremist groups in places such as Algeria, Sudan, and Afghanistan have been advocating a return to an idealized Islamic past by implementing traditional Islamic law.

Law: Shii Schools of Law *See* Jafari: Shii Legal Thought and Jurisprudence

Law: Sunni Schools of Law *See* Hanafi School of Law; Hanbali School of Law; Maliki School of Law; Shafii School of Law

Lawh Mahfuz Well-preserved tablet. Phrase used in Quran 85:22 to refer to the original codex or document on which the Quran, according to traditional commentators, was originally inscribed and which has always existed in heaven. Associated with another description of the divine archetype of revelation, "mother of the book" (Quran 3:6; 13:39; 43:3).

Laylat al-Baraah *See* Night of Power and Excellence

Laylat al-Qadr *See* Night of Power and Excellence

Leasing *See* Ijarah

Lebanon, Islam in There are five Muslim sects in Lebanon: Sunnis, Shiis, Druze, Alawis, and Ismailis. All but Ismailis enjoy proportional representation in parliament. About one-fifth of the Lebanese population is Sunni, concentrated in coastal cities. Shiis live mostly in the north and south; they generally hold lower social, economic, and educational status than Sunnis. By the 1980s Shiis constituted the largest confessional group in Lebanon, leading to demands for better educational and employment opportunities and redistribution of power based on actual numbers. Druze constitute about 7 percent of the population. Alawis are numerically insignificant but have risen in importance since the Gulf War of 1990–91 due to the growing influence of Syria, where Alawis dominate the government. Ismailis number only a few hundred and play no significant political role. Religious officials of each sect maintain jurisdiction over personal status law. The distribution of political power is based on religious affiliation: the president must be Maronite Christian, the prime minister must be Sunni Muslim, and the speaker of the parliament must be Shii Muslim.

Lepanto, Battle of Battle in 1571 between the Ottoman Empire and a coalition of the papacy, Venice, and the Austro-Hungarian Hapsburgs. The Ottoman defeat blocked their advance into the Mediterranean and was interpreted as a religious victory of Christian Europe over Muslim Turks.

Lesser Bayram *See* Id al-Fitr

Levant French term for the eastern Mediterranean.

Lexicography Arabic *ilm al-lugha.* Ibn Khaldun (d. 1406) defined it as "the science of instituted elements of language." Is primarily concerned with semiotic relations and contrasts between the elements of vocabulary.

Lian Mutual repudiation. A Quranic institution governing cases in which a husband accuses his wife of adultery without supplying witnesses. Quran 24:6–9 explicitly instructs the husband to swear four times that his accusation is true, followed by a fifth oath in which he invokes the wrath of God upon himself if he is lying. The wife may then neutralize this claim by responding with four oaths of her own, the fifth of which calls upon her the wrath of God if her husband is telling the truth. If she refuses to take the oath, she is presumed guilty and subject to the punishment for adultery. If she takes the oath, she is declared innocent and permanently divorced from her husband. Her husband, in turn, forfeits any paternity claims over children born subsequent to their sworn oaths.

Liberalism An ideology encompassing belief in electoral democracy, civil rights, gender equality, human progress, and/or the abolition of premodern social hierarchies. Introduced to the Islamic world in the nineteenth century by Europeans, then wielded against Europeans by Muslim intellectuals who noted the discrepancy between liberal ideals and colonial (and later postcolonial) practices. Takes several specifically Islamic forms: that divine revelation requires liberalism, that divine revelation allows but does not require liberalism, or that liberalism follows from the fallibility and multiplicity of human interpretations of divine revelation. Remains a controversial position among traditional Muslims, often vilified as inordinately Western or rationalistic.

Liberation Movement of Iran Iranian political party based on a moderate interpretation of Islam. Active in the 1963 opposition to the shah's regime, before its entire leadership was arrested and imprisoned. Reconstituted in 1977 and played a major role in the transfer of power from the shah to revolutionaries in 1979. Rejects both royal and clerical dictatorship in favor of political and economic liberalism.

Liberty See Hurr

Libraries The first library collections in the Muslim world appeared in the Umayyad era (661–750) and belonged to mosque libraries and private libraries. Historically, mosques provided the majority of public library services. The major classical library was Bayt al-Hikmah of Baghdad, founded under Caliph al-Mansur in the eighth century, which served as a major translation center and central clearinghouse for the learning of the Islamic world. Other major classical libraries were the Fatimid Dar al-Ilm in Cairo and the great library of the Spanish Umayyads in Córdoba, which held four hundred thousand volumes. The most notable libraries in the Islamic world today are Topkapi Sarayi and Suleymaniye Kutuphanesi in Istanbul, Turkey; the library of Ayatollah Marashi-Najati in Qom, Iran; and the Khuda Bakhsh Oriental Public Library in Patna, India.

Libya, Islam in Arabic-speaking Sunni Muslims of mixed Arab and Berber ancestry represent over 90 percent of the Libyan population; pockets of people practicing Berber folk religion and Sufis (primarily Sanusis) live in the rural areas. Independence and a monarchy were declared in 1951 after a particularly brutal Italian occupation; King Idris al-Sanusi (grandson of the Sufi order's founder) took the throne.

Al-Sanusi ignored the demands of a younger generation and those of a growing oil economy; the monarchy was dissolved in a military coup in 1969, with power going to Muammar Qaddafi. Qaddafi's "Green Book" sets forth his Third Universal Alternative to replace Communism and capitalism; unity, direct popular democracy, and Islamic socialism are considered the new bases of Libyan politics and society. Qaddafi weakened the ulama's power base through syncretic political, legal, and economic reforms. By the mid-1980s underground Islamic movements—the Hizb al-Tahrir and Ikhwan al-Muslimin—were targeted; with no legal means of protest, Islamist resistance against Qaddafi continues. Outside Libya, the National Front for the Salvation of Libya (NFSL) opposes Qaddafi's regime. Formed in 1981, its goal is a constitutional and democratically elected Libyan government.

Literature See Adab

Logic Arabic mantiq (a term etymologically related to nutq, "utterance"). In the Quran, mantiq is described as a means for justification and the expression of truth, hence connected with the ancient Greek logos. Is technically used to designate a science of logic adapted from Aristotle and the Neoplatonists. Was called a science of balance by al-Tahanawi (eighteenth century) because it is used to weigh arguments. For Ibn Sina (d. 1037), it designated rules for passing from the known to the unknown in the acquisition of knowledge. Was extended to an intuitive or speculative arrival at the truth and then adapted to the mystical illuminationist philosophy (hikmet al-ishraq). Some grammarians (ninth century onward) highlighted logic's dependence on its linguistic or civilizational contexts, a view later held by Ludwig Wittgenstein (d. 1951).

Lot Arabic Lut. Described as a prophet, righteous man, inhabitant of the city of Sodom, and, according to tradition, a nephew of Abraham. Lot was sent as a prophet to

Sodom and Gomorrah to warn of punishment for their sins. When Sodom was destroyed for its wickedness, exemplified by sexual perversity, Lot and his family alone were saved, except for his wife, who lagged behind. Biblical events such as Lot's impregnation of his two daughters and his wife's turning into a pillar of salt are not recorded in the Quran.

Loya Jirga Traditional tribal councils of Afghanistan.

Lubb *See* Qalb

Luqman Pre-Islamic sage-prophet, often referred to as al-Hakim (the wise). Surah 31 in the Quran bears his name and extols his wisdom and piety. His virtuous traits are manifested through his advice and admonitions to his son. Later compilers of maxims in Arabic attribute large portions of their collections to Luqman.

Lut *See* Lot

M

Maad *See* Day of Judgment; Resurrection

Maari, Abu al-Ala al- (d. 1058) Classical Arabic-language poet, blind, and well-known for composition of qasidah (panegyric) and ghazal (lyric) forms of poetry. Works include citations from the broad expanse of Arabic literature. His greatest collection of poetry is *Luzumiyyat*, named for self-imposed requirements in meter and rhyme. Al-Maari condemned the injustice and hypocrisy of rulers, ordinary citizens, and religious scholars alike. He regarded life as misfortune due to the extent of human shortcomings apparent in the world. Ridiculing formal religious dogmas, he claimed that the only truly religious people were those who helped their fellow human beings, regardless of what they believed privately.

Ma Ba (d. 1867) Senegalese religious leader whose 1862 declaration of holy war against "compromising" local Muslims inspired many Islamic converts and similar movements in West Africa. Although his revivalist efforts brought him into conflict with France, a local non-Muslim chief killed him to gain control of the West African kingdom of Salum. Today his tomb is a pilgrimage center.

Ma Hualong *See* New Sect

Ma Ming-Hsin *See* Ma Mingxin

Ma Mingxin (d. 1781) Major Muslim leader in China in the eighteenth century. Born in the Muslim community in Gansu, in northwest China, he traveled and studied in the Middle East, especially in Yemen and in Mecca and Medina. He was initiated into the Naqshbandi tariqah and returned to China in 1761 determined to purify Islamic life. His renewal movement, called the "New Teaching," practiced loudly spoken rather than silent litany and advocated reform of Muslim life. He came into conflict with Muslim and Chinese imperial establishments, and a rebellion broke out, during which he was killed by imperial forces.

Madani, Abbasi (b. 1931) Algerian Islamic activist and political leader. As a member of the National Liberation Front (FLN), Madani resisted the French colonizers. He was arrested and imprisoned for eight years. Later received a British doctoral degree in comparative education and was appointed professor at the University of Algiers (1978). He grew increasingly critical of the FLN's socialist orientation, and when a new constitution allowing the formation of political parties was adopted in February 1989, Madani established the Islamic Salvation Front (FIS). In the 1990 elections FIS won a majority of parliamentary seats. A new electoral law favoring the FLN was passed, and he and his deputy, Ali Bel Hajj, were arrested and sentenced to twelve years for leading an armed conspiracy against state security. Managing to integrate several Islamic parties into the FIS, Madani transformed the party into a potent political force in Algeria, challenging the historic monopoly of the FLN.

Madani, Husain Ahmad (d. 1957) Indian Deobandi alim, politically active in the debate over the role of regional and religious identity for statehood formation. President of group of ulama known as Jamiatul Ulama-i Hind, which opposed the creation of Pakistan and the ideology of Muhammad Iqbal. Allied with All-India National Congress. Well-known scholar of hadith.

Madhhab School of legal thought (pl. *madhabib*). *See also* Hanafi School of Law; Hanbali School of Law; Jafari: Shii Legal Thought and Jurisprudence; Shafii School of Law

Madinat al-Fadilah, al- The virtuous city. Title of a famous book written by Abu Nasr Muhammad ibn Tarkhan al-Farabi, the founder of Islamic political philosophy. Also refers to the city of Medina, originally called Yathrib, where Muhammad established the first community of Muslims.

Madjid, Nurcholish (b. 1939) Indonesian Islamic scholar and advocate of religious tolerance and pluralism. Interprets Islam to meet the spiritual needs of modern urban populations. More concerned with spirituality than ritual and social behavior. In the 1960s, challenged the traditionalist position advocating a literal interpretation of the Quran and hadith. Advocates instead a return to the spirit or underlying universal principles of early Islam as a guide for conduct in the cultural and historical context of contemporary Indonesia. In 1970, introduced the concept of "Islamic secularization," promoting the desacralization of aspects of human life and knowledge that are not properly religious. Emphasizes the concept of Islamic brotherhood, extending the boundaries of the Muslim community as broadly as possible. Has denounced sectarian and fundamentalist groups as cults. Defines Islam simply as submission to God, allowing him to use the word Islam when discussing Christians and Jews. Calls for an inclusive, tolerant Islam and dialogue with other faiths in order to resolve problems of bigotry and intolerance plaguing all major religions.

Madrasa Arabic madrasah. Establishment of learning where the Islamic sciences are taught; a college for higher studies. During the tenth and eleventh centuries the madrasa was devoted primarily to teaching law; the other Islamic sciences and philosophical subjects were optionally taught. At earlier stages instruction in the madrasa was linked with the mosque. With the advent of colonialism in Muslim countries, the introduction of Western curricula and teaching, and subsequent independence movements, madrasas experienced tremendous changes, varying throughout the Muslim world. In Turkey, most madrasas (medreses) were closed and state schools opened; at al-Azhar, secular faculties were introduced. After the introduction of a Western-influenced education system in Iran, the maktab or Quranic school declined; not until after the Iranian revolution (1979) did hozeh (religious schools) experience a revival. While originally the madrasa was contrasted with the kuttab or maktab, the children's schools in the Middle East, currently the term madrasa is sometimes used for establishments for elementary or secondary education, or any schools below university level for Quranic teaching. In recent years a significant Muslim migration from the Indian subcontinent to England, from North Africa to France, and from Turkey to Germany has been accompanied by the establishment of Muslim religious schools called madrasas for the European-born children of Muslim immigrants. See also Education: Educational Institutions

Madrasah Faiziyyah An important Shii theological college in the central Iranian city of Qom, adjacent to the shrine of Fatimah Masumah (d. 816), sister of the eighth Shii imam, Ali ibn Musa al-Rid (d. 818). It was initially built during the Safavid period (1501–1722) and was later named after a noted Shii theologian, Muhammad ibn Murtaza Kashani (d. 1679), known as Mulla Mohsen Faiz, who studied and later taught there. With the influx of Shii scholars following the collapse of the Ottoman Empire, Faiziyyah was revived and expanded under the intellectual leadership and administrative supervision of Ayatollah Abd al-Karim Haeri Yazdi (d. 1937). Since then it has been a major center of Shii learning. In 1963 Faiziah was the scene of confrontations between state security forces and demonstrators, leading ultimately to Ayatollah Khomeini's arrest and eventually his exile from the country.

Madrasah Nizamiyyah Madrasa founded in Baghadad in 1067. One of the most famous of those established by the great Seljuk vizier Nizam al-Mulk (d. 1092). This madrasa, like the others he founded, was primarily devoted to the teaching of law according to the Shafii school of Sunni Islamic law. The Nizamiyyah of Baghdad attracted noted scholars, of whom one of the most famous was the jurist, theologian, and mystic al-Ghazali (d. 1111).

Maghazi The military campaigns of the Prophet Muhammad. Writings about the maghazi are among the earliest records of the life of Muhammad. The *Book of Maghazi*, by al-Waqidi (d. 823), is a fundamental source of information about the life of the Prophet. Works on maghazi were important both as a source of the normative practice of the Prophet and in the development of Muslim theories on the conduct of war. *See also* Siyar

Maghreb *See* North Africa, Islam in

Magic The word *sihr* encompasses a wide range of subjects, from white and black magic to having contacts with jinn (non-human creatures). Its basic meaning is the same as the English word *magic*: falsification of reality, having contact with supernatural or psychic powers, and creating a transforming effect on the soul. The meaning, reality, and practice of magic have been dealt with in such diverse sciences as astrology, alchemy, law, and theology. Most of the Quranic references to magic are negative, since Muhammad was accused of being a magician (*sahir*, Quran 10:2) by his detractors. Even though white magic has been somewhat tolerated, its practice has been emphatically discouraged. *See also* Popular Religion

Mahamad Cabdille Hasan (d. 1921) Somali Islamic revivalist. Tribal leader and anticolonialist activist. His attempts to convert Somalis from the popular Qadiri Sufi order to the puritanical Salihi sect met with stiff resistance. His legacy was the recognition of the need to separate religious inspiration from secular power.

Mahaz-e Milli-ye Islami-ye Afghanistan *See* Gaylani Family

Mahdi Divinely guided one. An eschatological figure who Muslims believe will usher in an era of justice and true belief just prior to the end of time; an honorific applied to Muhammad and the first four caliphs by the earliest Muslims. Not mentioned in the Quran. The concept was developed by the Shiis and some Sunnis into that of a messianic deliverer who would return to champion their cause. Common themes run through both traditions: he will be of Muhammad's family; he will appear when the world is irretrievably corrupt; his reign will be a time of natural abundance; he will spread justice, restore the faith, and defeat the enemies of Islam. *See also* Eschatology; Messianism

Mahdi, Abd al-Rahman al- (d. 1959) Son of the Sudanese leader Muhammad Ahmad ibn Abd Allah, "the Mahdi." Regrouped his father's followers, the Mahdists, as a religious order in 1908. Built the family's mosque in Omdurman and cultivated lands on Aba Island, where the Mahdi had announced his mission in 1881. These actions enabled Abd al-Rahman to proclaim the imamate of Ansar and create a spiritual, political, and economic center for the movement on Aba. He was the patron of nationalists advocating a separate independent Sudan not united with Egypt. He established the Ummah Party in 1945.

Mahdi, Sadiq al- (b. 1936) Sudanese theologian and political leader. Great-grandson of the nineteenth-century Sudanese leader Muhammad Ahmad ibn Abd Allah, "the Mahdi." Head of the Ummah Party and prime minister 1966–67 and 1986–89. Was a leader of the opposition to the National Islamic Front government in the 1990s. Supports a modernist formulation of Islamic law. Defines the Islamic state as one abiding by the general constitutional principles of Islam with a legal system based on shariah. In economics, believes in social responsibility to provide for the poor, mandatory collection of zakah, implementation of traditional inheritance laws, and prohibition of usury. Islamic international relations are to be based on the principles of human brotherhood, supremacy of justice, irreversibility of contracts, and peaceful coexistence. *See also* Bashir, Omar Hassan al-

Mahdists *See* Mahdiyyah

Mahdiyyah Messianic movement founded in Sudan in the late nineteenth century by Muhammad Ahmad ibn Abd Allah, who proclaimed himself Mahdi (divinely appointed guide) in 1881 and called his followers ansar (helpers, supporters), after the Companions of Muhammad. Proclaimed a millenarian message of an age of justice and equity. Called for the overthrow of Turkish-Egyptian rule and jihad against its enemies; military activities against government troops were successful, enhancing the Mahdi's credibility among both sedentary and nomadic populations. The movement was in command of northern Sudan by early 1884, and Khartoum was captured in 1885. Mahdi died six months later. Though the movement was ultimately defeated by the Anglo-Egyptian army in 1889, it inspired nationalism and processes of Islamization and Arabization, and produced powerful symbols of common identity and national coherence. It also inspired the twentieth-century Ansar religious movement in Sudan and its political movement, the Ummah Party. Reverence for the Mahdi's family and observance of his collection of prayers are common throughout northern Sudan.

Mahfouz, Naguib (b. 1911) Egyptian writer who has produced over thirty-five novels and fourteen short-story collections and won the 1988 Nobel Prize in Literature. His first three novels in the early 1940s dealt with ancient Egypt, but his later ones deal with contemporary Egypt. *Al-thul al-hiyyah* (The Cairo trilogy), completed in 1952 but published in 1956–57, portrayed Cairene life between 1917 and 1944, chronicling generational and ideological conflicts, and established Mahfouz as a leading Arab novelist. His 1959 novel *Awlad haritna* (Children of Gebelaawi) tells the story of power struggles in a traditional Cairene neighborhood but

allegorically suggests the failure of religion and the potential success of science in establishing a better life. Mahfouz's later works continued to criticize Egyptian society and philosophically portray human foibles. In 1994 he was the target of an assassination attempt by militant Islamists.

Mahkamah Place of judgment. Refers to all forms of law court in the Arabic-speaking world. In traditional Islamic settings, emphasis was placed on the individual judge rather than the institution. The advent of colonialism and westernizing indigenous regimes accelerated an institutionalization of the judicial appartus, giving rise to the modern mahkamah.

Mahmal Palanquin symbolizing the protective role played by the sovereigns of Egypt, Syria, Yemen, and the Ottoman Empire for caravans of pilgrims from those countries on their way to Mecca. From 1266 until 1952 it also carried the kiswah (a cloth to cover the Kaaba, typically embroidered with verses from the Quran and encrusted with gold and jewels), extending the sovereign's protective role to the Kaaba and Islam.

Mahmud, Abd al-Halim (d. 1978) Egyptian Islamic leader who reasserted al-Azhar's independence from outside political control. Obtained a doctoral degree in philosophy from the Sorbonne in 1940. Appointed shaykh of al-Azhar by Anwar Sadat in 1973. Promoted Sufism based on the Quran and Sunnah. Called for the implementation of Islamic law in Egypt.

Mahmud, Mustafa (b. 1921) Egyptian Islamist philosopher, author, and scientist. Dedicated to the belief that Islam, science, and socioeconomic advancement are completely compatible and self-supportive. Founder of the Mustafa Mahmud Society, which provides sociomedical services, conducts tours to Islamic monuments, presents lectures and films, and sends relief abroad.

Mahmud, Zaki Najib (d. 1993) Egyptian liberal philosopher of positivism; writer and translator. Obtained a Ph.D. in philosophy from the University of London in 1947, then was a professor at the University of Cairo. Advocated the evaluation of the traditional Arab heritage in the light of modern scientific and rational thought.

Mahmud II (d. 1839) Ottoman sultan and reformer. Known for his Western-inspired reforms to consolidate his empire before grave internal and external threats. Faced a series of military defeats that cost him parts of the empire. During his reign, Muhammad Ali's son, Ibrahim, invaded Syria and advanced to Constantinople. The sultan's army attacked the Egyptians in Syria but was defeated at Nizip shortly before Mahmud's death in 1839. Established a modern army to replace the Janissary corps, introduced the cabinet system of government, undertook a census and a land survey, made primary education compulsory, established a medical school, and sent students on missions to Europe.

Mahmud of Ghazna (d. 1030) Ruler of Turkic origin who founded the independent Ghaznavid state in present-day Afghanistan and northeast Iran in 999. His raids into northern India laid the foundation for lasting Muslim rule there. In later Sufi traditions he became a symbol of devoted love because of his attachment to his young male slave Ayaz.

Mahr Dowry paid by a husband to his wife. Becomes the property of the wife to spend, save, or invest as she pleases, although in some countries it is often taken by the bride's family. Can be either money or property. May be paid all at once or split into two payments, one upon marriage and the other at a time stipulated in the marriage contract, such as upon the death of the husband or divorce. Required in order for the marriage contract and the marriage itself to be valid. *See also* Marriage and Divorce: Modern Practices

Mahram Forbidden, inviolable, holy, sacred. Traditionally used to refer to that part of the Bedouin tent, or bayt, reserved specifically

for women, where cooking was done and provisions stored. The plural, *maharim*, is used to refer to a man's close female relatives. In Islamic law, mahram connotes a state of consanguinity precluding marriage.

Mai Tatsine (d. 1980) Leader of a separatist sect involved in violent disturbances in Kano, Nigeria, in 1980. Especially known for his condemnation of all modern innovations, from bicycles to buttons. Accepted only the Quran as a valid source of religious teaching, but as a prophet, he reserved the right to reinterpret it.

Maimonides, Moses *See* Ben Maimon, Moshe

Majallah *See* Mecelle

Majd, Ahmad Kamal Abu al- (b. 1930) Egyptian Islamic intellectual, writer, professor of law, and former minister. Calls for a moderate, rational Islamic reform that links its program of change to the requirements of modern society. Believes in public and individual freedoms as a precondition for a lasting revival. Advocates gradualism in implementing the Islamic legislation and dialogue with intellectuals from non-Islamic currents. Believes Islamic rule should be based on the principles of shura (consultation), accountability of rulers, supremacy of Islamic-based rules, and respect for people's rights. Urges reconsideration of the concept of ahl al-dhimmah (people of the covenant) and promotes full equality between Muslims and non-Muslims.

Majlis Term initially meaning tribal council or council of tribes. After the advent of Islam, denoted a caliph's or sultan's audience chamber. Also referred to a gathering of a select group of people in the presence of a leading notable, religious dignitary, or well-known poet. In modern times, it generally refers to an institution set up to deal with matters pertaining to the public interest or domain. In the second half of the nineteenth century, it denoted an organization with clearly defined aims and precise internal regulations. In the twentieth century, it referred to a variety of official, private, and social institutions. Most frequently refers to parliamentary institutions endowed with legislative authority or deliberative functions.

Majlis-i Ahrar-i Islam A semireligious political organization that struggled for Muslim emancipation from British-Hindu oppression after the war of 1857. It was a revolutionary party that was formed at the call of Mawlana Abu al-Kalam Azad. The Majlis opposed the Ahmadis with full force, and in 1945 sided with with the Indian National Congress and opposed the creation of Pakistan. The state of Pakistan banned the party on 27 June 1957.

Majlis Sjuro Muslimin Indonesia *See* Masjumi

Majlisi, Muhammad Baqir ibn Muhammad al-Taqi al- (d. ca. 1699) Leading Iranian Shii scholar of the late Safavid period. Strongly opposed Sufism and attempted to popularize Shii thought among Iranians by writing in Persian rather than Arabic. In Shii thought and scholarship, represents the culminating point in the Ithna Ashari revival that began with the rise of the Safavids.

Makruh Reprehensible, detested, hateful, odious. Usually refers to one of the five legal values in Islamic law (the other four are fard or wajib, obligatory; mustahabb or mandub, preferred; halal, permissible; and haram, prohibited). Makruh acts are not legally forbidden but discouraged. Muslims are advised to avoid makruh acts because the continued and insistent commission of such acts will lead to sin.

Maktabah *See* Libraries

Maktub Written. The term frequently carries the meaning "decreed" or "established." Occurs once in the Quran at 7:157, a verse stating that Muhammad is clearly mentioned or "written" in the Torah and the Gospels.

In popular religion, it refers to fate or something that is predetermined.

Malaikah *See* Angels

Malaysia, Islam in Approximately 53 percent of Malaysia's population is Muslim. Islam spread to Malaysia between the twelfth and fourteenth centuries, largely through Sufi preachers and scholars. Malaysian Islam contains elements of other cultural and religious practices due to the variety of religions and ethnicities in the country. The early twentieth century witnessed the emergence of an Islamic reformist movement criticizing the socioeconomic backwardness and religious conservatism of traditional Malay society. Reformers pioneered the establishment of modern Islamic schools combining modern subjects with new methods of learning and teaching religion. Reformers called for greater exercise of ijtihad with direct reference to the Quran and Sunnah and less reliance on traditional interpretations of Islamic law. Demand for the establishment of more Islamic institutions was raised repeatedly in the 1970s and early 1980s, leading to the appointment of Malaysian Islamic Youth Movement's (ABIM) leader, Anwar Ibrahim, to Mahathir Mohamed's government in 1982. The creation of the Islamic Bank and the establishment of the International Islamic University (1983) and the International Institute of Islamic Thought and Civilization (1987) followed. Islamization also included the institutionalization of concrete Islamic programs, values, and intellectual discourse in government and educational institutions, support for the practice of Islamic law and the expansion of Islamic shariah court administration, and the establishment of an Islamic insurance company, the Institute of Islamic Understanding (1992), and interest-free banking facilities in conventional commercial banks (1993).

Malaysian Islamic Youth Movement *See* ABIM

Malcolm X (d. 1965) Also known as Malcolm Little and El-Hajj Malik El-Shabazz. African-American Muslim leader, civil and human rights advocate, pan-Africanist, and pan-Islamist. Introduced to Islam and Muslim heroic history while imprisoned for larceny, 1946–52. Converted in 1948 to the doctrines of Elijah Muhammad, leader of the Nation of Islam. Appointed to leadership of the Harlem-based Temple Number Seven in 1954. Inspired by Third Worldism and American political activism to denounce racism and publicly support African-American, African, and Muslim liberation. Instituted regular Arabic instruction, maintained close contact with Muslim diplomats, deemphasized the Nation of Islam's doctrine of the satanic nature of whites, and instructed assistant ministers in African and Asian cultures and current affairs. Withdrew from the Nation of Islam in 1964, although he continued to acknowledge Elijah Muhammad's spiritual leadership. Converted to Sunni Islam and performed the hajj in 1964. Assassinated on 21 February 1965 by members of the Nation of Islam. *See also* Nation of Islam

Malfuzat Written records of audiences and question-and-answer sessions of notable scholars or Sufis, providing historical context, teachings, and attitudes. Typically presented in chronological order and dated. Particular to Southeast Asia. Collections typically discuss the work's authenticity and the compiler's method of selection.

Mali, Islam in Islam entered West Africa over nine hundred years ago. Ninety percent of Mali's 10.6 million inhabitants are Sunni Muslim, 9 percent practice African traditional religions, and 1 percent are Catholic. The first independent government (1960–68), led by Modibo Keita, promoted radical state socialism; this regime dampened the emergence of an indigenous Islamic political organization. Dictator Moussa Traoré's nominally secular government (1968–91) was more tolerant of Islamic organizations. Despite efforts to co-opt Islamic reform, independent movements such as the Jamaat Ansar al-Sunnah (JAS) of the Gao region continue to exist on the margins of state control.

Malik ibn Anas al-Asbahi (d. 795) Eponymous founder of the Maliki school of Islamic law. Born and lived in Medina, leaving only to perform the pilgrimage to Mecca. Teachings reflect the scholarship of Medina. Author of the oldest surviving compendium on Islamic law. Compiled a collection of hadith of Muhammad, his Companions, and his followers, entitled *Al-muwatta*, which is widely used by Sunnis. Hadith-oriented and conservative in legal doctrines, declaring that he did not deviate from what he had been taught or the consensus of the scholars of Medina. Emphasized the importance of hadith as a basis for legal principles. Supported legal arguments and conclusions with citations from the Quran and hadith. In cases where differences of opinion existed, declared the local consensus of Medinan scholars authoritative. Used both ray (personal opinion) and qiyas (analogy) in legal thinking. Teacher of Muhammad Ibn Idris al-Shafii, founder of the Shafii school of Islamic law. Some scholars attribute to him the principle of public welfare (maslahah or masalih al-mursalah) as a guide to interpretation of Islamic law.

Malik Shah ibn Alp Arslan (r. 1072/73–92) Great Seljuk sultan. Third in the Sunni Turkish dynasty established by his great-uncle, Tughril Beg, that protected the Abbasid caliph as the spiritual leader of the Islamic community. His reign marked the fullest expansion of the dynasty's power, characterized by thorough assimilation to Persian/Arabic Muslim culture. He administered territories in Iran, Iraq, and Syria with the assistance of the vizier (Abu Ali Hasan ibn al-Hasan ibn Ali ibn Ishaq) who held the title nizam al-mulk (order of the kingdom) and established theological schools (nizamiyyah) in major cities; the jurist and mystic al-Ghazali headed the one in Baghdad. Malik Shah's death marked the beginning of the sultanate's decline, with his sons dividing the provinces among themselves.

Malika Arwa bint Ahmad al-Sulayhiyyah
See Women and Islam

Malika Asma bint Shihab al-Sulayhiyyah
See Women and Islam

Maliki School of Law School of law attributed to Malik ibn Anas al-Asbahi in the eighth century in the Arabian Peninsula. Originally referred to as the School of Hejaz or the School of Medina. Predominant in North Africa and significantly present in Upper Egypt, Sudan, Bahrain, United Arab Emirates, and Kuwait. Characterized by strong emphasis on hadith; many doctrines are attributed to early Muslims such as Muhammad's wives, relatives, and Companions. A distinguishing feature of the Maliki school is its reliance on the practice of the Companions in Medina as a source of law. Additionally, Malik was known to have used ray (personal opinion) and qiyas (analogy).

Malkom Khan (d. 1908) Iranian political and social reformer. His first treatise on political and administrative reform advocated the separation of powers, codification of law, equality before law, and freedom of belief. Sent into exile (1861); his influential newspaper Qanun, which was smuggled into Iran, attacked Qajar despotism, stressed westernization, and called for a constitutional government.

Mamluks A regime controlled by slave soldiers (mamluk means "owned" or "slave") that governed Egypt, Syria, southeastern Asia Minor, and western Arabia from 1250 to 1517. It flourished as the undisputed military power of the central Muslim world. The Mamluk sultan Baybars (r. 1260–77) spent much of his reign battling the Crusader states in Syria-Palestine and securing his frontiers against invasions from Ilkhanid Iran. Until 1340, when the Black Death decimated the population of Egypt and Syria, the regime enjoyed a prosperous reign.

Mamun, al- (r. 813–33) Abbasid caliph who encouraged the translation of scientific and philosophical texts of different civilizations into Arabic at Bayt al-Hikmah (House of Wisdom) in Baghdad. Supported Mutazilis.

Manaqib Hagiographical/biographical genre recounting the merits and miraculous deeds of holy persons. Muslim saints are typically portrayed in opposition to non-Muslim detractors, doubting Muslims, or other saints. Texts dealing with manaqib typically include hierarchies of saints and their territories and patronage. Discussions of Muhammad's virtues and miracles are particularly prominent. See also Hagiography

Manar, al- Influential Egyptian journal (the name means "the lighthouse") founded and published by Muhammad Abduh and Muhammad Rashid Rida in the early twentieth century. Hasan al-Banna took over the journal from 1939 to 1941. Published monthly between 1903 and 1935. Concentrated on Quranic exegesis and theological explication. Objectives were to articulate and disseminate ideas of reform and preserve the unity of the Muslim nation. Served as a voice for the Salafi movement, which promoted a return to the fundamental texts of Islam: the Quran and Sunnah. Sought to present reformist ideas in Quranic terms and reinterpret the Quran and Sunnah on their own, without the use of medieval texts.

Manasik Ceremonies, rituals, places for same. The word occurs twice in the Quran (2:128; 2:200), both times in connection with the duties of the pilgrimage. Plural of the Arabic noun of place mansik, referring to a place of sacrifice, a hermit's cell, and by association the actual sacrifice or ritual performed there. Among the various rituals of the pilgrimage are the wearing of special garments (ihram), circumambulation of the Kaaba (tawaf), various special prayers (dua), drinking from the well of Zamzam, the course between Safa and Marwah, the killing of an animal to be distributed later for food on the Day of Sacrifice (yawm al-nahr), and a symbolic stoning of Satan on the third day of the pilgrimage.

Manat One of three pre-Islamic goddesses worshiped at Kaaba in Mecca prior to the rise of Islam. Goddess of fate, she is identified in tradition as the "daughter of Allah"

since she was supposed to be the offspring of Allah's marriage to a jinn. The idol representing her was destroyed in 630 when Muhammad and Muslims conquered Mecca. Denounced in the Quran (53:19–20).

Mandub Recommended. One of the five classifications of actions in Islamic law. (The other four are fard or wajib, obligatory; makruh, discouraged; halal, permissible; and haram, prohibited). Refers to actions that are not required by law but are considered to be meritorious. Legal theorists generally contend that if one neglects these recommended acts, there is no punishment. Another common term used to denote the same category of practices is mustahabb.

Maneri, Sharif al-Din (d. 1381) Also called Sharafuddin Ahmad ibn Yahya Maneri. Sufi saint of Bihar, India. Initiated into Sufism after having a thorough education in traditional religious sciences. Most famous for his Hundred Letters, which are letters of spiritual advice written upon the request of his famous disciple Qazi Shamsuddin, the governor of Chausa in western Bihar.

Manfaluti, Mustafa Lutfi al- (d. 1924) Modern Egyptian writer. Advocated simplifying the complexities of earlier Arabic prose styles. Azhar-trained, he wrote moral tales, original essays, and versions of European works mostly characterized by disillusion and sentimentality. These remained immensely popular with the younger generations of Egyptians for several decades. Lacking knowledge of foreign languages, he managed to produce extremely popular versions of both Edmond Rostand's Cyrano de Bergerac (1921) and Bernardin de St. Pierre's Paul et Virginie (1923).

Manichaeism Religious doctrine professed by Mani in the first half of the third century in Mesopotamia, where a number of different religious and philosophical schools were active, including Christianity, Judaism, and Zoroastrianism. Only universal Near Eastern gnostic religion with missionary drive. Dualistic view holds that knowledge leads to salvation, achieved through the victory of good light over evil darkness. Permeated by pessimism about the world and a strong desire to free the divine and luminous principle from the bonds of physical matter and the body. Mani aspired to convert the Persian Empire; some successes in conversion were followed by persecutions by the Persian state after 277. The doctrine survived in secret until the fourteenth century.

Mansur, Abu Jafar al- (r. 754–75) Second Abbasid caliph. Built Baghdad as the new Abbasid capital. Established a translation bureau in Baghdad, which preceded Bayt al-Hikmah (House of Wisdom). Built a powerful state apparatus based on the army and bureaucracy. Introduced institution of hisbah, overseeing public duties and commerce.

Mantiq See Logic

Manzikert, Battle of Battle in 1071 between the Seljuk Turks and the Byzantine Empire. The Seljuks were victorious, capturing the Byzantine emperor and opening Asia Minor to Turkish expansion. The victory gave strength and added legitimacy to the Seljuk sultanate.

Maqam (1) Station (pl. maqamat). Used by Sufis to refer to the stages or degrees along the path to illumination. The goal of the path is personal experience of divine reality. A maqam is a stage that can be achieved through human effort, as opposed to hal (grace), which is a gift from God. The stages are to be achieved through the guidance and authority of a shaykh. The number and order of maqamat vary from order to order. The term also refers to physical locations where a saint has revealed his occasional presence, typically a tomb, which is then developed into a shrine and serves as a location for communication with that saint. (2) A system of pitch organization in traditional Arabic music for creating melodies and improvisation within a scale. The beginning, end, and main notes of a musical suite are determined by the maqam. See also Hal

Maqamah Arabic rhythmic prose genre, usually translated as "assembly" or "seance," commonly compared to the European picaresque genre. Its two most famous practitioners were al-Hamadhani and al-Hariri, from the tenth and eleventh centuries respectively. In the late nineteenth century Muhammad al-Muwaylihi successfully imitated the maqamah genre in his *Hadith Isa ibn Hisham*. *See also* Saj

Maqrizi, Taqi al-Din Abu al-Abbas Ahmad ibn Ali ibn al-Qadir al- (d. 1442) Egyptian historian, scholar, and judge. Assumed administrative, religious, and teaching positions in Cairo and Damascus. Dedicated the later years of his life to teaching and writing. Produced books on a wide variety of subjects, including the topography of al-Fustat and Cairo, the history of Alexandria and Egypt, geography, biographies of prominent Egyptians, and brief treatises on minerals and bees.

Marabout Westernized form of Arabic *murabit*, referring to a saint or to a person living in a Sufi hospice. Specific to North Africa. Refers to Sufi leaders or saints who are believed to have received barakah, or blessing, from God, which they are able to pass on to their followers when petitioned, whether they are dead or alive. Marabouts are at the center of popular Sufi shrine culture, which is considered heretical by modern reformers and orthodox movements.

Maraghi, Mustafa al- (d. 1945) Egyptian modernist reformer and rector of al-Azhar. Called for social, legal, and educational reforms. Pursued an aggressive campaign to integrate modern sciences into al-Azhar's curriculum. Called for the exercise of ijtihad (independent reasoning) and reconciliation of different schools of Islamic law. Participated in international religious conferences. Desired a greater role for clergy in government.

Marashi-Najafi, Ayatollah Sayyid Shihab al-Din (d. 1990) Iranian cleric. Studied at Najaf and Qom with Ayatollah Abd al-Karim Haeri Yazdi and later taught there. In addition to prolific scholarship, he was devoted to social and educational activities and was noted for collecting manuscripts on Shiism and Islamic studies in general. The Marashi Library in Qom, initially started in 1966, is now a significant collection. He was among a group of grand ayatollahs inside Iran who initially supported the revolution of 1979, demanding the return of Ayatollah Ruhollah Khomeini (d. 1989) from exile.

Marghinani, Ali ibn Abu Bakr al- (d. 1197) Leading Central Asian jurist of the Hanafi school of law. Best known as the author of the *Hidaya*, one of the most influential compendia of Hanafi law, which has been the subject of numerous commentaries and glosses.

Marifah Knowledge. Used by Sufis to describe mystical intuitive knowledge, knowledge of spiritual truth as reached through ecstatic experiences rather than revealed or rationally acquired.

Mariya the Copt *See* Maryam the Copt

Marja al-Taqlid Authority to be followed. Highest-ranking authorities of Twelver Shii community, who execute shariah. The term is usually applied to between four and eight high-ranking jurists (ayatollahs) locally or nationally; on the world scale, it is applied to only one or two jurists. The position is informally acquired and depends on patterns of loyalty and allegiance and the perceived conduct of the jurist. Two major ayatollahs holding this status after 1970 were Ayatollah Khomeini and Ayatollah Abu al-Qasim al-Khoi. Their followers included most Arabic-speaking Shiis in Iraq, the Gulf states, Lebanon, and Syria, and the majority of Shiis in India, Pakistan, East Africa, and Iran.

Maronite Eastern-rite community of the Roman Catholic Church. Originally monothelite, tracing its origins to St. Maron of Syria (late fourth and early fifth centuries) or St. John Maron (late seventh and early eighth centuries), but conformed to Roman doctrine in the sixteenth century. Until the mid-eighteenth century landlords appointed the patriarch and bishops. Eighteenth-century reformers tried to break lay control over the church hierarchy by establishing closer ties to Rome and promoting the idea of a church-led Maronite government. The result was a peasant revolt against feudal landlords and rising tensions with Druze, leading to civil war. The sect traditionally maintained close ties to France. It has been dominant in Lebanese politics due to the constitutional requirement that the president and the head of the military be Maronite.

Marriage and Divorce: Legal Foundations
In classical jurisprudence, the major schools (Maliki, Hanbali, Hanafi, Shafii, and Jafari) agreed that a contract is required for a juridically sound marriage, as is a dowry (mahr) for the bride, and that a Muslim woman needs a guardian (wali) to enter into marriage; they differ significantly as to the extent, nature, and duration of the wali's authority and on the nature and scope of the contract. Jurists generally agreed that the man held the right to divorce; they differed on whether the contract could stipulate that right to the woman. Shii jurisprudence allows for a temporary marriage (mutah), in which the parties stipulate to a predetermined end date. *See also* Kafaah; Khul; Lian; Mutah; Polygyny

Marriage and Divorce: Modern Practices
A contract and dowry are required for a marriage to be legally valid in most countries; local custom and laws set other conditions for validity. Tunisia and Turkey have outlawed polygyny; most other countries have imposed legal conditions. In most jurisdictions, men hold the right to divorce; women face legal impediments in divorce and child custody. All modern Muslim legislation permits men to marry non-Muslim women; Muslim women marrying non-Muslim men is illegal. The man is required to provide maintenance for his spouse(s) and children; married women have the right to own and dispose of private property. Temporary marriages are legal in Shii Iran. Mar-

riage and divorce laws and practices vary greatly from place to place depending on the historical context and on social, political, and economic circumstances. *See also* Family Law; Marriage and Divorce: Legal Foundations; Mutah; Polygyny

Marsiyyah Elegy. In Arabic *marthiyyah* or *marthat*. A poem written to commemorate the death of a person. The tradition of elegy has strong pre-Islamic roots and continues to flourish today in Arabic and other Islamic languages. The precursor of this tradition in Arabic is the poet al-Khansa, who was famous for her numerous elegies on the death of her brother. Today the function of *marsiyyah* has been extended to include elegizing entities such as cities, history, or nations.

Martel, Charles (d. 741) King of the Franks who stopped Muslim expansion into western Europe at the Battle of Tours in France in 732. *See also* Tours, Battle of

Marthiyyah *See* Marsiyyah

Martyr Arabic *shahid*. One who suffers or loses his or her life in the process of carrying out religious duty. Death during pilgrimage, from a particularly virulent or painful disease, or in childbirth is also considered an act of martyrdom. A martyr is believed to have been rendered free from sin by virtue of the meritorious act. Due to their purity, martyrs are buried in the clothes in which they died and are not washed prior to burial. They are entitled to immediate entry to paradise and enjoy special status there, since their faith has been sufficiently tested. Some Sunni theologians have declared ritual acts of fasting, regular prayer, Quran reading, filial devotion, and rectitude in tax collection types of moral and ethical martydom. Shiism in particular valorizes martyrs, beginning with the martyrdom of Husayn in 680.

Maruf *See* Justice, Concepts of

Marxism and Islam Diverse forms of Marxism agree that social ills result from oppression of the poor by the wealthy (class conflict) but differ on strategies to overcome poverty and establish social harmony. Marxism is also associated with atheism, based on Karl Marx's view that religion is used by rulers to legitimate the status quo, causing many Muslims to reject Marxism. But due to the affinity between Marxist and Islamic ideals of social justice, some Muslims adopted various forms of Marxism from the 1940s, reaching peak popularity in the 1960s and 1970s. Their analyses often ignored materialism and atheism, rejecting the idealist view that religion is independent of historical conditions and holding instead that many of its manifestations are related to the societies in which it operates. Islam in this view ideally meets the needs of society and can both accommodate and guide social change.

Mary Arabic *Maryam*. Mother of Jesus and cousin of Elizabeth. Similar to the biblical account, chapter 19 of the Quran (which is named for her) depicts Mary as a chaste woman whose miraculous virgin conception resulted in the birth of Jesus. Her relatives accused her of being unchaste, but she was vindicated when the infant Jesus came to her defense verbally. Mary's mother had dedicated her to God's service before she was born, and she was assigned to the care of the priest Zakariyya, Elizabeth's husband. Angels announced to Mary her role as chosen by God and commanded her to continue to pray, emphasizing her role as a servant of God.

Maryam *See* Mary

Maryam the Copt (d. 637) Muhammad's slave concubine. Mother of his son Ibrahim. Born in Upper Egypt. Sent to the Prophet as a gift by Cyrus (al-Muqawqas), the last Byzantine governor of Alexandria, in 628. Lived in a loft away from the Prophet's wives' chambers. After Ibrahim's birth, Muhammad released her from bondage, though she remained his concubine. His successors honored and maintained her on the same level as the Prophet's widows.

Masari, Muhammad al- Saudi opposition figure who leads the Committee for the Defense of Legitimate Rights, which was officially established in May 1993. The first communiqué was cosigned by his father, Abdullah. Muhammad rose to prominence, as his knowledge of Western languages made him accessible to Western media. Though his father was Saudi, his mother was Egyptian, which would later be used to discredit him as an impure Saudi. Studied in Germany in the 1960s and lived in the United States in the 1980s. Through the use of international media and communications (including the Internet), his group emerged as the best-known Saudi opposition group. By 1994 Muhammad was operating out of London, but his influence has waned as his movement has factionalized. *See also* Committee for the Defense of Legitimate Rights

Mashhad (1) Gravesites of Twelver Shii imams. All twelve imams were either murdered, persecuted, or poisoned, rendering them all martyrs. Their tombs have become sites of annual pilgrimage for Shiis. Shiis believe that devotion to martyred imams will win them forgiveness of sins and allow them to share in the final victory of the Mahdi (messianic imam). Pious Shiis also look on shrines as places where they can share in the imams' sanctity. The mashhads of all imams have been richly endowed and have received lavish gifts from Muslim rulers, particularly Shii dynasties. Towns, schools, and extensive cemeteries grew up around them. (2) City in Iran.

Mashriq Place of sunrise or east. Geographical term that refers generally to the eastern Arab lands: present-day Syria, Jordan, Lebanon, Palestine/Israel, and Iraq. Contrasts with *maghreb* ("place of sunset" or "west"), a geographical term that refers to the western Islamic empire, the lands of North Africa.

Mashriqi, Inayatullah Khan (d. 1963) Pakistani thinker and activist. Born in Amritsar in 1888, educated in English schools in India, and later attended Christ Church College at Cambridge, where he excelled in mathematics and natural sciences. Upon his return to India he devoted himself to Islamic scholarship, the most notable result of which was *Tazkirah*. He also became involved in Muslim politics and was particularly opposed to the Muslim League. He formed the Tahrik-i Khaksar (Movement of the Humble) in Punjab in 1931, a paramilitary organization that used agitation to undermine both the British government and the Muslim League. After partition the Tahrik-i Khaksar changed its name to the Islam League but continued to agitate. *See also* Tahrik-i Khaksar

Masih *See* Messianism

Masjid al-Aqsa *See* Aqsa, al-

Masjid al-Haram The Grand Mosque of Mecca in western Saudi Arabia. Along with the Prophet Muhammad's Mosque in Medina, it is one of the two holiest shrines in Islam, its spiritual center, and the focus of the hajj pilgrimage. A place of worship even before the time of Muhammad, the mosque is organized around the Kaaba, a pre-Islamic "House of God" founded by Abraham and Ishmael, toward which all Muslim prayer is directed. The present layout of the Grand Mosque evolved from a series of enlargements during the Umayyad and Abbasid periods, Ottoman refinements, and recent Saudi additions.

Masjid al-Qiblatayn *See* Mosque of the Two Qiblahs

Masjumi Also known as Majlis Sjuro Muslimin Indonesia (Consultative Council of Indonesian Muslims). One of Indonesia's main political parties during the period of parliamentary democracy in the 1950s. Founded in 1945 shortly following independence. All major Indonesian Muslim organizations joined. Masjumi constituted a major Muslim force in the new republic. As a Muslim party, it called for the establishment of an Islamic state and the obligation for Muslims to observe Islamic law. It participated in most governments from 1950 to 1957, though it suffered from internal rivalries. The party participated in a regional revolt in the mid-1950s, earning it the distrust of the military leadership under President Sukarno. It defended parliamentary democracy, opposing the Sukarno government's "guided democracy." Masjumi was banned in 1960 and its main leaders detained. It was later reformed as the Partai Muslimin Indonesia, but without the old leaders.

Maslahah Public interest; a basis of law. According to necessity and particular circumstances, it consists of prohibiting or permitting something on the basis of whether or not it serves the public's benefit or welfare. The concept of public interest can be very helpful in cases not regulated by the Quran, Sunnah, or qiyas (analogy). Here, equitable considerations can override the results of strict analogy, taking into account the public's welfare. Shafiis do not allow juridical opinions based on maslahah. *See also* Istihsan; Istislah

Masnavi *See* Mathnawi

Masnawi *See* Mathnawi

Masud, Ahmad Shah *See* Hizb-i Wahdat

Masudi, Abu al-Hasan Ali ibn al-Husayn al- (d. 957) Prolific writer and polymath. His known works number over twenty and deal with a wide variety of religious and secular subjects, including history (both Islamic and universal), geography, the natural sciences, philosophy, and theology. Only two of his works survive, both historical-geographical in scope: *Muruj al-dhahab wa maadin al-jawahir* (Meadows of gold and mines of gems) and *Akhbar al-zaman* (The history of time). Masudi wrote for an audience eager to acquire useful knowledge outside of the traditional religious sciences and appreciative of a fluent, nontechnical literary style. A native of Baghdad, he lived and worked in

Syria and Egypt, where he died. Associated in his early life with the Mutazilis, he is known for initiating the Arabic historiographic model of treating events topically (rather than strictly chronologically).

Masyumi *See* Masjumi

Mathal Pl. *amthal*. Usually a proverb, but also a maxim, adage, or aphorism. Medieval collections of amthal abound. Often short anecdotes accompany the proverb, tracing its origin. There are volumes of amthal from the Quran and the hadith. Proverb collections, some in dialect, are still widely popular in the Middle East

Mathematics Arabic *ilm al-hisab*. Drawing upon Indian and Greek sources, mathematicians in the medieval Islamic world developed the place-value system of decimal numbers (known as Arabic numerals), decimal fractions, irrational numbers, and use of zero (sifr), among other arithmetic notations and terms.

Mathnawi A genre of long poems, in Persian and other languages, written in rhyming couplets. Popular among mystics, often on epic themes of heroism, romanticism, and images of being separated from a lover. Some of the most famous mathnawi were written by Jalal al-Din Rumi (d. 1273), Abul Majd Majdud Sanai (d. 1131), Farid al-Din Attar (d. 1220), and Muhammad Iqbal (d. 1938).

Matn Content or text of a hadith report. Along with its chain of transmitters (isnad), one of the two main parts of a hadith report.

Maturidi, Abu al-Mansur al- (d. 956) Major Sunni theologian. Presented new methodological schemes to address theological disputes. Believed that divine justice flows from the nature and essence of God without limiting God's freedom. Human beings are distinct from animals due to their intellect, moral sense, and awareness of freedom. His method of Quranic interpretation was based on the principle that the Quran cannot be tested by any other source and that problems do not lie within texts but are due to human confusion when reading them. Consequently, unclear passages are to be compared with clearer passages in order to gain understanding. Modern thinkers such as Muhammad Abduh used al-Maturidi's methods to reinterpret traditions.

Maturidiyyah Sunni theological school founded in the tenth century in Transoxiana by Abu Mansur Muhammad al-Maturidi. Closely linked to the Hanafi school of Islamic law. Combined Sufi meditational and ethical exercises for emotional and spiritual awareness with correct external ritual and social behavior and the use of reason to understand religious truths. Stressed God's omnipotence, unity, and uniqueness, as well as the primal authority of the Quran, but also allowed for human freedom of will. Opposed to a literal interpretation of the Quran and anthropomorphism. Believed in assured salvation for those who sincerely fulfill their religious obligations as described in the Quran and Sunnah.

Mauritania, Islam in Merchants and traders introduced Islam to West Africa in the eighth century. Virtually all of the country is Sunni Muslim; the Tijani and Qadiri Sufi brotherhoods are predominant. Upon independence from the French (1960), the country's founders promoted a common Islamic culture to supplant ethnic constructions of national identity. The combined effects of the Sahara war, over twenty years of increasing drought, and resulting urbanization brought heightened internal tensions. Growing foreign debt is the most urgent domestic concern. Most threats to internal security are based on ethnic or racial tensions.

Mauritius, Islam in Indian Ocean island settled by French colonization in the seventeenth century. The population is a mixture of French, Africans (descendants of slaves), Creoles, Indians, and Chinese. About one-third of the Indian population, which is now the majority, are Muslims, forming an important Muslim minority of about 13 percent of the total population.

Mawali Sing. *mauda*. Non-Arab Muslims. Initially referred to those captured during the expansion of Islam throughout the Near East and parts of the Byzantine Empire who ultimately converted to Islam. Also refers to clients of Arab tribes. Under the Umayyad dynasty (661–750) mawali were not entitled to equal treatment with Arab Muslims, particularly with respect to taxes. Preferential treatment of Arab Muslims came to be a source of contention since it violated the Quranic declaration of equality of all believers. Under the subsequent Abbasid dynasty (750–1258), distinctions between Arab and non-Arab Muslims were not stressed.

Mawardi, Abu al-Hasan al- (d. 1058) Shafii jurist who wrote the most significant classical theoretical explanation of public law in relation to political theory, *Al-ahkam al-sultaniyyah* (Ordinances of government). Lived and wrote during the period of political transition from Shii Buwayhids to Sunni Seljuks, which brought into question the type of leadership appropriate for Muslim communities. Emphasized the authority of the caliph over that of the sultan in order to strengthen the caliph's hand against military commanders who held the power behind the throne. Conceded the possibility of having more than one executive organ of political power, but insisted on the unity of ummah and on the symbolic unity of the office of caliph. Distinguished between religious (millah) and sociopolitical (ummah) forms of human association.

Mawdudi, Sayyid Abu al-Ala (d. 1979) Indo-Pakistani Muslim revivalist thinker, prolific writer, politician, and founder of Jamaat-i Islami. Initially an ardent nationalist, activist in the Khilafat movement, and supporter of the Congress Party. After the 1924 collapse of the Khilafat movement, advocated an Islamic anti-imperialist platform. Believed the salvation of Muslim culture lay in the restitution and purification of Islamic institutions and practices. Advocated a separate cultural homeland for Indian Muslims but did not support the movement to create an independent Muslim state. Formed Jamaat-i Islami in 1941, combining model community with political party. After the foundation of Pakistan, campaigned to make it a religious state rather than a secular one. Soon identified as an enemy of the state and imprisoned several times. Advocated an Islamic state on the Prophetic model. Believed that social change would result from taking over centers of political power and effecting wide-scale reforms from the top down, rather than mobilizing the masses to overthrow the existing order. Intended for the Islamic revolution to unfold within the existing state structure rather than destroy it. Disparaged the use of violence in promoting the cause of Islam, preferring education as the keystone of Islamic activism. Author of more than 150 works. Influenced Islamic movements all over the Muslim world.

Mawla Protector, master. Also *mawlau*. From Arabic *waliya*, "to be close to," "to have power over." Has entered a number of languages as a loan word (e.g., Persian *mullah*). Can have reciprocal meanings depending on whether it is in the active or passive voice: master or slave, patron or client, and friend. In Sufism and Shiism, a spiritual protector or saint. Spelled *mawlay, moulay,* or *mulay* in the Maghreb and Andalusia. In Morocco, refers to descendants of Muhammad.

Mawlana My master. Honorific term originally reserved for addressing rulers. In Persian and Turkish it refers specifically to Jalal al-Din Rumi, and in South Asia to learned men of religion.

Mawlana Azad *See* Azad, Abu al-Kalam

Mawlawi Tariqah Turkish Sufi order known popularly as "whirling dervishes" after a special dance used as a meditation ritual. Created by descendants of Jalal al-Din Rumi (d. 1273). Most distinctive features are initiation through lengthy orientation, khal-wah (seclusion), and the importance given to sama (collective prayer chanting) as a form of meditation.

Mawlay See Mawla

Mawlid Birth. Commemoration of Muhammad's birthday, believed to be the twelfth day of Rabi al-Awwal. Celebrated as a holiday marked by popular festivities and state ceremonies in most Muslim countries except Saudi Arabia. In popular usage, also refers to the commemorative anniversary of a deceased holy person. Commemorative anniversaries take place around the holy person's tomb, the spot believed to shelter the body or a relic, or a site of an important event. This location serves as a center for annual pilgrimages by Muslims from throughout the world. Blends the mythical and mystical, ritual and scripturalist, religious and political/economic with popular traditional practices.

Mawlid al-Husayn Birthday of Husayn. Festival commemorating the birth of Husayn, Muhammad's grandson and the leader of the Shii rebellion against the Umayyad caliph Yazid. Celebrated annually in Cairo and among Shiis on the third day of Shaban. Devotees, many of whom are members of Sufi orders, visit the mosque-shrine where his head is said to be buried.

Mawlid al-Nabi Birthday of the Prophet. Celebrated on the twelfth day of Rabi al-Awwal. Popular celebration that includes readings from the Quran, poetry recitation, singing of songs commemorating Muhammad's virtues, and preparation of food dedicated to Muhammad and distributed to the poor. Also the occasion for state ceremonies except in Saudi Arabia. Some conservatives condemn the celebration since it was not celebrated during Muhammad's lifetime and is centered on a human being rather than God.

Maysir See Gambling

Mazahir al-Ulum One of the largest madrasas of Deobandi orientation in India. Founded in 1866 in Saharanpur, Uttar Pradesh, the institution was patterned largely on the madrasa at Deoband and run by people associated with the early history of the latter. Scholars associated with the Mazahir al-Ulum have been especially prominent in the study of hadith and have maintained close ties with the Tablighi Jamaat, a worldwide proselytizing movement that originated in India in the early twentieth century.

Mazalim Injustices.

Mazalim Courts Arabic dar al-mazalim. Courts that served as tribunals of administrative law where the public directly appealed to the ruler or his deputies against the abuse of or failure to exercise power by other authorities, as well as against decisions made by judges.

Mazari, Shaykh Ali See Hizb-i Wahdat

Mazdakism A dualist religion founded by Zaradust-e Khuragan and promulgated by Mazdak of Fasa in Iran during the late fifth and early sixth centuries. Though little is known of its teachings, Mazdakism appears to have been a reform movement within Manichaeanism or Zoroastrianism. Advocated social reform based on vegetarianism, pacifism, anticlericalism, and the abolition of private property. Suppressed by Zoroastrian authorities and eliminated by the eighth century.

M'Backe, Amadu Bamba See Muridi Tariqah

Mecca Holiest city of Islam, birthplace of Muhammad, site of the Kaaba and the annual pilgrimage, and the city Muslims face during prayer. Located in what is now Saudi Arabia. In pre-Islamic Arabia, Mecca was a major city on the trade routes, a pilgrimage site, and a site of worship of numerous pre-Islamic gods and goddesses. After the rise of

Islam, it lost commercial prosperity due to changes in trade routes. Its chief resources became endowment income, gifts by the faithful to the shrine and its overseers, and the annual pilgrimage. Became a major trading city again under the Mamluks of Egypt (1250–1517) due to a rise in Mediterranean and Red Sea trade. During the 1950s oil revenues brought new prosperity to Mecca, resulting in enlargement of the shrine, improvement of pilgrimage facilities, and the rapid growth and modernization of the city.

Mecelle The civil code in force in the Ottoman Empire from 1869 onward. The Mecelle-i Ahkam-i Adliye covers contracts, torts, and some principles of civil procedure. Derived from Hanafi jurisprudence, it represents the first attempt by any Islamic state to codify part of shariah.

Medical Ethics *See* Bioethics

Medicine of the Prophet *See* Medicine: Traditional Practice

Medicine: Traditional Practice Religious traditonal medicine focuses on Muhammad's practices. Early collections discuss a wide range of subjects, ranging from the curative power of honey to the medical properties of wolf's gall, whether or not one should flee from plague or use passages from the Quran as charms, and whether ritually unclean or forbidden substances are allowed if they could restore health. Incorporates natural/herbal and faith/magical remedies, extensive materia medica, and ethical and moral advice on topics ranging from doctor's fees to coitus and singing. In modern times, the medicine of the Prophet has enjoyed great popularity and engendered discussions of medicine from an Islamic perspective. *See also* Bioethics

Medina Second holiest city of Islam, to which Muhammad and early followers emigrated (hijrah) in 622 when persecuted by Meccans, and Muhammad's burial site. Originally known as Yathrib, it changed its name to "City of the Prophet" (madinat al-nabi). Place where Muhammad began to set the course for Islam to develop into a religious and political society; first he regulated the political problems of Medina by gaining assent to the Constitution of Medina, making all inhabitants into a single community. The early caliphs (successors to Muhammad) remained in Medina, making it the capital of the new Islamic empire until 661. A pilgrimage to Medina is often made in conjunction with the pilgrimage to Mecca in order to visit the tombs and shrines of Muhammad, his family, and the first three caliphs. Enjoyed little political importance in medieval times. Recovered political importance in the nineteenth century with the British occupation of Egypt and channeling of communication from Istanbul to Mecca via Medina. The Turks constructed a telegraph line to Medina and completed the Hejaz Railway through there in 1908. Medina thus became the chief communication center and chief garrison town of Ottoman Arabia. In the twentieth century, Muhammad's tomb and mosque were made larger and more ornate.

Mehmet II "The Conqueror" (r. 1444–46, 1451–81) Ottoman sultan who conquered Constantinople, renamed it Istanbul, and made it the capital of his empire. Established the oldest known Ottoman code of criminal and fiscal law. Established four millets (religion-based communities)—Greek Orthodox, Armenian Gregorians, Muslims, and Jews—to govern his subjects.

Mendaki Council for the Education of Muslim Children, a Singapore Islamic association established in 1981. Aims to improve the socioeconomic position of Malay Muslims through education. Funded by the government and through compulsory monthly contributions from every working Malay Muslim. Became controversial in 1989 when it agreed to the government's proposal to abolish free tertiary education for Malays.

Menstruation Monthly bleeding in women, causing a state of ritual impurity. During menses, women are prohibited from performing prescribed religious duties, including fasting; though they must perform the missed days of fasting at another time, they are not obligated to perform required prayers. Like men in a state of ritual impurity, they cannot touch the Quran nor remain in a mosque. Mentioned in the Quran, where men are instructed to refrain from having marital relations with menstruating women "until they are cleansed" (2:222). Women are therefore required to perform ritual cleansing (ghusl) before resuming religious duties or sexual relations.

Mesopotamia "Land between the two rivers." Region located in a position of great strategic and commercial significance in the fertile Tigris and Euphrates river valleys. Home of many great empires such as the Sumerian, Assyrian, and Babylonian. Site of the Abbasid capitals Baghdad and Samarra, as well as the Shii holy cities of Karbala and Najaf.

Messali al-Hajj (d. 1974) First Algerian nationalist leader to call for Algeria's independence from France. Joined the French army, moved to France (1923), and married a French woman. Returned to Algeria and founded the Party of the Algerian People (PPA) in 1937. After independence, he wrote his memoirs in France. Buried in Tlemcen.

Messenger *See* Rasul

Messiah *See* Messianism

Messianism Belief that a religio-political figure will appear at the end of time to lead society to justice. Shared by Judaism, Christianity, and Islam. Islamic messianism combines the belief that Jesus is the Messiah and will return at the end of time with the belief that a divinely appointed Mahdi (guide) will appear around the same time to deliver people from tyranny and oppression. *See also* Mahdi

Mevlevis *See* Mawlawi Tariqah

Michael Arabic Mikail. Archangel mentioned in Quran (2:98), often mentioned as one of the first angels to bow down to Adam, as commanded by God. Michael is believed to be among those who "opened Muhammad's breast" before his Night Journey (i.e., assisted in preparing Muhammad spiritually to receive revelation), and with Gabriel will weigh the record of human deeds on the Day of Judgment.

Middle East, Islam in Islam varies widely across the Middle East in practice, legal and theological orientation, attitude toward women, and role in government and society. The Middle East includes Turkey, Iran, Iraq, Jordan, Egypt, Palestine/Israel, Saudi Arabia, Kuwait, Yemen, Qatar, Oman, United Arab Emirates, Syria, and Lebanon. Islam has developed in four major periods in the Middle East: foundations (622–750), institutional formation (750–1050), classical period (1050–1800), and modern transformation (1800–present). The Middle East is the birthplace of Islam and the location where its major tenets, law, and many of its major historical dynasties (Ummayad, Abbasid, Ottoman, and Safavid) developed. The Middle East is also the heartland of religious scholarship and tradition, attracting scholars from throughout the Muslim world. Concerns about the perceived corruption of Islam and society and the need for reinterpretation of legal sources resulted in a major Islamic revival in the Middle East (and elsewhere in the Muslim world, especially in India) in the eighteenth century. The nineteenth century brought European colonial powers and Western science and technology to the Middle East. The result was the development of Islamic modernism, a reinterpretation of classical Islam to meet the needs of the modern world. Independence from European colonial powers resulted in the establishment of secular-oriented governments, adoption of state industrialization plans, and massive urbanization. The Islamic revival began in 1967 with losses in the Arab-Israeli War and the failure of modernization and development plans. Modernist and secular programs lost favor, and political

Islam or "Islamist" reformers gained popularity. They remain the dominant opposition to the surviving monarchies and military dictatorships. The most overtly religious states are Saudi Arabia and Iran, both of which claim to be Islamic states and implement Islamic law. Forms of states differ—Saudi Arabia is a Sunni monarchy, while Iran is a Shii republic that holds elections.

Midhat Pasha, Ahmad Shafiq (d. 1884) Ottoman grand vizier. Expanded local representative institutions and strengthened government in provinces. Introduced Western political institutions, constitution, and parliament. Worked to introduce contemporary European science and philosophy into education. Believed in progressive change through public education, rather than revolution. Led coup d'etat deposing Sultan Abdulaziz. Exiled in 1877. Murdered in exile.

Migration *See* Hijrah

Mihna Inquisition. Name given to program instituted by the Abbasid caliph al-Mamun (r. 813–33) to enforce the officially sponsored doctrine that the Quran was the created (rather than the uncreated or eternal) word of God. The principal targets were the traditionists (ashab al-hadith), led by Ahmad ibn Hanbal (d. 855). Though al-Mamun died shortly after the onset of the Mihna, it was continued with uneven enthusiasm by his two successors, who, like al-Mamun, supported the view of the rationalist theologians and jurists, several of whom belonged to the Mutazili school of theology and the nascent Hanafi school of law.

Mihrab Ornamental arched niche set into the wall of a mosque to indicate the direction of Mecca. Muslims face the mihrab during prayer so that they pray facing Mecca. *See also* Qiblah

Mikail *See* Michael

Military *See* Janissaries

Millah *See* Millet

Millet Religious community. From Arabic *millah*, "religion" or "religious community." Used by the Ottomans (1517–1922) to refer to self-governing non-Muslim religious communities. Under policy established by Mehmed II (r. 1451–81), major non-Muslim religious groups were allowed to follow their own civil and religious rules, subject to their own religious leaders, who were given official status in the administration. With the fall of the Ottoman Empire, *millet* came to mean "nation" in modern Turkish.

Milli Nizam Partisi *See* National Salvation Party

Milli Selamet Partisi *See* National Salvation Party

Minaret Beacon. Tower on a mosque from which the call to prayer is issued five times daily. Usually shaped like a cylindrical shaft with a spiral staircase on the inside or outside over a high, square base. An elevated passageway sometimes connects it to the mosque. Mosques may have up to six minarets.

Minbar Steps in a mosque or pulpit from which the Friday sermon is delivered. Emulates the stone platform that Muhammad used to ascend to deliver his sermons. Located next to the mihrab (niche indicating the direction of prayer).

Minorities: Muslim Minorities in Non-Muslim Societies More than a third of the world's 1.2 billion Muslims live as political and religious minorities. Early Islamic history yields two models for Muslim minorities to follow: the Meccan model, where Muslims facing persecution opted for emigration, and the Abyssinian model, in which the Muslim minority lived among a Christian majority in a state of tolerance and peaceful coexistence. In the modern world, Muslims living as minorities still consider themselves part of the worldwide family of Muslims.

Minorities: Non-Muslim Minorities in Muslim Societies The status and treatment of non-Muslim minorities in Muslim societies have varied over time and space. A contract of protection (dhimmah) guaranteed life, body, property, freedom of movement, and religious practice in return for submission to Muslim rule. Practice, however, was closely conditioned by economic and political circumstances and did not always conform to the law; there are historical instances of discrimination against non-Muslims, although these are considered deviations from orthopraxy. In the modern world, some reformers call for reimposition of traditional dhimmi regulations; others call for full legal and political equality between Muslims and non-Muslims. *See also* Ahl al-Kitab; Dhimmi; Mawali

Mir Damad (d. 1630) Also known as Mir Muhammad Baqir ibn Shams al-Din Muhammad Astarabadi. Persian philosopher and theologian of the Safavid period and a principal figure in the School of Isfahan, noted for his remarkable synthesis of Ibn Sina's peripatetic philosophy and Hikmat al-Ishraq's philosophy of illumination, and for his efforts to integrate Shiism and Sufism.

Miracles *See* Karamah

Miraj Ascension. Typically used to refer to Muhammad's Night Journey to heaven, which is a common theme in Sufi poetry and popular piety. Also used by Sufis to discuss their own progress along the path of spiritual ascension, which is typically modeled on Muhammad's miraj, organizing heaven into stages that correspond to emotional levels of the journey toward perfection in God. The traditional site of Muhammad's ascension in Jerusalem became a popular place for Muslim worship in the tenth and eleventh centuries. *See also* Night Journey

Mirath *See* Inheritance

Mirghani, Ali (d. 1968) Prominent religious and political leader in Sudan. The Mir-ghani family came to Sudan in the early nineteenth century and established the Khatmi tariqah. Ali assumed leadership of the family and the brotherhood early in the twentieth century. He was the patron of nationalist parties supporting the "unity of the Nile Valley" in competition with parties supported by the family of the Sudanese Mahdi. Following Sudanese independence, he was the major patron of one of the two largest political parties and during both military and parliamentary regimes was a significant political force until his death.

Mirghani, Muhammad Uthman al- (d. 1853) Sufi teacher and founder of the Khatmi (sometimes called Mirghani) Sufi order, influential in Nilotic Sudan in modern times. Born in Mecca to a prestigious family, and a student of Ahmad ibn Idris (d. 1837), a pivotal figure in the development of Sufi tariqahs in the early 1800s. He claimed that his devotional path was the "seal" (khatm) of all Sufi paths. His sons established his order in the Hejaz, Eritrea, and Egypt, but it was in Sudan that the movement had greatest success and is still an important force in social and political life. *See also* Khatmi Tariqah

Mirghani Tariqah *See* Khatmi Tariqah

Miriam *See* Mary

Mirza Husayn Ali Nuri *See* Baha Allah

Misbahah *See* Rosary

Misr Sing. of Arabic *amsar*. (1) In early Islam, referred to settlements that were established by Muslim warriors in conquered lands. The term is Semitic in origin; the original meaning is "frontier" or "border." For early Arab geographers, misr was a frontier outpost. Misr also referred to an administrative territorial unit run by an appointee of the caliph. The first such misrs were Kufa and Basra. (2) The land of Egypt. In colloquial usage in Egypt today the term refers to Cairo.

Mission *See* Dawah

Mithaq *See* Ahd

Mizan Balance. Held by Gabriel on the Day of Judgment. Weighs books containing earthly deeds against the phrase "la illaha ila Allah" (there is no god but God) written on a piece of paper. True faith will outweigh earthly deeds and ensure entry to heaven. Interpreted literally by orthodox opinion, by others as allegory.

MNP *See* National Salvation Party

Modernization and Development Western patterns of modernization and development, whether capitalist or socialist, are based on secularism, individualism, and commitment to progress through science and technology. In the perception of Islamists, they are also amoral and materialistic, perhaps even atheist. Islamists assert that Islamic approaches to development are superior to capitalism and socialism because of their attention to spiritual and material needs and concern for equity and social justice. Islamic theorists emphasize the connection between spiritual development and material improvement, concluding that institutionalization of religious goals and laws necessarily precedes development. Humans, as God's stewards, are custodians of God's resources, which must be distributed equitably. Personal wealth is permitted, but such accumulation is accompanied by responsibility for the basic needs of the less fortunate. An Islamic theory of development would thus be a set of modernized ethical standards to guide the economic, social, and political development of the Muslim world. *See also* Islamic Development Bank

Modesty Arabic *haya*. Islam calls for freedom from vanity. Muhammad is reported to have said that a person with vanity in his or her heart will not enter paradise. Muslims are not supposed to be arrogant in attitude, posture, or behavior. This includes a prohibition on racism, gender bias, and classism, as well as conspicuous consumption. Muslim men

and women are also enjoined to dress modestly, avoiding costly clothing and clothing that reveals the human figure. Some jurists demand that Muslim women veil their faces and avoid public life despite the fact that women in the time of Muhammad were not required to do so. *See also* Dress (Islamic)

Moghul Empire *See* Mughal Empire

Mohammad Tahir ibn Jalaluddin al-Azahari (d. 1957) Reformist thinker and journalist. Born in Sumatra, lived in Mecca, and studied at al-Azhar University, Cairo. Traveled between Malaya, Riau-Lingga, Sumatra, and the Middle East as religious teacher and scholar. Settled permanently in Malaya in 1906. Influenced by ideas of the Egyptian Wahhabi movement of the early nineteenth century. Identified with the reformist movement in Malaya known as Kaum Muda (Young Faction). Known for his journalistic writings as well as his editorship of the journal *Al-imam* (1906) and the newspaper *Saudara* (1934). Both publications criticized the backwardness of Malay society and advocated education as a means to achieve progress.

Mongiri, Sayyid Muhammad Ali *See* Nadwat al-Ulama

Mongols Tribal people of the inner Asian steppe who, under Genghis Khan and his successors in the thirteenth and fourteenth centuries, conquered most of Asia apart from India and established an empire from Korea to Hungary. In the Islamic Middle East, Mongol Ilkhanid rule was concentrated in Iran and Iraq, its spread further south and west halted by the Mamluk army at Ayn Jalut in Syria (1260). Mongol conquests were noted for their ferocity and great devastation. Later Ilkhanid rulers rebuilt cities and irrigation works, sponsored agriculture and trade, patronized traditional urban notables, and promoted monumental architecture, painting, and manuscript illumination.

Monotheism Belief in one god. Islam is a religion of strict monotheism, asserting a

Modernism

Islamic modernism—the reform of Islamic tradition through emphasis on the Quran and Sunnah to meet the needs of modern society, including its institutions and technology—arose in the nineteenth century. Its goal was to restore the strength, dynamism, and flexibility of Muslim societies. A selective approach to borrowing from Western developments was used to prevent Western culture from replacing Islamic culture. Modernists claimed that the adoption of modern science and technology actually meant reclaiming the Islamic heritage, since modern European science had its origins in classical Islamic learning. They distinguished between revealed knowledge and knowledge acquired through reason, but taught that reason did not clash with revelation.

The most important modernist movements arose in Egypt, India, and Indonesia, typically focusing on educational reforms to include the study of modern science and technology within the standard curriculum and legal reforms and codification of the law. Activism and resistance to European imperialism became part of modernist thought through the teachings of Jamal al-Din al-Afghani (d. 1897). Al-Afghani asserted that Muslims had to take charge of their own welfare rather than passively accepting foreign domination.

Islamic modernism underwent its richest development in the Middle East under al-Afghani's Egyptian disciple Muhammad Abduh (d. 1905). Abduh's teachings in law, education, and theology provided the intellectual basis for the assertion of the harmony of Islam and reason by demonstrating that all rational knowledge, including modern science, is in accord with Islamic principles. Abduh taught that Muslims could overcome European dominance only by embracing science and modern learning in conjunction with modernized religious education and a gradual reformation of society. Abduh's teachings created a tension between adherence to the authority of religion and a willingness to accommodate the demands of modernity. His followers called for a return to the dynamism, tolerance, and flexibility of the first generation of Muslims through close study of the Quran and Sunnah. Abduh's associate Muhammad Rashid Rida (d. 1935) sought to safeguard Islam's integrity and scriptural authority by demonstrating the compatibility of Islamic law and modern government.

In India, European domination after the 1857 Indian Mutiny and European missionaries' criticism of Islam sparked the development of the modernist movement. Indian modernism is exemplified by the works of Sayyid Ahmad Khan (d. 1898), who tried to convince the British to overcome their distrust of Muslims and to persuade the Muslims to open their minds to Western ideas. Typical of modernists, Ahmad Khan taught that Islam's teachings about God, the Prophet, and the Quran are compatible with modern science, and he placed a heavy emphasis on education. In the first half of the twentieth century Indian modernists had to address the question of how to sustain the Muslim community under a non-Muslim regime. One group, led by Muhammad Iqbal (d. 1938), argued that Indian Muslims comprised a distinct nation and must live in a Muslim state. This group struggled for the creation of Pakistan as a separate Muslim polity. The other group, led by Abu al-Kalam Azad (d. 1958), held that Muslims should join with Hindus in combating British rule and struggling for a unified, composite nation. Both sides supported democracy.

Similar to the Indian experience, Indonesian modernism was sparked by nineteenth-century Dutch domination and missionary activity. The most important Indonesian modernist movement, the Muhammadiyyah, was founded in 1912 by Hadji Ahmad Dahlan (d. 1923). Although the Muhammadiyyah established a network of

(continued)

Modernism (continued)

modernist schools for boys and girls to combine religious and modern scientific education and advocated legal reforms through a return to the Quran and Sunnah and the exercise of ijtihad (independent legal reasoning), its main focus was the purification of religious practices and beliefs.

Modernism's influence has diminished in the twenty-first century due to Islamist accusations of modernist compromise with European powers, which prolonged foreign rule, and the perception of modernism as an elitest, liberal intellectual response to Western power, rather than an indigenous ideology based on Islamic principles and culture. Modernist ideas remain alive, however, in the contemporary advocacy of the exercise of ijtihad in legal matters and the general principle of maslahah (public welfare) as a guiding principle in the evolution of Islamic law. The educational emphasis in modernism has gradually led to a degree of modern learning in some, although not all, religious schools.

---

single, unique God who has no associates and to whom no one and nothing else may be compared. Idolatry is strictly forbidden. Unlike Christianity, Islam has no doctrine of the Holy Trinity. Pre-Islamic monotheism existed in Arabia through hanifs, who are identified in Muslim tradition as descendants of Abraham and Ishmael, considered the original monotheists. Conservative interpretations of monotheism have led to criticism of Sufi and popular saint veneration. In the twenty-first century, common faith in a single, universal God for all of humankind has become the paradigm for transcending loyalty to geography, kinship ties, and national borders. *See also* Tawhid

Moon The Islamic calendar is structured according to lunar cycles. Sighting of the new moon marks the beginning of the period of required daytime fasting during Ramadan.

Whether the new moon must be visibly sighted or its position can be predicted in advance according to modern astronomical techniques remains a source of debate. The crescent moon became the symbol of Islam.

Moors Berbers from Northwest Africa who conquered the Iberian peninsula (711). The word *Moor* is a Middle French/Middle English term derived from the Latin *Maurus*, an inhabitant of Mauritania (fourteenth century). *See also* Berbers; Sri Lanka, Islam in

Moro Islamic Liberation Front A splinter faction of the Moro National Liberation Front formed in 1977 by Hashim Salamat. *See also* Moro National Liberation Front

Moro National Liberation Front A Muslim separatist group in southern Philippines led by Nur Misuari. Formed in 1969 to safeguard Moro interests in response to animosity between the Christian majority and the Muslim minority that resulted from the influx of Christian settlers into then Muslim-majority Mindanao, Sulu, and Palawan from the 1950s on. The party declared its intention to establish an independent Bangsa Moro Republik (1974), and civil war broke out. In January 1987 it tentatively accepted the government's offer of autonomy; by 1988 talks had deadlocked and fighting resumed on a much lower level. It refused to acknowledge the four autonomous Moro provinces created in a 1989 plebiscite. Since 1996 the party and the government have enjoyed an uneasy peace bolstered in part by economic rejuvenation in the region, but a radical splinter group, the Moro Islamic Liberation Front, continues to foment rebellion through guerrilla warfare and kidnappings. *See also* Moro Islamic National Front

Morocco, Islam in Ninety-nine percent of the population is Sunni Muslim; small Jewish and Christian communities exist in Casablanca and the coastal cities. Modern Islamic reformism began with Sidi Muhammad ibn Abd Allah (d. 1790). The Salifiyyah reform movement spread to Morocco (late nineteenth and early twentieth centuries) and merged with nationalism in Muhammad Allal al-Fasi's Istiqlal (Independence) Party. The reformist Abd al-Salam Yasin is the founder of the Justice and Charity Association (al-Adl wa'l-Ihsan), the strongest of a number of growing Islamist groups. He succeeded his father in July 1999. *See also* Fasi, Muhammad Allal al-; Yasin, Abd al-Salam

Mosaddeq, Mohammed (d. 1967) Appointed Iranian prime minister by Muhammad Reza Shah in 1951. Promoted nationalization of the oil industry to grant Iran independence from Western control. Ousted in 1953 by the shah's supporters aided by the CIA. The overthrow planted seeds of hostility between the Iranian people and the United States, which later exploded during the Islamic revolution.

Moses Arabic *Musa*. Prophet who led Israelites out of slavery in Egypt. The Quran records him having been placed in a basket in the Nile as a child, being taken into the house of Pharaoh, his appearance before Pharaoh, his encounters with court magicians, the plagues sent against Egypt when Pharaoh refused to let the Israelites go, the parting of the sea and the drowning of Pharaoh's army, Moses' forty days on the mountain, the receipt of the Tablets of Law, and the striking of his staff against a rock in the desert to obtain water. In the Quranic account Moses sets down the tablets containing God's commandments, rather than breaking them, after discovering the Israelites worshiping the golden calf.

Mosque of the Prophet Arabic *Masjid al-Nabi*. First mosque in Islam, originally built by the Prophet Muhammad when he moved from Mecca to Medina, both in Arabia. Originally an enclosure marked as a special place of worship and congregation. A small part of the space was used to house Muhammad and his family. Upon his death, Muhammad was buried in the mosque. The original structure was rebuilt and expanded several times. It served both as a model for all later mosques and as the second most sacred site

in Islam after the Kaaba sanctuary in Mecca. Though it is not obligatory, most Muslims include a visit to the Mosque of the Prophet as part of the pilgrimage rites to Mecca. *See also* Kaaba

Mosque of the Two Qiblahs One of the earliest mosques of Medina. Muhammad first prayed in Medina while facing Jerusalem. However, after a period of sixteen or seventeen months, Muhammad received a revelation (Quran 2:142–43) instructing him to turn the direction of prayer (qiblah) toward Mecca. One tradition indicates that Muhammad was performing the noon prayer at the mosque of Banu Salama in Medina when he changed direction in the middle of the prayer. Other traditions indicate that news of the change of the qiblah was brought to Muslims praying in the Quba mosque in an oasis just outside Medina, prompting them to change direction in the middle of prayer. The foundations for this mosque were laid by Muhammad himself; upon his emigration from Mecca, Muhammad first arrived at Quba, where he spent three days before continuing his trip to the center of Medina. The mosque wherein the direction was changed was thus known as the mosque of the two qiblahs, or the mosque where the same prayer was performed while facing the two qiblahs of Jerusalem and Mecca.

Moulay *See* Mawla

Mount Hira Mountain near Mecca, said to have been the scene of the first revelation given to Muhammad on the Night of Destiny (laylat al-qadr). The Prophet meditated in the cave at the summit of the mountain. Also known as Jabal al-Nur, the Mountain of Light.

Mourning In keeping with the basic ethos of Islam, death is viewed as a release, not necessarily something to be lamented. The afterlife is where the soul meets its ultimate destiny in the mercy of God. Loud lamentation for the deceased is discouraged in Islam, although culturally condoned in some

Mosque

The English word mosque comes from the Arabic word masjid, which means "place for (ritual) prostration." Jami designates the mosque used specifically for Friday communal prayer. Musalla is used for informal areas and open-air spaces for prayer. The mosque's main purpose is to serve as a place for formal worship in daily and Friday prayers. Both men and women attend, although women are typically segregated in a separate area. Mosques often sponsor Quranic recitations and Sufi dhikr (prayer) rites. They are the recommended location for retreats and voluntary vigils, especially during Ramadan. They serve as centers for the collection and distribution of alms and provide shelter and sustenance for the poor and homeless. Pilgrims often visit their local mosques prior to and upon returning from the hajj and lesser pilgrimages. Marriage and business agreements are frequently contracted there, and the dead are brought for funerary prayers. Mosques also serve as educational centers and central meeting points for government opposition in times of crisis. In principle, every knowledgeable Muslim is qualified to preside over ritual prayer and preach, but the leader, or imam, is supposed to be the most learned among them or his designated deputy. A woman may act as the imam where only other females are present.

Mosques are typically built wherever Muslims have settled in large enough numbers. In some cases they began as prayer spaces in military camps and evolved into buildings as cities developed. In other cases they were built over the sites of temples, churches, and palaces. There are two types of mosques: large state-controlled mosques used for Friday prayer and major communal assemblies, and smaller, private mosques built and operated by civilians. Most were founded and maintained by private charitable donations and waqf, or religious endowments. Shiis and Sufis have been particularly active in the construction of mosques over the tombs of Muhammad, his family, and other holy people. These sites serve as pilgrimage locations and congregational mosques. The mosques of Mecca, Medina, and Jerusalem hold special status. The Kaaba in Mecca became the center of the hajj, or pilgrimage, rites and the direction to be faced during prayer. Muhammad is buried in the mosque in Medina. The al-Aqsa Mosque of Jerusalem was identified as the site of Muhammad's miraculous Night Journey and ascent into heaven.

The mosque's central feature is the minbar, or steps from which the Friday sermon (khutbah) is delivered. The minbar emulates the stone platform that the Prophet ascended to give his sermons. It stands next to the mihrab, an ornamental arched niche set into the qiblah, or wall, that indicates the direction of Mecca. Mosques also contain ziyadahs, or walls that hold the ablution facilities, and minarets (towers from which the call to prayer is issued).

Mosques provide two types of religious education: talim, or instruction in the Quran, hadith, and sometimes law; and tarbiyah, or the building of a moral personality. Historically, scripture and law were taught by individual shaykhs, jurists, or ulama (religious scholars) to students assembled in circles around them according to their own choice. Students often traveled great distances to study with highly reputed scholars. For those coming from the countryside or urban lower classes, mosque education cost little and was the only path to upward mobility. For the urban upper classes and the ulama, mosque education provided access to important positions in the judiciary, state administration, and religious education. Lodging by region of origin and food for the students were provided by revenues from charitable endowments, gifts, donations, and legacies given by the wealthier classes. Upon completion of study, the

(continued)

Mosque (continued)

student was awarded an ijazah, or written statement certifying that the student had successfully studied certain texts with a particular teacher and was now allowed to teach these same texts. At the turn of the nineteenth century the major Sunni mosques providing education were the Great Mosques in Mecca and Medina, Cairo's al-Azhar mosque, Zaytunah in Tunis, and Qarawiyin in Fez. In modern times mosques have continued to serve as centers of religious instruction, inquiry, discussion, and debate, but religious education on the higher levels has been transferred to modern Islamic universities, institutes, and faculties of Islamic religious studies and shariah.

In modern times, governments have attempted to control mosque administration, the appointment of its officials, and the content of the khutbah in order to direct and control the nature of Islamic debate in society. Preachers are considered to be government employees and are encouraged to discuss religious topics, such as fasting, praying, and respect and obedience to those in authority, rather than current political issues. In contrast, the popular khutbah, which is uncontrolled by the government, is often a highly emotional and topical speech that combines discussions of mainstream Islamic thought and history with national problems and crises interpreted in the context of local politics and international crises related to Muslims. Common themes include the eternal, universal struggle between good and evil, where the West, especially the United States, symbolizes moral and spiritual decadence, and the necessity of jihad, or holy struggle, in the face of injustice. The analysis is usually presented in black and white terms and targets corrupt rulers, inequalities between rich and poor, and the inefficiency of government. Many of these popular preachers oversee large congregations and become prominent social and political voices.

Islamic societies. There is a period of forty days (iddah) during which a widow is considered to be in mourning for her husband. But Muslim jurists point out that this is really a period set aside to determine the paternity of any children born after the husband's death.

Mouvement de la Tendance Islamique *See* Hizb al-Nahdah (Tunisia)

Movement for the Restoration of Democracy (MRD) Opposition movement formed in Pakistan in early 1980s to protest then-president Zia-ul-Haq's indefinite postponement of elections. The movement included supporters of Zulfikar Ali Bhutto, members of the Pakistan National Alliance, and secular and religiously oriented parties; Jamaat-i Islami joined in 1984. The goals of the movement were restoration of democratic elections and political process and an end to martial law. The movement opposed and boycotted Zia's 1984 Islamization program. Despite a return to civilian rule in 1986, MRD continued to demand free elections of political parties and resignation of Zia as army chief of staff to ensure that the president was truly civilian.

Movement of the Dispossessed *See* Harakat al-Mahrumin

MQM *See* Muhajir Qaumi Movement

MSP *See* National Salvation Party

MTI *See* Hizb al-Nahdah (Tunisia)

Muamalat Dealings. Refers to commercial and civil acts or dealings under Islamic law. Islamic law divides all legal acts into either ibadat or muamalat. Ibadat are acts of ritual worship such as prayer or fasting, and muamalat are acts involving interaction and exchange among people such as sales and sureties. The distinction is important because the principle in all matters involving ibadat is that they are not susceptible to innovations or change (ittiba). In muamalat, however, there is considerably more room to develop and change the law to facilitate human interaction and promote justice. There is disagreement among Muslim jurists on whether certain legal acts, such as marriage or divorce, fall under the category of muamalat or ibadat.

Muawiyah ibn Abi Sufyan (r. 661–80) First Umayyad caliph and nephew of the third Sunni caliph, Uthman. Opposed Ali as caliph because he did not track down Uthman's murderer. This opposition led the Kharijis to break away from him since he had challenged the authority of a caliph they considered to be legitimate. He forced Hasan ibn Ali to abdicate the caliphate in his favor, and then moved the caliphate from Arabia to Damascus, symbolizing the transition to a new imperial age. The caliphate became an absolute monarchy under his rule.

Muawwadhatayn The last two surahs (chapters) of the Quran, or "surahs of refuge," often recited as prayers for protection against Satan, evil spirits, and the evil eye.

Mubaraah A form of divorce in which the wife comes before a judge and forsakes all her financial rights in return for divorce. The financial rights may include the dowry she has already received from her husband and the delayed dowry that she would have expected at the time of his death or if he divorced her. It could also include part of the financial support he gave her during their marriage as well as financial compensation over and above what she has received from him. Such a divorce is always a baynuna sughra, which does not prevent the couple from remarrying if they so wish. However, if the mubaraah divorce is the third time the couple has divorced, then it is baynuna kubra, which prevents their re-

marriage without an intervening marriage between the wife and a third party. In a baynuna sughra, the divorce is irrevocable, so the husband cannot take back his wife unless she has agreed, a new marriage contract is signed, and a dowry is paid to her. *See also* Khul; Marriage and Divorce: Modern Practices

Mudarabah Legal contractual arrangement under Islamic law between two partners for profit sharing—one provides capital and the other provides entrepreneurial or management skills. Islamic banks allow depositors to provide capital for borrowers to invest. Depositors may earn a share of either the bank's profit or the profit of a specified investment. If the investment or bank incurs a loss, no profit is paid to the depositors.

Muezzin A male Muslim who issues adhan (call to prayer) in Arabic from atop the minaret five times daily. In modern times, the call is often issued by a tape recording amplified through loudspeakers mounted on top of the minaret, rather than by an actual person, increasing the range and volume of the call.

Mufassir The writer of a commentary on the Quran. The word likely had its earliest usage in the tenth century, designating a specific group of people; prior to that other terms such as *ahl al-tawil* (people of interpretation) were used. Most significant religious scholars saw the role of mufassir as part of being a jurist, theologian, and grammarian. In modern times, the activity has become laicized and no longer necessarily designates someone with formal religious training or an exceptional ability in grammar and history.

Mufid, Muhammad ibn Muhammad ibn al-Numan al- (d. 1032) Preeminent Imami Shii jurist and theologian of his age in Buwayhid Baghdad. Through the work of al-Mufid and his students, Mutazili theology came to exert considerable influence on Shii thought. Al-Mufid is believed to have written some two hundred works, including *Al-irshad* (Book of biographies of the imams) and *Awil al-maqalat*.

Mufti Jurist capable of giving, upon request, an authoritative although nonbinding opinion (fatwa) on a point of Islamic law. These opinions are generally based on precedent and compiled in legal reference manuals. In Twelver Shiism an analogous role came to be played by a mujtahid. In some contexts, muftis are appointed by the state and serve on advisory councils. *See also* Faqih; Fatwa

Mughal Empire Muslim empire on the Indian subcontinent founded in 1526 by Babur (d. 1530), descended on his father's side from Timur Lang (Tamerlane) and on his mother's from Genghis Khan. The empire reached its zenith under four great emperors: Akbar (r. 1556–1605), Jahangir (r. 1605–27), Shah Jahan (r. 1627–57), and Aurangzeb (r. 1658–1707). Mughal rule embraced all of the subcontinent except the far south. After Aurangzeb died, power waned; former provinces became independent states. The British deposed the last emperor in 1857. Akbar introduced administrative systems of the empire, recruiting Persians, Indian Muslims, and Hindu rajputs; he also integrated Hindus throughout his administration and married rajput princesses. His policies of religious tolerance included abolition of the tax on non-Muslims and efforts to reconcile Muslim and Hindu belief. Aurangzeb reversed the policy of religious tolerance in the face of growing Hindu and Sikh opposition and under pressure from the religious scholars. Constant warfare and expansion of the official ruling classes led to a weakened empire. The Mughal Empire stands with the Safavids and Ottomans as one of the three great empires in which some of the highest expressions of Islamic culture were achieved, particularly in architecture.

Mughayyabat al-Khamis, al- The Five Hidden Things (or Mysteries). Technical theological term referring to things that only God knows: the hour of the Last Judgment, when

it will rain, the sex and number of unborn children in the womb, what a person will have for sustenance the next day, and when a person will die.

Muhaddithin Hadith collectors; traditionists.

Muhajir Qaumi Movement Refugee National Movement. Started by Pakistanis of north Indian descent in Karachi. Its goal is to eradicate feudalism from Pakistan; however, since the 1980s the movement has been implicated in various criminal activities. It was renamed Muttahida Qaumi Movement (Allied National Movement) in 1997.

Muhammad, Elijah (d. 1975) Leader of American Black Muslim organization, Nation of Islam, for more than forty years. Guided and mentored by Fard Muhammad and possibly Marcus Garvey. Emphasized black nationalism. Claimed that whites were descendants of the devil and that Fard Muhammad was God. Worked with Malcolm X to build the Nation of Islam into a powerful social movement in the prisons and inner cities of America. Success in reforming thousands of black men and women earned him the respect of some American sociologists. However, civil rights leaders opposed his views because of the damage they caused to race relations. Considered heretic by Muslim leaders. *See also* Nation of Islam

Muhammad, Warith Deen (b. 1933) Son of Nation of Islam founder Elijah Muhammad. Named leader of Nation of Islam after his father's death (1975); gradually reinterpreted Nation of Islam teachings concerning race, divinity, and prophecy, and revised the group's structure, moving it in the direction of orthodox Sunni Islam. Opened the movement to Muslims of all ethnicities. Restored use of the traditional Muslim declaration of faith (shahadah).

Muhammad Ali Dynasty Dynasty of Macedonian Ottoman origin that reigned in Egypt from 1805 until 1952. Founded by Muham-

Muhammad

Muslims believe that Muhammad (ca. 570–632) was God's Messenger sent to proclaim in Arabic the same revelation that had been proclaimed by earlier Jewish and Christian prophets, first to the Arabs and then to all people. The Quran provides some historical information about Muhammad's life, but fuller accounts are available in sirah (traditional biographies), hadith (reports of Muhammad's sayings and deeds), and general histories.

Muhammad grew up as an orphan in the tribe of Hashim under the guardianship of his uncle, Abu Talib. Details of his early life are not known with certainty. When he was twenty-five Muhammad was hired by a wealthy widow named Khadijah to oversee her caravan of goods to Syria. Muhammad later married her. They had four daughters who grew to adulthood and at least three sons, all of whom died in infancy. During her lifetime Khadijah was Muhammad's only wife. After her death, he married a widow named Sawdah. Khadijah and Sawdah were his only wives prior to the hijrah. Once in Medina, Muhammad contracted other marriages based on political alliances and his responsibilities as the head of the Muslim community.

Muhammad received his first revelation at about the age of forty when the angel Gabriel appeared and recited surah 96 to him. Accounts of miraculous foretelling of Muhammad's future prophethood in the sirah and hadith literature include recognition of Muhammad's prophetic status by Christian monks and a light shining from Muhammad's face and that of his mother during her pregnancy. Other miraculous accounts include Muhammad's Night Journey, or isra, from Mecca to the Temple Mount in Jerusalem and his ascension to heaven, or miraj.

The Quran does not specifically refer to Muhammad's public ministry in Mecca, but the biographical sources record the emigration of Muhammad's followers to Abyssinia (modern-day Ethiopia), the boycott of Muhammad's clan of Hashim, the deaths of his wife Khadijah and his uncle and protector, Abu Talib, the loss of his clan protection, his visit to al-Taif for refuge, and the hijrah to Medina. The Quran portrays Muhammad as fully human with no supernatural powers. His humanness is most apparent in the passages where he is told to be steadfast and patient in times of persecution, disappointment, or grief. Although he won many victories over the Meccans and succeeded in converting many of the tribes of Hejaz, the Quran records that Muhammad agonized over those who did not believe and remained humble, shy, and sincere. He constantly sought forgiveness for his own sins.

The Quran, sirah, and reports of Muhammad's military expeditions provide extensive information about the Medinan period. His victories over the larger forces of the Meccans were interpreted as signs of God's favor. By 627 Muhammad was in complete control of Medina, and Bedouin tribes in the surrounding area were making alliances with him and becoming Muslims. In the spring of 628 Muhammad negotiated a treaty with the Meccans for permission to perform the pilgrimage, or hajj, the following year, along with a ten-year truce. He led the first Muslim pilgrimage to Mecca in the spring of 629. When the truce was broken a year later, the leaders of Mecca agreed to surrender the city peacefully to Muhammad. As a result, Muhammad was in command of all of west-central Arabia by 630. In 631 envoys from all over Arabia came to him to surrender. Muhammad regarded the resulting treaties as an acceptance of Islam. In 632 he led the largest number of Muslim pilgrims ever assembled during his lifetime on his "Farewell Pilgrimage." On the return trip to Medina, Muhammad contracted a fatal illness. He died in June 632, at about the age of sixty.

(continued)

Muhammad (continued)

Muhammad served as administrator, legislator, judge, and commander-in-chief as well as teacher, preacher, and prayer leader of the Muslim community. For the scholars of Islamic law he is the legislator-jurist who defined ritual observance; for the mystic he is the ideal seeker of spiritual perfection; for the philosopher and statesman he is the role model of both a conqueror and a just ruler; for ordinary Muslims, he is a model of God's grace and salvation.

---

mad Ali (d. 1849). Supported by religious scholars of al-Azhar University. Responsible for major modernization and development programs and importation of European advisers to modernize the army, schools, technology and infrastructure, and bureaucracy. Although Egypt remained technically part of the Ottoman Empire, it came under de facto British control after 1882. The dynasty was overthrown in a military coup in 1952.

Muhammad ibn Ismail Also known as Muhammad al-Mahdi. Eighth Ismaili Shii imam. Grandson of Jafar al-Sadiq. His succession was accepted by a minority of Shiis; the majority recognized his brother, Musa al-Kazim. Muhammad ibn Ismail's descendants became the Fatimid caliphs of Egypt. Followers recognized him in the messianic role of the Mahdi due to the Ismaili belief that there were to be seven prophets in history, each followed by a cycle of seven imams. The Prophet Muhammad was believed to be the sixth prophet, followed by Ali as the seventh. Muhammad ibn Ismail was therefore the seventh imam and final prophet, who was supposed to return to reveal truth and justice.

Muhammad Marwa *See* Mai Tatsine

Muhammadi Tariqah Type of Sufi order that bases its authority on assimilation of the

spirituality of the Prophet Muhammad, includng visions of the Prophet. The term was first used by the Moroccan Jazuliyyah Shaykh Abdullah Ghazwani (d. 1529). Such tariqahs were most common in the early modern period and include the orders of Khwaja Mir Dard of Delhi (d. 1785), Sayyid Ahmad Reza Khan Barelwi in India (d. 1831), the Tijanis, and tariqahs in the tradition of Ahmad ibn Idris (such as the Sanusi). Mehmed Birgewi (d. 1573), an Ottoman scholar, used the term for his program of religious reform. In earlier periods, the term also applied to some extremist Shii subsects.

Muhammadiyyah Javanese Islamic reformist movement founded by Kiyai Hadji Ahmad Dahlan in 1912. One of the most important religious, educational, and social movements in Indonesia. Most powerful reformist movement in Muslim Southeast Asia today. Emerged as a means of coping with the pressures and alienation of colonial history. Established hundreds of branches with millions of members, missionary movements, clinics, orphanages, poorhouses, hospitals, publications, labor unions, farm cooperatives, factories, and schools. Has committees on Islamic law, politics, women's affairs, youth, education, library and archives, celebrations and evangelism, social welfare and health care, economic development, and property administration. Counts several million members, largely from the middle class. *See also* Aisyiyah; Dahlan, Kiyai Hadji Ahmad

Muhammadu Arab *See* Mai Tatsine

Muharram First month of the Islamic lunar calendar; the month when the qiblah (direction of prayer) was shifted from Jerusalem to Mecca. The first ten days are a period of intense ritual mourning during which Shiis engage in lamentation assemblies, public processions, and other activities, culminating in the anniversary of the murder of Husayn (Muhammad's grandson).

Muhsan Chastity. Legal concept describing the personal status of an individual who is free (not a slave) and who either has never committed an act of illicit intercourse or has consummated a lawful marriage to a free partner. In the latter case, the person is subject to the sentence of death by stoning if he or she commits adultery.

Muhtashimi, Ali Akbar (b. 1946) Student of Ayatollah Khomeini in Qom and Najaf. Trained in PLO guerrilla camps in Lebanon during the mid-1970s. Director of Iranian national radio and television, 1987. Member of parliament 1988–92. Opponent of cultural conservatives after 1992. Has strong ties with the Hasan Nasrallah faction of Lebanese Hizb Allah.

Muhtasib Holder of the office of al-hisbah, in classical Islamic administrations an executive falling roughly between the offices of judge (qadi) and court magistrate. Charged with enforcing public morality, overseeing the public welfare, and supervising the markets, the muhtasib had no jurisdiction to hear cases—only to settle disputes and breaches of the law where the facts were admitted or there was a confession of guilt. The muhtasib was vested with discretionary powers through which he could intervene in such matters as commercial fraud and public nuisances. Today there are few vestiges of this medieval institution. *See also* Hisbah

Mujaddid Renewer. Person who initiates tajdid (renewal). According to hadith, a mujaddid is to come at the beginning of each century to renew the faith and correct the practice of Muslims. Many puritanical reformers and revivalists have been identified by their followers as mujaddid because they have called Muslims back to the Islam of the early community as they interpret it, rejecting as innovations any later added practices or customs. Ahmad Sirhindi (d. 1624) of India, for example, who revived the Naqshbandi Sufi tariqah, was widely known as the mujaddid of the second thousand years of Islamic history.

Mujaddid Alf-i Thani *See* Sirhindi, Ahmad

Mujaddidi, Sibghat-Ullah (b. 1925) Scholar and important figure in the Naqshbandi tariqah in Afghanistan. Served two months as transitional president of the Islamic interim government of Afghanistan in 1992, between Mohammad Najibullah and Burhanuddin Rabbani. Head of conservative National Liberation Front.

Mujahidin (1) Plural of mujahid, "one who engages in jihad." Often translated as "warriors of God." Technically, the term does not have a necessary connection with war. In recent years those Muslims who engage in armed defense of Muslim lands call themselves or are called mujahidin. They are not a monolithic movement of one origin but rather are diverse. They see themselves as God-fearing people who are fighting against injustice, especially foreign domination, but also against unjust state oppression. The term became well known in the West in the early 1980s as the Afghan mujahidin battled against the Soviet invasion of Afghanistan. Muslim volunteers from many countries have been fighting under that name in conflicts such as those in Albania, Kashmir, Kosovo, Bosnia, and Chechnya. (2) Afghani guerrilla fighters who fought against Soviet occupation and Communist rule (1978–90). Supported by United States, Pakistan, and Saudi Arabia. They were divided into numerous political parties, following various ideological, ethnic, and sectarian loyalties. Dominant parties included the radical Hizb-i Islami, led by Gulbuddin Hekmatyar, and the moderate Jamaat-i Islami, led by Burhanuddin Rabbani and Ahmad Shah Masud.

Mujahidin-i Khalq (Iran) Better known as the Iranian Mujahidin. A religious but anticlerical organization that constitutes the main opposition to the Islamic Republic of Iran. Its ideology combines Shiism with Marxism and holds Islam as a divine message for social, economic, and political revolution. Ayatollah Khomeini pronounced the Mujahidin more dangerous than kafirs (unbelievers) and ordered the Revolutionary Guards to execute them (1981); their leader, Masud Rajavi, went into exile. The group's avowed goal is to replace the clerically dominated Islamic republic with a democratic Islamic republic. Although a significant force in exile, the group has lost most of its social basis in Iran.

Mujahidin Party *See* Hizb-i Wahdat

Mujtahid One who exercises independent reasoning (ijtihad) in the interpretation of Islamic law. Qualifications include training in recognized schools of Islamic law and extensive knowledge of the Quran and hadith. In Sunni Islam, the title is reserved for the founders of the four official schools of Islamic law, although modern Islamic reformers call for the revival of ijtihad as a means of accommodating new ideas and conditions.

Mukallaf *See* Taklif

Mukhtar *See* Umdah

Mukhtar, Umar al- (d. 1931) Libyan resistance leader. Unified the authority of the Sanusi Sufi order in Cyrenaica. Combining religious authority with military skill, inspired tribes to join the jihad against Italian occupation (1911–17). Was captured, tried, and hanged. Resistance crumbled after his death.

Mukhtasar Concise handbook of legal treatises, characterized by neatness and clarity. Originated during the Abbasid caliphate. Created as a method to facilitate the quick training of lawyers without the repetitiveness of lengthy volumes, yet evolved into a mode of access into the fundamentals of Islamic law for the educated layperson.

Mulay *See* Mawla

Mulhid *See* Ilhad

Mulk, Sitt al- *See* Women and Islam

Mulla Sadra *See* Shirazi, Sadr al-Din al-

Mullabashi Safavid institution designating a high religious functionary in Shii Islam. Served as foremost religious scholar and had a privileged seat next to the shah on formal occasions. Duties included soliciting pensions for students and men of merit, generally upholding virtuous conduct, and giving legal advice.

Mullah Title used to identify a religious functionary, cleric, learned man, or someone with religious education. A Persian construction from the Arabic *mawla* (master, leader, lord), the title is very similar to *akhund* in the range of meanings it invokes. As a class, mullahs are the principal interpreters of Islamic law for Shiis. *See also* Akhund; Mawla

Mullah Muhammad Omar (b. 1959) Reclusive, enigmatic supreme leader of the Taliban movement in Afghanistan. A fervent believer, with minimal education in a rural madrasa. Served as a mujahidin group subcommander in the jihad against Soviet occupation in the 1980s. Emerged as leader of the Taliban in 1994; declared amir al-muminin (commander of the faithful) in 1996. Strongly influenced by his rural Pushtun tribal background; adheres to a fundamentalist interpretation of Islam, including severe restrictions on the freedom of females. Politically isolated under his rule, Afghanistan became a safe haven for extremist groups, production and trafficking of narcotics, and a source of instability in the region.

Mumin Believer. Identified in the Quran as one who believes "in God and His messenger" (49:15). Mentioned over two hundred times in the Quran. Often used interchangeably with *muslim*, mentioned forty times in the Quran, referring to "those who submit" to the will of God.

Munafiq *See* Hypocrite

Munazarah A public debate using questions and answers, popular in classical Islam. Often held before an authority, who determined the victor. Originally theological in nature, the practice spread to other realms, such as jurisprudence, philosophy, and science. Also the name of a literary genre employing the format of debate in order to make points.

Mundhdhamat al-Mutamar al-Islami *See* Organization of the Islamic Conference

Munshi State scribe or secretary. Exponent of the writing style prevalent in Islamic chanceries from the eighth century onward. Secretary in the ruler's chancery in the Persian and Indo-Muslim worlds. Important official in the Safavid period. Europeans later applied the term to native teachers of local Indian languages.

Muntazar, al- *See* Shii Islam

Muntaziri, Husayn Ali (b. 1922) Born in Najafabad, Iran. Obtained his religious education in Isfahan, Burujird, and Qom. A student of Ayatollah Muhammad Husayn Burujirdi (d. 1962) and Ayatollah Ruhollah Khomeini (d. 1989). Imprisoned 1963–70; exiled to Najafabad, 1970–73, and then to Tabas (1973), Khalkhal (1974), and Saqqiz (1975); transferred to Evin Prison (1975). Released in 1978. Was acknowledged as Khomeini's successor in 1985 but dismissed from the succession by Khomeini four years later over policy differences. Currently an important voice of opposition to Iran's clerically dominated government.

Muqaddim Leader of a Sufi order; spiritual guide or shaykh.

Muqaddimah, al- Introduction. Refers to the lengthy introduction to the multivolume philosophical history of civilization, *Kitb al-ibar*, by Ibn Khaldun (d. 1406). The introduction explores human civilization in general and Bedouin civilization in particular, and investigates the basic kinds of political associations, the characteristics of sedentary civilization, the arts and crafts by which humans gain their livelihoods, and the different human sciences. Considered a forerunner of the modern discipline of historiography.

Muqarnas Three-dimensional architectural ornamentation, found from Spain to India, composed of superimposed ranks of small geometric niches, often interposed with pendant elements. Originally a structural form used in niches and in squinches under domes, the muqarnas later evolved into a highly characteristic form of architectural decoration in the Islamic world.

Muqasamah Tax system in use from 628 until the end of the Mamluk period (late sixteenth century). Usually known as muqasamah kharaj. Took the form of a sharecropping contract whereby the tenant entered into a lease agreement with the state or a private party, promising to pay a percentage of the crop yield in exchange for protection of the land. Most of the jurisprudential discussions focus on whether such contracts are unduly speculative.

Murabahah Islamic banking principle in which a bank purchases a good on behalf of the client and later resells it to the client at a marked-up price. The markup includes the bank's costs and allows return for risk taken during the period it owns the good being traded. The bank does not take delivery of the good but has responsibility of ownership. *See also* Banking (Islamic)

Murabit *See* Almoravids

Murabitun *See* Almoravids

Murid One who desires. Disciple or aspirant in Sufi order who submits to the direction, authority, and guidance of the murshid (Sufi master). Initiation into the order requires the murid to surrender his or her will to that of the murshid. Throughout the instruction period, the murid typically experiences visions and dreams during personal spiritual exercises. These visions are interpreted by the murshid. The murid is invested in the cloak of the order upon initiation, having progressed through a series of increasingly difficult and significant tasks on the path of mystical development. Murids often receive books of instruction from murshids and often accompany itinerant murshids on their wanderings.

Muridi Tariqah Best-known Sufi order in Senegal. Name comes from murid, referring to a postulant who seeks the path to spiritual knowledge. Founded in 1880s by Amadu Bamba M'Backe. Followers came into conflict with French colonialists in the 1890s. During the exile of the founder from 1895 to 1902, his family and friends encouraged members of the order to cultivate peanuts and acquire property in both rural and urban settings. Ultimately M'Backe endorsed the cause of the French in World War I. Members of the order are encouraged by leaders to work hard, particularly in peanut cultivation, and to allow marabouts to carry out intercession on their behalf. Recently followers have taken an interest in learning the teachings of Islam and the heritage of the founder.

Murjiah *See* Murjiis

Murjiis Postponers. Theological school that emerged in the eighth century as a reaction to the extreme puritanism of the Kharijis. Believed in postponing judgment on believers who committed grave sins. Emphasized promise, hope, and respite granted by God rather than threat and punishment. Opposed the doctrine of eternal punishment of sinners. Emphasized God's goodness and love for humankind. Held that a Muslim ruler should be obeyed, even if one disagreed with his policies or questioned his character. Believed in primary and authoritative status given to intention in faith. Preached tolerance toward other Muslims and equality of all believers, regardless of origins. Supported a spirit of unity within the Muslim community.

Murshid One who guides (Persian pir, "old man" or "respected elder"). Sufi master responsible for guiding and directing novices and disciples toward mystical knowledge of God through specified "way" or "path." Often bases decisions on interpretation of dreams and visions. Bestows practices, liturgy, formulas, and symbols of order on novices in the same manner in which he received them, preserving continuity of the order in the name of the original master. The murshid's name is listed in the silsilah (roster) of the order to verify that the transmittance is genuine and to trace the order back to the founder.

Murtadd Apostate; one who has renounced her or his religion. According to classical Islamic law, a murtadd is subject to the death penalty or banishment. Legal opinions vary regarding the status of an apostate's property but agree that an apostate's marriage is void and that he or she loses the right to a Muslim burial. Many modern thinkers reject the death penalty for apostasy, stressing instead the Quran's prohibition of coercion in matters of religion (2:257). *See also* Apostasy

Muruwwah Virility. Connotes a cluster of virtues—bravery, generosity, practical wisdom, and honor, all highly valued in both pre-Islamic and Arab tribal culture and literature.

Musa *See* Moses

Musa, Nabawiyyah (d. 1951) Egyptian feminist, nationalist, writer, and educator. Believed that education was the strongest weapon against colonial domination. Promoted education and work for women as a means of individual and national liberation within the framework of Islamic modernism.

Musaylima ibn Habib Seventh-century self-proclaimed prophet. Contemporary and opponent of Muhammad. Referred to as "the liar" in early Islamic sources. Became militarily aggressive against Muslims after the death of Muhammad. Formed an alliance against Muslims with Sajah, a female religious leader of Banu Tamim. Defeated by Khalid ibn al-Walid in 634.

Musharakah The generic term for business partnership or "participation financing," of which there are a variety of forms. The most popular in modern Islamic banking is inan, or limited liability partnership, in which partners share agency (not suretyship), contribute their work and their capital, divide profits in accordance with their agreement, and share losses in proportion to their contributed capital. The different legal schools treat the forms variously, affording an unusual degree of maneuverability to the contracts. *See also* Banking (Islamic)

Mushrikun *See* Polytheists

Music *See* Devotional Music

Muslim One who submits to the will of God. The plural form, *muslimun*, refers to the collective body of those who adhere to the Islamic faith and thus belong to the Islamic community of believers (ummah). To demonstrate that one has become a Muslim, one must recite the shahadah, witnessing that there is no God but Allah and that Muhammad is the messenger of God. The English term *Muslim* is used as an adjective attributing religious characteristics (e.g., Muslim faith), whereas *Islamic* generally connotes broader cultural meanings (e.g., Islamic art, Islamic literature).

Muslim (Ibn al-Hajjaj) (d. 875) Also known as al-Qushayri. Scholar and author of one of the six collections of hadith broadly recognized as authentic and canonical, known as *Sahih Muslim*, which, along with *Sahih al-Bukhari*, is considered the most authoritative hadith collection. Helped to establish the Islamic science of authentication of hadith transmission (ilm al-rajal). Divided hadith into three categories: those transmitted by upright people of skilled knowledge and free from contradictions or misrepresentations; those transmitted by people of lesser knowledge but upright in character; and reports that are suspect due to fabrication or error. His collection addresses requirements of faith, rituals, personal status, business transactions, crime and punishment, afterlife, knowledge, and the qualities of Muhammad and the Companions. *See also* Sahih Muslim

Muslim Brotherhood in Egypt Founded in 1928 in Egypt by Hasan al-Banna. Parent body and main source of inspiration for many Islamist organizations in Egypt and several other Arab countries, including Syria, Jordan, Kuwait, Sudan, and Yemen, and some North African states. Emerged as a reaction to the division of Arab countries into spheres of influence for European powers, the abolition of the caliphate in Turkey, and Western influence on Islamic culture. Promoted benevolence, charity, development, nationalism, independence, and social and governmental reform according to the letter and spirit of Islam. Tactics have ranged from activism and pro-regime political accommodation to militancy and anti-regime assassinations and violence, from philanthropy and economic institution building to accommodation with opposition political parties. Active in fund-raising for Palestinian Arabs resisting Zionism. In the 1940s was the most popular and respected of the nationalist forces fighting against British imperialism, military occupation, and Zionism in Palestine. Its leaders and theoreticians are among the most influential of Egypt's twentieth-century political figures; the most famous was Sayyid Qutb, whose principal concern was the use of jihad against ignorant or "pagan" societies, both Western and secular Islamic. The Muslim Brotherhood was initially allied with the Free Officers, who overthrew the Egyptian monarchy in 1952, but was ultimately persecuted by the new regime, headed by Gamal Abdel Nasser. Anwar Sadat rehabilitated the Muslim Brotherhood and sought its support in 1970s but refused to grant it unconditional legal status as a political party. In the 1980s it embraced nonviolence and became an opposition movement, accepting political pluralism and parliamentary democracy; more radical elements within the organization seceded. The Muslim Brotherhood has participated in and won elections in various political alliances since 1984 and has mass appeal across social classes. It is committed to educational publications.

Muslim Brotherhood in Jordan Islamic revivalist organization founded in 1946 by members of the Egyptian Muslim Brotherhood. Encouraged a return to Islamic values and the education of Jordanian society. Became increasingly politicized after the creation of Israel in 1948 and Jordanian annexation of the West Bank in 1950. During the 1950s it held close relations with the monarchy and the ruling regime. The relationship was further strengthened in 1967 after loss of the West Bank to Israel and the PLO's establishment of a stronghold among Palestinian refugees in Jordan but weakened due to its criticism of the monarchy in the 1980s, including charges of corruption of the ruling elite, public immorality, and insensitivity to religious life. King Hussein publicly distanced himself from the group in 1985, targeting it as a potential threat to the country's stability. The Muslim Brotherhood has participated in and won elections since the end of the 1980s. Its support for Iraq in the Gulf War of 1990–91 jeopardized its relationship with and financing from Kuwait and Saudi Arabia but preserved and legitimated its popular support. Its religious message remains popular.

Muslim Brotherhood in Palestine The Muslim Brotherhood in Palestine emerged from the efforts of Egyptian Muslim Brotherhood founder Hasan al-Banna in the early 1940s when he began setting up branches in Palestine. As Palestinian territory continued to be taken under the control of other countries—Egypt and Jordan in the late 1940s and then Israel after the Six-Day War in 1967—the Muslim Brotherhood of Palestine flourished under a partnership with other Brotherhood organizations. In 1973 the Palestinian version of the Brotherhood, under the leadership of Shaykh Ahmad Yasin and with the permission of Israeli authorities, developed social, religious, and welfare programs, which led to increased popularity.

However, by the 1980s the Brotherhood's apolitical path had caused its support to dwindle, especially among the increasingly politicized younger generation. As a result, Shaykh Yasin and others created Hamas, an offshoot, in 1987 during the Palestinian uprising (intifadah) against Israeli occupation and rule in Gaza and the West Bank. The Brotherhood continues as a separate organization primarily concerned with educational and social reform.

Muslim Brotherhood in Syria Islamic revivalist organization founded in the 1930s by Syrian students familiar with Hasan al-Banna's ideas. Its earliest goals were to spread Muslim education and ethics and inculcate anti-imperialist feelings among the urban populace. Its first published program sought to combat ignorance and deprivation and establish a political regime based on Islamic law. It briefly supported Islamic socialism, and it supported Syria's 1961 withdrawal from the United Arab Republic. The seizure of power by the Baath Party in 1963 focused the Muslim Brotherhood's opposition on the radical, secular, nationalist regime's socialist policies and introduction of large numbers of rural people into the state bureaucracy. The brotherhood split in 1970 over the 1967 military defeat and accession to power of Hafez al-Assad. During the 1970s it was the most visible and powerful opponent of the Assad regime, engaging in violence against it. In 1980 Assad declared any association with the Muslim Brotherhood punishable by death and initiated a government crackdown. The biggest blow to the group came in 1982 with the razing of Hama, its stronghold. Little has been heard of the organization since then. *See also* Sibai, Mustafa al-

Muslim Brotherhood in Sudan Islamic revivalist organization that originated among Sudanese students in Cairo in 1940s. Rejected union with the Egyptian branch, forming an alliance instead with the Sudanese Ansar-Ummah political bloc in support of Sudanese independence. Hassan al-Turabi emerged as its most effective spokesperson in 1964. The Muslim Brotherhood founded the Islamic Charter Front in 1964 to advocate Islamic constitution. It cooperated with the Ummah Party in an anti-Communist drive and the push for an Islamic constitution. The 1969 coup by Jafar al-Numayri and his Communist allies halted implementation of its goals. The Muslim Brotherhood preferred pragmatism to armed struggle and joined forces with the regime in 1977. Members were appointed to positions in the judiciary and the educational and financial systems, improving organization and finances. Insisted on the foundation of an Islamic state. Supported the implementation of hudud punishments in 1983 as part of an educational process to improve the morals of citizens. Formed the National Islamic Front in 1985 and participated in 1986 elections. Provided support for the regime established by a military coup in 1989 and has since dominated Sudanese politics.

Muslim-Christian Dialogue Intentional, structured encounters between Muslims and Christians in which two or more parties express their views and listen respectfully to their counterparts. The dialogue movement began during the 1950s, when the World Council of Churches and the Vatican organized meetings between Christian leaders and other faith representatives. By the 1980s and 1990s other regional and international bodies had developed their own programs: the Muslim World League, the World Muslim Congress, and the Middle East Council of Churches. Obstacles to successful dialogue include Muslim wariness because of the recent history of colonialism and the fact of Western hegemony and Christian perceptions of Islam as inherently threatening. See also Christianity and Islam; Dhimmi; Minorities: Muslim Minorities in Non-Muslim Societies; Minorities: Non-Muslim Minorities in Muslim Societies

Muslim Converts' Association of Singapore (Darul Arqam) Officially established in 1980; in the 1970s it was called Kampulan Saudara Baru (New Brothers Group). Provides Islamic religious courses in English and Mandarin for potential Muslim converts.

Concerned with the welfare and problems faced by new converts. Publishes a quarterly magazine, *The Muslim Reader*.

Muslim Council of Britain Federation of most major Sunni Muslim organizations in Britain, founded in 1997 and led by Iqbal Sacranie. Has specialist groups dealing with issues such as the media, education, politics, and the law. Prefers to avoid public confrontation and has successfully negotiated with the government concerning legislation and with newspapers to become aware of Muslim concerns.

Muslim Educational Trust Founded in Portland, Oregon, in 1993, to provide education about Islam for both Muslims and non-Muslims. Outreach efforts include advocacy for unbiased news coverage, workshops for public-school teachers, support for interfaith dialogue, public lectures, publications, and operation of Islamic schools.

Muslim League Successor of the All-India Muslim League. Established in 1906 in Dhaka. Led the movement for the creation of Pakistan. Sought to protect Muslim political rights in British India, achieve self-government, and cooperate with the All-India National Congress. Its first president, Mohammad Ali Jinnah, argued for creation of a separate Muslim province in Sindh and Muslim representation in Bengal and Punjab. In 1930 Muhammad Iqbal articulated the two-nation theory and the notion of Muslim self-determination. After the Lahore Resolution of 1940, it articulated a demand for a Muslim homeland. Jinnah finally agreed to the two-nation theory, which ultimately became the basis for the creation of the state of Pakistan. The Muslim League later splintered into factions; the primary surviving party is the Pakistan Muslim League. See also Jinnah, Mohammad Ali; Pakistan, Islam in; Pakistan Muslim League

Muslim Parliament Muslim organization founded in 1991 in London by Kalim Siddiqui, based on a proposal published in July

1989 with the title *The Muslim Manifesto*. The Muslim Parliament consists mainly of appointees, including many women and young people, and works through specialist committees. Its proposals have attracted public attention, and some have been copied by other Muslim groups. Since Kalim Siddiqui's death in 1996, the group has been mostly dormant.

Muslim Party of Indonesia *See* Partai Muslimin Indonesia (Parmusi)

Muslim Student Association (United States) Established in 1963 in Indiana to provide a sense of identity to foreign Muslim students and to give them an opportunity to learn about Islam in the modern context. Derives its constituency from all parts of the Muslim and non-Muslim worlds. Provides free access to Islamic literature and books for students, and provides global links through members and alumni. Representatives participate in conferences and conventions of other Muslim student organizations in other countries, making them increasingly aware of the variety of Islamic thought and identity.

Muslim Student Association (Nigeria) An organization of Muslim Nigerian college students founded in the 1960s that grew rapidly during the 1970s oil boom and the concomitant expansion of opportunities for higher education. Most members wanted to reform their Sufi orientation and were influenced by Abubakar Gumi, the grand kadi of northern Nigeria during the first republic (1960–66).

Muslim United Front An alliance of Islamic parties organized to contest the 1987 state elections in Indian-controlled Kashmir. The alliance won only three seats, allegedly due to massive electoral fraud. The group's poor showing in 1987 inspired a new phase of armed resistance to Indian rule in Kashmir that continues today.

Muslim World League Rabitat al-Alam al-Islami. Founded in 1962 in Saudi Arabia to discuss the affairs of the Muslim ummah in view of the threats posed to the Muslim world by Communism and irreligion. The intent was to promote the message of Islam, fight perceived conspiracies against Islam, and discuss all problems relevant to Islam. After 1972 it stressed a supranational, independent identity and concentrated on establishing a network of Islamic cultural and political organizations. During the 1970s it expanded activities in missionary work, jurisprudence, and social welfare. The group has acted as a mouthpiece for the Saudi Arabian government, which finances it. Since the beginning it has sought to establish a jurisprudence council entrusted with the elaboration and control of internationally accepted standards of Islamic law. *See also* International Islamic Relief Organization

Muslim Youth Movement of South Africa The Muslim Youth Movement of South Africa (MYMSA) was established in 1970 as a religious and cultural organization catering to the needs of young Muslims during the apartheid era. MYMSA at first drew inspiration from revivalist groups such as the Muslim Brotherhood of Egypt and the Jamaat-i Islami of Pakistan. Over time it developed an indigenous focus, changed its agenda to deal with issues of racial discrimination and gender justice, and adopted a more contextual approach to Islam. In the postapartheid period it has become representative of the diverse ethnic groups in the country.

Musnad Hadith or tradition of the Prophet, the transmission of which is traceable in an uninterrupted ascending order to the first person who transmitted or reported it, so as to corroborate its authenticity. *See also* Isnad

Mustadafin *See* Mustadafun

Mustadafun The lower classes; the downtrodden; the meek; "the barefoot." Ayatollah Ruhollah Khomeini (d. 1989) popularized this concept in revolutionary Iran. The term also refers to those who are deprived of the opportunity to develop their full potential.

Khomeini spoke of two diametrically opposed versions of Islam: that of the mutakbarun (the rich and arrogant) and that of the mustadafun. This group was Khomeini's popular base of support; he maintained that the Islamic revolution (1979) was made by the mustadafun and must serve their interests.

Mustafa, Shukri Ahmad *See* Jamaat al-Takfir wa'l-Hijrah

Mustafa Kemal *See* Atatürk, Mustafa Kemal

Mustahabb *See* Mandub

Mustansir, al- Eighth Fatimid Ismaili imam/caliph in Egypt (r. 1036–94); had a paradoxical career. Was considered the pinnacle of a religio-political hierarchy, with access to the inner truths of the Quran, but he was less powerful than his viziers, especially Badr al-Jamali. Unsuccessful in ousting Turkish invaders from Palestine, he tried to enlist the support of the Crusaders, later the Fatimids' enemies. He reputedly designated his elder son, al-Nizar, as spiritual and political heir; enthronement of his younger son split the Ismailis. Nizari devotees, whose imam was now "hidden," became the Assassins and ancestors of the largest modern Ismaili community.

Mustashriqun *See* Orientalists

Mutah Private and verbal marriage contract between a man and an unmarried woman for a specified period of time; a temporary marriage. A pre-Islamic tradition that still has legal sanction among Twelver Shiis, predominantly in Iran. The length of the contract and the amount of consideration must be specified. The minimum duration of the contract was hotly debated. Some required a three-day minimum; others required three months or one year. The object of mutah is sexual enjoyment and not procreation. After dissolution of the mutah, the wife must undergo a period of sexual abstinence (iddah); in case of pregnancy, iddah serves to identify a child's legitimate father. Sunni jurists reject the validity of this type of marriage.

Mutahhari, Murtaza (d. 1979) Iranian religious scholar and writer, one of the closest associates of Ayatollah Ruhollah Khomeini (d. 1989). Studied jurisprudence in Qom, where he met Khomeini and Muhammad Husayn Tabatabai (d. 1981). In 1954 he began teaching at Tehran University. Khomeini appointed Mutahhari to his Revolutionary Council, the interim legislature after the 1979 revolution. Assassinated in May 1979 by adherents of Furqan, a group that promoted an anticlerical interpretation of Shii Islam and who saw him as its most formidable intellectual opponent. Mutahhari's legacy lies in his writings, much of which philosophically refute materialism, cultural decline, and women's rights.

Mutanabbi, al- (d. 965) Also known as Abu al-Tayyib Ahmad ibn al-Husayn. Generally considered the greatest Arabic poet. Born in Kufa, Iraq. Became known as al-Mutanabbi, "the would-be prophet," after leading a Bedouin rebellion with religious shadings in 933. In his poetry are the greatest examples of pre-Islamic heroic motifs in the form of panegyrics during the Islamic era. *See also* Sayf al-Dawlah, Abu al-Hasan Ali

Mutawakkil, al- Tenth Abbasid caliph (r. 847–61). He brought to an end the Mihna, or "inquisition," that had been instituted by the caliph al-Mamun to test scholars' conformity with the state-sponsored doctrine that the Quran was the created word of God. He patronized the nascent Sunni traditionists (ashab al-hadith) and persecuted the Mutazili theologians, the Shiis, and non-Muslims. He tried to curtail the growing power of the Turkish soldiers but in the end was assassinated by them.

Mutawalli Manager or custodian of waqf (charitable endowment). The mutawalli is chosen by the founder of the waqf and is responsible for the administration of waqf property in the best interest of beneficiaries.

The mutawalli's first duty is preservation of property, then maximization of revenues for beneficiaries. The waqf document usually mentions how the mutawalli is to be compensated for this work, but if the document does not specify it, the mutawalli either works on a volunteer basis or seeks assignment of compensation by the court, which is the authority of reference with regard to all matters and disputes related to waqf. The mutawalli is often a member of the founder's family, typically a descendant, enabling the family to maintain some benefit from the waqf.

Mutawatir Successive. From *tawatur*, repetition, constancy. Highest classification of a tradition in hadith criticism; a hadith characterized by an established series of transmitters (isnad), at least two per generation, all of whom are deemed reliable. The number of reliable transmitters, along with other established criteria, ensures that the tradition is not fabricated. The Quran is considered authentic because all verses are mutawatir.

Mutawwadah *See* Diplomacy

Mutazilis Eighth-century theological school that emphasized God's absolute uniqueness, unity, and justice. Also known as Ahl al-Adl wa'l-Tawhid (People of Justice and Unity). Rejected anthropomorphism. Taught that the Quran was created rather than eternal. Preached human free will as a rational depiction of good and evil; preached harmony between human reason and revelation. Opposed the Ashari opinion that God's command is the sole criterion for determining the correctness of an act. Taught instead that the command by itself is insufficient as an agent for action. Additional factors, such as the nature of the agent issuing the command and the consequences of the act for the receiver of the command, must be taken into account. Use of logical arguments, materialism, and rationalistic ethics contributed to the development of philosophical methodology in Islamic theology.

Muttahida Qaumi Movement *See* Muhajir Qaumi Movement

Muwahhidun *See* Almohads; Druze; Wahhabi

Muwatta, al- Oldest surviving compendium of religious law by Malik ibn Anas al-Asbahi (d. 795), eponymous founder of the Maliki school of law. Cites various hadiths on specific topics but bases the final legal ruling on each issue on the practice of the Medinan school. Maintained strict standards in hadiths—if Malik quotes a hadith text on the authority of a narrator, the narrator is seen as reliable.

Muzaffar, Chandra (b. 1947) Malaysian intellectual and human rights activist. Born into a Hindu family. Actively campaigned on issues of human rights and intercivilizational dialogue. Detained by state security forces during the crackdown of 1987. Founder of Malaysian human rights NGO Aliran and president 1977–91; president of International Movement for a Just World beginning in 1991; deputy president of the National Justice Party (KeADILan) beginning in 1999. Author of *Universalism of Islam* (1979), *Islamic Resurgence in Malaysia* (1987), *Human Rights and the New World Order* (1993), and *Alternative Politics for Asia: A Buddhist-Muslim Dialogue* (1999). Awarded the Rockefeller Social Science Fellowship in Development Studies for Southeast Asia (1984–85) and the Harry J. Benda Prize for distinguished scholarship on Southeast Asia (1989).

Muzdalifa Narrow mountain pass just outside of Mecca where pilgrims on the hajj spend the night praying and resting in the open under the desert sky, without accommodations or facilities. One of the most ascetic experiences of the hajj, providing both spiritual inspiration and calm, since nothing stands between the believer and God. *See also* Hajj

Myanmar, Islam in Four percent of the population of Myanmar (Burma) are Muslim;

this proportion has remained stable over the last century. The majority are Sunni, but they are divided into three distinct Muslim communities. The longest-established community arrived in the thirteenth and fourteenth centuries from the West as court servants, traders, and mercenaries. British colonization of Burma encouraged significant numbers of Muslim immigrants, casual laborers, traders, and civil servants to settle in and around Yangon. The third Muslim community settled in Arakan (Rakhine), which borders Bangladesh. In the Shan state, bordering China, there is a small number of Muslims of Chinese descent.

MYMSA *See* Muslim Youth Movement of South Africa

Nabawiyyah *See* Prophethood

Nabhani, Taqi al-Din al- (d. 1977) Palestinian judge from Ijzin in northern Palestine. Founder and theoretician of Hizb al-Tahrir al-Islami (Islamic Liberation Party), established in 1953. It aimed at the restoration of Islamic rule and the liberation of Islamic lands from outside colonial rule. Stressed the need to restore the caliphate. Later influenced the rise of Islamic ideology among Palestinians in the West Bank and Gaza in the 1980s and 1990s. After the death of Nabahani, Shaykh Abd al-Qadhim Zallum assumed the leadership of the party. Nabahani's writings are widely circulated among fundamentalist activists throughout the region and in Europe, especially Britain. *See also* Hizb al-Tahrir al-Islami

Nabi Prophet; one who announces. Person called by God to communicate a divinely given message in the form of general moral teachings to humankind and the unseen world of spirits. Expresses the communicative nature of prophethood, rather than the emissary function of delivering a message in specific language (the role of rasul). The message is exemplified in the nabi's life. *See also* Rasul

Nabi al-Ummi, al- A term used to refer to the Prophet Muhammad and variably translated as "the unlettered prophet," "the prophet sent to a people without a scripture," or "the prophet of the community of Muslims" (Quran 7:157). The term ummi derives from the noun umm, which means "mother," "source," or "foundation," as in the Quranic umm al-kitab (sourcebook, primordial book). Ummi may also mean "motherly," "uneducated," or "illiterate." The most common meaning of al-nabi al-ummi is "the unlettered prophet," which refers to the Prophet Muhammad's inability to create a major literary work such as the Quran. Some commentators have traced the term to the noun ummah, which refers to a primary community sharing a common religious orientation. In this sense, al-nabi al-ummi means "the prophet sent to an unscripted community," or a community that has not yet received a scripture.

Nabidh *See* Intoxicants

Nadhir One who warns; Muhammad's self-described (Quran 22:49) position as messenger of the God of Jews and Christians who was called to recite the same revelations to Arabs. The Quran uses the word to refer to Muhammad and other prophets, since their role was to warn society that they had turned away from God and would be punished if they did not repent.

Nadir Shah Afshar, Muhammad (r. 1736–47) Founder of the Afsharid dynasty in Iran. Known for an attempt to end the sectarian hostilities between the Sunnis and the Shiis by having the latter give up some of the ritual practices that historically have been the cause of discord between the two communities, and sought to have the Shiis recognized by the Ottomans as a fifth school of law, alongside the four Sunni schools; the effort proved abortive on all fronts. Assassinated in 1747.

Nadwat al-Ulama Reformist school founded in India by Sayyid Muhammad Ali Mongiri in Lucknow in 1894. It aimed to train ulama who would promote traditional religious knowledge and national Muslim leadership using some Western learning. Among other Indian Muslim responses to Western hegemony and in the context of organized Hindu resurgence, the school sought to unify the ulama, connect Indian Muslims to the pan-Islamic community, reinvigorate pride in Islamic culture, and promote proselytization. Although self-identified later as Hanafi to the detriment of its original inclusivity, the diversity of its membership influenced future Muslim organizations and undertakings (e.g., the Khilafat movement). *See also* Nadwi, Abul Hasan Ali

Nadwatul Ulama *See* Nadwat al-Ulama

Nadwi, Abul Hasan Ali (d. 2000) A leading religious scholar and Muslim public intellectual of contemporary India and the author of numerous books on history, biography, contemporary Islam, and the Muslim community in India. Nadwi served as rector of the Nadwat al-Ulama in Lucknow, India, an institution of higher Islamic learning founded in the late nineteenth century. During the 1950s and 1960s he stringently attacked Arab nationalism and pan-Arabism as a new jahiliyyah (era of ignorance). A founding member of the Saudi-sponsored Muslim World League (Rabitat al-Alam al-Islami), Nadwi promoted pan-Islamism. He also had a lifelong association with the Tablighi Jamaat.

Nadwi, Sayyid Sulayman (d. 1953) A leading religious scholar of twentieth-century South Asia. He is the author, together with his teacher, Shibli Numani, of the multivolume *Sirat al-nabi* (Life of the Prophet) in the Urdu language, as well as of numerous other works on history, historiography, and Islamic studies in general. In 1915 he founded the Dar al-Musannifin (Writers Institute), a research academy devoted to the study of Islam, at Azamgarh in Uttar Pradesh, India. In 1952 he emigrated to Pakistan, where he contributed to the constitutional debates on the place of Islam in public life in the country.

Nafaqah Constitutes the financial obligation of a husband toward his wife during marriage and for a time after he divorces her. While married, a husband is expected to pay for housing, food, and his wife's clothes according to her social class or their agreement at the time the marriage was contracted. He generally is also expected to pay for all her medical expenses, although schools of legal thought differ on this point. Depending on social class and agreement, nafaqah could also include servants and a standard of living consistent with that of the wife's peers. If divorce takes place, the husband is expected to pay her the same financial support for the first three months following the divorce, a period known as iddah, during which the wife continues to live in her home and may not remarry; this is to ascertain that there is no pregnancy and to allow for a period in which the couple could reconcile. Nafaqah can also include support for family members such as father, mother, sisters, brothers, and children if they cannot support themselves.

Nafisa, al-Sayyida (d. 824) Great-granddaughter of Hasan, the older of the Prophet Muhammad's two grandsons. Wife of Ishaq al-Mutamin, son of the sixth Shii imam, Jafar al-Sadiq. Emigrated with him from the Hejaz to Egypt. Settled in Fustat. Famous for her piety and scholarship. Taught hadith to the jurist al-Shafii. Had a great reputation for possessing barakah (blessings from God) and performing miracles. Traditionally considered among the city's patron saints. Her shrine is located in Cairo's Southern Cemetery. It is said that she built it herself and read the Quran there long before her death. The shrine's prominence dates to the Fatimid period, and the structure has been repeatedly embellished and rebuilt. The present mosque dates to 1897. Miraculous cures and other signs of intercession are still attributed to her shrine. The land around it is a coveted place for interment.

Nafs Self or soul. Used in the Quran as a general designation for the self or true self; interpreted as the spiritual reality of all living creatures. In philosophy, the specifically human nafs is often described as the potential to actualize the fullness of self-awareness, often equated with the intellect (aql). In Sufism, often described as the "lower self," associated with physical rather than spiritual impulses, by contrast to ruh, understood as the "soul" or "higher self." Often understood primarily in a negative sense. In the more theoretical Sufi writings, also used in the neutral, philosophical meanings.

Nafzawiyah, Zaynab al- *See* Women and Islam

Nahdah Renaissance. Commonly refers to the revival of Arabic literature and culture in the Levant and Egypt from the mid-nineteenth century to World War I. Authors sought to revive classical forms of Arabic, develop language in ways appropriate to modern times, make compatriots aware of new ideas coming from Europe, and develop a common patriotism to transcend sectarian differences. This eventually developed into pan-Arab sentiment. The movement called for autonomy of Syria and Lebanon and recognition of Arabic as the official language there, and it published newspapers and periodicals. It began in Christian circles but was predominantly Muslim by the end of the nineteenth century. Nahdah laid the basis for the Arab national movement that followed World War I. In the twenty-first century the term often refers to the revival of Islam as the basis of sociopolitical life.

Nahdat al-Ulama *See* Nahdatul Ulama

Nahdatul Ulama One of the two largest Islamic traditionalist grassroots social organizations in Indonesia. Established in 1926 as part of the nationalist awakening and general Islamic reform. Its social basis is the pesantren (a traditional institution of Islamic learning), where students live and learn classical Arabic texts under tutelage of a spiritual leader. Reportedly in 2000, about six thousand pesantren and more than one million students were spread throughout mostly rural areas of the country. Its stated purposes are enhancement of relationships among ulama of various Sunni schools of Islamic law; examination of textbooks to determine whether they are appropriate for study; propagation of Islam based on the teachings of four Sunni schools of law; establishment

of schools; management of mosques, prayer houses, and dormitories; looking after orphans and the poor; and organization of Islamically lawful bodies for the advancement of agriculture, trade, and industry. It provides a forum for personal piety and spiritual solidarity through face-to-face communication. The group was headed by Abdurrahman Wahid from 1984 until his election as Indonesia's first democratically chosen president in 1999.

Nahhas, Mustafa al- (d. 1965) Egyptian statesman and politician. Leader of the nationalist Wafd Party from 1927 on. Five-time prime minister between 1928 and 1952. Tried to negotiate Egyptian independence from Britain. Clashed with the palace over control of the government. His image suffered after he was forcibly made prime minister by the British in 1942.

Nahj al-Balaghah The peak of eloquence. Collection of political discourse, sermons, letters, and wise sayings ascribed to Ali ibn Abi Talib, fourth caliph and cousin and son-in-law of Muhammad. Compiled in the eleventh century with detailed commentaries by Sunni and Shii scholars. Has served as ideological groundwork for establishment of an Islamic government. Contains a lengthy discussion of the balance between rights and duties, emphasizing that greater responsibilities result in greater rights. Proclaims the deficiencies of women and is often used to justify patriarchal social structures and the primacy of man over woman. At the heart of current Iranian clerical debates over the appropriate role and status of women in modern society.

Nahw Arabic grammar. The literal meaning of the word *nahw* is "way" or "manner," signifying the way language is used by its native speakers. One of the earliest sciences developed by Muslims, its origins are usually traced back to Abul Aswad al-Duali, who is said to have organized the rules of Arabic grammar at the request of Ali. Al-Sibawayh's *Kitab fil-nahw*, however, is considered to be the first authoritative text of the field. Arabic grammar is usually divided into two major parts: sarf or tasrif, the conjugation of verbs, and nahw or irab, modulations of words and declensions. The Baghdad and Basra schools of grammar are well known for their differences concerning Arabic syntax, semantics, and philosophy of language.

Naib Deputy or representative. In Sunni Islamic law, refers to the authorized representative of a qadi (judge) or local magistrate. Refers to a critical concept of agency in Shii Islam: al-naib al-amm is a general deputy during the occultation of the imam, al-naib al-imam is a deputy of the imam, and al-naib al-sidara is a deputy in charge of the state's religious administration. *See also* Niyabah

Naib al-Amm, al- *See* Naib

Naib al-Imam, al- *See* Naib

Naib al-Sidara, al- *See* Naib

Naini, Muhammad Husayn (d. 1936) Iraqi Shii cleric. Leading theoretician of the 1905–11 Constitutional Revolution in Iran. Led Iraqi nationalists in an independence movement against the British. Depicted those opposing Reza Shah Pahlavi's rule as enemies of Islam, opening the door to the deposing of the Qajar dynasty. Wrote a famous treatise justifying constitutional government from a Shii perspective. Aimed to reconcile the impossibility of legitimate rule in the absence of the Hidden Imam with the practical need for a government promoting the well-being of the Shii community. Did not advocate administration of government by ulama, but supported their participation in Iranian politics, Islamization of constitutionalist principles, and certain principles of democracy.

NAIT *See* North American Islamic Trust

Najaf One of Iraq's two holiest cities (Karbala is the other one). Reputedly founded by the Abbasid caliph Harun al-Rashid in 791. A Shii religious center located south of Baghdad and six miles west of Kufa. Site of Ali ibn Abi Talib's (the first Shii imam) tomb. Kufa retained its importance as the locus of Shii activities until the fifteenth century, when Najaf replaced it. Hospices, schools, libraries, and Sufi convents were built around the shrine. Late nineteenth-century Qom replaced Najaf as the center of Shii learning; this was reversed with the rise of Ayatollah Khomeini (d. 1989) and Muhammad Baqir al-Sadr (d. 1980).

Najibullah (d. 1996) Last Marxist president of Afghanistan. Known for his oratorical skills, political abilities, Pushtun nationalism, and ruthlessness as the head of the notorious State Security Committee or KHAD (1980–86). Soviet loyalist and a strongman of the Parcham (Banner) faction of the Communist Party (PDPA); became secretary general of the PDPA (1986–92) and president of Afghanistan (1987–92). Unable to flee the country when the mujahidin took over in April 1992, he took refuge in the UN compound in Kabul. Killed by the Taliban; his body was mutilated and hanged on a public square.

Namaz *See* Salat

Names and Naming The names given to a child often reflect the religious convictions of the parents. The Quran instructs that the only "given" name is the first name. The second name is to be the father's and the third name the grandfather's. This requirement traditionally applies to both boys and girls. Naming of a child may not occur until registration, which in some cultures is delayed if the actual birthdate is considered inauspicious or important family members are absent. The family typically discusses the name and assesses the child's personality and health to determine the name to be given. Traditionally, in the interim male children are called Muhammad and female children Fatimah. Celebrations herald the decision on a child's name in traditional societies. Converts are typically given Muslim names as a sign of conversion.

Names of God Encouraged by the Quran (7:180; 17:110; 20:8), Muslims selected ninety-nine attributes of God, describing His perfection, from the Quran and traditions. Referred to as "the most beautiful names of God," they describe a range of characteristics that balances the power of God (the Creator, the Sovereign, and the All-Knowing) with His love and mercy (the All-Loving, the Most Gracious, and the All-Forgiving). The names are frequently memorized and used in supplications. Preceded by the words *Abd* or *Amat* (male or female servant), they are often used in proper names (e.g., Abd al-Rahman, "servant of the Merciful").

Names of the Prophet A collection of over one hundred names for Muhammad, either specifically mentioned by him or developed from the Quran and traditions. The most noteworthy and theologically significant is Ahmad, derived from the same Arabic root as Muhammad, h-m-d (praise). Others include those derived from the mysterious unconnected letters at the beginning of Quranic chapters 20 (Ta-ha) and 36 (Ya-sin), as well as the frequently mentioned name al-Mustafa (the chosen one). Popular as names for Muslim children.

Namus *See* Honor

Naqib Guardian. Refers to the person in a Sufi order responsible for keeping the ritual liturgy and directing music. Typical of Syrian orders in particular. In some orders, also refers to the rank of saints within a hierarchical structure headed by the qutb (pole).

Naql Transportation. Refers to original sources, faithfully transmitted once their authenticity has been ascertained; often understood in contrast with aql (reason), which arrives at judgments through logic, experiment, and so on. Naql is therefore transmission of a special sort, and rational judgment is allowed only with regard to the method of verification of the authenticity of the source. Naql is usually a feature of Islamic law and religious scholarship but is occasionally found in other disciplines, such as theology, philosophy, and literary criticism.

Naqshbandi, Khalid al- (d. 1827) Kurdish shaykh who founded the Khalidi suborder of the Naqshbandi Sufi tariqah. After spending a year studying with Shah Gulam Ali in Delhi, Khalid returned home in 1811 and established a network of followers that differed from those of previous Naqshbandis by its centralization and focus on Khalid. He then built a network of 116 representatives and initiated many of the most senior Ottoman military, political, and religious leaders into his order. Following Khalid's death, the Khalidi order spread to Muslim territories from the Balkans to Indonesia. They are important today in Chechnya, Kurdistan, Lebanon, Syria, and Turkey.

Naqshbandi Tariqah One of the most widespread and vigorous Sufi orders. Originated in Bukhara in the fourteenth century. Leading characteristics are strict adherence to Islamic law, sobriety in devotional practice that results in shunning of music and dance and preference for silent dhikr, and frequent tendency to political activity. Active in Afghan affairs until the formation of the first post-Communist administration in 1991. Prominent in the resistance to Russian conquest and its aftermath throughout Asia. Headed rebellions against Chinese rule in Xinjiang. Passively resistant to secularism in Turkey. Influence is strongest in Turkey and Kurdish lands. A number of its leaders have been important spiritual and intellectual teachers, but in the twenty-first century, the order has not produced any leaders with universal appeal and the capability of reinvigorating the order. Instead, groups varying in size, influence, and emphasis operate separately across the Islamic world, from the United States to Indonesia.

Nar *See* Hell

Nasab Spiritual lineage or genealogy. Shows the descent of Sufi liturgy and the path from the founder. Sometimes used to demonstrate the descent of barakah (blessing) from a saint. An important means of identification for traveling Sufis who wish to be accepted by members of the same order in other locations.

Nasai, Abu Abd al-Rahman Ahmad ibn Ali al- (d. 915) Author of one of the six Sunni canonical compilations of hadith. Traveled extensively in order to hear tradition. Eventually settled first in Egypt, then in Damascus. His tomb is in Mecca. Among his other works is a collection of hadiths in praise of Ali, the fourth caliph.

Nasif, Malak Hifni (d. 1918) Egyptian feminist, Islamic modernist reformer, and writer. Protested male abuses of divorce and polygyny. Demanded that women be allowed to participate in congregational worship in mosques, study in all fields, enter all occupations and professions, and be permitted to develop themselves and contribute to the welfare of the ummah. Called for reform of the Muslim personal status code. Wrote under the pen name Bahithat al-Badiyyah (seeker of the desert).

NASIMCO *See* Organization of North American Shia Ithna-Ashari Muslim Communities (NASIMCO)

Nasir-i Khusraw, Abu Muin Nasur ibn Khusraw ibn Harith (d. 1088) Ismaili propagandist and poet. Much of his poetry is autobiographical, giving a full and detailed accounts of his moral and intellectual dilemmas at various stages of life. His poetry offers accounts of the sectarian, juridical, theological, philosophical, and interreligious divisions of his time and is a highly valued example of Iranian culture.

Naskh (1) Abrogation, revocation, repeal. Theoretical tool used to resolve contradictions in Quranic verses, hadith literature, tafsir (Quranic exegesis), and usul al-fiqh (roots of law), whereby later verses (or reports or decisions) abrogate earlier ones. Based on Quranic verse (2:106) according to which God occasionally replaces older verses with better ones. (2) A style of Arabic calligraphy.

Nasr, Seyyed Hossein (b. 1933) Iranian philosopher, theologian, traditionalist, teacher, and writer. Left Iran in 1979 for the United States. Advocates Safavid Islam as representing the real essence of Islamic and Shii thought. Claims that contemporary people, especially in the West, no longer understand or appreciate the sacred and have lost sight of what is essential and eternal. Hopes to revive the sacred quality of knowledge. Opponent of modernism, rationalism, materialism, and secularism as forces that alienate people from faith. Desires the integration of science, philosophy, and art, believing that the essential unity of all things reflects the unity of God. Sees true freedom as a matter of understanding one's relationship to God, as expressed in Islamic philosophy and Sufism.

Nass A statement that is fixed or explicit. Used in Islamic law to refer to an explicit statement within the Quran or hadith upon which a ruling is based. Finds a special usage in Shiism, referring to Ali being Muhammad's designated successor with the sense that it was clear and obvious. Used in modern Muslim writing to distinguish between text as a human production and revelation as a divine source of law and guidance.

Nasserism Political movement calling for the liberation of Arabs and all Afro-Asian states colonized or dominated by Western powers, with Egypt playing a key leadership role. Influence grew as Gamal Abdel Nasser led opposition to the pro-Western Baghdad Pact (established in 1955 between Turkey, Iran, Iraq, Pakistan, and England), bought Soviet arms, and declared neutrality in the Cold War and defiance of the old colonial powers. Most potent political force in the eastern Arab world in the 1960s. Declined after Egypt's defeat in the 1967 Arab-Israeli War. Essentially a secular pan-Arabist movement, although it never stood for total separation of religion and state or establishment of a secular republic. Proclaimed the necessity of socialism for economic security and equality of opportunity.

Nastaliq A hybrid form of Arabic calligraphy. First introduced by a Persian calligrapher as a lighter variation of writing. A compound word, *nastaliq* is derived from *naskh* and *taliq*, two more common styles of calligraphy. This hybrid form was frequently used by Persian artists in the production of non-sacramental texts. *See also* Calligraphy and Epigraphy

Nation of Islam Heterodox black religious movement in America, based on black nationalism. More than 90 percent of converts are African-Americans. The Nation of Islam was founded in 1930 by Wallace D. Fard. Elijah Muhammad assumed leadership in 1934 when Fard mysteriously disappeared. Muhammad taught that Fard was God, proclaimed himself God's messenger, and infused Fard's teachings with black nationalism. The group tried to help blacks develop economic independence and recover an acceptable black identity. Its ethic became one of hard work, frugality, avoidance of debt, self-improvement, and a conservative lifestyle. The group recruited actively in prisons and ghettoes and urged the formation of a separate black nation. The movement split after the death of Elijah Muhammad in 1975. The branch following Elijah Muhammad's son Warith Deen Muhammad has moved in the direction of orthodox Sunni Islam. The branch following Louis Farrakhan has maintained the black nationalist and separatist stances central to Elijah Muhammad's teachings. *See also* America, Islam in

National Congress Party Secularly oriented Indian political party. Founded in 1885 as a nationalist party, but came to be associated with Hindu interests. Routed Muslim League candidates in a landslide victory in the 1937 elections. Refused to establish Hindu-Muslim coalition governments in Muslim-majority areas in India, sparking calls for a separate Muslim state and ultimately leading to the foundation of Pakistan as a homeland for Indian Muslims.

National Council of French Muslims *See* Conseil National des Français Musulmans

National Front for the Salvation of Libya *See* Libya, Islam in

National Islamic Front (Afghanistan) *See* Gaylani Family

National Islamic Front (Sudan) Sudanese political party founded in 1985 by the Sudanese Muslim Brotherhood in collaboration with Jafar al-Numayri. Main supporters are university students and graduates. Took control of the country's Islamic banking system in the 1970s through connections with Saudi Arabia and collaboration with Numayri. Supported implementation of hudud punishments in 1983 as part of an educational process to improve the morals of citizens. After the 1989 coup, enhanced domination of banks, building industry, transport, media, and higher educational institutions. Serves as current state's chief financial institution. Has also successfully infiltrated the army due to its support for soldiers' demands for better pay and equipment. Founded the African Islamic Center to undertake missionary work among the non-Muslim majority in southern Sudan. Published a national charter in 1987, explaining its program for Islamizing the South. Has accepted the right of all citizens, regardless of religion, to hold any public office. Promises freedom of conscience and equality before the law, although it rejects secularism.

National Order Party *See* National Salvation Party

National Party *See* Kamil, Mustafa

National Salvation Party Milli Selamet Partisi. Islamist party founded in Turkey in 1972 as a regrouping of the Milli Nizam Partisi (MNP, National Order Party) after the latter was outlawed in 1971. Promoted a program of rapid industrialization and moral and spiritual reconstruction as a remedy to secularization and westernization. Reinterpreted Ottoman history to emphasize its contributions to Muslim civilization, with its decline beginning only with penetration of foreign cultural influences. Participated in three coalition governments between 1973 and 1978, with Necmettin Erbakan as deputy prime minister, permitting the spread of Islamists throughout the bureaucracy. Banned from political activity by the military junta that seized power in September 1980. Reorganized as the Refah Partisi (Welfare Party) in 1983 and then as the Fazilet Partisi (Virtue Party) in 1998.

Nationalism and Islam As premodern socioeconomic systems disintegrated and modern conditions developed, so did nationalism, the tendency to organize politically with people in one's homeland regardless of religion, social class, etc. As religious groups participated in the nationalist movements from the Maghreb and Egypt to India and Indonesia, Islam was often an integral part of nationalist discourse. It continues to be a major component of many independent Muslim nations' ideologies.

Natsir, Mohammad (d. 1993) Indonesian intellectual, writer, nationalist, journalist, and politician. Held that a return to the intellectual and scriptural tradition of classical Islam was essential for the modernization of Muslim societies. Understood the nation-state as a tool for constructing Islamic society. Emphasized the relationship between a just society and the rewards of heaven, using the Quran and Muhammad's example as a sociological model for achieving both. Devoted in his younger years to Indonesian nationalism, development, and the struggle to establish a more explicitly Islamic social system; later was the most outspoken proponent of fundamentalism in contemporary Indonesia. Blamed the Christian community for the establishment of Indonesia as a secular rather than Islamic state. Revered by Indonesian Muslim fundamentalists.

Natural Science Arabic *ilm al-tabiah*. Physics, in contemporary usage. Ranked as the lowest of the intellectual sciences by the Hellenized philosopher al-Farabi (d. ca. 950), who says that its subject matter is terrestrial bodies—animals, plants, and minerals; Ibn Khaldun (d. 1406) subsumes all sensible objects, including heavenly bodies, in the scope of this science. Islamic scientists made numerous advances in several branches of physics. For example, al-Kindi (d. 873) mathematized physical notions.

Nawafil Acts of supererogation. Often used to denote supererogatory (voluntary rather than obligatory) prayers, though it can refer to a broad range of other voluntary pious acts as well. Besides being meritorious in their own right, such acts are believed to assist in the expiation of minor sins.

Nawwab Ruler of a region, principality, or city. An elite whose nobility rests upon the virtues of magnanimity, valor, and honor. Title of the notables of the Mughal era in India, who helped the central authority govern different statelets within the subcontinent. During the British period, new nawwabs were created because of the allocation of arable land to the pro-British elite. However, old nawwabs continued to be the area elites.

Nawwab Safawi, Sayyid Mujtaba Mir Luhi (d. 1956) Known as Nawwab-i Safawi. Iranian religio-political activist. Published the newspaper *Parcham-i Islam* and established the organization Fadayan-i Islam (Martyrs of Islam), which was responsible for the assassination of a number of intellectuals and political leaders in the 1950s. Executed.

Nazr Vow. Considered a serious commitment in Islam. Failure to fulfill a vow is seen as a grievous offense for which expiation must be made, for example, by feeding or clothing the poor or fasting. Most common vows are those that are conditional upon the occurrence of an event, such as "If God heals my mother, I will prepare a feast for fifty people."

Necessary See Fard al-Ayn; Fard al-Kifayah; Wajib

Neo-Destour Party Tunisian political party founded in 1934 by members of the Destour Party. Promoted independence from France and boycotted French products. Supported democracy, modernization, development, socialism, and secularism. Used Islam as a value system to mobilize the Tunisian people. Drew its membership from the middle classes and rural masses. Came to power in 1957 upon achieving independence.

Neoplatonism The most influential philosophy for major Islamic thinkers such as al-Kindi (d. ca. 866), al-Farabi (d. 950), Ibn Sina (d. 1037), and Suhrawardi (d. 1191) and Sufis such as Ibn al-Arabi (d. 1240), Qunawi (d. 1274), and Iraqi (d. 1289). Hellenistic in origin. There are two versions of the philosophy, the first containing Enneads IV, V, and VI by Plotinus (d. ca. 270) and the second The Elements of Theology by Proclus (d. 485). Appealed to Muslims primarily through its doctrine of the One and a mystical emanationist theory that helped them expound upon the relationship between God and creation. The fundamental movement is downward, by force of the utterly transcendent One, successively through Intellect, World Soul, and Nature to particular beings in this world, and upward from these through desire for the One. Neoplatonism led to illuminationism (hikmat al-ishraq), especially in Iran, inspired by the vision of the luminous presence of the One through all levels of being, for instance in Mulla Sadra (Sadr al-Din al-Shirazi, d. 1641). Neoplatonism continues to this day in Iran. See also Gnosticism; Nur Muhammadi

Neotraditionalists Muslim reformers who advocate returning to the Quran, Sunnah, and shariah to renew Muslim society. Respect classical interpretations of Islam but reserve the right to reinterpret Islam for contemporary needs and issues. Believe that Islamic law historically incorporated many un-Islamic practices, necessitating a return to original sources for fresh interpretation.

Reject secularism and Islamic modernism but do accept science and technology as compatible with Islamic values. Emphasize Islam as a complete way of life. Promote Islamic alternatives to Western politics, economics, law, and education. Focus on solidarity of the broader Muslim community rather than nationalism or ethnic identities.

New Brothers Group See Muslim Converts' Association of Singapore (Darul Arqam)

New Sect Eighteenth-century Chinese revivalist Muslim group led by Ma Mingxin. Located in Gansu Province. Called for reform of local religious practices via the rejection of compromises with local customs and an emphasis on distinctive Muslim practices. Influenced by the Naqshbandi tariqah. Broke with the Old Sect, resulting in revolts in 1781 and 1783. Proscribed after 1783 but remained active. Participated in a major rebellion led by Ma Hualong in 1862, leading to Muslim control over many cities in the province. The revolt, which was crushed in 1873, was a combination of vigorous activism with a return to the fundamentals of Islam and rejection of the previous policy of adaptationism, and represented the assertion of a distinctive identity from within the context of Chinese culture.

Niche See Mihrab; Muqarnas

NIF See National Islamic Front (Sudan)

Niger, Islam in Eighty percent of Niger's multiethnic population is Muslim. Islam arrived in the region through different means: seventh- through ninth-century Saharan-Sahelian trade routes; Hausa, Malian, Songhay (ca. 1100–1300) dynasties; merchant missionaries; and Sufi orders. The Tijani tariqah is the most popular Sufi brotherhood; the Qadiri, Sanusi, and Shadhili tariqahs are also active. Major droughts in 1973–74 and 1984–85 brought many formerly marginal groups into contact with Islamic associations and communities in the urban areas. In the early 1990s tensions arose between adherents of various Sufi brotherhoods and the Association Izalatoul Bidah wa Ikamatou Sunnah (Association for Elimination of Innovations in the Religion and for Reinforcement of the Sunnah), also referred to as the Izal. Development of a coherent judicial process that incorporates customary and Islamic law on the issues of judicial rights, privileges, protection of women and the family, and land tenure rights is a significant challenge facing Niger today.

Nigeria, Islam in Nigeria's population is roughly split between Christians and Muslims. Nigerian Muslim religious identity is diverse: Sufi brotherhoods (Tijani and Qadiri), anti-innovation legalists, adherents of the caliphal/Medina model, women's groups, and national organizations. Civilian rule returned to Nigeria in 1999 with the election of Olusegun Obasanjo (a Christian) as president and Atiku Abubaker (a Muslim) as vice president. Early 2000 saw extensive intercommunal rioting after several northern Muslim-majority states announced the impending adoption of shariah. Nigeria's stability is viewed as critical in Africa. Obasanjo's government is widely credited with allowing far greater freedoms than previous military regimes, but corruption and abuses continue. *See also* Dan Fodio, Uthman; Sokoto Caliphate

Night Journey Also known as al-Isra and Laylat al-Miraj. Refers to the journey made by Muhammad from the Great Mosque in Mecca to the Temple Mount in Jerusalem on a winged horselike creature known as Buraq, followed by Muhammad's ascension into heaven. Briefly mentioned in the Quran (17: 1) but known primarily through hadith. During the journey, Muhammad traveled with Gabriel to see everything in heaven and earth and then to the Temple in Jerusalem, where he met with Abraham, Moses, Jesus, and other prophets there and led them in prayer. Then Muhammad was shown a ladder, which he climbed with Gabriel up to the Gate of Watchers in heaven, where he met Jesus, John the Baptist, Joseph, Idris, Aaron, Moses, and Abraham. Muslims de-

bate whether this journey was physical or mystical in nature. The result of the journey was the reduction of daily prayers to five from fifty after lengthy debate with Moses. Muhammad argued that fifty prayers per day would represent too great a hardship for believers. Daily prayers were instituted after this event. The Night Journey made Jerusalem the third holiest city in Islam and affirmed the continuity of Islam with Judaism and Christianity. It is celebrated annually on the twenty-seventh of Rajab and is a popular theme for Islamic artwork and legends.

Night of Power and Excellence Term for the night when Muhammad received the first revelation of the Quran, when the angel Gabriel commanded Muhammad to recite (Quran 96:1–5). Commemorated each year on the night between the twenty-sixth and twenty-seventh days of Ramadan. Also known as the Night of Destiny.

Nik, Abdul Aziz (d. 2002) Malaysian cleric and politician. A leader in Parti Islam Se Malaysia (PAS). Attended Darul Ulum Deoband, India, and obtained a master's degree from al-Azhar. Joined PAS in 1967 and won his first state legislative seat in 1969. Became PAS spiritual guide and served as chief minister of Kelantan from 1990 to 2002, working to make Kelantan a Malayo-Islamic state led by ulama.

Nikah Marriage ceremony.

Nimatullahi Tariqah Began as a Sunni Sufi order in the fourteenth century in southeast Iran but became Shii in the fifteenth century. Spread to the West in the mid-1970s. Emphasizes the universal, spiritual, and ethical aspects of Sufism and Islam, shariah, and the need to continuously practice silent remembrance of God (dhikr) while in the midst of productive activity in the world.

Niqabah Those who earn their living by practicing a common profession; similar to the French *syndicat*. Covers a range of occupations from medicine or law to craftsmen, skilled workers, and industrial employees.

Can refer to a branch of a union as well as to higher levels of association; the highest level of institutional coordination of many subordinate branches (referred to in the United Statse as the international union) is ittihad. The term was first used in this sense in the late nineteenth or early twentieth century; before that niqabah meant "guardianship" or "legal power." The modern meaning marks a significant change in attitudes toward power, responsibility, and the delegation of authority.

Nisam-i Islam *See* Pakistan Muslim League

Niyabah In modern Muslim law, "agency" (wakalah) or "mandate." A naib is a person authorized to represent another or act as his or her attorney in serving the interests of the principal. In modern law, there are many different types of agencies, including niyabah ammah (general agency), niyabat takhsis (an exclusive agency), niyabat tamthil fi amal (a power of attorney given to accomplish a specific act), niyabah dihamiyyah or zahiriyyah (ostensible agency), niyabah dimniyyah (implied agency), and niyabah nafiiyya (agency coupled with an interest in favor of the agent). Al-niyabah al-ammah is the office of public prosecution charged with representing the interests of the victims and society in criminal matters. Al-niyabah al-barlamaniyyah is parliamentary representation, and a delegate to the parliament is known as naib barlamani.

Niyyah *See* Intention

Nizam Order, organization, system, rule. Muslim Brotherhood doctrine held that Islam was the perfect nizam and was valid for all people at all times. Tablighi Jamaat, an important twentieth-century grassroots Islamic movement, is sometimes called Nizam or "system." In the 1970s Pakistan's Jamaat-i Islami spearheaded a religio-political program called Nizam-i Mustafa (System of the Prophet).

Nizam al-Mulk, Abu Ali al-Hasan ibn al-Hasan ibn Ali ibn Ishaq al-Tusi (d. 1092)

Longtime minister of the Seljuk sultans Alp Arslan and Malik Shah. Also known for his remarkable treatise on kingship, *Siyasat Nameh* (The book of government), which focused on the art of government, the requirements of majesty, and the threats that endangered the empire. Possessed immense power, as he controlled the administration of the Seljuk Empire for thirty years. Was strongly dedicated to Sunni Islam and severely suppressed heterodox religious movements, particularly the Shiis and the Ismailis. Established the Nizamiyyah madrasas, hospitals, and extensive public works. Was killed, allegedly by an Ismaili.

Nizam-i Mustafa Movement The System of the Prophet Muhammad. Nine-party popular movement in Pakistan begun by the Jamaat-i Islami in 1977 to overthrow the secular government of Zulfikar Ali Bhutto and establish an Islamic system of government in Pakistan. The movement was eclipsed after the military coup of Zia-ul-Haq.

Nizami, Jamal al-Din Abu Muhammad Ilyas ibn Yusuf ibn Zaki Muayyad (d. ca. 1209) Persian poet. Author of the *Khamsa* (also known as the *Panj Ganj*), which comprises the following five epic poems: *Makhzan al-Asrar*; the romances *Khusraw and Shirin* and *Layla and Majnun*; *Iskandar Nama*; and *Haft Paykar*. Nizami's work, strongly evocative of Sufi ideas, exercised great influence on the subsequent development of Persian verse.

Nizamiyyah College of Baghdad *See* Madrasah Nizamiyyah

Nizaris One of two branches of Ismaili Shiis (the other is the Mustalis). The Ismailis split in 1094 over the succesion to the Fatimid caliphate. The Nizaris, led by Hasan-i Sabbah, recognized Nizar as imam, although he was an infant, instead of his brother, al-Mustali bi Allah, and have maintained a lineage of "living imams" through the Aga Khans (a title introduced in 1843). Talim (divinely inspired teaching) through the imam offsets the insufficiency of human reason for understanding God. The Crusaders mistook the Nizaris' association with political murder with hashish addiction and spawned the Assassins legend. The third Aga Khan (d. 1957) began a move toward the Islamic mainstream that was continued by the fourth, Prince Karim Khan al-Husayni (b. 1936). Originally in Iran and Syria, Nizaris are found currently in Africa, the West, and South, Central, and West Asia.

Noah Arabic Nuh. In the Quran, prophet who, along with righteous members of his family, was saved from the Great Flood in an ark while the rest of the world was destroyed due to its unrighteousness. Noah preached faith in God for 950 years, according to the Quran.

Noble Drew Ali (d. 1929) Born Timothy Drew. Founded the Moorish Science Temple in 1913. The Quran used by this group is entirely different from the Quran of Islam. He preached that Christianity is the religon of whites and that the true religion for "Asiatics" (blacks) is Islam. The movement he founded spread to major American cities but weakened after his death.

Noor, Fadzil Mohamad (d. 2002) Malaysian thinker and religious activist. Educated at al-Azhar. Taught at the Faculty of Islamic Studies at the Technical University of Malaysia (UTM). Joined Angkatan Belia Islam Malaysia (ABIM) in the 1970s and later the Parti Islam Se Malaysia (PAS). In 1989 became president of PAS.

Noorani, Mawlana Shah Ahmad (Dates unknown) Leader of Jamiatul Ulama-i Pakistan during the 1960s. Made the Jamiat the most vociferous actor in the political arena, addressing issues of national concern. Initially chosen by opponents of Zulfikar Ali Bhutto's regime to succeed him as prime minister. In the 1990s his followers formed the Islamic Democratic Front as an offshoot of Jamiatul Ulama-i Islam.

North Africa, Islam in Islam arrived in the Maghreb soon after the death of Muhammad. Arab Muslim armies spread Islamic administration from Egypt to Tunisia by 647 and to the Atlantic by 710. The majority of the population converted relatively rapidly, but there were many revolts against central control, and by the tenth century Muslim northwest Africa was developing independently. States controlling most of the region, the al-Murabitun and al-Muwahhidun, set important patterns in the twelfth and thirteenth centuries. From then on, most Muslims in the region were Sunni and followed the Maliki school of Islamic jurisprudence. The influence of pious leaders and Sufi teachers was great. Islamic identification supported nationalism in the modern era, and the Islamic resurgence of the late twentieth century found expression in movements such as the Islamic Salvation Front of Algeria.

North American Islamic Trust Registered in 1975 in the state of Indiana as a nonprofit organization seeking to own and promote waqf (pious endowments) of Muslims in North America. Owns and maintains many mosques, Islamic centers, and Islamic schools in North America. A sister organization under the same name is registered in the province of Ontario in Canada.

Northern People's Congress (NPC) Nigerian political party founded in 1949. Aimed to unite the peoples of northern Nigeria, retain northern regional autonomy within Nigeria, and enhance the power of traditional Muslim rulers. Dominated northern Nigeria and was an important part of Nigeria's federal government from the 1950s until the military seized power in 1966.

NU *See* Nahdatul Ulama

Nuh *See* Noah

Numan, al-Qadi Fatimid jurist. Wrote extensively on the Islamic concept of guardianship, using historical and exegetical evidence to argue that Islamic political history had gone awry since Muhammad's death. Claimed that only in his time was there a rightful claimant in position to join force and guardianship to lead the Muslim community.

Numerology Practice of interpreting numbers in a mystical or magical sense. Popular in the traditional Islamic world. Assigning each letter of the Arabic alphabet a numerical value allowed practitioners to derive occult information from scripture by adding the values of the letters in key words or important phrases.

Nur Light. One of the names of God from the Quran (24:35). Also used by the Quran to refer to divine guidance (e.g., 5:44–46). Quranic and prophetic uses of the term have given rise to a number of philosophical and Sufi commentaries and to the mystico-philosophical school of illumination (hikmat al-ishraq) founded by al-Suhrawardi.

Nur Jahan (d. 1645) Mughal empress. Last and favorite wife of Mughal emperor Jahangir. Garnered government control during his decline and became a major power broker and patron of the arts. She held such influence that Shah Jahan, upon his ascension, sought to defame her and remove her image from coins.

Nur Muhammadi Muhammadan light; also called al-nur al-muhammadi. In the emanation scheme of cosmology characteristic of Sufi and Shii metaphysics, refers to the precosmic soul of Muhammad, which is equivalent to the active intellect of Neoplatonism and associated with the perfect person (al-insan al-kamil) and Muhammadan truth (haqiqah muhammadiyyah). Represents the first creation (or emanation) of God, the self-manifestation of divine consciousness. All prophets preceding Muhammad derived their prophetic ability from the Muhammadan light. The doctrine appears in the writings of such early Sufi writers as Sahl al-Tustari and Hakim al-Tirmidhi and was later developed by Ibn al-Arabi and his school. The concept plays an important role in both Sufi and Shii concepts of sainthood (walayah).

Nurculuk Modern Turkish religious movement named after its founder and leader, Bediuzzaman Said al-Nursi (d. 1960). The late-nineteenth-century Ottoman administration differentiated between the more modern Turks of western Anatolia and the Balkans and Nursi's own comparatively backward Kurdish region. Nursi's solution to this cultural bifurcation was to promulgate an Islam that brought all Muslims under a common faith but added the advantages of Western technology. The movement is popular among an increasingly educated, urbane population and is extremely active in publishing his writings and the newspaper *Yeni asya*. *See also* Nursi, Bediuzzaman Said al-

Nuri, Fazlullah (d. 1909) Also known as Hajj Shaykh Fazlullah ibn Mulla Abbas Mazandarani Nuri Tihrani. Distinguished Iranian Shii cleric. Issued anti-tobacco edict during the Tobacco Revolt of 1891–92. Initially one of the most active supporters of constitutional government but gradually shifted to the opposition as he became concerned by the perceived dangers of constitutional government for Islam in general and Islamic law in particular. Argued for tying the foundations of the secular form of government to the requirements of Shii law. Emphasized the necessity of the monarchy and clerical viceregency in matters of prophethood for Islam. Captured and executed by constitutionalist forces. *See also* Constitutional Revolution (Iran)

Nursi, Bediuzzaman Said al- (d. 1960) Turkish Islamic leader and thinker from Turkey's Kurdish region. Founder of the Nurculuk movement. His outlook was shaped by the Naqshbandi tariqah and westernization in the Ottoman administration. Realized that the Turkish modernization movement needed Islam to bring all Muslims under the umbrella of common faith, with the advantages of Western technology and knowledge. Hoped that this sociopolitical program would be carried out by Young Turks, but those efforts failed despite his collaboration with the Young Turk government and led to his exile. Later exiled by Atatürk when his program of religious revitalization clashed with Atatürk's aims. Proselytizing and influence over disciples led to additional exiles and imprisonments. *See also* Nurculuk

Nusayris *See* Alawis

Nusrat, Fatih Ali Khan (d. 1997) Pakistani musician. Started his career as a professional qawwali singer, performing at local Sufi shrines in Pakistan. Had a unique style of singing devotional poetry that, along with his oratorial and harmonium dexterity, brought him immense fame. Achieved unprecedented commercial success worldwide by fusing the tradition with pop music.

O

Oath *See* Ahd; Bayah

Occasionalism A theory adopted by Ashari theology, according to which events are the result of entities whose cause is God alone. Hence any causation of one event by another is denied. A human agent is properly said to be able to act only at the moment he or she actually performs the action; only at this instant does God create in the person the ability to perform it.

Occultation "Hidden" state of the twelfth Shii imam. Shiis believe that during the Lesser Occultation, the imam continued to communicate with the community through four successive appointed agents, the last of whom died in 944. During the Greater Occultation, which continues to the present, there is no special agent, although Shii jurists are recognized as his agents and the only legitimate interpreters of shariah.

OIC *See* Organization of the Islamic Conference

Omar Khayyam (d. 1131) Well-known author of the *Rubaiyat*. Arabic and Persian sources written before 1300 consistently describe him as a philosopher, astronomer, and mathematician, and he is known to have devised a new and more accurate calendar. Many of the hundreds of quatrains attributed to him, undoubtedly including some translated by Edward Fitzgerald, are spurious.

Opinion *See* Ray

Oppression *See* Zulm

Order *See* Tariqah

Organization of the Islamic Conference Founded in 1971 in the aftermath of a 1969 fire at the al-Aqsa mosque. Primary goals are the promotion of Islamic solidarity among member states; consolidation of cooperation in economic, social, cultural, scientific, and other fields of activity; carrying out consultations among member states in international organizations; elimination of all forms of racial segregation, discrimination, and colonialism (including that of Israel in Palestine); and support for international peace and security founded on justice. Has been more successful in cultural programs than in political matters. Based in Jeddah, Saudi Arabia, it currently has fifty-three member states and several observers. The most important affiliated institution is the Islamic Development Bank. *See also* International Islamic News Agency; Islamic Chamber of Commerce; Islamic Development Bank; Islamic Educational, Scientific, and Cultural Organization (ISESCO)

Organization of North American Shia Ithna-Ashari Muslim Communities (NASIMCO) Established in 1986 and comprises primarily the Twelver Khoja Muslim communities in Canada and the United States. The majority of the membership is immigrants who arrived from East Africa since the 1960s. The total membership (2002) includes eleven communities with some five thousand members. The mission statement includes promotion of the religious, educational, social, and economic uplift of the Shii community.

Orientalism *See* Orientalists

Orientalists Term designating those who study classical texts in Asian languages (Akkadian, Arabic, Aramaic, Greek, Hebrew, Persian, Sanskrit, etc.), requiring rigorous specialized training. Flourished in Western scholarship from the eighteenth to the twentieth century. Sought to uncover allegedly essential features of Asian civilizations through the critical philological study of cultural texts. Became associated with the romantic, exoticizing impulse of nineteenth-century European culture, influenced by ethnocentrism and imperialism. Because of the negative connotations of this association, developed in the late twentieth century, scholars no longer use the term.

Orphans Mentioned in the Quran twenty-three times, with the admonition that they must be protected and cared for by society. The Quran is particularly concerned with orphan girls, and their guardians are admonished to act justly toward their female wards, not to marry them or give them as wives to their sons. *See also* Adoption

Osman, Fathi (b. 1928) Egyptian-born academic, writer, and leading Muslim liberal thinker. Distinguished himself as a pioneering advocate of reform of Islamic thought based on the values of democracy and human rights within a genuine Islamic perspective. Participated in the 1960s reform of al-Azhar and later taught at Princeton and in Algeria and Saudi Arabia. Came to international prominence as editor of the magazine *Arabia* (London, 1981–87). Currently resides and teaches in California. Published numerous works on Islamic history, law, and doctrine, most notably *Huquq al-Insan bayna shariaht al-Islam wa'l-fikr al-gharbi* (Human rights in Islamic law and Western thought) (1978) and *The Children of Adam* (1996).

Osmania University Established in 1917 in Hyderabad by Rafat Yar Jung and Jamal al-Din al-Afghani, it is one of the oldest and largest institutions of higher learning in India and the first to use an Indian language (Urdu) as a medium of instruction. It has trained generations of the Muslim elite of South India.

Ottoman Empire Vast state created by Central Asian Oghuz Turks (or Osmanlis, after the dynastic founder Osman I) from ca. 1300 to 1923; its territories ultimately encompassed southeastern Europe, Anatolia, the Middle East to Iran, and North Africa. Mehmed II conquered Constantinople (1453), which had been ravaged and depopulated by the Latin Crusaders since 1204; he rebuilt and repopulated the city. Thousands of persecuted Jews emigrated from Christian Europe to Ottoman lands at the behest of Sultan Mehmed and the chief rabbi of Edirne, providing substantial support to Mehmed's massive effort to rebuild Istanbul. The reign of Suleyman the Magnificent, 1520–66, marked the peak of Ottoman power and prosperity as well as the highest development of its government, social, and economic systems. Ottoman Islam was a syncretistic system combining the practices and beliefs of Sunnism, Sufism, and indigenous Christianity. Muslims, Christians, and Jews were organized into millets, which were responsible for both religious and secular duties in their communities. The empire eventually weakened due to large-scale corruption and nepotism, overtaxation, and misrule. Extensive reforms were implemented between 1808 and 1909; democracy flourished from 1909 to 1918 with an active parliament, multiple political parties, and enactment of major secular and liberal reforms. Austria's annexation of Bosnia and Bulgaria's conquest of east Rumelia encouraged Christian minorities throughout the empire to rebel; the Turkish war for independence (1918–23), led by Mustafa Kemal Atatürk and Ismet Inono, resulted in the establishment of the Turkish Republic in Anatolia and eastern Thrace.

P

Pacific Region, Islam in The presence of Islam in the Pacific Basin is the result of postwar immigration, with the majority of immigrants from Turkey, the Levant, Egypt, and the Balkans and a small representation from the Indian subcontinent and Indonesia. The main areas of Muslim population are in Australia and New Zealand, but there are increasing numbers in Japan, Korea, Solomon Islands, Vanuatu, Western Samoa, and Papua New Guinea. Muslim missionary work has been carried out vigorously since the 1970s, resulting in a small but steady stream of local converts. In more developed states, Muslims are supported by administrative structures, including various councils and advisory bodies. No serious political problems face Islam or Muslims in these countries.

Pact of Umar Treaty attributed to the second caliph, Umar ibn Khattab (d. 644), regulating the activities of non-Muslims. Serves as a model for contemporary revivalist groups seeking to control non-Muslim social and religious life.

Padri Movement Sumatran revivalist movement (1803–37) associated with commercialization of the coffee industry; worked to reform local religious practices, Islamize Muslim villages, and resist Dutch imperialism. It was started by three scholars returning from pilgrimage to Mecca and studies in Mecca and Medina who tried to bring local religious practices into accord with traditional Islamic law. The movement created a peasant resistance led by ulama, upsetting the local balance between chiefs and ulama. It expanded by both persuasion and force; targeted villages were reorganized into communities where popular religious practices were forbidden. Adherents adopted distinctive dress. The Dutch assisted leaders opposed to the Padris, hoping to expand their own power and influence; the result was a relatively united Muslim front supporting indigenous interests and denouncing the Dutch as infidel foreigners. The Dutch were ultimately victorious and retained control over the administration. Some descendants of the leaders became rigorous religious teachers who played an important role in the Islamic modernist movement in Indonesia.

PAGAD *See* People Against Gangsterism and Drugs

Pahlavi, Muhammad Reza Shah (d. 1980) Last ruling monarch of the Iranian Pahlavi dynasty. Placed on the throne by the British and Russians in 1941 and again in 1953 by the British and Americans, leading to charges that he served foreign, rather than Iranian national, interests. Implemented the "White Revolution," designed to secularize, modernize, and develop Iran economically and socially. Particularly emphasized the need for land reform and expansion of women's participation in Iranian society. Criticized by Ayatollah Khomeini for alleged worship and imitation of the West and emphasis on continuity with pre-Islamic rule and history at the expense of Islamic heritage. Overthrown and exiled in the 1979 Islamic revolution.

Pahlavi, Reza Shah (d. 1944) Iranian monarch and founder of the Pahlavi dynasty. Initiated numerous reforms, particularly in education and the legal system, encroaching on privileges of the clergy. Outlawed the veil in 1936. Inspired by nationalism based in and glorifying the pre-Islamic era. He was forced to abdicate by the Allied occupation in 1941.

Painting Most painting in the Islamic world consists of illustration of manuscripts of histories, folktales, romances, epics, poetry, and animal fables, and production of single-page paintings that were collected and assembled into albums by individual patrons. Traditionally, painting was done in miniature format on paper and was generally produced in royal ateliers or for elite patrons. Some manuscripts that contain religious subjects have been illustrated, such as events in the life of Muhammad, despite traditional prohibitions on religious imagery.

Pakistan, Islam in Second largest Muslim nation in the world and the only country established in the name of Islam. Founded in 1947 as a homeland for Indian Muslims. The resurgence of Indian Islam began with Sir Sayyid Ahmad Khan and the Aligarh movement of educational and religio-political reforms, which insisted on political autonomy and protection of the rights of Indian Muslims. The All-India Muslim League worked with the Hindu-dominated Indian National Congress for independence from the British but became convinced that the religious, cultural, and political interests of the Indian Muslim community could not be safeguarded in a postindependence India dominated by a Hindu majority. Thus it adopted the goal of creating a separate state for Muslims. Mohammad Ali Jinnah, the founder of Pakistan, envisioned the new state to be a liberal Muslim democratic state. Major debates since independence have concerned the appropriate role of Islam in the state, the exercise of Islamic law, and the Islamization of society and economy. Islamization measures were introduced between 1977 and 1988 by Zia-ul-Haq, including hudud punishments, compulsory collection and distribution of zakah and ushr taxes, establishment of shariah courts, partial elimination of interest from the banking system, and revision of school textbooks to reflect an Islamic slant. Numerous Islamically oriented political parties participate in the political process and agitate for the further implementation of traditional Islamic law in Pakistan. Approximately 97 percent of Pakistanis are Muslim. The majority are Sunnis following the Hanafi school of Islamic law. Between 10 and 15 percent are Shiis, mostly Twelvers. Privately managed mosques and madrasas have provided a base for an independent, and often oppositional, role by the religious establishment.

Pakistan Democratic Alliance Political coalition consisting of the Pakistan People's Party and the Shii party Tahrik-i Nifaz-i Fiqh-i Jafariyyah; formed in 1990 to run in elections. Opposed by the Islamic Democratic Alliance, led by the Muslim League and Jamaat-i Islami. *See also* Pakistan, Islam in

Pakistan Muslim League Successor of the (All-India) Muslim League, which led to Muslim independence in parts of the Indian subcontinent. Established in 1906 in Dhaka, it championed self-rule in the Muslim provinces of India until 1930. After the Lahore Resolution in 1940, it articulated a clear demand for a Muslim homeland. Pakistan was created with the effort of Indian Muslims for which the Muslim League served as a vital platform. After the creation of Pakistan in 1947, the Muslim League ruled Pakistan from 1947 to 1958 and also in the 1960s, 1980s, and 1990s. *See also* Muslim League

Pakistan National Alliance (PNA) Nine-party coalition formed in March 1977, using Islamic symbolism and slogans to oppose the secular, socialist regime of Zulfikar Ali Bhutto. Parties included Pakistan Muslim League, National Democratic Party, Tahrik-i Istiqlal, Jamaat-i Islami, Jamiatul Ulama-i Pakistan, and Jamiatul Ulama-i Islam. Promoted the establishment of an Islamic system of government, elimination of moral and political corruption, and support for business and industrial interests. Developed a network of mosques, religious schools, seminaries, and ulama for political activities and communications. The membership was largely urban- and town-based and middle-class. Some parties joined with Zia-ul-Haq's regime after it seized power in July 1979.

Pakistan People's Party (PPP) Political party founded in 1967 by Zulfikar Ali Bhutto, emphasizing secularized Islamic principles of social justice. Gradually embraced the Islamization of society due to popular demand. Tried to balance secularist tradition with public demands for Islamization. In power from 1971 until 1979, when it was overthrown by Zia-ul-Haq. Opposed by conservatives and Islamic parties as too radically socialist and un-Islamic. Resurfaced in 1988 as a major opposition party. Its leader, Benazir Bhutto, was elected prime minister in 1988 and 1993.

Pakistani Revolutionary Guards See Tahrik-i Jafariyyah Pakistan

Palestine and Israel, Islam in The liberation of Palestine from Israeli occupation is often projected as a duty for all Muslims because of the important Muslim shrines and mosques in Jerusalem, Islam's third holiest city. Israeli military occupation of the West Bank and Gaza since 1967 has resulted in major restrictions on and suppression of many Muslim organizations and activities and has been accompanied by the establishment of Israeli settlements in violation of international law. Some Muslims have become radicalized, although the majority of their work, funding, and activities is centered on social services. The Islamist movement is currently the opposition party in Palestinian politics. Muslims in Israel also face legal restrictions, but Islamic political organizations have had success at local levels. See also HAMAS; Islamic Jihad of Palestine

Palestine Liberation Organization (PLO) Umbrella organization established in 1964 to represent Palestinian interests. Immediate goals are the liberation of Palestine from foreign control, political independence from Arab regimes, and securing the return of Palestinian refugees. It is dominated by the Harakat al-Tahrir al-Filistin (Palestine Liberation Movement, also known by its Arabic acronym Fatah), led by Yasir Arafat. In 1993 it signed a Declaration of Principles with Israel in Washington to facilitate the peace process. See also Arab-Israeli Conflict

Palimbani, Abd al-Samad al- See Sammani, Muhammad ibn Abd al-Karim al-

Pancasila Indonesian. Five principles. Core ideology of the Indonesian government consisting of belief in God, Indonesian nationalism, humanitarianism or just and civilized humanity, democracy, and social justice. Formulated by Sukarno in 1945. Intended to alleviate religious tensions and promote pluralism, since specific religious practice is the individual's choice. Some Muslim activists contest that Pancasila is responsible for the rising number of conversions to Christianity and does not give Islam a sufficiently prominent place in Indonesian national ideology.

Pan-Islamism Ideology calling for sociopolitical solidarity among all Muslims. Has existed as a religious concept since the early days of Islam. Emerged as a modern political ideology in the 1860s and 1870s at the height of European colonialism, when Turkish intellectuals began discussing and writing about it as a way to save the Ottoman Empire from fragmentation. Became the favored state policy during the reign of Sultan Abdulhamid II (r. 1876–1909) and was adopted and promoted by members of the ruling bureaucratic and intellectual elites of the empire. With the rise of colonialism, became a defensive ideology, directed against European political, military, economic, and missionary penetration. Posed the sultan as a universal caliph to whom Muslims everywhere owed allegiance and obedience. Sought to offset military and economic weakness in the Muslim world by favoring central government over the periphery and Muslims over non-Muslims in education, office, and economic opportunities. Ultimately failed and collapsed after the defeat and dismemberment of the Ottoman Empire after World War I. Resurrected during the resurgence of Islam after World War II. Expressed via organizations such as the Muslim World League and the Organization of the Islamic Conference, which seek to coordinate Islamic solidarity through political and economic cooperation internationally. Has also served as an important political tool in recruiting all-Muslim support against foreign aggressions.

Pan-Turanism Nationalist ideology that emerged in Ottoman Turkey during the Young Turk era (1908–18) in response to the failure of Ottomanism in the face of other nationalisms (Greek, Arab, Armenian) in the Ottoman Empire. Also known as Turkism, Pan-Turkism, or Turanianism.

Parmusi *See* Partai Muslimin Indonesia (Parmusi)

Parsis *See* Zoroastrianism and Islam

Partai Islam Se-Malaysia (PAS) Islamic Party of Malaysia. Formed in 1951 by members of three political parties (Malay Nationalist Party, Hizbul Muslimin, and United Malays National Organization) and registered as a political party in 1956. The party advocated formation of an Islamic state. During the decade after 1956 it gave priority to radical Malay nationalism and pan-Indonesianism. During the 1970s it symbolized conservative Malay nationalism coupled with support for the goals of traditional Islam. In the late 1970s it called for alterations in the federal constitution to bring it more into line with traditional Islamic law and administration, and criticized the government's policies as being devoid of spiritual values. Since 1982 it has given priority to reformist Islamic goals and downplayed Malay nationalism. Led by Islamists today, its strength lies in rural Malay peasants and traditional village leaders, who are not always receptive to fundamentalism. Main rival to the United Malays National Organization. Formed governments in Kelantan and Trengannu in the 1990s.

Partai Muslimin Indonesia (Parmusi) Indonesian Muslims Party. Indonesian political party formed in 1960 after the popular Islamic modernist party Masjumi was banned by the Sukarno government. Many Masjumi members joined Parmusi, but they were prohibited from taking leadership positions in the new party by the military-led government, which sought to limit the power of Muslim parties. Following a poor election showing in 1971, when it received only

5.36 percent of the vote, Parmusi joined with other Muslim parties to form the Partai Persatuan Pembangunan (PPP, Development Unity Party) in January 1973.

Parti du Peuple Algérien Populist party formed in Algeria in 1937 by Messali al-Hajj, two months after the French government dissolved a prior party, Etoile Nord-Africaine. Sought to use tactics of spontaneous mass uprisings in the quest for national independence. Banned in 1945 by French authorities for activities against the government and was powerless to bring about political reforms and national independence, despite membership of ten thousand by 1940.

Parti Islam Se-Malaysia (PAS) *See* Partai Islam Se-Malaysia

Parti Orang Muslimin Malaya *See* Hizbul Muslimin

Party of God (Iran) *See* Hizb Allah (Iran)

Party of God (Kashmir) *See* Hizbul Mujahidin

Parvez, Ghulam Ahmad *See* Parwez, Ghulam Ahmad

Parwez, Ghulam Ahmad (d. 1986) Pakistani modernist Islamic thinker. Born and educated in Punjab, in the 1930s Parwez began a modernist exegesis, whose distinctive mark was rejection of the hadith as a source for Islamic law. He was influential in Islamic debates in Pakistan in the 1950s and 1960s, mainly through his lectures and written work and his *Idara Tulu-i Islam* (Bureau of the Dawn of Islam), which continues to propagate his views.

PAS *See* Partai Islam Se-Malaysia (PAS)

Pasdaran *See* Sipah-i Pasdaran-i Inqilab-i Islami

Pasha Turkish abbreviation of Persian *padishah*, "sovereign" (Arabic *basha*). Title of honor awarded in the thirteenth to nineteenth centuries mostly to generals, governors, and viziers in the Ottoman administration, rarely to religious officials or women. After the mid-nineteenth-century Tanzimat reforms it was given to the highest four grades in the civil and military hierarchies, and from 1923 to 1934 only to soldiers.

Passion See Ishq

Patani United Liberation Organization Muslim separatist organization in Thailand, established in 1968. Its goal is to create an independent Islamic state from the current Thai provinces of Pattani, Narathiwat, Yala, and Satun. Creation of this state is considered essential to the preservation of "Malayness" and the Islamic way of life of local Malay Muslims. The group considers Thailand an occupying power, from whom independence can be wrested only through the use of armed force. Popular with younger, more militant Malay Muslims, and has attracted moral, financial, and other support from Malay individuals, organizations associated with the Islamic Party of Malaysia (PAS), and the Middle East.

Patrona Halil (Rebellion of) Rebellion in Istanbul in 1730. Urban groups protesting new taxes were joined by the poor and leading religious officials in a rebellion against Sultan Ahmet III and his grand vizier, Ibrahim. The sultan was deposed, and conservative groups exercised greater influence. Patrona Halil was a small-scale merchant who was a street leader of the rebellion.

PBUH See Sala Allah Alayhi wa-Salaam

Peace See Salaam

Peace and Blessings Be upon Him See Sala Allah Alayhi wa-Salaam

Peace Be upon You See Salaam(u) Alaykum(u), al-

People Against Gangsterism and Drugs (PAGAD) Grassroots South African movement that arose in 1996 to draw attention to runaway drug addiction and rising crime in the "colored" townships and Muslim residential neighborhoods of Cape Town. The original aim of fighting crime soon gave way to vigilante activities. PAGAD has close alliances with the Islamic Unity Convention and Qibla, two groups that are highly critical of the postapartheid democratic government. However, following highly visible acts of urban terrorism, support from Muslim groups and public approval rapidly dwindled.

People of the Book See Ahl al-Kitab

PERKIM Acronym for Pertubuhan Kabajikan Islam Se-Malaysia, or All Malaysia Muslim Welfare Association, founded in 1960 as religious and social welfare organization. Its principal goal is promotion of Islam as a national religion, with particular emphasis on voluntary conversion of the non-Malay population. It came to public attention following the ethnic and political conflicts of 1960s, which resulted in growing ethnic and religious polarization between Malay Muslims and other groups. Provides a wide range of social services, including hostel accommodation, religious instruction, counseling, educational services, clinics, and drug rehabilitation. Publications include instructional books on Islam and social problems, as well as regular newsletters in Malay, Chinese, and English.

Permitted See Halal

Persatuan Islam (Persis) Islamic Union. Indonesian modernist organization founded in Bandung in 1923. Prior to World War II, the group opposed nationalism based on the belief that it divided Islam. In 1939 it joined the Supreme Islamic Council of Indonesia, which became a central coordinating body for Islamic affairs. Has a history of support for religious education, promotion of Islamic values, and concern with contemporary political and social questions.

Persian See Farsi

Persis *See* Persatuan Islam (Persis)

Pertubuhan Kabajikan Islam Se-Malaysia
See PERKIM

Pesantren Secondary-level Islamic education system in Southeast Asia offering training in Islamic subjects. Historically, scholars provided education, gave advice to villagers, and legitimized local ceremonies. Villagers supported the schools with food and labor, supplemented in some places with a poor tax, alms, and pious endowments. Fees were seldom charged for learning. Contemporary Indonesian Muslim intellectuals have lauded the anti-Dutch stance of pesantren scholars, seeing them as preservers of Indonesian and Islamic values during the colonial period. In the twentieth century, pesantren is waning as an educational choice as Muslims feel increasingly compelled to send their children to modern government schools.

Peter the Venerable (d. 1156) Abbot of Cluny who began a movement for better Christian understanding of Islam. Commissioned Robert of Ketton to translate the Quran into Latin.

Pharaoh *See* Firawn

Philippines, Islam in Five percent of the population of the Philippines is Muslim, mostly living in the western and central parts of Mindanao island and the Sulu Archipelago, a region with little industrial base and an agri-fishing economy. Conflict between the Christianized north and southern Muslim populations has been exacerbated by severe land conflicts, with government-supported Christian resettlement in Muslim areas, and neglect of Moro (Muslim) economic and educational aspirations. These led to increased armed clashes and Ferdinand Marcos' proclamation of martial law in 1972. The Moro National Liberation Front (MNLF) split into three factions, but negotiations led to limited autonomy and some sociocultural concessions in 1987. President Gloria Arroyo announced a unilateral ceasefire with the Moro Islamic Liberation Front (MILF) in 2001, hoping that the consequent stability would allow economic development to undermine the desire for Muslim independence. An extremist Islamic separatist movement, Abu Sayyaf, continued to terrorize foreign nationals and Philippine government officials into 2002.

Philosophy Arabic *falsafah*. Muslim scholars integrated certain elements of Greek philosophy into Islamic perspectives, creating new schools of thought. Al-Kindi (d. 873) founded the early Peripatetic school, combining Aristotelian and Neoplatonic elements and attempting to harmonize faith and reason. The father of formal logic and Islamic political philosophy, al-Farabi (d. 950), synthesized Plato's political philosophy and Islam. Ibn Sina's (Avicenna, d. 1037) stress on the distinction between necessary and contingent existents became central to Islamic thought and deeply influenced Judeo-Christian philosophy and theology. Major medieval theologians such as al-Ghazali (d. 1111) composed treatises against philosophy, thus curtailing rationalism, although he was refuted by the renowned Aristotelian philosopher Ibn Rushd (Averroës, d. 1198). His influence in the West was greater than that in the Islamic world. Ibn Khaldun (d. 1406) established a philosophy of history. The twelfth through sixteenth centuries marked the ascendancy of philosophy in Persia, particularly hikmat al-ishraq (the wisdom of illumination), initiated by al-Suhrawardi (d. 1191) and culminating in the work of Sadr al-Din al-Shirazi (Mulla Sadra, d. 1641). Philosophy continues to play an important role in Iranian intellectual life.

Physics *See* Natural Science

Pickthall, Muhammad Marmaduke (d. 1936) British translator of the Quran into English. First editor of the journal *Islamic Culture*, published in India. Works include a commentary on the Quran, a collection of folklore from the Holy Land, travel memoirs from trips to Palestine and Syria, several novels, and works on Islamic culture. Supported Ottomans and Young Turk reformers.

Pilgrim *See* Hajji

Pilgrimage *See* Hajj; Umrah

Pillars of Islam The five pillars of Islam (arkan al-Islam; also arkan al-din, "pillars of religion") comprise five official acts considered obligatory for all Muslims. The Quran presents them as a framework for worship and a sign of commitment to faith. The five pillars are the shahadah (witnessing the oneness of God and the prophethood of Muhammad), regular observance of the five prescribed daily prayers (salat), paying zakah (almsgiving), fasting (sawm; siyyam) during the month of Ramadan, and performance of the hajj (pilgrimage during the prescribed month) at least once in a lifetime.

The first pillar, the shahadah, consists of two declarations. The first, "There is no god but God," affirms belief in a single divine reality (tawhid). The second, "Muhammad is the messenger of God," affirms submission to God via acceptance of His message as revealed to humanity through Muhammad. This declaration of faith signifies entrance of the believer into the broader community (ummah) of Muslims and is required of converts to Islam.

The second pillar, the five daily prayers, signifies the believer's submission to God and serves as public, physical evidence of the believer's adherence to Islam. Prayers are to be performed just before dawn, at noon, in midafternoon, just after sunset, and in the evening, between an hour after sunset and midnight. Prayers are to be made in the direction of Mecca and must be carried out in a state of ritual purity, achieved by either ritual ablutions or a bath. Movements during prayer imitate entrance into the presence of a great ruler (symbolized by the raising of the hands to the ears and proclamation of the glory and majesty of the ruler for all to hear), bowing reverently, and then uttering the opening chapter of the Quran, the

Surat al-Fatihah. Worshipers then utter other Quranic verses while completing the ritual bowing, which is followed by prostration, performed on the knees with both hands on the ground and the forehead touching between them. Worshipers repeat their glorification of God and prostration three times. The entire cycle of prayer (rakah) is then repeated. After every two cycles and after the third cycle in the sunset prayer, the worshiper sits back on the heels and addresses God with a ritual prayer calling forth God's blessings upon Muhammad. After completing all cycles of canonical prayer, the worshiper sits back on the heels and recites the shahadah, formally reaffirming the truth of Islam and engaging the worshiper in direct communication with God. Private petitions are then offered. Formal blessings are requested upon Muhammad and Abraham. The prayer ends with an invocation of peace. Every canonical prayer requires between two and four rakahs. In total, seventeen rakahs are performed daily.

The third pillar is the zakah (alms tax), typically paid to a religious official or representative of the Islamic state or to a representative of a local mosque. This amount is traditionally set at one-fortieth, or 2.5 percent, of the value of all liquid assets and income-generating properties owned by the believer. It is used to feed the poor, encourage conversion to Islam, ransom captives, help travelers, support those devoting themselves to God's work, relieve debtors, defend the faith, and any other purpose deemed appropriate. The zakah serves as a reminder of one's broader social responsibilities to the community.

The fourth pillar is observation of the monthlong fast (sawm) of Ramadan (the ninth month of the lunar Islamic calendar), from sunrise to sunset. The believer is supposed to abstain from food, drink, and sexual activity during the daylight hours, demonstrating affirmation of ethical awareness and serving as a purifying act of sacrifice of one's bodily desires for the sake of God. The direct experience of pain and hunger over a prolonged period of time reminds the believer of the pain and hunger experienced by the poor.

The fifth pillar is the pilgrimage to Mecca during the first ten days of the month of Dhu al-Hijjah. Every Muslim who is physically and financially capable of making the trip and performing the prescribed rites is required to make the hajj. The nine essential rites of the hajj are the putting on of the ihram (unsewn cloth symbolizing the humility and equality of all believers), circumambulation of the Kaaba, standing at the plain of Arafat, spending the night at Muzdalifa, throwing stones at three symbols of Satan, sacrifice of an animal at Mina, repetition of the circumambulation of the Kaaba, drinking of water from the well of Zamzam, and performance of two cycles of prayer at the Station of Abraham. The hajj can be considered complete without performing all of the required rites, but the pilgrim must pay expiation for the failure to complete them. During the hajj, the pilgrim is to avoid thinking about anything but the remembrance of God and the rites of pilgrimage, since the circumambulation of the Kaaba, like canonical prayer, symbolizes the believer's entrance into the divine presence.

Both Sunnis and Shiis agree on the essential details for carrying out the five pillars. In popular Sufi piety, the five pillars were personally internalized as acts of devotion and spiritual exercises. The shahadah became a constant recollection (dhikr) of God and the obligatory prayers became a life of continuous prayer and meditation.

Pir See Murshid

Plato (d. 347 B.C.E.) Arabic *Aflaton*. Hellenistic philosopher, some of whose writings (*Timaeus, Republic,* and *Laws*) were partially translated into Arabic during the Middle Ages. Much was known of Plato's works through oral transmission as well. Thus, in his *Philosophy of Plato*, al-Farabi (d. 950) provided an extensive account of Plato's philosophy, identifying all of the dialogues now accepted as authentic and providing a reasonable explanation of the topic covered in each. Either because of his penchant for metaphysical

investigations or due to the acknowledged enigmatic character of his writings, Plato was accorded the title "divine" and thus distinguished—at least for popular discussions—from the more sober Aristotle. Al-Farabi, along with Ibn Sina (Avicenna, d. 1037) and Ibn Rushd (Averroës, d. 1198), considered Plato's *Laws* especially important for understanding the significance of lawgiving within the framework of revelation. Others, such as Ibn Bajjah (Avempace, d. 1138) and Ibn Tufayl (d. 1185), relied heavily on Plato to explore what they held to be the necessary tension between philosophy and politics.

PLO See Palestine Liberation Organization

Pluralism Arabic *taaddudiya,* Persian *takththur qara'i.* Inclusiveness that acknowledges the legitimacy of other faiths. In general, Muslim pluralists stress that the Quran recognizes salvific value in other religions, particularly Judaism and Christianity, with whom it is linked through shared prophets. Some Muslims accept other faiths as not merely inferior manifestations of religiosity, but variant forms of individual and communal responses to the presence of the transcendent in human life. Proponents of this view find support in the Islamic teaching that all persons are created by God with a disposition that potentially leads to knowledge of God (fitrah). The mainstream Islamic viewpoint, however, is that Islam is superior to other religions; while protecting individuals' rights to practice the religion of their choice privately, Islam sees itself as the final revelation, perfect and complete, which corrects the errors of earlier religious communities. Its law must therefore remain dominant and may not be challenged by other legal systems.

PNA See Pakistan National Alliance (PNA)

Poetry See Devotional Poetry

Poll Tax See Jizyah

Polygamy See Polygyny

Polygyny Practice according to which one man may have several wives simultaneously; a controversial issue in modern Islamic societies. Polygyny is a pre-Islamic practice from Mesopotamia and the Mediterranean that continued in Islam. However, the Quran limited the number of wives a man may marry simultaneously to four. Shiis debate whether the limitation applies only to permanent marriages or mutah (temporary marriages) as well. Many modern Islamic nations have either outlawed or regulated polygyny (Egypt, 1920; Sudan, 1929; India, 1939; Jordan, 1951; Syria, 1953; Tunisia, 1956; Morocco, 1958; Iraq, 1959; Pakistan, 1961; Turkey, 1971; and South Yemen, 1974), although many traditionalists consider a man's right to four wives essential to the Islamic concept of marriage.

Polytheists Arabic mushrikun. Those who associate [other things with God]. Persons or societies who ascribe divinity to objects and beings other than or along with God. Muhammad's prophetic mission was to teach the Arab polytheists monotheism (Quran 6:137; 29:41; 43:15,16). The Quran classifies Jews and Christians as "People of the Book" but also labels them as polytheists—Jews for adhering to concepts of divine national selection, and Christians for their doctrines of the Trinity and Incarnation (Quran 2:94–95; 5:18; 62:6; 98). Muslim reformers denounce the Sufi practices of seeking intercession of saints and veneration of their tombs as polytheistic.

Poole, Paul Robert See Muhammad, Elijah

Popular Religion Combination of pre-Islamic local culture and practices (adat) with Islamic meanings, terms, and interpretations. Includes pilgrimages (ziyarah) to tombs and shrines of saints, descendants of Muhammad, religious teachers, founders of Sufi orders and Shii imams (often accompanied by presentation of gifts or offering of sacrifices for requests for blessing, mystical knowledge, resolution of daily problems, and/or intercession by God); popular celebrations of Muhammad's birthday; reenactment of events surrounding martyrdom of Husayn; Quran recitations at major life events; curing sick; exorcism of demons; use of Quranic verses as charms and amulets for protection, prevention, and medical cures; use of numerology and astrology to predict the future and defend oneself from evil and misfortune; dhikr (chanting) performance; use of popular accounts of lives of Muhammad, his descendants, and other holy people as instructive literature; participation in ritual meals and distribution of blessed foods; belief in the Mahdi (messianic figure); and belief in and invocation of jinn (nonhuman creatures) for magical purposes. Scripturally oriented reformers typically reject popular practices as heretical innovations, although many movements use popular imagery and language and have maintained ties with popular leaders or movements to attract more adherents. *See also* Magic

Pork Consumption of pork is prohibited by the Quran. Many modern Muslims explain the prohibition on scientific grounds, claiming that pigs are susceptible to diseases such as trichinosis, which can be transmitted to human beings, and that pigs consume unclean or rotten food, although the Quran tends to associate the prohibition with following the law of God as revealed in the Torah (e.g., 5:66).

Postmodernism and Islam Postmodernism questions the modernist reliance on reason as the basis of certainty, just as modernism questioned the traditional or premodern reliance on revelation. Rejecting neither revelation as such, nor the validity of human reason, postmodernism rejects instead the notion that any human being or group is privileged with the ability to interpret revelation or nature authoritatively for all time and circumstances. Postmodernists analyze all texts in terms of their socioeconomic, political, and cultural contexts and assert that all readings are interpretations likewise contextualized and therefore subject to reinterpretation. Contemporary Muslim thinkers using postmodernist theories and methods

of interpretation (hermeneutics) characteristically question traditional interpretations
of religious teaching, recognizing their relevance to certain historical contexts but seeking interpretations of eternal truths more
suitable to changing contemporary realities.
This hermeneutic is often identified with the
Islamic legal reasoning process known as
ijtihad.

PPP *See* Pakistan People's Party (PPP)

Prayer *See* Salat

Prayer Rug *See* Sajjadah

President *See* Rais

Prince *See* Amir

Profit Sharing *See* Mudarabah

Proof *See* Dalil

Property Islamic law considers property
rights as God-given and regulated. The
owner of personal property is vested with
the exclusive right of its use, enjoyment, and
disposal, except when legally restricted. For
example, ownership of pork and alcoholic
beverages by Muslims is forbidden.

Prophet *See* Nabi

Prophethood Arabic *nabawiyyah*. Calling by
God to communicate a divinely given message to humankind and to the unseen world
of spirits. A nabi is the recipient of divine
revelation in the form of general moral
teaching, exemplified in the prophet's own
life. A rasul is a prophet whose revelation
contains God's specific commands and prohibitions in the form of an ethical code

(shariah) recorded in scriptural form as
guidance for a particular community and as
a standard by which its members will be
judged on the Last Day. The Quran presents
belief in prophethood as a corollary of belief
in God, providing a means by which humans
can respond individually and collectively to
God. The prophet is a witness of God's unity,
announces the righteous conduct God wills
for this world, and warns of God's judgment
on the Last Day. Prophets are believed to
have been infallible in their fidelity to divine
commands and their ability to communicate
what God gave them to convey, and wise in
understanding its meaning. In Islam, prophethood is always defined in terms of Muhammad's experience, since his is considered the final, perfected message sent to
confirm all previous revelations.

Prophetic Traditions *See* Hadith

Prostitution *See* Zina

Proverb *See* Mathal

Psalms Arabic *zabur*. In the Quran the Psalms
of David are said to be revelation sent to
David, who is considered a prophet (4:163;
17:55; 21:105). God is considered the author of the psalms. Surah 21:105 is a direct
counterpart of the biblical Psalm 37:29.

Puberty Rites *See* Rites of Passage

Public Interest *See* Istislah; Maslahah

Pulpit *See* Minbar

Punishment *See* Hadd

Purdah *See* Seclusion

Purification *See* Ghusl; Wudu

Q

Qabaliyyah See Qabilah

Qabd Contraction or compression. One of the stages of mystical or spiritual development in Sufism, characterized by feeling of constriction and sadness. Typically seen as a response to the display of the divine attributes of majesty and severity. Contrasted with *bast* (expansion), a response to divine beauty and gentleness. *See also* Bast; Sufism

Qabilah Tribe. Basis of the type of social organization typical of the premodern world and still dominant in regions where state or other civil organization has not taken effect. Tribal identities are neither exclusive nor fixed, since tribal peoples can demonstrate varied linguistic, ethnic, religious, regional, class, residential, and occupational categories and traits. The Islamic ideal was to overcome tribal loyalties and divisions through membership in a broader Muslim community, which proclaimed the equality of all believers.

Qabr See Tombs

Qada Court judgment. Binding and enforceable, unlike a fatwa, which is merely a legal opinion. Issued by a qadi (judge) in response to a specific case and circumstances. The qadi may request a fatwa to help determine the legal outcome of a specific case but is not bound to follow it. The decision is based on recognized legal precedent.

Qadar See Jabr

Qadari Tariqah Sufi order founded posthumously by followers of Abd al-Qadir al-Jilani (Gilani) in fourteenth-century Damascus. Hanbali in legal orientation. Spread throughout Sub-Saharan Africa and the Arab world, enjoying particular prominence in Egypt and Syria by the end of the fourteenth century

and extending from West Africa to Southeast Asia by the nineteenth century. Prominent in India, North Africa, and the Malay peninsula. Its leaders played an important role in resistance to European imperialism throughout Africa in the nineteenth century.

Qadariyyah Classical Islamic theological school, seventh to ninth century, which asserted human free will in decision making and as justification for God's power to blame or punish humans. Humans' capacity to make choices makes them responsible for the outcome of their actions and absolves God of responsibility for evil in the world. Many of this school's doctrines were adopted by Mutazilis. The position was rejected by the dominant Ashari theology.

Qaddafi, Muammar al- (b. 1942) Libyan political leader. Rose to power after a coup that overthrew the monarchy in 1969. Put forth idiosyncratic religio-political views in his Green Book. Argued that democracy must be direct and participatory. Viewed Islam as the natural religion for meeting the individual's and humanity's needs. Critical of the ulama and Sufi orders. Actively supported various self-styled liberation struggles in the 1970s and 1980s and Islamic activism in the 1990s.

Qadhf Slander, defamation, or accusation. To accuse someone without proof is a serious offense in Islam; in particular, baselessly accusing a woman of committing an immoral act is punishable by flogging.

Qadi A judge.

Qadi Askar The two highest-ranking qadis of the Ottoman judiciary. As senior members of the royal court, they supervised judicial affairs, heard legal cases, oversaw legal matters of the military-administrative personnel, and handled campaign duties.

Qadianis *See* Ahmadis

Qadisiyyah, Battle of Battle in 637 between Arabs and Persians. The Arabs seized the Persian capital and forced the last pre-Islamic emperor, Yazdagird, to flee to Inner Asia, marking the collapse of the Sasanian empire and the opening of Persia to Arab-Muslim conquest. The battle was used as a symbol by Saddam Hussein to justify the war against Iran (1980–88) and the 1990 invasion of Kuwait.

Qadiyyah A legal proceeding, an action in law, a case, a lawsuit, or a legal dispute. In civil proceedings, it is also called a dawah. The claimant is known as al-mudai and the respondent is al-muda alayh. In criminal proceedings, the defendant is called the muttaham (accused). In all the legal disputes, the burden of proof is against the claimant or prosecutor and there is a presumption of innocence (baraat al-dhimma or al-baraah al-asliyyah) in favor of the defendant or respondent. After the presentation of evidence and witnesses (shuhd), a judge (qadi) renders a decision. The judge's decision is called a qada or hukm. In modern law, the judiciary as a whole is known as al-qada.

Qaeda, al- The base. Militant organization formed circa 1986 by Osama bin Laden to channel fighters and funds for the Afghan resistance movement. Became a vehicle for the declaration of international military struggle against governments and Western representatives and institutions in the Muslim world, America, and other parts of the West. Influenced by the fundamentalist worldview and militant piety of seventh-century Kharijis, Wahhabism, and contemporary Egyptian extremist movements. Allied with the Taliban regime of Afghanistan; the alliance became a base for a network of organizations and cells throughout the Muslim world. Transnational in identity and recruitment; global in ideology, strategy, targets, economic transactions, and network of organizations. Embraces extremist militant views that are rejected by mainstream Muslims.

Qahira, al- *See* Cairo

Qahtani, Muhammad al- (d. 1979) Self-declared Mahdi of the 1979 seizure of the Grand Mosque in Mecca. Denounced the House of Saud for impiety and irreligious innovations. Believed the government modernization program was heretical and the ulama had been co-opted by the state. Announced the end of Saudi reign and sought to establish an Islamic state. Killed by government military forces during the storming of the Grand Mosque. *See also* Utaybi, Juhayman al-

Qaid al-Azam *See* Jinnah, Mohammad Ali

Qajar Dynasty Turkic tribal dynasty that ruled Iran between 1796 and 1925. Began as a tribal federation founded by Muhammad Khan (d. 1797). Qajar unification ended eighteenth-century civil strife. In 1919 Reza Khan led a coup, ended the Qajar dynasty, and established the Pahlavi dynasty (1925).

Qalandar Persian term for a general type of mendicant Sufi unattached to any specific shaykh or order and known for having a disheveled appearance and flouting public opinion. Although qalandars lacked tangible organization, they carried their own linkages and rules. They were particularly known for public demonstrations of devotion.

Qalb Heart. Also *fuad, lubb.* Central concept of Sufi epistemology and psychology, based on frequent Quranic references to it as an intuitive faculty by which the inner reality of things is perceived. Sufis consider qalb superior to logical reasoning in grasping the divine mysteries.

Qamar *See* Moon

Qanun Laws and regulations enacted by a government. Qanun were meant to be supplements to Islamic law in matters it left insufficiently regulated. Under the Ottoman sultans, qanun became an integral part of the legal system, especially in the administrative, fiscal, and penal domains. The sultan's prerogative to enforce customary practices deemed publicly beneficial was a main justification of qanun. In the modern era, qanun gradually became a generic name for all laws and regulations. Similar developments took place in other Muslim countries under such different names as dustur and nizam.

Qanun al-Dawli *See* Siyar

Qarafi, Shihab al-Din (d. 1285) Abu al-Abbas Ahmad ibn Idris. Maliki jurist of Berber origin who lived in Ayyubid and Mamluk Egypt. The greatest Maliki legal theoretician of the thirteenth century, his writings and influence on Islamic legal theory (usul al-fiqh) spread throughout the Muslim world. His insistence on the limits of law underscores the importance of nonlegal (not to be confused with illegal) considerations in determining the proper course of action, with significant implications for legal reform in the modern Islamic world. His views on the common good (maslahah) and custom provide means to accommodate the space-time differential between modern and premodern realities. The most important of his many works are *Al-dhakhirah* (The stored treasure), *Al-furuq* (Differences [between apparently identical legal precepts]), *Nafais al-usul* (Gems of legal theory), and *Kitab al-ihkam fi tamyiz al-fatawa an al-ahkam wa tasarrufat al-qadi wa'l-imam* (The book of perfecting the distinction between legal opinions, judicial decisions, and the discretionary actions of judges and caliphs).

Qaramanli Dynasty Turkish dynasty founded by Ahmed Bey, which controlled Ottoman Tripolitania, Cyrenaica, and Fezzan (present-day Libya) from 1711 to 1835. Tripoli became a base for pirates who enjoyed the patronage of Qaramanli pashas. Entered into bilateral trade agreements with France and England that recognized the dynasty's autonomy from Istanbul; then pressed pirates not to attack maritime traders operating under its trade allies' flags. This led to diplomatic clashes with pirate victims such as the neighboring Italian states and the United States. Sultan Mahmud II sent armed forces to end the dynasty (1835) in part due to pressures from the British, who opposed a French-sympathizing Qaramanli successor.

Qaramita The popular nickname of a group of Ismaili Shiis who founded the Fatimid dynasty in the tenth century. Initially, the Qaramita challenged the Abbasids in the Iraqi and Syrian deserts. Although defeated in 906, they later established an Ismaili republic in eastern Arabia. From there, the Qaramita carried out extensive raiding in western Arabia and Iraq and stole the Black Stone of the Kaaba. In 909 their caliphal candidate al-Mahdi, with the help of a Berber tribal bloc, overthrew the Rustomids of Tahert and the Aghlabids of the eastern Maghreb, thereby establishing the Fatimid dynasty.

Qarawiyin University Celebrated university associated with the mosque of the same name at Fez, Morocco, built by a pious woman, Fatimah bint Muhammad al-Fihri, in 859, as a center for Islamic education. Considered the oldest Islamic university, where religious disciplines were taught in addition to natural sciences. Followed an open system of education until 1789, when the educational program was regulated. Reorganized in 1931 into three divisions for primary, secondary, and higher levels of education; a section for girls was also added. After Morocco's independence from France, the university was placed under the Ministry of Education and restructured into shariah, Arabic studies, and theology faculties. Its library contains a large number of rare manuscripts.

Qardawi, Yusuf (b. 1926) Egyptian Islamic activist and ideologue. Calls for collective awakening of Arab-Islamic identity and reestablishment of the universal caliphate as a visible sign of Muslim unity. Calls on Muslims to reject corruption and Western ideologies. Sees the contradiction between Islamic ideals and un-Islamic reality as the cause of rebellion and violence in youth. Rejects both religious and secular extremism as distortions of the image of Islam. Condemns violence. Proposes moderate leadership, both spiritually and politically, directed toward broader Islamic goals. Opposed to recognition of Israel or giving up any part of Jerusalem.

Qasida Polythematic poem, usually translated as "ode," composed according to strict metrical requirements. Four main themes (aghrad) may be identified within qasidas: panegyric (madih/madh), lampooning (hija), love (ghazal), and threnody or lamentation (ritha). The most famous collection of poems of this genre is called the Muallaqat from pre-Islamic Arabia.

Qassam, Izz al-Din al- (d. 1935) Syrian Islamic activist who organized armed resistance to the Zionist movement and British authorities among predominantly peasant communities. Encouraged peasants to reestablish the basic principles of Islamic faith. Followers continued the campaign after his death and were key figures in the Palestinian uprising of 1936–39. The militant Qassam Brigades of Hamas are named after him.

Qat Addictive narcotic plant consumed widely in Yemen and East Africa. In Islamic law, qat falls into the category of things not prohibited but discouraged (makruh).

Qawwali Group song genre of Hindustani light classical music that presents mystical poetry in Persian, Hindi, and Urdu. Performed in Chishti Sufi assemblies to produce religious emotion and ecstasy. Performers are hereditary specialists patronized by Sufis. Popularized as a world music genre in the late twentieth century.

Qiblah (1) Direction Muslims face during prayer (toward the Kaaba in Mecca), or a prayer wall in the mosque into which the mihrab (niche) is set, indicating the direction of prayer. Numerous astronomical treatises have been composed on methods for determining qiblah placement based on

mathematical geography. (2) South African Islamist organization. *See also* Mihrab

Qimar *See* Gambling

Qiraah *See* Tajwid

Qisas Retribution. Prescribed in Islamic law for murder, voluntary manslaughter, involuntary killing, intentional physical injury, and unintentional physical injury. In cases of intentional killing and physical injury, the family or victim may waive retribution and exact monetary compensation. In other cases, only monetary compensation can be exacted. The perpetrator's clan is responsible for payment of compensation, which is divided by the victim's clan.

Qismah Destiny or fate foreordained by God. The doctrine of qismah holds that the overall fate of human beings is governed by the foreknowledge of God. The individual makes meaningful choices between good and evil, so that individual fate is a matter of ongoing and continuous interaction between human will and God's will.

Qissah One of several Arabic terms meaning "narrative" or "story" (from the verb qassa, "to narrate, recount a story," found in the Quran). During medieval times, it referred mainly to short, dramatic, nonfictional narrative accounts. Today, the term refers primarily to narrative fiction, especially the short story (qissah qasirah).

Qist *See* Justice, Concepts of

Qiyamah *See* Resurrection

Qiyas In Islamic law, the deduction of legal prescriptions from the Quran or Sunnah by analogic reasoning. Qiyas provided classical Muslim jurists with a method of deducing laws on matters not explicitly covered by the Quran or Sunnah without relying on unsystematic opinion (ray or hawa). According to this method, the ruling of the Quran or Sunnah may be extended to a new problem provided that the precedent (asl) and the new problem (far) share the same operative or effective cause (illa). The illa is the specific set of circumstances that trigger a certain law into action. For example, the operative cause for the prohibition against alcohol is that it intoxicates the mind. Therefore, anything that intoxicates the mind, such as narcotics, is also prohibited by the use of analogy. Although various schools of thought in Islamic history have vigorously debated the legitimacy of the use of analogy, qiyas has played a central role in the development of Islamic law. The four main Sunni schools of law consider it one of the four main sources of law, the other sources being the Quran, Sunnah, and consensus (ijma). The Jafari Shii of school of law, however, counts aql (reason) as a separate source of law instead of qiyas. Other methods of deducing the law, such as mafhm al-nass (the clear implication of the text), tamthil (similarity or likeness), istihsan (juristic preference), or istislah (consideration of public interest), either explicitly rely on qiyas or use methods of analysis that are similar in their approach to qiyas.

Qom Leading center of Shii theological seminaries and site of Hazrat-i Masumah, which is the second most important Shii shrine in Iran. Burial site of numerous shahs of the Safavid and Qajar dynasties and many religious scholars. Major center of political activity in 1963, 1975, and 1977–79. The shrine and the Borujerdi mosque are important places for leading communal prayers and sermons. The shrine has been an economic and state institution, the focus of endowments and commercial rents dedicated to its upkeep, and a symbolic site whose opening and closing each day are accompanied by state-appointed guards extolling the sovereignty of the reigning government under God. Qom's madrasas in particular were a major center of resistance to the Pahlavi monarchy. When Ayatollah Khomeini returned to Iran from exile, he went immediately to Qom, which remains a key seat of the ulama's educational and political organizations.

Qubbah See Shrine; Tombs

Qubbat al-Sakhra Dome of the Rock. Muslim shrine erected circa 692 in the Haram al-Sharif, Jerusalem. Symbolically placed as an Islamic visual challenge to the nearby dome of the Holy Sepulcher, the domed structure was built by the Umayyad caliph Abd al-Malik on the site of the rock (sakhra) where, according to Muslim tradition, the Prophet Muhammad departed for his mystical journey (miraj) to heaven and hell. The annular plan, closely related to Roman and Byzantine antecedents, consists of two ambulatories around the central domed space. Complex vegetal decoration and Arabic inscriptions in mosaic decorate the interior.

Quds, al- See Jerusalem

Quduri, al- (d. 1037) Ahmad ibn Muhammad Abu al-Husayn al-Baghdadi al-Quduri. A leading Hanafi scholar of Baghdad from the classical period of Islamic law, best known for his *Mukhtasar*, a much-commented-on handbook of law that is still studied in Hanafi institutions of traditional Islamic learning.

Queen of Sheba See Bilqis

Qum See Qom

Qummi, al- See Ibn Babawayh Muhammad

Quran Commentary See Tafsir

Quraysh Powerful Meccan tribe at the time of the Prophet Muhammad; descendants of Qusayy, who united them. The Quraysh were prosperous merchants controlling Mecca and trade in the region. Muhammad was born into the Hashemite clan of the Quraysh tribe. Presently the keys to the Kaaba are held by the Quraysh clan. Surah 106 in the Quran is directed at them.

Qurayshi, al- See Muslim (Ibn al-Hajjaj)

Qurban See Hajj

Qusayy Ancestor of Muhammad. Spent time in Syria, then took possession of the sanctuary of Mecca, becoming ruler of the town.

Quran

The book of Islamic revelation; scripture. The term means "recitation." The Quran is believed to be the word of God transmitted through the Prophet Muhammad. The Quran proclaims God's existence and will and is the ultimate source of religious knowledge for Muslims. The Quran serves as both record and guide for the Muslim community, transcending time and space. Muslims have dedicated their best minds and talents to the exegesis and recitation of the Quran. Because the Quran is the criterion by which everything else is to be judged, all movements, whether of radical reform or of moderate change, whether originating at the center or at the periphery of the Islamic world, have grounded their programs in the Quran and used it as a support.

Revelation of the Quran to Muhammad began in 610 with the first five verses of surah 96. No further revelations followed for a period of up to two years, at which point Muhammad received reassurance that the revelation was from God, not the devil. Thereafter, revelation continued without interruption until his death in 632, at which time the Quran was considered complete. Partial collections of the Quran were made during Muhammad's lifetime by his wives, companions, and scribes. The final, authoritative version was completed and fixed under the direction of the third caliph, Uthman, within twenty years after Muhammad's death. The Quran consists of 114 surahs (chapters), varying in length from 3 to 286 ayat (verses). Surahs are arranged by length, with the latest and longest surahs at the beginning and the earliest and shortest surahs at the end. Very early commentators classified these chapters into Meccan surahs (received while Muhammad lived in Mecca) and Medinan surahs (received after the hijrah, when Muhammad and his followers moved to Medina).

The fundamental message of the Quran may be summarized in the term tawhid, the oneness of God. Both men and women are held to be rational and ethically responsible creatures whose duty is to submit to the divine truth expressed in revelation. This act separates islam, surrender and submission to the one God, from kufr, disbelief. Men and women who trust in God and live moral lives in thought, word, and deed become God's stewards, responsible for caring for the rest of God's creatures on earth. The society composed of such witnesses to the truth appears in history as the community created by Muhammad and his Companions in Medina in 622–32.

The revelation of the Quran as a book to be read emphasized the importance of literacy and the recording of scriptural text, leading to the development of the Islamic sciences. Hadith reports recording the words of Muhammad not contained in the Quran came to be regarded as authoritative for explication of the Quran. The sciences of the Arabic language, from lexicography to grammar and rhetoric, were developed in order to gain a precise and accurate understanding of the Quranic text. The need to understand the legislative content of the Quran gave rise to Islamic law and legal theory. Historiography originated with the aim of elaborating the Quranic view of religious history, according to which Adam was the first bearer of the divine message and Muhammad the last.

The Quran is considered to be the ultimate authority in all matters pertaining to religion. It furnishes the basic tenets of the faith, the principles of ethical behavior, and guidance for social, political, and economic activities. It is used in the five obligatory daily prayers and for special prayers during Ramadan, when it is recited in its entirety. It is a basic vehicle of education, since most Muslim children learn the Arabic alphabet in order to be able to read the Quran. The Quran is used to invoke God's blessing, and verses from it are often

(continued)

Quran (continued)

recited at the death of a loved one, at the beginning of public political and social meetings, at conferences, and sometimes at government or official functions. The Quran is the focus of rhythmic chanting and the art of calligraphy—the most highly developed artistic skills in Islamic culture.

Modern Quranic exegesis emphasizes the use of classical analytical tools such as ijtihad to reform both religious practice and society as a whole and to achieve social and intellectual development. Modern exegetes use the Quran to interpret and explain itself, rather than relying on external sources. Although the Quran is considered authentic only in Arabic, scholars in the twentieth century have produced translations of the Quran into local and regional vernaculars in order to make the text available to non-Arabic-speaking audiences. These translations also provide commentary, so as to clarify the meaning of the text. Important contemporary translations of the Quran include those by the Indian modernist Abdullah Yusuf Ali in English, the Pakistani reformer Sayyid Abu al-Ala Mawdudi in Urdu, and the Indonesian scholar, poet, and independence activist Hamka in Bahasa Indonesia.

Held the keys to the Kaaba and the well of Zamzam, and fed pilgrims. The Quraysh, the leading clan of Mecca during the time of Muhammad, claimed Qusayy as their founder. His descendants inherited his power.

Qushashi, Ahmad al- (d. 1660) Sufi mystic and scholar whose family originated from a village near Jerusalem, then settled in Medina. He spent his early life as a soldier, then turned to the study of religion. In Medina he studied under two renowned mystics of Indian origin, al-Shinnawi and Sibghat Allah, developing and transmitting the theosophical ideas of al-Jili. He was affiliated with a number of tariqahs, including the Naqshbandi and Shattari, of which he became khalifah. He attracted numerous students, some from Sumatra and Java, including Abd al-Rauf al-Sinkili, who was his student for twenty years. A distinctive feature of his writings is his mystical interpretations of hadith.

Qushayri, al- *See* Muslim (Ibn al-Hajjaj)

Qutb Axis, pivot, or pole. In Sufi thought, a human manifestation of divine consciousness, only one of which exists in any age, and around whom the spiritual life of the age revolves, that is, through whom spiritual knowledge is gained. It is the highest rank in the Sufi hierarchical structure of saints or walis, equivalent to the Shii understanding of the role of the imam. The shaykh of the Sufi order symbolizes qutb. The identity of the qutb is revealed to a few chosen mystics in every age due to the human need for direct knowledge of God in every age. Popularly has come to refer to any holy man. Associated with the notion of al-insan al-kamil (perfect person).

Qutb, Muhammad (b. 1915) Important intellectual of the Egyptian Islamic movement. Brother of Sayyid Qutb. Author of more than a dozen books, of which *Jahiliyyah of the Twentieth Century* and *Our Contemporary Reality* are the most important. Studied English literature and teaches Islamic studies at Umm al-Qura University in Mecca.

Qutb, Sayyid (d. 1966) Egyptian literary critic, novelist, and poet who became an important Islamist thinker and activist. Brother of Muhammad Qutb. Believed that Islam is a timeless body of ideas and practices forming a comprehensive way of life, rendering nonadherence to Islamic law inexcusable. Interpreted Islam as a call to social commitment and activism. Initially believed that violence against the government was justified only in cases where the government used violence, but later taught that Muslims who are actively engaged in a dynamic community of faith are mandated to apply God's laws as revealed, as well as to replace any leaders who fail to do so. Regarded leaders of whom he disapproved and societies they governed to be living in a state of jahiliyyah (ignorance), which he perceived to have pervaded contemporary life throughout the Islamic world. Called for resistance by turning away from existing society and creating a model community, which would eventually establish a truly Islamic state. Acknowledged the economic and scientific achievements of American society but was appalled by its racism, sexual permissiveness, and support for Zionism in view of the violation of Palestinian rights. Said to have been a key liaison between the Muslim Brotherhood and the Free Officers, who overthrew the monarchy in 1952. Tried and executed in 1966 for calling for armed overthrow of the Egyptian state. His writings advocating revolutionary change are influential among both Sunni and Shii Islamists.

R

Rabb Lord, master, owner. The term is found over nine hundred times in the Quran as a name for the deity. Usually translated "lord." Never used with the definite article unless it refers to God. Some modern translators render it "sustainer," reflecting its root meaning, "to bring something gradually to its perfection."

Rabbani, Burhanuddin Former president of Afghanistan. Head of Afghani Jamiat-i Islami (formerly part of the Afghani branch of the Muslim Brotherhood). A former professor of Islamic studies, he favored Hasan al-Banna's moderate populist approach seeking to effect change from the bottom up. Hoped to create a broadly based movement dedicated to fundamentalist goals and bringing together modern intellectuals with tribal and traditional elements.

Rabiah al-Adawiyah (d. 801) Female mystic of slave origin from Basra, often called the first Islamic saint. Introduced the doctrine of selfless love into Sufism. Demonstrated the importance of attitude and spiritual motivation for actions, rather than mere ritual correctness. Emphasized ascetic detachment, renunciation of the world, meditation, and love of God. Taught that people should worship God out of love, rather than the fear of hell or promise of paradise. Wrote passionate poems about the desire to be joined to God, permanently influencing the development and nature of Sufism. She symbolizes the importance of spiritual excellence over gender and serves as a historical example of female autonomy and freedom from male authority.

Rabitat al-Alam al-Islami *See* Muslim World League

Radd To send back or take back; to refute or respond. In Islamic law, it most often refers to taking back a repudiated wife. A new contract or dowry is not necessary as long as the radd takes place during the prescribed waiting period. Radd al-mahr is the return of a dowry by a woman in exchange for a divorce. The term also refers to a response to a complaint in a civil case, and to the act of returning products in a sales contract. *See also* Marriage and Divorce: Legal Foundations; Marriage and Divorce: Modern Practices

Radicalism Ideologies and actions not recognized as consistent with mainstream values. In Islam, the term often refers to the appeal to religion in order to legitimize violence, terrorism, and represssion. Distinguishing between radicalism and legitimate resistance is often difficult in contemporary circumstances. However, Islamic law regulates the use of violence, restricting it to self-defense and warfare initiated by a duly constituted government, with due warning, holding noncombatants immune, etc. *See also* Jihad; Terrorism

Radiyyah *See* Women and Islam

Rahain *See* Hostages

Rahim, al- The Merciful One. One of the ninety-nine names of God, reflecting the belief that God provides for human beings, guides them to the truth, furnishes them with a code of conduct, rewards them for their good deeds, and forgives their sins. Grammatically, the name signifies the permanence of divine mercy.

Rahmah Mercy. In the Quran, rahmah represents the all-encompassing divine concern for humanity, reflected, for example, in divine revelation (Muhammad is called "a [reflection of] mercy for the worlds") and the kindness that ought to characterize human conduct.

Rahman, al- The Compassionate One. One of the ninety-nine names of God, reflecting the belief that God sustains the universe, sends down revelation to guide human beings, and gives refuge against evil. Grammatically, the term signifies the superabundance of divine mercy.

Rahman, Fazlur (d. 1988) Pakistani philosopher, educator, and liberal reformer of Islam. Director of Pakistan's Central Institute of Islamic Research (1962–68). Educated at the University of Punjab and Oxford University, he taught Islamic studies at McGill University and the University of Chicago. Believed that those who try to maintain the status quo in religious tradition and interpret the Quran literally are as misguided as secularists who deny Islam's relevance to political and economic spheres. Believed in the necessity of going beyond a literal or traditional interpretation of the Quran to understand its spirit, requiring the study of the historical context in which each verse was revealed. Promoted the study of the specific circumstances of one's own time in order to apply principles derived from revelation. Devoted to educational reform and the revival of ijtihad (independent reasoning). Respected by Islamic reformers but criticized by conservatives as being overly liberal in his interpretation of the Quran, Sunnah, and classical Islamic law and his insistence on judging the weight of hadith reports in light of the overall spirit of the Quran.

Rahman Khalil, Mawlana Fazlur See Harakat ul-Ansar/Harakat ul-Mujahidin

Rahmani Tariqah Suborder of the Khalwati tariqah, founded in the Kabyle region of Algeria in the eighteenth century by Abu Abd Allah Muhammad ibn Abd al-Rahman al-Gishtuli al-Jurjuri. Al-Jurjuri was initially the focal point of a popular saint cult. Established in Algeria and Tunisia, the order came to be associated with the province and city of Constantine, a major center of religious learning and scholarship in Algeria. It was the most prominent Sufi order in Algeria by the twentieth century. It used the widespread suffering caused by the 1805 famine in Algeria to guide the population toward sociomoral reconstruction and to quell popular rebellions in the region. Used networks of zawiyahs (Sufi hospices) in Algeria and Tunisia to resist the French occupation in the nineteenth century. Responsible for preparing the way for a major popular rebellion against French rule in the 1870s—the only major rebellion in North Africa after the defeat of Abd al-Qadir, although it too failed. The local administrators and leaders of the Rahmani tariqah in eastern Algeria joined forces to oppose French rule. After French occupation, several zawiyahs served as centers for revolts either supported or led by Sufi notables. The Hejaz branch was founded by Muhammad ibn Muhammad ibn Masud ibn Abd al-Rahman al-Fasi in the nineteenth century.

Rai See Ray

Raids See Ghazw

Rais Head, leader, or president of a social or political organization; president of a state. One who has been bestowed with enormous material wealth and laurels. Colloquially understood as someone with hereditary endowment and family wealth. Feminine is *raissa*, meaning a woman of wealth, princess, or leader of the people.

Rajah Return. Associated with the Shii doctrine of the Hidden Imam, who is expected to return as a messianic imam, or Mahdi, who will rule the earth in justice and equity. In the twentieth century, Imam Musa al-Sadr has been associated with this role, having vanished during a trip to Libya in 1978.

Rajavi, Masud (b. 1947) Leader of Mujahidin-i Khalq in Iran. Opposed the Pahlavi regime. His organization grew into a major force after the Iranian revolution

(1979). During the 1980s the group countered the new regime's state terror with its own brand of revolutionary terror, including assassinations and bombings. Its leadership was forced into exile in Iraq. After 1986, sought to replace the Islamic republic with a democratic Islamic republic. By the summer of 1990, was powerful enough to constitute a significant threat to the existing government, but had declined in significance by the late 1990s. *See also* Mujahidin-i Khalq (Iran)

Rakah Act of prostration accompanying ritual prayers. Often used broadly to include words and actions surrounding prayer, particularly in Sufi orders. Prayers are begun with the supplicant facing Mecca. The supplicant kneels and then leans forward to touch the forehead to the ground during prayer or Quranic recitation, returning to knees upon conclusion. There are two to four prostrations, depending on time of day. *See also* Pillars of Islam; Salat

Ramadan Ninth month of the lunar calendar, during which fasting is required. *See also* Fasting

Ramla bint Abi Sufyan (d. 664) Better known as Umm Habiba. Meccan aristocrat and wife of the Prophet Muhammad. Emigrated to Abyssinia with her first husband, who died there. The Prophet proposed to her through the Negus, the ruler of Abyssinia, who paid her dowry (628).

Raniri, Nuruddin al- Seventeenth-century Indian scholar who traveled to the sultanate of Atjeh in Sumatra from 1637 to 1644. Translated Arabic and Persian texts into Malay. Proposed an orthodox interpretation of the Quran and Sunnah, opposing the adaptation of Islam to local custom. Defended orthodox mysticism. Works are still read today in Indonesian and Malaysian religious schools.

Rashid Rida, Muhammad (d. 1935) Syrian Islamic revivalist, reformer, and writer. Lived in Egypt from 1897 until his death. Close associate and disciple of Muhammad Abduh. Published the journal *Al-manar* to articulate and disseminate reformist ideas and preserve the unity of the Muslim nation. Concerned with the preservation of Muslim identity and culture. Viewed original Islamic sources—the Quran, Sunnah, and ijma (consensus) of Muhammad's companions—as the basis for reform. Believed that matters of worship (ibadat), intended to organize human behavior, were revealed in the Quran and authentic hadith, making them unchangeable. Human relations (muamalat), in the absence of an explicit, authentic, and binding text, can be reinterpreted according to the interest of the community (maslahah). Ijtihad (independent reasoning) is to be exercised to achieve the common good of the Muslim community. Believed the decline of the Muslim nation was due to the stagnation of scholars and tyranny of rulers. Viewed European dominance over Muslims as a result of Muslim weakness due to a lack of mastery over the sciences, an inability to form organized political institutions, and a lack of restrictions on the power of government. Considered education a precondition for political reform and independence. Urged Muslims to acquire the commendable aspects of Western civilization, such as science, technical skill, and wealth. Tried to combine modern education with religious teachings. Supported revival of the caliphate as essential to the unity and coherence of the Muslim community.

Rashidi, Muhammad ibn Salih al- *See* Salihi Tariqah

Rashidi Tariqah *See* Yusufi Tariqah

Rashidun *See* Rightly Guided Caliphs

Rashti, Sayyid Kazim (d. 1844) A student of Shaykh Ahmad Ahsai (d. 1826) and a leading figure in the Shii Shaykhi movement. Born and educated in Rasht, Iran, and developed an early interest in Sufism and Shii debates on gnosticism. Succeeded Ahsai as the head of his pupils in Karbala. The mainstream ulama soon labeled the Shaykhis as heterodox.

Rasul Messenger (of God). One of two Quranic terms to refer to Muhammad and other prophets. The other is *nabi*, usually translated as "prophet." Some scholars describe a rasul as a nabi who has delivered a written revelation (scripture), although the Quran appears to use the terms interchangeably. It describes a coherent chain of prophets and messengers (and scriptures associated with them) sent by God, including Adam, Noah, Abraham, David (the Psalms are considered his scripture), Solomon, Moses (who brought the Torah), Jesus (the Gospels are considered his scripture), and Muhammad (who brought the Quran). The Quran states (10:47) that a rasul has been sent to every spiritual community (ummah). All messengers call humanity to worship the one God and renounce evil. Muslims are asked to believe in all the messengers. The Islamic testimony of faith (shahadah) comprises witnessing the oneness of God and the fact that Muhammad is God's messenger. *See also* Nabi

Rawafid Those who refuse. Derogatory term historically applied by the Sunnis to describe the Shiis, who refused to accept the early caliphate of Abu Bakr, Umar, and Uthman as legitimate. The term had a connotation of militancy and struggle engaged in by the Shiis against the ruling power that oppressed them. In modern times, the term is still used in Sunni polemics against the Shiis, but also by some Shiis themselves in places such as Lebanon and Iraq as a source of pride, signifying revolt against all tyranny.

Rawdah, al- (1) Area in the Mosque of the Prophet in Medina, near the Prophet Muhammad's tomb, referred to in hadith literature as a paradisaical garden (rawdah). (2) Island and residential area on the Nile River, located between al-Fustat on the eastern bank and al-Gizah on the western side. Also known as Jazirat al-Miqiyas and Jazirat al-Hisn. During medieval times hosted a naval arsenal, fortresses, splendid buildings, and gardens. Al-Malik al-Salih Najm al-Din Ayyub built his famous fortress on the island (1240–49) to accommodate his Bahari Mamluks. Successive rulers removed materials from its palaces to erect buildings on other sites.

Rawdah Khaneh *See* Rawzah Khani

Rawzah Khani Narrative accounts of Imam Husayn's martyrdom; remembrance through recitations and chanting of the suffering and death of Husayn and other Shii martyrs at the Battle of Karbala on the tenth of Muharram (Ashura) in 680, while fighting against the forces of the Umayyad Yazid, whom the Shiis consider an illegitimate, oppressive usurper of the caliphate. Recitations are performed at various types of religious gatherings throughout the year, especially on the anniversaries of the death dates of the imams and other saintly figures such as Fatimah, the daughter of the Prophet Muhammad and wife of Ali, the first imam.

Ray Expedient and free reasoning in the field of Islamic law. Practiced as a means of exercising ijtihad in the early years of Islam but was soon replaced by emphasis on careful analogical or syllogistic reasoning (qiyas). *See also* Ijtihad; Qiyas

Rayhana bint Zayd ibn Amr (d. 632) Wife of the Prophet Muhammad. From the Jewish al-Nadir tribe. Captured with her husband's tribe, the Banu Qurayza, in 627. Thereafter the Prophet freed and married her. May also have retained the status of concubine. Died shortly before he did.

Razi, Abu Bakr Muhammad ibn Zakariyya al- (d. ca. 925) Persian scientist, physician, and Platonist philosopher, known in the West as Rhazes. Focused on expansion of empirical medical knowledge and practical procedures for treatment, rather than theoretical reflections on illness and health. Emphasized method, practice, observational diagnosis, and therapy. Criticized extant medical knowledge on the basis of empirical observation. Wrote two compendia of clinical medicine, *Al-kitab al-mansuri* and *Al-hawi*, discussing diseases, symptoms, treatments, and clinical observations, that were translated into Latin in the Middle Ages and were influential in the development of European medicine. Believed that reason was a competent means of discovering the truth and cultivating morals; thus revelation and prophethood were superfluous.

Razi, Fakhr al-Din al- (d. 1209) Iranian philosopher and Quranic exegete, learned in Shafii legal method and Ashari theology. Sought to demonstrate the compatibility of reason and revelation. His extensive Quran commentary, *Mafatih al-ghayb* (The keys of the unseen), is still often cited.

Recitation, Quranic *See* Tajwid

Refah Partisi *See* Welfare Party

Reform *See* Islah; Tanzim

Refugees The Islamic model for granting asylum to refugees is the unreserved welcome that the Medinans accorded Muhammad and his followers at the time of the hijrah. It is reflected in the Quranic verse "Whoever emigrates for the sake of God will find much refuge and abundance of the earth" (Quran 4:100). Over the centuries there have been large influxes of refugees within the Muslim world, including Jews escaping the Spanish Inquisition and the Holocaust.

Regional Islamic Dawah Council of Southeast Asia and the Pacific Nongovernmental, nonprofit organization formed in 1980 in response to the need to bring together area Muslims and coordinate their Islamic missionary activities. Headquarters are in Kuala Lumpur, Malaysia. Funded largely by Malaysia and Saudi Arabia. Seeks to forge links among various voluntary Islamic organizations in the spirit of brotherhood and to coordinate policies and actions for the benefit of Muslims in the region; responsibilities include supervising mission-

ary activities, training individuals for Islamic social work, providing experts to teach Islam, the establishment of mosques and Islamic centers, and publication and distribution of Islamic literature. Provides prayer leaders, religious teachers, and advisers to new converts. Established a women's movement in 1986 to encourage the participation of Muslim women in the development of society. Helps Muslim minorities emphasize the Islamic basis of life, facilitates their observance of Islamic rituals and customs, and creates a hospitable environment for them.

Relics Things associated with holy people, which serve as objects of veneration and of devotional practices. Some of these may be the physical remains of the holy person, such as hair, teeth, or clothing. According to folk belief, relics possess particular spiritual powers (barakah), and as such, they may be objects of visitation by devotees and pilgrims (ziyarah). The veneration of relics has often been condemned as idolatry by Muslim reformers.

Religious Education *See* Education; Educational Institutions

Religious Scholar *See* Akhund; Mullah; Ulama

Remembrance *See* Dhikr

Renaissance Party *See* Hizb al-Nahdah (Tunisia)

Reorganization *See* Tanzim

Repentance Arabic *tawbah*. A major theme of the Quran, mentioned over seventy times and with an entire surah (9) titled for it. Usually described as turning toward God, asking forgiveness, and being forgiven. Islam has no concept of original sin, need for atonement, or ecclesiastical confession. Repentance and forgiveness are a direct matter between the individual and God, requiring no intercession. In cases of sin against another person, restitution is required. In cases of sin against God, repentance, remorse, and resolution to change one's behavior are considered sufficient. Although classical scholars emphasized the individual dimension of repentance, many revivalists and reformists have tied individual actions to larger issues of public morality, ethics, and social reform, arguing for reimplementation of the Islamic penal code as public expiation for sins. Sufis understand repentance as a process of spiritual conversion toward constant awareness of God's presence. Muhammad reputedly requested God's forgiveness several times daily.

Republican Brothers Sudanese Islamic renewal movement formed in the 1960s. Led by Mahmud Muhammad Taha. Defined religion as a behavioral system of morals employed to attain peace, genuine freedom, and ever-growing, eternal happiness. Advocated federal democracy with economic socialism and equal political rights for all, regardless of gender or religion. Opposed implementation of traditional Islamic legal codes since they reflect fundamental political, economic, and social inequalities. Promoted use of ijtihad in reinterpreting and implementing Meccan, rather than Medinan, verses of the Quran. Had a small membership but was well known internationally. Dormant as an organization since Taha's execution in 1985.

Republican People's Party (Turkey) Cumhuriyet Halk Partisi. Major Turkish political party 1923–80. Formally terminated in 1982 by decision of the National Security Council. Obedient to Kemal Atatürk's charismatic authority and modernization program. Held dictatorial single-party rule 1923–46 and continued in power under the multiparty system until 1950, when it lost free general elections and became an opposition party. Led several coalition governments in the 1960s and 1970s. Ideology was Ottoman patriotism and Islamism, rather than Turkish nationalism. Sought to preserve the offices of caliphate and sultanate, secure the integrity of the Ottoman motherland, and safeguard national independence. Rallied people through religion.

Resurrection The bringing back to life of human beings for final judgment. Contrary to the belief of pre-Islamic Arabs that physical death is final, the Quran affirms that on the final day all persons will be resurrected and must account for how they have lived their lives. A series of dramatic events will signal the coming of the resurrection. Tradition says Muhammad will be the first to be brought back to life. While bodily resurrection has never seriously been contested by orthodox Islam, some modern commentators interpret the final reckoning to be more spiritual than physical.

Retribution *See* Qisas

Revivalist *See* Mujaddid

Revolution From a classical Muslim perspective, the term *revolution* (Arabic *thawrah*) has pejorative connotations, signifying impious attempts to overthrow an order established by believers who are following God's commands. The general rule was a reluctance to advocate resistance in all but the most reprehensible instances of misrule. Modern use of the term generally has a positive connotation when used by nationalists resisting the despotism of unjust secular rulers. In order to distinguish the two connotations, modern thinkers use the Arabic *inqilab* instead of *thawrah*. This term is used by revivalist movements to condemn what they perceive to be heretical deviations from Islam. Movements have been largely spurred by a deep antipathy to Western colonialism and imperialism. In the contemporary world, those seeking the overthrow of regimes they believe to be corrupt, such as Sayyid Qutb and Ayatollah Khomeini, emphasize revolutionary action as jihad, providing religious legitimation of the quest for justice and emphasizing Islam as din wa-dawlah (both religion and state).

Rhazes *See* Razi, Abu Bakr Muhammad ibn Zakariyya al-

Riba Interest or usurious interest. Quranic verses prohibit riba, a practice that doubled a debt if the borrower defaulted and redoubled it if the borrower defaulted again. Islamic legal scholars have historically inter-

Revival and Renewal

The Arabic terms *ihya* (revival) and *tajdid* (renewal) are typically used in the context of modern Islamic movements, although they have premodern roots. Premodern renewal was usually associated with a designated renewer (mujaddid) who, according to hadith, would come at the beginning of each century to renew Muslim faith and practice. The modern call for revival and renewal derives from perceptions of backwardness and stagnation in Muslim societies in the eighteenth and nineteenth centuries. Islamic thinkers encourage a renewed commitment to Islamic values and practice as the means to achieve development and progress.

The eighteenth-century revivalist trend is represented in India by Shah Wali Allah (d. 1762) and in the Arab world by the Wahhabis of Arabia. Rather than concerning themselves with competition with the West or adapting to modern life, they focused instead on the purity of religion and cleansing it of alien elements and bidah (innovations). Muhammad ibn Abd al-Wahhab (d. 1787) believed that Muslims in his time had strayed from the correct path of Muhammad's example. His proposed solution was to return to the simplicity of early Islam and the religious texts. He sought to revive Islam's role in society through an emphasis on tawhid (the unity and uniqueness of God). Sufi and popular religious manifestations, such as visitations of tombs and veneration of saints, were dismissed as un-Islamic and polytheistic. Other late-eighteenth- and nineteenth-century revivalist movements stressing that Islam alone should guide the lives of Muslims include the Sanusis of North Africa, the Mahdists in Sudan, and the Barelwis of India. The nineteenth- and twentieth-century reformist strand is represented by Islamic thinkers and activists such as Muhammad Abduh (d. 1905), Jamal al-Din al-Afghani (d. 1897), and Muhammad Iqbal (d. 1938). Recognizing that Muslim society was underdeveloped in comparison to Europe, they declared the necessity of a revival and rejuvenation of Islamic thought and practice in order to restore dignity and greatness to Muslims. They did not call for imitation of Western ways, however, instead stressing the compatibility of science and Islam, pointing to the contributions from Islamic civilization evident in European progress and modernity. By teaching that reason and faith are compatible, such reformers encouraged the rejection of taqlid, or imitation of traditional thought and practice, declaring it a major factor in the stagnation of the Muslim world. They advocated the continuous process of interpretation of texts through ijtihad, or independent reasoning in legal matters, in order to regain Islam's dynamism and ability to deal with changing circumstances. They taught that Islam was flexible and creative enough to adapt to modern times. Like the revivalists, they opposed practices considered superstitious (such as visiting saints' shrines), politically passive, or compromised by colonial governments.

In the twenty-first century, reform efforts have centered on questions of major political reform, the establishment of a new caliphate in order to unify Muslims throughout the world, the need to improve the status of women in Islamic societies, legal reforms guided by the principle of public interest, and educational reforms requiring the inclusion of modern science and technology in school curricula as the vehicle for the revitalization of the Muslim world. In many cases, advocates of Islamic revival and reform have found themselves in opposition to official government policies, sometimes resulting in government crackdowns against the movements. Revival and renewal are often understood in national terms, including elements of national independence and national resistance. The major names in the contemporary history of revival and renewal are

(continued)

Revival and Renewal (continued)

associated with struggle against foreign control and occupation.

The political popularity of movements and leaders calling for revival and renewal stems from public awareness of the depth of social, economic, and political problems that afflict the Muslim world. Political, social, and economic underdevelopment, the increased influence of the West, and the plight of people in disputed areas such as Palestine and Kashmir have increased the calls for revival and renewal.

---

preted this as prohibiting any loan contract that specifies a fixed return to the lender, since it provides unearned profit to the lender and imposes an unfair obligation on the borrower. In the modern world, most Muslim countries allow the charging of moderate interest, prohibiting only usurious or compound interest, although some reformers condemn all interest as an impediment to social justice. Prohibition of interest is considered by them as critical to Islamic economic reform.

Ribat Fort or stronghold. Initially founded by Muslims in non-Muslim areas, simultaneously fulfilling defensive and missionary purposes. Over time, their character changed and they became centers of Sufi teaching and devotion, usually combined with a hostel or hospice capacity. Sometimes they were supported by charitable endowments, enabling them to become permanent structures. During the nineteenth century, Sufi centers used the ribat structure to stockpile arms and hide dissidents during the struggle for independence, earning the distrust of colonial governments. The ribat is also a place where the ascetic withdraws to engage in internal spiritual jihad (struggle). *See also* Khanaqah

Rida, Ali al- (d. 818) Eighth imam in the reckoning of the Twelver Shiis. The Abbasid caliph al-Mamun (d. 833) designated him as his successor to the caliphate in 816,

provoking a revolt in Iraq. But al-Rida predeceased the caliph and was buried near Tus (now Mashhad), which, because of his tomb, has remained one of the most important shrine cities of the Shii world.

Rif Coastal mountain region in northern Morocco extending from the Straits of Gibraltar to the mouth of the Moulouya River. Site of the Rif Rebellion (1921–26), an important anticolonial movement led by Islamic reformer Muhammad ibn Abd el-Krim al-Khattabi (d. 1963) against Spanish and French protectorate forces. In 1921 Rifian forces inflicted as many as nineteen thousand casualties on Spanish forces in the greatest single defeat suffered by a European power in the colonial history of North Africa. The Rifian Republic (1923–26) emphasized modern self-determination and the application of Islamic law. The idea of a Rifian republic, while inspirational, has been seen as potentially divisive in modern-day Morocco.

Rifai Tariqah Sunni Sufi order that played an important role in the institutionalization of Sufism; until the fifteenth century it was the most prevalent order. Ahmad ibn Ali al-Rifai's (d. 1182) disciples are largely responsible for its promulgation outside southern Iraq. New orders branched out, the most important of which were the Badawi, Dasuqi, and Alwani. Although found elsewhere, the Rifai order is most significant in Turkey, southeastern Europe, Egypt, Palestine, Syria, and Iraq, with a nascent presence in the United States. In Turkey Kenan Rifai (d. 1950) was a Rifai shaykh whose circle included many highly cultured and educated Turks, including women and Christians; he taught a Sufism of universal love. In southeastern Europe the Rifai order has been recently active in Albania, Bulgaria, Greece, and Yugoslavia. Currently at least three Rifai branches are active in the United States: that of Shaykh Taner Vargonen, based in northern California; that of Mehmet Catalkaya (Serif Baba) in Chapel Hill, North Carolina, and New York City; and another also located in New York. The Rifai order exhibits a wide variety of practices and teachings that have not been adequately studied.

Rightly Guided Caliphs For Sunnis, the first four successors of Muhammad: Abu Bakr al-Siddiq, Umar ibn al-Khattab, Uthman ibn Affan, and Ali ibn Abi Talib. All were prominent Companions of Muhammad and belonged to the tribe of Quraysh. The period of their rule is considered a golden age, when the caliphs were consciously guided by Muhammad's practices. The period saw the establishment of Arab Muslim rule over the heartlands of the Middle East and preparation for conquests and expansion carried out under subsequent dynasties. Umar is portrayed as the dominant personality among the caliphs, establishing many of the fundamental institutions of the classical Islamic state. Uthman is generally held responsible for the canonization of the Quran as it is known today. He is described as personally pious but lacking the character needed to withstand unscrupulous relatives. Uthman's murder by malcontents opened a period of fitnah (disorder, civil war), which brought about the disintegration of the previously united community, the takeover of the caliphate by the Umayyad family, and the end of the era of Arabia-centered Islam. *See also* Abu Bakr al-Siddiq; Ali ibn Abi Talib; Umar ibn al-Khattab; Uthman ibn Affan

Risalah Message (oral or written); letter, epistle; essay, treatise, monograph. A literary/scholarly form of varying length and content found in a wide range of fields, including theology, grammar, law, and belles-lettres. Scholars often used the risalah form to publish their own opinions and ideas framed as responses to questions. Literary risalahs were often composed in highly stylized, rhyming, and rhythmic prose (saj), and at times in verse. *Rasail*, the plural of *risalah*, can refer to published collections of the correspondence of famous literary figures.

Rites of Passage The most important Islamic rites of passage are circumcision and marriage, signaling the end of childhood and initiation into the culturally and religiously defined roles of adulthood. Although not mentioned in the Quran, male circumcision is the most widely observed rite of passage throughout the Muslim world. Circumcision usually occurs between the ages of three and fifteen years, depending on regional custom, and may follow some achievement, such as a boy's first Quran recitation from memory. It is commonly held during the month of Muhammad's birthday and is accompanied by festive celebrations and Quranic recitations. Circumcision signals the boy's entrance into full participation in Islamic ritual world and into the gendered world of men. The wedding is the equivalent puberty rite for a girl, marking her movement from girl and daughter to woman and wife. After marriage, a girl may move to the home of her husband's family, her movements may be restricted, and she may receive greater respect and authority. Processions, special clothing, and feasts often accompany a wedding.

Ritual *See* Hajj; Salat

Riwayah Premodern meanings include "telling," "recounting," and "version," with reference both to literary works and historical events. While still used in these senses, *riwayah* is also currently the principal term used for the novel, a literary form that first emerged in Arabic during the nineteenth century and which has now achieved great popularity and literary sophistication.

Roger II of Sicily (r. 1130–54) Grandson of Tancred of the Crusades, and king of Sicily. Sponsored the translation of Arabic and Greek scientific and philosophical works into Latin, restoring classical knowledge to the Western world and its universities. Sponsored al-Idrisi, the most noted geographer of the Muslim world, as chief geographer and compiler of the contributions and ideas of Ptolemy, al-Khwarizmi, and al-Masudi.

Rosary Arabic *misbahah; tasbih; subhah*. String of thirty-three beads used by Muslims since the ninth century to count repetition of prayers and recite the names of God. Probably adapted from similar devices used by Eastern Christian monks since the third century.

Rubai In four. Also *rubaiya*. An intensely lyrical and subjective form of poetic writing. Close but not identical to the quatrain, the form varies considerably among Arabic, Persian, and Turkish traditions. It is most elaborate in Persian. Omar Khayyam's *Rubaiyyat* is the most famous collection.

Rubaiyyat *See* Rubai

Ruh Spirit, breath (of life). Used in the Quran twenty-one times, referring to the divine spirit in the sense of communication of life force. Often interpreted as an immaterial, immortal element of a living being, as well as the true self, or soul, apart from the body. Also a designation for Jesus and the angel Gabriel. Often used interchangeably with *nafs* (self), although Sufis distinguish between ruh as the higher principle of soul and nafs as the "lower" or "animal" self.

Ruhaniyyat Spiritual beings. The term was used by Muslim philosophers and mystics to designate the angels who rule the heavenly spheres of ancient cosmology and mediate between the spiritual world and humanity; even referred to the communication of supernatural powers on occasion. The singular, *ruhaniyya*, is used in the modern sense of "spirituality."

Rukhsah An exception to a general law, granted to preserve life or remove hardship, such as the allowance for a pregnant woman to refrain from fasting during Ramadan. In Sufism rukhsah is contrasted with azimah (determination). It is considered to be an inferior state, since one who follows rukhsah practices what is allowable for the weak, while the strong choose the path of self-denial. Certain Sufi orders emphasize their commitment to azimah. However, it is not considered appropriate to criticize those who opt for rukhsah, which, some religious scholars assert, is equally valid in the eyes of God.

Rumi, Jalal al-Din al- (d. 1273) Born in Balkh (in modern Afghanistan) but lived in Qonya, Anatolia (Turkey). Initially followed existing Sufi paths, but became a visionary ecstatic in 1244 after being inspired on a new path of aesthetic and emotional mysticism, which developed into the Mawlawi (Mevlevi) order after his death. Created an aristocratic organizational structure, with hereditary succession and wealthy corporate status. Taught that the Master of the Way was to serve as a medium between God and humanity. Played an important role in Turkish culture and the reconciliation of some Christians to Islam. Sought identification of the human self with divine Being. Famous for humanism, devotion to music, and dhikr exercises incorporating dance where dervishes imitate the order of the universe by spinning in circles around the shaykh like planets revolving around the sun; this gave rise to the European expression "whirling dervishes." Wrote more than seventy thousand verses of Persian poetry in ordinary language, expressing the experience of God's presence in creation and inspiring joy in the listener; common themes are the trials of separation from the Beloved and the joys of union with Him. Most famous poem is *Mathnawi*, a compilation of spiritual outbursts, anecdotal ruminations, and parables expressed in poetic form. Followers believe it to reveal the inner meaning of the Quran.

Ruqayyah bint Husayn Daughter of Husayn ibn Ali and granddaughter of Muhammad. The shrine over her tomb in Damascus is an important pilgrimage site for both Shiis and Sunnis.

Rushdie Affair Incident arising from the publication of a novel entitled *The Satanic Verses*, by British author Salman Rushdie, in 1988. Many Muslim authorities decried the novel as blasphemous. Its sale and distribution were forbidden in India, Pakistan, South Africa, and Iran. Reactions became dramatic in early 1989 when Muslims in England burned copies of it and protest demonstrations in Pakistan ended in killings and injuries. On 14 February 1989 Ayatollah Khomeini issued a fatwa placing a death sentence on the author and publishers for blasphemy against Islam, calling on Muslims everywhere to execute those associated with the novel. The sentence has never been carried out. The fatwa was revoked under the Khatami regime in the late 1990s.

Russia, Islam in Eight to 12 percent of Russians are Muslim, comprising over twenty ethnic groups. The largest groups are the Turkic Tatars, Bashkirs, and Kazakhs, and the Caucasian Chechens, Avars, and Kabardinians. Despite frequently hostile relations with the rulers of the Russian Empire, Soviet Union, and Russian Federation, Islam has survived and expanded in Russia. Although *glasnost* and the fall of the USSR facilitated the expansion of Islamic organizations in Russia, the Gorbachev and Yeltsin administrations contained no Muslims. The 1993 constitution stipulates that Russia is a secular state, but the 1997 Religion Law places Islam in a second-tier classification, below Russian Orthodoxy. The several independent, countrywide Islamic political organizations established since 1989 work to defend Muslim culture in Russia rather than to establish an Islamic state.

Ruzbihan Baqli (d. 1209) Persian Sufi, born in Pasa and buried in Shiraz. Best known for his ecstatic and visionary life and his writings on Sufi expression of ecstasy (shath). His works in Arabic and Persian cover Quranic commentary, poetry, theology, jurisprudence, and grammar. Among his Sufi writings, the most important are *Kashf al-asrar* (The unveiling of secrets), *Abhar al-ashiqin* (Jasmine of the lovers), and *Sarh al-shathiyyat* (Commentary on ecstatic sayings).

S

Sabbah, Hasan-i Eleventh-century founder of a branch of Ismaili Shiis known as Nizaris or Assassins. Initially worked as an Ismaili missionary. Established base of command in the mountain fortress of Alamut in 1090. Became the de facto leader of the new order, although he did not assume the title of imam. The group engaged in assassination of political and cultural leaders to advance the Ismaili revolution.

Sabil Way, road, path. Used in the Quran over 150 times in reference to correct belief and behavior—the right way, the way of God, the path upon which one struggles for the sake of God. May consist of spiritual discipline, altruistic works, scholarship, or warfare. Jihad is often described as a struggle on sabil Allah (the path of God).

Sabr Steadfastness, perseverance, endurance, patience. The Quran calls for steadfastness in fulfilling religious obligations and patience in sorrow, defeat, or suffering. In Sufism, patience in accepting God's will is a cardinal virtue.

Sacrifice The most common sacrificial ritual is the compulsory slaughter of an animal as part of the obligatory pilgrimage (hajj) and the optional slaughter of an animal by non-pilgrims on the occasion of Id al-Adha (Feast of the Sacrifice), which commemorates Abraham's sacrifice. More recently the ritual has been interpreted as fulfilling the needs of social welfare and charity: the meat of sacrifices during the hajj is distributed to disadvantaged Muslim communities. Aqiqah is the optional traditional sacrifice of animals on the occasion of a birth. Animal sacrifice may also be made in fulfillment of a vow or as expiation of a sin during the pilgrimage.

Sad ibn Abi Waqqas (d. ca. 671) Early convert to Islam and one of the ten eminent

Companions of the Prophet Muhammad to whom he is believed to have promised paradise. Considered among the six people appointed by the second caliph, Umar, to elect his successor (644). Known for fighting in all of the Prophet's battles and for being appointed by Umar as commander of the army that defeated the Persian Sasanid empire circa 636. Although a well-respected pious leader of early Islam, he did not contend for the caliphate. Seeing no way for humans to judge the faith of others, he remained neutral during the strife between the fourth caliph, Ali, and Muawiyah.

Sadaqah Charity, alms, freely made offering. Sometimes used synonymously with *zakah*, which refers to the alms required of all Muslims of means. Can also be a supererogatory charity, expiation for offenses (e.g., Quran 2:271; 9:104), or a way of making up for not having performed certain rituals (e.g., cutting the hair or shaving the head after pilgrimage).

Sadi, Musharrif al-Din Muslih (d. ca. 1291) Persian mystic poet. Lived and wrote in Shiraz. A member of the Suhrawardi tariqah, he is best known for spiritual and moral teachings. He traveled throughout the Islamic world as a Sufi dervish. His two major works, *Bustan* (The orchard) and *Ghulistan* (The [flower] garden), are characterized by garden and floral imagery in the context of scriptural admonitions to live a moral life. Known as a master of the Persian language.

Sadiq, Jafar ibn Muhammad al- (d. 765) Sixth Shii imam. The dispute over which son was to succeed him led to the split between the Twelver (Ithna Ashari) Shiis and the Sevener (Ismaili) Shiis. He founded the Jafari school of Islamic law, the most important in Shiism. Taught that the true caliph and ruler of the Muslim community had to be a descendant of Ali, designated by his predecessor to inherit secret knowledge and the exclusive authority to interpret the Quran and hadith, and to elaborate the legal system. He shifted the emphasis of Shiism from political issues to religious teachings and highlighted the sacred origins of craft corporations. Patron saint of the Bektashi Sufi order.

Sadiqi College Tunisian college founded in 1875 by Khayr al-Din al-Tunisi. Original purpose was to train a new corps of government officials in both Islamic and modern scientific topics. Broke the control of ulama over secondary education, thus limiting their actual, although unofficial, power in government and society. Became the model for French-Arab schools during the French colonial period. Reorganized in 1911 as a diploma-granting institution and again in 1930 to follow the format of French lycées. Along with students from Zaytunah Mosque, its graduates became the heart of the Tunisian nationalist movement.

Sadr Originally an Arabic honorific; has been used since the tenth century to denote a prominent member of the ulama. The title became hereditary in some Twelver Shii families and is often used as a surname. As an official religious or political title, it occurs with significant variation according to place and period.

Sadr, Muhammad Baqir al- (d. 1980) Iraqi Shii intellectual and political leader. Authored books on philosophy, Quranic interpretation, logic, education, constitutional law, and economics, as well as more traditional works on jurisprudence, compilations of devotional rites, commentaries on prayers, and a history of early Sunni-Shii controversies. His work on economics, *Iqtisaduna* (Our economics), remains among the most scholarly twentieth-century studies of Islamic economics as an alternative ideological system to capitalism and Communism. His philosophical treatise, *Falsafatuna* (Our philosophy), is a notable exercise in philo-

sophical exegesis. Sadr's works on the Islamic state influenced the development of the Iranian constitution (1979); he grafted an Islamic component derived from a combination of Shii scholarship and Platonic philosophy onto the traditional separation between the executive, legislative, and judicial powers. Sadr's influence among Iraq's Shiis combined with the threat that Iran's revolution posed to Iraq led to his arrest and execution in 1980. *See also* Hizb al-Dawah al-Islamiyyah

Sadr, Musa al- (d. 1978?) Iranian cleric and leader of the Shii movement Harakat al-Mahrumin in Lebanon. Educated in Qom, Iran. Moved to Lebanon in 1959, where he took on the role of charismatic mullah. Asserted the need for social and political activism rather than quiet scholarship and prayer. Used the central myths of Shiism, particularly the martyrdom of Husayn, to spur his followers to action, transforming the Lebanese Shiis from a passive persecuted minority to a politically active and assertive social force seeking to confront tyranny and injustice, particularly poor schools, nonexistent public services, and government neglect. Linked the peasant majority with the upperclass minority in the formation of Harakat al-Mahrumin as the largest and most effective Shii political organization in Lebanon. Supported ecumenism, particularly with the Maronite Christians of Lebanon. His mysterious disappearance in 1978 during a visit to Libya led to his symbolic association with the Shii Hidden Imam. *See also* Harakat al-Mahrumin

Sadr al-Din al-Shirazi *See* Shirazi, Sadr al-Din al-

Sadr-i Azam Grand vizier; title given to the chief minister in Safavid and Qajar Iran and in Ottoman Turkey. As chief of the "Outer Service" in the Ottoman court structure, the sadr-i azam had overall responsible for all aspects of the Ottoman system beyond the palace. He chaired the imperial council (diwan), which consisted of other officials holding the rank of vizier and the title pasha.

Saduq, al- *See* Ibn Babawayh Muhammad

Saeed, Hafiz Muhammad *See* Lashkar-i Taiba

Safavid Dynasty Ruling dynasty of Persia (Iran) from 1501 to 1722. Descendants of Shaykh Safi al-Din (d. 1334) of Ardibil, head of the Safawi tariqah. Founded by Ismail I. Early on, fostered heterodox popular religious belief; later, Shii assumptions became the main distinguishing element of Persian religious life, in comparison to Sunni Ottomans, Uzbeks, and Mughals. A literary and philosophical renaissance occurred under the influence of Shiism.

Saffah, Abu al-Abbas al- (d. 754) First Abbasid caliph (r. 750–54). Many factions participated in the Abbasid revolt against the Umayyads. Although al-Saffah's personal role in establishing the early Abbasid caliphate is ambiguous, his reign is known for its brutal suppression of opponents and its declaration of the descendants of Prophet Muhammad's uncle, Abbas, as the ruling faction of the revolution.

Safi, Ghulam Mohammad *See* Hizbul Mujahidin

Sahaba *See* Companions

Sahih See Sahih al-Bukhari; Sahih Muslim

Sahih al-Bukhari One of six canonical collections of hadith. With Sahih Muslim, considered the most authoritative among Sunni Muslims. Compiled and codified in the ninth century by Muhammad ibn Ismail al-Bukhari. Contains approximately 7,275 traditions in nine books, arranged thematically, recounting Muhammad's statements on issues related to faith, belief, prayer, purification, alms, fasting, pilgrimage, monotheism, commerce, inheritance, crimes, judicial procedures, murders, wills, vows, oaths, war, wine, and hunting. Al-Bukhari was noted for careful testing of genuineness of hadith and tracing genealogies, giving rise to the methodology of ilm al-rijal ("study of men," i.e., study of authorities in hadith

transmission) and definitive shape to the body of hadith. *See also* Bukhari, Muhammad ibn Ismail ibn Ibrahim ibn al-Mughirah al-

Sahih Muslim One of six canonical collections of hadith. With Sahih al-Bukhari, considered particularly authoritative among Sunni Muslims. Compiled and codified in the ninth century by Muslim (Ibn al-Hajjaj). Consists of forty-two books arranged by topic, covering faith, purification, prayer, almsgiving, personal hygiene, fasting, pilgrimage, marriage and divorce, business transactions, inheritance, gifts, bequests, oaths, punishments, judicial decisions, jihad, travel, government, sacrifices, food and drink, clothing, adab, greetings, qualities of Muhammad and his Companions, destiny, dhikr, repentance, knowledge, hell, paradise, Judgment Day, piety, and tafsir. Divides hadith into three categories according to the knowledge and character of the transmitter and the degree to which the hadith is free from contradictions, falsehoods, or misrepresentations. *See also* Muslim (Ibn al-Hajjaj)

Sahnun (d. 855) Abu Said Abd al-Salam ibn Said ibn Habib al-Tanukhi. A Maliki scholar and teacher from Kairouan (Qayrawan), he compiled *Al-mudawwanah*, on the authority of Ibn al-Qasim, among the most comprehensive and authoritative sources of Maliki law. The most illustrious and influential Maliki of his age, he played a major role in spreading Malikism in North Africa and Spain. Elevated to the post of qadi (judge) later in life, he was a champion of Sunni orthodoxy, particularly against the Mutazilis.

Sahu Sobriety. Stage of mystical or spiritual development characterized by careful observance of shariah, manifestation of wisdom, and clarity of spiritual vision. Contrasted with *sukr*, spiritual "intoxication." In negative terms, refers to closure to spiritual influences.

Said, Hakim Mohammed (d. 1998) Prominent philanthropist and dignitary of Pakistan, tabib (physician) in the traditional Greco-Arabic (Yunani) medical system, and vice president of the Islamic Organization for Medical Sciences. He was president of Hamdard Foundation Pakistan, a large business enterprise manufacturing herbal medicines and other natural products in innovative modern ways and running a chain of clinics. Founded Madinat al-Hikmah (City of Wisdom), which was conceived as providing a comprehensive educational network from primary school through university, with a high-level research institution and a grand library. Held a number of high government positions, including the governership of Pakistan's Sindh province. Murdered in Karachi.

Said Halim Pasha, Mehmed (d. 1921) Ottoman grand vizier and Islamic reformer. Leader of the Islamist faction of the Committee of Union and Progress (CUP) and spokesman for the conservative Islamist faction of Young Turks. His appointment as grand vizier was intended to appease Arab/Islamic sentiment in the Ottoman Empire. He argued that Islam was a rational religion encouraging scientific thought. He believed it was damaging to blindly borrow Western ideas such as constitutionalism, since the problems of Western society differ from those of Islamic society and the Islamic world should look for answers in the context of its own traditions and heritage, especially shariah. Assassinated by an Armenian nationalist.

Sainthood *See* Walayah

Saj Usually translated as "rhyming prose," a style that involves not only rhyme but also rhythm and cadence. Makes full use of the musical and morphological potential of the Arabic language. First encountered in the magical utterances of soothsayers in the pre-Islamic period. The majority of the Quranic text utilizes the conventions of saj, but the style finds its most widespread literary exposition in the later emergence (tenth century) of the maqamah genre. *See also* Maqamah

Sajah *See* Musaylima ibn Habib

Sajjadah Derived from a root meaning "to prostrate." Refers to the rug used for the five daily prayers. Typically measures 1 by 1.5 meters. Modern rugs often include a compass pointing to Mecca, the direction supplicant is to face while praying. In Sufi orders, the shaykh inherits the prayer rug of the order's founder as a symbol of authority.

Sakinah The presence or peace of God. As mentioned in the Quran (48:4) and elsewhere, it was sent by God into the hearts of believers and upon His messenger, Muhammad, as support and reassurance. Associated with piety and moments of divine inspiration, sakinah in Islamic mysticism signifies an interior spiritual illumination.

Sala Allah Alayhi wa-Salaam Peace and blessings be upon him (abbreviated PBUH). Epithet used by pious Muslims in speech and writing as a sign of respect and honor after the name of a prophet or holy person, especially Muhammad.

Salaam The root of the term connotes safety, but the word generally means "peace." One of the divine names of God. The most common Quranic usage is as a salutation: "al-salaam(u) alaykum(u)" (peace be upon you). Also appears in Quran as "salvation," both in this world and the next. Although from an early period the salaam greeting was considered an Islamic institution, it was a greeting before Islam, corresponding to the Hebrew greeting *shalom*. In prayer, salaam is conferred upon the prophet prior to the confession of faith (al-salaamu alayka, ayyuha al-nabiyyu).

Salaam(u) Alaykum(u), al- Peace be upon you. Used by Muslims as a greeting. Response is "wa-alaykum al-salaam" (peace be upon you also). Hadith portray use of the greeting as a good work.

Saladin *See* Salah al-Din

Salaf Predecessors or ancestors. Usually used in the sense of "pious ancestors," especially the first three generations of the Muslim community, who are considered to have lived the normative experience of Islam. Often referred to in works by Hanbali jurists, particularly Ibn Taymiyyah and Muhammad ibn Abd al-Wahhab. Wahhabis called for implementation of the social organization of salaf as a means of restoring Islamic ethics and piety to original purity. The same principles are followed by the twentieth-century Salafi movement, leading many to characterize it as traditionalist. The writings of Muhammad ibn Abd al-Wahhab suggest a return to the values of the salaf, rather than literal implementation of their practices, as the purpose of reform. See also Salafi

Salafi Name (derived from salaf, "pious ancestors") given to a reform movement led by Jamal al-Din al-Afghani and Muhammad Abduh at the turn of the twentieth century. Emphasized restoration of Islamic doctrines to pure form, adherence to the Quran and Sunnah, rejection of the authority of later interpretations, and maintenance of the unity of ummah. Prime objectives were to rid the Muslim ummah of the centuries-long mentality of taqlid (unquestioning imitation of precedent) and stagnation and to reform the moral, cultural, and political conditions of Muslims. Essentially intellectual and modernist in nature. Worked to assert the validity of Islam in modern times, prove its compatibility with reason and science, and legitimize the acquisition of Western scientific and technological achievements. Sought reforms of Islamic law, education, and Arabic language. Viewed political reform as an essential requirement for revitalization of the Muslim community. Its influence spread to Algeria, Morocco, Tunisia, Syria, India, Indonesia, and Egypt in particular. The most influential movements inspired by Salafi were the Muslim Brotherhood of Egypt and Jamaat-i Islami of Pakistan. In the late twentieth century, the term came to refer to traditionalist reformers.

Salah See Salat

Salah al-Din (d. 1193) Also known as Saladin. Commander of Muslim forces during the third phase of the Crusades. Legends of his military and diplomatic successes circulated widely in Europe. He brought an end to the Fatimid caliphate in 1171 when he established the Ayyubid dynasty. Salah al-Din unified Egypt, Syria, and Mesopotamia into a single state, enabling him to defeat the Christian Crusaders at the Battle of Hattin in 1187 and end Latin occupation of Jerusalem. At the siege of Acre in 1192 he made a truce with Richard the Lionhearted that allowed crusading principalities to maintain a foothold on the coasts of Palestine and Syria. He is known for his humane treatment of the Christian population of Jerusalem, which is typically contrasted to the way Christian Crusaders had dealt with Muslims and Jews upon their arrival in Jerusalem. He restored the Muslim holy sites of the Dome of the Rock and the al-Aqsa mosque to Muslim use and raised Muslim appreciation of Jerusalem as the third holiest city of Islam. Regarded Shiis as potentially more subversive enemies than Christians.

Salat Prayer, worship (Persian namaz). The second pillar of Islam is the prayers required of Muslims five times daily: daybreak (salat al-fajr), noon (salat al-duhr), midafternoon (salat al-asr), sunset (salat al-maghreb), and evening (salat al-isha). The times of prayer are determined by the sun's position and are announced in a human voice by the muezzin (prayer announcer) from the minaret (tower) of a mosque. Can be performed in any clean space, either individually or communally (preferable), although Friday noon prayer (jumah) should be performed communally in the mosque by men. Must be preceded by ritual purification (wudu) and declaration of proper intention (niyyah). Consists of recitations from the Quran and formulas in praise of God (takbir); must be done facing the direction of the Kaaba in Mecca (qiblah). Each prayer has two to four cycles (rakah), each containing a series of postures, most characteristic of which is prostration. See also Dua; Pillars of Islam

Salat al-Asr Midafternoon prayer. Third of five mandatory daily prayers (salat), containing four cycles (rakah). Performed when the sun reaches the point in the sky when the shadow of an object is as long as its height. The Jafari (Shii) school allows for combining this prayer with the noon prayer (salat al-duhr). See also Pillars of Islam; Salat

Salat al-Duhr Noon prayer. Second of five mandatory daily prayers (salat), containing four cycles (rakah). Performed immediately after the sun reaches its zenith. Given the restrictions of modern business hours, it is increasingly being performed in the work-place during lunch breaks. On Fridays it is part of the communal prayers (jumah). See also Pillars of Islam; Salat

Salat al-Fajr Dawn prayer. First of five mandatory daily prayers (salat), containing two cycles (rakah). The time for this salat begins at "true dawn" (preferable) and ends at sunrise. The call to prayer (adhan) for salat al-fajr, a distinctive and frequently noted feature of Muslim societies, adds the line "Prayer is better for you than sleep!" See also Pillars of Islam; Salat

Salat al-Hajah Prayer of need, addressed to God through intermediaries. Legal sources describe the source of the prayer as a blind man who approached the Prophet Muhammad, asking to have his sight restored. The Prophet instructed him to call on God and ask for Muhammad's intercession as the Prophet of Mercy. Intercession is a controversial topic in reformist Islam. See also Pillars of Islam; Salat

Salat al-Isha Night prayer. Fifth of the five mandatory daily prayers (salat), containing four cycles (rakah). Performed after the salat al-maghreb. Some schools of law maintain that it must be done no later than midnight; others allow until dawn. The Jafari (Shii) school allows for combining this prayer with the salat al-maghreb. See also Pillars of Islam; Salat

Salat al-Jumah Friday congregational prayer required of all Sunni men but not generally of women. For Shiis, it is required of every

man only when an imam is present. If no imam is present, it is required only of the community in general. Salat al-jumah is held in the mosque and performed in straight lines, with men in front and women and children either behind or in a separate area. The khutbah (sermon) is a feature particular to the Friday service.

Salat al-Khawf "Fear" prayer, performed in times of danger, usually warfare. Based on the Prophet Muhammad's example during military battles. See also Salat

Salat al-Maghreb Sunset prayer. Fourth of five mandatory daily prayers (salat), containing three cycles (rakah). To ensure that it is not misunderstood as being addressed to the setting sun, it is performed after sunset. There is some debate among different schools of law as to how long after sunset one can or should wait to begin the prayer. See also Pillars of Islam; Salat

Salat al-Tarawih Recommended (but not obligatory) prayers performed in the month of fasting, Ramadan. Usually twenty or more cycles (rakah), done preferably in a group setting. Done anytime after the night prayer (salat al-isha) and before dawn. Performing these prayers is often taken as an indication of piety. See also Salat

Salihi Tariqah Branch of the revivalist/reformist Sanusi tariqah that broke off from the main order 1887. Founded by Muhammad ibn Salih al-Rashidi in Mecca. Became influential in Somalia through agricultural settlements for runaway slaves and detribalized people. Declared a holy war against British imperialism in the early twentieth century. Originator of the nineteenth-century movement of Muhammad ibn Abdallah al-Hasan, the "Mad Mullah." Promoted personal piety and advocated the foundation of a society based on a comprehensive application of Islamic principles. Clashed with the Uwaysi tariqah due to the Salihis' political militance, opposition to visitation of saints' tombs, and declaration that deceased saints could not serve as mediators between people and God. *See also* Ibn Idris, Ahmad

Salman the Persian Iranian Companion of the Prophet Muhammad and popular figure of Muslim legend. Became mawla of the Prophet in Medina. Credited with the idea of digging a ditch that led to Muslim victory over the Meccans in the Battle of the Ditch. Renowned in Shii tradition and a major personage in the Shuubi movement.

Salvation *See* Inqadh

Sama Spiritual concert; a public recital of poetry, typically accompanied by music, as part of a Sufi dhikr ritual. Liturgical means of inducing ecstasy. Often held on the same day of each month. In early Sufi orders, sama involved three physical actions—dancing, whirling, and jumping—by participants, giving rise to the phrase "whirling dervish." After the eleventh century, some tariqahs added a teaching session for interpretation of texts as a critical component of the ritual preceding the poetry recitation and singing. Use of music is often attacked by orthodox and legalistic interpreters as an irreligious innovation, constituting a major source of criticism of Sufism. *See also* Mawlawi Tariqah

Samarra Ancient town on the east bank of the Tigris River in Iraq. Was the capital of the Abbasid empire between 836 and 892. Had a golden age under the reign of the caliph al-Mutawakkil (r. 847–61). Famous for its architectural and artistic remains, including the extant spiral minaret of the Great Mosque.

Sammani, Muhammad ibn Abd al-Karim al- (d. 1775) Celebrated Egyptian Sufi. Was a pupil of Mustafa ibn Kamal al-Din al-Bakri (d. 1749), a Syrian who was a member of the Khalwati tariqah. After his master's death he developed a sub-branch of the order that became known by his name, the Sammani tariqah. Al-Sammani spent the latter part of his life in Mecca. There he became a teacher of the South Sumatran Sufi Abd al-Samad al-Palimbani (d. ca. 1788). He inducted him

into his tariqah, which through Abd al-Samad's pupils became popular in South Sumatra and other areas of Indonesia. It is distinguished by its dhikr, a recitation of Quranic verses followed by the recitation of divine names and concluding with prayers.

Sammani Tariqah Activist, reformist branch of the revivalist Khalwati tariqah. Founded by Muhammad ibn Abd al-Karim al-Sammani in the eighteenth century. Committed to formal Islamic law. Opposed to the traditional veneration of saints. Provided an organizational framework and inspiration for more militant revivalist movements. Spread into Sumatra, Indonesia, Egypt, and Sudan in the eighteenth century and became a major order in the Malay peninsula and throughout Africa in the nineteenth century. In Southeast Asia, writings by shaykhs of this order provided inspiration for nineteenth- and twentieth-century jihads against the Dutch colonial occupiers. Famous adherents include Muhammad Ahmad ibn Abd Allah (the Sudanese Mahdi), who used the tariqah's teachings to denounce the corruption of faith in Sudan and to declare himself the expected Mahdi (messiah). In Sudan, a widespread network among the local population permitted it to become the basis for local organization and opposition to Egyptian rule, along with the Khatmi and Majdhubi orders.

Sanad *See* Isnad

Sangalaji, Mirza Riza Quli Shariat (d. 1944) Reformist Iranian theologian. Chief representative of a radical notion of modernity who tried to advance ideas such as discarding the institution of taqlid (emulation of the exemplary conduct of religious authorities). Proposed a return to absolute monotheism, the rejection of the Shii cult of saints, and stress on rationalism to rescue the Shii faith from medieval absolutism while equipping it for confrontation with the perceived evils of the West. Rejected the Shii belief in the return of the Twelfth Imam to earth prior to resurrection in order to avenge Muhammad's descendants of all prejudices and violence inflicted on them throughout the ages. Most of his stances were rejected by his colleagues.

Sanhuri, Abd al-Razzaq al- (d. 1971) Egyptian jurist and legal scholar. French- and Egyptian-educated, al-Sanhuri proposed modernizing Islamic law based on the historical, social, and legal experience of the respective countries. He was involved in the construction of the civil codes of Iraq and Egypt. Legacy also lies in his extensive works on Islamic law.

Santri Indonesian term for a student of Islam. Characteristics of a santri include being a devout and correct Muslim, dedication to the five pillars of Islam, rigid adherence to rituals such as prayer and fasting, and little concern for animistic and mystical beliefs. Lifestyle of travel and trade adopted by the Muhammadiyyah movement in Java, founded in 1912.

Sanusi, Muhammad ibn Ali al- (d. 1859) Algerian disciple of Ahmad ibn Idris and founder of the Sanusi Sufi tariqah. A reformist and revivalist who, after study in Fez and Mecca, advocated return to the Quran, Sunnah, and the practice of ijtihad. Rejected legal principles of ijma, qiyas, and taqlid. Promoted contemplation of Muhammad and a devotional, quietist mode of dhikr and meditation. Rejected inclusion of music and dancing in Sufi practice but permitted popular practices honoring saints. Tried to establish a theocratic state by peaceful means in Libya. Encouraged missionary activities, particularly in West and Central Africa. Developed the zawiyah (Sufi lodge) into a center for agriculture, education, and worship. Author of a work detailing the rituals, dhikrs, and organization of numerous Sufi orders. *See also* Sanusi Tariqah

Sanusi, Muhammad Idris ibn al-Mahdi al- (r. 1951–69) First king of independent Libya and grandson of Muhammad ibn Ali al-Sanusi. His legitimacy as king was based on his leadership of the Sanusi Sufi order and unification of the struggle against Italian imperialism (1911–51). He developed the Sanusi order into the politically activist, ideologically conservative core of Libyan nationalism. As king, he promoted progams for economic development and worked to create national institutions such as the army and parliament. He based the country's legal system on French and Italian legal codes, except for family law, which fell under Islamic law, and incorporated ulama into the bureaucracy, leading to state control of religion. He was overthrown in 1969 by a coup d'etat led by Muammar Qaddafi.

Sanusi Tariqah Revivalist Sufi order based in Libya and the central Sahara. Founded in 1841 by Muhammad ibn Ali al-Sanusi. Well known for its role in the resistance to French and Italian colonialism. Supported the right to jihad. Disapproved of excesses in ritual, such as dancing and singing. Its founder placed great emphasis on the role of Muhammad and on following his example. Its core supporters were Bedouin of Cyrenaica, although there were some urban lodges. In its early period, it promoted learning and piety among adherents. The tariqah had a strong work ethic, particularly with respect to the building and upkeep of lodges (zawiyahs) and development through agriculture. It became an important factor in the development of trans-Saharan trade. The French saw the Sanusis as an activist force and initiated hostilities against them in 1901; the Sanusis took up arms in response. The regional population fought the French in the name of and under the leadership of the brotherhood. The Sanusi leader also called for jihad and led a largely Bedouin force against Italian invaders. The ensuing struggle for control of Libya led to destruction of the organizational structure of Sanusi lodges. Muhammad Idris, the head of the order, was the first amir and king of the modern state of Libya; he was overthrown by Muammar Qaddafi in 1969. Most of the organization was destroyed in conflicts in Egypt, Chad, and Cyrenaica. The order is not tolerated in Libya today. *See also* Salihi Tariqah; Sanusi, Muhammad Idris ibn al-Mahdi al-

Sapa Tresno *See* Aisyiyah

Sara *See* Sarah

Saracens Name first used by Romans for nomadic groups in Syria, later applied to Arabs, and then extended by medieval Christian writers to all Muslims.

Sarah Wife of Abraham and mother of Isaac. Not mentioned by name in the Quran but prominent in hadith. Known for her physical beauty, faithfulness to God, and fidelity to her husband. Her barrenness led her to offer her handmaid, Hagar, to Abraham. After the birth of her own son, she became jealous of Hagar's son Ishmael (Ismail) and had Abraham send them away.

Sarakhshi, Muhammad ibn Ahmad al- (d. 1090) Great Hanafi jurist and legal specialist predating the more famous al-Ghazali (d. 1111). Wrote a commentary on the seminal *Siyar al-kabir* of Shaybani (ca. 740–804). His two-volume *Muharrar fi usul al-fiqh* (Studies in the fundamentals of Islamic law) is influential.

Sarekat Islam Indonesia's first mass political party, which at one time claimed more than one million adherents. In the early twentieth century it was set against local Chinese economic power and capitalism; it was nationalistic against Chinese and Dutch colonialism. The party tended to reflect Islamic socialist and modernist views, but the organization was never strongly centralized and declined in power. After 1955 it continued to be active in Muslim politics as a splinter party; it was absorbed into the Partai Persatuan Pembangunan when Suharto consolidated all Muslim parties into one coalition in the 1970s.

Sariqah Theft. Traditional Islamic penal ordinances (hudud) distinguish between two kinds: al-sariqah al-sughra (simple theft), requiring amputation of the right hand, and al-sariqah al-kubra, the meaning of which is contested but which requires the amputation of the right hand and left foot. Any amputation is carried out only after stringent evidentiary requirements are satisfied. In the opinion of most jurists, a theft induced by hunger is not subject to amputation. Repeat offenders may be subject to additional amputations and imprisonment. Murder during the commission of theft results in the death penalty. Hudud ordinances are considered primarily deterrant and, due to their strict evidentiary requirements, are rarely invoked. *See also* Hadd

Sarraj, Abu Nasr al- (d. 988) Major historian and theorist of Sufism from Tus in northeastern Iran. His *Kitab al-luma* (Book of light flashes) is an important source of the sayings and thought of early mystical personalities and movements. Sought to demonstrate that Sufism was fully compatible with mainstream Islamic belief and practice.

Sasanians Dynasty (205–641) founded by Ardashir, son of Papak or possibly Sasan. Possible distant relation of the former Persian Achaemenid dynasty. Conquered and replaced Parthian rule in Iran. Established a main administrative capital in Ctesiphon, Iraq. Enjoyed centralized administration, bureacracy, and legal system. Language was Pahlavi. State religion was Zoroastrianism, which regarded the king (shahanshah) as chosen by God, with a divine right to rule as protector and impartial judge of subjects. Fought sporadic and debilitating wars with the Roman Empire throughout its period of power. Was conquered and overthrown by Islamic armies in the major Battles of Qadisiyya (636) and Nihavand (642). Yazdegird III was the dynasty's last ruler (651).

Satan Devil. The Arabic term *shaytan* means "adversary." Used in the Quran in both the singular and the plural, often interchangeably with Iblis (considered to be a particular satan), the disobedient angel ejected from heaven for disobeying God. Iblis tempts Adam and Eve into disobedience, in which story he is referred to as *shaytan*. Also sometimes referred to as a jinn, giving rise to scholarly speculation concerning the exact nature of Satan and Iblis. Scholars agree only that the term represents at least a principle (if not personification) of evil.

Satanic Verses Term coined by Sir William Muir in his Life of Mahomet (1858), used in reference to the report recorded by al-Tabari (d. 923) that Satan interjected in surah 53: 19–20 words recognizing the intercessory powers of the pre-Islamic Arabian deities al-Lat, al-Uzzah, and al-Manat. According to the report, these "Satanic verses" were later repealed (see Quran 22:51–52). Also the name of a controversial novel by Salman Rushdie (1989).

Saud, Abd al-Aziz ibn Abd al-Rahman al- (d. 1953) Founder and first ruler of present kingdom of Saudi Arabia. His religio-political legitimacy and the foundation of the kingdom were rooted in the promotion and protection of Wahhabi doctrines. He brought the nomadic tribes under control by settling them in permanent hujjar (paramilitary settlements), where they were instructed in the principles of faith by religious tutors.

Saud, Faisal ibn Abd al-Aziz al- (d. 1975) King of Saudi Arabia during its transformation into an oil-producing power. Known for personal piety. During the 1960s and 1970s, emphasized Islamic values in response to rising Arab nationalism in Egypt. Rejected secularism and socialism. Implemented a ten-point reform program to abolish slavery, modernize the administration, reorganize religious and judicial institutions, revamp labor and social laws, utilize natural resources soundly, build efficient infrastructure, and establish consultative and local councils. Established the Ministry of Justice to integrate the judiciary into the government and the Council of Senior Ulama to provide the ruler with appropriate religious opinions and approvals. Assassinated by his nephew in 1975.

Saud, Khalid ibn Abd al-Aziz al- (r. 1975–82) King of Saudi Arabia during the seizure of the Grand Mosque in Mecca and the Shii uprising in Eastern Province in 1979. Or-

dered a controversial military assault on the mosque to liberate it, violating the mosque's role as sanctuary and earning opposition and criticism of other Muslim leaders. Was accused of impiety and innovation due to his modernization projects within the kingdom.

Saud, Muhammad ibn al- (r. 1746–65) Founder of the first Saudi dynasty in Arabia. Formed a politico-religious pact with Muhammad ibn Abd al-Wahhab in 1744 to found the country based on purification of Islamic practices from popular religion and an emphasis on strict monotheism. Ibn al-Saud was responsible for political and economic affairs; Ibn Abd al-Wahhab provided religious guidance. Used a combination of religious ideology and lineage to unite disparate tribes in the first political expression of eighteenth-century Islamic reform. The Saud family has maintained its role of political and military leadership in the modern-day kingdom of Saudi Arabia, with the descendants of Ibn Abd al-Wahhab continuing to serve as religious advisers.

Saudi Arabia, Islam in Islam is the religion of state in Saudi Arabia and is interpreted according to the conservative Wahhabi ideology. The legitimacy of the monarchy rests on an alliance between the Saudi royal family and the ulama, who serve as consultants. The monarchy has institutionalized religious organizations within the state power structure. The most powerful religious body is the state-funded Council of Senior Ulama, which provides religious approval for policies determined by the government. Religious police enforce public morality guidelines as determined by the Council. The population of fifteen million to twenty million is overwhelmingly Sunni. A Shii minority, located mostly in Eastern Province, constitutes about 2 percent of total population. Islam's two holiest cities and major pilgrimage sites, Mecca and Medina, are located in Saudi Arabia.

Saul Arabic Talut. The Quran records that he was anointed by the prophet and priest Samuel as king of the Jews. Under his reign, the

Ark of the Covenant was restored to Israel. He led troops against Goliath and his forces out of faith in God, even though they were outnumbered, and achieved victory through David.

Sawda bint Zama (d. 674) Second wife of the Prophet Muhammad. Emigrated to Abyssinia with her first husband, who died in Mecca after their return. In Abyssinia she had a vision of her future marriage to the Prophet. Became the Prophet's wife shortly after Khadijah's death (620). Emigrated to Medina.

Sawit *See* Marabout

Sawm *See* Fasting

Say *See* Hajj

Sayf al-Dawlah, Abu al-Hasan Ali (d. 967) Hamdanid ruler of Aleppo (r. 945–67). Famed for the illustrious scholars of his court and his fearless battles against Byzantine aggressions on Muslim frontiers. His military successes were modest but noticeable in a fragmented caliphate unable to mount a viable defense. They became legendary in the poems of his panegyrist, al-Mutanabbi, who found in him the ideal qualities of a pre-Islamic Arab nobleman.

Sayyid Honorific title used by those claiming descent from Muhammad, especially through his second grandson, Husayn. Sayyids receive the proceeds from a special Islamic tax, khums, to prevent financial hardship and maintain dignity. They are considered both spiritually and socially supreme, particularly in Iran and the Indian subcontinent. The founders of many Sufi orders and most Sufi masters claimed sayyid status. *See also* Ahl al-Bayt

Sayyid, Ahmad Lutfi al- (d. 1963) Writer and editor, scion of landowning Egyptian family. Studied law at King Fuad University (Cairo); served as a prosecutor and edited the first Egyptian law journal. Member of the secret society that became the National

Party. Lived in Europe; influenced by Muhammad Abduh (d. 1905). Gained fame by defending the accused in the famous Dinshaway incident (1906). Beginning in 1907, was editor of the liberal newspaper *Al-jaridah*; later became spokesperson of the Ummah Party. Was a leading early member of the Wafd Party, with ideas that stressed educational reforms and Egyptian patriotism, but then distanced himself from it, abandoned politics, and focused on translations and writing.

Sayyid Shaykh ibn Ahmad al-Hadi (d. 1934) Reformist, writer, publisher and educator. Of Hadrami descent, he was born and raised in Malaya. He belonged to the reformist group Kaum Muda (Young Faction), was cofounder of the journal *Al-imam* (1906–8), and founded the Jelutong Press, which published the monthly journal *Al-ikhwan* (1926–31) and the biweekly newspaper *Saudara* (1928–41) as well as his own translations and literary works. All publications were aimed at encouraging Malays to modernize their society. As headmaster of the Madrasa Masyhur Islamiah (1918–26), he strongly promoted a modern religious education with a curriculum comprising Islamic themes, Arabic, English, and modern scientific subjects.

Saziman-i Mujahidin-i Khalq-i Iran *See* Mujahidin-i Khalq (Iran)

Science Arabic ilm, pl. ulum. Refers to all systematic knowledge, both religious and secular. Between the ninth and thirteenth centuries, Islamic civilization made major original contributions to the development of premodern science and transmitted Greek learning to Europe through extensive translations. The introduction of post-Renaissance science, technology, and thought into Islamic societies was pioneered by modernizing rulers and academic exchanges from the eighteenth through the twentieth centuries. The introduction of modern science has led many to recognize the need to synthesize traditional Islamic education with a modern curriculum. Many Muslim countries have developed major scientific research institutes and sponsored programs designed to Islamize science and knowledge. Islam recognizes no conflict between revelation and reason, believing that they are compatible. See also Aesthetics; Alchemy; Astrology; Astronomy; Cosmology; Ethics; Geomancy; Geometry; History; Ilm al-Huruf; Ilm al-Rijal; Lexicology; Mathematics; Medicine: Traditional Practice; Natural Science

Science, Attitudes Toward Seeking religious knowledge is of such importance that it is deemed an act of worship. Muhammad is quoted as having said, "Acquire knowledge from the cradle to the grave," and "Seek knowledge everywhere, even in China." Attitudes toward science in the Muslim world have varied enormously over the centuries. They have vacillated between comprehensive embrace, as in the work of al-Biruni (d. 1048), Ibn Sina (d. 1037), and Ibn al-Haytham (d. 1039), to a very cautious and sometimes negative position, as seen in the writings of the orthodox ulama and in al-Ghazali's (d. 1111) Tahafut al-tahafut (Destruction of the philosophers). The general view among the rejectors of the scientific point of view (that of Greek natural philosophy) was that it was dangerous to religion. This view was shared by Ibn Khaldun (d. 1406), who devoted a long section of his Muqaddimah to a "refutation of philosophy" and cited the hadith "Muslims do not do what does not concern them." This follows the view that "useful" knowledge is that which enhances religious piety. Religious conservatives periodically gained the upper hand in Islamic society, with the resultant condemnation of the study of logic, philosophy, and the natural sciences. The paradoxical nature of attitudes toward science in the Muslim world is reflected in the fact that Muslims made major contributions to the development of the natural sciences, yet mainstream educational institutions tended to ignore modern science. Currently, there is no opposition to the natural sciences in the Muslim world, although there is great caution about such issues as genetic engineering and organ transplants. In some Muslim circles there is concern about the use of

sociological descriptions of human society because these suggest that factors other than Islamic beliefs govern human interactions. The general view today is that there is nothing in the Quran that explicitly opposes scientific inquiry.

Seal of the Prophets See Khatam al-Nabiyyin

Seclusion Term referring to various practices designed to protect women from men in traditional Muslim societies, including confining women to the company of other women and close male relatives in their home or in separate female living quarters, veiling, self-effacing mannerisms, and the separation of men and women in public places. These practices reflect both social and religious custom. Seclusion practices were well established in pre-Islamic societies of the Mediterranean, Mesopotamia, and Persia and are reinforced in Islamic scripture and law. Female seclusion declined precipitously in the early twentieth century due to education and increased economic opportunities for women, particularly in urban areas. In traditional and rural societies, such as some of the Gulf states, value is still placed on the rigid separation of women from unrelated men. Since the early 1980s sermons and fatwas of conservative preachers and theologians have encouraged female modesty, veiling, and seclusion practices; the positive response of many young women is often a reflection of a desire to assert an Islamic identity distinct from Western standards. For professional working women, wearing the veil is a way to claim space in an arena traditionally reserved for men; it is a strategy for coping with men who are uncomfortable working with women; and for religious women, it is a means of emulating their grandmothers' generation and preserving religious and cultural heritage. See also Haram; Hijab

Sectarianism Although the Quran warns against sectarianism (e.g., 30:31–32), divisions and sects emerged within the Muslim community as early as the first civil war (656–61). Questions about legitimate authority and about the proper attitude toward those involved in this civil war were central to the subsequent emergence of Shii and Sunni Islam as well as to other, shorter-lived groups (e.g., the Kharijis). Relations between the majority Sunnis and the various communities of the Shiis (today some 10–15 percent of the Muslim population) have varied widely in Muslim history. There have been long periods of peace and relatively harmonious coexistence as well as sharp polemical exchanges and bitter conflict. In recent times, the success of the Iranian revolution of 1979 has contributed to a resurgence among the Shiis in the Middle East and South Asia, which, in many cases, has led to strained relations with apprehensive Sunni communities. In the Arab Middle East, the Iranian revolution was viewed with deep suspicion by the ruling elite, who sometimes supported the activities of rival Sunni organizations as a means of countering the spread of Iran's revolutionary influence. In Pakistan, militant Sunni and Shii organizations emerged in the 1980s and have remained active since then in recurrent cycles of sectarian violence. Sectarian tensions in South and West Asia were exacerbated with the emergence of the anti-Shii Taliban in Afghanistan. *See also* Ahmadis; Ismailis; Shii Islam

Secularism Derived from European historical experience, which sought to remove coercive power from ecclesiastical authority and thus safeguard freedom of religion; separation of religion and state. Often interpreted by Muslims as the removal of religious values from the public sphere, and therefore condemned. Muslim theologians have long distinguished between matters of din (religion) and dawlah (state) but insist that public life must be guided by Islamic values. Historically, Muslims have experienced secularism as an ideology imposed from outside by invaders and colonialists, thus as an extension of foreign culture. The battle perceived by Islamists between religion and secularism pits secularist attempts to define Islam as a matter of personal belief against those for whom reimposition of Islamic law and Islamic political authority is essential.

Seljuk Dynasty A Turkic family of Central Asian origin that ruled much of the eastern Islamic world from 1038 to 1194. Their ascendance marked a Sunni revival after a period in which Shiism (Fatimid Egypt, Buwayhid Iraq, and Iran) dominated; it also was the beginning of centuries of Turkic political and military dominance throughout the Middle East and Central Asia and introduced a major new ethnic element in the region. The Seljuk administrative legacy lies in Nizam al-Mulk's governmental and educational systems, which prevailed in Iran until the nineteenth century.

Seminary *See* Madrasa

Senegal, Islam in Ninety-two percent of the population is Muslim and 2 percent Christian, with 6 percent other. Nineteenth-century Sufi brotherhoods such as the Tijani and Muridi fought against French and British colonization. French colonists established a secular state, which the independent Senegalese government (1960) has maintained. The Muridi tariqah is based in Touba, a state within a state in which there is no governor, no administration, and no police force. Veiling is not required, and criminal activity is rare. Alcohol, cigarettes, sports, loud music, and politics are banned. *See also* Futa Toro; Umar Tal

September Laws Laws implemented in Sudan from 1983 to 1985 under Jafar al-Numayri as part of his Islamization program, to buttress his political legitimacy, and to justify authoritarian rule. Numayri declared Sudan an Islamic republic with shariah as law. The move was intended to unify the country, but it led to civil war between Muslims in the north and Christians and practitioners of traditional religions, opposed to these measures, in the south.

Sermon *See* Khutbah

Servant *See* Abd

Servant of God *See* Abd Allah

Sevener Shiis *See* Ismailis

Sexuality Islam rejects asceticism; sexual fulfillment within marriage for both partners is the ideal state. Sexual relations are permitted only within a legal and normative marriage or, among the Shii, in a temporary marriage contracted between an unmarried woman and a married or unmarried man. Sexual intercourse is prohibited during menstruation, for forty days after childbirth, during the daylight hours of Ramadan, and on pilgrimage. Women must be chaste for a period of three months after divorce (iddah) to determine paternity in the event of pregnancy. Various legal arguments allow or oppose specific forms of sexual activity and mandate that wives submit sexually upon their husbands' request. Homosexuality is acknowledged in the Muslim world; it is variously considered unlawful, abnormal, and punishable under religious law, or tolerated in areas where homosexuals are viewed as a third sex. The pre-Islamic practice of female circumcision (and/or infibulation) is practiced in Egypt, Sudan, parts of the Gulf, Libya, Chad, and other Muslim areas of Africa in order to control female sexuality. *See also* Birth Control/Contraception

Shaban, Said (d. 1998) Lebanese Sunni political and religious activist. Graduated from al-Azhar University. Active in Tripoli in the Muslim Brotherhood. Came to prominence in the 1980s after he founded the militant Harakat al-Tawhid al-Islami (Islamic Unity Movement). Asserted control over the city of Tripoli in the 1980s, but after the Syrian army intervened he aligned himself with Syria and Iran. Was the Iranian government's strongest Sunni ally in Lebanon.

Shabazz, al-Hajj Malik al- *See* Malcolm X

Shabestari, Mahmud (d. 1288) Also known as Shaykh Sad al-Din. Persian mystic poet, born in the town of Shabestar, near the northeast shore of Lake Urumia in Azerbaijan. Prominent religious scholar in Tabriz, Iran. Famous for the mystical poem "Golshan-i raz" (The rose garden of the secret).

Shadhili, Abu al-Hasan Ali ibn Abd Allah al- (d. 1258) Born in Morocco, educated in Tunis and Morocco, and died in Egypt. Founded the Shadhili Sufi order, combining formal scholarship with mystical exercises. The opposition of establishment Tunisian ulama to his preaching led him to move to Alexandria, Egypt, in 1244, where he gathered students and followers, founded a zawiyah (Sufi lodge), and created the distinctive organization, devotional activities, and social life of the order. He avoided close relations with the government. Passed down popular prayers and Sufi terms. The movement he inspired is one of the four oldest Sufi tariqahs and became the most important in North Africa. Buried at Humaythra near the Red Sea.

Shadhili Tariqah One of the four oldest Sufi orders in Muslim world. Has numerous branches in North Africa, Egypt, Sudan, Comoros, Sri Lanka, Yemen, China, Bulgaria, Romania, Yugoslavia, Kosovo, Macedonia, and Sub-Saharan and East Africa. Founded in the twelfth century by Moroccan-born Abu al-Hasan Ali al-Shadhili. Its founder left no scholarly works, but passed down a number of enduringly popular prayers, one of which, Hizb al-Bahr, was widely used as a prayer for safety at sea; these prayers have been compiled and translated into English. The order's doctrines were systematized in the thirteenth century under the third shaykh, Ahmad ibn Ata Allah al-Iskandari. Biographies of other shaykhs were also recorded at this time. Ibn Ata Allah's aphorisms guaranteed the popularity of the order and became a major instrument for expansion. The order is known for its pragmatic approach to worldly comforts; it did not believe that wealth precluded piety. The order was active in Turkey during the Ottoman period. It is prominent among modern reform-minded Sufis, especially in Egypt. Branches inspired by the order include Fasi, Darqawi, and Yusufi in North Africa; Burhani Disuqi in Sudan, Egypt, and Syria; Hamidi and Ashirah Muhammadi in Egypt; and Azami Shadhili in Sudan. *See also* Yashruti Tariqah; Yusufi Tariqah

Shadow of God Arabic *zill Allah*. Pre-Islamic Persian concept of divine right kingship popularized by Muslim rulers as part of their claims to be vicegerents (caliphs) of God on earth and descendants of Muhammad and the imams. Many kings considered the concept to be justification of their accountability only to God, thus removing them from public scrutiny. It is particularly prominent among Shiis, especially in Iran. The Safavid dynasty used it to declare themselves divine incarnations. Some Qajar rulers and the Pahlavi dynasty formally carried title to bolster power. The epithet created the image of a divine protector, binding the nation together and validating its mission. The divine right of kings served to personalize and sacralize monarchy as well as personify the nation-state.

Shafaa To intercede. The Quran generally rejects all kinds of intercession with anyone but God (2:48, 254; 39:44). None can barter or pay ransom for redemption from the sin of rejection of faith, idolatry (6:94; 30:13; 36:23; 39:43), or the commission of grave sins (2:48, 123, 254; 3:91; 5:36; 10:54; 13:18; 39:47; 40:18; 57:15; 70:11). In other places, the Quran mentions that God will permit intercession in some instances (10:3; 20:109; 34:23; 53:26), such as by the angels on behalf of believers (40:7; 53:26). These verses have led some to conclude that Muhammad will intercede on behalf of his community. This was further developed into belief in mediation by the Shii Imams and Sufi saints.

Shafii, Muhammad ibn Idris ibn al-Abbas ibn Uthman ibn (d. 819/20) Jurist, theologian, and founder of the Shafii school of Islamic law. Born in Gaza. Died in Egypt. Educated in Quran, hadith, and fiqh in Mecca, Medina, and Iraq. Systematized the theoretical bases of Islamic law and outlined the doctrines and differences of Islamic law schools; thus often called the architect of Islamic law. First jurist to insist that hadith were decisive source of law over customary doctrines of earlier schools. Rejected use of ray (personal opinion) in favor of qiyas (analogy). Argued for grounding all legal deductions in the Quran and Sunnah, defined as hadith reports. Authorized the practice of consensus (ijma) and rejected juristic preference (istishan) as a source of law. Taught that penal sanctions lapse in cases where repentance precedes punishment.

Shafii School of Law School of Islamic law founded by Muhammad ibn Idris ibn al-Abbas ibn Uthman ibn Shafii in the eighth century. Prominent in Egypt, Palestine, and Jordan with a significant number of followers in Syria, Lebanon, Iraq, Hejaz, Pakistan, India, and Indonesia and among Sunnis in Iran and Yemen. Official school for Ayyubid dynasty in Egypt, and prominent during the Mamluk regime that followed. Displaced by the Hanafi school there when the Ottomans occupied Egypt in 1517. Combined knowledge of fiqh as practiced in Iraq with that of Hejaz. Considers hadith superior to customary doctrines of earlier schools in formulation of Islamic law. Denies preference (istishan) as source of law.

Shafiq, Durriyah (d. 1976) Also known as Doria Shafiq. Egyptian scholar, teacher, journalist, and feminist activist. Worked for female literacy and full political rights for women. Argued that Islam speaks for the equality of women and requires neither veil nor domesticity. Achieved gains for women's rights but faced opposition from conservative Muslims and was placed under house arrest due to her opposition to the Nasser regime. Ultimately experienced an emotional breakdown and committed suicide.

Shah One of the most common titles used by the dynastic rulers of Iran and the Turko-Persian cultural area; often used in a compound form such as padishah (emperor) or shahanshah (king of kings). In its original and most distinctive usage, connotes sacred kingship.

Shah Abbas I (r. 1587–1629) Major ruler of the Safavid dynasty in Iran. Secured the borders of the empire, consolidated the institutions of the state, and reduced the power of the original military forces of the state, the Qizilbash, by creating a special royal guard. Transferred the capital from Qazvin to Isfahan, where he constructed many major buildings and created a magnificent center for the empire. His support for the religious schools and institutions helped make them more independent of political control, and the arts flourished under his patronage.

Shah Bano Begum Case Refers to a lawsuit in India (Mohammed Ahmed Khan v. Shah Bano Begum AIR 1985 S.C.945) regarding support for a divorced Muslim woman, as well as to a successful movement among conservative elements of the Muslim minority in India. Ulama and Muslim politicians who conducted this campaign argued against the court's decision in favor of the wife as an invasion of Muslim Personal Law in violation of Article 30 of the Indian constitution.

Shah Ismail (d. 1524) Founder of the Persian Safavid dynasty in 1501. Self-proclaimed reincarnation of Ali, spirit of Jesus and al-Khidr, and Hidden Imam of Shii tradition. Claimed status as both shah and messiah to legitimate rule. Used a combination of militance and millenarianism to expand the Safavid empire. Established Twelver/Ithna Ashari Shiism as the state religion of Iran.

Shahadah Witness. Recitation of the Islamic witness of faith, "There is no god but God and Muhammad is the messenger of God"; the first of the five pillars of Islam. Shahadah is accepted as a declaration of acceptance of Islam by a convert: the convert has only to repeat it twice in the presence of at least one other Muslim.

Shahid *See* Martyr

Shahid, Shah Ismail (d. 1831) Prominent scholar-activist of Muslim South Asia. In 1819 he became a follower of the reformer Sayyid Ahmad Barelwi. Together they produced a number of tracts condemning Muslim integration of Hindu rituals and formulating a new practice of Sufism called the Way of Muhammad. He and Barelwi died in the Battle of Balakot (North-West Frontier Province, pre-partition India) during an unsuccessful jihad against Sikh forces.

Shahrastani, Abu al-Fath Muhammad ibn Abd al-Karim al- (d. 1153) Scholar, philosopher, theologian, and historian of religions from the Iranian province of Khurasan. Mainly concerned with religious and philosophical worldviews. Best known for a history of the religious ideas of Muslim sects and other peoples of the world, *Kitab al-milal wa'l-nihal* (The book of sects and systems of thought). Although self-identified and generally perceived as an Ashari Sunni in this work, his sectarian affiliation has come under dispute, raising questions about the assessment of his contributions to the Muslim tradition. A few of his contemporaries accused him of covertly being an Ismaili. Some modern scholars affirm this, citing, among other evidence, similarities between the vision of Divine Order espoused in his Quran commentary and Ismaili doctrines.

Shahrur, Muhammad Syrian engineer and author of works on the Quran and Islamic jurisprudence, of which the best-known is his 1990 book *Al-kitab wa'l-Quran: Qiraa muasira* (The book and the Quran: A contemporary reading). Shahrur seeks to build a new Islamic jurisprudence with a radical rereading of the Quran, rejecting much of the work of medieval Muslim jurists as well as such sources of Sunni law as ijma (consensus) and qiyas (analogic reasoning).

Shaltut, Mahmud (d. 1963) Egyptian religious scholar who worked to reform al-Azhar, reversing its decline and recapturing its previous role as an active participant in Egypt's educational, cultural, and political destiny. Best known for his knowledge of Islamic jurisprudence and Quranic interpretation. Envisaged a reformed Islam and shariah capable of becoming a source for modern legislation. Promoted an activist international role for al-Azhar in fighting religious fanaticism and uniting Islamic ummah and various schools of thought. Reorganization and budgetary allowances allowed him to engage in ijtihad (independent legal reasoning) in an effort to reform education through introduction of modern subjects and end religious fanaticism by narrowing the differences between the different legal schools (madhhabs).

Shamil, Imam (d. 1871) Muslim leader of resistance to the Russian conquest of the Caucasus in the nineteenth century. He had a formal Islamic education in Daghistan and became a leader in the Naqshbandi tariqah of the Khalidi branch, which advocated reform of Muslim life. Tariqah leadership organized military opposition to Russian expansion. Shamil became leader of the movement in 1834 and led military resistance in Daghistan and Chechnya until defeated in 1859. He created an effective administrative structure whose core was the murids (followers) in the tariqah. Following his defeat, he lived in comfortable retirement until his death.

Shams al-Din, Muhammad Mahdi Lebanese Shii leader. Deputy chairman of the Supreme Islamic Shii Council, which serves as the representative body for Shiis independent of Sunni Muslims in Lebanon. Was trained in Najaf, Iraq, in the reformulation of Shiism as an ideology of political activism and protest. Opposed Ayatollah Khomeini by condemning hostage taking as un-Islamic and illegal.

Sharaf *See* Honor

Sharafuddin Ahmad ibn Yahya Maneri *See* Maneri, Sharif al-Din

Sharawi, Huda (d. 1947) Egyptian feminist leader. Promoted critical examination of customary practice and religious prescription, particularly veiling and seclusion. Active in the early Egyptian independence movement. Led the first organized feminist movement in Egypt and the Arab world, bringing together Muslim and Christian women. Although secular in orientation, her agenda was articulated within the framework of modernist Islam.

Sharawi, Shaykh Muhammad Mutawali al- (d. 1998) Popular Egyptian religious scholar, writer, and former minister of endowments. Resigned from his ministerial post after one year (1978) and kept a distance from politics. His publications included an interpretation of the Quran; the Great Fatwas (religious opinions), which covered four hundred issues; and books on other religious subjects. Best known for his weekly session of Quran interpretation, which is still aired on Egyptian and Arab television. Followed a lexicographical exegesis of the Quran and made its meanings readily accessible to average Muslims. Respected for his forceful logic and undisputed popularity.

Sharh Commentary on a summary or interpretation of a specific legal or religious text. The eleventh century saw a gradual concentration of literary education in madrasas and the substitution of encyclopedic compilation and supercommentary for original composition.

Shari From the word *shira*, which means "sell," "vend," or "buy." *Shari* (also occurs in legal sources as *mushtari*) in classical legal usage refers to the seller or buyer. In modern legal usage it always refers to the buyer. The legal discourses focus on the warranties, options, and rights that accrue to the benefit of the buyer. Generally the risk of loss remains with the seller until the buyer takes possession. According to the majority view, the buyer has the right to inspect the object of a contract and enjoys an implied warranty of merchantability.

Shariah God's eternal and immutable will for humanity, as expressed in the Quran and

Muhammad's example (Sunnah), considered binding for all believers; ideal Islamic law. The Quran contains only about ninety verses directly and specifically addressing questions of law. Islamic legal discourse refers to these verses as God's law and incorporates them into legal codes. The remainder of Islamic law is the result of jurisprudence (fiqh), human efforts to codify Islamic norms in practical terms and legislate for cases not specifically dealt with in the Quran and Sunnah. Although human-generated legislation is considered fallible and open to revision, the term *shariah* is sometimes applied to all Islamic legislation. This was supported by formal structures of juristic literature and many specific statements from the tenth through the nineteenth centuries. Modern scholars have challenged this claim, distinguishing between shariah and fiqh and calling for reform of fiqh codes in light of modern conditions. *See also* Renewal and Reform; Usul al-Fiqh

Shariah Courts In premodern times, the primary judicial institution presided over by a judge, called a qadi or hakim, and empowered to adjudicate legal disputes in private (e.g., marriage, divorce, inheritance), civil (e.g., contracts and torts), and public (e.g., criminal activity) matters on the basis of the Islamic legal codes. In the earliest period, the qadi ruled in accordance with his own legal interpretations. But by the eleventh century, judicial discretion was essentially limited to choosing appropriate precedents. In traditional shariah courts the plaintiff and defendant represent themselves, without a jury. The qadi passes judgment on all evidence in accordance with strict rules of evidence and testimony meticulously laid out in the schools of law. He retains the right, however, to impugn the integrity of any witness and to refuse to admit that witness' testimony.

The nineteenth century witnessed a number of far-reaching changes for shariah courts, as Muslim lands came under the direct rule of the European powers and the influence of European legal codes and concepts. There was concern over the hostility of Muslim jurists toward the admission of circumstantial evidence (insisting instead on the testimony of eyewitnesses), for example, and the unequal treatment of non-Muslims. Massive social, economic, demographic, and political changes in the modern era also pressured the traditional legal system. As a result, under the Ottomans and then the colonial powers, many issues were removed from the jurisdiction of the shariah courts and placed under that of special foreign tribunals, so-called mixed courts, and/or secular national courts. Shariah courts were left presiding only over cases of personal status (marriage, divorce, custody, and inheritance) and waqf (pious endowments). This trend continued in the twentieth century.

Shariat Madari, Ayatollah Muhammad Kazim (d. 1986) Iranian legal scholar from Tabriz. Studied in Qom with Abd al-Karim Haeri Yazdi (d. 1937), founder of the modern seminary there, and went to Najaf for higher studies in law with Muhammad Husayn Naini (d. 1936), Abu al-Hasan Isfahani (d. 1946), and Diya al-Din Iraqi (d. 1942). Returned to Tabriz to teach until 1949, and then went back to Qom to teach fiqh. Said to have interceded with the shah in 1963 to spare the life of Ayatollah Ruhollah Khomeini (d. 1989). In 1970 the shah sought to influence Shariat Madari's elevation to the position of marja al-taqlid. In the early 1970s Shariat Madari established in Qom the Dar al-Tabligh-i Islami, an institution of Islamic education and missionizing. He advocated constitutional monarchy and sponsored the Muslim People's Party as a counter to the Khomeini-influenced Islamic Republican Party. He opposed Khomeini's doctrine of vilayat i-faqih and was accused of treason in an assassination plot against Khomeini in April 1982; he was "defrocked" by the regime and spent his last years under house arrest in Qom and Tehran.

Shariati, Ali (d. 1977) Iranian Shii thinker and political activist. Influenced by Marxian thought, he argued that scripture required adaptation to changing historical circumstances and that religion must be transformed from a purely private set of ethical injunctions into a revolutionary program to change the world and bring about social justice and freedom for the downtrodden and oppressed. Exhorted the masses to action according to Husayn's example in consciously sacrificing his life on behalf of the political and social liberation of his followers. Advocated a fresh reading of Islamic scripture in order to reconstruct Islam's concepts into a modern, progressive ideology of mobilization to enfranchise and empower the masses.

Shariatullah, Hajji *See* Faraidi Movement

Sharif Pl. *ashraf.* Honorable, noble, high-born, or high-bred. Associated with honor, high position, nobility, and distinction. Man claiming descent from prominent ancestors, usually Muhammad through his grandson Hasan. Particularly important in but not limited to Shii Islam, where veneration for Muhammad and his family has led to particular eminence of Muhammad's descendants. Usually wear green or white turbans to distinguish themselves from others. Revered and respected historically, although not necessarily wealthy, and not subject to the same religious stipulations that apply to other Muslims. Believe that their sins will be forgiven by God due to their special status. The Sunni rulers of Jordan and Morocco claim sharif status. *See also* Ahl al-Bayt; Sayyid

Sharif Husayn ibn Ali (d. 1931) Grand sharif of Mecca who led the Arab Revolt against the Ottoman Empire in 1916. His legitimacy was based on his religious prestige as a descendant of Muhammad and his role as custodian of Mecca and Medina. Declared himself caliph in 1924 when the Ottoman caliphate was abolished. Was overthrown and exiled by Abd al-Aziz ibn Saud, but his sons established Hashemite rule in Iraq and Trans-Jordan.

Sharq *See* Mashriq

Shart Condition or stipulation existing in law or contract. In law, it often refers to a condition without which the religious or legal act is rendered invalid. The shart is an element (rukn) that must be fulfilled in order for the legal act to be valid. For instance, a condition of valid prayer is purity, and a condition of a valid contract is consent. The term also refers to contractual stipulations either implied by law or expressly mandated by the contracting parties. Under classical and modern Islamic law, there are various options and warranties mandated by law into a contractual obligation. Furthermore, parties may expressly dictate conditions into the contract as long as such conditions are lawful. Classical and modern Islamic law vigorously debate which, if any, conditions may be dictated by the parties in a marriage contract. For instance, it is debated whether a woman may stipulate that her husband not move her away from her present residence or not take a second wife, otherwise the marriage is rendered invalid. Many Muslim countries permit women to insert such stipulations.

Shath Sufi term referring to ecstatic expression or utterance, often of an apparently blasphemous nature. An example cited in the ninth century is Abu Yazid al-Bistami's exclamation of "Glory be to me, how great is my majesty," viewed by some Sufi authors as evidence of profound experience of the divine but attributed by others to intoxication, immaturity, or madness; some, such as al-Ghazali, are ambivalent about the apparent blasphemy of shath but admire the spiritual status of their authors. Due to the ambiguous definition of blasphemy in Islamic law, shath utterances are treated variously by legal authorities as beyond shariah jurisdiction or as a clear indication of heresy.

Shatibi, Abu Ishaq Ibrahim al- (d. 790) Andalusian Maliki scholar and reformer. Wrote on a variety of subjects including usul al-fiqh, grammar, and poetry. Was critical of fiqh of his age and disagreed with Maliki contemporaries on many points, including taxation and the significance of taqlid (precedent). Reemphasized the principle of Quranic supremacy as the ultimate source for making rules among Muslims. Argued that the individual's interests and common good (maslahah) constitute the prime purposes of Islamic law. In modern times Muhammad Abduh and his student Muhammad Rashid Rida resurrected Shatibi's scholarship, especially regarding the purposes of law.

Shattari Tariqah Important Sufi order in India and Indonesia. Its foundation in the fifteenth century is attributed to Abdullah Shattari, who maintained a close relationship with the Timurid sultans and provided them with spiritual guidance. The tariqah embraced the Indian cultural milieu and Hindu, particularly yogic, ideas. Shattari studied yoga and composed songs in Indian vernaculars. Later leaders of the order allowed disciples to use Sanskrit and Hindi formulas in dhikr. Meditation exercises involving yoga postures and breath control were also introduced.

Shauq Desire or longing; in Sufi Islam, a mystical or spiritual state associated with the longing to contemplate the divine beloved. In early Arab Islamic poetry the term was used primarily in the sense of profane love for an earthly object; in the later mystical tradition it refers to the mystic's ardent desire to reach union with the divine or achieve the vision of God in the afterlife.

Shawkani, Muhammad al- (d. 1834) Yemeni scholar, jurisprudent, and reformer. Rejected the Shii Zaydi school of law into which he was born. Influenced by Salafi thought; called for a return to the textual sources of the Quran and hadith. Viewed himself as a mujtahid mutlaq, an authority to whom others had to defer in religious law. Developed a series of syllabi for attaining various ranks of scholarship. Used a strict system of legal analysis based on Sunni thought. Despite his Shii background, he is regarded as a great revivalist of Sunni Islam in his time by various Salafi and Wahhabi movements and has influenced contemporary Islamist movements in other parts of the Muslim world such as the Ahl-e-Hadith in India. His legal decisions and discussions

are frequently used in contemporary debate among Muslim scholars.

Shaybani, Abu Abd Allah Muhammad ibn al-Hasan ibn Farqad al- (d. 804) Jurist and student of Abu Hanifah and Malik ibn Anas. Trained in jurisprudence of both the Iraqi and Medina schools. Insisted on the decisive role of hadith in Islamic law. Held a high position in the Abbasid court, enabling him to spread the writings and ideas of the Hanafi school. First jurist to write down Hanafi legal thought. Wrote a detailed work on inheritance law and the first comprehensive treatise on the law of jihad. Formulated the doctrine of international law (siyar), helping to rationalize relations with the outside world and discuss the rights of non-Muslims in Islamic law. Supported equality of Muslims and non-Muslims under Islamic law, except in family matters.

Shaykh A pre-Islamic honorific title. Meaning embraces concepts such as "leader," "patriarch," "notable," "elder," "chief," and "counselor." The term "shaykh al-din" has been applied to men who possess scriptural learning. Heads of religious orders are called shaykhs, as are Quranic scholars, jurists, and those who preach and lead prayers in the mosque. A shaykh's reputation traditionally depended on his ability to resolve disputes, a detailed knowledge of customary law (urf), an ability to dispense hospitality on a grand scale, and an ability to lead in times of raiding and warfare. Among tribespeople, the title is not inherited, and one can attain or lose that rank. See also Murshid

Shaykh al-Akhbar, al- See Ibn al-Arabi, Muhyi al-Din

Shaykh al-Islam Originally an honorific title for ranking Sufis among others or denoting formal office. In the Ottoman system, the shaykh al-Islam (Turkish seyhulislam) was the chief mufti (juriconsult) and head of the state hierarchy of ulama. Often served as adviser to the sultan's court on political affairs.

Shaykhis A branch of Twelver Shiism named after Shaykh Ahmad al-Ahsai (d. 1826), a Bahraini mystic and theologian. He spent fifteen years in Iran, where he won the esteem of the Qajar ruler Fath Ali Shah and attracted many followers. Al-Ahsai was eventually condemned by traditional ulama because of his doctrine of spiritual rather than physical resurrection; he retired to Mecca. Al-Ahsai was influenced by the Akhbari school, which stresses the importance of Shii traditions (akhbar) and opposes Usulis, the mainstream of clerical Shiism. After the Iranian revolution (1979), the Shaykhis were persecuted and the leader, Sayyid Ali Musawi Basri, moved the community's headquarters to Iraq. *See also* Akhbaris

Shaytan *See* Satan

Shibli Numani, Muhammad (d. 1914) Founder of Urdu historiography. Wrote several biographies of heroes of Islam. Convinced that Islam needed to be revived from within and that Muslims of his time could learn valuable lessons from past heroes. Established Dar al-Musannifin to organize a school of writers who would engage in the highest traditions of Islamic scholarship.

Shiraz Capital of the province of Fars in south-central Iran. In the twelfth and thirteenth centuries, Shiraz attained a remarkable literary status, to the extent that it was referred to as the "city of poets." Classical poets such as Sadi and Hafez were both from Shiraz. In 1387 and again in 1393, Shiraz was occupied by Timur (Tamerlane). In 1724 the city was sacked by Afghan invaders. Several times in the course of Persian history Shiraz became the Iranian capital. During the Zand period (1757–94) Shiraz was the seat of the government of Karim Khan Zand (r. 1757–79). Buildings in the new city include a modern university (founded in 1945) and the Namazi medical center, named after its benefactor. Shiraz is noted for a variety of traditional crafts such as woodwork. Its modern industry includes cement, fertilizer, and sugar factories, as well as textile mills.

Shirazi, al- *See* Hafiz, Shams al-Din Muhammad

Shirazi, Mirza Hasan (d. 1896) Nineteenth-century Iranian jurist, cleric, and marja al-taqlid. Issued a fatwa against the shah's grant of the tobacco monopoly to a British subject in the early 1890s. The fatwa mobilized thousands in protest, resulted in cancellation of the concession, and led to a crisis between the British and Iranian govenrments.

Shirazi, Sadr al-Din al- (d. 1641) Also known as Mulla Sadra. Iranian philosopher and theologian. Synthesized elements of the Peripatetics, illuminationists, mystics, and Muslim theologians. Replaced the influence of Aristotelian philosophy on Shii theology with Neoplatonic emanationism. Drew on the philosophical tradition of Ibn Sina and on the illuminationist theories of Suhrawardi. Greatly influenced by Ibn al-Arabi's cosmology, but attempted to create his own synthesis of cosmological ideas. Highly influential in Persia, Muslim India, and Shii Iraq. His philosophy was taught in eighteenth-century India and revived in Qajar Persia. The message of his magnum opus, *Al-asfar al-arbaah* (The four journeys), came gradually to be known as "divine wisdom." This powerful intellectual tradition has continued into the late twentieth century and remains the subject of theological commentaries today.

Shirazi, Sayyid Ali Muhammad (d. 1850) Also known as Bab. Messianic religious leader. First individual in Islamic history to make a serious attempt to break away from Islam in order to found a separate religion with distinct books and laws. Initially claimed to be the gate (bab) or spokesperson for the Hidden Imam of Imami Shiism and an interpreter of the Quran; later he claimed to be the imam in person, and then a divine manifestation. Most of his prophetic career was spent under house arrest or in prison in northwest Iran. Shirazi was shot by a firing squad in 1850. His followers declared a formal break with Islam in 1848, and the movement became known as Babism. Bahais

Shii Islam

Shii Muslims, the followers or party of Ali, believe that Muhammad's religious leadership, spiritual authority, and divine guidance were passed on to his descendants, beginning with his son-in-law and cousin, Ali ibn Abi Talib, his daughter, Fatimah, and their sons, Hasan and Husayn. The defining event of Shiism was the martyrdom of Husayn, his male family members, and many companions at Karbala (Iraq) in 681 by the Umayyads, granting an element of passion and pathos to Shiism.

There are three main branches of Shiis today: the Zaydis, the Ismailis (Seveners), and the Ithna Asharis (Twelvers or Imamis). The Zaydis (followers of Zayd ibn Ali ibn al-Husayn) are located in Yemen, Iraq, and parts of Africa. They represent the activist groups who believe that the imam ought to fight for his rights and be a ruler of state. The Ismailis (Seveners) are named after the seventh imam, Ismail. They founded the Fatimid Empire (909–1171) and represent esoteric Shiism. The Ithna Asharis (Twelvers or Imamis) are the largest and most moderate group. They believe in twelve imams, beginning with Ali and ending with Muhammad al-Mahdi, who went into occultation and is expected to return at the end of time as the messianic imam who will restore justice and equity on earth. He is therefore referred to as the imam al-muntazar, the expected or awaited imam.

Historically, the Shiis enjoyed the most favorable conditions under Buwayhid rule (945–1055) in Baghdad and Iran. During this period, major collections of Shii hadith were compiled and Shii legal thought was formulated. Two popular Shii commemorations were instituted in Baghdad at this time: the remembrance of the martyrdom of Husayn on the tenth day of Muharram and the festival of Ghadir al-Khumm, commemorating the Prophet's nomination of Ali as his successor, on the eighteenth day of Dhu al-Hijjah. It was also at this time that public mourning ceremonies for Husayn were initiated, shrines were built for the imams, and the custom of pilgrimage to these shrines was established at the popular level. Scholars of the Mongol, Safavid, and Qajar periods also made major contributions to Shii literature, philosophy, theology, and law.

Shii political thought entered its modern phase during the Iranian Constitutional Revolution of 1905–11, when Shiis were divided between the forces of constitutionalism, modernism, reason, and secularism, on one hand, and more traditional interpretations of faith, religious law, and the role of clerics, on the other. The clerical establishment ultimately joined with secular revolutionaries in opposing European colonialism. By the 1940s and 1950s Shii political thought was addressing issues such as Communism and nationalism, often presenting Shiism as an alternative. During the 1960s the institutional bases for the propagation of modern Shii political thought were formed through Quranic schools and voluntary associations of Muslim university students and professionals. Informal gatherings led by clerics and intellectuals also promoted Shii political mobilization. The most important event of the 1960s was the 1963 uprising led by Ayatollah Ruhollah Khomeini (d. 1989), who called for the ouster of the shah.

The most effective ideologue of modern Shiism was Ali Shariati (d. 1977). In the late 1960s and 1970s Shariati combined Islam with Third Worldism and revolution into an activist political ideology. He identified Western imperialism, cultural colonialism, social injustice, and political repression as the greatest contemporary challenges. In contrast to the passive, suffering role typically assumed by Shiis, Shariati cast Shiism as activist, radical, revolutionary, classless, and opposed to tyranny and repression. Shariati inspired the Iranian clerics Ayatollah Khomeini, who

(continued)

Shii Islam (continued)

emerged at the head of the Iranian Islamic revolution, and Imam Musa al-Sadr
(d. 1978), who encouraged the Shiis of
Lebanon to take an activist role in struggling for better socioeconomic conditions and political representation.

Khomeini was the most rhetorically
successful revolutionary Shii. Opposed to
the increasing secularization of Pahlavi
society and American domination of Iranian political, social, economic, and cultural life, Khomeini introduced the principle of *vilayat-i faqih* as the foundation
for Islamic government. According to
this principle, in the absence of an imam,
the leadership of Muslim nations is to be
entrusted to Shii jurists, who are to rule
by virtue of their knowledge of sacred
law and their ability to regulate the daily
affairs of Muslims. The resultant Islamic
revolution of 1979 and constitution of
the Islamic Republic of Iran represent the
ideological institutionalization of modern Shii political ideas. In the postrevolutionary period, such reformist thinkers
as Abd al-Karim Soroush have tried to
move ideological debates beyond factionalism toward serious engagement of
the consequences of the success of the
Islamic revolution.

consider Shirazi a forerunner of the founder
of their faith, Baha Allah. *See also* Babism;
Bahais

Shirk Association. Theological term referring to the association of someone or something with God, that is, putting someone or
something in the place of God, thus deviat-
ing from monotheism. *See also* Polytheists

Shrine Arabic *qubbah*. Site considered a locus
of spirituality, often dedicated to deceased
descendants of Muhammad or saints or associated with natural phenomena. A visit to
a shrine is believed to offer spiritual blessings. Major shrines have annual festivals that
attract tens of thousands of pilgrims. Some
shrines, particularly Shii ones, have religious
schools associated with them, along with
bureaucracies to accept donations, support
humanitarian works, and administer endowed properties that produce revenue for
the upkeep of the shrine. Because of their
marginal status in mosques, women tend to
visit shrines to make requests or offer prayers
more frequently than do men.

Shubha Sophism. In Islamic law, an illicit
act that seems like a licit one. Often used by
jurists to reduce severity of punishment in
criminal cases.

Shughni-Rushani Language group within
the family of Pamir languages, which belong
to the Modern Eastern Iranian languages.
Languages of the Shughni-Rushani group are
spoken in the Central Asian republic of Tajikistan, particularly in the autonomous region of Badakhshan; in the Afghan province
of Badakhshan; and in Xinjiang in China.
The Shughni-Rushani language group consists of five languages: Shughni, with the
Bajuv and Shahdara dialects; Rushani, with
the Xuf dialect; Bartangi; Roshorvi; and Sar-
iqoli, which is spoken in China. Shughni is
the most important language in the Shughni-
Rushani group, being the language of the
capital of Tajik Badakshan, Khorog, and a
lingua franca within Badakhshan. None of
the languages of the Shughni-Rushani group
has achieved the status of a written language,
although recently attempts have been made
to design a suitable script for Shughni; Tajik
or Persian is generally used for writing. The
majority of the speakers of Shughni-Rushani
are Ismailis, for whom Persian is also
important as a language of religion. There
are no recent reliable data regarding the
number of speakers of Shughni-Rushani: a
very rough estimate is around three hundred
thousand people. Descriptions of these languages and most of the dialects are available
in Russian.

Shura Consultation. Based on Quranic in-
junction to Muhammad to consult with his
followers (3:159) and to Muslims to consult
with each other in conducting their affairs

(42:38). Modern scholars consider shura to be the basis for the implementation of democracy. Liberal scholars argue that shura declares the sovereignty of people in electing representative leaders to democratic instutitions designed to act in the public interest. For conservative thinkers, shura must be based on the principle of the ultimate sovereignty of God and geared toward implementation of traditional Islamic law.

Shuubiyyah Movement Name given to a literary movement that arose during Abbasid times, stressing the merits of non-Arab and particularly Persian linguistic traditions. The movement arose in reaction to the perceived privileging of Arab over non-Arab linguistic traditions and, by extension, Arabs over non-Arabs. Gave rise to the characterization of Arabs and Arabic as relatively uncivilized and unrefined.

Shuyuiyyah *See* Communism and Islam

Sibai, Mustafa al- (d. 1964) Syrian political thinker, educator, writer, and founder of the Syrian Muslim Brotherhood. Involved in political activism in Egypt, where he was a member of the Muslim Brotherhood and associated with Hasan al-Banna. Demonstrated against the British in Egypt and was imprisoned. Founded Shabab Muhammad (Muhammad's Youth) upon his return to Syria. Arrested and tortured by the French. Formed the Muslim Brotherhood in Syria in 1946 through a merger of different Islamic organizations; was elected as its general guide. Conceived of the movement as ruh (spirit) intended to raise public consciousness to achieve comprehensive Islamic reform, rather than as an organization or political party. Argued in *Socialism of Islam* that Islam teaches a unique type of socialism conforming with human nature based on five natural rights: life, freedom, knowledge, dignity, and ownership. Viewed the role of the state as that of a regulator, through nationalization of essential public services, implementation of Islamic laws on mutual social responsibility, and sanctions.

Sibawayhi, Abu Bishr al- (eighth century) Pioneering Arab grammarian of the school of Basra (Iraq) and the author of the definitive work on Arabic grammar, known as *Kitab fil-nahw* (The book of grammar). His background is unknown, although it is clear that al-Sibawayhi died young. Most likely born to Persian parents and probably died in Persia. While the science of Arabic grammar has evolved since al-Sibawayhi, his work remains the definitive starting point for contemporary studies of Arabic grammar and continues to inspire pride in the uniqueness of the Arabic language.

Siddiqui, Kalim (d. 1996) Indian British writer and activist. Founded the Muslim Institute in London in 1972. Campaigned through his writings for political Islam, declaring his support for the revolution in Iran and Ayatollah Khomeini's fatwa against Salman Rushdie. In 1989 founded the Muslim Parliament, which he led until his death.

Siffah, al- Characteristic, attribute, or capacity. Used in theology to describe the divine attributes, which are usually understood metaphorically rather than literally since Islam rejects assignment of human characteristics to God. Usually listed as seven in number: knowledge, power, life, will, speech, hearing, and sight.

Siffin, Battle of Battle in 657 between two Muslim armies, the Iraqi forces of Caliph Ali ibn Abi Talib and the Syrian forces of the governor, Muawiyah. The two were reluctant to fight each other initially but engaged in battle after a seventy-seven-day stalemate. The battle ended in extensive bloodshed on both sides followed by an arbitration agreement. The Kharijis split from Ali due to the lack of a decisive victory. A major step toward the establishment of the Umayyad caliphate.

Sijistani, Abu Daud al-, Sulayman ibn al-Ashath (d. 889) Collector of one of six Sunni canonical sources of hadith, *Kitab al-sunan*. The collection particularly focuses on what is commanded, permitted, or forbidden by Islamic law. It also addresses violence, disruption of order, and eschatology. The work contains notes by its author indicating the relative strength or weakness of tradition in question, which encouraged the development of systematic criticism of individual traditions. The believed transmitters were trustworthy unless formal proof existed indicating otherwise. The work was highly acclaimed by eleventh-century scholars. He was the teacher of al-Tirmidhi (the author of another canonical collection) and traveled widely for his studies, gaining a reputation for piety and scholarship. He settled and taught near Basra in present-day Iraq.

Sijistani, Abu Yaqub Ishaq ibn Ahmad al- (d. ca. 971) Prominent early Ismaili dai (missionary) and author, who also carried the curious nickname Panbah-danah (Arabic *khayshafuj*), meaning "cotton seed." Eventually succeeded to the leadership of the Ismaili dawah (missionary) activities in his native Sistan (Arabicized to Sijistan), as well as Khurasan and other parts of Iran and Transoxiana. Influential early member of the Iranian school of philosophical Ismailism characterized by complex metaphysical systems in which Ismaili theology was amalgamated with a variety of philosophical traditions, notably Neoplatonism. Writings provide a main source for understanding the early development of this distinctively Ismaili tradition of philosophical theology and its cosmological doctrines.

Silsilah Formal chain of spiritual descent in Islamic mysticism (Sufism); the process of transmission of ritual from original teacher to students. The origin is usually traced from Muhammad through the founder of the order to the present student. Linking to the chain is believed to occur when the student is initiated into the tariqah, swearing an oath of allegiance to the founder and to the founder's current earthly deputy, and receiving the order's secret litany (wird), which transmits the spiritual power of the chain. Silsilah also is used to determine leadership within some orders, as well as spiritual seniority. It reflects the rise of the more formal

organization of Sufi orders and the greater authority of shaykhs over disciples.

Simnani, Ala al-Dawlah (d. 1336) Iranian mystic and philosopher. A member of the Kubrawi Sufi order; maintained that strict adherence to the Quran and Islamic law was the basis of the mystic path. He was critical of Ibn al-Arabi's monism and systematized Kubrawi meditations, focusing on visions of light and color.

Sin A breach of the laws and norms laid down by a religion. The sin may be one of omission or commission; any violation of a religious law or ethical norm is a sin, but one is held accountable only for those intentionally committed. It arises from a willful misuse of humans' God-given freedom. Islam recognizes major and minor sins; holding someone or something equal to God (shirk) is the most serious and unforgivable sin. Islam does not accept the theory of original sin; Adam and Eve ate the forbidden fruit, then sought and received forgiveness.

Sinai Mountain and peninsula in Egypt. The mountain is also known as Jabal Musa (the mountain of Moses). Highlighted in the Quran as the place where God delivered the tablets of law (7:139), assembled the prophets, and took a compact from them (3:75).

Sinan, Rashid al-Din (d. 1193) Medieval Nizari Ismaili missionary in Syria. He reorganized the Nizari community in Syria and played a prominent role in the regional politics of his time, entering into shifting alliances with Salah al-Din (Saladin), the Crusaders, and others to safeguard the independence of his community. Sinan was the original "Old Man of the Mountain" of the Crusaders, who made the Nizari Ismailis famous in medieval Europe as the Assassins together with a number of tales regarding their secret practices. An outstanding organizer and statesman, Sinan led the Syrian Nizaris for some three decades, to the peak of their power, until his death.

Sinan Abdul Menan (d. 1588) Also known as Mimar Sinan. Chief architect to the Ottoman court. Emerging from the devshirme system, Sinan began his career as a military engineer, eventually becoming chief architect in 1538. Biographers attribute to him over 350 buildings, including mosques, madrasas, bridges, hospitals, palaces, baths, and mausoleums. His masterpieces include the mosques of Suleyman I in Istanbul (1559) and of Selim II in Edirne (1572), where the mature Ottoman style reached its zenith. Sinan's buildings are characterized by elegance and clarity of interior space.

Sindhi, Ubaydullah (d. 1944) Indian Sikh convert to Islam and a leading exponent of the ideas of Shah Wali Allah. Joined Deobandi movement. Forged links between ulama and students at Aligarh University. Emphasized the reformist, progressive tendencies of Islam. Taught that Islam preaches social revolution and overthrow of imperialism and feudalism. Advocated peaceful jihad. Exiled by the British.

Sindi, Shaykh Muhammad Hayya al- (d. ca. 1750) Major hadith teacher in Medina. Born in India. Member of the Naqshbandi Sufi order. Encouraged the practice of independent reasoning (ijtihad) in legal matters, rather than adherence to medieval interpretations. Opposed to popular religious practices associated with saints and tombs. Taught and influenced several major eighteenth-century revivalists and reformists.

Sinf *See* Guilds

Singapore Muslim Religious Council Established under the Administration of Muslim Law Act of 1966. Inaugurated in 1968. Supreme Islamic religious authority in Singapore. Advises government on matters relating to Islam. Administers a mosque-building program, manages mosques and endowment properties, and coordinates the annual pilgrimage to Mecca. Forms an appeals board for divorce proceedings and inheritance disputes.

Sinkili, Abd-al-Rauf al- (d. 1693) Acehnese (North Sumatran) scholar who played a major role in translating Islamic texts into Malay. Born in Singkel, North Sumatra, he studied in Arabia between 1641 and 1660 under scholars such as Ahmad al-Qushashi and Ibrahim al-Kurani. Returned to North Sumatra and taught under the patronage of the Acehnese court. His best-known work is an adaptive Malay rendering of al-Suyuti's *Tafsir al-Jalalayn* (The tafsir of the two Jalals). It is the earliest complete explication of the Quran in Malay, still widely used in local madrasas.

Sipah-i Pasdaran-i Inqilab-i Islami Islamic Revolutionary Guard Corps. Iranian military force formed after the Islamic revolution of 1979 to purge the existing armed forces of elements considered un-Islamic and a threat to the revolutionary regime. Its role as guardian of the revolution is affirmed in the constitution. Includes mlitary command units for army, air force, and navy, and cabinet-level ministry. Activities have included restoring order to cities and dislodging opposition groups from government positions in the early days of revolution, suppressing ethnic uprisings throughout the country in 1979, helping Ayatollah Khomeini's efforts to monopolize power during attacks by leftist mujahidin in 1981, and actively participating in the Iran-Iraq War.

Sipah-i-Sahaba Army of Prophet's Companions. A militant Sunni group in Pakistan blamed for a stream of anti-Shii violence in the country. Founded by a Sunni cleric, Mawlana Haq Nawaz Jhangvi, in the mid-1980s. The group wants Pakistan to be declared a Sunni Muslim state and Shiis to be designated in the constitution as a non-Muslim minority. Jhangvi was assassinated in 1990 in a sectarian attack and was succeeded by Mawlana Azam Tariq. The group was banned in December 2001 by Pakistan's government for its involvement in sectarian violence.

Sipahsalar, (Mirza) Husayn Khan Mushir al-Dawlah (d. 1881) Iranian statesman and modernizing politician under Nasir al-Din Shah Qajar (d. 1896). Served in India and Russia. Appointed ambassador to Istanbul, minister of justice, minister of war, then prime minister (1871–73). Believed in the modernization and westernization of Iran. Introduced administrative, military, and legal reforms. Promoted the railroad concession to Baron Julius de Reuter. Removed from office under pressure from opponents of reforms and the concession.

Sirah Literary genre that developed out of narrative histories of Muhammad's life and activities, often comparing him to other prophets. Similar to Jewish and Christian traditions, sirah chronicles the creation and history of the world up through the time of Muhammad, showing Muhammad's life and work as the fulfillment of divine revelation and providing a basis for Muslim views of history. Sirah has been expanded to encompass the lives of Muhammad's Companions and of saints, treated in similar format. Used as sources for models for interacting with non-Muslims, processes of conversion, correct behavior in the face of adversity, and a guide for social and legal reforms. *See also* Hagiography

Sirat al-Mustaqim, al- The right way; the straight path. Phrase used thirty-three times in the Quran to describe proper conduct and correct religious belief and practice. The "right way" is also applied to the Quran itself, as it reveals broad moral directives, with some legal prescriptions, as guidance for humanity.

Sirhindi, Ahmad (d. 1624) Indian Sufi whose ideas shaped the second (Mujaddidi) phase of the Naqshbandi order. Prolific writer who addressed the need for revival of orthodoxy, suppression of superstitious Sufi practices, and humiliation of infidels. Prime concern was to integrate Sufi ideas within a Sunni framework. Promoted the concept of wahdat al-shuhud (unity of appearance) over Ibn al-Arabi's wadat al-wujud (unity of Being). New emphasis focused on worldly action, rather than just otherworldly con-

templation, forming a basis for involvement with political power and emphasis on orthodoxy. Titled "mujaddid-i alf-i thani" (renewer of the second millennium of Islam). His notion of obedience to Islamic law as a means of achieving spiritual realization was widely accepted by the Naqshbandis and carried by his successors into Central Asia, Turkey, and Arab lands

Sirr Mystery, secret, heart-secret. The innermost part of the heart. In Islamic mysticism, the locus for spiritual revelation and witnessing the divine presence. The designation "secret" alludes to the intimate relation between the mystic and God.

Siyam *See* Fasting

Siyar (1) Arabic term connoting a particular manner of conduct as recorded in the biography of an exemplary person. The singular form (sirah) usually refers to the biography of Muhammad. The plural form (siyar) is used for the exemplary lives of saints, typically found in collective biographies or biographical dictionaries, as well as for the history of political campaigns. (2) Conduct of state in relation to other communities. Technical meaning acquired by the term in the second century of Islam, as popularized by scholars of Hanafi jurisprudence, especially al-Shaybani (d. 804). Includes conduct of war, conduct of believers in their relations with nonbelievers in enemy territory, and conduct of believers with whom they have entered into treaties. Today the term refers generally to international law (Arabic qanun al-dawli).

Siyasat Nameh *See* Nizam al-Mulk, Abu Ali al-Hasan ibn al-Hasan ibn Ali ibn Ishaq al-Tusi

Slave *See* Abd

Slavery Slavery was common in the pre-Islamic communities of the Mediterranean basin, Africa, and Asia. Early Islam mitigated the conditions of human bondage: it forbade the enslavement of Muslims and non-Muslims living under Muslim rule. The only legal slaves were non-Muslims who were imprisoned or bought beyond the borders of Islamic rule, or the sons and daughters of those already in captivity. Manumission was recommended as a meritorious act. Since the mid-twentieth century, slavery has been virtually extinct in the central Islamic lands, though reports from Sudan and Somalia reveal that slavery is still practiced in border areas as a result of continuing warfare.

Social Justice *See* Maslahah

Socialism and Islam Although generally considered to be of European origin, socialism (Arabic *ishtirakiyyah*) also has roots in the Arab Middle East. Jamal al-Din al-Afghani believed that socialism was an indigenous Arab doctrine located in pre-Islamic Arabian Bedouin traditions. He claimed that the framers of the initial Islamic state in the seventh century adopted these traditions as a structural basis from which to organize and regulate society. Islamic reformists began articulating religiously based ideas of social justice in the 1930s and 1940s. They asserted Islam's universality and commitment to comprehensive human and economic justice, returning to the Quran for confirmation of Islam's spiritual and material compatibility with social progress. Islamic socialism took root in the Middle East and North Africa and was most successfully used as an ideology in Egypt, Syria, and Iraq. Reformists saw Islamic socialism as a cure for colonial control, economic backwardness, human exploitation, and moral bankruptcy. Spiritual and economic improvement were not possible until the lives of people could be improved and the decent treatment and justice stipulated by the Quran could be provided to them. Islamic socialism allows the public sector to exist side by side with the private sector, advocating harmonious relations between social groups, not class warfare. The basis of social solidarity in the Islamic socialist model is a combination of equality, justice, mutuality, and responsibility. *See also* Arab Socialism; Sibai, Mustafa al-

Society for the Victory of Islam *See* Jamatul Nasril Islam

Society of Call and Guidance *See* Jamiat al-Dawah wa'l-Irshad

Society of Islamic Students *See* Islami Jamiat Tulaba

Society of Militant Clergy *See* Jamiah-yi Ruhaniyat-i Mubariz

Society of Muhammad's Youth *See* Jamiah Shabab Sayyidna Muhammad

Sokoto Caliphate Founded in the nineteenth century in Nigeria by Uthman Dan Fodio, who led a holy war against rulers of Hausa states in order to unite the populace under the caliphate, which was a loose confederation of emirates that recognized the leader as "commander of the faithful." Many descendants of the founder became part of the first generation of national leaders after Nigeria achieved independence in 1960. The sultan of Sokoto is still regarded as the spiritual leader of the Muslim community, although the legislative and executive functions of government have passed to local, state, and federal bodies. *See also* Dan Fodio, Uthman; Fulani Dynasty

Solomon Described in the Quran as the son of David, king renowned for his wisdom, and builder of the Temple in Jerusalem. Inherited both his father's kingdom and his spiritual insight and prophetic office. Impressed the Queen of Sheba with his glorious kingdom and converted her to Islam, in the Quranic account.

Somalia, Islam in Ninety-nine percent of Somalia's population is Muslim; the Qadiri, Ahmadi, Salihi, and Rifai Sufi orders have greatly influenced Somali Islam. General Mohamed Siyad Barre's coup (1969) and his repressive regime's execution of ten religious leaders caused a dramatic Islamic renewal and the emergence of Islamic opposition groups. During the period he was in power, Barre's troops massacred hundreds of religious leaders and their followers. Barre's fall (1990) resulted in chaos, civil wars, banditry, and famine, leading to a humanitarian intervention by the United Nations under American leadership in December 1992. The main Somali Islamic revivalist movement, al-Ittihad al-Islami (Islamic Unity), which operates in the northeast, is known to be linked with Sudan and Iran.

Son *See* Ibn

Soroush, Abd al-Karim (b. 1945) Iranian intellectual and political activist. Studied pharmacology in Iran, and chemistry, history, and the philosophy of science in England. He participated in the Iranian revolution of 1979, serving as one of its ideologues. Later he criticized theocracy and advocated the distinction between religion as the sacred and immutable body of beliefs and doctrines and religious knowledge as historically constructed by its practitioners; this led to serious tensions between his followers, mostly university students and young intellectuals, and their opponents. He was censured and barred from public teaching. He is currently associated with the Iranian Academy of Philosophy.

Soul *See* Nafs; Ruh

South Africa, Islam in Under 2 percent of the population is Muslim, 2 percent Hindu, and 68 percent Christian; the rest practice African traditional religions. Muslims arrived in two groups: involuntary immigrants such as slaves, political prisoners, and criminals brought by Dutch colonists to the Cape region (1652–1807), and indentured laborers and free passengers from India and Malaya brought by British colonists to Natal and Transvaal (1873–1880). In the 1990s some Muslims supported the African National Congress (ANC), while others supported the Pan-African Congress (PAC); conservative groups such as the Jamiat al-Ulama remained neutral. Many individual Muslims participated actively in the struggle against apart-

heid and became national heroes, such as Imam Haron. Few Muslim parties politically participate in South Africa—the African Muslim Party and the Islamic Party wield no significant national power. In 1994, the ANC appointed a Muslim, Abdullah Omar, to its cabinet as minister of justice.

South Asia, Islam in Nearly 390 million people of the Indian subcontinent and Sri Lanka either define themselves as Muslims or are so defined by others. They belong to myriad groups whose members speak different languages and confront disparate socioeconomic circumstances. Islam arrived in India through two different routes: military campaigns by Turko-Afghans in the north, and southern Arabian traders in the south. The dominant political power from the thirteenth to the nineteenth centuries was the Mughal Empire, which left a rich tradition of Islamic scholarship in Arabic, Persian, Urdu, and English. British colonial control ended Mughal power in 1857. The subcontinent was partitioned into Hindu-dominated India and Muslim Pakistan in 1947, reflecting sectarian hostilities engendered during Muslim dominance. East Pakistan became independent Bangladesh in 1971 following a bloody civil war. Religious-based conflicts continue on the subcontinent, and 120 million Indian Muslims feel threatened by the rise of militant Hinduism and a weakening of the secular foundations of the state. *See also* Afghanistan, Islam in; Bangladesh, Islam in; India, Islam in; Kashmir; Khilafat Movement; Mughal Empire; Pakistan, Islam in

Southeast Asia, Islam in About 220 million Muslims live in an archipelago that stretches from southern Thailand through Malaysia, Singapore, and Indonesia and north to the southern Philippines. Additional isolated pockets of Muslims live in Burma (Myanmar), northern and southern Thailand, and Cambodia. The majority of Muslims in the archipelago speak Malay or one of its variants. Islam spread to the region in the twelfth century via Arab-controlled trade involving the Mediterranean, Central Asia, and the Indian subcontinent. Islamic philosophy and accounts of the great Muslim kingdoms of West and Central Asia offered indigenous rulers both justification and model for rule. Islam was successful in the archipelago despite preexisting Hinduism and Buddhism because it was initially accepted and later imposed by rulers on the population. Islam was transmitted in Malay, which was the language of all classes. Thus, Islam came to be associated with the state and the Malay language. An extensive and complex literature inspired by Islam developed. During the colonial period, religion was divorced from the state. Islam became a vehicle of protest and anticolonial agitation. West Asian reform movements arrived in the late nineteenth century, sparking an Islamic revival. In the postindependence period, Islam has been institutionalized in governmental ministries and offices of religious affairs in Malaysia, Singapore, Borneo, and Indonesia. Islamic parties are contributors to the political process in all but Thailand and the Philippines, where Muslim minorities sometimes resist the government in the name of Islam.

Spain *See* Andalus, al-

Spirit *See* Nafs; Ruh

Sri Lanka, Islam in Sri Lankan Muslims are often called Moors and are largely Sunni Muslims following the Shafii school of law. The small Muslim community, numbering about 1.2 million out of a total population of 15 million, is largely urban. They trace their ancestry through migration and conversion dating back to the seventh century. Sri Lankan Muslims were forced to develop in isolation from the subcontinent's other Muslims for three centuries during occupations by the Portuguese and British. A revival of Islamic learning, observance, piety, scriptural norms, and ritual activities was brought by Sufi orders in the nineteenth century. Muslims supported the nationalist movement and have been included in governments that have ruled Sri Lanka since 1947.

State *See* Islamic State

Stevens, Cat *See* Islam, Yusuf

Struggle *See* Jihad

Suavi, Ali (d. 1878) Journalist and political activist in the Ottoman Empire. Briefly involved in the establishment of the Young Ottoman movement but broke with more liberal reformers. Emphasized the Islamic dimensions of reform and was a pioneer in articulating Turkish nationalism and pan-Turkish ideology. Killed while participating in a revolt.

Subannu al-Muslimin West African educational association formed in 1949. Advocated ideas and practices similar to those of Salafi movements in other countries. Identified by ideological position rather than ethnicity or social class. Founded numerous schools throughout West Africa, reviving interest in locally led, rather than French-style, education. Focused on the teaching of religious studies and the Arabic language. Not politically oriented as a whole, although individual members were politically active in the anti-French resistance. Worked to build a sense of a broader Islamic community. Allied with the Rassemblement Démocratique Africain (RDA) in political matters. Led to the 1957 creation of a cultural association called the Union Culturelle Musulmane.

Subhan Allah Praise be to God. An expression similar to *hallelujah*. Glorification (tasbih) of God is essential to the practice of divine remembrance (dhikr). The expression is frequently employed in the daily language of Muslims. It forms part of an optional litany after each prayer; it is uttered in the various postures of the five daily ritual prayers (salat) and is also commonly used as an expression of surprise or admiration if something good has occurred.

Sub-Saharan Africa, Islam in Four of the most populous countries in Africa—Nigeria, Egypt, Ethiopia, and Zaire—account for well over 160 million Muslims; nearly half of the continent is now Muslim. There were five primary modes by which Islam entered Sub-Saharan Africa: conquest (eleventh-century al-Moravid invasions of West Africa); Muslim migration and settlement in non-Muslim areas (Yemeni, Omani, and Indian Muslims settled in East Africa, and Malay slaves were imported into South Africa); trans-Saharan trade among modern-day Guinea, Mali, Senegal, Niger, and parts of Uganda, Zaire, Malawi and Mozambique; dawah (mission-ary activities); and periodic revivalist move-ments. The last two modes of transmission were sometimes internal, as part of a puri-fying jihad or conducted by self-proclaimed Mahdis. Muslim-Christian relations vary markedly throughout the region, depending on history and culture: relations in Senegal, South Africa, Malawi, and Tanzania reflect the liberality of indigenous African culture; relations in Nigeria, Sudan, and Ethiopia re-veal ethnoreligious cleavages, the roots of which can be traced to colonial rule.

Successors Refers to those Muslims of the second generation who came after the gen-eration of personal Companions of the Prophet. People designated as successors (tabiun) personally knew at least one of the Companions. The next generation of Mus-lims who knew at least one of the first suc-cessors is known as the "successors of the successors." The successors played an im-portant role in hadith transmission. Among the best-known successors is the pious trad-itionist Hasan al-Basri (d. 728).

Sudan, Islam in Seventy percent of Sudan's thirty-five million people are Muslims, mostly living in the northern two-thirds of the country; 5 percent are Christians, and the rest practice African traditional religions. Modern Sudanese history begins with the Ottoman Turkish-Egyptian invasion of 1821. Nineteenth-century Sudanic Africa wit-nessed successful jihad movements in re-sponse to foreign intervention. The most famous uprising occurred with the procla-

mation of Muhammad Ahmad as the Mahdi (Expected One) in 1881–89; Turkish troops were forced out, leaving the British to estab-lish Anglo-Egyptian Sudan between 1898 and 1902. Sufi brotherhoods (Qadiri, Khatmi, Sanusi, and Shadhili) flourished, blending local customs and traditions into an egalitarian Islam. Postindependence Su-dan (1956) was governed by civilian re-gimes, based on Muslim political parties, and military regimes. The period was marked by sporadic fighting between the North and South. In 1983 the military dic-tator Jafar al-Numayri (r. 1969–85) issued decrees establishing Islamic law as the law of the state. Southern Sudanese activists organized the Sudan People's Liberation Movement (SPLM) and resumed the 1950s civil war. A 1989 coup d'etat brought to power an Islamist regime formally headed by Omar al-Bashir but guided by Islamist leader Hasan al-Turabi. Its Islamist agenda isolated Sudan, and its severe repression of dissent drove many moderates and Muslim Nubians into the opposition National Dem-ocratic Alliance (NDA) with the SPLM. Omar al-Bashir was reelected in January 2001; Tur-abi's own party ousted Turabi in favor of Bashir's allies.

Sufism in America Various Sufi orders, such as the Mawlawi, Nimatullahi, Khalwati-Jarrahi, Naqshibandi, Shadhali, and Qadiri, are to be found today in the United States and Canada. The earliest appearance of Su-fism in America goes back to the migration of some Albanian Muslims to North America in the first part of the twentieth century, and to such South Asian Sufis as Hazrat Inayat Khan and Bawa Muhyiddin. They were fol-lowed by Sufi masters from Turkey, Iran, and some Arab countries. The Mawlawi or-der (Mevlevi in Turkish, known popularly as the whirling dervishes) is among the best-known Sufi orders, due largely to the unprec-edented popularity of its founder, Jalal al-Din Rumi, the celebrated Persian Sufi poet and mystic, and the spiritual concert (sama) per-formed by his followers. In addition to nu-merous Sufi centers throughout the country,

Sufism

Islamic mysticism, often referred to as the internalization and intensification of Islamic faith and practice. Sufis strive to constantly be aware of God's presence, stressing contemplation over action, spiritual development over legalism, and cultivation of the soul over social interaction. In contrast to the academic exercises of theology and jurisprudence, which depend on reason, Sufism depends on emotion and imagination in the divine-human relationship. Sufism is unrelated to the Sunni/Shii split, schools of jurisprudence, social class, gender, geography, or family connections. It is closely associated with both popular religion and orthodox expressions of Islamic teachings. It has been both opposed and supported by the state.

Sufi rituals typically consist of the recitation of prayers, poems, and selections from the Quran, and methodical repetitions of divine names (dhikr) or Quranic formulas, such as the shahadah. In communal gatherings, Sufis perform dhikr aloud, often with musical accompaniment. The specific structure and format of the daily devotional exercises and activities were set by each order's founder as a special spiritual path. The founder was the spiritual guide for all followers, who swore a special oath of obedience to him as their shaykh (teacher). The record of the transmission of the ritual was preserved in a formal chain of spiritual descent (silsilah) extending back to the founder and then usually to Muhammad. Leadership was passed down either within a family line or on the basis of spiritual seniority within the tariqah (order). The typical initiation rite transmits a blessing (barakah) to the disciple, transforming his or her soul.

Tariqahs had become major social organizations by the twelfth century and enjoyed mass popularity by the fifteenth or sixteenth century. Orders range in form from simple preservation of the tariqah as a set of devotional exercises to vast interregional organizations with carefully de-

fined structures. Historically, Sufi orders have facilitated interregional interaction, education, and travel, and have supported reform, spiritual revival, and missionary activities. They have also provided organization and support for movements resisting foreign rule throughout the Islamic world.

Written expressions of Sufism include hagiographies, poetry, and literature describing the stations (maqamat) of spiritual ascent on the path to God and their accompanying psychological transformations. Sufis use terms such as sukr (intoxication) and sahu (sobriety) to describe their experiences. "Intoxicated" expressions of Sufism predominate in Sufi poetry, expressing joy and ecstasy. "Sober" Sufism offers methodical, specialized discussions of ritual, behavior, morality, Quranic exegesis, and the nature of God and the world. Intoxicated Sufism is popular among Muslims of all classes and persuasions. Sober Sufism tends to appeal to intellectuals.

Some modern observers have proclaimed the effective end of the Sufi orders, claiming that mystical religious experience and modernity are incompatible. Politically minded Muslims have made Sufism the scapegoat for Islam's alleged backwardness in comparison with the West, claiming that Sufism, as the religion of the common people, embodied superstition and un-Islamic elements adopted from local cultures. Eradication of Sufism was believed necessary in order for Islam to reclaim its birthright, including modern science and technology. However, by the end of the twentieth century, it was clear that Sufi orders remained a dynamic part of the religious life of the Islamic world and were active in the expansion of Islam in both rural areas and modern societies in the West and among the modernized intellectual elites within the Muslim world. Sufi organizations provide social cohesion in an increasingly mobile society, emphasizing

(continued)

Sufism (continued)

communal activities such as dhikr. They have helped to shape responses to the challenges to Muslim faith in the modern era by providing organizational bases for activist reformist programs and modern-style political parties. They have assisted in developing modernization programs and providing a framework for Islamic communal identity in the face of official efforts to suppress religion. Popular participation in Sufi gatherings and support for various types of tariqahs remain high throughout the Muslim world. Estimates of membership in Sufi orders in Egypt alone are in the millions, in contrast to the hundreds or thousands in the more militant Islamic revivalist organizations.

---

there is also a sizeable subculture of Sufi practices, with music, poetry, and even healing methods.

Suhrawardi, Shihab al-Din Yahya (d. 1191) Sufi philosopher who sought to synthesize philosophy and mysticism. Credited with founding illuminationism with his integration of Islam, Neoplatonism, and the wisdom of the ancient Persians, contained in his *Hikmat al-ishraq* (The wisdom of illumination). Wrote more than fifty works in both Arabic and Persian, including commentaries on Plato and Aristotle. Was opposed by orthodox ulama and executed, earning the nickname al-Shaykh al-Maqtul, "the slain shaykh." The Ishraqi and Nurbakhshi tariqahs trace their origins to him. *See also* Hikmat al-Ishraq

Suhrawardi Tariqah Orthodox Sufi order founded by Shihab al-Din Umar Suhrawardi in Baghdad in the twelfth century. Aristocratic order tied to religious scholars (ulama), Abbasid court, wealth, and urban living. Oriented toward classical Sufi doctrine and the Shafii school of Islamic law. Emphasized canonical prayer, fasting during Ramadan, preservation of the Prophetic tradition, and the superiority of prophethood

over sainthood. Widespread in India and Kashmir. Served as a mediator between the Delhi sultanate and tribal and frontier peoples. Rejected music, poetry, and the practice of prostration before the head of the order. Supported the forced conversion of Hindus and Buddhists. Inspired the sixteenth-century reformer Ahmad Sirhindi and reformers of the seventeenth and eighteenth centuries.

Suhur Last meal prior to daybreak during the month of Ramadan. Marks the beginning of the fast. After suhur, Muslims abstain from food, drink, and sex until the sun sets.

Suicide One phrase in the Quran mentions suicide (4:29), forbidding it, and the subject is little discussed in the exegetical literature. The Prophetic traditions clearly and frequently forbid suicide, reflecting the Islamic ethic of forbearance and patient acceptance of hardship as well as the belief that God, not humankind, has absolute power over human affairs and the term of human life. Despite this disapprobation, some Muslims in the Middle East and Islamic Southeast Asia have recently become known for their suicidal military missions. Some Muslims perceive these actions as a necessary part of active armed struggle and view the death that results as martyrdom, not suicide.

Sujud Prostration with forehead, palms, knees, and feet touching the ground. In every unit of prayer, two prostrations are mandatory while "Glory to my Lord, the Most High" is uttered or other similar praises of God recited. Sitting is required between the two prostrations. Also seen as an act of penitence and humility. The name of Muslim houses of worship (sing. *masjid*) is derived from the same root.

Sukr Intoxication. Stage of mystical or spiritual development characterized by ecstasy, loss of discernment. Occurs when the person is overcome by divine love. Although highly praised in poetry, it is generally considered a stage that needs to be surpassed by sober wisdom (sahu) and respect for shariah.

Sulaiman, Ibrahim Influential northern Nigerian intellectual. Considered to be part of a new generation of Muslim thinkers in the 1980s who actively affirm the Islamic identity of Nigeria and advocate activist religious renewal. Participated in a major effort to study the early-nineteenth-century jihad; his historical studies of the jihad of Uthman Dan Fodio and the subsequent Sokoto caliphate have been influential in shaping current historical understanding. Associated for many years with the Centre for Islamic Legal Studies of Ahmadu Bello University, Zaria, Nigeria.

Sulayman *See* Solomon

Sulaymanis *See* Bohras

Suleyman, Mawlay Abu al-Rabi ibn Muhammad (r. 1792–1822) Alawite sultan of Morocco, known for his piety, justice, and magnificent buildings. Proclaimed the sultan of Fez and Meknas in 1792, he subdued his rival brothers and extended his authority over the entire country by 1797. He confronted rebellions from Berber tribes and some Sufi orders and engaged in successive expeditions against his opponents in different parts on the country. By the end of his reign, the people of Fez rebelled against the sultan, who recaptured the city (1822). In an expedition against the Sharradi zawiyah (Sufi lodge) near Marrakesh, the sultan was captured and sent back to Marrakesh, where he died the same year. Erected several mosques, gates, bridges, and palaces in Morocco.

Suleyman, Sultan (d. 1873) Also known as Du Wenxiu. Led a Hui rebellion against the Chinese state in the southern Chinese province of Yunnan, near the Burmese border, in 1855, seeking independence for a new Muslim state, "the state that pacifies the south" (Pingnan Guo). The revolt represented an assertion of identity separate and distinct from that of the Chinese imperial administration and combined vigorous activism with self-assertion on the part of Hui Muslims, who previously had been more adaptationist in their approach. The movement may have had ties to earlier Naqshbandi revivalist movements in northwest China. The state he founded lasted until 1873, when it was crushed by Qing troops.

Suleyman the Magnificent Tenth and greatest sultan of the Ottoman Empire (r. 1520–66). As messianic "lord of the age" and "Grand Turk," he extended Ottoman sovereignty from Hungary (Mohacs, 1526) to Iraq, Moldavia to Yemen; exerted naval power in the western Mediterranean and the Indian Ocean and threatened the gates of Vienna (1529). Enforced Sunni Islam to counter Safavid Shiism in Iran. As lawgiver (kanuni), he reconciled dynastic and Islamic law, enforced justice, and organized provincial administration, land tenure, taxation, and educational/religious hierarchy. Presided over a revival of the arts, literature, and the Ottoman literary language; patronized the architect Sinan and wrote poetry for his wife Hurrem (Roxelana), the first of the dynasty's powerful women. Executed two viziers and two sons whose power grew excessive but was succeeded by the weakest, Selim II. Suleyman's reign was later considered a golden age and he "the second Solomon."

Sultan Arabic term denoting possession of power, might, or authority. In Quran, refers to divinely granted authority, usually in the context of prophecy. In hadith, denotes worldly power or possession of governmental authority. Used as a title by the Seljuk rulers of Baghdad, Ottomans, and rulers of Oman, Brunei, and Yang Di-Pertuan Agong of Malaysia.

Sultan Selim III (d. 1807) Ottoman sultan who implemented sweeping reforms, known as Nizam-i Jedid (new system), in civil administration and education. Established a new military corps armed and organized according to modern European principles and techniques of warfare. Introduced gun making, printing presses, and translation of Western works into Turkish. Introduced algebra, trigonometry, ballistics, mechanics, and metallurgy into school curricula in order to sustain the army. Imported teachers from Europe to implement the new curriculum. Deposed by a coalition of ulama and Janissaries who represented conservative forces opposed to Western influences. His reforms laid the foundation for the nineteenth-century Tanzimat reforms.

Sultanate Political office possessing real political power, created by the Seljuks (1038–1194). The sultan governed, adjudicated, and administered power in the name of the Abbasid caliph; as forces of power, the sultan and caliph legitimated each other. The caliph became the symbol of the religio-political unity of Sunni Islam against the political claims of the Shii Buwayhid amirs (r. 945–1055). The sultanate was not necessarily a territorial title. The dissolution of the Abbasid caliphate (1258) saw the rise of numerous sultanates in the form of courts and monarchies in Africa, Turkey, India, and the Indo-Malay archipelago. Some of the Deccan sultanates were Shii in orientation. The colonial era saw a reduction in the powers of the sultanates to that of representing the heads of Muslim colonies, responsible for administrating the religious and personal aspects of Islamic law. This political arrangement was either dissolved or further reduced with the rise of Muslim nation-states. Currently, only Brunei Darussalam and Oman use the sultanate as an official title.

Sumaa See Khanaqah

Sumayah bint Khubbat Also known as Sumayah Umm Ammar. Regarded as the first martyr in Islam. One of the early converts to Islam before the emigration to Abyssinia (ca. 615), she was tortured to death, along with her husband, Yasir, in Mecca by the notorious Qurayshi opponent of Islam, Abu Jahl.

Sunnah Established custom, normative precedent, conduct, and cumulative tradition, typically based on Muhammad's example. The actions and sayings of Muhammad are believed to complement the divinely revealed message of the Quran, constituting a source for establishing norms for Muslim conduct and making it a primary source of Islamic law. In the legal field, Sunnah complements and stands alongside the Quran, giving precision to its precepts. Sunnah encompasses knowledge believed to have been passed down from previous generations and representing an authoritative, valued, and continuing corpus of beliefs and customs. Early Muslim scholars developed and elaborated the concept of Prophetic Sunnah in order to capture as complete a picture of Muhammad's exemplary life as they could authenticate on the basis of hadith reports. The quest to memorialize Muhammad's life and ground it in historically verifiable process led to the biographical tradition known as sirah. This literature informed and inspired Muslim communities' interpretations of Islam as they sought to ground their own juridical, doctrinal, and historical identities in what they perceived to be normative Sunnah. Sunnah serves as a common template for Muslim groups and individuals, permitting them to represent a connection with the beginnings of Islam and acting as a common referent in the religious discourse of community formation and identity. It fosters self-identity and enhances the private moral lives of Muslims. See also Hadith

Supplication See Dua

Supreme Council of the Islamic Revolution in Iraq (SCIRI) Shii resistance group established in 1982 against the Iraqi regime. SCIRI, whose Arabic name is al-Majlis al-Ala li-Thawra al-Islamiyya fi'l-Iraq, is centered in southern Iraq, where the majority of the Shii population of Iraq lives. Headed by Ayatollah Mohammad Baqir al-Hakim and supported by Iran, SCIRI continues to lead a resistance movement with the aim of toppling Saddam Hussein's military rule. Part of the armed revolt orchestrated by the United States against Saddam after the Desert Storm

Sunni Islam

The Sunnis are the largest branch of the Muslim community, at least 85 percent of the world's 1.2 billion Muslims. The name is derived from the Sunnah, the exemplary behavior of the Prophet. All Muslims are guided by the Sunnah, but Sunnis stress it, as well as consensus (ijma; the full name of Sunnis is Ahl al-Sunnah wa'l-Ijma, people of the Sunnah and consensus). The other branch of Islam, the Shiis, are guided as well by the wisdom of Muhammad's descendants, but through his son-in-law Ali.

Sunni life is guided by four schools of legal thought—Hanafi, Maliki, Shafii, and Hanbali—each of which strives to develop practical applications of revelation and the Prophet's example.

Although Sunni Islam comprises a variety of theological and legal schools, attitudes, and outlooks conditioned by historical setting, locale, and culture, Sunnis around the world share some common points: acceptance of the legitimacy of the first four successors of Muhammad (Abu Bakr, Umar, Uthman, and Ali), and the belief that other Islamic sects have introduced innovations (bidah), departing from majority belief.

Sunni Islamic institutions developed out of struggles in early Islam over leadership of the Muslim community. Political and religious positions, articulated by scholars, arose out of disputes over the definition of "true" belief, the status of those who profess Islam but commit a great sin, freedom, and determinism. Sunnis tend to reject excessive rationalism or intellectualism, focusing instead on the spirit and intent of the Quran.

Reform movements within Sunni Islam began to appear during the eighteenth century in the works of scholars seeking to revive the dynamism of Islamic thought and life in order to meet the demands of the modern world. These movements gained momentum with the imposition of European colonial control throughout the Muslim world. The nineteenth and twentieth centuries witnessed the revival of Quranic studies as well as renewed commitment to science and education as the path to independence and development within the context of Islamic values and identity. Sunni thought of the eighteenth through twentieth centuries has also reexamined traditional Islamic law. Many modern reformers believe that fiqh (jurisprudence), as a human interpretation of divine law, should be open to reinterpretation in accordance with present circumstances and community needs. Almost all twentieth-century Muslim countries are debating the role of Islamic law and civil codes in modern society and the implications for constitutional law and the organization of the state. Many Islamic thinkers reject the notion that Islam requires a particular form of state and government, looking instead to Quranic principles such as shura (consultation) for guidance. Some believe that religion and the state are intended to be separate entities, while others, such as the Muslim Brotherhood and Jamaat-i Islami, believe that an Islamic state is necessary to the development of an Islamic social order. Many thinkers have studied in the West and are open to dialogue with the West and commitment to a common struggle for the causes of humanity. They have examined the impact of European imperialism, Western neocolonialism, exploitation by socialist-bloc countries, the Cold War, the displacement of Palestinians, the lack of democracy in the Muslim world, and other crisis factors. Most Muslim thinkers today stress the importance of justice, especially social justice, in Islam. A Universal Islamic Declaration of Human Rights has been propounded, next to that of the United Nations. Increasing attention is also being given to subjects such as women and gender, the family, religious freedom, pluralism, the status of minorities, and religious tolerance. Islam is increasingly em-

(continued)

Sunni Islam (continued)

phasized as a total way of life, encompassing both religious and worldly issues. Human beings are seen as God's stewards on earth, and the Muslim community is intended to reflect God's will. In this view, secularism is often rejected as being antithetical to religious values. Instead, Islam is presented as perfectly suited for human society, individually and collectively.

---

operation. Saddam's forces crushed the Shii uprising, killing and executing large number of SCIRI soldiers, members, and scholars.

Supreme Islamic Shii Council (Lebanon) Established by an act of the Chamber of Deputies (Lebanese parliament) in 1967 to form a representative body for Shiis independent of Sunnis. Came into existence in 1969 under the leadership of Musa al-Sadr. Demanded improved defenses in southern Lebanon, provision of development funds, construction and improvement of schools and hospitals, and an increased number of Shii appointees to senior government positions in order to improve living conditions and prospects for future employment for Shiis and provide more proportional representation in government. The Shii intelligentsia, emerging middle class, and traditional elites were actively involved.

Surah Usually translated as "chapter." The Quran is divided into 114 surahs, arranged by descending length rather than chronological order. These were divided by early commentators into the Meccan and Medinan periods of Muhammad's ministry. The Meccan surahs are broadly universal, while the Medinan surahs were often revealed in response to specific situations faced by the early Muslim community.

Surrogate Motherhood Contractual agreement whereby a woman agrees to be impregnated by a man or implanted with a fertilized embryo and then surrenders the baby to the man and his wife after birth. Infertility treatments, including in vitro fertilization, are permitted by some Muslim jurists, but not the use of donor sperm, eggs, or surrogate arrangements.

Suyuti, Abu al-Fadl Abd al-Rahman ibn Abi Bakr ibn Muhammad Jalal al-Din al-Khudayri al- (d. 1505) Prolific Egyptian scholar of virtually all disciplines—Quran commentary, jurisprudence, hadith, belles-lettres, biography, philology, Sufism, history, theology, and geography. Held teaching and legal positions within the Shafii school of law. Member of the Shadhili Sufi order, for which he wrote an apology offering praise of Sufi techniques, such as dhikr. Completed al-Mahalli Jalal al-Din's Quran commentary, which has come to be known as *Tafsir al-Jalalayn* (The commentary of the two Jalals) and is still widely in use for its conciseness and practicality.

Syndicate *See* Guilds; Niqabah

Syria, Islam in The Muslim population of Syria is composed of a Sunni majority and four minority Shii sects: Alawis, Druzes, Ismailis, and Twelver Shiis. In March 1963 a military coup installed a secular, socialist regime with an Alawi ruler (former president Hafez al-Assad; his son Bashir is the current president). The most intractable challenge to Baathist rule has come from Islamic groups, most notably the Muslim Brotherhood. The first Islamic uprising was in 1964 in Hama; other sectarian disturbances followed in 1967. Discontent lay mainly in the cities; rural areas had witnessed unprecedented economic progress under the Baathists, and Syria's religious minorities—Druze, Alawis, Christians, and Ismailis—were unsympathetic to Islamist aspirations. Insurrections by Islamic groups between 1979 and 1982 were quelled violently. Hafez al-Assad's regime demanded a strict separation of religion from politics; it is unclear how this policy might change under the current president.

Syrian Islamic Front Coalition of Syrian Islamic opposition groups led by the Muslim Brotherhood. Founded in 1980, it called for a number of legal, political, and economic reforms and the establishment of an Islamic state in Syria. Severely repressed by the Syrian government in the wake of the Hama uprising of 1982.

T

Tabaqah Cell in Sufi hospice (zawiyah or khanaqah) used for individual meditation, contemplation, and lodging. Usually located along the sides of a central courtyard and close to the mosque area. Adherents of many orders are required to engage in periodic individual retreats in these cells as part of their personal spiritual journey. *See also* Khalwah

Tabaqat Biographical dictionary. Arranged by rank, class, or generation. The selection of biographies can be thematic by religious profession, geographical by city or region, or chronological. Entries typically include the person's genealogy, marriage(s), child(ren), acceptance of Islam, declaration of allegiance to Muhammad (bayah), reports about the person's contributions to Islam, and information about death, funeral, and attending mourners. *See also* Hagiography

Tabari, Abu Jafar Muhammad ibn Jarir al- (d. 923) Early Muslim historian and collector of hadith. Shariah scholar and jurist. Inspired a short-lived school of Islamic law named after him that sought to develop a more perfect system of law. Traveled throughout the Fertile Crescent prior to settling in Baghdad to teach. Wrote a substantial commentary on the Quran, collecting the chief interpretations and offering his own perspective. His monumental *The History of Rulers and Kings* outlined the successes and failures of various groups called to follow God, with particular emphasis on the Muslim community; it records the personal decisions of individual Muslims, rather than the actions or decisions of rulers or institutions. The history is largely chronological, with little personal commentary or interpretation, but the selection, arrangement, and documentation of reports offer insight into his views. The inclusion of various versions of the same story and different perspectives and interpretations make the work appealing to a broad audience. Al-Tabari developed history as a field secondary to hadith study. He taught that history could only be transmitted, not deduced or inferred. *See also* Ibn al-Athir, Abu al-Hasan Ali Izz al-Din

Tabatabai, Muhammad Husayn (d. 1981) Also known as Allamah Tabatabai. One of the foremost Quranic commentators and traditional Persian philosophers of the twentieth century, prolific author, and renowned teacher. Resuscitated Islamic philosophy despite the opposition of many ulama. Among his most influential works are *The Quran in Islam* and *Shii Islam*. Since his death, a university in Iran has been named after him; his works continue to enjoy great popularity.

Tabiun *See* Successors

Tabligh Communication of a message or revelation; fulfillment of a mission. Interchangeable with *dawah* (propagation of faith) in modern usage. The Quranic use of related words signifies that proclamation of the message is sufficient for fulfillment of the mission; a preacher is not responsible for conversion. Muhammad Rashid Rida (d. 1935) believed that tabligh was a duty of all Muslims; Abu al-Ala Mawdudi (d. 1979), the founder of the Jamaat-i Islami, stressed that humans are free to choose between truth and falsehood and that tabligh does not entail coercion (prohibited in Quran 2:256). It forms the spiritual imperative behind the largest contemporary Muslim transnational movement, the Tablighi Jamaat.

Tablighi Jamaat Indian reform movement founded by Mawlana Muhammad Ilyas in 1927 in Delhi. Popular with villagers and peasants. Called for reform of personal religious practices and defense of Islam and Muslim minority populations. Focused on religious, rather than political, aspects of Islam. Spread throughout the Muslim world from 1950 on. *See also* Ilyas, Muhammad; Kandhalavi, Muhammad Zakariyya

Tadhkirah Memorial. Refers to biographical collections of the lives of mystics and scholars. Sometimes includes nonreligious figures. Common in Iran, the Ottoman Empire, and South Asia. Lives are presented through anecdotes accompanied by narrative biographical material. Order is generational or alphabetical, rather than by rank. Occasionally organized by affinity or family relationship. *See also* Hagiography

Tafsir Quranic exegesis. Elucidation, explanation, interpretation, and commentary carried out in order to understand the Quran and its commandments. Muhammad is considered the most authoritative interpreter of the Quran, but Quranic interpretation through reports from acknowledged Companions of the Prophet or by their successors is also considered authoritative. Tafsir is carried out in linguistic, juristic, and theological fields.

Taftazani, Sad al-Din Masud ibn Umar ibn Abd Allah al- (d. 1390) Renowned scholar from distinguished scholarly family, born in the village of Taftazan in the northeastern Iranian province of Khurasan. Author of works on Arabic grammar, rhetoric, theology, logic, law, and Quranic exegesis (tafsir). His commentaries on well-known works in various fields of Islamic sciences were widely used in madrasas until modern times.

Tafwid In Islamic theology, relegation of matters to God (tafwid al-amr li Allah). In law, delegation of power, authorization of an act, or issuance of a warrant for arrest. Often indicates a delegation of power in a procurement contract. It also indicates a type of legal partnership (sharikat mufawadah) in which the partners make an equal investment and share an equal interest in the profits and decision-making power. Also used to describe a type of divorce (talaq al-tafwid or

tafwid al-talaq) in which the husband delegates a power of divorce (ismah) to his wife. The delegation may be made at the time the marriage is contracted, or upon the occurrence of certain circumstances, or at any time during the marriage. For instance, the parties may specify that if the husband takes a second wife, the first wife will automatically have the power to initiate a divorce, or that the wife has the power to initiate a divorce at any time without reason. Classical Muslim jurists debate the various types of delegations and the validity of each. Most Muslim countries permit this type of divorce in one form or another.

Taghut Quranic term for false god or idol. Also applied to tyrannical rulers who arrogate God's absolute power and use it to oppress people. In modern Iran it is applied to the fallen shah and all those who supported him. In the same way that *jahiliyyah* is used in Islamic history to refer to the pre-Islamic age of paganism, *taghut* stands for the pre-Islamic-revolution period in the history of modern Iran.

Taha, Mahmud Muhammad (d. 1985) Islamic reform theorist and founder of the Republican Brothers in Sudan. Trained as an engineer; a self-taught expert in religion. Jailed in the 1940s for nationalist activities, he later led a group advocating a socioeconomic system based on an understanding of Islam that distinguished between the universal application of the revelations of the Meccan period and the specific revelations said to be valid only for life in Medina. His group was small and had little power, but his ideas received much attention. During the final days of the Numayri regime he was executed for heresy.

Taharah *See* Circumcision

Tahlil In Islamic law, the process of contracting a second marriage after a triple (final) repudiation or divorce. If a husband has divorced his wife three times, then the couple cannot remarry unless the wife first marries another man and consummates the marriage. Thereafter the wife may divorce the second husband, complete her waiting period (iddah), and then remarry the first husband.

Tahreek-i Khilafat *See* Ahmad, Israr

Tahrif Corruption of a text. The term does not occur in the Quran, but three verses claim that people have tampered with the sacred texts (2:75; 4:46; 5:13; 5:41). Tahrif is generally understood as a charge that previous religious communities, through actual textual alteration or through false interpretation, have expunged references to the advent of Muhammad contained in the Hebrew Bible and the Gospels. The term also is used to refer to the Shii charge that parts of the Quran in which Ali's authority is given divine sanction have been removed.

Tahrik-i Jafariyyah Pakistan The leading Shii political organization in Pakistan. The Tahrik-i Jafariyyah was founded under the name Tahrik-i Nifaz-i Fiqh-i Jafariyyah in 1980 to protect the interests of the Shiis against the Sunni-dominated Islamization policies of Zia-ul-Haq. It reached its height of prominence under Allamah Arif Husayni. In championing the rights of the Shiis and in maintaining close ties with Iran, the Tahrik-i Jafariyyah provoked strong suspicions on the part of Sunni religio-political groups, leading to a drastic radicalization of the sectarian landscape in Pakistan.

Tahrik-i Khaksar Movement, based in Lahore, Pakistan, established by Inayatullah Khan Mashriqi in 1930 to improve the conditions of the Muslims of the Indian subcontinent. The movement was based on the premise that Muslims and Hindus could not live together, and it demanded a separate homeland for Muslims. The movement played an important role in the creation of Pakistan.

Tahrik-i Nifaz-i Fiqh-i Jafariyyah *See* Tahrik-i Jafariyyah Pakistan

Tahtawi, Rifaa al- (d. 1873) Egyptian religious scholar trained in Islamic disciplines at al-Azhar by a shaykh sympathetic to the reform program of Muhammad Ali. Went to Paris as a religious teacher for the diplomatic mission there, gaining familiarity with European ideas. Helped develop a new educational system in Egypt and encouraged language instruction and translations. Worked to develop an intellectual framework for the integration of European and Islamic ideas, laying the foundation for Islamic modernist thought. Also laid the foundation for Egyptian nationalism.

Taif Oasis in the South Hejaz, Arabia. In 619 Muhammad sought support from this oasis, which is close to Medina; he was ridiculed and driven out.

Taj Mahal Mausoleum created for Mumtaz Mahal, wife of the Mughal emperor Shah Jahan, in Agra, India, completed circa 1648; the name means "crown palace." With its huge dome inspired by Central Asian antecedents, small octagonal pavilions (chatri) on the roof, four minaret-like towers in the corners, and white marble lavishly inlaid with semiprecious stones in floral and calligraphic designs, it is the most famous Mughal architectural monument. Inscriptions indicate it was intended as an architectural metaphor for the Throne of God.

Tajammu al-Yamani li'l-Islah, al- Yemeni Society for Reform. Often called Islah. Founded in 1990 as the product of an alliance between Muslim Brotherhood ideologues and the Hashid tribal confederation. Became the second most important political party in opposition to the ruling People's General Congress. In the first postreunification Yemeni multiparty elections in 1993 the Islah Party gained 62 out of 301 parliamentary seats; its leader, Shaykh Abdallah Ben Hussein al-Ahmar, was elected speaker of the parliament, and the party contributed nine ministers to a coalition government. After a more modest showing in the 1997 parliamentary elections (fifty-four seats), the party withdrew from the government but supported President Ali Abdullah Saleh in the first universal suffrage presidential elections in September 1999.

Tajdid *See* Revival and Renewal

Tajikistan, Islam in With the collapse of the Soviet Union (1991), Tajikistan emerged as an independent state in Central Asia. The overwhelming majority of Tajikistan's population (6.5 million) belongs to historically Muslim ethnic groups: Tajiks 65 percent, Uzbeks 25 percent, and Tatars, Kyrgyzes, and Turkmens each 2 percent. Most are Hanafi Sunnis; a small percentage is Ismaili Shii. Sufism, particularly the Naqshbandi order, has strong historic roots in Tajikistan and adjoining republics, especially in the Ferghana Valley. In the early years of independence, Soviet anti-Islamic measures disappeared, and citizens became more openly religious. The presidents of Kazakhstan, Kyrgyzstan, Tajikistan, and Uzbekistan are working together to quell radical Muslim unrest in the Ferghana Valley; the Islamic Movement of Uzbekistan (IMU) frequently crosses from its Afghani base into Tajikistan to conduct military activities. *See also* Islamic Movement of Uzbekistan (IMU)

Tajsim *See* Incarnation

Tajwid Art of Quran recitation. Also known as qiraah (reading, recitation). Intended to be performed only by people in a ritually pure state. Typically heard in mosques but often included in celebrations such as weddings, funerals, business openings, conferences, and government functions.

Takbir *See* Allahu Akbar

Takfir Pronouncement that someone is an unbeliever (kafir) and no longer Muslim. Takfir is used in the modern era for sanctioning violence against leaders of Islamic states who are deemed insufficiently religious. It has become a central ideology of militant groups such as those in Egypt, which reflect the ideas of Sayyid Qutb, Maw-dudi, Ibn Taymiyyah, and Ibn Kathir. Mainstream Muslims and Islamist groups reject the concept as a doctrinal deviation. Leaders such as Hasan al-Hudaybi (d. 1977) and Yusuf al-Qaradawi reject takfir as un-Islamic and marked by bigotry and zealotry.

Taklif A legal charge or obligation; to entrust or charge someone with a task. A person who meets the legal prerequisites becomes a mukallaf (a person obligated by law to discharge a legal duty). For instance, prayer is a taklif imposed upon those who reach the age of discernment (bulgh). A woman who is menstruating does not have a taklif to perform prayer. Hardship or incapacity will relieve a person from certain obligations or impose less demanding obligations, for instance, praying while sitting down in the case of a sick person. A taklif imposed upon property is an encumbrance.

Talaq *See* Marriage and Divorce: Modern Practices

Taleqani, Mahmud (d. 1979) Iranian cleric and a key ideologue of the Islamic revolution. Advocated pursuit of social justice as a religious vocation. Collaborated with Mehdi Bazargan in formulating an ideological alternative to Communism, repression, and traditional religion, resulting in foundation of the Liberation Movement of Iran in 1961. Prominent public activist. Elected to the Assembly of Experts in 1979 with the highest number of votes, but died prior to the passing of the final constitution.

Talfiq Piecing together. Legal term describing the derivation of rules from material of various schools of Islamic law. In modern times talfiq was advocated by Muhammad Abduh (d. 1905) and his student Muhammad Rashid Rida (d. 1935) as a means to reform Islamic law. Ikhtilaf (differences of opinion) were a source of intellectual wealth, they reasoned, that ought to be utilized for the benefit of the whole community.

Talhah ibn Ubayd Allah al-Taymi (d. 656) Early convert to Islam and one of the ten eminent Companions of Prophet Muhammad to whom he promised paradise. Appointed by the second caliph, Umar, to the council electing his successor (644). Contender for the caliphate who unsuccessfully fought the fourth caliph, Ali, in the Battle of the Camel in 656 to avenge the murder of the preceding caliph, Uthman.

Taliban Militant group of students and religious leaders who established the Islamic Republic of Afghanistan in 1994–96 in order to end the lengthy civil war following the withdrawal of the Soviet Union from the region in 1989. Led by Mullah Omar. Promotes Islam as a moral, stable, and orderly alternative to civil war, ethnic divisions, and warring tribal chiefs. Follows strict, literal, and conservative interpretations of Islam and Sunni Islamic public standards, including the implementation of hudud punishments. Influenced primarily by Wahhabi teachers and Pashtun tribal traditions. The regime was denounced by international human rights organizations for its refusal to allow the practice or presence of any other religion besides Islam in Afghanistan and for the absolute segregation of women. It was supported and recognized by only Pakistan, Saudi Arabia, and the United Arab Emirates. It provided shelter for Osama bin Laden and his associates, who ran training camps for international terrorists. Forcibly removed from power by United States forces after the 11 September 2001 attacks on the World Trade Center and Pentagon.

Talim (1) Instruction in Quran and hadith and sometimes Islamic law, typically provided in the mosque. Students form a circle around the instructor of their choice. Upon completion of study, the student is awarded a certificate, or ijazah, certifying the successful study of certain texts with a particular teacher, enabling the student to teach these same texts. Remains an important part of education in the Islamic world. Sometimes added as a supplement to the required curriculum. Muslims living in non-Muslim-majority countries often desire to continue this type of education for their children and

are working to establish local institutions to offer instruction. Also used for informal lessons in the mosque on Thursday evenings or after communal prayer. (2) In Nizari Ismaili Shiism, divinely inspired teaching through the imam.

Taliq A style of Arabic calligraphy.

Talut See Saul

Tamerlane See Timur Lang

Tanasukh See Naskh

Tanzania, Islam in Tanzania's mainland population is 45 percent Christian, 35 percent Muslim, and 20 percent indigenous religions. Islam spread from the coast to the interior through trade; in the twentieth century, Sufi orders thoroughly popularized Islam. About 70 percent of Tanzanian Sunnis are affiliated with Sufi orders; the Qadiri accounts for 75 percent of all brotherhood followers. Shadhili, Askari, Ahmadi-Dandarawi, and Rifai are other active brotherhoods. After independence (1961) Tanzania and Zanzibar united as a republic; today Zanzibar enjoys limited autonomy. Tensions between the pro-capitalist, pro-Western government and the African Muslim population have risen against a backdrop of economic uncertainty.

Tanzeem-i Islami See Ahmad, Israr

Tanzih Doctrine of divine exemption according to which God is unique and in no way like anything created. The basis of the prohibition of anthropomorphism (tashbih). Sufis interpret the doctrine as necessitating that one purge oneself of all images and preconceived notions about God in order to allow mystical experience to fully reveal God. This doctrine is linked to the concept of tawhid and formed the basis for the eighteenth-century Sufi concentration on union with the spirit of Muhammad, rather than God, since union between two unlikes is considered impossible (although some early mystics had claimed that such communion was possible due to the special relationship between creator and created).

Tanzil The transmission of divine guidance for humanity through prophets, beginning with Adam and culminating in the mission of Muhammad, "the seal of prophets," according to the Quran. Since the message is given to guide human affairs, intellectual understanding and practical implementation through reliable example are also necessary. Prophets serve as both messengers and models. Recent Muslim thinkers have expressed the need to free interpretation of the Quran from the narrow literalism and verse-by-verse, atomistic methods of earlier exegetes, focusing instead on the universal relevancy of revelation in a world of rapid and radical change. Throughout Muslim history, debates have raged over the relative value of knowledge received from divine revelation and knowledge arrived at through independent reasoning. Acceptance of the Quran as revelation of God's will means that it is unchallengeable and without equal. Orthodox Islam, in particular, opposes the idea that all things can be known by human reason alone. Thus humanity requires revelation for clear information about the mysteries of existence, which inform us of the relationship between the absolute and the manifest. Revelation is considered a unique and necessary kind of knowledge.

Tanzim Early-twentieth-century movement in northern India that called for reform of personal religious practices and defense of a beleaguered Islam and an abused Muslim minority.

Tanzimat Turkish. Reforms or regulation. Denotes a period of social and political reform that transformed the Ottoman Empire by integrating institutions deliberately copied from Western Europe; a response to both internal and external political pressures. Tanzimat began with the proclamation of the quasi-constitutional Gulhane Rescript or Charter of Gulhane (1839); the terminal date is harder to determine. The Edict of Reforms (1856) guaranteed Muslims and non-Muslims equal rights and obligations regarding military service, the administration of justice, taxation, education, and employment. Modernization of Turkey under the Young Turks (1980–18) and the republic (established 1923) is an uninterrupted movement proceeding from the Tanzimat. *See also* Gulhane Rescript of 1839

Taqi Khan, Muhammad (d. 1852) Known as Amir Kabir. Reformer and chief minister of Qajar court in Iran, 1848–51. Visited the Ottoman Empire, studying the Tanzimat reforms. Instituted reforms in finance, administration, and education. Closely associated with Dar al-Fanun, a new college for training administrators and introducing modern subjects. Murdered while in exile in Kashan.

Taqiyah Precautionary denial of religious belief in the face of potential persecution. Stressed by Shii Muslims, who have been subject to periodic persecution by the Sunni majority. The concept is based on Quran 3: 28 and 16:106 as well as hadith, tafsir literature, and juridical commentaries.

Taqlid Imitation. Conformity to legal precedent, traditional behavior, and doctrines. Often juxtaposed by reformers with ijtihad, independent reasoning based on revelation. Traditionally, legal precedent is considered binding in Islamic law, but taqlid has acquired a negative connotation among modern reformers, who use the term to refer to cultural and intellectual stagnation and unwillingness to experiment with new ideas. Reformist criticism has taken both fundamentalist and modernist directions.

Taqwa God-consciousness or God-fearing piety. Also rendered as "god-fearing," "right conduct," "virtue," "wariness." *Taqwa* and its derivatives appear more than 250 times in the Quran; Abu al-Ala Mawdudi (d. 1979) identified taqwa as the basic Islamic principle of God-consciousness, together with brotherhood, equality, fairness, and justice, on which the true Islamic society is established. Sayyid Qutb (d. 1966) systematically elaborated the significance of taqwa in his

Quranic commentary, which is characterized by an emphasis on political activism. Fazlur Rahman (d. 1988) identified it as "perhaps the most important single concept in the Quran," an inner vision that helps humans overcome their weaknesses.

Tarbiyyah Upbringing, education. In medieval Islam, a proper education for the upper classses included both religious and humanistic disciplines (adab). In the contemporary world, refers to child rearing, education (usually secular), and pedagogy. *See also* Adab

Tariqah Path or way; Sufi order or spiritual regimen of specific teacher or master, including devotional practices, recitations, and literature of piety. Also refers to the Sufi order as a social organization that can extend across several regions. Can be a short-lived organization developed around an individual or a longer-lasting structure with institutional coherence. *See also* Sufism

Tariqah-i Muhammadiyyah *See* Ahl al-Hadith

Tarjuman al-Quran A partial Urdu translation of and commentary on the Quran by Abu al-Kalam Azad (d. 1958), a prominent religious scholar and political leader of twentieth-century South Asia. The translation was meant to introduce the Quran to ordinary Muslims, though it did not advance beyond the first twenty-three surahs. The most significant part of this work is Azad's extensive commentary on the Fatiha, the first chapter of the Quran. Azad saw the Fatiha not only as encapsulating the teachings of the entire Quran but, in line with his commitment to a united Hindu-Muslim nationhood in India, also as testifying to the essential unity of all religions.

Tarwiyah Satisfying thirst. Name for the eighth day of the hajj pilgrimage, either because on that day pilgrims water their camels or because Abraham heeded the vision wherein he was instructed to sacrifice his son Ishmael.

Tasawwuf *See* Sufism

Tasdiq Affirmation of the truth of God's existence and knowledge of divine attributes, prophets, and divine will. State of devotion stemming from love of God. Reflects submission to and trust in God, dedication to what God expects people to do, and opposition to anything God has forbidden.

Tashahhud Attestation of faith, recited in the second and final unit of prayer. After the second prostration, the worshiper testifies while sitting that there is no god but God, He has no partner; the worshiper also proclaims Muhammad as the servant and messenger of God. The index finger of the worshiper's right hand is raised to emphasize God's uniqueness. *See also* Shahadah

Tashbih *See* Anthropomorphism

Taslim Noun from the Arabic root s-l-m, which means "to surrender" or "to be safe." The words Islam and salaam (peace) are derived from the same root. Taslim indicates an acceptance of fate or divine will.

Tatars A group of Turkic peoples found mainly in the Tatar Republic of Russia and parts of Siberia who converted to Islam in the late twelfth and early thirteenth centuries.

Tawaf Sevenfold counterclockwise circumambulation of the Kaaba as the earthly House of God by pilgrims on the pilgrimage (hajj) to Mecca. Believed to be in imitation of angels and all created beings circumambulating the throne of God, symbolizing the entrance of the pilgrim into God's presence. First major ritual of the hajj. Performed again after standing on the Plain of Arafat, spending the night at Muzdalifah, throwing stones at Mina, and the sacrifice of an animal. The second circumambulation is the minimum requirement of the hajj. Pilgrims try to touch or kiss the Black Stone of Kaaba while performing tawaf, or at least salute the Black Stone as a gesture of their renewed covenant with God.

Tawakkul Trust. Refers to the Sufi practice of complete self-abandonment in God in order to do His will. Also indicates the Sufi's total reliance on God to provide for daily needs. Sufis traditionally state that a Sufi should be like a corpse in the hands of God, without resistance to the divine will. Such trust leads to a state of tranquility, which precedes contentment and illumination. Tawakkul is achieved through training, guidance, submission to the shaykh of the order, dhikr, and/or sama.

Tawassul *See* Intercession

Tawbah *See* Repentance

Tawhidi, Abu Hayyan al- (d. ca. 1023) Baghdadi writer and philosopher. Studied jurisprudence, grammar, philosophy, belles-lettres, and Sufism. Through his broad knowledge and commentaries on his contemporaries, his work illustrates the lively intellectual milieu and diffusion of philosophical ideas in Baghdad during the late tenth and early eleventh centuries. He explored philosophical issues through ornate prose. He did not view philosophy as the sole means to truth, asserting that revelation, not reason, is the source of religious belief.

Tawil Interpretation or allegorical interpretation. The term occurs in Quran 3:5–7 in the context of distinguishing between those verses of the Quran that are precise in meaning (muhkamat) and those that are ambiguous (mutashabihat). Subsequent verses assert, according to one reading, that "only God and those well grounded in knowledge" know the interpretation of the ambiguous parts of the text, whereas according to another, more popular reading, only God knows the interpretation or hidden meaning of those parts. Historically, from the seventh century on, scholars were divided into those who rejected interpretation in any guise or form and those who were willing to apply the discursive methods of reading the text in varying degrees. The former or literalist group included such scholars as Malik ibn

Anas (d. 795), Ahmad ibn Hanbal (d. 855), and Ahmad ibn Hazm (d. 1086); the latter included such liberal scholars as Hasan al-Basri (d. 728), the Mutazili theologians, and the philosophers in general. The most enthusiastic advocate of allegorical interpretation in the twelfth century was the great Aristotelian philosopher and Maliki judge Ibn Rushd (Averroës) (d. 1198).

Tawrat *See* Torah

Taxation Payment of Islamic taxes is considered a religious duty. The most important tax is zakah, which is based on wealth and paid annually. Cash holdings, asset disposals, and inventories are subject to tax at a standard rate of 2.5 percent. Zakah is to be paid by those with surplus liquid wealth for the benefit of the poor and needy, typically via spending on social and humanitarian causes. The collection of zakah is usually organized separately from that of state taxes. Another traditional Islamic tax was the jizyah, or poll tax, paid by non-Muslim residents of a Muslim state to the government in exchange for government protection. The Islamic land tax (kharaj) is applied to both Muslims and non-Muslims according to acreage of land, with the rate depending upon output potential and a maximum rate of half of the crop value.

Taxes *See* Jizyah; Kharaj; Khums

Tayyibi Tariqah Reformist branch of the Sammani tariqah founded by Mulay Abdullah ibn Ibrahim al-Sharif in northwestern Algeria in the seventeenth century. Named after the fourth shaykh, Mulay al-Tayyib. Also known as the Wazzani tariqah (named after the zawiyah founded in Wazzan in 1670) and Tihami tariqah (named after the grandson of the order's founder). Has zawiyahs throughout Morocco, Algeria, and Tunisia. Was dominant in Tangiers in the eighteenth and nineteenth centuries, where members were recognized by the sultan as allies and held autonomy in local affairs. Opposed to the popular veneration of mar-

Tawhid

Tawhid is the defining doctrine of Islam. It declares absolute monotheism—the unity and uniqueness of God as creator and sustainer of the universe. Used by Islamic reformers and activists as an organizing principle for human society and the basis of religious knowledge, history, metaphysics, aesthetics, and ethics, as well as social, economic, and world order.

During the classical period, discussions of tawhid focused on philosophical considerations about God's essence and attributes and the validity of the political institution of the caliphate. The thirteenth-century Hanbali jurist Ibn Taymiyyah shifted the emphasis of tawhid to sociomoral issues. He interpreted tawhid as a declaration that God is the sole creator, ruler, and judge of the world, rendering human beings responsible for submitting to and carrying out His revealed will through religious practice, ritual, and actions. True faith is expressed in both individual and collective virtuous behavior, linking the private and public (i.e., spiritual and political) spheres. Social organization is to be guided by religion.

The eighteenth-century Arabian reformer Muhammad ibn Abd al-Wahhab (d. 1792) reasserted tawhid as a remedy for spiritual stagnation and excesses. He denounced those who compromised Islamic unity by promoting sectarianism; by praying to saints and requesting intercession by saints, angels, and prophets; and by claiming knowledge based on sources other than the Quran, Sunnah, and results of logical processes. He sought to establish a state based on divine and Islamic unity, replacing tribal solidarity with religious solidarity and purifying Islam from extraneous and popular practices. That state became the basis of the modern state of Saudi Arabia.

The nineteenth-century Egyptian reformer Muhammad Abduh (d. 1905) synthesized tawhid, human free will, and obedience to God's revealed word. He justified rational inquiries into the Quran through tawhid by claiming that there could be no conflict between reason and revelation, so the Quran validates and encourages humans' exercise of reason. Like Muhammad Ibn Abd al-Wahhab, he attacked traditionalism, focusing instead on knowledge of God and reliance upon proof rather than tradition as evidence. The two most influential themes of Abduh's work for twenty-first century activists are the need to revive the spirit of ijtihad (independent reasoning) by rejecting taqlid (strict adherence to tradition) and pursuing practical goals in the creation of Islamic society rather than contemplating the nature of the divine essence and attributes.

Abduh's interpretation of the centrality of tawhid in directing human pursuits became more important as the Islamic world suffered political setbacks, particularly as secular ideologies such as Nasserism, socialism, capitalism, and nationalism failed to achieve independence from the colonial powers, prosperity, and unity throughout the Islamic world. Sayyid Qutb articulated an Islamic worldview based on tawhid as a human response to God, whereby society is to reflect divine unity through unanimous submission to God's revealed will, both privately and publicly. He asserted that governments should be based on Islamic law.

The Palestinian scholar Ismail al-Faruqi (d. 1986) discussed the practical implications of tawhid, focusing on Muslim responsibility for all of humanity and the entire cosmos since Muslims are the beneficiaries of perfect and complete revelation. Such responsibility demands an Islamic world order oriented toward human activity in public action, rather than excessive legalism, materialism, or spirituality alone. Tawhid commands that all life must be ordered according to divine will, so Islamic law must both legislate every

(continued)

Tawhid (continued)

aspect of life and be the dominant legal system throughout the world.

The major ideologue of the Iranian Islamic revolution, Ali Shariati (d. 1977), popularized tawhid for Shiis. He stressed the purpose of human existence as agreement or trust between God and creation, whereby human beings are responsible for caring for all of creation with tawhid as the foundation for social action; for the rejection of legal, class, social, political, racial, national, territorial, genetic, and economic distinctions; and for the requirement for all believers to work for justice. Tawhid is, therefore, designed to transform a religion that justifies and accepts the status quo into a religion of awareness, activism, and revolution.

Ayatollah Ruhollah Khomeini (d. 1989) also placed tawhid at the center of Islamic spiritual and material life, calling for unity of all Muslims and particularly stressing political unity as the only way to resolve the lack of harmony among Muslim countries, which he blamed on the West. He called for revolution and the elimination of specific leaders, based on tawhid and true Islam, to ensure the unity of all Muslims throughout the world.

Tawhid is at the forefront of Islamic thought today due to a concern with the practical manifestations of Islamic unity in a world fragmented by colonialism and nationalism. Tawhid has emerged as a powerful symbol of divine, spiritual, and sociopolitical unity.

---

abouts. Cooperated with the French protectorate in the nineteenth century as a means of resisting the power of the sultan.

Tazir Punishment for crime not measuring up to the strict requirements of hadd punishments, although they are of the same nature, or those for which specific punishments have not been fixed by the Quran. Punishments range from the death penalty for espionage and heresy to flagellation, imprisonment, local banishment, and a variety of fines. Determination of punishment is left to the judge or chief executive, who can vary the punishment according to a number of criteria including who has inflicted the crime and upon whom. *See also* Hadd

Taziyah Shii passion play, performed mainly in Iran, that reenacts the passion and death of Husayn, Muhammad's grandson and the third imam. Husayn was murdered along with his male children and companions while contesting his right to the caliphate on the Plain of Karbala (in present-day Iraq) in 680. The massacre is viewed as martyrdom and has been mourned ever since by Shiis worldwide. In Iran, taziyah received royal patronage when Shii Islam was established as the state religion in the sixteenth century.

Tekke Turkish term for Sufi residence, hospice, or lodge. Typically a building where Sufi activities, such as teaching, rituals, and worship, occur. The head of the order may live there. They became suspect during the colonial era as potential sites for arms stockpiling and dissident activities, and were targeted for abolition under Atatürk following the declaration of the secular Turkish state. *See also* Khalwah; Khanaqah; Zawiyah

Tentera Islam Military wing of the Darul Islam movement in Aceh, Indonesia. The group's adoption of guerrilla tactics in the 1950s led to a split in the Darul Islam leadership between those agitating for an Islamic state in northern Sumatra and those seeking accommodation with the Jakarta government.

Terrorism Deliberate use of violence against noncombatants for political ends. Perpetrators can be states, agents of states, or individuals or groups acting independently or in cells. Does not apply to all acts of politically inspired violence. Islamic law condemns the use of violence except to combat injustice, particularly where acts of aggression have occurred, such as people being driven out of their homes, and even then circumscribes the use of violence with careful regulations concerning who may initiate violence, warning prior to the initiation of violence, the immunity of noncombatants, and requirements for the cessation of hostilities. Violence not sanctioned by Islamic law is called hirabah.

Thaalibi, Abd al-Aziz (d. 1944) Tunisian nationalist leader and Islamic reformer. Founded the Destour (Constitution) Party in 1920 to lead the demands for independence from the French protectorate. Exiled by France for fourteen years. Unable to revive the Destour Party after his return to Tunisia, Thaalibi retreated from politics. Influenced by the reformist ideas of the Salafi movement, he stressed the Arabo-Islamic identity of Tunisia. Advocated a constitutional government, the modernization of the judicial system, the development of social services, and the redirection of the economy.

Thaalibi, Abu Mansur Abd al-Malik ibn Muhammad al- (d. 1038) Renowned Arabic writer of the premodern era. From the Iranian province of Khurasan. Of the numerous works attributed to him, those generally considered authentic include anthologies of Arabic literature; philological discussions of grammar, lexicography, and literary tropes; and compilations of entertaining anecdotes from Islamic political and cultural history intended for the lettered society. Left a lasting mark on the history of Arabic literature through his critical literary taste, exemplified in a widely emulated multivolume biographical anthology of poets and artistic writers that was intended as a comprehensive survey of the Arabic Islamic world during the preceding decades.

Thailand, Islam in About 95 percent of the Thai population practices Theravada Buddhism; the largest religious minority is Muslims (4 percent) in two broad, self-defined categories: Malay Muslims, residing primarily in the south, and Thai Muslims, in central and northern Thailand. Despite government assimilationist policies, most Malay Muslims maintain strong ethnic and cultural affinities with Muslims in Malaysia; assimilationist policies have resulted in separatist ethnic and religious movements in the South. The heterogeneous Thai Muslim population includes descendants of Iranians, Chams, Indonesians, Indians, Pakistanis, Chinese, and Malays. Muslims increasingly participate in Thai political, cultural, and educational activities.

Thamud Pre-Islamic Arabian community, successors of Ad. According to the Quran, the prophet Salih was sent to guide and warn Thamud; he miraculously conjured a pregnant she-camel out of a rock. Thamud rejected him, slew the camel, and persisted in idolatry. The community was destroyed by earthquake and thunderbolt because of its disbelief.

Thanawi, Ashraf Ali (d. 1943) Indian scholar and author. Student of the Deoband theological school who sought to bring Islamic values to less-educated Muslims. His most famous work, the ten-volume Bihishti zevar (Heavenly ornaments), provided a guide in Urdu for the education of Muslim women that demonstrated a new concern that they learn Islamic values. Although he considered women inherently equal to men in ability, Thanawi upheld subordinate familial roles for women as part of a stable social order. Supporter of the Muslim League and the movement to create the state of Pakistan. Practiced a reformed Sufism.

Thanawi, Ihtishan ul-Haq (d. 1980) A prominent religious leader and nephew as well as a student of Ashraf Ali Thanawi. Trained at the madrasa of Deoband, he was best known for his moving sermons. He participated in the movement to establish the state of Pakistan. After independence he migrated to Pakistan and was active in Islamic politics.

Thanawiyyah See Dualism

Thawrah See Revolution

Theft *See* Sariqah

Theodemocracy *See* Democracy

Theology Philosophical, rational, or mystical discussions of revealed truths. Called "disputation" (kalam) in Arabic. Theological controversies in Islam focus on seven major issues: the concept of God; ontological and cosmological proofs of God's existence; the cosmology of the relationship between God and the world; the ethics of theodicy of God's order with respect to free will, determinism, fate, good, evil, punishment, and reward; the pragmatics of the language of religion and the peculiar function of the faculty of imagination that is special to prophets, mystics, and prophet-statesmen; the relationship between reason and revelation; and the politics of the application of divine rule to the community.

Thiqali Trustworthy, reliable. In hadith studies, *thiqa* is a reference to the one informant of whose trustworthiness a particular muhadith (narrator of the Prophet's reports) is personally confident.

Third Universal Alternative Libyan leader Muammar Qaddafi's interpretation of Islam as outlined in his Green Book. Intended to be an alternative to capitalism and Communism. Proposes direct popular rule, equal distribution and ownership of wealth and resources, and economic equality of all. Relegates the Quran to religious observances, leading many Muslims to consider it heretical.

Throne Verse *See* Ayat al-Kursi, al-

Tibb al-Nabawi, al- *See* Medicine: Traditional Practice

Tijani, Ahmad al- (d. 1815) Algerian founder of the Tijani Sufi order. Initially introduced a revived Khalwati order into the Maghreb. Had a visionary encounter with Muhammad in 1782 in which he was taught a new, independent tariqah and instructed to sever relations with other orders and shaykhs. Warmly received by those seeking to eradicate popular Sufism, since his order combined strict observance of Islamic law with the rejection of asceticism and withdrawal from the world. Claimed rank of khatm al-awliyah (seal of the saints), implying that he was a link between Muhammad and all past and future saints. Promised access to paradise without the need to give up possessions, attracting rich merchants and senior officials.

Tijani Tariqah *See* Tijani, Ahmad al-

Timar Turkish; same as Arabic iqta. Right granted to free cavalrymen to collect taxes directly in return for their military service in the Ottoman Empire; taxes from land grants paid to support cavalry. By the eighteenth century, the timar system was replaced by tax farming (iltizam).

Timur Lang (d. 1405) "Timur the Lame," known in the West as Tamerlane. Military adventurer who came to power in Iran by defeating other chiefs. He was supported by local Muslim elites and Sufis. Religious leaders were later incorporated into the state administrative structure, with Naqshbandis holding leading positions. His conquests included Iran, northern India, Anatolia, and northern Syria. Relics of Timur Lang in Samarqand became a pilgrimage site.

Tirmidhi, Abu Isa Muhammad ibn Isa ibn Sawra ibn Shaddad al- (d. 892) Compiler of one of six Sunni canonical sources of hadith, *Sahih al-Tirmidhi*. Traveled in Khurasan, Iraq, and Hejaz to collect traditions. Studied with Ahmad Ibn Hanbal, al-Bukhari, and Abu Daud al-Sijistani. Numerous works were ascribed to him, but not all survived. Addresses law, theology, devotion, popular beliefs, manners, education, and hagiology. Records a smaller number of traditions than Muslim and al-Bukhari but is less repetitive and has more variety in transmitters. Includes critical discussions of chains of transmitters and points of difference between Islamic law schools. Collections include personal notes discussing the currents of thought and practice in the Islamic world of his time.

Toaddud See Pluralism

Tobacco Protest (Iran) (1891–92) Popular Iranian protest against the shah's granting of a monopoly to the British in the sale and export of tobacco. Led by religious scholars, merchants, liberal intellectuals, officers, and Islamic modernists, who encouraged resistance to economic concessions that could serve as a prelude to foreign rule. Smoking was prohibited, the bazaars were closed, and strikes and demonstrations were held. Religious legitimation was provided by Ayatollah Hasan al-Shirazi, a spokesman for the ulama, who issued a fatwa against smoking tobacco. Mosques offered sanctuary to protesters and served as centers of resistance and political organization. The protest set a precedent for cooperation between the ulama and merchants in limiting the shah's power.

Tombs In popular Islam and some Sufi orders, places where believers gather to request barakah, or blessing, from the departed. Shrines are often built over the tombs of famous Sufi leaders and saints who are believed capable of working miracles. Elaborate tombs, mosques, screens, mausoleums, and funerary sculptures mark the graves of Muhammad's descendants, Shii imams, and government officials throughout the Islamic world. Revivalist and reformist movements, especially eighteenth-century Wahhabis and twentieth-century Salafis, condemn the practice as a heretical innovation (bidah). Muslim tombs are generally unadorned and take the form of flat grave markers that carry only personal details of the deceased or Quranic verses. See also Shrine

Tombstones Typically flat, plain pieces of rock adorned with only personal details of the deceased or Quranic verses. Many Muslim jurists disapprove of marking graves due to concerns about visitation and requests for intercession with God.

Torah Arabic tawrat. Mentioned in the Quran eighteen times as true revelation that preceded the Gospels and the Quran. Confirmed by the Quran (5:46, 61:6), it is described as a source of wisdom (3:48, 5:110) and guidance (5:46). Muslims believe that the Torah, unlike the Quran, has not been preserved in its original, true, and complete form. See also Bible; Judaism and Islam

Tours, Battle of Also known as the Battle of Poitiers. Occurred in 732 between the Franks, led by Charles Martel, and Muslims. The victory by the Franks became a symbol of the halting of Muslim expansion in western Europe.

Trade Financing, Islamic See Murabahah

Traditionists See Muhaddithin

Treasury See Bayt al-Mal

Treaty of Hudaybiyah Truce in 628 between the Meccan tribe of Quraysh and Muhammad. The Meccans agreed to allow Muslims to make the pilgrimage but refused to recognize Muhammad's claim to prophethood. Muhammad agreed that children who left Mecca to become Muslims without parental consent would be returned to their parents, but Muslim apostates would not be returned. The treaty eased Meccan hostility toward Islam and confirmed recognition of Muhammad's political and military power. Allowed Muhammad to subdue one of Mecca's key allies, the oasis of Khaybar, opening the door to the eventual conquest of Mecca in 630. Mecca ceased trying to defeat Muhammad after the treaty was concluded.

Trench, Battle of the Battle fought in 627 by Abu Sufyan's forces against Muslims in a last attempt to stop Muhammad by force. The Muslims dug a trench across exposed areas leading to their settlement, deterring attack. Members of the clan that plotted against the Muslims were sold into slavery or executed.

Tribe *See* Qabilah

Trinidad and Tobago, Islam in Muslims in Trinidad and Tobago constitute only 8 percent of the population and are mostly of East Indian descent, but they play an important political, economic, and social role: numerous elected officials are Muslim, and many businesses are Muslim-owned. In 1990 Trinidad was briefly thrust into the world spotlight when an obscure Black Muslim group attempted to overthrow the democratically elected government by force. There are about eighty-five mosques on Trinidad but only one or two on Tobago. The government officially recognizes several Muslim holidays and sponsors an annual Id al-Fitr celebration. Islamic leaders have begun to join with Christians and Hindus in calling attention to growing problems with alcoholism, drug abuse, violent crime, and AIDS.

Tulunids Founded by Ahmad ibn Tulun (d. 884), the Tulunids ruled Egypt from 868 to 905. Originally a subgovernor of Egypt under the Abbasid empire, Ibn Tulun took advantage of weakened authority in Baghdad to build up a private slave army, seize control of Egypt's finances, and establish his own dynasty with its capital northeast of Cairo. The Tulunids extended their power to Syria but were later defeated by the caliphate, which reconquered Egypt in 905, destroying the Tulunid capital in the process. The major surviving monument of the Tulunid period is the mosque Ibn Tulun built in Cairo between 876 and 879.

Tunisia, Islam in Virtually all Tunisians are Sunni Muslims of the Maliki school of legal thought. During the French protectorate (1883–1956), Sufi brotherhoods (Qadiri, Rahmani, Isawa, and Tijani) were popular, though politically impotent and declining in religious significance—a continuing trend today. Tunisia became independent in 1956,

and President Habib Bourguiba instituted a controversial personal status code replacing traditional Islamic law on marriage, divorce, and children; it was the first Arab country to outlaw polygyny. Zine el-Abidine Ben Ali ousted Bourguiba in 1987 on the grounds of ill health and senility. An Islamist reform party, the Islamic Tendency Movement (MTI), was founded in 1981 by Rashid al-Ghannoushi, a Tunis university professor, and Abd al-Fattah Muru, a lawyer; after its leaders' prosecution and imprisonment, MTI emerged as Hizb al-Nahdah (Renaissance Party) in 1988. Ben Ali forbade Hizb al-Nahdah's participation in the 1989 local elections; al-Ghannoushi went into voluntary exile in Europe. Seven political parties, including the Communist Party, are legal today. Ben Ali's rule has been marked by both prosperity (5 percent growth per year from 1995 to 2000) and repression. Communications are tapped, and encrypting e-mail is illegal. Open dissent or criticism of the government is illegal.

Turabi, Hassan al- (b. 1932) Sudanese Islamist and political leader. Educated in law at the University of Khartoum, the University of London, and the Sorbonne. Joined Sudan's Muslim Brotherhood in the 1950s, coming to prominence during the popular uprising of October 1964. Advocated an Islamic constitution through the Islamic Charter Front. Went into exile after the military coup of 1969. Reconciled with the Numayri regime in 1977. Became attorney general and encouraged members of the Muslim Brotherhood to move into public life, especially new Islamic banks and the armed forces. Reportedly behind Numayri's introduction of Islamic law in 1983. Currently head of the National Islamic Front (2001). Since 1989 he has been seen as the mastermind behind Sudan's effort to establish an Islamic state. He held positions of importance in the government but was relieved of these posts by President Bashir in 1999–2000. His writings present a relatively liberal interpretation of Islam, unlike the National Islamic Front regime of the 1990s.

Turban A headdress worn by men from northern Africa to western and southern Asia consisting of a cap around which a long cloth is wound. The term comes from Persian *dulband* and/or Turkish *tulbent*.

Turkey, Islam in One of the successor states of the Ottoman Empire, and the first secular state in the Islamic world. Led by Mustafa Kemal Atatürk, the secular republic was declared in 1923, and the caliphate was abolished in 1924; all educational institutions were placed under government jurisdiction. By 1929 Kemalists had effectively removed Islam from political and public life: Sufi orders and shrines were closed, the fez was outlawed and men were required to wear hats, and the Gregorian calendar and twenty-four-hour clock were adopted. A Swiss-based civil code replaced Islamic legal codes, and Ottoman script was replaced with a modified Latin alphabet. Kemalism advocated six fundamental principles: republicanism, nationalism, populism, statism, secularism, and revolutionism. The Turkish military became the safeguard of secular democracy, and in May 1960, March 1971, and September 1980 it removed the government, curbing political activity until such time as democracy could be restored. This history of state-imposed secularism along with an unrestrained military has collided with the aspirations of practicing Turkish Muslims. In 1998 the National Board of Higher Education banned head scarves for women students; women cannot attend classes, take exams, or graduate wearing the veil. Religious freedom in Turkey is rapidly becoming an international human rights issue.

Turkmenistan, Islam in Eighty-nine percent of Turkmenistan's population is Sunni Muslim; 9 percent is Orthodox Christian. Prior to independence (October 1991), the Soviets defined and controlled institutionalized Islam; popular (unofficial) Islam consequently flourished, centered around the tombs of Sufi saints and Muslim holy places. After the Soviet Union's collapse, Hajji Nasrullah ibn Ibadullah registered the Kaziate Administration of Turkmenistani Muslims with the Turkmen Ministry of Justice; it received full juridical powers, and law enforcement officials maintain a working relationship with religious representatives. Religious organizations are precluded from registering as political parties, and the Turkmen legal system is based on civil law.

Tusi, Muhammad ibn al-Hasan (d. 1067) Eminent Twelver/Ithna Ashari/Imami Shii theologian, jurist, traditionist, bibliographer, and Quran commentator from the Iranian province of Khurasan. Compiled two of the four canonical books of Twelver traditions. Made major contributions to the structuring of a Twelver system of jurisprudence and theology independent of the imam during the critical century following the Great Occultation (the disappearance of the last imam, 940). Sought a middle ground between rationalism and traditionalism. Known as Shaykh al-Taifah, "master of the sect," for his definitive collections of hadith as well as his index of Shii works (fihrist) and numerous other works.

Tusi, Nasir al-Din al- (d. 1274) Shii astronomer and theologian. Author of numerous works, including commentaries on Euclid, extensive commentaries on Ibn Sina's theodicy, and comprehensive texts on logic, astronomy, mathematics, practical ethics, philosophy, theology, and mysticism. Served as an official in the court of Mongol leader Hulagu Khan and used his influence to oust the last Sunni caliph in Baghdad. His major work on Islamic ethics is *Akhlaq-i nasiri* (The Nasirean ethics); his *Tajrid al-itiqadat* (Definition of the articles of faith) is his best-known work of Twelver theology.

Twelvers *See* Ithna Asharis

U

Uganda, Islam in Sixteen percent of the population is Sunni Muslim; their ancestors arrived in nineteenth-century Uganda from the east through Kenya and from the north through Egypt and Sudan. The Shafii legal school predominates in the central region of Buganda; the Maliki legal school is found in the north. Islamization was not accompanied by Arabization, as it was in North Africa, and Arabic is not widely spoken. Independent of Britain since 1962, postcolonial Uganda has been consistently ruled by Protestant Christians, except for the Idi Amin years (1971–79). Uganda joined the Organization of the Islamic Conference (OIC) in the early 1970s; both Id al-Fitr and Id al-Adha have been national holidays since the Amin era.

Uganda Muslim Student Association Founded in the 1970s by Ugandan president Idi Amin Dada (r. 1971–79) to promote Islam in Uganda and close ties with Libya and Saudi Arabia.

Uhud, Battle of Battle fought in 625 against Muslims by Meccan forces seeking revenge for the Muslim victory in the Battle of Badr. Muhammad was injured and seventy of his followers and allies were killed. The loss deflated Muslim elation over their victory in the Battle of Badr.

Ukaz Marketplace and site of pre-Islamic fairs and poetry contests in Mecca. Location was tied to the pilgrimage season in pre-Islamic times and served as a place where warring tribes could come together peacefully to worship and trade together. A similar practice was adopted by Muslims on the hajj.

Ulama: Shii Professional although unofficial clergy of Shii Islam. Most important center for education is in Qom, Iran. Historically, ulama have exercised the right of ijtihad (independent reasoning) in interpretation of Islamic law, setting the stage for engagement in social issues. They are believed to serve as agents of the Hidden Imam during his absence, lending them religious authority and placing them in a position to care for the poor, infirm, widows, and orphans and to supervise religious and charitable expenditures. This relationship has provided the basis for social mobilization and collective protest, both socially and politically, as well as financial autonomy. Ulama became an important social force in Iran during the European imperial era in the nineteenth century. They served as major critics of the Qajar shahs on foreign concessions, tax policies, loans, territorial losses, and autocratic conduct—charges that were later leveled against Reza Shah Pahlavi. Ayatollah Ruhollah Khomeini taught that clergy are appropriate rulers in order to ensure implementation of Islamic law. The centralization of power in the hands of Shii ulama since the Iranian revolution is unprecedented in history.

Ulama: Sunni Men of knowledge (sing., *alim*). Refers to those who have been trained in religious sciences (Quran, hadith, fiqh, etc.). In the colonial and postcolonial world, *alim* can also mean a scientist in the secular sense. Formulators of Islamic theology and law in the classical age. In the modern era, the ulama's sphere of operation is confined to the mosque and the madrasa. As imam of the local mosque, an alim leads daily prayers, delivers the Friday sermon, and teaches children the basics of Islamic law and Quranic recitation. On occasions of birth, death, and marriage, he may also be called upon for prayers or for help in performing the rituals themselves. In rural areas, an alim may be the most educated or wisest man in the area, but not necessarily formally trained; in urban centers, ulama generally possess some sort of credentials or formal education.

Ulum *See* Science

Ulum al-Tabiah, al- *See* Natural Science

Umar ibn Abd al-Aziz (r. 717–20) Also known as Umar II. Umayyad caliph who introduced measures to create a uniform judicial system. Shifted the emphasis of the empire from Arab to Muslim, recognizing all Muslims as equal. Made rules of taxation more egalitarian, revising kharaj tax to consider the status of land rather than the religion of its owner. Preserved nominal state ownership of land by preventing kharaj lands (owned by state but cultivated by individuals) from becoming ushri lands (owned by individuals and taxed according to yield). Sought to convert West Asia to Islam.

Umar ibn al-Khattab (r. 634–644) Second Sunni caliph and Companion of Muhammad. Oversaw major expansion of the Islamic empire. Great military leader who adopted the title "Commander of the Faithful." Transformed Arab conquerors into a separate elite military class who ruled newly conquered regions but were not permitted to engage in agriculture or commerce. Permitted conquered peoples to continue to practice their own religions, rather than insisting that they convert to Islam, provided that they paid a poll tax. Transmitted numerous hadith; considered a particularly authoritative source. Instituted the method of appointing a committee to select the next caliph; the election was to be accompanied by the clasping of hands and the exchange of oaths of allegiance to the successor.

Umar Tal (d. 1864) Islamic militant leader and intellectual. Initiated into the Tijani tariqah and became its most prominent leader in West Africa. After making the pilgrimage to Mecca and studying with the son of Uthman Dan Fodio, he began a jihad in 1852. His conquests created an empire that included much of modern-day Senegal, Guinea, Mali, and Mauritania. He faced local resistance and French imperial expansion in the region. His state collapsed soon after his death. This jihad marked an important phase in the Islamization of West Africa, and his writings influenced Tijani and general Islamic thought at the time.

Umayyad Caliphate Dynasty that ruled the Islamic caliphate from the death of the fourth Sunni caliph (first Shii imam), Ali, in 661 until 750. Its founder was Muawiyah ibn Abi Sufyan of the Meccan clan of Umayyah. By the time of Muawiyah's death in 680, he had established Damascus as the capital and a system of administration for the caliphate that gave it a degree of stability. A later caliph, Abd al-Malik, strengthened the organization of the empire, making Arabic the official language of government and replacing Byzantine and Sassanian coinage with coins with Arabic inscriptions. At times tribal rivalries threatened the unity of the empire. The dynasty was responsible for the expansion of the Islamic state westward through North Africa to the Atlantic Ocean. In 711 the Umayyads crossed into the Iberian peninsula and rapidly conquered most of it, establishing a forward base in southern France. They were defeated between Tours and Poitiers in 732 by Charles Martel, halting the expansion of Islam into western Europe. In the East, they moved from Iran into Central Asia and northwest India. Little progress was made in the North due to the strength of the Byzantine Empire. The Umayyads' great expansion was primarily military and political, not religious; conversion to Islam was discouraged for some time since it would reduce the treasury's intake of taxes on non-Muslims. Its armies were originally exclusively Arab and Muslim, but clients were ultimately included, mostly of Iranian and Berber origin. Later Muslim historians accused the Umayyads of transforming the Islamic state into an Arab kingdom. The Umayyads did rely largely on the traditional political ideas of Arabs, but they also claimed to be upholders of Islam. Overthrown by Abbasids in 750.

Umdah (1) Village chief or magistrate. (2) Veteran master in a guild. (3) Basic argument in a debate.

Umm al-Qura *See* Mecca

Umm al-Walad Mother of the son. Refers to a slave woman impregnated by her owner, thereby bearing a child. In the opinion of many classical jurists, such a slave woman cannot be sold. In sociohistorical practice, slave girls used their beauty and intelligence to attract the attention of powerful men and then used the birth of male children to place themselves in positions of power. In some cases they were raised to the rank of queen after giving birth to a son, especially under the Abbasids and Ottomans. Children, male or female, born of this union are legally free and enjoy all rights of legitimate parentage, including inheritance and use of the father's name.

Umm Habiba *See* Ramla bint Abi Sufyan

Umm Salama *See* Hind bint Abi Umayya

Ummah Muslim community. A fundamental concept in Islam, expressing the essential unity and theoretical equality of Muslims from diverse cultural and geographical settings. In the Quran, designates people to whom God has sent a prophet or people who are objects of a divine plan of salvation.

Ummah Party Founded by Abd al-Rahman al-Mahdi, son of the Sudanese leader Muhammad Ahmad ibn Abd Allah, the "Mahdi," in 1945 as a nationalist movement demanding Sudanese independence from Egypt and Britain. Was an alliance between rural followers of the Mahdist tradition and the emerging modern-educated class. Has contested elections in every era of civilian politics in Sudan since 1956 and has headed coalition governments in each era as well. It took an active role in the opposition to the military regimes of Abboud, Numayri, and Bashir. Heads of the party have been descendants of the Mahdi. *See also* Mahdi, Abd al-Rahman al-; Mahdi, al-Sadiq al-; Mahdiyyah

UMNO *See* United Malays National Organization

Umrah Pilgrimage to Mecca at a time other than that designated for the obligatory hajj. Often called the lesser pilgrimage. Umrah is not required of Muslims, but it is considered meritorious. Many of the basic rituals that comprise the hajj are part of the umrah as well: walking around the Kaaba seven times, running or walking between the hills of Safa and Marwa, and cutting the hair or shaving one's head.

Union des Organisations Islamiques de France Created in 1983 as a federation of local Islamic associations. Receives financial assistance from the Muslim World League and private individuals in Saudi Arabia, Kuwait, and United Arab Emirates. Particularly active in the center and east of France. Its leaders are influenced by the ideology of Egyptian and Tunisian Islamist movements and seek to support local associations in managing religious and educational activities specifically tailored to the needs of Muslims living in France, such as children's holiday camps providing Quranic teaching. In 1991 the group created the first Muslim seminary in France to train imams. It seeks to improve knowledge of Islam among the French.

Unitarians *See* Wahhabis

United Kingdom–Islamic Mission Founded in 1962 to promote missionary work in Britain through lectures and hospitality, distribution of the Quran, and establishment of Islamic bookshops. Concentrates on strengthening religious knowledge among immigrants of Muslim background through organization of classes on the Quran and on the basic teachings and practices of Islam for the children of Muslim families. Regular lectures and short courses on Islamic studies are organized for adults. Training camps and activities are organized for young people. Local branches organize pastoral visits to prisons. During the 1980s it started offering legal advice. In 1981 it established a marriage bureau. The group works closely with the Islamic Foundation and is influenced by Jamaat-i Islami of Pakistan.

United Malays National Organization Ethnic Malay party founded in 1946. Has been a dominant political force in Malaysia. Seeks to protect and promote Malay political, sociocultural, religious, and economic interests. Under the leadership of Mahathir Mohamed, has promoted an Islamization program to uphold Islamic values while modernizing.

Universal Islamic Declaration of Human Rights (UIDHR) Islamic counterpart to the UN's Universal Declaration of Human Rights (UDHR). Prepared by the Islamic Council, affiliated with the Muslim World League. Ratified in 1981 and presented to UNESCO. Outlines human rights in criminal cases, marriage, inheritance, divorce, and economic activities, and supports freedom of religion based on traditional Islamic law.

Universities (Islamic) The first Islamic university, Qarawiyin, was founded in Fez in 859. After that, universities were established across the Muslim world with classical Islamic curricula. In the nineteenth century secular educational systems entered Muslim societies. Colonial powers established modern secular schools to train a new elite to govern and modernize society, resulting in resistance from traditional Muslim ulama. Today most universities incorporate the traditional Islamic sciences and curricula as well as modern sciences. New Islamic universities, endorsed by the Organization of the Islamic Conference, operate in Kuala Lumpur, Malaysia, and Islamabad, Pakistan. With a diverse student body and teaching staff, they seek to combine access to classical subjects with reliance on scientific methodology and nontraditional disciplines. *See also* Azhar, al-; Education: Educational Institutions; Education: Educational Reform

Urabi, Ahmad (d. 1911) Egyptian colonel of peasant background and national hero in the struggle for independence from Britain. Appointed Egyptian war minister in 1882 with the slogan "Misr lil-misriyyin" (Egypt for the Egyptians). Led a failed revolt against the British in 1882.

Urf Custom. In the central Islamic countries, it is the common name for unwritten customary law, in contrast to written Islamic law codes or other legal canons. *Adat* is a synonym used in other parts of the Islamic world, especially Indonesia. Urf often refers to three different types of legal categories: the way common people maintain order, engage in social interactions, or conduct business locally, for example, in the marketplace or in wedding ceremonies; the legal decisions made by a ruler and his representatives; and the practices of local courts. According to the Malikis and some Hanafis such as Ibn Abidin, urf is considered to be a source of law. *See also* Adat

Urs (1) Marriage or wedding. In Islam, a contract of civil law. The signing of a marriage contract is typically accompanied by processions, special clothing, and feasts. In some countries it is accompanied by music and dancing. (2) In Sufism, the union of a saint with God, the ultimate goal of Sufi experience. In India it refers to commemoration of the death date of a Sufi saint. *See also* Marriage and Divorce: Legal Foundations

Urwat al-Wuthqa, al- The strongest bond; from the Quran 2:256. Name of a journal jointly published by Muhammad Abduh and Jamal al-Din al-Afghani in Paris in 1884. Was used to disseminate Afghani's reformist reinterpretation of Islam and advocacy of resistance to European colonialism in the Muslim world. Greatly influenced later Muslim reformists, most notably Muhammad Rashid Rida. Was published for seven months, a total of eighteen issues. Marks the debut of Islamic periodical literature.

Ushr Tithe or tenth; the land tax levied on the produce of agricultural land owned by Muslims in the premodern era. Ushr was revived in Pakistan in the 1980s as part of the Islamization regime.

Usman Dan Fodio See Dan Fodio, Uthman

Ustadh Teacher. Honorific title of respect popularly assigned to those who are widely recognized for their learning. Can also be a person in an official capacity at a school or university. In Sufism, refers to the master of a tariqah, who is responsible for imparting the special devotional practices and teachings of the order to disciples.

Usul al-Fiqh Roots of law. The body of principles and investigative methodologies through which practical legal rules are developed from the foundational sources. The primary base of law is the Quran. The second source is the Sunnah, reports about the sayings, actions, or tacit approvals of the Prophet. The third source is the consensus (ijma) of all Muslim interpretive scholars in a specific age on a legal rule about an issue not covered in the Quran or Sunnah. Most Sunni scholars consider consensus binding; others, including Shii scholars, say such consensus is impossible. The fourth source is analogy (qiyas), or rule by precedent. Some Hanafis, such as Ibn Abidin and Maliki jurists, consider urf (custom) to be an additional source of law. In addition to these basic sources, several presumptions and principles aid the jurist in deriving interpretive rules: preference (istihsan), unregulated interest (maslahah mursalah), and the presumption of continuity (istishab). This field is also concerned with hermeneutic and deductive principles

Usulis Shii school of Islamic law relying on a series of rational processes dating to at least the twelfth century. Opposed to traditionist Akhbaris. Favored the exercise of ijtihad (independent reasoning) by those qualified to carry it out and obedience to these rulings (taqlid) by those not capable of exercising ijtihad themselves. The most important legacy of the movement is the selection of scholars to be imitated, known as marja altaqlid; the teachings of the most respected scholar of the time are to be adhered to. Obedience to practitioners of ijtihad became a religious duty for Shiis, elevating the status

of jurists and profoundly impacting Iranian history and society by setting the stage for the political activism of Shii ulama in the nineteenth and twentieth centuries. The movement can be regarded as the precursor to the Islamic revolution of 1978–79.

Usury See Riba

Utaybi, Juhayman al- (d. 1980) Leader of a militant group that seized the Grand Mosque in Mecca in November 1979, protesting the corruption and excesses of the Saudi royal family and demanding a return to a purer Islam. Proclaimed the coming of the Mahdi and the end of the Saudi state. Attacked the religious legitimacy of the Saudi family, declaring them unfit to serve as custodians of holy cities. Executed by the state. His messianic message reflected a growing dissatisfaction with the Saudi state and pressured the royal family to accede to demands for a consultative assembly (majlis); this did not materialize until after the Gulf War, 1990–91. See also Qahtani, Muhammad al-

Uthman Dan Fodio See Dan Fodio, Uthman

Uthman ibn Affan (d. 656) Companion of the Prophet Muhammad, third caliph in the succession of early leaders. From the powerful Umayyad clan. Despite his family's opposition to Muhammad, Uthman was among the first converts and married two daughters of Muhammad, first Rukayya and then Umm Kalthum. Uthman was elected caliph by a committee appointed by his predecessor, Umar, on his deathbed. Under his leadership, the text of the Quran was standardized, with variant collections being destroyed. He appointed many relatives to high positions. Popular discontent led to a mutiny of troops, who killed him in 656. The nomination of Ali as his successor led to the first major civil war in Islam.

Uwaysi Tariqah Branch of the Qadiri tariqah founded by Shaykh Umar Uways al-Barawi. Active throughout East Africa, particularly Somalia. Based in Zanzibar. Active in missionary activities in Tanzania, Kenya, and eastern Congo. Ability to transcend tribal loyalties helped it to unite and lead Muslim anti-German resistance in southern Tanganyika during the early part of the colonial era. Known for revivalism and for tolerance of visitation of saints' tombs and requesting intercession with God from deceased holy people. Acceptance of popular practices brought it into conflict with the more fundamentalist Salihi tariqah. Shaykh Uways was assassinated in 1909.

Uzayr See Ezra

Uzbekistan, Islam in Eighty-eight percent of the population is Sunni (Hanafi) Muslim; 9 percent is Eastern Orthodox. Ethnic breakdown: Uzbek 80 percent, Russian 5.5 percent, Tajik 5 percent, Kazakh 3 percent, Karakalpak 2.5 percent, Tatar 1 percent, other 2.5 percent. Active Sufi orders include Naqshbandi, Qadiri, Kubrawi, and Qalandari. Islam arrived in Uzbekistan via trade and itinerant preachers in the seventh cen-

tury. The modern capital, Tashkent, was the dominant political center during the tsarist and Soviet periods. Many Muslims defied or circumvented Soviet strictures by continuing to observe rituals and making forbidden pilgrimages to saints' tombs. Since independence (1991), unresolved social and economic problems and severe political and religious oppression have fueled radical elements such as the Islamic Movement of Uzbekistan. The government has responded with mass arrests, detainment, and torture of Muslims unaffiliated with approved state Muslim organizations.

Uzzah, al- One of three pre-Islamic goddesses worshiped at the Kaaba in Mecca prior to the rise of Islam. Goddess of strength, she is identified as a daughter of Allah, since she was supposed to be the offspring of Allah's marriage to jinn. Usually represented as a sacred tree. The idol representing her was destroyed in 630 when Muhammad and the Muslims conquered Mecca. Denounced in the Quran (53:19–20).

V

Vazir *See* Vizier

Veil *See* Chador; Hijab

Verses *See* Ayah/Ayat

Vezir *See* Vizier

Vicegerent *See* Khalifah

Vilayat-i Faqih Rule or guardianship by a jurist. The concept gained wide currency in the Shii world when it was used as the title of a published series of lectures given by Ayatollah Khomeini in 1969. It became the form of Islamic government in Iran when Khomeini came to power in 1979 and became the supreme arbiter of all matters of government in Iran. The concept derives from the historical understanding that the exclusive right of interpretation of Islamic law belongs to religious scholars.

Virtue Party Short-lived successor to the Welfare Party (Refah Partisi) in Turkey. Founded in 1998. Became the leading opposition party. Led by Recai Kutan. Proclaimed a softer Islamic profile than Refah, emphasizing Turkey's Islamic traditions and culture; this change was symbolized by the appointment of three non-Islamist, non-hijab-wearing women to the party's executive board. Favored full integration with the West to ensure civilian rule and democracy in Turkey. Fared well in the 1998 municipal elections and proved successful in providing social services. Came in third in the 1999 parliamentary elections. Became controversial later that year after a female deputy, Merve Kavakci, was forced to leave the swearing-in session of the parliament because she wore a head scarf. Accused of being an illegal Islamic organization and was banned in 2001, making it the sixteenth political party to be outlawed in Turkey since 1983.

Vizier Arabic and Persian *wazir, vazir;* Turkish *vezir.* Sovereign's chief deputy or minister. Acted for the caliph in military and civil matters. Under the Ottoman Empire (1300–1923), the grand vizier presided over the ordinary ministers and other officers of state. He resided in the Bab-i Ali (Sublime Porte), which became synonymous with the state itself. *See also* Grand Vizier

W

Waad *See* Infanticide

WABIL *See* World Ahl al-Bayt Islamic League

Wadud, Amina (b. 1952) Muslim academic and activist. Trained in Islamic studies, but her scholarship and activism center on gender jihad (struggle for Islamic gender parity). Active with the Women in Islam group in Malaysia. In her *Quran and Woman* (1996), creates a female-inclusive hermeneutical approach to the Quran based on ijtihadist methods articulated by Fazlur Rahman (d. 1988).

Wahdat al-Shuhud Oneness of appearance, as opposed to oneness of Being (wahdat al-wujud), as taught by Ibn al-Arabi. Doctrine taught by the Indian Sufi Ahmad al-Sirhindi as an attempt to integrate reformist Sufi ideas into a Sunni framework.

Wahdat al-Wujud The unity of Being. Doctrine formulated by the school of Ibn al-Arabi, which postulates that God and His creation are one, since all that is created preexisted in God's knowledge and will return to it, making mystical union with God possible. This was a problematic doctrine for legalist interpreters of Islam such as the Wahhabis, who held to a strict interpretation of tawhid that did not permit anyone or anything to be associated or in union with God.

Wahhabis Eighteenth-century reformist/revivalist movement for sociomoral reconstruction of society. Founded by Muhammad ibn Abd al-Wahhab, a Hanbali scholar, in Arabia. Proclaimed tawhid (uniqueness and unity of God) as its primary doctrine. Began in response to the perceived moral decline and political weakness of the Muslim community in Arabia. Proposed a return to an idealized Islamic past through reassertion of monotheism and reliance on Quran and hadith, rejecting medieval interpretations of Islam and jurisprudence. Emphasized education and knowledge as weapons in dealing with nonbelievers. Known for its sometimes violent opposition to the popular cult of saints, idolatry, and shrine and tomb visitation, as well as the sacking of Shii shrines in Najaf and Karbala in 1802. Formed an alliance with Muhammad ibn Saud in 1747, which served as the basis for the consolidation of the present-day kingdom of Saudi Arabia. Referred to as Wahhabis by opponents, but referred to themselves as Muwahhidun, or those upholding the doctrine of tawhid.

Wahhabiyyah *See* Wahhabis

Wahid, Abdurrahman (b. 1940) Also known as Gus Dur. Indonesian Islamic thinker, writer, and politician. Elected president of Indonesia in 1998 and replaced by parliamentary vote in 2000. Chair of the Executive Council of Nahdatul Ulama (NU) from 1984 to 1998. Promoted pesantren (rural Islamic boarding schools) as an agent for the development of rural community and democratic society at the grassroots level. Desires reconstruction of socioethical guidelines for contemporary Muslims through reinterpretation of the Quran and Sunnah in historical perspective. Known for his moderate politics and support of religious pluralism and tolerance. Argues that the principles underlying values such as human rights, social justice, fair development, and democracy are inherent in Islam, rather than an ideological compromise or cultural mixture with Western liberalism. Maintains that rediscovery of the values and dynamism of the methodology for jurisprudence has been hindered by traditionalist ulama, who are focused on legal formalism and ritual correctness. Opposed to both secularization of the Indonesian state and Islamic fundamentalism's claims to be a comprehensive way of life superior to existing secular regimes. Believes that neither Islam nor any other religion should be in confrontation with the state or another religion. *See also* Nahdatul Ulama

Wahy Inspiration, particularly the divine inspiration of the Quran and other scriptures. Islam teaches that God periodically reveals His will, providing precise information to guide human affairs and to lead to a happy afterlife. Wahy is the direct transmission of the specific words of revelation (not simply the ideas) through prophets.

Waiting Period *See* Iddah

Wajib In Islamic jurisprudence, an obligatory act, with failure to perform it being sinful. Wajib acts can be obligatory on every individual (fard al-ayn), such as prayer, or on the entire community (fard al-kifayah), such as burying the dead. In the latter case, if some members perform the act, the obligation on the rest of the community is removed. *See also* Fard al-Ayn; Fard al-Kifayah

Wakalat al-Ammah, al- Concept in Twelver Shiism that justifies assumption by the ulama of the leadership role and the prerogatives of the Hidden Imam as his collective deputy. Because all spiritual and political authority rests with the imam in Twelver Shiism, the legitimacy of any political or judicial position must derive from him, and all revenues from religious taxes must go to him. The concept gave Shii ulama legitimacy and a source of income independent of secular appointments or state support, enabling them to build a separate base of power from which to challenge secular authorities; it formed the basis for Ayatollah Khomeini's vilayat-i faqih, which has been enshrined in the Iranian constitution.

Wakalat al-Khassah, al- In Twelver Shiism, the designation of four successive persons to act as deputies of the Hidden Imam. When the twelfth imam went into occultation, a lesser occultation period followed in which four successive persons claimed to be his deputies. In 944 the last one declared that there would be no more specific representatives until the Hidden Imam returned, marking the beginning of the period of greater occultation. The only figure since then to claim special deputy status was the founder of the nineteenth-century Bab movement in Iran. Ayatollah Khomeini concentrated the general deputyship in himself, rendering him the de facto if not de jure vicegerent of the Hidden Imam.

Wakil In Islamic law, a duly delegated agent who acts on behalf of the principal in legal matters, such as in contracting marriage or conducting business. Under the law, there are different types of agencies, each one enjoying certain rights and powers. Wakil can refer to the custodian or administrator of a mosque (particularly those in Mecca and Medina) or of a Sufi order, often responsible for finances, collection of dues and contributions, and organizing mawlid and other celebrations.

Walad Descendant, offspring, child, son, boy, or young one. From the Arabic *walada*, meaning "to bear," "to give birth to," "to beget," "to produce."

Walayah Sometimes translated as "sainthood." State of being of one chosen by God to interpret the inner meaning of God's revelation to human beings, providing an ongoing link between humankind and divine revelation. In Shiism, denotes the characteristics required for succession to the imamate. Successors must be descendants of Muhammad who are appointed based on their esoteric knowledge. They are expected to provide political leadership, be actively involved in upholding religious law, and possess special knowledge of the esoteric dimension of Quranic revelation. In Sufism, a person chosen by God to fulfill the duty of walayah is known as a wali, or friend of God. The wali is believed to have been given divine protection against error in order to preserve God's religion intact.

Wali *See* Walayah

Wali al-Ahd Guardian of the covenant. The heir to a kingdom or state. Crown prince.

Wali al-Amr Male legal guardian, usually the father. Responsible for overseeing minors' and unmarried females' marriage contracts and property interests, and for the maintenance and welfare of wards. In cases where the father is not present, male guardianship passes first to the paternal uncle or paternal grandfather. In some cases, the court may be petitioned to assume guardianship.

Wali Allah, Shah (d. 1762) Most prominent Muslim intellectual of eighteeenth-century India and a prolific writer on a wide range of Islamic topics in Arabic and Persian. He was accepted into the Naqshbandi tariqah at fifteen and performed the hajj when he was twenty-eight. Upon his return to India, Wali Allah taught in a madrasa and served as a Sufi guide. His most influential work, *Hujjat Allah al-balighah*, sought to reform Islamic studies through the new exegetical literature in hadith studies; this book is still studied from the Arab Middle East to South and Southeast Asia. After his death, Wali Allah's teachings were carried on by his sons and grandson. Today all major religious movements in Muslim South Asia claim Wali Allah as an intellectual progenitor. Groups such as the Deobandis assert his teachings on intellectual and mystical Islam. Puritanical and anti-Sufi movements such as the Ahl-i Hadith stress his return to shariah's fundamentals and rejection of Sufi excesses and foreign elements. Politically oriented Islamic groups emphasize his ideas on socioeconomic justice and political activism.

Walid, Khalid ibn al-Mughira Makhzumi al- (d. ca. 641) Commander of Muslim army. Conquered Damascus in 635, ending Byzantine rule in Syria and Palestine and leading to Muslim control over Jerusalem. Nicknamed "Sword of God" by Muhammad. Crushed a tribal revolt, known as the Wars of Apostasy, following Muhammad's death,

defeating the contemporary self-proclaimed prophet Musaylima, consolidating Muslim control over the entire Arabian peninsula, and preserving the unity and solidarity of the Islamic community.

Wansharisi, Ahmad al- (d. 1508) Maliki jurist and scholar born in Tlemcen (present-day Algeria). Principally known for his compilation of North African and Andalusian legal opinions (fatwas) in his multivolume *Al-miyar al-murib*. By the sixteenth century his *Al-miyar* had become an integral part of the educational curriculum in North Africa; today it is studied as a source of information on the social, cultural, economic, and juridical practices of medieval al-Andalus and the Maghreb. In addition to *Al-miyar*, another fourteen of his known works are extant; almost all concern Islamic jurisprudence.

Waqf Confinement or prohibition; pl. *awqaf*. Generally used to mean the endowment of a certain property for the sole benefit of a certain philanthropy with the intention of prohibiting any use or disposition of the property outside that specific purpose; applies to nonperishable property whose benefit can be extracted without consuming the property itself. The three most typical kinds of waqf are religious (mosques, as well as real estate that exclusively provides revenues for mosque maintenance and service expenses), philanthropic (support for the poor and the public interest at large by funding such institutions and activities as libraries, scientific research, education, health services, and care of animals and the environment), and posterity or family awqaf (whose revenues are first given to the family's descendants; only the surplus, if any, is given to the poor).

Waqidi, Abu Abd Allah Muhammad ibn Umar al- (d. 823) Historian and judge from Arabia. Famed for popular histories of the military expeditions of the Prophet Muhammad and the early caliphs. Among the first to use hadith traditions to develop a chronology of events in early Islam. Many of his traditions were viewed with suspicion under later traditionists' strict standards of authenticity.

War See Harb; Jihad; Terrorism

Waraqah ibn Nawfal ibn Asad Christian cousin of Muhammad's first wife, Khadijah. According to tradition, assured Muhammad that his call to prophecy and message were genuinely from God. Acknowledged that Muhammad's recitation of revelation was identical to the revelation given to Moses. Prophesied that Muhammad, like other prophets before him, would be rejected, fought against, and lied about.

Wasat Party See Hizb al-Wasat

Washing, Funerary See Funerary Rites

Wasi The legatee of religious knowledge and esoteric truths in Shiism. According to Shii belief, Muhammad designated his cousin and son-in-law, Ali ibn Abi Talib (d. 661), as his legatee and successor. The knowledge given to Ali as wasi and imam was then passed on to the latter's successors through formal designation (nass).

Wasil ibn Ata (d. 749) One of the putative founders of the Mutazili school of theology. Studied with theologian Hasan al-Basri. Declared that grave sinners were neither believers nor unbelievers but occupied "a position between these two" (manzilah bayna al-manzilatayn). This story was often used to explain Mutazilis' refusal to take a position on which of those involved in the first civil war (656–61) were right or wrong. He died in 749.

Wasiyyah See Bequest

Wataniyyah See Nationalism and Islam

Wazifah (1) Something that is assigned or appointed. The principal meaning refers to the apportioning of sections of the Quran for orderly recitation. The simplest mode of division arranges the reading into seven sections, so that the entire scripture can be recited in one week. An alternative recitation divides the Quran into thirty parts so that it can be read in one month. (2) In the system of waqf, denotes a portion of the financial provision to be assigned to maintenance of religious functionaries. (3) In the language of Islamic taxation, a major source of public revenue based on the potential of a piece of land for production, whether or not it was actually cultivated.

Wazir See Vizier

Weddings See Marriage and Divorce: Legal Foundations; Marriage and Divorce: Modern Practices

Weiss, Leopold See Asad, Muhammad

Welfare Party Refah Partisi (RP). Turkish Islamist political organization established in 1983 as heir to two earlier parties, Milli Nizam Partisi (National Order Party, MNP) and Milli Selamet Partisi (National Salvation Party, MSP), which were successively banned from politics. Each of the three parties was led by Necmettin Erbakan. MNP was banned before it could stand for elections; MSP participated in two coalition governments before being shut down following the 1980 military coup. The RP participated in elections and in 1995 won more parliamentary seats than any other party. Erbakan became prime minister in 1996 at the head of a coalition government but was forced out of power by the military in 1997. The RP was outlawed in 1998. The Fazilet Partisi (Virtue Party, FP) was soon organized and became identified as the Islamically oriented party. The RP advocated stronger ties with other Muslim countries and an economic system based on Islamic morals rather than global capitalist ideas.

West Bank and Gaza, Islam in Palestinian territories, including the west bank of the Jordan River, taken over by Jordan in 1952 and lost to Israel in 1967, and a narrow strip of land on the Mediterranean coast lost by Egypt to Israel in the same war. Considered the "Palestinian entity" and are the basis of negotiations for the creation of a Palestinian state. Historically, they are only part of Palestine. Ninety-nine percent of the population of Gaza is Sunni Muslim, and .07 percent is Christian; 75 percent of the West Bank and East Jerusalem is Sunni Muslim, with 17 percent Jewish and 8 percent Christian or other. Since the imposition of military rule by Israel in 1967, Palestinians have been denied civil and political rights, and Israel has confiscated significant portions of the occupied land to establish settlements for Israeli citizens (some 250,000 in 2002), diverted water resources, and annexed East Jerusalem, all in violation of international law. The West Bank, including East Jerusalem, and the Gaza Strip are considered occupied territory under international law. UN Security Council resolutions 242 (1967) and 338 (1973) call for the withdrawal of Israel from these territories. *See also* Arab-Israeli Conflict; Jerusalem

Westernization Refers to economic, legal, social, cultural, and political modernization and development following Western models of law, political systems, finance, dress, language, education, ideas, and behavior. Typically accompanied European colonial activities throughout the Islamic world and resulted in the devaluation of local languages, culture, and economic and social structures, as well as alienation, marginalization, and the perceived loss of cultural identity. Political failures as well as the failure to achieve development, public order, and modernization led some to conclude that Western models had failed and to call for religio-cultural revival, returning to Islam and its accompanying cultural values as a more authentic and historically powerful identity.

Westoxification Persian *gharbzadegi*. Term coined by the Iranian secular intellectual Jalal al-e Ahmad to describe the fascination with and dependence upon the West to the detriment of traditional, historical, and cultural ties to Islam and Islamic world. Defined as an indiscriminate borrowing from and imitation of the West, joining the twin dangers of cultural imperialism and political domination. Implies a sense of intoxication or infatuation that impairs rational judgment and confers an inability to see the dangers presented by the toxic substance, that is, the West. The West's inherent dangers are described as moral laxity, social injustice, secularism, devaluation of religion, and obsession with money, all of which are fueled by capitalism; the common result is cultural alienation. The term was adopted by Ali Shariati, ideologue of the Iranian revolution, to describe the results of Iran's modernization program.

Whirling Dervishes *See* Mawlawi Tariqah

White Revolution Social, economic, and legal reforms undertaken by Shah Reza Pahlavi in the 1960s and 1970s to modernize Iran. The benefits went largely to elites in urban environments; the reforms failed to achieve results in rural areas or among the more traditional sectors of society. Administration of the reforms was often corrupt. The presence of Western corporations and banks fueled concerns about Western economic imperialism. The government tried to control the ulama by controlling seminaries and religious schools and introducing state-trained, secular-oriented teachers into rural schools. Critical religious leaders and intellectuals were harassed, tortured, exiled, arrested, and sometimes killed. The reforms' failures fueled popular dissatisfaction, leading to the Islamic revolution of 1979.

Wilayah *See* Guardianship

Wilayat al-Faqih *See* Vilayat-i Faqih

Wird Devotion or liturgy specific to a particular Sufi order. Prayers in which the substance of the tariqah is defined. Originally designated specific times Sufis devoted to God and the specific dhikr recited on these occasions. An initiate is given the secret wird of the order upon completion of training, transferring the spiritual power of the chain of transmission from the founder of the order and Muhammad to the initiate. Taking wird is equivalent to full initiation into the tariqah.

Wisdom *See* Hikmah

Wives of the Prophet According to the biographer Ibn Hisham (d. 834), the Prophet married thirteen women. Khadijah bint Khuwaylid, Sawda bint Zama, Aishah bint Abi Bakr, Hafsah bint Umar, Zaynab bint Khuzaymah, Hind bint Abi Umayya (known as Umm Salama), Zaynab bint Jahsh, Maymuna bint al-Harith, and Juwayriyah bint al-Harith were Arab; six of them were from Quraysh, and the rest were from other tribes. Safiyah bint Huyay was from a Jewish tribe. Rayhanah bint Zayd was from a Jewish tribe as well, although there is some doubt regarding her marriage to the Prophet; Asma bint al-Numan and Amra bint Yazid were both divorced by the Prophet before consummation. At the time of his death in 632 the Prophet left behind nine wives and a consort, Maryam the Copt. The wives of the Prophet are called "Mothers of the Faithful" (Umm al-Muminin) in the Quran (33:6) and forbidden in marriage to other men after the Prophet's death (33:53). They are regarded as moral exemplars for Muslim women. Aishah and Umm Salama in particular reported numerous hadiths from Muhammad and thus played a decisive role in the shaping of the Sunnah.

Wolcott, Louis Eugene *See* Farrakhan, Louis

Women's Action Forum Formed in 1981 in response to the Pakistani government's implementation of the traditional Islamic penal code. Members feared that new laws would discriminate against women and compromise their civil status. The group has played a central role in the public exposure of controversy regarding various intepretations of Islamic law, its role in the modern state, and ways in which women can play a more active role in political matters. Current goals include securing women's representation in parliament; working to raise women's consciousness, particularly with respect to family planning; and countering suppression and raising public awareness of women's issues by taking stands and issuing statements on events as they occur.

World Ahl al-Bayt Islamic League International Shii organization headquartered in London. Oversees performance and registration of marriages and divorces, distribution of authoritative opinions, assignment of teachers and religious leaders to Shii communities, assistance to Shii victims of natural disasters, financial aid to Shii students wishing to study in madrasas, and responses to propaganda against Shiis.

World Assembly of Muslim Youth Founded in 1972 in Riyadh, Saudi Arabia, to help Islamic youth organizations around the world implement planned projects. International meetings are held approximately every three years. Publishes a newsletter in English and Arabic. Headquarters are located in Riyadh with regional offices in Jeddah (Saudi Arabia), Malaysia, Spain, Nigeria, and Kenya.

World Community of Islam in the West Reformist group headed by Warith Deen Muhammad that split from the racial supremicism and nationalism of the Black Muslims in 1976 in favor of a closer connection to mainstream Sunni Islam. Aimed to increase international awareness of Islam and its practice on a global scale. Changed its name to the American Muslim Mission in 1978. *See also* American Muslim Mission; Nation of Islam

World Council for Islamic Call Suborganization of the Libyan Islamic Call Society. Established in 1982 as a competitor to the Saudi-based World Muslim League. Advocates for Muammar Qaddafi's Third Universal Alternative and Libyan foreign policy. Meets annually. Thirty-six members are elected by the Conference for the Islamic Mission. Concerned with the international impact of the Islamic Call Society's role as point of contact for Islamic communities worldwide.

World Council of Mosques The Muslim counterpart to the Christian World Council of Churches. Founded in 1975 as a suborganization of the Muslim World League.

Women and Islam

In Islam, men and women are moral equals in God's sight and are expected to fulfill the same duties of worship, prayer, faith, almsgiving, fasting, and pilgrimage to Mecca. Islam generally improved the status of women compared to earlier Arab cultures, prohibiting female infanticide and recognizing women's full personhood. Islamic law emphasizes the contractual nature of marriage, requiring that a dowry be paid to the woman rather than to her family, and guaranteeing women's rights of inheritance and to own and manage property. Women were also granted the right to live in the matrimonial home and receive financial maintainance during marriage and a waiting period following death and divorce.

The historical record shows that Muhammad consulted women and weighed their opinions seriously. At least one woman, Umm Waraqah, was appointed imam over her household by Muhammad. Women contributed significantly to the canonization of the Quran. A woman is known to have corrected the authoritative ruling of Caliph Umar on dowry. Women prayed in mosques unsegregated from men, were involved in hadith transmission, gave sanctuary to men, engaged in commercial transactions, were encouraged to seek knowledge, and were both instructors and pupils in the early Islamic period. Muhammad's last wife, Aishah, was a well-known authority in medicine, history, and rhetoric. The Quran refers to women who pledged an oath of allegiance to Muhammad independently of their male kin. Some distinguished women converted to Islam prior to their husbands, a demonstration of Islam's recognition of their capacity for independent action. Caliph Umar appointed women to serve as officials in the market of Medina. Biographies of distinguished women, especially in Muhammad's household, show that women behaved relatively autonomously in early Islam. In Sufi circles, women were recognized as teachers, adherents, "spiritual mothers," and even inheritors of the spiritual secrets of their fathers.

No woman held religious titles in Islam, but many women held political power, some jointly with their husbands, others independently. The best-known women rulers in the premodern era include Khayzuran, who governed the Muslim Empire under three Abbasid caliphs in the eighth century; Malika Asma bint Shihab al-Sulayhiyya and Malika Arwa bint Ahmad al-Sulayhiyya, who both held power in Yemen in the eleventh century; Sitt al-Mulk, a Fatimid queen of Egypt in the eleventh century; the Berber queen Zaynab al-Nafzawiyah (r. 1061–1107); two thirteenth-century Mamluk queens, Shajar al-Durr in Cairo and Radiyyah in Delhi; six Mongol queens, including Kutlugh Khatun (thirteenth century) and her daughter Padishah Khatun of the Kutlugh-Khanid dynasty; the fifteenth-century Andalusian queen Aishah al-Hurra, known by the Spaniards as Sultana Madre de Boabdil; Sayyida al-Hurra, governor of Tetouán in Morocco (r. 1510–1542); and four seventeenth-century Indonesian queens.

Nevertheless, the status of women in premodern Islam in general conformed not to Quranic ideals but to prevailing patriarchal cultural norms. As a result, improvement of the status of women became a major issue in modern, reformist Islam.

Since the mid-nineteenth century, men and women have questioned the legal and social restrictions on women, especially regarding education, seclusion, strict veiling, polygyny, slavery, and concubinage. Women have published works advocating reforms, established schools for girls, opposed veiling and polygyny, and engaged in student and nationalist movements. Nationalist movements and new states that emerged in the post–World War II period perceived women and gender issues as crucial to social development. State policies

(continued)

Women and Islam (continued)

enabled groups of women to enter the male-dominated political sphere and professions previously closed to them, although these policies often caused popular and religious backlash.

Debates continue over the appropriate level of female participation in the public sphere. Women are typically viewed as key to either reforming or conserving tradition because of their roles in maintaining family, social continuity, and culture. Women's status has also been used as a means of defining national identity. Although governments of twentieth-century Muslim nation-states have promoted education for both boys and girls as a means of achieving economic growth, the percentage of girls enrolled in schools in developing countries with large and rapidly growing populations remains low. Concern for men's jobs has given added incentive to the conservative call for women to adhere to traditional roles as housewives and mothers, although economic necessity has led women to undertake whatever work they can find, usually low-paid, unskilled labor. War and labor migration have increased the number of female-headed households.

Women today are active participants in grassroots organizations; development projects; economic, education, health, and political projects; relief efforts; charitable associations; and social services. Modern reforms have made polygynous marriages difficult or illegal; permitted wives to sue for divorce in religious courts, particularly in cases of cruelty, desertion, or dangerous contagious diseases; provided women with the right to contract themselves in marriage; required husbands to find housing for a divorced wife while she has custody over the children; increased the minimum age for spouses; limited the ability of guardians to contract women in marriage against their wishes; provided opportunities for minor girls wed against their wishes to abrogate the marriage upon reaching majority; enhanced the rights of women with regard to child custody; and allowed women to write clauses into marriage contracts that limit the husband's authority over them.

In the contemporary era, women have again assumed leadership roles in the Muslim world. Benazir Bhutto was prime minister of Pakistan (1988–90, 1993–96), Tansu Çiller was prime minister of Turkey (1993–96), and Shaykh Hasina is the current prime minister of Bangladesh (1996–). Nonetheless, tensions remain between traditionalists, who advocate continued patriarchy, and reformists, who advocate continued liberation of women. *See also* Hijab; Seclusion

Specializes in coordination of missionary activities. Supports the establishment of a jurisprudence council entrusted with the elaboration and control of internationally accepted standards of Islamic law. Supported the opening of the Islamic Fiqh Academy in Saudi Arabia in 1976.

World Federation of Khoja Shia Ithna-Ashari Muslim Communities Established as a nonprofit organization in 1976 in London to serve the Khoja Shii communities around the world. Operating under a constitution, it is run by elected officeholders and the executive council. It derives its policies from a conference held every three years. The secretariat is at the Islamic Centre in Stanmore, England. With twenty-four member communities, four regional federations in Africa, Europe, North America, and India, and a total memberhsip of over a hundred thousand, it is regarded as one of the key organizations in the wider Shii world. The organization has served as an important catalyst for capital projects and a venue for channeling humanitarian and other welfare services around the world.

World Islamic Council for Propagation and Relief Founded in 1988 to integrate missionary activities with relief work supported by the Muslim World League. Aimed at communities and localities affected by natural disaster, unemployment, or poverty, motivated by the conviction that the Islamic ummah is a singular expression of solidarity and humanity.

Worship *See* Ibadah

Wudu Obligatory cleansing rituals performed in order to render the believer ritually pure. Required prior to prayer for both men and women. Consists of washing the hands, mouth, face, arms up to the elbows, and feet. Water is usually poured over the top of the head as well. Among the things that defile purity are sleep, sex, menstrua-

tion, and toilet operations. Major ritual impurity (incurred by, e.g., sexual intercourse, menstruation, childbirth) necessitates a ritual bath (ghusl). In the absence of water, ablutions might be performed by rubbing one's hands against clay or sand and passing them over the face and arms (tayammum).

Wuquf (1) Ceremonial pause or halt during the hajj pilgrimage to Mecca; prescribed prayers performed on the ninth day of Dhu al-Hijja in the Plain of Arafat from noon until sunset. (2) In Naqshbandi Sufism, a pause in or stopping of the performance of a verbal, rhythmic dhikr. Baha al-Din al-Naqshbandi classified three types: temporal pause (wuquf-i zamani), numerical pause (wuquf-i adadi), and heart pause (wuquf-i qalbi).

Y

Yahya ibn Muhammad (d. 1948) Zaydi imam and political ruler of North Yemen (1904–48). Succeeded his father, Muhammad, as imam of the Zaydis. Led the struggle of North Yemeni tribes against Ottoman rule to create a kingdom in North Yemen. Accepted the British presence but attempted to insulate Yemen from the rest of the world. Was autocratic, rejected political and economic modernization, and favored preservation of a traditional Islamic society. The Free Yemeni Movement revolted against his despotic rule. He was killed in 1948. His son Ahmad ruled North Yemen until 1962; after his death it became a republic, ending the rule of Zaydi imams over the country.

Yahya ibn Zakariyya See John the Baptist.

Yakan, Shaykh Fathi See Jamaah al-Islamiyyah, al-

Yaqin, al- Certainty; certain faith. Muslim mystics often distinguish three ascending levels of certainty in spiritual matters: certainty based on proof, certainty derived from exposition, and certainty attained by direct vision or experience. The first level belongs to theologians, the second to gnostics, while the third belongs to those loving God alone.

Yaqub See Jacob

Yarmuk, Battle of Battle in 637 between Muslim forces led by Khalid ibn al-Walid and the Byzantine emperor Heraclius. The decisive Muslim victory led to the Byzantine withdrawal from Syria and Palestine, which surrendered to the Muslims between 637 and 647. Jerusalem also surrendered to the Muslims in 638, one of the most peaceful conquests in Jerusalem's history.

Yasa Written code of general laws said to have been laid down by Genghis Khan in 1206 and thereafter regarded as binding on rulers throughout the Mongol Empire. No complete copy survives, and purported quotations from it in other sources have been shown to derive not from a general code but from an assortment of Genghis' decrees regarding taxation and military training, written down for purposes of consultation only. A formal written code may never have existed, although rulers continued to respect Genghis' maxims and Mongol customary law in general. See also Mongols

Yasa, al- See Elisha

Yashruti Tariqah Reformist branch of the Shadhili tariqah founded by Ali Nur al-Din al-Yashruti. Centered in Palestine, but spread throughout Syria and North and East Africa. Particularly active in East Africa, where it established centers and performed missionary work along the eastern coastal region. Active in the pan-Islamic movement supported by the Ottoman sultan in the nineteenth century. The order was significant for establishing a rigorous interpretation of Islam in the region. It did not become a major political force, although leaders sometimes attacked policies of local rulers and sometimes faced European controls.

Yasin, Abd al-Salam (b. 1928) Moroccan Islamic activist, leader, and ideologue of the movement of al-Adl wa'l-Ihsan. Produced several books and published a now-banned monthly periodical, Al-jamaah. Known for his harsh criticism of the monarchical institution, the official religious scholars, and the westernized elite, whom he accuses of de-Islamizing society. Imprisoned for several years and then placed under house arrest from 1989 to 2000. Calls for a reconciliation of the state and dawah (call) and the implementation of the Prophetic Paradigm, a comprehensive process of organization, socialization, and mobilization that reflects Yasin's Sufi influences and prepares for the restoration of the caliphate. Yasin's movement represents the most influential Islamic opposition in Morocco.

Yasin, Shaykh Ahmad (b. 1936) Founder of Hamas as an alternative to the PLO. Declared the goal of restoring Islamic principles and character to Palestinian society. Inspired by the Egyptian Muslim Brotherhood. Initially resisted violence, focusing instead on religious education. Later sanctioned violence as a means of eradicating oppression, corruption, and injustice. Became a popular leader in the late 1970s with the general resurgence of political Islam. Worked to reform the Palestinian community from within by combating secularism and developing social service institutions. Turned mosques into centers for education and political organization. Declared that all Palestine is Muslim land and no one has the right to give any portion away.

Yathrib See Medina

Yawm al-Din See Day of Judgment

Yawm al-Qiyama See Day of Judgment

Yazid (r. 680–83) Umayyad caliph who sent forces against Husayn and his followers in Karbala, Iraq, in 680, resulting in their martyrdom. Personification of evil and oppression for Shiis. In the twentieth century the Husayn/Yazid paradigm was used to describe the relationship between the oppressed Iranian people and the Pahlavi regime, and between the oppressed Shiis of Lebanon and the landlords, state, and police.

Year of the Elephant (ca. 570) According to tradition and the earliest biographical accounts of Ibn Ishaq and Ibn Saad, the year of Muhammad's birth. Name comes from the expedition led by Abrahah of southern Arabia into northern Arabia, during which he rode an elephant. Historians today believe that this event occurred at least a decade prior to Muhammad's birth.

Yemeni Society for Reform See Tajammu al-Yamani li'l-Islah, al-

YMMA See Jamiat al-Shubban al-Muslimin

Young Men's Muslim Association See Jamiat al-Shubban al-Muslimin

Young Ottomans Liberal movement that developed the first constitutional ideology of the Ottoman Empire; influential from circa 1800 to 1876. Alliance of reformist ulama and intellectuals whose ideas were partially instrumental in inspiring the overthrow of Sultan Abdulaziz (r. 1861–76), though they never opposed the monarchical principle in theory. Contributed to the elaboration of the first Ottoman constitution (1876) and a short-lived parliament. Namik Kamel was a leading figure. See also Tanzimat; Young Turks

Young Turks Successor movement to the Young Ottomans. Opposed Sultan Abdulhamid II's regime (1876–1908) that restored the constitution on 23 July 1908 and ruled the Ottoman Empire until its destruction in 1918. Divided into two groups, both determined to maintain the integrity of the Ottoman Empire: unionists, who emphasized modernization under a centralized state, and liberals, who favored a decentralized policy with substantial autonomy for the non-Turkish, non-Muslim communities.

Yuldeshev, Tahir See Islamic Movement of Uzbekistan (IMU)

Yunus See Jonah

Yusuf See Joseph

Yusufi Tariqah A Sufi order, also known as Rashidi, founded by Ahmad ibn Yusuf al-Milyani al-Rashidi (d. 1524). The Yusufi order is in the Shadhili tradition predominant in North Africa. Like other Shadhili-influenced orders, the Yusufis emphasized the barakah (blessing) of the Sufi shaykhs, called sharifs, and, upon their death, the veneration of their tombs. See also Ibn Idris, Ahmad

Z

Zabidi, Muhammad Murtada al- (d. 1160) Yemeni grammarian and scholar of the Hanafi school of Islamic law. Author of a polemical treatise entitled *Refutation of Those Who Deviate in the Mighty Book*, condemning materialists, skeptics, and atheists as mentioned in the Quran. Attacked rationalist theologians of the Abbasid period.

Zabur *See* Psalms

Zachariah Arabic *Zakariyya.* Identified in the Quran as the father of John, the husband of Elizabeth, and the priest entrusted with the care of Mary, mother of Jesus. Prayed to God in his old age for a child, since he had no heir and was concerned about what would happen to his relatives and property after his death; he was also concerned that he needed someone to represent him in continuing service to God. Prayed that the child would be pleasing to God. Angels announced to him the coming birth of John.

Zahid *See* Ascetic

Zahir Apparent, external, manifest. In esoteric interpretations of Islam, contrasted with the inner or hidden (batin) aspects of reality. The outer or apparent meaning of the Quran is made known traditionally through the discipline of tafsir (exegesis), while the hidden meanings of the text are accessed through the esoteric hermeneutical process known as tawil. *See also* Batin

Zahir al-Riwayah Manifest meaning of a text. Refers to the canons of a legal school's eponyms and their disciples, which constitute the structural basis of the school of thought (madhhab). Arguments contradicting zahir al-riwayah are thus discredited.

Zahiri School of Islamic law founded by Abu Sulayman Daud al-Zahiri in the ninth century. Flourished in Spain, particularly under the leadership of the jurist Ibn Hazm. Extinct by the fourteenth century, although it is recognized by four extant Sunni schools. Declared the Quran, hadith, and consensus of Companions as the only acceptable sources of authority. Rejected the practice of taqlid (imitation of precedent). Based its legal principles on a literal (zahir) interpretation of Quran and hadith, rejecting analogy (qiyas) and juristic preference (istihsan). Emphasized the importance of applying the rules of grammar to the text in order to determine the revealed meaning. Objected to the use of reason in favor of revelation.

Zahiriyyah *See* Zahiri

Zaim Political leader who provides both general and personal services. The leader's power is based on the loyalty of his clientele and the relationship held with the state or central authorities. The style of leadership is personal rather than party-based. Such a leader may have a religious or community base or transcend confessional boundaries by having a local or geographic base. Particularly prominent in Lebanon.

Zakah Required almsgiving that is one of the five pillars of Islam. Muslims with financial means are required to give 2.5 percent of their net worth annually as zakah. To practicing Muslims, zakah connotes the path to purity, comprehension of material responsibility, and an enhanced sense of spirituality. Zakah is used for the needy, for propagation of the faith, to free slaves, to relieve debtors, to help travelers, and for the administration of zakah, as well as other efforts approved by religious authorities. The primary forms of wealth subject to zakah include gold, silver, livestock, agricultural produce, articles of trade, currency, shares and bonds, and other liquid assets.

Zakariyya See Zachariah

Zallum, Abd al-Qadhim See Nabhani, Taqi al-Din al-; Hizb al-Tahrir al-Islami

Zamakhshari, Abu al-Qasim Mahmud ibn Umar (d. 1144) Mutazili theologian, Arabic philologist, and Quran exegete of Persian origin. His Quran commentary, *Al-kashshaf an haqaiq al-tanzil*, exhibits his Mutazili dogmas with little attention to tradition and elaborates on lexical, grammatical, and rhetorical elements while interpreting the Quran and highlighting its miraculous inimitability. His *Al-mufassal* is an exhaustive exposition of Arabic grammar, and his *Asas al-balagha* is a dictionary of Arabic. His literary works include *Maqamat*, containing moralizing discourses; his diwan of poems; and *Al-mustaqsa fi-l-amthal*, a popular collection of proverbs.

Zamzam Well in Mecca revealed by God to Hagar and Ishmael after Abraham abandoned them. Hagar ran seven times between two small hills looking for water to save her son from thirst. This action is reenacted each year during the hajj pilgrimage as the say ritual. Pilgrims drink water from this well as part of the ritual. *See also* Hajj

Zand Dynasty Branch of chieftains who ruled western and southern Iran from 1751 to 1794. The founder, Karim Khan Zand, mastered all of Iran except Khurasan. The dynasty began as a Safavid restoration but soon became an independent effort to restore peace and prosperity. It rebuilt and rerouted trade through Iran, issued coins in the name of the Hidden Imam, and built a mosque in Shiraz, but never sought clerical endorsement of power. Karim Khan Zand holds an enduring reputation as the most humane Iranian ruler of the Islamic era. His descendants were overthrown by the Qajars.

Zandaqah Arabic term for every sort of socially abhorred heresy. Historically applied to anyone suspected of undermining orthodoxy by cloaking an esoteric faith beneath a profession of Islam. Hence a zindiq is a heretic who subscribes to sectarianism and threatens the unity of the community by dissension. In modern Arabic the term is used for atheists and secularists, whereas *ilhad* and *mulhid* are used for heresy and heretics.

Zann Suspicion; in law, probability. In the hadith literature, lack of certainty concerning the authenticity and meaning of hadith supported by only a single reporter.

Zanzibar, Islam in The population of Zanzibar is almost entirely Muslim. Arab Muslims arrived in the eighth century, followed by Muslim merchants from many Indian Ocean lands. The Muslim community was cosmopolitan and developed its own distinctive Swahili culture. Following a period of Portuguese domination, the sultans of Oman established control, and the Bu Said dynasty moved its center to Zanzibar in the nineteenth century. A British protectorate, established at the end of the nineteenth century, maintained control until independence in 1963. A violent revolution in 1964 killed or drove out many of the Arabs, and Zanzibar joined Tanganyika to form Tanzania. Zanzibar has maintained substantial autonomy.

Zawiyah Sufi place of worship and welfare institution. May be identified with the mausoleum of a saint. Location where the five daily prayers are said, litanies of the Sufi order are recited, offerings are brought, food and sanctuary may be sought, and social activities requiring religious blessing are conducted. Also the designated place for achievement of various spiritual states. Under the direction of a spiritual guide, an aspirant isolates himself in zawiyah, eating minimally and reciting dhikrs in the hope that they will bring him to spiritual fulfillment. Zawiyah has also served as a unit of politico-religious organization; it often has a school attached. Its social and economic significance have eroded in the modern period. *See also* Khalwah; Khanaqah; Tekke

Zayd ibn Ali (d. 740) Grandson of Muhammad's son Husayn, son of Ali Zayn al-Abidin. Shii sect of Zaydis believed he was the fifth imam. He rejected the notion of the Hidden Imam, pursuing instead a more activist revolutionary position against the Umayyad dynasty. Led a rebellion against them in 740. First descendant of Husayn to rebel openly against the Umayyads. His leadership resulted in his followers declaring that any descendant of Fatimah and Ali could claim the imamate; the determining factor was not birth order but a public assertion of the imamate. He died violently in rebellion. Today he serves as a symbol for Shiis, encouraging activism, rather than passive acceptance, in response to suffering, injustice, and oppression.

Zaydis Moderate branch of Shii Islam that diverged from other Shii denominations in a dispute over succession to the imamate. The Zaydis favored Zayd ibn Ali, grandson of Husayn, as fifth imam due to his activist revolutionary position against the Umayyad dynasty. Its first state was founded in northern Iran in 864 and lasted until 1126. A longer-lasting state was established in northern Yemen in 893, where it endured until 1962. It is the closest of all Shii factions to Sunnis. It has its own law school and differs from other Shii denominations due to its acceptance of the legitimacy of Abu Bakr and Umar, with partial acceptance of Uthman. It does not view the imam as a supernaturally endowed person representing God on earth. The only qualifications for the imamate are descent from Ali and Fatimah, absence of physical imperfections, and personal piety. The imam must be able to take up the sword, either offensively or defensively, ruling out the legitimacy of infants and hidden imams. Members tend to be puritanical in moral teachings and to disapprove of Sufism. *See also* Yahya ibn Muhammad; Zayd ibn Ali

Zayn al-Abidin, Ali (d. ca. 713) Fourth Shii imam, great-grandson of Muhammad, and the only son of Husayn who survived the massacre of Shiis at Karbala. Was protected by Husayn's sister, Zaynab, who convinced Yazid's troops not to kill him, leaving an heir to the imamate. Became a noted scholar in Hejaz and devoted himself to prayer. Quiescent in attitude toward the Umayyad dynasty, leading many Shiis to abandon him in favor of Ali's third son by a Hanafi woman,

marking a break in the prior belief that only descendants of Ali and Fatimah could serve as imams. Reinterpreted in the twentieth century as an example of patience and perseverance when numerical odds are against the Shii community.

Zaynab bint Ali (d. 681) Daughter of Fatimah and Ali. Married Abd Allah ibn Jafar, with whom she had three sons and two daughters. Zaynab accompanied her brother Husayn to Karbala in 680; after his tragic death there, she was instrumental in saving the life of Husayn's young son, Ali Zayn al-Abidin, who became the fourth imam of the Twelver Shiis. For her bravery during the battle of Karbala she earned the title "the heroine [batalah] of Karbala."

Zaynab bint al-Khuzaymah (d. 625) Married the Prophet after the death of her husband at the Battle of Uhud in 625. She died after only eight (according to some versions, three) months of marriage to the Prophet. She is described as extremely charitable, on account of which she earned the sobriquet "Mother of the Poor" (Umm al-Masakin). *See also* Wives of the Prophet

Zaynab bint Jahsh (d. ca. 641) Married the Prophet Muhammad, her cousin, in 627. Described as a proud woman from a noble tribe, she was divorced from Zayd ibn Haritha, the Prophet's former bondsman and adopted son, whom she regarded as her social inferior, and married Muhammad soon thereafter. These events are alluded to in the Quran (33:37). *See also* Wives of the Prophet

Zaynab bint Muhammad (d. 630) Daughter of the Prophet Muhammad. Married to Abu al-As ibn al-Rabia. A pregnant Zaynab left for Medina circa 624; pursued by some hostile Qurayshis, she suffered a miscarriage. In 629 Zaynab was joined by her husband, who had finally accepted Islam, but she died a year later.

Zaytunah A mosque and center of higher learning in Tunis since the early eighth century. When the Hafsid dynasty (1207–1534) came to power and made Tunis its capital,

Zaytunah emerged as one of the most important Islamic institutions of higher learning in North Africa. In 1534 the Spaniards occupied Tunis, ransacked its libraries and mosques, and burned or removed many of its books and manuscripts. It was restored under the Muradids and the Husayids from 1631 to 1957. In 1965 its role as an independent educational institution was officially abolished; it became the school of theology and Islamic studies of the University of Tunis.

Zechariah See Zachariah

Zia-ul-Haq, Mohammad (d. 1988) President of Pakistan, 1979–88. Led the 1977 military coup d'etat against Zulfikar Ali Bhutto. Legitimized his rule by promoting the "Islamization" of state and society via the introduction of Islamic taxes (zakah and ushr), an interest-free economy, the traditional Islamic penal code, and reforms in culture and education. Was a close ally of the United States and conduit for U.S. support for Afghani resistance to the Soviet occupation. Killed in a suspicious plane crash.

Zikr See Dhikr

Zina Unlawful sexual intercourse; fornication or adultery. A criminal offense in Islamic law for which the Quran prescribes three possible punishments: stoning to death, whipping, or exile. Zina must be established by the testimony of four adult male witnesses of established character and integrity. There is considerable disagreement as to the conditions under which the prescribed punishments may be waived. Historically, these sentences have been rarely applied, though stonings have occurred in late-twentieth-century Afghanistan, Algeria, Saudi Arabia, and Sudan. The Quran also mandates eighty lashes for one who falsely accuses another of zina and who fails to produce four witnesses to the alleged incident.

Zindiq See Zandaqah

Ziyarah Visitation. Refers to visiting gravesites for the purpose of praying for the dead or visiting the tombs of holy people (saints), seeking blessings. Rituals require that one should turn toward the dead when approaching the grave, offer a greeting, and pray for that person. The Wahhabis of Saudi Arabia (Hanbali school of law) forbid women from entering the historic Baqi cemetery, where the Prophet's family, wives, and prominent Companions are buried. Shafii and Shii jurists allow women to visit all gravesites.

Zoroastrianism and Islam The state religion of pre-Islamic Persia. Not mentioned in the Quran. Islam shares Zoroastrianism's ethical monotheism based on a supreme, transcendent creator who will administer a final judgment and who governs an afterlife of heaven and hell. Zoroastrians were therefore legally tolerated after the seventh-century Muslim conquest of Persia. Nevertheless, Zoroastrians suffered persistent persecution in Iran, so the contemporary Parsi (Persian) community of India, founded by tenth-century refugees, far outnumbers the Zoroastrian population of its homeland, where discrimination occurs despite constitutional protection.

Zuhd Asceticism. Rejection of material comforts to pursue personal contemplation and meditation. Encompasses notions of piety, asceticism, and renunciation. Practiced in some Sufi orders. Some orders adhering to this principle adopted a special manner of dress as a visible sign of asceticism. Prominent in the Darqawi tariqah.

Zuhri, Muhammad ibn Muslim ibn Shihab (d. 742) Arab historian and hadith scholar of the preliterary period in Medina. Transmitted material about Muhammad and his Companions and frequently appears in the isnads of works by historians, biographers, and hadith collectors. A large quantity of material is ascribed to him, providing the basis for books by Ibn Ishaq (d. 767) and al-Waqidi (d. 823), especially in detailing Muhammad's battles. Alleged by some to have been the first to write down hadith material.

Zulaykha Popular traditions identify her as the wife of the Egyptian who bought Joseph as a slave from his brothers. She became enamored of Joseph and tried to seduce him, causing chaos in her home. Considered by Sufis to be a paradigm of piety because she eventually abandoned the love of Joseph for the love of God.

Zu'l-Janah Possessor of wings. Refers to the horse used by Husayn ibn Ali in the battle at Karbala. According to popular Shii literature, the horse either belonged to Muhammad originally or was a descendant of Muhammad's horse. Shii literature on Karbala does not have a name for the horse. In popular culture, a horse symbolizing Zu'l-Janah is led through cities and venerated during Muharram processions.

Zulm Wrongdoing against God, others, or self. Since the Middle Ages the term has been used to mean oppression and tyranny, par-ticularly by rulers over their subjects. Frequently used as the opposite of justice, particularly in Islamic political treatises and books of counsel for princes and rulers. In jurisprudence, it refers to that which exceeds legal limits. In Shii tradition zulm expresses the traditional ethos of suffering, oppression, and tyranny under the Sunni community.

Zurkhaneh Traditional gymnasium in Iran dedicated to the development of men's physical strength and promotion of ethical values. Usually privately owned; membership was traditionally informal but restricted to adult men. During the Qajar period, served as centers for the performing arts and sports and as gathering places for guilds and merchants. Exercises are geared toward body-building, acrobatic jumping, and wrestling and are accompanied by the rhythmic beating of drums and chanting of epic verses.

Chronology of Key Events

ca. 570 Birth of Muhammad

610 Muhammad receives first revelation

613 Muhammad begins public preaching in Mecca; first emigration of Muslims to Abyssinia; Muhammad remains in Mecca to continue preaching against polytheists

619 Deaths of Muhammad's wife, Khadija, and uncle, Abu Talib, leaving Muhammad without a protector; Muhammad tries to leave Mecca

621 Muhammad's first contact with Medina

622 Migration (Hijra) of early Muslims to Medina; Islam takes form of political state; first year of Islamic calendar

624 Battle of Badr—Muslims outnumbered, but victorious; serves as symbol for Muslims of divine intervention and guidance

625 Battle of Uhud—Muhammad and Muslims attacked and defeated by Meccans

627 Battle of the Trench—Muhammad and Muslims victorious over Meccans and Bedouin mercenaries; Muhammad consolidates leadership in Medina

628 Treaty of Hudaybiyah permits Muslims to make pilgrimage to Mecca

630 Muhammad occupies Mecca

632 Death of Muhammad; Abu Bakr becomes first Caliph

634 Death of Caliph Abu Bakr; Umar ibn al-Khattab becomes second Caliph

638 Muslims occupy Jerusalem

644 Caliph Umar ibn al-Khattab stabbed; dies one week later after appointing committee to select successor, setting precedent for orderly transfer of caliphate; Uthman ibn Affan becomes third Caliph; Quran is collected and put in final format during reign of Uthman

656 Caliph Uthman ibn Affan assassinated; Ali ibn Abi Talib becomes Fourth Caliph

656–661 First Muslim civil war over succession, leading to Sunni-Shii split; Battle of the Camel with Aisha leading Muslim opposition forces against fourth caliph, Ali ibn Abi Talib; Ali victorious; first instance of Muslim caliph involved in military action against other Muslims

661 Caliph Ali ibn Abi Talib assassinated; Muawiya ibn Abi Sufyan founds Umayyad Dynasty

670 Muslim conquest of northwest Africa

680–692 Second Muslim civil war— Husayn, son of Ali, leads rebellion against Umayyad Caliph Yazid and is martyred, creating paradigm of protest and suffering for Shiis

711 Berber converts to Islam cross Straits of Gibraltar and enter southern Iberia, expanding Islam into Europe

732 Charles Martel defeats Muslims at Battle of Tours, France, halting expansion of Islam into Europe

744–750 Third Muslim civil war and defeat of Umayyads by Abbasids

750–850 Consolidation of Abbasid Muslim empire in Iraq, Western Iran, Khurasan, Mesopotamia, Egypt and Syria by caliphs al-Mahdi, Harun al-Rashid, and al-Mamun

756 Emirate of Cordoba founded by Umayyad prince Abd al-Rahman

762 Baghdad founded as Abbasid capital

765 Death of sixth Shii Imam and founder of Jafari school of Islamic law, Jafar al-Sadiq; succession disputed, creating split between Sevener and Twelver Shiis

786–809 Harun al-Rashid caliph (legendary exploits recounted in *The Thousand and One Nights*), height of Abbasid caliphate

830 Caliph Mamum establishes "House of Wisdom" (Bayt al-Hikmah) in Baghdad, responsible for translating manuscripts from other languages and cultures into Arabic

836 Abbasid capital transferred from Baghdad to Samarra

874 Twelfth Imam goes into occultation; end of direct rule of Shii Imams

1031 End of Andalusian caliphate

1071 Battle of Mankizert—Turkish nomads defeat Byzantine emperor and enter Anatolia

1095 Pope Urban II calls Crusade against Islam at Council of Clermont

1099 Crusaders capture Jerusalem and establish Latin Kingdom

1143 First translation of Quran into Latin commissioned to Robert of Ketton by Peter the Venerable, Abbot of Cluny

1171 Saladin conquers Egypt, restoring Sunni rule

1187 Saladin defeats Franks at Battle of Hittin and recovers Jerusalem for Islam

1219 Francis of Assisi attempts to convert Muslims to Christianity

1258 Mongols sack Baghdad—end of Abbasid Caliphate

1260 Mamluks defeat Mongols at Ayn Jalut

ca. 1280 Ertugrul begins Ottoman expansion

1295–1304 Ghazan—first Mongol Khan to convert to Islam

12th century Sufi orders begin to provide organizational framework for social movements

1326 Ottomans take Bursa

1345 Ottomans cross straits of Gallipoli

1370–1405 Conquests of Tamerlane

1389 Ottomans defeat Serbs at Battle of Kosovo

1444 Last anti-Ottoman European crusade defeated at Varna

1453 Ottomans capture Constantinople

1478 Islamic conquest of Majapahit kingdom in Java

1492 Granada—last Muslim stronghold in Spain—falls to Christian rulers Ferdinand and Isabella

1511 Portuguese capture Melaka

1514 Ottomans defeat Safavids at Battle of Chaldiran

1517 Ottoman conquest of Egypt, Syria, Mecca and Medina

1520 Ottomans capture Belgrade

1520–1566 Rule of Suleyman the Magnificent, high point of Ottoman Empire

1526 Battle of Panipat, beginning of Mughal rule

1529 Failed siege of Vienna by Ottomans

1534 Ottoman occupation of Baghdad

1556–1605 Akbar rules India, high point of Mughal Empire

1571 Battle of Lepanto—Europeans block Ottoman advance into Mediterranean

1580 End of Mediterranean wars; Ottoman-Habsburg truce defines Muslim and Christian boundaries

1583 British negotiate first trade treaty with Ottoman Empire

1588–1629 Shah Abbas ruler of Persia, high point of Safavid Empire

1606 Treaty of Zsitva Torok—Habsburgs recognize Ottoman rule in Romania, Transylvania and Hungary

1639 Treaty of Qasr Shirin—permanent borders of Iraq and Iran established

1658–1707 Aurangzeb rules Mughal Empire, implementing religious rule

of ulama and Islamic basis for character of state and society

1703 Edirne Incident in Ottoman Empire—Shaykh al-Islam Feyzullah dominates government and grand viziers; high point of ulama influence over affairs of state; ousted by Janissaries and lower-level religious leaders and students

1774 Treaty of Kuchuk Kaynarja—Russians take control of Black Sea from Ottomans

1792 Treaty of Jassy—Russians consolidate control of Georgia, Black Sea and Romania; beginning of Ottoman reforms

18th century Rise of reform Sufism and renewed interest in hadith scholarship as means for socio-moral reconstruction of society; Akhbari vs. Usuli debate over proper source of guidance for Islamic community

1722 Afghans seize Isfahan, bringing end to Safavid rule in Iran

1737–1815 Ahmad al-Tijani, founder of Tijaniyah Sufi order, major reformist Sufi order in Morocco, which inspired West and North African jihad and resistance movements

1745 Beginning of Wahhabi movement in Arabia

1754–1817 Uthman Dan Fodio, leader of Northern Nigerian reformist opposition to Hausa states

1757–1790 Sultan Muhammad ibn Abdallah ruler of Morocco; encourages revival of Islamic scholarship and study of hadith

1785–present Naqshbandiyah movement leads anti-Russian resistance in Caucasus

1786–1831 Sayyid Ahmad Barelwi, leader of jihad movement in India against Sikhs and British

1787–1859 Muhammad Ali ibn al-Sanusi of Libya, founder of Sanusiyah Tariqah and Islamic state

1789–1807 Sultan Selim III rules Ottoman Empire and tries to implement reforms in civil administration and education; resisted due to Westernization inherent in reforms

1798 French occupation of Egypt under Napoleon; Muhammad Ali comes to power, initiating period of reform of political and economic structures along Western lines

19th century European imperial expansion in the Muslim world

1803–1837 Padri Movement in Sumatra

1817–1898 Sir Sayyid Ahmad Khan, leader of Islamic modernist movement in India

1818–1845 Faraidi of Bengal opposes Hindus and British

1822–1895 Ahmad Cevdet Pasha Shaykh al-Islam of Ottoman Empire; formulates civil code combining Islamic legal principles with new legal ideas and influences Tanzimat

1825–1830 Dipanegara leads revolt in Java

1830 French invade Algeria; Abd al-Qadir, leader of Qadiriyah tariqah, leads resistance until 1847 and tries to establish Islamic state

1838–1897 Jamal al-Din al-Afghani, father of Islamic modernism

1848–1885 Muhammad Ahmad, Mahdi of Sudan and founder of Islamic state

1849–1905 Muhammad Abduh, Islamic modernist and reformist and co-founder of Salafiyah movement in Egypt

1851–1914 Ismail Gasprinski, sponsor of schools combining Russian and Muslim education to achieve modernization

1856–1873 Yunnan leads rebellion against Chinese rule and tries to establish Muslim state

1862–1867 Jihad in Senegal led by Ma Ba against French

1865–1935 Muhammad Rashid Rida, co-founder of Salafiyah movement in Egypt and Islamic modernist movement

1873–1908 Ulama lead resistance to Dutch occupation of Acheh

1875–1938 Muhammad Iqbal, Islamic modernist who developed ideology for foundation of Pakistan

1876 Deobandi school founded to combine hadith studies and Sufism

1876–1909 Sultan Abdulhamid II rules Ottoman Empire and pursues pan-Islamic ideal as caliph

1879–1882 Urabi revolt against European influence in Egypt, leading to British occupation and later rise of nationalism in Egypt

1891–1892 Tobacco Protest in Iran—*ulama* and merchants opposed to Shah's government granting tobacco concessions to Europeans; sets pattern of cooperation between two social classes later used during 1979 Iranian Revolution

1897–1975 Elijah Muhammad, leader of Black Muslim movement in United States

1898 Mahdist state of Sudan defeated by British; Muhammad Rashid Rida begins publishing *al-Manar* in Egypt—journal becomes leading publication for Islamic reformist ideas

1899–1920 Muhammad Abdallah Hasan leads resistance to British in Somalia

1905–1911 Constitutional Revolt in Iran places limits on Shah's power; local religious leaders play key role in opposition to Shah

1908 Young Turk revolution in Ottoman Empire

1912 Muhammadiya founded in Southeast Asia to promote educational and social reform

1919–1924 End of Ottoman Empire following World War I and creation of Turkish Republic

1919–1925 Khilafat movement in India in support of caliphate

1924 Ottoman/Turkish caliphate and *shariah* court system abolished by Mustafa Kemal Ataturk

1926 Islamic law replaced by Swiss and Italian-based system in Turkey

1927 Tablighi Islam founded by Mawlana Muhammad Ilyas in India

1928 Muslim Brotherhood founded in Egypt by Hasan al-Banna; reference to Islam as religion of state eliminated in Turkey

1932 Kingdom of Saudi Arabia founded on basis of alliance between religion and politics with *sharia* as law

1933–1977 Ali Shariati, ideologue of Iranian Revolution of 1979

1941 Jamaat-i Islami founded in India/Pakistan by Mawlana Abu al-Ala Mawdudi

1943 National Pact of Lebanon agreed upon, assuring dominance of Christian Arabs in political process based on numerical superiority in 1932 census; president of country to be Maronite Christian, prime minister Sunni Muslim, and speaker of chamber of deputies Shii Muslim; other key government positions distributed proportionally along confessional lines

1947 Pakistan founded as independent state for Muslims of India

1948 State of Israel declared

1949 Religious education reintroduced in Turkish schools as elective course; Hasan al-Banna assassinated by Egyptian police

1950 Religious education mandatory in Turkish schools unless parents object

1951 Idris ibn al-Mahdi, grandson of Muhammad ibn Ali al-Sanusi, becomes king of newly created Libya, highlighting leadership and nationalistic roles of Sanusiyah Tariqah

1952 Gamal Abd al-Nasser seizes power in Egypt under banner of pan-Arabism and Arab socialism, supported by shaykhs of al-Azhar; religion restricted to personal status and beliefs

1954 Muslim Brotherhood founded in Sudan, advocating Islamic political and social order via adoption of Islamic constitution based on the

Quran and introduction of Islamic
law

1956 Pakistan adopts constitution
declaring itself an Islamic Republic
with a Muslim head of state and
based upon Islamic principles;
Islamic research center deemed
necessary for reconstruction of
Muslim society on Islamic basis

1965 Crackdown on Muslim Brotherhood
in Egypt after Nasser accuses them
of plotting to assassinate him

1966 Execution of Sayyid Qutb, prominent
writer for Muslim Brotherhood who
gave movement radical, militant
tone, by Nasser in Egypt

1967 Arab-Israeli war—Arab forces routed
by Israel, leading to Arab
disillusionment with secular policies
like nationalism and socialism and
sparking Islamic revival

1969 Muammar al-Qadhdhafi seizes power
in Libya, later implementing own
version of Islamic state as "Third
Universal Alternative"; Jafar al-
Numayri seizes power in the Sudan;
al-Aqsa Mosque in Jerusalem
burned, leading King Faisal of Saudi
Arabia to call for jihad against Israel
and to organize an Islamic summit
conference combining pan-Islamism
with Arabism

1970 Organization of the Islamic
Conference founded—first official
pan-Islamic institution for
cooperation among Islamic
governments

1970–1971 East-West Pakistan civil war
results in declaration of independent
state of Bangladesh (formerly East
Pakistan)

1971 ABIM (Malaysian League of Muslim
Youth) founded in Malaysia as

mission movement and political
party, rejecting capitalism and
socialism and promoting Islam as an
alternative political and economic
system

1972 National Salvation Party founded in
Turkey by Necmettin Erbakan; goal
is Islamic state and Islamization of
Turkish life

1973 "Operation Badr"—second Arab-
Israeli war, with Egypt recovering
some of territory lost to Israel in
1967 war; Arab oil embargo against
West renders Arabs world economic
power

1974 Musa al-Sadr founds Movement of
the Disinherited, a populist
movement for social and political
reform in Lebanon favoring
redistribution of power and
resources to include Shii majority of
Lebanon otherwise excluded;
militant wing develops into AMAL.

1975 Outbreak of civil war in Lebanon,
resulting in radicalization of Shii
population; Muammar al-Qadhdhafi
of Libya publishes *The Green Book*,
outlining his interpretation of Islam
and the world

1977 Zulfikar Ali Bhutto's government in
Pakistan ousted by General Zia ul-
Haq, who introduces Islamization

1978 Disappearance of Musa al-Sadr
during trip to Libya, giving him
popular "hidden imam" status
among Shiis of Lebanon; Israel
invades Lebanon; Pakistan announces
creation of *Shariah* Courts

1979 Iranian Revolution—Islamic Republic
of Iran founded; American Embassy
seized by militant supporters of
Khomeini protesting US ties to Shah;
seizure of Grand Mosque of Mecca
by militants led by Mahdi in Saudi

Arabia; Shii riots in Eastern Province of Saudi Arabia, calling for fairer distribution of oil wealth and services; Soviet Union invades Afghanistan, launching decade-long war

1980 Hizbollah founded in Lebanon; Islamic Jihad founded in Palestine by Muslim Brotherhood

1981 Anwar al-Sadat of Egypt assassinated by militant Tanzim al-Jihad; Habib Bourguiba of Tunisia cracks down on Tunisia's Islamic Trend Movement

1982 Hafiz al-Asad of Syria levels city of Hama to put down opposition movement led by Muslim Brotherhood; Israel invades Lebanon for second time; massacre of inhabitants of Sabra and Shatilla in Lebanon

1983 September Laws implemented in Sudan, reintroducing Islamic laws and military courts; commission established by Gulf states to study and develop unified code of *shariah* law

1987 Crackdown on Tunisia's Islamic Trend Movement by Habib Bourguiba government; *intifada* declared in Palestine; HAMAS founded in response to *intifada*

1988 Benazir Bhutto elected Prime Minister of Pakistan, first elected female head of state in Muslim world; end of Iran-Iraq War; Islamic Trend Movement becomes Tunisia's leading opposition group, performing impressively in national elections

1989 Death of Ayatollah Ruhollah Khomeini, first ruler of Islamic Republic of Iran and author of doctrine of *vilayat-i faqih*; Ayatollah

Sayyed Ali Khamenei suceeds Khomeini as *faqih*; Omar Hassan al-Bashir seizes power in Sudan—tied to National Islamic Front; FIS (Islamic Salvation Front) in Algeria sweeps municipal elections; Tunisia refuses to allow Renaissance Party (formerly Islamic Tendency Movement) to participate in elections in order to keep religion and politics separate; liberation of Afghanistan from occupation by Soviet Union, largely due to efforts of *mujahidin*

1990–1991 Persian Gulf War results from Iraq's invasion of Kuwait

1990 Islamists win 32 out of 80 seats in Jordanian Parliament and member of Muslim Brotherhood is elected Speaker of national parliament; FIS (Islamic Salvation Front) wins municipal and regional elections in Algeria, coming to power through democratic process, rather than revolution

1991 FIS (Islamic Salvation Front) wins parliamentary elections in Algeria

1992 Iranian elections place conservatives in control of parliament, marginalizing hard-liners and paving way for limited liberalization of political participation and dissent; all mosques in Egypt placed under government control; military prevents FIS (Islamic Salvation Front) from coming to power in Algeria, cancelling results of democratic parliamentary elections; Algerian government crack-down on FIS, leading to civil war which has claimed over 150,000 lives; slaughter of thousands of Bosnians by Serbs in civil war in Yugoslavia

1993 Bombing of World Trade Center in New York City, tied to Shaykh Umar Abd al-Rahman

1994 Baruch Goldstein (Jewish settler) kills 29 worshippers at Mosque of the Patriarch in Hebron, provoking suicide bombings by Qassam Brigade (military wing of HAMAS); Taliban, composed of religious leaders and students, appears in Afghanistan, claiming mantle of moral leadership; Refah (Welfare) Party wins mayoral elections in more than a dozen major cities in Turkey, including Ankara and Istanul

1995 Refah (Welfare) Party wins enough seats in National Assembly to make its leader, Necmettin Erbakan, Turkey's first Islamist prime minister; Dayton Peace Agreement for resolution of the Bosnian conflict

1996 Bombing of US Army barracks at Khobar Towers in Saudi Arabia, tied to al-Qaeda network; Taliban in control of majority of Afghanistan

1997 Mohammad Khatami elected president of Iran in landslide victory, defeating candidate supported by clerical establishment and opening door to United States for cultural, scholarly and economic exchanges; Khatami appoints woman as one of vice-presidents; Algeria resumes parliamentary elections, although FIS (Islamic Salvation Front) barred from participating; alternative Islamic movement MSP (Movement of Society for Peace) wins second highest number of votes; Islamist Prime Minister Necmettin Erbakan forced to resign by Turkish military

1998 Islamist-oriented Rifah Party declared unconstitutional and banned from political activity and assets seized by state in Turkey; Deputy Prime Minister and leader of ABIM, Anwar Ibrahim, removed from power in Malaysia; bombings of US embassies in Kenya and Tanzania; increasing violence in Kosovo leads to international sanctions against Yugoslavian (Serbian) government

1999 Female MP, Merve Kavakci, ousted from Turkish Parliament for wearing headscarf, sparking debate about meaning of democracy and right to religious freedom in Turkey; General Pervez Musharraf comes to power in bloodless coup in Pakistan, promises economic and political reforms, end of sectarian violence and corruption, respect for Constitution; Emir of Bahrain announces plan to gradually establish fully elected parliament and hold municipal elections; Islamic activist Abdurrahman Wahid elected president of Indonesia

2000 Rahmat Ruhani Sarvestani appointed district governor in Iran, marking first time woman has served in this capacity since Iranian Revolution; attack on USS Cole off coast of Yemen; Israeli Prime Minister Ariel Sharon visits and asserts Israeli control over Haram al-Sharif, sparking outbreak of new Palestinian *intifada*; Slobodan Milosevic, former head of Yugoslavia, placed on trial for crimes against humanity due to slaughter of Bosnians in 1992; Egyptian women win equal divorce rights with men; local elections resume in Pakistan with 1/3 of seats reserved for women and 1/3 for poor in order to break former power blocs

2001 U.S. Postal Service issues stamp commemorating Muslim Id holidays; Sept. 11 attacks on World Trade Center and Pentagon by extremists affiliated with al-Qaeda and Osama bin Laden; US declares war on terrorism and pursues Osama bin Laden, al-Qaeda network and Taliban regime in Afghanistan; Khatami re-elected president of Iran in landslide victory; clerical establishment of Iran intensifies crackdown against

opposition calling for more open
society supported by Khatami; plot
by Jewish Defense League to bomb
two US mosques and offices of Arab-
American congressman foiled;
Islamic Virtue Party banned in
Turkey due to Islamic orientation,
resulting in expulsion of two
members from Parliament; Pakistan
successfully tests nuclear bomb,
becoming first Muslim nuclear
power; publication of memoirs of
Algerian military officer blaming
massacres of Algerian civilians on
military and government, rather
than Islamists